THE TRUSTEES OF THE FELLOWES ATHENAEUM
INCORPORATED
FEBY. 21, 1866
IN ROXBURY

Peter Fryer was born in Yorkshire in 1927. His interest in black history began in 1948, when as a reporter he was sent to cover the arrival at Tilbury of Jamaican workers on the *Empire Windrush*. He has written several books, including *Hungarian Tragedy*; *Mrs Grundy: Studies in English Prudery*; and *The Birth Controllers*. Peter Fryer lives in London and is currently working on an historical anthology of black writing in Britain, which will also be published by Pluto.

Peter Fryer

Staying power

Black people in Britain since 1504

HUMANITIES PRESS
ATLANTIC HIGHLANDS, N.J.

First published in 1984 in the United States of America
by Humanities Press Inc., Atlantic Highlands, NJ 07716

Library of Congress Cataloging in Publication Data
Fryer, Peter.
Staying power.
Bibliography: p.
Includes index.
1. Blacks—Great Britain—History. 2. Great Britain—Race relations. 3. Slavery—Great Britain—History.
I. Title.
DA125.N4F78 1984 941'.00496 84–12841
ISBN 0–391–03167–8

Printed in Great Britain

To Emily, Frances, and James

Contents

Preface

Black people – by whom I mean Africans and Asians and their descendants – have been living in Britain for close on 500 years. They have been born in Britain since about the year 1505. In the seventeenth and eighteenth centuries thousands of black youngsters were brought to this country against their will as domestic slaves. Other black people came of their own accord and stayed for a while or settled here. This book gives an account of the lives, struggles, and achievements of men and women most of whom have been either forgotten or, still more insultingly, remembered as curiosities or objects of condescension.

Can such an account be written by a white writer in a way that is acceptable to black readers? This question has been much discussed in the United States. Robbed in the past of all they had, from their freedom to their very names, Afro-Americans have made up their minds never to be robbed again – and no longer to tolerate the pillage of their history by ignorant and superficial white writers out for fame and gain.[1] On the other hand, it is accepted that white writers who make the effort to 'think black' – i.e. to grasp imaginatively as well as intellectually the essence of the black historical experience – may have something worthwhile to offer. But they are warned that this may entail a painful rethinking of basic assumptions.[2] I have written with these considerations in mind.

This however, though peopled to a large extent by Africans, West Indians, Afro-Americans, and Asians, is a history of the black presence in Britain. And it is written, not just for black or just for white readers, but for all who have a serious interest in the subject.[3] Serious readers will want to know first of all what keys to understanding this book has to offer. It offers two. One is the contribution made by black slavery to the rise of British capitalism and, in particular, to the accumulation of wealth that fuelled the industrial revolution. That's why there is a chapter on Britain's slave ports. The other key is the effect English racism has had on the lives of black people living in this country. That's why there is a chapter on the rise of English racism. These two chapters are not 'background'. They go to the heart of the matter. Black slave labour on sugar plantations in the West Indies was British industry's springboard. And racism not only justified plantation slavery and, later, colonialism but also poisoned the lives of black people living in Britain. It is still doing so. Without these two chapters this book would be like a history of the Jews in Germany that stayed silent about antisemitism and extermination camps.

Readers familiar with Eric Williams's classic, *Capitalism and Slavery,* will see that I have made use of it. But not uncritically. Much work has been done in that area of economic history since Williams's book first came out 40 years ago. Some of it supports his case; some argues against him. I haven't seen it as part of my job to defend Williams against his critics; on essentials, no such defence is needed. In any case, when I have used other people's work I have gone, wherever I could, to the original sources and judged for myself. In quoting such sources I have retained archaic spelling and punctuation, explaining whatever might be obscure or misleading.

For the rest, the method is as far as possible biographical, the scope comprehensive but not exhaustive. It seemed best to tell the earlier part of the story, about which the least is generally known, in the greatest detail. So the book becomes more selective as it approaches the present day. Thus music, dance, and sport are covered to the start of the twentieth century only. And the two final chapters, treating of the past 35 years, are purposely restricted to a bare outline. To be sure, the great majority of black people who have ever lived in Britain have done so in this recent period; but to write their history on the scale of the rest of the book would require a perspective, and an access to documents, that will not be available for a long time.

It is a pleasure to thank those who urged me to take on this task and have helped and encouraged me along the way. It was a chance remark by Bob Supiya of the British Library, during the 1981 'riots', that finally led me to lay aside other work and start writing this book instead. I learnt much from the 'Roots in Britain' exhibition assembled by Ziggi Alexander and Audrey Dewjee. Ziggi Alexander has kindly made time to read much of my manuscript; her criticisms saved me from many blunders and she gave me a number of valuable leads. Paul Gilroy read a draft of the last two chapters and made helpful comments. Jeffrey P. Green gave me a lot of information about black people in Britain in the early years of this century. Bill Elkins, Elisabeth Ingles, Walter Kendall, John Lipsey, Douglas Lorimer, Norma Meacock, Ron Ramdin, John Saville, A. Sivanandan, Nicolas Walter, and Ken Weller have sustained me with advice and encouragement. I was privileged to attend the International Conference on the History of Blacks in Britain (1981), and the scholars I met there were unstinting with information and suggestions; my particular debts to them, and to others who have so generously shared their knowledge with me, are specified in the notes. I am grateful to Pluto Press Limited: for being so patient with an author whose project took four and a half times as long as promised; and for the skill and care with which Paul Crane and Angela Quinn pruned a bulky MS. of irrelevancies and obscurities. I am grateful to the staffs of the British Library (Colindale as well as Bloomsbury), Institute of Commonwealth Studies, Institute of Race Relations, London School of Economics, Public Record Office (Chancery Lane as well as Kew), School of Oriental and African Studies, and University of London Library who met my requests for books and documents with such efficiency and courtesy. Not least, I thank the three people to whom this book is dedicated; it is, I fear, an inadequate return for their forbearance and love.

It seems to me now that I began work on this book with an arrogance that has been deservedly humbled by what I have learnt while writing it. Above all, I have learnt how little I know and can hope to know. All who venture into this field must sooner or later ponder the West African saying: 'Knowledge is like the baobab tree; one person's arms cannot encompass it.'

The blacks will know as friends only those whites
who are fighting in the ranks beside them.
And whites will be there.

C.L.R.James, *The Black Jacobins* (1938)

1. 'Those kinde of people'

Africans in Britannia

There were Africans in Britain before the English came here. Some were soldiers in the Roman imperial army that occupied the southern part of our island for three and a half centuries. Others were slaves. Among the troops defending Hadrian's wall in the third century AD was a 'division of Moors' (*numerus Maurorum Aurelianorum*) named after Marcus Aurelius or a later emperor known officially by the same name. Originally raised in north Africa, this unit was stationed at Aballava, now Burgh by Sands, near Carlisle. It was listed in the *Notitia Dignitatum*, an official register of the Roman administrative system,[1] and there is an inscription referring to it on a third-century altar found in 1934 built face down into a cottage wall at Beaumont, not far from Burgh.[2]

Though the earliest attested date for this unit's presence here is 253–8, an African soldier is reputed to have reached Britain by about the year 210. 'Of great fame among clowns and good for a laugh any time' (*clarae inter scurras famae et celebratorum semper iocorum*), this 'Ethiopian' has gone down in history as a man daring enough to mock the emperor who, in all probability, had brought him to Britain. It happened near Carlisle. Septimius Severus, the Libya-born emperor who spent his last three years in what was then a remote province, had been inspecting Hadrian's wall. He had just defeated the wild Caledonians who lived on the other side and, being very superstitious, was hoping for a good omen. He was far from pleased to encounter a black soldier flourishing a garland of cypress boughs. Sacred to the underworld god Pluto, the cypress could mean only one thing to a Roman: death. Severus was troubled, not only by the ominous nature of the garland, but also by the soldier's 'ominous' colour. 'Get out of my sight!' he shouted. The soldier replied sardonically: 'You have been all things, you have conquered all things, now, O conqueror, be a god!' Matters were hardly improved when, wishing to make a propitiatory sacrifice,

Severus was provided with victims who also happened to be black. Abandoning the sacrifice in disgust at this further bad omen, he found that his attendants had carelessly brought these slaves to the very door of the palace.[3] It was a black day, as we say, for the emperor – we share some puns with the Romans, and some superstitions – and he died not long afterwards, at York.

Besides African soldiers and slaves, there may well have been officers (*praefecti*) from the flourishing towns of north Africa serving in Roman Britain in the second and third centuries.[4] And, though no remains have yet been positively identified, there can be little doubt that Africans were buried here. Among 350 human skeletons found in an excavation at York in 1951–9 – the greatest number yet exhumed in any Romano-British cemetery – were several of men whose limb proportions suggest that they were black Africans.[5]

Africans in Scotland

There are traces of an African presence in the British Isles some 400 or 500 years after the Romans left. An ancient Irish chronicle records that 'blue men' (*fir gorma*) were seized by Vikings in Morocco in the ninth century and carried off to Ireland, where they stayed for a long time.[1] And the remains of a young African girl were recently found in a burial, dated *c.* 1000, at North Elmham in Norfolk, about 25 miles north-west of Norwich.[2] Then the records are silent until the early sixteenth century, when a small group of Africans was attached to the court of King James IV of Scotland, experiencing in the royal service what has been called a 'benevolent form' of the black slavery that had become common and fashionable in southern Europe during the preceding 200 years.[3] These Africans were probably taken from Portuguese slavers by the Barton brothers, Scottish privateers whose father's ship, loaded with rich merchandise, had been seized by a Portuguese squadron and who had been authorized by James IV to seize Portuguese ships until the equivalent of 12,000 ducats was recovered.[4]

One of the Africans in Edinburgh was a drummer ('taubronar') and choreographer. For the Shrove Tuesday festivities in 1505 he devised a dance with 12 performers in chequered black-and-white costumes, specially made at a cost of £13 2*s.* 10*d.* The king loved music, himself played both lute and clavichord, and was generous to other musicians; and he seems to have liked the drummer. He bought him a horse costing £4 4*s.* and took him at least once, with four Italian minstrels and three falconers, on the annual royal pilgrimage to the shrine of St Duthac in Tain.[5] He bought him clothes (a yellow coat, for instance), spent 28*s.* on having his drum painted ('to pay for paynting of his taubron'), paid his doctor's bills, and gave money to his wife and child – perhaps the same 'Moris barne' whom the king asked specially to see, tipping the nurse 28*s.* for bringing the baby to him.[6]

There were several young women ('More lasses') among the Africans in Edinburgh. On 11 December 1504, one of them was baptized – 'the More las wes cristinit', says the account.[7] A few years later one of these women had a poem written about her by the great Scottish poet William Dunbar, according to whom she had recently disembarked ('landet furth of the last schippis'). Dunbar describes her participation in the tournament of the black knight and the black lady, one of the spectacular shows that James IV loved as much as he loved music. The king himself played the part of the black knight – some sources say 'wild knight' – who championed the black lady in the lists, and the event was so successful in 1507 that it was repeated, more elaborately still, in the following year. The poet says the black lady had full lips and a snub nose, and skin that shone like soap; in her rich costume she gleamed as bright as a barrel of tar; when she was born the sun had to tolerate eclipse.[8] Her tournament gown alone cost £29, a tidy sum in those days. It was made of damask flowered with gold, trimmed with green and yellow taffeta; her gauze-covered sleeves and her gloves were of soft black leather and about her arm she had a gauze kerchief. Her two female attendants wore gowns of green Flemish taffeta trimmed with yellow and her two squires were dressed in white damask. She was carried in a 'chair triumphale' covered with white, yellow, purple, green, and grey Flemish taffeta – altogether £88 was spent on this stuff, which in those days was always pure silk.[9] One of her tasks was to guard the Tree of Esperance, a great artificial tree of chivalry on which the shields of challenge were hung.[10] As black knight the king beat all challengers, whether with spear, sword, or mace[11] – which was just as well since, if Dunbar's ribald poem is to be believed, the winner was rewarded by the black lady's kiss and close embrace, while losers had to 'cum behind and kis her hippis'.[12] After the 40-day tournament there were three days of feasting, culminating in a display by a conjuror who caused a cloud to descend from the roof of the Holyroodhouse banqueting hall and, as it seemed, snatch up the black lady so that she was seen no more.[13]

In 1513 there were still at least 'twa blak ladeis' at the Scottish court, and the king spent £7 on ten French crowns as a new year gift for them.[14] Clothing and shoes were bought for 'Elen More', otherwise referred to as 'Blak Elene', and she was given five French crowns in 1512, while a gown for 'blak Margaret' in the following year cost 48*s.*[15] The Scottish queen's attendants included a 'blak madin', who was given four and a quarter ells (just under five yards) of French russet, at a cost of £3 16*s.* 6*d.*[16] In the same period the bishop of Murray too had a black servant ('the Bischop of Murrais more'), who earned himself a tip of 14*s.* when he carried a present to the king.[17] In 1527 'Helenor, the blak moir' was paid 40*s.*,[18] and in 1567 and 1569 'Nageir the More' had clothing bought for him.[19]

A generation later there was still at least one African living in Edinburgh. By standing in for a lion as a pageant performer in 1594 he helped celebrate the birth of Henry Frederick, eldest son of James VI of Scotland (soon to be England's James I). It had been planned to use a lion to pull a chariot, 12 feet long and 7 feet across, bearing a 'sumpteous couered Table, decked with all sortes of exquisite delicates and dainties, of pattisserie, frutages [i.e. decorative arrangements of fruit], and confections'. But at the last minute it was feared that the lion might frighten the spectators or worse, especially if startled by the torches. So 'a Black-Moore', 'very richly attyred', pretended to haul on 'great chaines of pure gold' attached to a chariot in fact propelled by 'a secreet convoy'. Grouped around the sumptuously decked table were 'six Gallant dames', representing Ceres, goddess of agriculture, Fecundity, Faith, Concord, Liberality, and Perseverance.[20] Nothing whatever is known about the black man who 'pulled' the chariot, not even his name, but he could well have been a descendant of the group that had arrived in Scotland some 90 years earlier.

Africans in England

Around the same time as that group of Africans reached Edinburgh, a solitary black musician was living in London, employed by Henry VII and his successor, Henry VIII. Whether he came straight from Africa or from Scotland – or, indeed, as is quite possible, from Spain or Portugal – is not recorded. Nor do we know his real name. The accounts of the treasurer of the Chamber, who paid the king's musicians their wages, refer to him as John Blanke – but this, since it means 'John White', was surely an 'ironic jest'.[1] We know however that he played the trumpet, that Henry VII paid him 8*d.* a day, and that he had to wait a week for the 20*s.* due to him for the month of November 1507.[2] This 'blacke trumpet', as the accounts call him, is pretty certainly the man who is twice portrayed in the painted roll of the 1511 Westminster Tournament, held to celebrate the birth of a son to Catherine of Arragon. The most precious treasure of the College of Arms, the roll shows a black trumpeter mounted on a grey horse with black harness; his five white companions are also on horseback. All six wear yellow halved with grey and have blue purses at their waists. The white trumpeters are bare-headed, but the black trumpeter is wearing a brown turban latticed with yellow. The double-curve fanfare trumpets are decorated with the royal quarterings, fringed white and green.[3]

Forty years later, the first group of black Africans came to England. It was the summer of 1555 – before we had potatoes, or tobacco, or tea, and nine years before Shakespeare was born. Queen Mary was on the throne, had recently married Philip of Spain, and was much occupied with having heretics burnt. Some of her subjects were more interested in getting rich than in arguing about religion, and it was the pursuit of riches that caused them to bring here a group of five Africans. The visitors came from the small town of Shama, which can be found in any large atlas, on the coast of what nowadays we call Ghana. Three of them were known as Binne, Anthonie, and George; the names, real or adopted, of the other two have not come down to us. A contemporary account speaks of 'taule and stronge men' who 'coulde well agree with owr meates and drynkes' although 'the coulde and moyst ayer dooth sumwhat offende them' (tall and strong men [who] could well agree with our kind of food and drink [although] the cold and damp air gives them some trouble).[4]

The same account refers to these five Africans as slaves. Whatever their status, they had been borrowed, not bought. Englishmen were not to start trafficking in slaves for another eight years. For the time being, English merchants were simply after a share in the profits to be gained from African gold, ivory, and pepper. The Portuguese had been hogging this lucrative West African trade for more than 100 years and had long managed to keep their rich pickings secret from their European neighbours. Now the secret was out. Portugal had ardent competitors to face. But the English needed African help if they were to succeed in breaking the Portuguese monopoly. That was why John Lok, son of a prominent London merchant and alderman, brought the group of West Africans over here in 1555. The idea was that they should learn English and then go back to Africa as interpreters and, as it were, public relations men.[5]

In fact, three of them were taken home after a few months by another London merchant, William Towerson, whom they were soon helping by persuading fellow-Africans that it was safe to venture on board the *Hart* and the *Tiger* for trading purposes: the going rate for three ounces of gold was 39 brass or copper basins and two small white saucers. An eyewitness account tells how the three returning travellers were welcomed by their countrymen. At Hanta, not far from Shama, 'our Negroes were well knowen, and the men of the towne wept for joy, when they saw them'. And at Shama itself one of them was greeted by an aunt, another by a sister-in-law, and these ladies 'receiued them with much ioy, and so did all the rest of the people, as if they had bene their naturall brethren' (received them with much joy, and so did all the rest of the people, as if they had been their blood relatives).[6]

If we can detect a note of surprise here at Africans' behaving with such human warmth, that is because sixteenth-century English people were poorly informed about Africa and those who lived there. Of course, as more and more Englishmen went to Africa, were surprised and impressed by the riches and living standards of the rulers and merchants they met, and started publishing their findings in travel books, sober facts began to get mixed with the accepted myths. When Vice-Admiral Thomas Wyndham reached Benin in 1553 he found the king (*oba*) able to speak good Portuguese, which he had learnt as a child, and perfectly willing to let the Englishmen have 80 tons of pepper on credit until their next voyage.[7] Yet the same books that contained matter-of-fact reports providing accurate details of the Africans' houses, manners, dress, crops, and crafts – of their civilization, in short – gave equal weight to the fabulous Prester John, King of Ethiopia, who had attained the age of 562 back in the twelfth century. And these books reprinted, virtually unchanged, the ancient folklore of the elder Pliny (AD 23–79), a popular English version of whose description of Africa and Africans was published in 1566, entitled *A Summarie of the Antiquities, and wonders of the Worlde.*

What kind of light did this throw on the 'dark' continent? Readers were told that some Ethiopians had no noses, others no upper lips or tongues, others again no mouths. The Syrbotae were eight feet tall. The Ptoemphani were ruled by a dog. The Arimaspi had a single eye, in the forehead. The Agriophagi lived on the flesh of panthers and lions, the Anthropophagi on human flesh. There were people in Libya who had no names, nor did they ever dream. The Garamantes made no marriages; the men held the women in common. The Gamphasantes went all naked. The Cynamolgi ('dogmilkers') had heads like dogs' heads. The Blemmyes had no heads at all, but eyes and mouths in their breasts.[8] 'The laste of all the Affriens Southewarde', according to another book of the time, were the Ichthyophagi, or fish-eaters. 'Like vnto beastes', after a meal of fish washed up on the shore and baked by the sun, they would 'falle vpon their women, euen as they come to hande withoute any choyse; vtterly voide of care, by reason they are alwaye sure of meate in good plentye' (like animals . . . [they would] fall upon their women, even as they come to hand, without any choice; utterly free from care because they are always sure of plenty of food).[9]

Such fantasies tended to cement in the minds of English people the notion that Africans were inherently carefree, lazy, and lustful. By the middle of the sixteenth century this notion was taken for granted,[10] just as some English people took it for granted that every male African had an enormous penis; the tiny naked figures of Africans on more than one fifteenth-century map attest to the antiquity of that belief.[11]

We can be sure that the five Africans who visited England in 1555 were stared at very hard indeed by the local inhabitants, as was the elephant's head brought over on the same voyage – along with about 250 tusks, 36 casks of malaguetta pepper, and over 400lb of 22 carat gold[12] – and put on display in the house of Sir Andrew Judd, a prosperous London merchant and alderman. The English were prepared to swallow all kinds of yarns about elephants, too – for instance, that they were continually at war with dragons, 'which desyre theyr bludde bycause it is very coulde' (which desire their blood because it is very cold).[13] Having live Africans in their midst, and finding them human enough to tolerate English food and drink while complaining of the weather, must have taught their hosts more about Africa than staring at a dead elephant's head. From that time on, those mythical carefree, lazy, lustful cannibals were always, so to say, beyond the next river or the next mountain range.

So, although knowledge about African peoples and cultures was increasing, the pale-skinned islanders disposed to make ethnocentric generalizations about dark-skinned people from over the sea found the persistent folk myths a convenient quarry. Such myths eased English consciences about enslaving Africans and thereby encouraged the slave trade. To justify this trade, and the use of slaves to make sugar, the myths were woven into a more or less coherent racist ideology. Africans were said to be inherently inferior, mentally, morally, culturally, and spiritually, to Europeans. They were sub-human savages, not civilized human beings like us.

So there could be no disgrace in buying or kidnapping them, branding them, shipping them to the New World, selling them, forcing them to work under the whip. English racism was born of greed. (The rise of racism as an ideology is discussed in chapter 7.)

The first Englishman to line his pockets by trafficking in black slaves was an unscrupulous adventurer called John Hawkyns. On that first English triangular voyage, in 1562–3, he acquired at least 300 inhabitants of the Guinea coast. Some he bought from African merchants whose wares included domestic slaves; some he hijacked from Portuguese slavers; some he simply seized. He took these people to the Caribbean island of Hispaniola (now Haiti and the Dominican Republic), where he sold them to the Spaniards for £10,000 worth of pearls, hides, sugar, and ginger. His profit on the venture was about 12 per cent.[14] Queen Elizabeth I is said, on rather slender authority, to have warned him that carrying off Africans without their consent would be 'detestable, and would call down the Vengeance of Heaven upon the Undertakers'.[15] However that may be, she was quite happy to lend Hawkyns, for his second slave-hunting voyage (1564–5), the *Jesus of Lubeck*, a 600-ton vessel with a complement of 300 men that had been bought for the English navy and was valued at £4,000.[16] And Clarenceux King-of-Arms lost no time in augmenting Hawkyns's coat of arms with a crest showing 'a demi-Moor proper [i.e. a half-length figure in natural colouring] bound captive, with annulets on his arms and in his ears'.[17] Three black men shackled with slave-collars were displayed on the coat of arms itself – a singular honour for the city of Plymouth, whose freeman Hawkyns was, and for the English navy, whose treasurer and comptroller he was soon to become.

Though it would be another 100 years before English merchants were trafficking in slaves in a really organized way, and longer still before they succeeded in dominating the slave trade, they had started dabbling. And, as a by-product of this dabbling, African slaves were brought to England from the 1570s onwards. In the late sixteenth century they were used here in three capacities: as household servants (the majority); as prostitutes or sexual conveniences for well-to-do Englishmen and Dutchmen; and as court entertainers. There is no evidence of black people being bought and sold in this country until 1621,[18] which is not to say that it did not happen before that year. But there is clear evidence that black people were living here – and not only in London – in the last 30 years of the sixteenth century. In 1570 one Nicholas Wichehalse of

Barnstaple in Devon mentioned 'Anthonye my negarre' in his will.[19] The illegitimate daughter of Mary, described as 'a *negro of* John Whites', was baptized in Plymouth in 1594; the supposed father was a Dutchman.[20] An assessment of 'Strangers' in Barking (All Hallows parish, Tower ward) about the year 1598 shows two 'Negras' – Clare, at Widow Stokes's, and Maria, at Olyver Skynnar's – and two 'Negroes', one called perhaps Jesse or Lewse (the manuscript is hard to decipher) at Mr Miton's, the other called Marea at Mr Wood's. In the following year Clare is still at Widow Stokes's and 'Mary a Negra' is at Richard Wood's, while there is an unnamed 'blackemore, seruant to Jeronimo Lopez' also resident in the parish.[21]

Towards the end of the sixteenth century it was beginning to be the smart thing for titled and propertied families in England to have a black slave or two among the household servants. One of the first to acquire such an exotic status symbol was Lady Ralegh, wife of the Sir Walter Ralegh who figures in the history books for other innovations.[22] Her example was soon followed by the Earl of Dorset[23] and others, but the practice was not to become general until the second half of the seventeenth century. In 1599 one Denis Edwards wrote to the Earl of Hertford's secretary: 'Pray enquire after and secure my negress: she is certainly at the "Swan", a Dane's beershop, Turnbull Street, Clerkenwell.'[24] This cryptic reference has been read as suggesting the presence of black prostitutes in Elizabethan London, and there is, perhaps, supporting evidence in the fact that the part of the 'Abbess *de Clerkenwell*' – 'abbess', in this context, means brothel-keeper – in the Gray's Inn revels at Christmas 1594 was played by a woman called Lucy Negro (whom one authority identifies as Shakespeare's Dark Lady).[25] There were certainly black entertainers at court well before the turn of the century, like the 'lytle Blackamore' for whom, not long after 1577, a 'Gascon coate' was made, of 'white Taffata, cut and lyned under with tincel, striped down with gold and silver, and lined with buckram and bayes, poynted with poynts and ribands'.[26] In the 1570s Queen Elizabeth was shown with a group of black musicians and dancers entertaining her courtiers and herself. The seven musicians and three boy dancers dressed in scarlet can be seen on a painted panel supposed to depict *Queen Elizabeth and her court at Kenilworth Castle*, attributed to Marcus Gheeraerts the elder and dating from about 1575;[27] it clearly isn't Kenilworth, but such a group was by now a standard feature of every self-respecting European court, as will appear. To disguise themselves as black women in masquerades became a favourite pastime among the queen's ladies-in-waiting.[28]

Queen Elizabeth's response

However entertaining she may have found them at court, the queen was soon expressing strong disapproval of the presence of black people elsewhere in her realm and, indeed, ordering that 'those kinde of people' should be deported forthwith. This episode rarely figures in the history books, and it is easy to see why. Elizabeth's professed reasons were that there were enough people in England without 'blackmoores' (the population was around 3,000,000); that they were taking food out of her subjects' mouths (there had been a series of bad harvests); and that in any case most of them were 'infidels'. A further reason has been suggested: the widespread belief, more firmly held than ever in the reign of a virgin queen of exceptional pallor, that whiteness stood for purity, virtue, beauty, and beneficence, whereas anything black was bound to be filthy, base, ugly, and evil.[1] Like Septimius Severus, many English people did tend to think that way. But was Elizabeth's action merely crude xenophobia? To answer this question we have to examine the documents, which have rarely been printed (and the most accessible version of one of which is marred by errors of transcription).

On 11 July 1596, Elizabeth caused an open letter to be sent to the lord mayor of London and his aldermen, and to the mayors and sheriffs of other towns, in the following terms:

> Her Majestie understanding that there are of late divers blackmoores brought into this realme, of which kinde of people there are allready here to manie . . . Her Majesty's pleasure therefore ys that those kinde of people should be sent forth of the lande, and for that purpose there ys direction given to this bearer Edwarde Banes to take of those blackmoores that in this last voyage under Sir Thomas Baskervile were brought into this realme the nomber of tenn, to be transported by him out of the realme. Wherein wee require you to be aydinge and assysting unto him as he shall have occacion, therof not to faile.

> (Her Majesty understanding that several blackamoors have lately been brought into this realm, of which kind of people there are already too many here . . . her Majesty's pleasure

> therefore is that those kind of people should be expelled from the land, and for that purpose instruction is given to the bearer, Edward Banes, to take ten of those blackamoors that were brought into this realm by Sir Thomas Baskerville on his last voyage, and transport them out of the realm. In this we require you to give him any help he needs, without fail.)[2]

But that was only the beginning. A week later an open warrant was sent to the lord mayor of London and all vice-admirals, mayors, and other public officers, informing them that a Lübeck merchant called Casper van Senden, who had arranged for the release of 89 English prisoners in Spain and Portugal, was asking in return 'lycense to take up so much blackamoores here in this realme and to transport them into Spaine and Portugall' (licence to arrest the same number of blackamoors here in this realm and to transport them to Spain and Portugal). Her Majesty,

> considering the reasonablenes of his requestes to transport so many blackamoores from hence, doth thincke yt a very good exchange and that those kinde of people may be well spared in this realme . . . [Public officers] are therefore . . . required to aide and assist him to take up such blackamores as he shall finde within this realme with the consent of their masters, who we doubt not, considering her Majesty's good pleasure to have those kinde of people sent out of the lande . . . and that they shall doe charitably and like Christians rather to be served by their owne contrymen then with those kinde of people, will yielde those in their possession to him.

> (considering the reasonableness of his requests to transport so many blackamoors from here, thinks it a very good exchange and that those kind of people may be well spared in this realm . . . [Public officers] are therefore . . . required to aid and assist him to arrest such blackamoors as he shall find within this realm, with the consent of their masters, who we have no doubt – considering her Majesty's good pleasure to have those kind of people sent out of the land . . . and that, with christian love of their fellow-men, they will prefer to be served by their own countrymen rather than by those kind of people – will yield those in their possession to him.)[3]

This was an astute piece of business, which must have saved the queen a lot of money. The black people concerned were being used as payment for the return of 89 English prisoners. The government simply confiscated them from their owners – there is no mention of compensation – and handed them over to a German slave-trader.

In so far as this was a serious attempt to deport all black people from England, it failed completely. For within four years the English queen and her advisers were engaged in a second deal of the same kind. In 1601 Elizabeth issued a proclamation in which she declared herself

> highly discontented to understand the great numbers of negars and Blackamoores which (as she is informed) are crept into this realm . . . who are fostered and relieved [i.e. fed] here to the great annoyance of her own liege people, that want the relief [i.e. food], which those people consume, as also for that the most of them are infidels, having no understanding of Christ or his Gospel.

The queen had therefore given 'especial commandment that the said kind of people should be with all speed avoided [i.e. banished] and discharged out of this Her Majesty's dominions'. And, once again, Elizabeth commissioned handy Casper van Senden to arrest and transport them.[4] But this second attempt to get rid of black people was no more successful than the first. From that day to this, there has been a continuous black presence in Britain.

A Khoi-khoin in England

A 'Hottentot' known as Coree the Saldanian was one of the earliest African visitors to London – against his will, for he was kidnapped and brought here by the crew of an English ship. Hans Werner Debrunner suggests that Coree (it was spelt in many other ways too) means 'Man of the Kora (or Gorachoqua) clan';[1] Saldania was the old name for the regions round the Cape of Good Hope, where the Khoi-khoin lived. That was what they called themselves; it was the Dutch who called them 'Hottentots', a derogatory reference to the 'clicks' in their language. Coree and another Khoi-khoin were captured in 1613 when they ventured on board the *Hector*, commanded by Gabriel Towerson of the East India Company. Soon after the ship set sail Coree's companion died, 'meerly out of extreme sullenness'. When Coree reached London four months later he was put up in the house of Sir Thomas Smith, merchant and governor of the East India Company. The company wanted information from Coree that would help its trading ventures. So he was given 'good diet, good clothes, good lodging, with all other fitting accommodations', as well as a chain, armour, and buckler of brass, a metal he had not seen before and much admired.

In spite of his captors' good treatment of Coree, they were surprised to find 'none ever more desirous to return home to his Countrey than he'. After he had picked up a little English he would prostrate himself before Sir Thomas Smith, exclaiming: '*Cooree home goe, Souldania goe, home goe.*' And as soon as his foot touched his native shore he tore off his European clothes and threw them away. He did however agree to act as middleman between English traders and local people with cattle for sale. His loyalty to the English cost him his life, for in 1627 he was publicly put to death by the Dutch for refusing to trade with their ships.[2]

According to Debrunner, Coree's visit to London helped change Europe's image of the Khoi-khoin. Instead of being seen as dangerous savages they were now seen as strange and mostly harmless savages.[3]

2. 'Necessary Implements'

Sugar and slavery

Throughout the first half of the seventeenth century England's black population remained very small. Scattered from Devon across to Kent was a handful of black pages and laundrymaids and the like: young slaves used as household servants and status symbols in the mansions of English noblemen and gentry. Then, in the 1650s, their numbers began to rise steadily. Having a black slave or two in one's household soon became a craze for all who could afford it. And what started the process was the simple, everyday act of putting a spoonful of sugar into a dish of tea or coffee or chocolate.

Each of these three new beverages that English people began to drink in the 1650s had a rather bitter natural taste. So there was a growing demand for sugar, even among the very poor.[1] The increasing popularity of rum punch also promoted sugar consumption in England, which went up fourfold between 1660 and 1700 – and about twentyfold between 1663 and 1775.[2] How was a reliable and increasing supply of sugar to be obtained? The planters of St Kitts, England's first successful Caribbean colony, made no bones about it. In 1680 their council told the Lords of Trade in London: 'It is as great a bondage for us to cultivate our plantations without negro slaves as for the Egyptians to make bricks without straw.'[3] A planter on the neighbouring island of Nevis said the same thing nearly 100 years later (it must have been received wisdom in the Leeward Islands): 'It is as impossible for a Man to make Sugar without the assistance of Negroes, as to make Bricks without Straw.'[4] John Pinney knew what he was talking about, for he and his family had made a vast fortune out of the sugar produced for them by black slaves.[5] They had plenty of straw, and it made them bricks of gold. They were not the only ones.

Ships left London, Bristol, and Liverpool loaded with textiles made in Lancashire; muskets, brass rods, and cutlery made in Birmingham; copper rods and manillas (bronze rings used as a medium of exchange) made in Glamorgan, Bristol, Warrington, St Helens, and Flintshire. Cargoes also included gunpowder, felt hats, silk pieces, sailcloth, green glass, beads, spirits, tobacco, and beer brewed by Samuel Whitbread and Sir Benjamin Truman.[6] On the African coast these commodities were bartered for slaves, who were shipped across the Atlantic in the notorious middle passage. In Barbados, the Leeward Islands, Jamaica, and Surinam these young Africans were exchanged for sugar, spices, molasses, rum, and tobacco, which were carried back to Britain and sold. With a proportion of the profit more manufactured goods were bought, and the cycle began afresh. It was an ingenious system, for the ships never needed to travel empty.[7] And it was an enormously profitable system for the planters whose slaves produced the sugar, the merchant capitalists who sold them the slaves, the industrial capitalists who supplied the manufactured goods with which the slaves were bought, and the bankers and commission agents who lent money to all of them.

'The Effects of this Trade to Great Britain are beneficial to an infinite extent', declared the Committee of the Company of Merchants Trading to Africa in 1788, adding:

> In it's immediate Effect it employs about 150 Sail of Shipping which carry Annually from this Country upwards of a Million of property the greatest part Our Own Manufactures and in it's more remote Effects there is hardly any Branch of Commerce, in which this Nation is concerned that does not derive some advantage from it.[8]

Manchester and the textile industry prospered. The British Linen Company was chartered in 1746 mainly to supply merchants trading in Africa and the New World plantations 'with the like Kinds of Linen-cloth as they hitherto were obliged to purchase from foreign Nations'.[9] The Lancashire cotton manufacturers did their best to capture the market by copying Indian fabrics, popular on the African coast.[10] Cotton piece goods worth £4,381 were marketed in Africa in 1739; within 30 years the trade had soared to £98,699, or almost half of Britain's total exports in this line.[11] In 1788 the manufacturer Samuel Taylor told the Lords of Trade that the value of goods supplied each year to Africa from the Manchester area was about £200,000, of which £180,000 was for the sole purpose of buying black slaves; about 18,000 men, women, and children were employed in this manufacture, which had a capital of at least £300,000.[12] Birmingham and its gun-making, brass, cutlery, and wrought iron industries prospered, as did the copper industry in the Swansea area and elsewhere; exports to Africa of guns, unmanufactured brass, brass rods and rings, cutlery, hardware, copper rods, and manillas increased enormously (see appendix F, pp. 417–20).

Thus, at the dawn of the factory system in Britain, the trade in black slaves directly nourished several important industries and boomed precisely those four provincial towns that, in the 1801 census, ranked immediately after London: Manchester, Liverpool, Birmingham, and Bristol.[13] Still more widespread were the trade's indirect effects. There is controversy about the extent to which the threefold profits of the triangular trade as a whole financed Britain's industrial revolution. The evidence marshalled by the late Eric Williams shows that they gave it, at the very least, a shot in the arm.[14] Funds accumulated from the triangular trade helped to finance James Watt's steam engine,[15] the south Wales iron and coal industries,[16] the south Yorkshire iron industry,[17] the north Wales slate industry,[18] the Liverpool and Manchester Railway,[19] and the Great Western Railway.[20] Rising British capitalism had a magic money machine, an endless chain with three links: sugar cultivation; manufacturing industry; and the slave trade. And the slave trade was the 'essential link'.[21] The whole system 'was frankly regarded as resting on slavery'.[22]

Sir Henry Bennet, secretary of state, received a letter in 1663 from a friend visiting Surinam, then in English hands, who told him plainly: 'Were the planters supplied with negroes, the strength and sinews of this western world, they would advance their fortunes and his Majesty's customs.'[23] 'Of all the Things we have occasion for, *Negroes* are the most necessary, and the most valuable', wrote Edward Littleton, agent for Barbados and former judge there, in 1689.[24] The mercantilist MP Charles Davenant – the mercantilists based their thinking on the principle that only money is wealth – supported Littleton's view in his *Discourses on the Publick Revenues* (1698):

> So great a part of our Foreign Business arising from these Colonies, they ought undoubtedly to have all due Encouragement, and to be plentifully supply'd, and at reasonable rates, with *Negroes* to meliorate and cultivate the Land. The labour of these Slaves, is the principal Foundation of our Riches there; upon which account we should take all probable Measures to bring them to us at easie Terms . . .
>
> Slaves are the first and most necessary Material for

> Planting; from whence follows, That all Measures should be taken that may produce such a Plenty of them, as may be an Encouragement to the industrious Planter.[25]

In 1729 the merchant Joshua Gee whole-heartedly agreed:

> OUR Trade with *Africa* is very profitable to the Nation in general; it has this Advantage, that it carries no Money out, and not only supplies our Plantations with Servants, but brings in a great Deal of Bullion for those that are sold to the *Spanish* West-Indies . . . The supplying our Plantations with Negroes is of that extraordinary Advantage to us, that the Planting Sugar and Tobacco, and carrying on Trade there could not be supported without [t]hem; which Plantations . . . are the great Cause of the Increase of the Riches of the Kingdom . . . All this great Increase of our Treasure proceeds chiefly from the Labour of Negroes in the *Plantations.*[26]

The mercantilist writer Malachy Postlethwayt put it like this:

> If we have no *Negroes*, we can have no *Sugars*, *Tobaccoes*, *Rice*, *Rum*, &c. . . . consequently, the Publick *Revenue*, arising from the Importation of *Plantation-Produce*, must be annihilated: And will this not turn many hundreds of Thousands of *British Manufacturers* a Begging . . . ?[27]

In other words:

> The extensive Employment of our Shipping in, to, and from *America*, . . . and the daily Bread of the most considerable Part of our *British Manufacturers*, are owing primarily to the Labour of *Negroes* . . .
>
> The *Negroe-Trade* therefore . . . may be justly esteemed an inexhaustible Fund of Wealth and Naval Power to this Nation.[28]

To a later writer, the slave trade was 'the first principle and foundation of all the rest; the main spring of the machine, which sets every wheel in motion'.[29]

Everything, in short, depended on a plentiful supply of black labour in the great Caribbean sugar-bowl. The planters looked on black slaves as replaceable tools for producing sugar, an attitude summed up in such remarks as 'the Negroes come here ready made, the bags of sugar have yet to be made'.[30] And, as the demand for these 'ready made' tools became more insistent and the British slave trade flourished, the black population of Britain itself grew.

For close on 150 years young black slaves were brought to Britain as household servants by planters who, having made their fortunes, came back home to spend them and lead the sweet life of the absentee sugar baron. It was estimated in 1774 that as many as 2,000 Jamaican annuitants and proprietors were non-residents. There were said to be 100 gentlemen from Barbados constantly in England, and growing absenteeism was reported from Britain's other Caribbean colonies.[31] In 1778 the Earl of Shelburne remarked in a Lords debate that 'there was scarce a space of ten miles together, throughout this country, where the house and estate of a rich West Indian were not to be seen'.[32] 'As rich as a West Indian' was an everyday saying. In the next chapter we shall be looking at the powerful West India lobby, which exerted 'an influence over British politics far greater than any of its contemporaries'.[33] Here we are concerned with the West Indians' social life. Their grand dinner-parties were so well attended that Londoners complained about the carriages blocking the streets for some distance around.[34] Many West Indians lived in Bristol and Southampton, and they were familiar figures in such fashionable resorts as Bath, Cheltenham, and Epsom. People laughed at these parvenus as they dissipated their fortunes at the gaming table and on the race-course. We read about them in Smollett's *Humphry Clinker* (1771):

> Every upstart of fortune . . . presents himself at Bath, as in the very focus of observation – . . . planters, negro-drivers, and hucksters, from our American plantations, enriched they know not how . . . Knowing no other criterion of greatness, but the ostentation of wealth, they discharge their affluence without taste or conduct, through every channel of the most absurd extravagance.[35]

Noblemen and royals looked on the West Indians with a cold eye. King George III and Pitt, on a visit to Weymouth, came across the imposing equipage of a Jamaica planter, with outriders and other attendants in pretentious livery. Very put out, the king exclaimed to his prime minister: 'Sugar, sugar, eh? all *that* sugar! How are the duties, eh, Pitt, how are the duties?'[36] Dr John Fothergill, first person to recognize diphtheria in England, recognized another disease in the West Indians and described it with a sharp pen:

> Bred for the most part at the Breast of a Negro Slave; surrounded in their Infancy with a numerous Retinue of these dark Attendants, they are habituated by Precept and Example, to Sensuality, Selfishness, and Despotism. Of those sent over to this Country for their Education, few totally emerge from their first Habitudes . . . Splendor, Dress, Shew, Equipage, every thing that can create an Opinion of their Importance, is exerted to the utmost of their Credit . . . An opulent West Indian vies in Glare with a Nobleman of the first Distinction.[37]

In the 1670s about 300 sons of West Indian planters were coming to England every year for their education. A hundred years later, three-quarters of the planters' children – daughters as well as sons by now – were doing so.[38] It was in order to continue living in the grand way they had got used to on their plantations[39] that the West Indians and their offspring brought back to England their 'numerous Retinue of . . . dark Attendants'.

Young black slaves were also brought to Britain by the officers of slave-ships. In Bristol and Liverpool and Shadwell you could tell a slaver captain by the 12- or 14-year-old black lad who trudged through the streets at his heels. Captains, mates, ships' surgeons and, sometimes, ordinary seamen were allowed a few 'privilege Negroes' from each cargo as perks. Many of these people were sold off in the West Indies. Those brought to this country were sold privately to rich families or bequeathed to friends[40] – or, as we shall see later, exposed for public sale. In 1702 the Royal African Company ordered its factor in Sierra Leone to 'put on board every one of the Company's ships trading to and from England or the West Indies Two Negroe Boyes Between Sixteen and Twenty Years of Age for the use of the Ships',[41] and many of these young men jumped ship when they got to Britain. Other black slaves, Asians as well as Africans, were brought by government officials and army and navy officers returning from service abroad and by the captains of ordinary merchant ships. Lastly, there were Africans who came here as free seamen, recruited to take the place of English crew members who had died or deserted on the African coast; though intending to go home on a later voyage, they often found themselves stranded in Britain.[42] But the great majority of black people who came here were brought as slaves, and most of these were very young.

Chattels and status symbols

For some Englishmen the idea of buying and selling human beings went against the grain. Trading up the Gambia river in 1620, Captain Richard Jobson was offered young female slaves but refused point-blank to buy. He told the Manding merchant that the English were 'a people who did not deale in any such commodities, neither did wee buy or sell one another, or any that had our own shapes'. When the merchant protested that slaves were sold to other 'white men, who earnestly desired them, especially such young women, as hee had brought for vs', Jobson explained that those white men 'were another kinde of people different from vs'.[1]

Even in 1620, Jobson's principles must have seemed rather old-fashioned. As it turned out, English traders were not all that different – just slower to get organized than, say, the Dutch, whose West India Company was formed in 1621 and on whom the English largely but not exclusively depended for their supply of slaves over the next 40 years.[2] Evidence of English trafficking in slaves before the 1660s is scrappy, but it does exist. In 1626 the London trader Maurice Thompson, in association with Thomas Combe of Southampton, equipped three ships that conveyed 60 slaves, presumably Africans, to St Kitts.[3] Four years later two English merchants complained to the Privy Council that their slave-carrying ship the *Benedictine* had been seized by the French, and they wrote of their 'accustomed trade'. This could imply the slave trade, or it could simply mean that their ship was carrying an unusual cargo in its usual place.[4] By 1637, when the *Talbot* was fitted out by John Crispe and his partners to take 'nigers' in Guinea and 'carry them to foreign parts' – under pretext of trading licitly on the Barbary coast – there is nothing to suggest that this was at all out-of-the-way. The Privy Council put a stop to this venture, not because Crispe and his collaborators were slaving but because they were interlopers. Gradually, the English were 'becoming habituated'.[5] With rare exceptions, such as Jobson, slavery 'caused liberty-loving Englishmen no serious searchings of conscience'.[6]

Not until 1663 did an English company, the Royal Adventurers into Africa, obtain a charter specifying slaves as an objective. 'How necessary it is', declared the company's prospectus, 'that the *English* Plantations in *America* should have a competent [i.e. sufficient] and a constant supply of *Negro-servants* for their own use of Planting, and that at a moderate Rate.'[7] The Royal Adventurers were incorporated for 1,000 years – though they were to collapse rather sooner through mismanagement and be succeeded by a new monopoly, the Royal African Company. And the grandest and richest people in England were eager for a slice of slave pie. The Royal Adventurers included the king and queen, the queen mother, a prince, 3 dukes, 7 earls, a countess, 6 lords, and 25 knights. Aristocracy and gentry held about a quarter of the stock; the rest was snapped up by merchants and City men.[8] For this august company, a new gold coin was struck: from 1663, English wealth would be measured in *guineas*.

A Company of Adventurers of London Trading into the Parts of Africa had been created by James I as early as 1618. Better known as the Guinea Company, it was reconstructed in 1631 or 1632. Its early history is very obscure, but by 1651 its administrators could ask their 'Loving Freind' and chief factor, James Pope, on the eve of his departure for West Africa, to do a bit of shopping for them: 'Wee pray you buy for us 15 or 20 young lusty Negers of about 15 years of age, bring them home with you for London, laying in that Countrey provisions for them, as you shall see needful.'[9] A few weeks later they were instructing the master of the frigate *Supply* that he would have to take on board, when he reached the Guinea coast, 'so many negers as yo'r ship can cary'. Their letter added an important warning. They had provided him with '30 pairs of shackles and boults for such of your negers as are rebellious and we pray you to be veary carefull to keepe them under and let them have their food in due season that they ryse not against you, as they have done in other ships.'[10]

So not all the black people who, as Queen Elizabeth I had put it, 'crept into this realm' were brought here in chains – just the openly 'rebellious' ones. But they were brought, these children and teenagers from Africa and the West Indies, as menials or body-servants or pets. The Guinea Company, as we have just seen, preferred 15-year-olds despite the problems caused by that age-group's hunger, for food and freedom. Sometimes, along with a gaudy parrot or two and other exotic gifts, a rich traveller would bring back a black child as a present for his own children, to be their page and plaything. The diarist Samuel Pepys records how, in 1662, the Earl of Sandwich, who had been abroad on government business, brought his daughters 'a little Turke and a negro' besides 'many birds and other pretty noveltys'.[11] The official record of the arrival of the *Fountain* at Spithead from Guinea in December 1667 says: 'An agent formerly there has returned, and brought with him a great many small blacks.'[12] In 1701 the Royal African Company ordered its agent-general at Cape Coast to buy boys and girls of 12 to 15 years in preference to adults over 30;[13] and, as we shall see, this preference was often expressed in the eighteenth century.

Advertisements raising a hue and cry after escaped black slaves appeared in England as soon as there were newspapers to publish them.[14] Printed alongside advertisements offering canaries for sale, or puffing 'the famous Oyl for giving Ease in the Gout' or quack remedies for pox and clap, they rarely speak of runaways over 20. Most are in their teens; now and again, a child as young as eight or nine has made a dash for freedom. Indeed, 'a Negro-boy about nine years of age, in a gray Searge-suit' is the subject of one of the earliest of these advertisements, in a newspaper (technically speaking, a 'news-book') of 1659.[15] In 1686 Lady Broughton of Marchwhiel Hall near Wrexham in Denbighshire offers a guinea reward for the return of her black boy, about 14 years old, who has been 'taken away . . . by a Person on Horse back'.[16] A 'Negro Boy about 9 years old' is reported missing in 1687,[17] and three years later an anxious owner is offering 20*s*. reward for the return of 'a Guinea Negro Boy, about 8 years old, named Jack, straight Limb'd', who has 'strayed away'.[18] More was offered for strayed and stolen dogs and horses.[19]

These advertisements also show that black slaves in England, though not normally kept in chains,[20] were customarily obliged to wear metal collars riveted round their necks. Made of brass, copper, or silver, the collar was generally inscribed with the owner's name, initials, coat of arms, or other symbol. In 1686 we read of a black boy of about 15 years of age, named John White, who had run away from Colonel Kirke: 'he has a Silver Collar about his Neck, upon which is the Colonel's Coat of Arms and Cipher.'[21] A 16-year-old runaway, said to have made off from the Tower of London with about £10 in silver and a guinea (it sounds quite an achievement) had 'a Silver Collar about his Neck, Engraven, Thomas Dymock at the Lyon Office'.[22] Another advertisement tells of 'a Negro Man of a Tawny Complexion . . . with a down cast look . . . he walks with his Chin in his Bosom, a piece of one of his Ears cut off, with a Brass Collar about his Neck, he talks very bad English, and is called Ned'.[23] In 1690 'a Negro Boy, named Toney, aged about 16, was lost from Ratcliff . . . He has a Brass Collar on, with directions where he liv'd'.[24] In the following year, 'a black Boy, called John Moor, aged 10 years', was wearing a 'Silver Collar about his Neck' when he ran away.[25] William III, King of England from 1689 to 1702, had a favourite black slave, a bust of whom used to be on display at Hampton Court, complete with 'carved white marble collar, with a padlock, in every respect like a dog's collar'.[26]

These metal collars were taken for granted in the literature of the time. When Dryden wrote a prologue for the stage in 1690, he included a satirical proposal that the English troops then fighting in Ireland should

> Each bring his Love, a *Bogland* Captive home,
> Such proper Pages, will long Trayns become;
> With Copper-Collars, and with brawny Backs,
> Quite to put down the Fashion of our Blacks.[27]

And a character in Cibber's comedy *The Double Gallant*, printed in 1707, speaks of Lord Outside's 'frightful *Blackamore* Coachman, with his Flat-nose, and great Silver Collar'.[28]

Again and again in the advertisements for runaway slaves there are references to scars, especially on the head; and it doesn't take a great deal of imagination to guess how they came there. The 15-year-old John White who ran away from Colonel Kirke in 1686 had 'upon his Throat a great Scar, bare in Habit'[29] (I take these last three words to mean that it was visible when he was dressed). A runaway called Tom Black, about 15 or 16 years old, had 'a scar in his Head lately broken'.[30] Another, about 21 years old, had 'a scarr on his Temple, a great many scarrs on his Neck'.[31] 'A Negro Boy, about 15 years old', who 'went away on Christmas day in the morning', had 'a Scar on the left-side of his Forehead, and a Scratch between his Eye brows'.[32] Another, 'about 9 years old', had 'a Scar on the left side of his Forehead'.[33] A runaway 'black Boy, well-favour'd, call'd Peter, speaks pretty good English, having been from Surinam almost 3 years', was 'about 12 years old' and had 'a small Scar on his upper Lip'.[34] Though slaves were normally branded on the body, a 26-year-old advertised for in 1691 had '2 Rings burnt in his Forehead almost wore out'.[35] The politician Sir John Reresby was accused of castrating the 'fine More about sixteen years of age', given him by a Mr Drax who had brought the lad from Barbados; a post-mortem examination showed that this charge was false.[36]

These young black slaves were almost entirely at their owners' mercy. The case of Katherine Auker shows how much protection the law gave them. She asked the Middlesex sessions in 1690 to discharge her from her master, a Barbados planter called Robert Rich, who had brought her to England about six years before. When she had herself baptized – a ceremony widely but wrongly supposed to confer freedom on slaves – her master and mistress 'tortured her and turned her out; her said master refusing to give her a discharge, she could not be "entertained in service elsewhere" '. Her master, now back in Barbados, had caused her to be arrested and imprisoned. The court maintained a neat balance between property rights and the rights of the individual by ordering that she be free to serve anyone – until her master returned to England.[37]

It would be nonsense to suggest that all masters and mistresses treated their black chattels with brutality. In general, the higher up the social scale the owner was, the less did the slave have to fear physical violence, if only because the rich paid good money for their slaves and were careful to protect their investment. King Charles II paid £50 for a black slave he bought from the Marquis of Antrim in 1682.[38] And when we find Pepys writing in glowing terms of his new cook-maid, 'a black-moore of Mr. Batelier's (Doll), who dresses our meat mighty well, and we mightily pleased with her',[39] we cannot imagine him or his wife beating a cook that gave such satisfaction – though, Pepys being Pepys, he may have subjected her to other forms of harassment.

But black people fortunate enough not to be struck on the head, whipped, or otherwise brutalized were nevertheless denied elementary human dignity. Their own African names, filled with meaning, were taken from them. It was the fashion for black slaves owned by titled families, by high-class prostitutes, and by others with social pretensions to be given high-sounding Greek or Roman names: Zeno, for instance, or Socrates, or Scipio – or even Scipio Africanus. Commonest was Pompey, which by the 1750s had virtually become a generic term for a black servant;[40] from black servants 'it descended to little dogs'.[41] But not every titled family followed this convention. The Sackvilles, Earls (afterwards Dukes) of Dorset, defied it and established a tradition of their own. They had a black page at Knole, their huge mansion in Kent, from the days of Lady Anne Clifford, who became countess in 1609, and he was always called John Morocco 'regardless of what his true name might be'.[42] The Sackvilles' black laundrymaid, acquired some time between 1613 and 1624, was called Grace Robinson.[43] The politician and satirist George Villiers, second Duke of Buckingham, gave the name Tom to the 'poor Ignorant Lad just come from *Guinea*' whom he took with him as servant when appointed English ambassador to Paris in 1670. Though this 'young *Black-a-more* Boy . . . cou'd just make a shift to be understood in *English*', the duke found his comments on the mass he saw in Notre Dame diverting and thought-provoking enough to be quoted in an argument with an Irish Jesuit.[44]

Even in death, a black slave in Britain might be denied human dignity. One at least, in place of burial, was preserved as a curiosity and talking-point for guests. When Pepys was entertained in 1665 by the goldsmith-banker Sir Robert Vyner, one of England's richest men, he was shown 'a black boy that he had that died of a consumption; and being dead, he caused him to be dried in a Oven, and lies there entire in a box'.[45]

Rich people would often display their wealth and good taste by dressing their black slaves in special costume: either obviously expensive garments or some kind of showy livery. This can be studied in the many portraits of aristocrats that conventionally include a black child – no doubt as a foil or status symbol or both. Tucked into a corner of the painting, the child might be shown with jewelled eardrops and a fillet to bind the hair, as in the portrait of Sir Thomas Herbert, friend of Charles I, that hangs at Upper Helmsley Hall, near York.[46] Or, if female, she might be wearing a necklace, laced bodice, and laced cuffs, and holding a branch of coral and her mistress's jewel-case, as in Pierre Mignard's 1682 portrait of Louise de Kéroualle, Duchess of Portsmouth and friend of Charles II, that hangs in the National Portrait Gallery. This duchess, complete with black page, was also painted by Sir Godfrey Kneller, who included black servants in his portraits of the Duchess of Ormonde, the Duke of Schomberg, and Captain Thomas Lucy, too.[47] As early as 1628 Sir James Bagg of Plymouth ordered that his newly arrived 'negrowe' should be 'handsomely clothed'.[48] That might mean a blue livery suit trimmed with a narrow, closely woven braid of silk or gold or silver thread called galloon and lined with orange cloth, with silk-fringed sleeves and gold galloon on the facing;[49] or maybe 'a Fustian Frock with yellow Mettal Buttons, a blue Livery Coat lined with red, with yellow Mettal Buttons, a red Waistcoat, Breeches and Stockings', and a 'Hat laced with Silver Orris'[50] – a kind of fine gold or silver bobbin-lace.

Pageant performers

More decorative still were the costumes chosen for the black people who often performed in the Lord Mayor's Pageant, the annual festival of London's merchant capitalists, demonstrating the wealth of the metropolis and showing how a lot of it was obtained. The pageant replaced the Midsummer Show or Watch, in which a 'King of the Moors', played by a white actor, had traditionally symbolized Africa, that rich, exotic, and mysterious continent. In 1521 this character (played by one John Wakelyng, whose fee was 5*s.* for the two nights) was dressed in red and black satin, with shoes made of silver paper and a canopy held over his head. His 50 attendant male 'morians' (at 4*d.* each for the two nights) and one female 'morian' (at 8*d.*) seem to have performed as tumblers. He was supplied with fireworks, probably to clear the way for the pageant. He appeared again in the 1536 Midsummer Show, mounted on horseback with 12 attendant 'morians'.[1] A 'Luzerne' or lynx, carried by two lads and led by a 'moryne' and two wildmen armed with clubs and squibs, figured in the 1551 pageant; a player 'apparelled like a Moore' rode on the effigy of a lynx in 1585. 'Two Moores rydeing vppon vnicornes' took part in the 1611 pageant;[2] these may have been black performers.

Continuing many of the traditions of the Midsummer Show,[3] the Lord Mayor's Pageant was paid for by the livery company to which the incoming lord mayor belonged and was staged, often very elaborately and expensively, on the day he took his oath of office. The livery company responsible would commission a dramatist or 'City poet' to write a libretto, complete with detailed description of the scenes, florid speeches, songs and even, sometimes, music. In the pageant written by the dramatist Thomas Middleton for the Grocers' Company in 1613, the 'King of the Moores, his Queene, and two Attendants of their owne colour' made an appearance on 'a strange Ship'. The king, who seemed much astonished 'at the many eies of such a multitude', made a long speech beginning with the words:

I see amazement set vpon the faces
Of these white people, wondrings, and strange gazes,
Is it at mee? do's my Complexion draw
So many Christian Eyes, that neuer saw
A King so blacke before?

Soon he was announcing that he had been converted to christianity by the '*Religious Conuersation/Of English Merchants*', and he and his companions, infidels no longer, were 'bowing their bodies to the Temple of Saint *Paul*'.[4] In 1616 he appeared again, with six 'tributarie Kings on horse-backe', in a pageant written for the Fishmongers' Company by the dramatist Anthony Munday. This time he was 'gallantly mounted on a golden Leopard' and 'hurling gold and siluer euery way about him'. A contemporary coloured picture of the scene makes it clear that these were white performers.[5] The dramatist John Webster, son of a tailor and a freeman of the Merchant Taylors' Company, included 'a Moore or wild *Numidian*' riding on a lion in the pageant he wrote for that company in 1624.[6]

The first pageant performer that can be positively identified as black appeared in the pageant written for the ironmongers by the dramatist Thomas Dekker in 1629. Dekker's libretto refers to 'an Indian boy, holding in one hand a long *Tobacco pipe*, in the other a dart', and riding on a wooden ostrich with a horseshoe in its mouth.[7] In the University of Utrecht library there is a contemporary sketch by a visiting Dutchman of this black performer and his horseshoe-biting steed.[8] In the 1656 pageant there were 'two Leopards bestrid by two Moors';[9] by this date, these were certainly black performers, too; so, most likely, were the four attendants who represented Africa in the following year and heard the lord mayor informed that

> The Ill-
> -Complexion'd *Affrican* into your Breast
> Poures forth his Spicie Treasure.[10]

Africa was also personified, riding on a griffin – an imaginary creature with lion's body, eagle's beak, and wings – in the next year's pageant.[11]

In 1663 there were 'two Negroes, habited [i.e. dressed] very costly after their manner', seated on the backs of 'two Leopards richly set out'.* Each of the two black riders held two banners, one with the arms of the City of London, the other with those of the Skinners' Company.[12] The same company was responsible for the 1671 pageant, written by the City poet Thomas Jordan, which opened with a scene depicting 'two *Negro* Boys, properly Habited [i.e. handsomely dressed], and mounted upon two Panthers, bearing the Banners of the Lord Mayor's and the Companies Arms'. At the top of a 'stately' pyramid with four triumphal arches sat a 'female Negra richly and properly adorned with Silver, Gold, and Jewels, representing *Africa*'. A later scene included '*two Negroes richly adorned with Oriental Pearl and Jewels, mounted upon two Panthers*'.[13]

The next year came the first of the many spectacular shows staged

* It should be borne in mind that the word *Negro* in this period could mean an Asian as well as an African (or person of African descent). Sometimes a performer is identified as one or the other, or the costume provides a clue – though black performers were often required to personate American 'Indians'.

by the Grocers' Company in which, to give yet more spice to the proceedings, black performers were used for the traditional custom of throwing foreign fruits and spices into the crowds to be scrambled for. Jordan's pageant opened with a scene showing a black youth mounted on a model of the Grocers' Company crest (a 'Camel artfully Carved, and properly painted, which is neer as big as the life, and sheweth very Magnificently'), scattering raisins, almonds, dates, figs, and prunes from two baskets 'with a plentiful hand':

> This *Negro* holds in one hand a Banner of the Kings Arms, his Bridle is of red and white Ribon, (being the Companies Colours,) on his head he wares a Garland or rather Wreath of Feathers, at each side of him stand a Goddess; the one representing *Plenty* . . . On the other hand standeth a young Virgin representing *Concord.*

Two black performers representing 'Princes of *West-India*' were 'attired properly in diverse colour'd Silks, with Silver or Gold Wreaths or Coronets upon their Heads, . . . adorned with Necklaces, pendants, and Bracelets of Jewels and Pearls, and Javelins in their Hands'. Near them sat 'three other *Black-Moors*, in antick [i.e. bizarre] attire, their habits all consisting of diverse delightful colour'd Silks and gaudy Feathers'; these were holding the banners of the king, the City, the lord mayor, and the Grocers' Company. Two more banner-bearing black performers, in Indian costume, were mounted on 'large Gryphons', the supporters of the company's arms. And in a 'Wilderness or Desart', somewhere in '*West-India*', the crowds saw a group of

> Tawny *Moors*, who are laborious in gathering, carrying, setting, sorting, sowing, and ordering the Fruits and other Physical Plants of their Country . . . there are also three Pipers, and several Kitchen Musicians, that Play upon Tongs, Gridiron, Keys, and other such-like confused Musick; whilst others are Dancing and shewing Tricks.

Then the crowds heard 'a proper Masculine Woman [i.e. a woman who was handsome and had the qualities – such as, for instance, strength – thought proper to a man], with a tawny Face' declare:

> THat I the better may Attention draw,
> Be pleas'd to know I am *America*.

At the end of her speech, the labourers and pipers sang:

We labour all day, but we frollick at Night,
With smoaking and joking, and tricks of Delight.[14]

Jordan's 1673 pageant, performed before Charles II and his queen, Catherine of Braganza, again opened with 'a *Negro*-Boy, beautifully Black', mounted on 'a Camel of magnitude, lively carved, and aptly painted', and scattering foreign fruit from two silver panniers as before. Once again the crowds were entertained with 'the Effigies of two great Gryphons . . . on whose backs are two *Negroes* properly mounted', holding London's and the grocers' armorial banners. A 'Scene of Drolls' showed 'a Garden of Fruits and Spices, where the Black and Tawny Inhabitants are very actively imployed, some in Working and Planting, others Carrying and re-carrying; some are Drolling, Piping, Dancing and Singing' – to the accompaniment of three pipes, tongs, a key, a frying-pan, a gridiron, and a salt-box. (Jordan punningly calls this 'very melodious Musick, which, the worse it is performed, the better it is accepted'. But the carefully chosen texture of contrasting sonorities – clappers, gong, scraper, and rattle – strongly suggests that these players in 1672 and 1673 were black musicians using the best available local substitutes for African vernacular instruments.)[15] A 'Lady of comely Proportion and pleasant Complexion', representing Pomona, goddess of plantations, orchards, and fruits, began her speech with the lines:

I Am the Pregnant Goddess of these Brutes,
That Plant and Gather all delicious Fruits.[16]

In Jordan's 1674 pageant for the goldsmiths, '*AFFRICA*' was represented by 'a tall Person, with a Face, Shoulders, Breast and Neck, all black'. She wore pearl necklaces and jewelled ear-rings, and 'a Coronet of upright Feathers' on her 'black woolly-curl'd Hair'; at her back was a quiver of arrows, in her right hand she held a bow, in her left the lord mayor's banner.[17] 'Two Negro's in Robes of Silver', astride 'large and lively carved Lions in Gold', figured in the 1675 pageant, staged by the Drapers' Company. Wearing feathered head-dresses, they represented Strength and Concord.[18] Three years later, when it was the grocers' turn again, their armorial camel was

> so curiously Carved and Exquisitely Gilded that it appeareth like a live Animal in a Hide of Massy Gold . . . This Camel is back'd by a young Negro-Boy, sitting betwixt two Silver Hampers plentifully stored with all sorts of Fruits and fragrant

> Spices, and what ever else is pertinent to Grocery; which . . . the Negro with a Prodigal hand, scatereth abroad in the Tumult, where you might see an hundred persons confusedly scrambling in the dirt for the Frail Atchievement of a Bunch of Raisins, or a handful of Dates, Almonds, Nutmegs: This Negro-Boy is habited in an Indian Robe of divers Colours, a wreath of various-colour'd Feathers on his black woolly head. Silver Buskins [i.e. high boots] laced and surfled [i.e. embroidered] with Gold, a Bridle of white and red Ribon . . . at each hand of him sitteth a Virgin, one of them representing *Industry* . . . The other Person is a beautiful young Lady representing *Fortune*.

The camel's supporters also returned: 'two great Golden Gryphons . . . on which are Vigorously mounted two Active Negro's, in rich *East-Indian* Vestments' and the customary feathered coronets.[19] 'Two *Negro's*, richly and properly habited' rode on the drapers' golden lions that drew a royal chariot in the next year's pageant;[20] and in 1680 the merchant tailors also had a golden lion, ridden by 'a Young *Negro* Prince' representing Power.[21] In 1681 the grocers' camel was once more ridden by 'a young *Negro* betwixt two Silver Panniers, who representeth *Liberality*, as appeareth by his Bountiful distribution of those Delicates which are . . . the delicious Traffic of the *Grocers* Company'. The incoming lord mayor was called Sir John Moore, and Jordan did not let slip the opportunity to include some puns on his name. In a garden of spices were 'several Planters, Tumblers, Dancers and Vaulters, all Blacks, Men and Women, who are supposed to be brought over . . . to celebrate the Day, and to delight his Lordship with their ridiculous Rusticity'. One of the performers sang these words put into his mouth:

> A Merchant of Fame,
> Let's love him for shame,
> For *Moor* is our Nature, and *Moor* is his Name;
> They feast him with Dainties, in peace let him Reign;
> The *More is his* Honour, the *More* is our *Gain*.[22]

In the 1687 pageant, written by the City poet Matthew Taubman, 'two beautiful young *Negroes*', attired in 'the richest Dress' of Barbary and Guinea, rode on the 'excellently carv'd and painted' golden unicorns of the Goldsmiths' Company.[23] The dramatist Elkanah Settle's 1691 pageant for the drapers opened with 'two *Negroes* in their Native Habit' riding on golden lions.[24] In the following year Settle had 'a Negro habited according to the *Indian* Manner' throwing fruit into the crowds from the back of the grocers' golden camel;[25] while in 1693 an Asian and an African on camel-back, 'in their Richest Robes', intimated their 'Submission to the Heroick Monarch of *Great Britain*, the sole Soveraign of the Sea'.[26] A plantation scene in 1695 showed 'several Persons in Rural Habits, as *Negroes*, *Tawneys*, *Virginia-Planters*, *&c.*'[27] The 1708 pageant, the last of its kind, was written but not performed. Cancelled because of the death of Queen Anne's husband, it was to have featured a temple of Apollo drawn by 'Six stately Horses, each Horse mounted by a Negroe, sumptuously drest after the *Moorish* Garb in white Feathers and other Ornaments', and a chariot of Justice, with 'Two Negroes, as Charioteers' mounted on the goldsmiths' golden unicorns – a scene which, though it did not take place, was illustrated in anticipation in Settle's libretto.[28]

A black woman entertainer at London's Bartholomew Fair towards the end of the seventeenth century is briefly referred to by Ned Ward in his boisterous classic *The London Spy* (1698–9). This '*Negro* Woman' was a rope dancer, half acrobat, half posture girl. Ward describes how 'with much Art and Agility, she . . . exercis'd her well-Proportioned Limbs, to the great satisfaction of the Spectators', and how a 'Countrey Fellow' – a west countryman by his accent – 'Cackled' to see '*the Devil going to Dance*'. A little later

> up steps the *Negro*, to the top of the Booth, and began to play at Swing Swang, with a Rope, as if the *Devil* were in her, Hanging sometimes by a Hand, sometimes by a Leg, and sometimes by her Toes; so that I found, let her do what she would, Providence or Destiny would by no means suffer the Rope to part with her.[29]

Since possession of a black slave was such an emblem of riches, rank, and fashion in England, and had such desirably exotic overtones, it is not surprising that innkeepers and tobacconists should have cashed in on the vogue by using portraits or caricatures of black people as commercial signs. Between 1541 and the middle of the nineteenth century 61 taverns called 'Black Boy' are recorded in the capital and many more in the provinces; and in the same period London had 51 establishments known as 'The Blackamoor's Head'.[30] It also became fashionable to give English ships names like *Black Boy* and *Ethiopian* (both seized by the Dutch in 1661).[31] But perhaps the status of London's black population in the second half of the seventeenth century is best conveyed in a little book published in 1675, called *The Character of a Town Misse*. 'Town miss' was a euphemism for the fashionable high-class whore of the period, who the book says 'hath always two necessary Implements about her, a *Blackamoor*, and a little *Dog*; for without these, she would be neither *Fair* nor *Sweet*'.[32]

Though their largest concentration was in London, black people were scattered all over England in the second half of the century. Parish records, far from exhaustive, show a black presence in Plymouth, Bedfordshire, Essex, and Cumberland.[33] Twelve black slaves were living with their families in Nottinghamshire in 1680; in the same period the Jenkinsons of Claxby, near Market Rasen, in Lincolnshire owned a black slave whose master killed him in a fit of drunken rage, and a black slave called Richard Zeno was living with his master in Friston, east Suffolk.[34] In 1704 Charles Mason, MP for Bishop's Castle, Shropshire, had a black page-boy from the West Indies, 'aged about 10', who was baptized Charles Hector.[35]

The earliest indication of black people living in Bristol comes in 1645, when a '*Blackymore maide*' called Frances, 'a servant to one that lived upon ye Back of Bristoll', joined a Bristol church.[36] In 1677 Ann Atkins, a 'Dark woman', was baptized and joined the same church; she died 18 years later.[37] In 1687 there was a court case involving an African woman known as Dinah Black, who had been living as a slave in Bristol for five years. Her mistress, Dorothy Smith, wanted to send her to the plantations. The law was not yet clear about whether this could be done against a slave's will. Dinah Black was rescued from the ship just in time, 'but her mistress (who had doubtless sold her) refused to take her back; and it was therefore ordered that she should be free to earn her living until the case was heard at the next sessions.'[38] Unfortunately the sessions book is lost, so it is not known how this case was decided. Another black woman, baptized in a west-country church and given the name Queen Anstis, became known locally as 'the Black Queen'; she died young, 'and to this day her spirit is supposed to haunt Church Lane near the site of her tomb'.[39]

By the turn of the century Bristol and London were both thriving slave ports. But Liverpool was beginning to challenge and would soon overtake both of them. Ahead of these British ports lay 100 years of gigantic profits from the transportation and sale of millions of Africans. Several thousands from among those millions, mostly very young, were spared from the plantations. These youngsters made the third leg of the triangular voyage and were landed on the cobbled quaysides of London, Bristol, or Liverpool.

3. Britain's slave ports

A profitable business

A bill of sale of slaves, formerly on display in a Bristol pub for tourists to goggle at, turned out to have come from Jamaica. And 'enthusiasts' persist in showing unwary visitors some caves near the city which, they say, were used for the reception of slaves – though there is no evidence that slaves were ever kept there. Such regrettable imperfections of the folk memory permit the comforting thought that Bristol never witnessed the sale of slaves 'on a large scale'.[1]

Bristol's involvement in the slave trade cannot usefully be discussed at this level. Bristol was built on the trade in slaves and the trade in slave-produced sugar. Its rival Liverpool was built on the trade in slaves and the trade in slave-produced cotton. With belated rhetoric, it was said of each in the nineteenth century that every brick in the city had been cemented with a slave's blood.[2] Slavery, in one way or another, put both Bristol and Liverpool on the map. It gave them a transfusion of wealth that, in a few decades, turned them into boom towns and great world ports. In 1833 a prominent Bristol merchant admitted that without the West Indian trade in slaves and sugar his city would have been a mere fishing port.[3] Thanks to slaves and sugar, the eighteenth century was Bristol's golden age; for three-quarters of the century it ranked as Britain's second city.[4] Without the slave trade, Liverpool would have remained much as it had been towards the end of the seventeenth century: 'an insignificant seaport', 'a small port of little consequence . . . a few streets some little distance from the creek – or pool – which served as a harbour'.[5] The slave trade was 'the pride of Liverpool', for it flooded the town with wealth

> which invigorated every industry, provided the capital for docks, enriched and employed the mills of Lancashire, and afforded the means for opening out new and ever new lines of

> trade. Beyond a doubt it was the slave trade which raised Liverpool from a struggling port to be one of the richest and most prosperous trading centres in the world.[6]

Liverpool's population grew five times as fast as Bristol's. The population of Bristol rose from about 20,000 at the start of the eighteenth century to 64,000 at its close, that of Liverpool from 5,000 to 78,000.[7] Yet Bristol's merchants had been quicker off the mark than those of Liverpool. They had entered the slave trade illegally and energetically well before the end of the seventeenth century, in flagrant breach of the Royal African Company's monopoly.[8] There is little doubt that they bribed Customs officials to accept false declarations about where their ships were bound; their Liverpool rivals certainly did so later, and it explains some of the gaps in the records.[9] In 1688 the *Society* of Bristol, 'laden with negroes and elephants' teeth from the Guinea Coast', was seized and condemned in Virginia as an interloper, and the merchandise, human and otherwise, was 'sold on the King's behalf'. In the same year the *Betty* of Bristol also violated the Royal African Company's monopoly by landing black slaves on Montserrat, and 'the King's share of the condemned negroes' was put up for sale.[10] But the company did sometimes license non-members to trade. In 1690 it sanctioned the fitting out of a slaver in Bristol and five years later it voluntarily threw open the region east of the river Volta (the 'Slave Coast') to any Englishman on payment of 20*s.* for every African transported.[11] Then in 1698 the African trade was finally opened up to all who paid 10 per cent on goods imported into and exported from Africa – except for redwood, which carried only 5 per cent, and three commodities free of all duty: gold, silver, and slaves.[12] The ending of the monopoly was welcomed by the Bristol merchants, one of whom, John Cary, had recently been eulogizing

> a trade of the most Advantage to this Kingdom of any we drive, and as it were all Profit, the first Cost being little more than small Matters of our own Manufactures, for which we have in Return, *Gold*, [elephants'] *Teeth*, *Wax*, and *Negroes*, the last whereof is much better than the first, being indeed the best Traffick the Kingdom hath, as it doth occasionally [i.e. incidentally] give so vast an Imployment to our People both by Sea and Land.[13]

For all the energy and enterprise displayed by the Bristol merchants, Britain's leadership in the Atlantic slave trade 'was not gained quickly or without effort or design'.[14] The turning-point came in 1713, when the treaty of Utrecht gave Britain the coveted assiento, the right to supply slaves to Spain's American colonies – not for the first time, though it was the first time the government had been concerned in the formal contract to do so. The privilege of supplying 4,800 African slaves a year to south and central America, the Spanish West Indies, Mexico, and Florida was conferred on the newly created South Sea Company – 'those voracious robbers', as they were called in Bristol.[15] The British now emerged as the world's foremost slave-traders, responsible for about a quarter of the Atlantic slave trade up to 1791 and for more than half the trade between 1791 and 1806.[16] In the words of James Ramsay, the abolitionist, they were 'honourable slave carriers' for their European rivals.[17]

When did Liverpool enter the slave trade? Almost always the first voyage is dated 1709, when a tiny slaver of 30 tons sailed to West Africa; after which there is supposed to have been a gap until 1730.[18] But the first recorded voyage in fact took place in September 1700, when the *Liverpool Merchant* sailed under Captain William Webster. This vessel delivered 220 slaves to Barbados, where they were sold for £4,239. The next month the *Blessing* sailed from Liverpool under Captain Thomas Brownhill, whose instructions suggest that this was a new kind of trade for the two merchants concerned. One of these, Richard Norris, was mayor of Liverpool and younger brother of one of its Members of Parliament; the other, Thomas Johnson, was a former mayor and future MP. Their *Blessing* was fitted out for the Gold Coast, Ouidah, and Angola, the slaves to be sold in the West Indies or at Cartagena in Colombia. In the following year this ship made another such voyage and in 1703 sailed again, only to be captured by a privateer after a fight two leagues off Angola. Another Liverpool ship, the *Rebecca*, also made a slaving voyage in 1703.[19] It is by no means certain that even these were Liverpool's first slaving ventures. As we have seen, the records were falsified. The merchants 'were very largely evading the ten per cent. export duty by concealing their destination, probably with the connivance of the Customs officers'.[20]

As for the supposed gap, in 1718 the seven owners of the Liverpool brigantine *Imploy* sued the ship's doctor because of his neglect of the slaves in his care; out of 123 who had left the African coast healthy, 64 died before the ship reached Virginia, as did a baby born on board, and the owners lost £1,900.[21] There were sailings from

Liverpool in 1720 (the *Farlton* and the *Filsby*), 1724 (the *Elizabeth*, slaving in Madagascar under Captain John Webster), and 1726. In this latter year there were perhaps 15 voyages; Liverpool's slaving fleet was by now 21 strong.[22]

Bristol peaked in 1738–9 with 52 sailings to Africa. In 1748–9 Bristol sent 47 ships that transported 16,640 slaves. But by mid-century Liverpool had decisively overtaken Bristol.[23] The ships varied considerably in size, and Liverpool's tended to be smaller than Bristol's. The 88 slavers trading from Liverpool in 1752 ranged from the *Ferret* (owned by John Welch & Co. and commanded by Joseph Welch), which carried only 50 slaves, to the exceptionally large *Sarah* (owned by Thomas Crowder & Co. and commanded by Alexander Lawson) and *Eaton* (owned by John Okill & Co. and commanded by John Hughes), each of which held eleven times as many. Altogether the Liverpool fleet in that year could carry 25,820 slaves, packed in the holds 'like books upon a shelf', each person allowed less than half the space granted, in the same period, to a transported convict.[24] In 1771 Liverpool sent 106 ships, carrying 28,200 slaves; Bristol sent 23, carrying 8,810; and London sent 58, carrying 8,136. In 1787 the score, in sailings, stood at: Liverpool, 73; London, 26; Bristol, 22.[25] By the 1780s Liverpool accounted for three out of four of the slaves transported to Jamaica; of the 19 British firms that transported the most slaves to Jamaica after 1781 – the top 10 per cent of the trade – all but three were located in Liverpool.[26] By the 1790s a quarter of Liverpool's total shipping was employed in the slave trade and Liverpool, according to a contemporary estimate, accounted for 60 per cent of the British trade and 40 per cent of that of Europe as a whole.[27]

According to the most recent estimate, Britain's slave-merchants netted a profit of about £12,000,000 on the 2,500,000 Africans they bought and sold between *c.*1630 and 1807, and perhaps half of this profit accrued between 1750 and 1790.[28] The profit from an averagely successful Bristol voyage in the 1730s, with an average cargo of about 170 slaves, came to between £7,000 and £8,000, not counting the proceeds from ivory. One 'indifferent cargo', in the same period, brought in a mere £5,746; but the disappointed merchants were lucky, as it turned out, for when more than one in three of the merchandise died a few weeks after being sold, this loss fell on the buyers.[29] (It was taken for granted that one transported African in three, at least, would either die of dysentery or commit suicide during the three-year 'seasoning' or acclimatization period.)[30]

The Liverpool merchants soon found ways to undersell their London and Bristol rivals. The latter paid their captains monthly, granted them daily port charges and primage (an allowance for loading and care of the cargo), engaged full crews of adults, paid them monthly, and gave their agents 5 per cent on all transactions. Liverpool merchants cut such expenses to the bone. They paid officers and crews once a year, granted few allowances, hired as many boys as was practicable in preference to adult seamen, and paid their agents salaries instead of commissions. So they were able to undercut their rivals by about 12 per cent, or £4 to £5 per slave.[31] Whereas London and Bristol captains in port between voyages could eat on shore occasionally and even enjoy a bottle of Madeira with their meals, their unfortunate Liverpool colleagues had to make do with a shipboard meal of salt-beef and hard biscuit washed down with rum punch.[32] A contemporary estimate put Liverpool's net proceeds from the entire African trade in 1783–93 at £12,294,116 or £1,117,647 per year; in those 11 years the net profit from the 303,737 slaves bought and sold by the Liverpool merchants was estimated at £214,677 15*s.* 1*d.* per year, or about £7 10*s.* per slave.[33] Profits per voyage were very variable. There were occasional ruinous losses, balanced by occasional bonanzas of as much as 300 or 400 per cent; 100 per cent was 'not uncommon'.[34] Recent estimates of the annual rate of return on investment, between 1761 and 1808, put it at about 10 per cent,[35] which was 'distinctly good by the standards of the time'[36] and better than anything that Britain's competitors managed to secure.

But the Liverpool merchants still weren't satisfied. So they devised an ingenious twist to the triangular system. They took to bringing back from the West Indies either ballast or small freight for other merchants, the proceeds from the sale of slaves being remitted in the form of post-dated bills of exchange. These bills were discounted in Liverpool and elsewhere. Such a system enabled merchants who owned ships better equipped for carrying inanimate cargoes to engage directly in the West Indies trade. This in turn stimulated both the creation, as we shall see, of banking facilities in Liverpool and the rise of the Merseyside shipbuilding industry.[37] In any case, by the 1780s Liverpool was 'the single largest English construction site for slave ships'; of every five British-made slavers, two were built in Liverpool dockyards.[38]

Some of Liverpool's loot was siphoned off for the needs of Manchester's burgeoning cotton industry, and Manchester textile manufacturers in turn helped the Liverpool slave-merchants by granting them up to 18 months' credit.[39] Samuel Touchet and his brothers, who owned one of the leading check-making firms in Manchester, were engaged in both the Liverpool slave trade and the London sugar trade and also owned plantations in the Caribbean. In 1751 the brothers had an interest in about 20 West India ships. Samuel helped equip the expedition that captured Senegal in 1758, was MP for Shaftesbury (1761–8), and left a large fortune when he died in 1773.[40] Another Manchester family, the Hibberts, started out by supplying the Royal African Company with checks and imitation Indian cottons, came to own Jamaica's biggest slave factorage business (which sold 16,254 slaves to the island's planters between 1764 and 1774), acquired Jamaican sugar estates, and set up a leading West India commission house in London.[41]

The slave-merchants of Bristol and Liverpool

In both Bristol and Liverpool, very small speculators had their snouts in the trough alongside the big merchants. It was a Bristol tradition for small shopkeepers to go in for bold trading ventures. Roger North, attorney-general in the reign of James II, found it 'remarkable' that in Bristol

> all Men, that are Dealers, even in Shop Trades, launch into Adventures by Sea, chiefly to the *West India* Plantations and *Spain*. A poor Shopkeeper, that sells Candles, will have a Bale of Stockings, or a Piece of Stuff for *Nevis*, or *Virginia*, *&c.* and, rather than fail, they Trade in Men.[1]

There was in fact, until 1685, a local traffic in white slaves. That too was traditional: Bristol had been notorious as a slave market in the eleventh century.[2] In the seventeenth century, reprieved local felons were transported to the West Indies and sold into slavery, and successive mayors and magistrates either took a huge rake-off or simply connived. The magistrates also arranged for 'small Rogues, and Pilferers' to be advised privately by court officials that their only chance of escaping the gallows was to beg for transportation. This racket went on for years, until Judge Jeffreys publicly scolded the mayor, Sir William Hayman, as a kidnapping knave and fined him £1,000.[3] With black slaves, both small and municipal enterprise continued. According to a satirist of the 1740s, Bristol boasted

> swarming Vessels, whose Plebeian State
> Owes not to Merchants, but Mechanicks Freight.[4]

In Liverpool likewise, 'many of the poorer townsfolk had a share, however slight, in the smaller slavers'.[5] A local historian wrote in 1795:

> Almost every man in Liverpool is a merchant, and he who cannot send a bale, will send a bandbox . . . The attractive African meteor has . . . so dazzled their ideas, that almost every order of people is interested in a Guinea cargo . . . It is well known that many of the small vessels that import about an hundred slaves, are fitted out by attornies, drapers, ropers, grocers, tallow-chandlers, barbers, taylors, &c. some have one-eighth, some a fifteenth [*sic*], and some a thirty-second.[6]

The clergy were scarcely less eager than the grocers, barbers, and tailors. 'The very Parsons at *Bristol* talk of nothing but Trade, and how to turn the Penny', observed the government spy and travel-writer John Macky in 1732.[7] But in this respect, as in so many others, Liverpool left Bristol standing. In the 1750s one of Liverpool's younger slave-ship captains was studying for the ministry. His name was John Newton, he had experienced a sudden religious conversion in 1748, and he commanded, first the *Duke of Argyle*, then the *African*, which was owned by Joseph Manesty & Co. and carried 250 slaves.[8] He put a stop to swearing by his crews (in front of him, at any rate), read them the liturgy twice on Sundays,[9] and on one occasion tortured four recalcitrant black youths with thumb-screws, though only 'slightly', to be sure, and only to force them to confess to planning a mutiny.[10] Newton became rector of St Mary Woolnoth, wrote the hymn 'How Sweet the Name of Jesus Sounds',[11] and was a friend of the poet William Cowper, author of the lines:

> I OWN I am shock'd at the purchase of slaves,
> And fear those who buy them and sell them are knaves;
> What I hear of their hardships, their tortures, and groans,
> Is almost enough to drive pity from stones.
>
> I pity them greatly, but I must be mum,
> For how could we do without sugar and rum?[12]

When Cowper included in another poem a line about 'merchants rich in cargoes of despair'[13] he may well have had in mind Newton's first-hand account of the middle passage.[14]

Besides the small investors with their 3 per cent shares in 50- and 100-slave vessels – some of these sloops were later converted into pleasure-boats[15] – there were of course the big battalions of the rich and powerful. The slave trade was always very closely connected with local government and it was tolerably well represented in Parliament, too. In the early part of the eighteenth century it was the practice for merchants to gain first-hand experience in the plantations before setting up in business in Bristol, and several who did so became aldermen and one, William Jefferis, became mayor.[16] (By mid-century the leading Bristol houses had permanent representatives stationed in the chief colonial slave ports; these were often junior members sent out to learn the ropes.)[17] Jefferis and Robert Armitage, mayor of Liverpool, were among the 'Traders . . . to the Coast of Africa' who signed a petition to the king in 1739 asking for naval protection against the Spaniards.[18] Fifty years later a committee set up in Bristol to oppose abolition of the slave trade included nine former mayors, five former sheriffs, and many other worthies. Leading light on this committee was Alderman John Anderson, who had been captain of a slaver for 12 years, sheriff of Bristol in 1772, and mayor in 1783.[19] A prominent local slave-merchant, Onesiphorus Tyndall, was senior partner in Bristol's first bank, established in 1750; when he died seven years later he left at least £16,000 and some land in Gloucestershire.[20] Another Bristol success story was that of the Miles family. William Miles arrived in the port around 1760 with three-halfpence in his pocket, sailed to Jamaica as ship's carpenter, bought a couple of casks of sugar, sold them in Bristol at a large profit, repeated his investment, and became Bristol's leading sugar refiner, an alderman, and one of the leading local bankers. His son Philip John Miles dealt chiefly in sugar and slaves, received £5,481 2*s.* compensation for his 293 slaves in Jamaica plus a share of £8,782 for others emancipated in Trinidad, and died in 1848 leaving property worth more than £1,000,000.[21]

We met Thomas Johnson of Liverpool as part-owner of the *Blessing*. Despite the ship's mishap in 1703, it was, for Johnson, aptly named. Described as 'founder of the modern town of Liverpool',[22] he had been mayor in 1695 and sat as MP from 1701 to 1723; in 1708 he was knighted. In the House of Commons this pioneer of the Liverpool slave trade proved himself 'a zealous servant of the trading interests'.[23] His son-in-law Richard Gildart (mayor, 1714, 1731, and 1736; MP for Liverpool, 1734–54) and another relative, James Gildart (mayor, 1750), were among the big names in the Liverpool slave trade in the 1750s,[24] along with John Welch, John Knight, George Campbell, Edward Forbes, and Foster Cunliffe and Sons.[25] Originally destined for the church, Foster Cunliffe became Liverpool's leading merchant – some said the biggest businessman in the whole country – and was three times mayor (1716, 1729, and 1735). In mid-century he and his sons Ellis and Robert owned or part-owned at least 26 ships, at least four of them slavers: the *Bulkeley*, *Bridget*, *Foster*, and *Ellis and Robert*. Altogether these four ships held 1,120 slaves, and they brought the Cunliffe family enough profit to load a dozen ships a year with sugar and rum for sale in England. When Foster Cunliffe was invited to stand for Parliament he put his son Ellis up instead. Ellis Cunliffe was returned unopposed, held one of the Liverpool seats in the Commons for 12 years (1755–67), and was made a baronet. Foster Cunliffe's elder sister married Charles Pole, who traded with Africa and the West Indies, was director and chairman of Sun Fire Insurance, and held the other Liverpool seat for five years (1756–61).[26] Foster Cunliffe's younger sister married Bryan Blundell (mayor, 1721 and 1728), who was treasurer and trustee of the Blue Coat hospital and 'found in his philanthropy no argument against joining in the slave-trade'.[27] Ralph and Thomas Earle, mayors of Liverpool in 1769 and 1787 respectively, were sons of the local slave-trader John Earle, who started out as an ironmonger. Arthur and Benjamin Heywood, two brothers who made their fortunes in the slave trade, built with some of the proceeds two adjoining houses that served as both residences and business premises; behind the houses was a tennis court where they would relax after their labours. Each of the brothers married a rich heiress and each became a banker. When Benjamin Heywood died in 1796 he left legacies of several thousand pounds, apart from real estate; and his son Nathaniel left about £50,000 in legacies when he died in 1815. Arthur Heywood Sons & Co. was in 1883 absorbed by the Bank of Liverpool, afterwards Martin's Bank and then, in its turn, absorbed by Barclay's Bank.[28]

A list, compiled in 1752, of 101 Liverpool merchants trading to Africa included 12 who had been, or were to become, mayor of the town,[29] and 15 who were pewholders in the fashionable Benn's Garden Presbyterian chapel.[30] At least 26 of Liverpool's mayors, holding office for 35 of the years from 1700 to 1820, were or had been slave-merchants or close relatives.[31]

By 1795, though there was still ample scope for the small investor, ten firms had secured control of more than half the port's slaving fleet and accounted for almost two-thirds of the cargoes; in the years 1789–91 over half the total number of slaving ventures were accounted for by the seven largest firms.[32] The leading names were now William Neilson, John Shaw, William Forbes, Edward Philip

Grayson, Francis Ingram, Thomas Rodie and, above all, Thomas Leyland.[33] A self-made and very stingy man – his dearest love was money – Thomas Leyland started out as a dealer in wheat, oats, peas, and bacon, won some government stock in a lottery, married his former employer's daughter, and found that dealing in Africans brought him more of what he loved best than did any other branch of commerce. It made him, in fact, one of Liverpool's three richest men, with an income estimated locally at tens of thousands of pounds a year. In the years 1782–1807 he transported 3,489 slaves to Jamaica alone.[34] The surviving records of his 11 ships' slaving voyages are 'beautifully written books'.[35] Co-opted to the Liverpool town council, he served as bailiff in 1796 and mayor in 1798, 1814, and 1820. In 1798 he 'contributed a handsome £300 to the Tory fund in support of the Government's vigorous prosecution of war with France'; after all, 'Liverpool, probably including its mayor, derived considerable profit from privateering activities'.[36] No doubt judging that abolition of the slave trade was inevitable and that diversification of his money-making activities would be a prudent step, Leyland joined Liverpool's oldest bank in 1802 as a senior partner. (Curiously, one of his new associates, William Roscoe, was an abolitionist.) Leyland presumably learned all he could about banking before withdrawing in 1806 and launching his own bank, Leyland and Bullin, in 1807. His nephew and partner Richard Bullin was also a merchant and shipowner in the slave trade, both before and after his formal entry into banking. Within eight years the new bank had assets of over £1,000,000 sterling and rivalled the larger London banks in importance.[37] By 1826 Leyland's private fortune totalled £736,531 9*s.* 8*d.*, including £384,374 11*s.* 7*d.* in government stock. He died in the following year. Leyland and Bullin was absorbed by the North and South Wales Bank in 1901, and that in turn by the Midland in 1908.[38]

The Heywoods, Thomas Leyland, and Richard Bullin were not the only Liverpool slave-merchants who gravitated towards banking. The Bolds, the Gregsons, and the Staniforths did the same.[39] It was a natural progression. The growth of banking and insurance in the port coincided with the involvement of merchants in the slave trade:

> Merchants and shipowners very largely insured their own ventures themselves, but the need for discounting facilities arose after 1750 with the growing volume of bills drawn against West Indian merchants. Thus some of the more

important Liverpool merchants began to exercise the functions of banking.[40]

Ten prominent local slave-merchants helped to found ten of the fourteen important Liverpool banks listed after 1750.[41] Many other local bankers were West India merchants or, like John Moss of Moss, Dale, and Rogers, owned immense sugar plantations in Demerara (afterwards part of British Guiana).[42] Each of the Liverpool banking houses associated with the slave trade could command assets of between £200,000 and £300,000.[43]

In a trade studded with self-made men, the name of Peter Baker, of Baker & Dawson, stands out. Originally a joiner's apprentice, he became a shipbuilder and died in 1795 during his year of office as Liverpool's mayor. He and his son-in-law John Dawson were credited with shipping more than 20,000 Africans to the West Indies in the years 1783–9.[44] Dawson was 'perhaps the biggest operator' in the port, 'but in a highly specialised way'. From 1783 he was under contract with Spain to supply its colonies with slaves, providing a minimum of 3,000 per year, and as many more as possible, to Cuba, Santo Domingo, Carácas, and Savannah. His ships were the largest and most specialized in the trade. And when, in 1787, a new contract was negotiated, Messrs Baker & Dawson laid out nearly £2,000 in Spain in bribes.[45]

Not only the self-made men, but all the 'grand old Liverpool families' too were 'more or less steeped'[46] in slavery, either trading or owning or both. One celebrated Liverpool slave-owning family bore the name Gladstones, from which the final *s* was dropped by royal letters patent in 1835. John Gladstone's slaves in British Guiana and Jamaica made his sugar, his rum, and his fortune, which he invested in land and houses in Liverpool and in profitable trade links with Russia, India, and China. He was chairman of the West India Association and, under the pen-name Mercator, carried on a long controversy with a local abolitionist in the *Liverpool Mercury*.[47] An MP from 1818 to 1827, he was created a baronet in 1846. He proved himself 'especially influential in adjusting with Lord Stanley, then Secretary for the Colonies, the terms of negro emancipation' in 1833 – and in procuring for the West Indies planters a grant of £20,000,000 by way of compensation.[48] His own share was 'adjusted' to £93,526, awarded for the loss of 2,039 slaves.[49] At his death in 1851 his estate was valued at about £600,000.[50] When his son William Ewart Gladstone first stood for Parliament in 1832, at Newark, opponents mocked the 23-year-old candidate as a schoolboy and, more unkindly, reminded him that a large part of his father's gold had sprung 'from the blood of black slaves'.[51] That did not prevent the future Liberal prime minister from devoting his first substantial speech in the Commons to a defence of slavery on the family estates in British Guiana.[52] The younger Gladstone was to make several other speeches in defence of the slave-owners. He and his father took the view that immediate emancipation would not be in the slaves' best interests; if the ground were not first well prepared, emancipation would prove 'more fleeting than a shadow and more empty than a name'.[53]

London as a slave port: the West India lobby

By the beginning of the eighteenth century the Royal African Company had sent to Africa 500 ships carrying goods worth £500,000, transported 100,000 black slaves to the plantations, imported 30,000 tons of sugar, coined 500,000 guineas, and built eight forts on the African coast.[1] Fifteen of London's lord mayors and 25 of its sheriffs between 1660 and 1689 were shareholders in the company, as were 38 of the City's aldermen between 1672 and 1690.[2] In fact London was 'as deeply involved in the slave trade as . . . Liverpool'[3] – but not merely through sending out ships. It was the London commission agents that greased the wheels by financing the entire system. By 1750 London merchants were handling almost three-quarters of the sugar imported into England, and their profits played a crucial sweetening role.[4] They had become money-lenders of a highly specialized kind. 'Acting in the dual capacity of broker and banker', they 'reaped lucrative commissions and interest for accommodating the peculiar needs of planters and slave merchants'.[5]

The foundations of this commission or 'factorage' system were laid in the last 40 years of the seventeenth century. It was the means whereby credit, 'the very life-blood of the West Indies in the eighteenth century', was transmitted from Britain.[6] Because of the long seasonal delays, and the time needed to convert newly acquired slave labour into produce, a complex system of long-term credits was evolved. The agents in the West Indies paid for slaves and supplies with bills drawn on their London connections, payable after 18 months or even two or three years. The slave-ship captains conveyed these bills to their employers. The commission agents took 5 per cent commission on gross sales and a further 5 per cent on the sums remitted to Britain: 10 per cent on gross turnover, in other words. They also raked in large sums as interest from the planters. In their role as acceptance houses or quasi-bankers, these London West India houses 'stood at the centre of this web of trade'. They were 'the focus of the system'.[7]

One of the first commission agents was John Bawden, absentee planter and part-owner of ships plying for hire. From time to time he dabbled directly in the slave trade. In 1687 he was knighted and became an alderman of the City of London. By then he and John Gardiner, his partner from 1682, had 'the largest Commissions from Barbadoes of any Merchants in *England*, and perhaps the largest that ever were lodg'd in one House in the *West-India* Trade': so wrote Bawden's brother-in-law, John Oldmixon.[8] Bawden's chief competitors in this lush field were John and Francis Eyles, sons of a Wiltshire mercer and wool stapler, who made their fortunes as London merchants and founded 'one of the great mercantile dynasties of eighteenth-century London'. Active in the West Indies commission business at least as early as 1674, John Eyles sat as MP for Devizes (1679–81), became an alderman and lord mayor of London (1688), and ended with a knighthood. He lent £29,000 to the government in 1689 and 'died a wealthy man'. His brother Francis became an alderman and a baronet.[9]

The system pioneered by men like Bawden and the Eyles brothers was developed more profitably still by the Lascelles family, connected with Barbados from the end of the seventeenth century. 'Big business was slave business, especially in Barbados . . . an island of great slave merchants',[10] and Lascelles and Maxwell, sugar factors, stood security on behalf of these great slave-merchants, receiving the customary 5 per cent on the money advanced. They also lent large sums to the slave-merchants of other islands and received interest on those loans, too. The loans were used partly to buy slaves and partly to buy plantations.[11] As Customs collectors for Barbados, Henry Lascelles and his brother Edward had earlier found another way of enriching themselves. Henry had pocketed about a third, Edward over half, of the sugar duty they collected on the government's behalf. Systematic fraud and money-lending to slave-merchants eventually made Henry rich enough to buy himself a seat in the Commons for somewhat under £13,000 (about three or four times the going rate, apparently). He got rid of the sitting member, William Smelt, by procuring a Customs post for him in Barbados.[12] He sat for his native town of Northallerton from 1745 to 1752, when he resigned in favour of his younger son Daniel, who held the seat until 1780 and then retired to let in the elder son,

Edwin. Chief fixer for the house of Lascelles was the powerful John Sharpe, MP, solicitor to the Treasury and agent for Barbados and other islands.[13] When Henry Lascelles died in 1753 he left £284,000 besides annuities; £166,666 went to Edwin, whose share was 'enough by itself to found one of the noble families of England'.[14] And that was what happened. Edwin was created Baron Harewood in 1780. Some 40 years later, on the eve of emancipation, his cousin's son the Earl of Harewood owned two plantations and 344 slaves in Jamaica, three plantations and 745 slaves in Barbados.[15] When these slaves were emancipated, the earl received compensation totalling £22,473 17*s.* 11*d.*[16]

Slave-merchants' and sugar planters' special financial needs led, in London as in Bristol and Liverpool, to close connections between these trades and the banks. Alexander and David Barclay – theirs was not yet a household name – were among the 84 Quaker slave-traders in 1756.[17] Another prominent London banker, Sir Francis Baring, seems to have made his first money out of dealing in slaves when he was only 16. It evidently gave him an excellent start in life, for this 'prince of merchants' earned nearly £7,000,000 over 70 years, sat as MP for 18 of them, was made a baronet in 1793, and left property worth £1,000,000.[18] City of London financiers with interests in the West Indies included the Lloyds underwriter John Julius Angerstein, whose choice collection of pictures formed the nucleus of the National Gallery.[19]

The bank that might justly have been called the 'Bank of the West Indies' in the eighteenth century was the Bank of England. Black slavery augmented, in one way or another, the family fortunes of many of its directors and governors. Humphry Morice, MP, director of the bank from 1716, deputy governor in 1725–6, and governor in 1727–9, personally owned six slave-ships, four of them named after members of his family: *Anne*, *Katherine*, *Sarah*, and *Judith*. After Morice's sudden death in 1731 he was found to have had his hand in the Bank of England's till: he had discounted fictitious bills to the tune of over £29,000, had embezzled trust funds left to his daughters by an uncle, and was said to have taken poison to forestall discovery.[20] Sir Richard Neave, Bt, director of the Bank of England for 48 years, deputy governor in 1781–3, and governor in 1783–5, was chairman of the Society of West India Merchants and of the London Dock Company (which built the London Docks in Wapping, opened in 1803). Neave's daughter married Beeston Long junior, son of Neave's predecessor as chairman of the West India Merchants; Beeston Long junior in his turn became chairman of the West India Merchants and the London Dock Company – and director (1784–1820) and governor (1804–6) of the Bank of England.[21] Thomas Boddington, director of the Bank of England (1782–1809) and of the London Dock Company, financed the purchase of estates for the Pinneys in the late 1780s.[22] Thomas Raikes, director (1776–1810), deputy governor (1795–7), and governor (1797–9) of the Bank of England, dandy, and friend of Beau Brummell, had a nephew, Job Mathew Raikes, who was partner in a prosperous family firm of West India merchants. This nephew married the eldest daughter of Nathaniel Bayly, ex-MP and rich Jamaican plantation-owner, who died in 1798 leaving well over £100,000; the two families linked by this marriage later acquired a connection with the banking firm of Glyn, Mills & Co.[23] William Manning – whose father had acquired by marriage two estates on St Kitts – was agent for St Vincent and Grenada, 'eclipsed the older families to become the most eminent of West India merchants', amassed a 'handsome fortune', and served as director (1790–1831) and governor (1812–14) of the Bank of England. His brother-in-law Abel Smith was a partner in the banking house of Smith, Payne and Smiths; his youngest son was to add a different kind of lustre to the family name by becoming a cardinal and archbishop of Westminster.[24]

No wonder that the 'sugar and slave men', as one historian of the Bank of England calls them, were favoured customers:

> Including the discounting done for bankers, the aggregate for persons 'in Discount with the Bank', as reported on 1 January 1800, was £6,603,000 . . .
>
> At the head of the merchants, with £581,000 of bills under discount on that day, came the great West India Interest – the sugar and slave men. Because of the 'extraordinary situation of their trade' in war time, they had recently been given specially favourable terms.[25]

London's immensely rich and powerful West India lobby was made up of three closely associated and often overlapping elements. First, there were the commission agents, already referred to. Second, there were the absentee proprietors, many of whom played an active part in local and national politics. 'I need not, I suppose, observe to you', wrote a pamphleteer in 1760, 'how many Gentlemen of the *West Indies* have seats in the *British* House of Commons.'[26] Jasper Mauduit, agent for Massachusetts (then a British colony) wrote in 1764 that the West Indians had a 'very formidable number of votes' in the Commons,[27] and his brother Israel declared in the same year that '50 or 60 West India voters' in the Commons 'can turn the balance on which side they please'.[28] Two years later a writer in the *Gentleman's Magazine* reckoned that 'there are now in parliament upwards of 40 members who are either *West-India* planters themselves, descended from such, or have concerns there that entitle them to this pre eminence'.[29] Two prominent slave-traders who sat in the Commons in the early part of the eighteenth century were the Barbados merchants Robert and William Heysham. The former was an alderman of the City of London (1720) and master of the Drapers' Company (1720–1).[30] Other early West Indian MPs were Sir William Stapleton and Sir William Codrington, both baronets. One of Stapleton's grandfathers had been captain-general of the Leeward Islands, the other, governor of Nevis. Codrington's grandfather had migrated to Barbados in 1628 and he and his two sons made great fortunes there, which the grandson inherited.[31] Sir William Pulteney, MP, who served as secretary at war (1714–17), and was afterwards created Earl of Bath, owned large estates in the West Indies and Scotland that brought him in about £10,000 a year.[32] Richard Pennant, MP, first Baron Penrhyn, who inherited the largest estate in Jamaica, summed up the slave-owners' views when he wrote to his agent there in 1783: 'I am glad to hear the Negroes are well. The Hearing a good account of them, and of the Cattle, always gives pleasure.'[33]

Perhaps the most famous, and probably the richest, of this group of MPs was William Beckford, uncrowned king of Jamaica, where he held 22,022 acres in 1750. Born on the island, he became a successful London merchant and a City alderman. He served as sheriff (1755–6), as lord mayor twice (1762–3 and 1769–70), and as MP for Shaftesbury (1747–54) and London (1754–70). One of his brothers, Richard, who owned 9,242 acres in Jamaica, sat for Bristol (1754–6); another brother, Julines, who owned 8,198 acres in Jamaica, sat for Salisbury (1754–64). William Beckford's illegitimate son Richard was also a West Indian planter-MP (Bridport, 1780–4; Arundel, 1784–90; Leominster, 1791–8), and his legitimate son William, author of *Vathek* (1786) and, in Byron's phrase, 'England's wealthiest son', sat for Wells (1784–90) and Hindon (1790–4 and 1806–20) and squandered a huge fortune.[34]

The West Indians could well afford to buy their seats in the Commons. In 1767 a borough-jobber – a dealer in rotten and pocket boroughs – laughed at Lord Chesterfield's offer of £2,500 for a seat in Northampton, explaining that

> there was no such thing as a borough to be had now; for that the rich East and West Indians had secured them all at the rate of three thousand pounds at least; but many at four thousand; and two or three, that he knew, at five thousand.[35]

The West Indian colonies' political agents resident in London made up the third element in the West India lobby. These representatives of the island planters and merchants were paid by the various colonial legislatures. Barbados appointed an agent as early as 1671; he seems to have been the first. Jamaica and the Leeward Islands followed suit in 1677.[36] Like John Sharpe, one of the most successful, many of these agents were also British government employees; others had formerly been in government service or would later enter it. So this was politically the most powerful element in the lobby – more so than even the planter- and merchant-MPs. Charles Delafoye, agent for Jamaica, was a government clerk and became an under-secretary of state. John Pownall, agent for the Virgin Islands, had been secretary to the Board of Trade and Plantations. George Chalmers, agent for the Bahamas, had the main responsibility for administrative work at the Board of Trade for many years. Sir John Stanley, agent for Barbados, was commissioner of the Custom House. Thomas Beake, agent for St Kitts, was a clerk in the Council Office. Lovel Stanhope, agent for Jamaica, was law clerk to the secretaries of state.[37]

Several important measures were adopted under the determined pressure of the West India lobby. One was the Molasses Act of 1733, hitting at the north American colonies' trade with the French islands; in 1764 this was reinforced by the Sugar Act. It was on the lobby's demand that Canada was annexed to the British Empire in 1763 instead of Guadeloupe or Martinique, whose huge crops would have brought sugar prices crashing down.[38] The lobby also succeeded, against much opposition, in having the West India Docks, in the Isle of Dogs, constructed and opened in 1802. Prime movers in the scheme were George Hibbert, son of a West India merchant, agent for Jamaica, alderman of the City of London, and later an MP and author of a pamphlet opposing abolition of the slave trade; and Robert Milligan, a West India merchant.[39]

Nobody sat down and planned the West India lobby. It took shape piecemeal. Informal gatherings in coffee-houses achieved more than formal meetings. A Committee for the Concern of Barbados was set up in London in 1671. The Planters' Club of London was formed before 1740, but its membership was confined to proprietors and, in any case, it seems to have been more social than political in character.[40] A co-ordinated Society of West India Merchants did not come into existence until the 1760s.[41]

From 1788 the entire strength of the West India interest in London would be mobilized to defend the slave trade against the mounting campaign for abolition. By then London's pro-slavery network had behind it more than 100 years' experience in running pressure groups, presenting and managing petitions, transmitting information, getting letters into the newspapers, organizing lobbying of every kind – including, as we shall see in a later chapter, having a quiet word with the attorney-general and solicitor-general after dinner to persuade them to give an official ruling that a slave who was brought to this country remained a slave and could lawfully be shipped back to the plantations. Here is a remarkably modern-sounding example of the lobby's cosmetic operations. 'The vulgar are influenced by names and titles', said a letter published in the *Gentleman's Magazine* in 1789. 'Instead of SLAVES, let the Negroes be called ASSISTANT-PLANTERS; and we shall not then hear such violent outcries against the slave trade by pious divines, tender-hearted poetesses, and short-sighted politicians.'[42]

Those who wanted the slave trade abolished had formidable enemies. Agents, planters, and merchants had built up a powerful system. And so 'the history of the abolition movement . . . was one of continuous fighting against the almost overwhelming power of interest.'[43]

Competition

Britain's three main slave ports had to face competition, chiefly in the 1750s, 1760s, and 1770s, from ten other ports. But only three of these – Lancaster, Whitehaven, and Portsmouth – ever made a significant contribution to the trade, and even then their role was minor compared with that of Liverpool, Bristol, and London. Slave-trading ventures from the remaining seven – Chester, Preston, and Poulton-le-Fylde (near Blackpool) in the north-west; Plymouth, Exeter, and Dartmouth in the south-west; and Glasgow – seem to have been quite rare. In 1750, in fact, Lancaster, Chester, Plymouth, and Glasgow were reported to have only six slave-ships between them.[1]

In a certain sense, though, Lancaster had entered the trade 30 years earlier. The slaver *Penellopy* was built there in 1720 but was registered at Liverpool, in 1724, with four north Lancashire owners.[2] There was an intricate connection between Lancaster and Liverpool, especially in the years 1759–76, with some Lancaster slavers clearing from the larger port and some Lancaster merchants holding shares in Liverpool slavers in the 1760s.[3] Occasional slaving voyages are recorded from Lancaster itself from 1736 onwards, but regular trade did not begin until 1748.[4] By 1754 Lancaster could boast nine slave-ships of its own, and in the years 1757–76 an average of four ships a year were cleared from the port for slaving voyages. Lancaster's slave-ships were extremely small: 40 to 80 tons, with some even smaller that were probably used as tenders. Favourite destinations were Sierra Leone and the Gambia, where in 1761 the slaves on board the Lancaster ship *Mary*, commanded by Captain Sandys, rose and killed most of the crew.[5] Two years later the Lancaster merchants were petitioning the Commissioners for Trade and Plantations, 'setting forth the prejudice arising to their Interests . . . from some of His Majesty's Subjects having entered into Contracts for supplying the French with Negroes'.[6] Lancaster's slave trade dwindled to a trickle after 1781 and ended altogether, formally speaking, with two voyages in 1792 – though three later examples are known of Lancaster-owned vessels clearing from Liverpool.[7]

The other small north-western ports seem to have entered the slave trade in the 1750s because they thought they could undercut their bigger rivals; but it does not seem to have done them much good. Chester tried twice, in 1750–7 and 1773–5, registering a total of only nine voyages altogether.[8] Two of Chester's ships were lost and not replaced – one of these, the *Black Prince*, was destroyed by French men-of-war[9] – and two were advertised for sale in Liverpool newspapers. Chester was probably too close to Liverpool to compete successfully.[10] Preston and Poulton started regular trade in 1753, but between them managed only five slaving voyages by three ships before dropping out four years later. At least one of these ships was owned by a Kirkham firm of linen manufacturers that also had shares in five Liverpool slavers between 1767 and 1771.[11]

Whitehaven was more successful. It entered the trade in 1750 and sent out an average of four slave-ships a year between 1758 and 1769. Portsmouth managed two such voyages a year between 1758 and 1774.[12] Glasgow took part very occasionally, though 'many of its merchants waxed fat on the direct trades in sugar and tobacco' and 'some made fortunes directly by becoming planters in the West Indies'.[13] The Glasgow slave-trading firm of Alexander Grant

Junior & Co. went bankrupt in 1807 after the passing of the Abolition Act.[14]

There was also occasional competition from the Royal Navy. In 1703 Vice-Admiral John Graydon, described as a 'brutal' man, was accused by the Jamaica merchants and planters of stealing their slaves and cattle to sell on the Spanish American coast. He was dismissed the service, for another offence, by resolution of the House of Lords.[15] In 1711 a complaint was made to the Admiralty that Captain Matthew Elford had been taking black slaves to Antigua to sell and provisioning them at Queen Anne's expense.[16] Two years later, 42 Jamaica merchants petitioned the Council of Trade and Plantations about the conduct of Rear-Admiral Sir Hovenden Walker, who was letting his captains carry black slaves and other merchandise to sell duty-free on the Spanish American coast, thus stealing 'the most considerable and advantageous branch' of their trade. Indeed, in order to render this 'private trade' more convenient, the admiral had considerately shifted his base from Port Royal to Bluefields, about 200 miles to the west. The merchants asked that the captains be restricted to guarding the coast and protecting trade instead of appropriating it.[17] There were similar complaints in 1718.[18] The Admiralty often sent out warships to the West Indies by way of the west coast of Africa, and this gave naval officers a chance to supplement their pay by dealing in slaves. King George II promised in 1732 that he would put a stop to this improper behaviour but, in spite of complaints by the French, 'it does not seem to have stopped'.[19]

Naval officers sent to the West African coast to guard British slavers from foreign privateers were also sometimes tempted to do a little trading themselves, and they could not always resist temptation. In 1737 the officers and crews of the warships *Diamond*, *Greenwich*, and *Spence*, lying off the African coast for the protection of British merchant vessels, were actively engaged in buying gold dust, ivory, and slaves. Each of his Majesty's three ships had on board large stores of cotton goods, liquor, gunpowder, and other merchandise, which they were offering at prices far below normal. At the same time they were paying £4 per head above the usual rate for slaves. The slaver captains found themselves unable to procure cargoes except at an outlay involving ruinous losses for their employers. A Bristol affidavit complained that HMS *Greenwich* had sailed for Barbados with 200 slaves, while HMS *Spence*, a mere sloop-of-war, had taken between 50 and 60 more.[20]

Quality control

The reputation of those who traded in black slaves depended on their ability to supply customers with first-class goods. Here was the one area where they could not afford to cut costs. The Liverpool brand, DD, burnt with red-hot irons into the living flesh of African men, women, and children, was famous among West Indian planters as a guarantee of prime quality.[1] Merchants and planters alike exercised strict quality control by careful examination at the point of purchase on both sides of the Atlantic. A naval surgeon who watched slavers at work in West Africa in the 1720s compared the scene to a cattle market. The people offered for sale were 'examined by us in like manner, as our Brother Trade do Beasts in *Smithfield*; the Countenance, and Stature, a good Set of Teeth, Pliancy in their Limbs, and Joints, and being free of Venereal Taint, are the things inspected, and governs our choice in buying'.[2] It was the same at the other end of the middle passage. Richard Ligon described the scene in Barbados: 'The Planters . . . choose them as they do Horses in a Market; the strongest, youthfullest, and most beautiful, yield the greatest prices.'[3] John Oldmixon's account was similar: 'The Slaves are purchased by Lots, out of the *Guinea* Ships. They are all view'd stark naked, and the strongest and handsomest bear the best Prizes.'[4] 'Selling these Slaves', the author of a book-keeping manual assured his readers in 1754, 'differs in nothing from selling other Merchandize.'[5]

If merchants were to be sure of 'Prime Healthy Negroes'[6] they had to keep their employees up to the mark. So they sent detailed instructions to every captain, sometimes more than once during a single voyage. These were the instructions sent by the Bristol firm of Isaac Hobhouse & Co. to William Barry, commander of the *Dispatch*, in 1725:

> Let your endeavours be to buy none but what's healthy and strong and of a Convenient Age – none to exceed the years of 25 or under if posible, among which so many men, and stout men boys [i.e. strong male adolescents] as can be had seeing such are most Valuable at the Plantations . . . So soon as you begin to slave let your knetting be fix'd breast high fore and aft and so keep 'em shackled and hand Bolted fearing their rising or leaping Overboard.[7]

The same house wrote to one of its agents in 1733:

> We hope this will find you safe arrived on the coast of Angola and with a fine Parcell of Negroes ready to putt on board our ship *Union* . . . You must in the best manner of which you are capable exert yourself in the purchase of a parcell of fine Men and Women, that you may not loose the good caracter you have already gott. And as you are obliged to take at times some boys and Girls, you must endeavour . . . to purchase about 100, aiming chiefly at the females from 10 to 14 years of age . . .
>
> Observe that the Boys and Girls you buy be very black and handsome.[8]

Cargoes often included a high proportion of children. When Sir William Young, afterwards governor of Tobago, visited the Windward Islands in 1791 he went on board the *Pilgrim* of Bristol and the *Aeolus* of Liverpool and found that 'a full half of either cargo consisted of children (and generally as fine children as I ever saw) from six to fourteen years of age'.[9] Thomas Leyland's firm instructed the master of the *Earl of Liverpool* when it sailed in 1797: 'In your selection of the slaves, we desire you will not purchase any exceeding eighteen to twenty years of age, well formed, and free from any disorder.'[10] John Pinney was one of the many planters who preferred to buy 'men–boys' and 'women–girls' rather than adults.[11] In the 1720s, one in six of the slaves the Royal African Company landed in Barbados, one in three of those it landed in Jamaica, was a child. Seventy years later, about 13 per cent of the slaves taken on board British slavers were children, officially defined as those under 4ft 4in. tall. Of the slaves landed in Jamaica in the same period, 7 per cent were children. The difference is to be accounted for partly by the uniformly high mortality rate among the children, for three boys in twenty and one girl in five did not survive the middle passage.[12]

The overall death rate of slaves in transit gradually dropped from one in four in the 1680s to one in twelve 100 years later.[13] During the ships' long absences some of the merchants were inclined to fret about the possibility that captains were risking a higher than average death rate by buying Africans who were diseased or infirm or past their first youth. This fear obsessed the Liverpool merchant Robert Bostock. During a single voyage one of his captains received ten separate sets of instructions from him. Bostock wrote in 1789 to Edward Williams, commander of the *Jemmy*: 'I hope you will be very careful about your Slaves and take none on Board but what is

Healthy & Young.' In the following year he warned another of his captains, named Flint, not to buy slaves of 'Old Spider Leged Quality'.[14] In 1803 Captain Cæsar Lawson, master of the Liverpool slaver *Enterprize*, was instructed to obtain 'prime Negroes, Ivory and Palm Oil', and the owners added: 'In the choice of the Negroes be very particular, select those that are well formed and strong; and do not buy any above 24 years of Age.'[15]

These slave-ship captains were the elite of their calling, identifiable not only by their 'privilege Negroes' but also by their gaudy laced coats with big silver or gold buttons, their cocked hats, the silver or gold buckles on their shoes.[16] Most of them, whatever they had been like when they entered the trade, turned into brutal tyrants. But it was a trade that tended to attract sadists. Slaves were flogged with a cat-o'-nine-tails on the slightest pretext, and it was often the captain himself who did the flogging and took a visible delight in it. In 1764 the newly promoted captain of the Liverpool slaver *Black Joke*, whose name was Marshall, flogged to death a baby less than a year old for refusing food, then forced the mother to throw the corpse overboard.[17] Uprisings were put down with horrible reprisals, partly because they sent officers and crews into paroxysms of terror. But the need to satisfy their employers' lust for profit did tend to put a check on the captains' lust for inflicting pain. Unable to torture the slaves freely, sadistic captains had to make do with their own seamen. To these they were so cruel that by the 1780s it was growing hard to recruit men for slaving voyages. Such voyages were unpopular for two other reasons: they could last a year or more; and the death rate among crews as well as cargoes was notoriously high. The seamen used to sing:

> Beware and take care of the Bight of Benin
> There's one comes out for forty go in.[18]

That was an exaggeration – but from 1784 to 1790 the death rate among seamen on slaving voyages was one in five, more than twice as high as the death rate among slaves in transit in that period. One authority writes, with agreeable irony: 'If the Africans suffered hardships and the mortality rate among them was high, it must be acknowledged that the same was true with respect to the white seamen removing them to their new homes.'[19] According to Hugh Crow, master of the last slaver to sail from an English port, many of these seamen were 'the very dregs of the community':

> Some of them had escaped from jails; others were undiscovered

> offenders, who sought to withdraw themselves from their country lest they should fall into the hands of the officers of justice. These wretched beings used to flock to Liverpool when the ships were fitting out, and after acquiring a few sea phrases from some crimp [i.e. agent who recruited seamen] or other, they were shipped as ordinary seamen, though they had never been at sea in their lives. If, when at sea, they became saucy and insubordinate, which was generally the case, the officers were compelled to treat them with severity: and, never having been in a warm climate before, if they took ill, they seldom recovered . . . Amongst these wretched beings I have known many gentlemen's sons of desperate character and abandoned habits, who had either fled for some offence, or had involved themselves in pecuniary embarrassments.[20]

But not all the seamen employed on board the slavers were white. And the free black seamen, who often signed on as cooks, bore their full share of the captains' frustration. In 1786 Joseph Williams, commander of the Bristol slaver *Little Pearl* (later renamed the *Ruby*), 'appeared to enjoy a particular Pleasure in flogging and tormenting' his cook, a free black seaman who spoke Portuguese: 'He often amused himself with making the Man swallow Cockroaches alive, on pain of being most severely flogged, and having Beef Brine rubbed into his Wounds.' The black cook, who sometimes opted for a flogging rather than swallow 'the nauseous Vermin', was chained by the neck night and day to the copper in which he prepared food for the slaves and crew; and 'the Body of this poor Wretch, from the Crown of his Head to the Soles of his Feet, was covered with Scars and Lacerations, intersecting each other in all Directions, so that he was a most miserable Object to behold'. The ship's surgeon said afterwards that not a man on board had escaped the captain's fury.[21]

In the previous year the *Brothers* had limped home to Bristol with 32 of the crew dead through their captain's ill-treatment and another crew member, a free black seaman called John Dean, sickeningly mutilated. The captain had tied him face down on the deck, poured hot pitch over him, and cut his back open with hot tongs – all for 'a trifling circumstance, for which he was in no-wise to blame'. When the abolitionist Thomas Clarkson visited Bristol to gather ammunition for the campaign against the slave trade, he investigated this case and had the details confirmed by a 'respectable ship-builder' called Sydenham Teast.[22] He also investigated the case of the slaver *Alfred*, which had just docked, and whose captain had chained the surgeon's mate to the deck for days and nights on end. Yet another free black seaman, a cook on board the *Juno*, was beaten with handspikes and other implements by the captain and surgeon and forced to work in chains.[23]

Such atrocities were the talk of Bristol. The deputy town clerk, Daniel Burges, confided to Clarkson 'that he only knew of one captain from the port in the Slave-trade, who did not deserve long ago to be hanged'.[24] Public opinion was turning against the trade. Bristol seamen had to be dead drunk before they would sign on – or, for a consideration, obliging publicans would falsely accuse them of debt, offering them the choice of 'a slave-vessel, or a gaol'.[24]

In Liverpool, too, Clarkson found that 'horrible facts' about the trade were 'in every body's mouth', though Liverpool people seemed 'more hardened' than Bristol people. While he was investigating the case of a Liverpool captain who had flogged a seaman to death, some of the owner's bully-boys tried to throw him off the end of the pier.[26] The campaign against the trade had the merchants badly rattled. Soon after Clarkson's visit the Liverpool council conferred the freedom of the borough on Charles Jenkinson, Lord Hawkesbury, 'in gratitude for the essential services rendered to the town of Liverpool by his Lordship's late exertion in Parliament in support of the African Slave Trade'; he was later created Earl of Liverpool.[27] And the council commissioned a Spanish-born Jesuit, the Reverend Raymund Harris (his real name was Hormasa), to write a 77-page pamphlet, *Scriptural Researches on the Licitness of the Slave-trade, shewing its conformity with the principles of natural and revealed religion, delineated in the sacred writings of the word of God.* As their 'most obedient And most humble Servant', Harris 'most respectfully inscribed' this work to the mayor, recorder, aldermen, and bailiffs of the town.[28] According to Harris, the trade was 'in perfect harmony with . . . the principles and decisions of the Word of God respecting *Right* and *Justice*'.[29] Even in Liverpool it was just as well to know that God was on your side, and the council awarded the author £100 out of the public purse 'for his late excellent publication on the subject of the Slave Trade', in recognition of 'the advantages resulting to the town and trade of Liverpool from the said publication'.[30] Liverpool sentiment was summed up in a 1790 election squib:

> If our slave trade had gone, there's an end to our lives,
> Beggars all we must be, our children and wives;

No ships from our ports their proud sails e'er would spread,
And our streets grown with grass, where the cows might be fed.[31]

While in Liverpool Clarkson saw, on public display in a shop window, the devices used by the slavers' crews to manacle, punish, and forcibly feed their cargoes. He bought specimens of them: iron handcuffs; leg-shackles; thumb-screws; and a speculum oris, a surgical instrument for wrenching open a locked jaw, used on the slave-ships to force open the mouths of slaves who refused to eat.[32] (Other expedients were to shove hot coals against the lips of those refusing food or pour molten lead on them[33] or flog them unmercifully.)[34] Branding-irons, too, were openly exhibited for sale in eighteenth-century Liverpool.[35] In 1756, at an auction in the Merchants' Coffee-house there, 83 pairs of shackles, 11 slave-collars, 22 pairs of handcuffs, 4 long chains, 34 rings, and 2 travelling chains were among the apparatus offered for sale, and shackles, chains, slave-collars, and handcuffs were advertised for sale in 1757.[36] An 'Iron Gag Muzzle' specially designed for use on Africans was offered for sale by London ironmongers in the 1760s.[37]

Black people in the slave ports

There is no positive evidence that such instruments were exposed for sale in Bristol, where Clarkson says he 'entirely overlooked' them, the implication being that he would probably have found them had he known about such things at that stage of his inquiries.[1] But there is plenty of evidence that slaves themselves were bought and sold in Bristol. Many a captain, mate, or ship's surgeon, short of funds, decided to convert his 'privilege Negro' into a spot of ready cash before the next voyage. 'To be sold, a black boy' is a cry that punctuates the pages of Bristol's eighteenth-century newspapers.

Here, for instance, in 1728, is Captain John Gwythen with 'a Negro man about 20 years old' to dispose of; so he inserts a genteel advertisement in *Farley's Bristol Newspaper*, where it is sure to reach a good class of person. It describes the slave as 'well limb'd', which has an elegant ring; 'fit to serve a gentleman', which flatters any prospective buyer; and apt for instruction in any handicraft trade, which is a highly practical recommendation.[2] Here, in the *Bristol Journal* of 1750, a black boy 'of about 12 years of age' is advertised for sale.[3] In 1754, 'any gentleman or lady who wants a Negro Boy' can buy a 14-year-old, recently landed – as most of those offered for sale in this way probably were.[4] In 1760 Bristol citizens are invited to buy 'A Negroe BOY, about ten Years old', and the advertisement adds reassuringly: 'He has had the SMALL-POX.'[5] 'To be sold, a Black Boy, about 15 years of age; capable of waiting at table', announces an advertisement of 1767.[6] And in 1768 there is offered 'a healthy Negro Slave named Prince, 17 years of age; extremely well grown'.[7]

One Liverpool street – the sources do not identify it – witnessed so many sales of black children and youths that it was nicknamed 'Negro Row' or 'Negro Street'. They were sold by auction in shops, warehouses, and coffee-houses, and on the front steps of the Custom House, on the east side of the Old Dock (afterwards Canning Place).[8] An 8-year-old black girl was publicly auctioned in Liverpool in 1765, the auction being announced in a local newspaper in these terms:

> To be sold by Auction at George's Coffee-house, betwixt the hours of six and eight o'clock, a very fine negro girl about eight years of age, very healthy, and hath been some time from the coast. Any person willing to purchase the same may apply to Capt. Robert Syers, at Mr. Bartley Hodgett's, Mercer and Draper near the Exchange, where she may be seen till the time of sale.[9]

A 'fine negro boy' offered for sale by auction at the Merchants' Coffee-house, Old Church Yard, was 11 years old; the sale was 'by order of Mr. Thomas Yates, who hath imported him from Bonny'.[10] In 1757 a flour merchant called Joseph Daltera offered for sale '10 pipes of raisin wine, a parcel of bottled cyder, and a negro boy'.[11] In the same year two black youngsters were offered for sale in the same advertisement:

> For Sale immediately, ONE stout [i.e. strong] NEGRO young fellow, about 20 years of age, that has been employed for 12 months on board a ship, and is a very serviceable hand. And a NEGRO BOY, about 12 years old, that has been used since Sept. last to wait at a table, and is of a very good disposition, both warranted sound. Apply to Robert Williamson, Broker.[12]

A Liverpool advertisement of 1766 offered the unusually high number of 11 black slaves for sale: 'To be sold At the Exchange Coffee House in Water Street, this day the 12th inst. September, at one o'clock precisely, Eleven negroes Imported per the Angola.'[13] Two years later, a 'fine Negroe Boy' offered for sale in

Liverpool was said to be 'about 4 Feet 5 Inches high, Of a sober, tractable, humane [i.e. willing] Disposition, Eleven or Twelve Years of Age, talks English very well, and can Dress Hair in a tolerable way'.[14] Sometimes an advertisement was inserted by a prospective buyer. 'Wanted immediately a negro boy', said one such advertisement in a Liverpool newspaper in 1756, specifying that he must be 'of a deep black complexion, and a lively, humane disposition, with good features, and not above 15, nor under 12 years of age'.[15]

Not all the young Africans to be seen about the streets of Liverpool in the last quarter of the eighteenth century were slaves. By the 1780s there were always at least 50 African schoolchildren, girls as well as boys, in Liverpool and the villages around. Most of them came from the Windward and Gold Coasts (i.e. present-day Liberia, Ivory Coast, and Ghana), and they were sent by their well-to-do parents to receive the advantage of a European elementary education. They were taught reading, writing, arithmetic, and religion. The girls, in addition, were instructed in 'domestic Duties' and needlework. African children were also educated in Bristol in the same period.[16]

What about London? Were black slaves bought and sold publicly in Britain's capital? The Admiralty judge Lord Stowell answered this question in 1827:

> The personal traffic in slaves resident in *England* had been as public and as authorised in *London* as in any of our *West India* islands. They were sold on the Exchange and other places of public resort by parties themselves resident in *London*, and with as little reserve as they would have been in any of our *West India* possessions. Such a state of things continued without impeachment from a very early period up to nearly the end of the last [i.e. eighteenth] century.[17]

Most of the slaves sold in London were children. An advertisement of Queen Anne's reign offered the purchaser 'a Negro boy about 12 years of age, that speaks English'.[18] 'To be Sold, A NEGRO BOY, aged about Eleven Years', proclaimed a 1728 advertisement, adding: 'Inquire at the Virginia Coffee-House in Threadneedle-street, behind the Royal-Exchange.'[19] 'A Pretty little Negro Boy, about nine Years old, and well limb'd' was offered for sale in 1744. He could be inspected at the Dolphin tavern in Tower Street and, 'if not dispos'd of', was to be 'sent to the West Indies in six Days Time'.[20] Two 'fine Negro Boys', offered for sale in 1756, were stated to be 'on Board the Molly . . . from Africa, now lying at Horsleydown Lower Chain'.[21] 'To be disposed of', said a 1762 advertisement, 'A Negro Boy 12 Years old, extremely well made, good-natured, sensible, and handy, speaks English well, and has had the Small-Pox'.[22] In the following year, a young black slave who had belonged to a forger – the forger was hanged at Tyburn and his property was therefore forfeit to the Crown – was put up for auction and sold for £32, and the *Gentleman's Magazine*, rather behind the times, supposed it to be 'perhaps the first instance of the kind in a free country'.[23] 'To be disposed of, a fine healthy Negro-Boy, between ten and eleven Years of Age', said a 1769 advertisement, adding: 'He has been five Years in England, is very good-natured and tractable, and would be very useful in a Family, or a Lady's Foot-boy . . . No Objections to lett the Boy be a Week on Trial.' The price was 50 guineas, which may explain why the advertisement was reinserted seven weeks later, this time with no price stated: the child was now said to have been born in America.[24] In the same year there was offered for sale in London 'a Black Girl, the Property of John Bull, Eleven Years of Age, who is extremely handy, works at her Needle tolerably, and speaks English perfectly well; is of an excellent Temper, and willing Disposition'.[25] Here is another 1769 advertisement (a timwhisky, usually so spelt, was a kind of carriage):

> HORSES, TIM WISKY, and BLACK BOY.
>
> To be SOLD, at the Bull and-Gate Inn, Holborn, A very good Tim Wisky, little the worse for wear, with good harness, and, if desired, a Horse also, that goes well in it.
>
> A Chestnut Gelding, 14 hands and a half high, is very sightly, and would suit a lady in every respect, extremely well, as he goes safe, pleasant, and steady.
>
> A very good Grey Mare, 15 hands high, mistress of 12 stone, and a very pleasant goer. The above are just come out of the country, are rising five years old, and will be warranted sound.
>
> A well made, good-tempered Black Boy,; he has lately had the small-pox, and will be sold to any gentleman. Enquire as above.[26]

As in Liverpool, prospective buyers in London advertised their wants sometimes: 'WANTED, A Blackamoor Boy of eight or nine Years of Age: Whoever has such a one to dispose of, may hear of a Purchaser at Mrs. Cranwell's, over-against [i.e. opposite] the Chapel in Conduit-Street.'[27]

Seventeenth-century hue-and-cry advertisements for runaway slaves were quoted in the previous chapter. Such advertisements were often inserted in Bristol's local newspapers in the eighteenth century and, with odd scraps of evidence of other kinds, such as an epitaph, they throw light on the development of the black community in the port and its hinterland. In 1713 Captain Foye of Bristol offered £5 for the return of 'a Negro called Scipio (his Negro Name Ossion), of middle Stature aged about 24 Years, speaks imperfect English, somewhat Splayfooted'.[28] Two years later another Bristol 'Scipio' ran away, and the local postmaster undertook to pay two guineas and expenses for his recovery; he belonged to a privateer captain called Stephen Courtney and was described as 'about 20 years of Age, well sett, having 3 or 4 marks on each Temple, and the same on each Cheek'.[29] Yet another local black youth of the same name – Scipio Africanus, in fact – served the Earl of Suffolk, died in 1720 at the age of 18, and is buried in Henbury churchyard, four miles from Bristol. The inscription on his tombstone reads:

> I who was Born a PAGAN and a SLAVE
> Now Sweetly Sleep a CHRISTIAN in my Grave
> What tho' my hue was dark my SAVIOUR's Sight
> Shall Change this darkness into radiant light
> Such grace to me my Lord on earth has given
> To recommend me to my Lord in heaven
> Whose glorious second coming here I wait
> With saints and Angels Him to celebrate[30]

In 1746 Captain Eaton announced in Bristol that his slave Mingo had run away after eight years, offered a guinea reward for his recapture, and warned: 'All persons are hereby forbid entertaining the said Black at their peril.'[31] Such a warning, which was not unique, suggests that there were people in Bristol prepared to give shelter to runaway black slaves. Josiah Ross, a Redcliff Street soapmaker, advertised the escape of his '*Black-Boy*' in 1748: 'He is about 12 or 13 Years of Age, a stocky round favour'd well-set Boy, and goes by the Name of *Somerset*. Whoever shall help the said Mr. Ross to the Boy again, shall be rewarded and all Charges thankfully Repaid, by directing a Letter to him at Bristol.'[32] In 1757 a young black slave called Starling, who 'blows the French horn very well', ran away from a publican in Prince's Street, and a guinea reward was offered for his capture;[33] a week later a black slave owned by Captain Bouchier, of Keynsham, escaped;[34] and six months after that Captain Ezekiel Nash was advertising the escape of his black slave and threatening to prosecute anyone that sheltered him.[35] A £5 reward was offered in 1758 for the recapture of a 'Malotta Boy' who had run away from his master in St Philip's Plain.[36] And in 1759 Captain Holbrook advertised a 'handsome reward' for the recovery of his 'Negro man named Thomas'.[37]

Similar hue-and-cry advertisements were frequently to be found in London newspapers of the eighteenth century. In Queen Anne's reign a guinea reward was offered for the return of 'a Negro Maid, aged about 16 Years, much pitted with the Small Pox, speaks English well, having a piece of her left Ear bit off by a Dog; She hath on a strip'd Stuff waistcoat and Petticoat'.[38] Two similar advertisements from the same period: 'A Tall Negro young fellow commonly known as Jack Chelsea, having a Collar about his Neck (unless it be lately filed off), with these Words; Mr. Moses Goodyeare of Chelsea his Negro, ran away from his Master last Tuesday evening';[39] 'Run away from his Master about a Fortnight since, a lusty Negroe Boy about 18 years of Age, full of pock holes, had a Silver Collar about his Neck engrav'd Capt. Tho. Mitchel's Negroe, living in Griffith Street in Shadwel'.[40] On three consecutive days of 1756, the *Public Advertiser* carried a notice offering a guinea reward for 'a Negro Boy, named *Torrie*, the Property of William Lessley, Commander of the Ship Johnson'. This 'Property' was 'about fourteen Years of Age, not tall, but well-set, walks in-toed, is thick-lipp'd, and flat-nosed . . . He sometimes calls himself Liverpool, and has a Scar on the Top of the upper Joint of his Arm'.[41] Two guineas was offered in the *Public Ledger*, in November 1761, for the return of 'a BLACK Fellow, about five Feet six Inches, aged 16 Years', who had 'RUN AWAY from Mr. STUBBS'; he had 'a scar in his Face'.[42] Almost two months later, this runaway not having been recaptured, his Ratcliff master inserted a longer and more detailed advertisement:

RUN AWAY.
From Captain STUBBS

A Yellowish Negro Man, about Five Feet Seven Inches, very flat Nose, and a Scar across his Forehead, he had when he run away, a white Pea-Jacket, a Pair of black Worsted Stockings, and a black Wig. Whoever will bring the said Negro Man to his abovementioned Master, Capt. STUBBS, in Prince's Square, Ratcliff Highway, shall receive Two Guineas Reward.

N.B. The abovementioned Master, Capt. STUBBS, desires

> that no Commander, Merchants, or any other Gentlemen will employ the abovementioned Negro; he goes by the Name of Stephen Brown, and if he will return to his Master, nothing will be [done to] him.[43]

In those last two months of 1761, the pages of the *Public Ledger* fairly bristled with hue-and-cry advertisements. Four guineas was offered for the capture of 'a Negro Man, called YORK', who had run away from the *Lovely Betsy*, commanded by Matthew Darke and lying in Church Hole. The absconder was 'about five Feet six inches high, thick-set, and well-made, aged about 21 Years, and says he was born in New York or Bermudas, and speaks good English'.[44] Another runaway was described as 'a Negro Man about 24 Years of Age, Five Feet eight Inches . . . remarkably bad legg'd and stoops much, and speaks tolerable good English'. The reward offered for his return was two guineas.[45] On Christmas Day of that year two black slaves ran away together from the *Britannia*, commanded by Captain Scott. One, named Lewis, was nearly six feet tall and had two holes in his ears; the other had 'two or three Particular Scars between his Eyebrows, and his Teeth are filed down like a Saw between every Tooth'.[46] And soon after Christmas 'a New Negro Fellow, about 20 Years of Age, five Feet eight or thereabouts' ran away from the brig *Madeira Merchant*, commanded by Captain Goodhand, which had brought him from Guadeloupe. There was a guinea reward for this runaway, who could not speak English and was scarred on both sides of his face.[47] One final advertisement from the end of the same decade: a 'pot-belly'd' black boy, aged about 12 or 13, had bad scurvy and a shaven head, could talk some English, answered to the name of Mark, or Batchelor, 'and whoever detains him, shall be prosecuted'.[48]

The slave ports' self-image

When the Commons turned down Wilberforce's first motion to bring in a Bill abolishing the slave trade, in 1791, Bristol's church bells were rung, workmen and sailors were given a half-holiday, cannon were fired on Brandon Hill, a bonfire was lit, and there was a fireworks display.[1] Sixteen years and many cargoes later the trade was at last abolished. Did abolition hit the slave ports hard, as had been forecast?

Bristol's slave trade, in fact, was already in decay. Its merchants had been severely hit by the 1793 economic crisis and their ranks had been thinned by bankruptcies.[2] Those left could see the writing on the wall and had largely transferred their capital to safer fields. The need to diversify had been clear for some time to Liverpool's more far-sighted businessmen, too. Some, like Thomas Leyland, had chosen banking as the next best thing to slave trading. Most of them simply switched their attention to another profitable commodity – one that happened to be produced by slave labour. For the next quarter of a century cotton, slavery, and Liverpool made up a trinity no less rewarding, and no less important to British capitalism, than the triangular trade it replaced. Liverpool, says a recent writer,

> gained greatly in importance even as the slave trade on which it was founded was officially abolished. The city's slave-trading past . . . was smugly overlaid by a respectability based on cotton. Yet by a cruel irony, slavery remained one of the bases of the wealth of Lancashire, and of Liverpool's prosperity, which together provided such a large component of Britain's nineteenth-century supremacy. For a further 27 years . . ., as for the previous two centuries, the black slave remained the prop, and victim, of the British economy.[3]

Apart from folklore – which, as we have seen, is sometimes imprecise – London, Bristol, and Liverpool have almost entirely forgotten their past as slave ports. When it is remembered the tone is usually one of oily complacency. This chapter began with an example of such complacency from Bristol; it ends with three from Liverpool.

Ten years before the British slave trade was abolished, a Liverpool surgeon justified it in these words:

> While the Africans continue in the same untutored, and consequently defenceless state, they must remain a prey to their more skilful neighbours – such *is* the character of man. Will the enlightened and refined European say, why his Creator doomed the mind of the African to remain as dark and naked as his body? . . . The ignorance of the African slave makes him unconscious of being so . . . The thousand wants and cares of the *free* and opulent European are unknown to him; the few he has, which his nature and education require, are gratified. Why then is his lot so very miserable? . . . Since slavery has existed in all ages, and this particular part of it for a long time and to its present extent, instead of aiming to

> subdue it by violence, let us rather endeavour, as human prudence will suggest, to meliorate it to the utmost in our ability; and thus endeavour to palliate what it is not in our power to remove.[4]

We go forward nearly 100 years. In 1893 a Liverpool writer declared that there was nothing derogatory in the fact that their ancestors had dealt in 'niggers'; that the horrors of the slave trade were exceeded by the horrors of the Liverpool drink traffic; that, after all, 'it was the capital made in the African slave trade that built some of our docks' and 'the price of human flesh and blood that gave us a start'; that some of those who made their fortunes out of the slave trade had soft hearts under their waistcoats for the poor of Liverpool; and that the profits from slave trading represented 'an influx of wealth which, perhaps, no consideration would induce a commercial community to relinquish'.[5]

Sixty years later the same tune was being sung. A history of Liverpool, written in 1957 by the city's then public librarian, and sponsored by the city council to celebrate the seven-hundred-and-fiftieth anniversary of Liverpool's charter, dismissed the slave trade in just 28 lines (in a book of 515 pages) that ended with this remarkable sentence: 'In the long run, the triangular operation based on Liverpool was to bring benefits to all, not least to the transplanted slaves, whose descendants have subsequently achieved in the New World standards of education and civilisation far ahead of their compatriots whom they left behind.'[6]

Well might a city governed and memorialized by Panglosses display on its town hall, built in 1749–54, the symbolic heads of African elephants and African slaves.[7] For all its past and present wealth, Liverpool remains at its heart what a poet called it in 1909: a 'City of festering streets by Misery trod'.[8]

4. The black community takes shape

Early black organizations

So far we have been looking at Britain's black population exclusively through the eyes of the natives of the country they were brought to against their will. We have had no alternative. Until about 1750 the traces left by their presence here – royal proclamations, entries in parish registers, instructions to slave-ship captains, offers of slaves for sale, advertisements for runaways – were the documents of native rulers, administrators, merchants, noblemen, and ships' officers. But from about the middle of the eighteenth century there is something new in the records. There is evidence of cohesion, solidarity, and mutual help among black people in Britain. They had developed a lively social life. And they were finding ways of expressing their political aspirations. Black self-awareness took literary shape in autobiography, political protest, journalism, and other published writings by Africans who lived in or visited England and wrote in English. The lives and work of these writers and leaders of Britain's black community will be described in the next chapter.

How many black people lived in Britain in the eighteenth century? In estimating the size of the black population we must bear in mind that it was constantly being reinforced. For the first three-quarters of the century at least, black slaves were brought here, not merely by slaver captains, but also by returning planters, government officials, and army and navy officers. However rich they might be, such people objected to paying wages to English servants when there were black slaves available to work for nothing but food and clothing.[1] So they brought their slaves here as personal and household servants. Richard Bathurst, planter and colonel in the Jamaica militia, returning to England about the year 1752, brought back with him a young black slave called Francis Barber, whom he set free in his will and who became valet-cum-secretary to Samuel Johnson and ended his days as a village schoolmaster.[2] Mrs Valentine Morris, wife of the governor of St Vincent, returned to England with a black slave who later served the painter Sir Joshua Reynolds.[3] The politician and poet Robert 'Doughty Deeds' Graham, returning from Jamaica after a stint as a tax collector, brought back his black slave Tom, who had been left as a legacy by his former owner.[4] Admiral Lord Romney brought over a black slave he acquired in the West Indies, who served him for many years and cared for him on his death bed.[5] A subordinate of Pitt's favourite admiral, Edward 'Old Dreadnought' Boscawen, turned up one day with a surprise present for the admiral's wife: a 10-year-old black boy. She told her husband that their son, aged four, 'took to him immediately and whispered he should be his servant' – and soon the black child was waiting on the white one at table.[6] The 'little negro boy . . . pretty, and very good humoured' given to the first Lady Shelburne by Richard Wells in 1768 was only five years old.[7]

In 1772 there was a legal decision which, while not stemming this flow of black people into Britain, did slow it down. After a long and perhaps embarrassed delay, Lord Chief Justice Mansfield handed down his famous but often misinterpreted judgment in the Somerset case. We shall see later that he did not rule against the institution of slavery as such, but simply that slaves could not lawfully be shipped out of England against their will. In the course of the hearing Mansfield accepted, and based certain delicate calculations on, an advocate's estimate of 14,000 or 15,000 for the number of black people in the country.[8] This is the figure generally cited by historians. Some contemporary estimates were much higher. Eight years before Mansfield, the *Gentleman's Magazine* had come up with an estimate of 20,000 for London alone;[9] Granville Sharp, the energetic humanitarian campaigner against slavery, privately accepted that figure for the country as a whole.[10] But F.O. Shyllon has recently argued that Britain's black population must have fluctuated constantly during the eighteenth century, since ill-treatment, starvation, disease, and poverty checked the growth of its permanent core, and that it is unlikely to have exceeded 10,000 at any given time.[11] By the turn of the century the total population of England and Wales had reached almost 9,000,000.

More important, of course, than its size, which can never be calculated precisely, is how the community conducted its affairs, reacted to the atrocious circumstances so many of its members had to endure, and took part in the movement for the abolition of the slave trade and of slavery. In London at least, black servants were able to gather informally in small groups from time to time, no doubt to exchange information and discuss matters of common concern. One of Samuel Johnson's visitors stumbled across such a gathering about the year 1760. Johnson was away from home, 'and when Francis Barber, his black servant, opened the door to tell me so, a group of his African countrymen were sitting round a fire in the gloomy anti-room'.[12] Barber was no longer a slave, and in Johnson – who once scandalized 'some very grave men at Oxford' with the toast: 'Here's to the next insurrection of the negroes in the West-Indies'[13] – he had an employer who treated him as a human being. So the meeting was more probably a regular event that had Johnson's blessing than one hastily convened while his back was turned. (For Francis Barber, see pp. 424–6 below.)

But London's black community organized very much bigger and more elaborate affairs, with music and dancing, at various taverns – 'the wonted haunts of Moormen and Gentoos', as the author of *The Servants Pocket-Book* (1761) called them, noting that black servants invariably tended to 'herd together' there.[14] 'Among the fashionable routs or clubs, that are held in town, that of the Blacks or Negro servants is not the least', reported a newspaper in 1764, telling how black domestics of both sexes 'supped, drank, and entertained themselves with dancing and music, consisting of violins, French horns, and other instruments, at a public-house in Fleet-street, till four in the morning. No Whites were allowed to be present, for all the performers were Blacks'.[15] The black community attentively followed the long-drawn-out Somerset case and sent representatives to attend the hearings. At the lord chief justice's fateful words, 'The man must be discharged', they bowed to the judges, then clasped each other's hands in joy and relief.[16] A few days later this partial victory was celebrated by a gathering of about 200 blacks, 'with their ladies', at a Westminster public house. Tickets of admission cost 5*s*., so these were either better-off servants, whose masters paid them wages, or else delegates each of whom represented many others. Lord Mansfield's health was 'echoed round the room' and the evening ended with dancing.[17]

Besides small private meetings and more elaborate gatherings with music and dancing there was also community observance of christenings, weddings, and funerals – precisely those events in the human life-cycle which, if we take christening as a special case of name-giving, figure so largely as social occasions throughout black Africa. A christening at the parish church of St Giles, London, in 1726 assembled 'well-drest' black people of both sexes. The two godmothers and their half-dozen attendants are described in a newspaper report as 'all Guiney Blacks, as pretty, genteel Girls, as could be girt with a Girdle, and setting aside the Complexion, enough to tempt an old frozen Anchorite to have crack'd a Commandment with any of them'.[18] At least one black kinsman of Jack Beef, footman to the Leeward Islands solicitor-general John Baker, attended Beef's funeral in Bloomsbury in 1771;[19] and Samuel Bowden, physician and versifier, in 'An Epitaph, On a Negro Servant, who died at Governor Phipps's, At Haywood near Westbury', recorded that

> Black guests, and *Æthiopian* night,
> Sit round this funeral room.[20]

And when, in 1773, two black men were imprisoned in the Bridewell house of correction for the crime of begging, they were 'visited by upwards of 300 of their countrymen' and the black community 'contributed largely towards their support during their confinement'.[21]

It is tempting to speculate about these black organizations in eighteenth-century London in the light of what is known about their counterparts in, for example, Buenos Aires, where seven neo-African societies were flourishing legally as late as 1827, some taking their names (Angola, Bangala, Conga, Mina) from the regions of Africa to which members traced their descent.[22] The differences are obvious. Most black Londoners were very young. Most of them had been torn from their parents and ethnic groups while still children. They were atomized in separate households, cut off from the cultural nourishment and reinforcement made possible by even the most inhumane plantation system. These circumstances could not but limit severely those neo-African forms of organization that found their richest expression in Brazil, Cuba, and Haiti. All the more value, therefore, attaches to the details about London's black clubs provided by three hostile witnesses.

The quarrelsome eccentric Philip Thicknesse, whom we shall meet later as a vehement racist, complained in 1778 that 'London abounds with an incredible number of these black men, who have clubs to support those who are out of place'.[23] 'Out of place' means out of work, but the reference here is clearly to black people who had escaped from servitude and in many cases, no doubt, were living under cover. The father of English racism, Edward Long, had complained in 1772 that those blacks who had escaped and not been recaptured were influencing the rest, especially newcomers:

> Upon arriving in *London*, these servants soon grow acquainted with a knot of blacks, who, having eloped from their respective owners at different times, repose themselves here in ease and indolence, and endeavour to strengthen their party, by seducing as many of these strangers into the association as they can work to their purpose.[24]

But the most interesting and informative of these hostile witnesses is Sir John Fielding the 'Blind Beak', magistrate and half-brother of the novelist. He noted in 1768 that it was the practice of blacks *'intoxicated with Liberty'* and *'grown refractory'* to *'enter into Societies, and make it their Business to corrupt and dissatisfy the Mind of every fresh black Servant that comes to England'*. Worse still, it was often hazardous, according to Fielding, for an owner to try to recapture a runaway. For the blacks had succeeded in getting *'the Mob on their Side'*. That made it *'not only difficult but dangerous'* for owners to recover possession of their black chattels *'when once they are spirited away'*. When blacks were brought to England, *'they no sooner come over, but the Sweets of Liberty and the Conversation with free Men and Christians, enlarge their Minds'*. So they grew *'restless, prompt to conceive, and alert to execute*[,] *the blackest Conspiracies against their Governors and Masters'*.[25] And to this fact Fielding, authentic voice of the English governing and master class, attributed the frequent slave rebellions in the West Indies.

Now, when Fielding says the blacks had the 'Mob' on their side, what exactly does he mean by 'Mob'? He himself had identified them, ten years earlier, as the 'infinite . . . Number of Chairmen [i.e. carriers of sedans], Porters, Labourers and drunken Mechanics in this Town'.[26] And he himself, in the Gordon riots of 1780, was to have his house sacked by them. The 'Mob' were the working people of London, the pre-industrial craftsmen and labourers who, in the very year that Fielding wrote of their support for runaway black slaves, poured onto the streets of the capital in their thousands to demonstrate for 'Wilkes and Liberty'. Groups marched or ran through Shoreditch, the City, Westminster, and Southwark, 'captained' by men like the journeyman wheelwright William Pateman and the coach-master Thomas Taplin, gathering numbers as they went, smashing lamps, windows, and accessible woodwork in the Mansion House and the big town houses of the nobility. Among them were apprentices, journeymen, labourers, servants, waiters, craftsmen, shopkeepers, small traders, Spitalfields weavers, east London coal-heavers, tanners, brewers' draymen, and sailors.[27]

Ever since the political upheavals of the seventeenth century, this 'Mob' had been impregnated (or, as Fielding had it, 'intoxicated') with a love of liberty, a hatred of slavery, and a spirit of 'sturdy independence and hostility to the executive'.[28] No wonder it was not merely difficult but dangerous for masters to try to recapture people who had such formidable allies. And allies they were. London's working people were not trying to make use of the black community or usurp its leadership. Their attitude to slavery had nothing in common with the sentimentality of many middle-class abolitionists. They saw black people as fellow-victims of their own enemies, fellow-fighters against a system that degraded poor whites and poor blacks alike. With their help, London had by the 1760s become a centre of black resistance.

Black people at work

The majority of the 10,000 or so black people who lived in Britain in the eighteenth century were household servants – pages, valets, footmen, coachmen, cooks, and maids – much as their predecessors had been in the previous century. Among the aristocracy and those who aped them, the fashion for black servants in metal collars and showy livery continued – although, with the mid-century vogue of *chinoiserie*, it became for a time 'more original' for the trend-setting upper class to go in for Chinese servants.[1] As in the seventeenth century, judging by the large number of contemporary portraits in which they appear, many of the black pages could not have been more than nine or ten years old.[2] Andrea Soldi's portrait of Catherine, Countess of Fauconberg, which hangs at Newburgh Priory in north Yorkshire, shows a black child holding the countess's coronet. Some of Johann Zoffany's family groups include a black servant. So do George Morland's *The Fruits of Early Industry and Œconomy* (*c.*1785–90) and William Redmore Bigg's *The Charitable Lady* (1787), and both a black page and a black footman figure in the fourth plate of Hogarth's *Marriage à la Mode* (1745).[3] Using his own as a model, Reynolds painted black servants into a number of portraits: holding the Marquis of Granby's horse, for instance.[4] For a portrayal of a black child in service lower down the social scale we must turn to Hogarth again: in the third plate of *A Harlot's Progress* (1732) a small boy, wearing a jewelled, feathered turban, is carrying a kettle or large teapot.[5]

Associated in many English people's minds with the immense riches of Africa and India, and the immense riches amassed by the West and East Indians, black servants conferred on their masters and mistresses 'an air of luxurious wellbeing'.[6] They were at once charming, exotic ornaments, objects of curiosity, talking-points, and, above all, symbols of prestige.[7] In the phrase of a minor poet of the 1790s, who wrote when the fashion was past its peak, a black attendant served as the 'Index of Rank or Opulence supreme'.[8] One gains the impression that there was scarcely a titled woman in eighteenth-century England who would have been seen dead without one. Elizabeth Chudleigh, for instance, the profligate Duchess of Kingston, had a black servant called Sambo, whom she brought up from the age of five or six, and of whom she was so fond that she took him, elegantly dressed, to most of the public places she frequented. He sat with her in her box at the theatre, watching *The Beggar's Opera*. Unfortunately, when he reached the age of 18 or 19 he began staying away for several days and nights at a time and associating with 'a set of whores and ruffians', so she packed him off to the West Indies.[9] Catherine Douglas, eccentric Duchess of Queensberry, who died from eating too many cherries, had a black servant whom she called Soubise. Son of a woman slave on St Kitts, the young man was an accomplished fencer, horseman, and musician. He was taken up by fashionable society, became a fop among fops, used expensive scent, was a favourite of Garrick, was sketched by Gainsborough, and was accused of raping one of his mistress's maids – though he seems to have found no shortage of willing female partners, being indeed 'as general a lover as Don Juan'. Eventually he was sent to India, where he ran a riding academy, became government horse-breaker, and was killed in a fall from a horse.[10] Georgiana Cavendish, Duchess of Devonshire, was an exception to the general rule, since the duke for some reason objected to her accepting a black boy, 'eleven years old and very honest'. So she offered the child to her mother: 'I cannot bear the poor wretch being ill-used; if you liked him instead of Michel I will send him, he will be a cheap servant and you will make a Christian of him and a good boy; if you don't like him they say Lady Rockingham wants one.'[11] The fashion still extended right to the top: according to Thackeray, when King George I came over to England from his duchy of Hanover in 1714 he brought with him his two black servants, Mustapha and Mahomet.[12]

What were the duties of a page waiting upon a lady of quality? He had to attend his mistress's person and her tea-table; carry her train as she moved to and fro; take charge of her fan and smelling-salts and produce them when required; feed her parrots; and comb her lapdogs.[13] From a black youngster's point of view it was no doubt better to serve a slightly dotty duchess until she grew tired of you than a sadistic captain of a slave-ship or a rum-sodden absentee planter. Between the extremes of petting and brutality there must have been an infinite number of gradations. But all were servitude. As the hue-and-cry advertisements showed us and those complaints by Thicknesse, Long, and Fielding reminded us, a great number of black people resisted servitude in the only way open to them: by running away. There was liable to be about even the most docile, well-trained, and well-treated of black servants something that unimaginative English gentlefolk interpreted as an ungrateful restlessness, an itchiness of the feet. Some took it to be an inherent racial characteristic. Few realized just how bitterly the black members of their households loathed servitude and longed for freedom.

Higher-minded masters and mistresses had their black slaves taught to read and write, had them taught christian doctrine, even had them baptized, once it became fairly clear that baptism did not mean freedom. The two black slaves of the Duke of Marlborough were schooled in 1734 by one Charles Beesley, at a cost to the duke of £10 15*s.* for four months' tuition, plus 2*s.* for '2 Writing Books for ye Blacks', 3*s.* for Thomas Dyche's *Guide to the English Tongue*, and 5*s.* for a history of England.[14] Lord Chesterfield, while ambassador at The Hague, had his 'Black-a-Moor boy' instructed in the christian faith by his chaplain, personally catechized him, then had him christened.[15] To those who had done their christian duty in this way the slaves' itch for liberty came as a sore disappointment, a blow to pride as well as pocket.

Some runaways got a bit of their own back by taking with them some money or a few portable household goods. Black youths came up at the Old Bailey from time to time, charged with petty theft,[16] and the hue-and-cry advertisements sometimes complain of theft. Not that freedom was an easy option, even if you had the 'Mob' to help you avoid recapture, a network of sympathizers to find you shelter, and a pair of your master's silver candlesticks or a bolt of your mistress's linen for sale to keep you from starving. To be young, black, and on the run meant scraping an existence at the very bottom of the social heap. Especially in London, where black people were not, after 1731, allowed to learn a trade. On 14 September of that year the lord mayor issued a solemn proclamation prohibiting apprenticeship for black people, some of whom had evidently been trying to acquire a useful skill:

It is Ordered by this Court, That for the future no *Negroes* or

> other *Blacks* be suffered to be bound Apprentices at any of the Companies of this City to any Freeman thereof; and that Copies of this Order be printed and sent to the Masters and Wardens of the several Companies of this City, who are required to see the same at all times hereafter duly observed.[17]

This is the earliest known instance of an employment colour bar in this country, and it seems to have been effective.

There is said to have been a concentration of destitute black people in the St Giles or Seven Dials district, then on London's northern outskirts; it was a mass of insanitary hovels where beggars, whores, criminals, and other outcasts congregated. According to one late eighteenth-century source, black mendicants, conspicuous among London beggars, were dubbed 'St Giles black birds'.[18] Other black people lived in the unfashionable riverside hamlets of Ratcliff (as early as 1690) and Limehouse (long before any Chinese settled there),[19] and local tradition has it that two riverside inns at Wapping were used as markets for the sale of black youths as domestic servants.[20]

A number of free black men, scattered all over the country, managed to earn their bread as labourers or craftsmen of various kinds, or in other ways. There were black agricultural labourers[21] and, as we have seen, black seamen.[22] A black fencing-master called George Turner, described as 'tall, well-made and pretty', was making a living in 1710 by sword-fighting at the Bear Garden in Southwark; his brother had been fatally wounded in the same occupation four years before.[23] A 'surprising Negro, or African Prince' was performing as fire-eater and contortionist at Charing Cross in 1751–2,[24] and a black actor was playing on the Dublin stage in the 1770s.[25] In 1785 John Marrant, a black man from Nova Scotia, was ordained a minister of the Countess of Huntingdon's Connection, a dissident Anglican sect; he died at Islington in 1791.[26] At least one black hairdresser was working in London in 1788.[27]

Joseph Banks's two servants, Thomas Richmond and George Dorlton (or Dalton) accompanied their master on Captain Cook's first voyage round the world, in 1768. With a white seaman, they went up a mountain to gather rare plants for scientific purposes. All three froze to death in the snow-covered wastes of Tierra del Fuego.[28]

What of black girls and women in eighteenth-century Britain? Some found work as laundrymaids, seamstresses, and children's nurses.[29]

Two London sculptors of the eighteenth century had black maidservants: Mary, servant to Roubiliac, died of smallpox; Elizabeth Rosina Clements, known as 'Black Bet' and 'Bronze', went grey in the service of the thrifty Nollekens, amused him on occasion by dancing his favourite cat round the studio, and was left 19 guineas in his will.[30] A black actress performing in Lancashire as Polly in *The Beggar's Opera* was reported to be 'excellent as to figure, and speaking, but remarkably so as to singing';[31] her name has not come down to us.

It is clear that many black women were forced into prostitution as the only alternative to starvation. A German who visited London in 1710 noted that 'there are . . . such a quantity of Moors of both sexes in England that I have never seen before'. He observed black women whom he described, naïvely or prudishly, as beggars. They wore European dress, 'and there is nothing more diverting than to see them in mobs or caps [*Cornetten oder Hauben*] of white stuff and with their black bosoms uncovered'.[32] These were merely the fashionable low-cut dresses of the period. A black woman is shown among a group of whores in the third plate of Hogarth's *A Rake's Progress* (1735).[33] One who was comparatively successful in this occupation in the 1770s was known as 'Black Harriot'. Bought on the Guinea coast when very young, she was taken to Jamaica and sold to a planter who fathered two children on her. Then he brought her to England, where he died of smallpox and left her practically penniless. 'Very alluring . . . tall, well made, and genteel', she had 'many attractions that are not often met with in the Female World who yield to prostitution'. Having educated herself by reading, she had attained 'a degree of politeness [i.e. intellectual culture], scarce to be paralleled in an African female'. After only a few months she had acquired more than 70 regular clients, at least 20 of whom, according to a contemporary account, were members of the House of Lords.[34] Titled patrons also frequented a black brothel in London in 1774, so Boswell was informed by the Earl of Pembroke.[35] Mrs Lowes, of 68 Upper Charlotte Street, Rathbone Place, Soho, born in the West Indies, was working as a prostitute in 1788, charging clients three guineas for a whole night, one guinea for 'a short visit'. She is described as short and plump, with 'a sweet chearful disposition, fine dark hair, and eyes of the same friendly hue; fine teeth'.[36] Five years later a Jamaican known as Miss Wilson was exercising the same profession at 27 Litchfield Street, Soho. She had 'very pleasing' features and was 'a girl of considerable taste and fashion', who danced well and sang 'with much sweetness and science' and whose 'conversation denotes her to be a girl of sound sense'. She was generally to be found of an evening at the Covent Garden Theatre, and was friendly with the actors there.[37]

Asians in Britain

Some of the black performers in the seventeenth-century Lord Mayor's Pageant were Asians, and some of the black servants in Britain in the eighteenth century were 'Moormen and Gentoos': Mohammedans and Hindus, in other words. Most of these came from Bengal, but there were some from Madras and elsewhere in India. They were brought back from the east by the nabobs. Sons of London merchants, army officers, country parsons, and petty gentry, the nabobs made their fortunes as writers and factors in the service of the East India Company. Like the West Indians, they came back to England to live luxuriously.[1] During their stay in India they had grown used to personal service on a stupendous scale. When the barrister William Hickey left India in 1808 he doled out 2,000 rupees in farewell presents to his 63 servants, among them two bakers, two cooks, eight waiters, three grass-cutters, four grooms, a coachman, a hairdresser, and nine valets.[2] But that was nothing out of the ordinary. Alexander Mackrabie, sheriff of Calcutta, lived with three friends in a household employing 110 servants, and the Revd William Tennant, a chaplain, lived with a family that employed 105.[3] An English captain serving in the 1780 Mysore campaign had with him his steward, cook, valet, groom, groom's assistant, barber, washerman, and 'other officers', plus 15 'coolies' to carry his luggage, wine, brandy, tea, live poultry, and milch-goats.[4]

If a nabob hankered after a really expensive status symbol he could easily buy an African slave on the spot. Known in Calcutta as 'Coffrees', Africans were used by the English and French in their wars in India, chiefly 'to stop a bullet from some more valuable life'. Before long the enterprising East India Company was running a regular service of armed slavers from Madagascar, mainly to supply its settlements on the west coast of India. Two-thirds of the cargoes were males aged 15 to 40; the rest were females aged 15 to 25 and children. Purchase price was £15 per head for adults; children were half-price; and captains, mates, and surgeons received a few shillings' bonus for each slave landed alive. Judging by press advertisements, some Englishmen in Calcutta bred Africans for the slave market. Profits were slow but enormous. The selling price of an African butler and cook in Calcutta in 1781 was 400 rupees. Since African slaves in India cost about ten times as much as boys and girls from Dacca, most English expatriates preferred to acquire Indian domestics. And it was those they took home with them.[5]

Governor-general Warren Hastings and his wife brought back to England a handsome all-black tiger, two Indian boys of 13 or 14, and four Indian maidservants. The boys, who spoke no English, were described by a German visitor as having 'longish faces, beautiful black eyes, fine eyebrows, sleek black hair, thin lips, fine teeth, a brownish complexion and kindly, intelligent faces'. But Mrs Hastings, formerly the Baroness von Imhoff, complained that her four maids 'refused to work any harder than in India, and wanted to lead exactly the same life'. So she got rid of them.[6] In 1789, at Godalming, Fanny Burney's friend Mrs William Lock watched the arrival of several post-chaises containing 'East Indian families with their Negro servants, Nurses and Children'. She found it 'touching . . . to see these poor negro women taken away from their country'. Her own servant met one on the stairs in tears.[7] Hickey was given a 'little pet boy', a Bengali nicknamed Nabob, whom he brought back to England and dressed as a hussar. The boy was sent to school and baptized, betrayed his master's whereabouts to a bailiff, and was at length reclaimed by his former owner.[8]

Many of the Englishwomen who travelled to the east brought Asian servants back with them. Returning from Bengal in 1774, a Mrs Gladwin was allegedly poisoned by her two Indian maids.[9] Eliza Fay, returning from Calcutta in 1782, stranded her Anglo-Indian maid Kitty Johnson on St Helena, and to her embarrassment was called to account for it on a subsequent visit.[10]

Like African slaves in Britain, Asians were sometimes ill-treated. In 1800 a Surrey woman was accused of cruelty to her Indian maid-servant during the absence of her husband, 'who had brought the poor girl from her native country'.[11] And, like African slaves, many of the Asians ran away and were the subject of hue-and-cry advertisements. An 'East-India Tawny Black' ran off and was advertised for in 1737, a 'Runaway Bengal Boy' in 1743.[12]

Asian slaves were sometimes advertised for sale. Steele's and Addison's *Tatler*, in 1709, carried an advertisement offering 'a Black Indian Boy, 12 Years of Age, fit to wait on a Gentleman, to be disposed of at Denis's Coffee-house in Finch-Lane near the Royal Exchange'.[13] Indian servants were often sought by people planning to go to India,[14] but other prospective employers sometimes advertised for them, like the advertiser who wanted to hire 'a young female East-Indian Servant' in 1758.[15]

Free Asians occasionally advertised their availability for work. In 1750 an East Indian who could speak six languages, among them Portuguese and German, and had been 'christen'd according to the Establishment of the Church of England', was looking for a place as a footman.[16] Such advertisers often expressed a wish to return to India: 'A Female Black Servant would be glad to wait on any Lady or Children going to India; she came from thence . . . to attend a Gentleman's Child'; 'A Young Man, a Native of Madras, and who understands shaving and dressing Gentlemen, and all other requisites necessary for a Valet, would be glad to engage with any Captain or private Gentleman going to that place the ensuing season in that capacity'; 'WANTS a passage to attend on a Lady going to India, a Black Girl, who came home [*sic*] as a lady's servant; has been in England some time; can dress hair; works well at her needle; get up small linen, &c'.[17]

But not all the Asians in Britain in the eighteenth century were servants. An 'East Indian Gentoo' conjuror, whose repertory included card tricks and thought-reading, was performing at Bartholomew Fair in 1790.[18] And, as we shall see in a later chapter, the plight of stranded Lascars – Indian seamen – first troubled the public conscience in 1785.

Black musicians

Music played such an important part in the daily lives of Africans and their descendants – which is not the same thing as saying that all black people were born musicians – that the early appearance of black musicians in the British Isles is not surprising. It was in fact part of a general European phenomenon. As early as the thirteenth century the German emperor Frederick II had five young black trumpeters at his splendid court in Palermo, on the island of Sicily. Aged between 16 and 20, they wore purple livery and played on silver trumpets. The imperial decree sending for them was dated 28 November 1239, and three years later they were being listened to in amazement by an English visitor. Richard, Earl of Cornwall, son of King John of England and afterwards King of the Romans, was passing through Sicily on his way back home from the crusades, and he was given a brilliant reception at Frederick's court. He was enchanted by the acrobatic dances of Saracen dancing-girls, noted that the page-boys were blacks, and heard strange music played by black musicians on instruments he had never seen or heard before.[1] His account of his travels must have helped spread to England the fame of black musicians as part of the rich trappings of a feudal court far more sophisticated than his father's. Other returning crusaders brought back to Europe, not only black musicians,[2] but also 'the particular combination of instruments in the Islamic military band':[3] the buisine, or herald's trumpet, and the *naqqāra*, the medium-sized Arabian kettledrum that the Italians adopted as the *nacchera*, the French as the *nacaire*, and the English as the naker.[4] The British Library has an illuminated manuscript of the late fourteenth century, attributed to the Genoese miniaturist known as 'the Monk of Hyères', showing a black cymbalist who is humping a pair of these laced kettledrums on his back. They are slung round his neck by means of a red strap and are being played with two small knobbed beaters by a white musician standing behind him.[5] Seville's black community were allowed to keep their dances and festivals in the reign of Enrique III of Castille (1390–1406).[6] African singing was heard at Lagos in Portugal on 8 August 1444, when the slaves taken back by Lançarote 'made their lamentations in song, according to the custom of their country' (*faziam suas lamentaçooẽs em maneira de canto, segundo o costume de sua terra*).[7] Black dance music was heard in Lisbon on 31 October 1451, during the triumphs honouring the imperial ambassadors sent by Frederick III to fetch his bride Princess Leonor; highlighting the reception was an African in a dragon mask.[8]

Half a century later, as we have seen, black musicians had reached the royal courts of the British Isles. Early in the sixteenth century the English king had his black trumpeter, the Scottish king his black drummer. Queen Elizabeth I is portrayed as having seven black musicians and three black dancers. What could well have been a group of black musicians performed in the 1672 and 1673 Lord Mayor's Pageants. Pinpointed in the hue-and-cry advertisement for a young black runaway in 1757 was his proficiency on the French horn. Black musicians performed on violins, horns, and other instruments at a social gathering of black servants in 1764. So much has been said in previous chapters.

Some black musicians were highly regarded. When the seventh Earl of Barrymore went stag-hunting he had in his train 'four Africans, superbly mounted, and superbly dressed in scarlet and silver, who were correct performers on the French horn'.[9] The musician said to 'blow the best French Horn and Trumpet' in eighteenth-century England was Cato, slave first to Sir Robert Walpole then to the Earl of Chesterfield, who gave him as a present to the Prince and Princess of Wales in 1738. Cato became the Prince's head gamekeeper; his portrait, in a group of hunting celebrities, was painted by the landscape painter John Wootton.[10] Others were less highly regarded. A satirical complaint in 1785 referred to two black musicians who 'never do a turn except playing on the French horn, and sometimes making punch, when it is wanted particularly nice'.[11]

By as early as 1787 white Londoners as well as black were dancing to black dance music at what a contemporary account describes as 'an innocent amusement, vulgarly called *black hops*, where twelve pence will gain admission'.[12] In the same year an ex-slave from Virginia, blinded in the American War of Independence, was scraping a living with his violin around the London streets, as we shall see in a later chapter; and a black musician was leading an itinerant concert party round the country. Parson Woodforde's diary tells how, one summer evening, a covered cart drew into his yard with three men in it, 'and one of them, the principal, was a black with a french Horn, blowing it all the way up the Yard to the Kitchen Door'. After hearing songs from 'a little Woman only 33 Inches high', Woodforde asked the horn-player where he came from and was told that he had formerly served the Earl of Albemarle. Woodforde gave his visitors a shilling for the entertainment.[13]

The use of black musicians as military bandsmen in the British army, a tradition that reached its height towards the end of the eighteenth century, seems to have started in the second half of the seventeenth. Black drummers were first acquired by English regiments serving in the West Indies. There are several seventeenth-century records of a colonel 'presenting a slave' to his regiment to act as drummer.[14] According to Sir Walter Scott, six black trumpeters were attached to the Scottish Life Guards in 1679. He describes them as wearing 'white dresses richly laced' and 'massive silver collars and armlets'.[15] A black kettledrummer can be seen in the background of Sir Godfrey Kneller's portrait (*c.*1689) of *Frederick, 1st Duke of Schomberg*, who served as a cavalry general in the English army. This drummer wears a scarlet coat with gold-laced seams, embroidered back and front with the royal cipher and crown, and a small white turban bound round a blue cloth cap with a hanging hood or bag.[16] At least one black drummer was present at the Battle of Blenheim in 1704, serving under Marlborough in the English army that defeated the French and Bavarians.[17] In 1713 a black trumpeter and kettledrummer called Brown, in 'Col. La

Boucheterre's Regiment of Dragoons', petitioned for an increase of pay, but this petition was turned down on the ground that neither trumpeter not kettledrummer was allowed by the establishment to dragoons, and 'the petitioner constantly received above the pay of Hautbois which the establishment allows'.[18] A contemporary account of a parade of the 4th Dragoons at Stirling in 1715 said: 'This was a show we could not pass by without looking at and to say truth I scarse think there is a more showy regiment in Europe . . . The six drumers were mores with bres [i.e. brass] drums . . . and they roade upon gray horses.'[19] In 1755 the 4th Dragoons' inspection returns recorded that 'the Drummers are all blacks'.[20] An 1802 painting of this regiment shows a black trumpeter in a white jacket with red collar, cuffs, and wings, all laced yellow with blue centre. He is wearing white breeches and, instead of the regulation fur cap, a white turban with cords or chains and an unusual green and red plume; his rolled cloak is red, and on the rear of his saddle is a small red box in which his trumpet was apparently kept when not in use. The 4th Dragoons' black trumpeters are also shown in an 1821 picture.[21] The Household Cavalry had its black trumpeters by about 1720,[22] and a black trumpeter in oriental dress can be seen in the background of a portrait (*c.*1735) of Captain Gifford of the 4th troop of Life Guards.[23] A contemporary engraving of the 12 musicians ('His Majesty's Trumpets') at the installation of the Knights Companions of the Order of the Bath in 1725 shows that one of them was black.[24]

This established tradition was greatly boosted by the craze for 'Turkish' military bands that swept across Europe in the eighteenth century. Poland led the way with a full military band imported from Constantinople. Russia followed suit in 1725; Austria, in 1741, when Franz von der Trenck marched into Vienna preceded by a Turkish band; France was not far behind. By about 1770 the new style of military band, augmented by some new and very loud percussion instruments, was customary all over Europe.[25] The kettledrum and long trumpet of the earlier military band had been borrowed, as we have seen, from the east. The fashion for what was often called 'Janissary' music – the word means, basically, a Turkish soldier – entailed the addition of five more oriental instruments. There were now large cymbals.[26] There was now a large bass drum – sometimes twice as long as the diameter of the head. This was carried at the waist, not on the chest, and was beaten on one skin with a heavy felt-tipped stick while the other skin (or the shell) was rubbed on the off-beat with a kind of broom or switch held in the drummer's left hand.[27] There was now a large triangle, much heavier than its modern counterpart, and often having metal jingles threaded on the lower bar.[28] Also added was a large tambourine, anything up to 90cm. in diameter, and often with many small bells as well as jingling plates in the rim.[29] Most spectacular, and by far the noisiest of the innovations, was the Turkish crescent or *chapeau chinois*, the impressive stick jingle that the Turks called *chaghána* – a word soon anglicized to 'johanna' in the Royal Artillery Band.[30] Usually known as the jingling johnny, this sonorous rhythm instrument consisted of a pole some six feet high surmounted by several crescents from which hung a myriad of bells; red horsehair plumes hung from its sides.[31] The 'Turkish' rage spread both to popular music, with composers writing special parts for triangle and tambourine as an accompaniment to the pianoforte,[32] and to orchestral music, as in the last movement of Beethoven's Choral Symphony.

But in fact the musicians who played in these 'Turkish' military bands, and whose playing inspired instrumental and rhythmical innovations by composers, were more often Africans and people of African descent than Turks. In Britain, indeed, Turkish musicians were never used. Elsewhere, when Turkish musicians died or were discharged they were usually replaced by black men[33] – so that when Frederick II of Prussia commanded his 'Turkish' band to perform before the Turkish ambassador, the latter complained: 'That's not Turkish.'[34] Black musicianship had a far earlier influence on European concert music than most historians of music and compilers of musical encyclopedias have been prepared to admit.[35] The outstanding exception is H.G. Farmer, who writes:

> It should not be forgotten that these negro drummers not only gave a tremendous fillip to regimental music . . ., but it was their contribution in this so-called 'Turkish music' that opened the eyes of the great composers, beginning with Mozart and Beethoven, to the possibilities of a new tone colour and fresh rhythmic devices in the wider realm of orchestral music.[36]

Public money was not provided for the creation or upkeep of British army bands until 1757, when the Duke of Cumberland succeeded in getting funds voted for six enlisted musicians in each battalion.[37] From then on, every British regiment with any pretension to smartness had its corps of black musicians, gorgeously dressed[38] and often – cymbalists and triangle-players especially – very young, though the bass drummer, if only because of the weight of his massive drum, tended to be 'of imposing physique'.[39] In 1759 eight or ten black drummers were 'procured' for the 29th Foot (afterwards The Worcestershire Regiment) by Admiral Boscawen, apparently in Guadeloupe. Thinking they would be 'very ornamental' in the regiment, which was commanded by his brother, he took them home with him. The 29th were then stationed in Ireland, and special permission had to be obtained from the king before the drummers were allowed to join them. Fifteen years later the regiment had ten black drummers, at least three of whom were survivors of the original group. The black drummers of the 29th always came in for high praise by the top brass at inspection time. They 'beat and play well', said a major-general in 1774, and another said the same in 1791. In 1797 a lieutenant noted in his diary that the black bandsman who beat the big drum was 'a handsome man, 6 feet 4 inches'. In 1821 there were '4 men of colour' in the band, and three years later it was reported that 11 vacancies in the band were 'reserved for black boys, who are on their way from Africa for the purpose'. In 1831 the band still had three black musicians: George Carvell, big drum; Peter Askins, kettledrum; and George Wise, tambourine. The last of The Worcestershire Regiment's black drummers died on 15 July 1843.[40]

Having been stationed in the West Indies for almost 60 years, the 38th Foot (afterwards the 1st South Staffordshire Regiment) brought back three black drummers when it returned home in 1765.[41] By 1772 the Grenadier Guards had black 'time-beaters' playing bass, tenor, and side drums and cymbals.[42] Three black drummers of the Grenadier Guards are shown marching out of St James's Palace with their white comrades in a 1790 engraving;[43] the regiment's black drummer, wearing a turban, is shown in an 1829 engraving by E. Hull;[44] and 'Francis, the last of the blacks in the Grenadier Guards, was discharged in 1840'.[45] An army inspection return in the Public Record Office shows that the 3rd Hussars had a black kettledrummer in 1776, and the regiment is said still to possess the solid silver collar he wore, presented in 1775 and worn by a mounted drummer of the regiment at the Edinburgh Military Tattoo a few years ago.[46] The 1st Life Guards had black drummers and trumpeters in the last quarter of the eighteenth century,[47] and the 2nd Life Guards had three black trombonists in its mounted band until 'just before the Crimean War' (1853–6).[48]

About the year 1784 the Duke of York, colonel-in-chief of the Coldstream Guards, imported a band from Germany to replace the regiment's British band, and the newcomers included two black tambourinists and a black player of the jingling johnny.

> This band became very popular, and attracted crowds of persons to St. James's Park to listen to its performances . . . The Africans . . . produced such effect with their tambourines, that those instruments afterwards, under their tuition, became extremely fashionable, and were cultivated by many of those belles of distinction who were emulous to display Turkish attitudes and Turkish graces.[49]

The Coldstream Guards spent £3 9*s.* 2*d.* on 'Boots for the Black Musicians' in 1792, and there were similar disbursements in 1803 and 1804; in the latter year £24 15*s.* 2*d.* was spent on 'silver collars for the Black Musicians'. Boots were again provided in 1807, and in 1808 'Turbans for the Band' cost £55.[50] The Coldstream Guards retained their black musicians until about 1840.[51] There is a well-known half-length mezzotint portrait of Fraser, their black tambourine-player.[52]

During the last decade of the eighteenth century all the drummers of the 7th Royal Fusiliers were black men.[53] The Buckinghamshire Militia had a black tambourinist and a black cymbalist in their band about the year 1790,[54] the Middlesex Militia two black tambourinists and a black cymbalist in 1793.[55] Two years later the Scots Guards' band had 'three black men performing on the tambourine, Turkish bells and cymbals',[56] and Martinique-born Jean Baptiste, the last black to serve in that regiment, was discharged on 22 December 1841.[57] A black musician was discharged from the King's Light Dragoons in 1803.[58] Black musicians were members of the Royal Artillery Band in 1812, and probably earlier; in that year jackets, waistcoats, pantaloons, caps and trimmings, feathers, gaiters, shirts, stockings, and leather stocks were ordered for their use.[59] Gaiters were bought for the black musicians of the 1st Foot Guards in 1802 and 1803, and those of the 3rd Foot Guards had breeches bought for them in 1809 and boots in 1810.[60] A 'native of the West Indies', aged 23, was discharged from the 1st Foot Guards in 1823 'in consequence of not being of a sufficiently black complexion'.[61] A print of the East India Company Volunteers being reviewed by George III (who died in 1820) shows that quite small units had black bandsmen.[62] And there was even a black drummer in the West Essex Yeomanry Cavalry, a regiment not raised until 1830 (and disbanded in 1877); he is said to have served previously with the Coldstream Guards.[63]

As the army agents' ledgers and contemporary portraits show, black military bandsmen were smartly and colourfully dressed, often in oriental style. They had gorgeous braided and slashed tunics with sashes, high-plumed turbans or bearskins or cocked hats, top boots or gaiters, and jewelled dirks, 'each regiment striving to outdo others in unconventionality and *bizarrerie*'.[64] This, for instance, was how the black 'time-beaters' of The Worcestershire Regiment were dressed in 1831:

> A muslin turban with a silver crescent in front, surmounted with a scarlet hackle feather 12 inches long, with silver cord and tassels, entwined round the turban. A silver-plated stock for the neck which opened with clasps and fastened behind. Yellow cloth jacket, hussar fashion, trimmed with black fur on collar and cuffs, the breast was embroidered with black silk cord, and three rows of silver buttons in front. The jacket was worn open. – The waistcoat was of white cloth embroidered with crimson silk cord, and had a row of silver buttons down the front. – A yellow and crimson silk sash round the waist.
>
> They also wore Turkish scimitars, brass scabbards with sling waist belts. The pantaloons were scarlet with a broad silver stripe on the outside seams, and fitted tight at the knee. Yellow Hessian boots with large black silk tassels in front.[65]

But if the black bandsmen's uniforms were a joy to the eye, their playing was a joy to both eye and ear. For they made vigorous bodily movements as they played. In Farmer's words, 'they capered rather than marched, and flung their drumsticks and tambourines into the air, adroitly catching them in discreetly measured cadence. Their agility with fingers, arms and legs was only equalled by their perfect time in the music.'[66] Drummers would throw a drumstick up in the air after the beat and catch it with the other hand in time for the next. Players of the jingling johnny would shake it, in perfect time, under their arms, over their heads, under their legs. Players of cymbals would clash them 'at every point they could reach'.[67] And their white comrades loved the display as much as the music. Regiments returning from service in the West Indies 'were the objects of envy in proportion to the number of "blacks" they could muster in the ranks of their bands'.[68] 'No other type of music demands such a firm, precise, and overwhelmingly dominant beat', wrote a musicologist. 'Every bar is so strongly marked with a new positive accent that it is almost impossible to get out of time.'[69] Or, as a military historian puts it, 'they were rattling good drummers'.[70] Farmer calls the practical results in the military sphere 'simply amazing'. Troops were said never to have marched better than they did to those 'rhythmic crashes and accented drummings'. And the effect on the general public was 'astounding'. Crowds thronged to see the latest craze.[71]

These army musicians probably had a better life than most other Africans and persons of African descent in Britain. When they worked, they played. They were valued for something they did outstandingly well. Ordinary soldiers enjoyed the energizing beat, exciting cross-rhythms, and justified swagger of black musicianship. And black military bandsmen were clearly popular with officers who found that they added a new dimension of smartness to a regiment. By sheer excellence, and long before the stereotype of 'the black as entertainer' arose, they won a special place for themselves within a privileged sub-culture of an alien society. In this achievement they echoed both the functionality of African traditional music and the pride and professionalism of its performers.

But they were not saints. Musicians, like other people, get into trouble sometimes. Toby Gill, a black drummer in the 4th Dragoons, described as 'a very drunken profligate Fellow', went to the gallows in 1750 for murdering a woman, and afterwards they hanged his corpse in chains at Blythburgh, Suffolk.[72] Eleven years later a black drummer in the same regiment killed his horse. He was tried by court martial, sentenced to 1,000 lashes, and had his pay docked by 2*s.* a week until the value of the horse – £23 – was made up.[73] In 1790 Othello and Carter, two of the 4th Dragoons' trumpeters, went absent without leave. They were recaptured and locked in the guard-house. One of them tried to escape by shinning up the chimney, but it was too narrow for him to get out. A court martial sentenced them both to be flogged and next day they 'entered on board a man of war'.[74] In 1796 William Russell, a black drummer in the 63rd Foot (afterwards the West Suffolk Regiment), was committed to jail at Ipswich on a charge of burglary.[75]

After all, these men were soldiers as well as musicians. In battle, their place was not on some distant hill:

> When the regiment was in line the band normally formed in rear and played during the action – probably a more exacting demand on courage than standing in the ranks with a musket. When a battalion formed square the band moved to the centre, taking post near the Colours – a particularly dangerous position.[76]

And the musicians' task, in the thick of the action, was not merely to encourage their comrades, and transmit signals, with trumpet and drum. Farmer spells out what else was expected of them: 'It is highly probable that many a bandsman, bugler, fifer and drummer – whose positions were *within* the square – not only cared for the wounded and dying who were carried into the square, but even handled musket and bayonet so as to close a breach in the ranks.'[77] Like other British troops, the black bandsmen were taught how to look after themselves. And they did not take racist insults lying down. That no doubt explains the riot at Plymouth Dock in 1780 when a large crowd took sides in a quarrel between two black bandsmen from the Somerset Militia and some white soldiers from the Brecknock Militia. What started the quarrel we can only guess, but in no time at all a serious riot was going on, and the 'piquet' (or, as we would say, military police) fired on the rioters, killing one and wounding ten.[78]

An anecdote tells how a black military bandsman was strolling down the Strand when he was accosted with the question: 'Well, blackie, what news from the devil?' He knocked the questioner down, remarking: 'He send you that – how you like it?'[79]

5. Eighteenth-century voices

Ukawsaw Gronniosaw

What was it like to be a black settler in Britain in the second half of the eighteenth century? A vivid account was published at Bath about the year 1770.

The author's real name was Ukawsaw Gronniosaw, but after coming to England he took the name James Albert. His birthplace was Borno, west of Lake Chad, in the north of present-day Nigeria. His mother was the eldest daughter of the king of Zaara. He was the youngest of her six children, and he tells us that 'my grandfather almost doated on me'.[1] Taken from his homeland by a Gold Coast ivory merchant when he was about 15, Gronniosaw was sold to a Dutch captain for two yards of check cloth. An American bought him in Barbados for \$50, then sold him for £50 in New York to 'a very gracious, good Minister'[2] who taught him to pray and sent him to school, where he learnt to read. His master died of a fever: 'I held his hand in mine when he departed: he told me he had given me my freedom. I was at liberty to go where I would . . . My master left me by his will, ten pounds and my freedom.'[3] But Gronniosaw chose to stay with his mistress and then, after her death, with her sons. When they died he was left destitute and friendless, and was persuaded to join a privateering expedition as cook. Cheated of his share of the prize-money, Gronniosaw worked as servant to a wine-merchant, then enlisted in the British army's 28th Foot (afterwards The North Gloucestershire Regiment), served in Martinique and Cuba (probably in 1762), received his discharge, and came to England.

He had expected to find nothing but 'goodness, gentleness and meekness in this Christian land',[4] but he was soon disabused. First, the cursing of the citizens of Portsmouth astonished him. Then, when he took lodgings at a public house and left 19 guineas with his landlady for safe keeping, she denied that he had ever given it to her. 'I could scarcely believe it possible that the place where so many eminent Christians had lived and preached could abound with so much wickedness and deceit . . . I cried like a child.' Eventually the landlady coughed up four guineas, 'which she said she gave me out of charity'.[5]

Moving to London, Gronniosaw met and married a weaver called Betty, a poor English widow with a child: 'I firmly believed that we should be very happy together, and so it proved.'[6] Before they had been married a year, fear of the consequences of industrial unrest led the couple to move to Colchester, where Gronniosaw worked for a time as a labourer on the roads. But, during a severe winter, both husband and wife were unemployed, 'and we were reduced to the greatest distress imaginable'. Gronniosaw tried to get a job helping a gentleman's gardener, but managed to obtain only a gift of four big carrots. These were welcome enough, but the family had to eat them raw since they had nothing to make a fire with. And they had to eke them out: 'We allowed ourselves but one every day, least they should not last till we could get some other supply.'[7] A Colchester lawyer, 'a sincere good Christian', gave Gronniosaw a guinea: 'I went immediately and bought some bread and cheese, and coal, and carried it home. My dear wife was rejoiced to see me return with something to eat . . . The first nobility in the land never made a better meal.'[8] The lawyer then employed him for more than a year to help pull down a house and rebuild it.

Gronniosaw was offered regular work in Norwich, but his new employer failed to pay his wages regularly. Betty hired a loom and wove in her leisure time, and all was going well when their three children were stricken with smallpox. Threatened with eviction, the family were saved by a Quaker who paid their arrears of rent. When their daughter died of a fever various ministers of religion refused to bury her, since she had not been baptized and was not a member of their own congregation.

> At length I resolved to dig a grave in the garden behind the house, and bury her there; when the parson of the parish sent for to tell me he would bury the child, but did not choose to read the burial service over her. I told him I did not care whether he would or no, as the child could not hear it.[9]

After pawning their clothes and feeling 'ready to sink under our troubles',[10] the family moved to Kidderminster, first selling all they had to pay their debts. Gronniosaw's *Narrative of the Most remarkable Particulars in the life of . . . an African prince* (*c.*1770), '*committed to* *paper by the elegant pen of a young* LADY *of the town of* LEOMINSTER', ends when he '*appears to be turn'd of sixty*'.[11]

> Such is our situation at present. – My wife, by hard labour at the loom, does every thing that can be expected from her, towards the maintenance of our family; and GOD is pleased to incline the hearts of his people at times to yield us their charitable assistance, being myself through age and infirmities able to contribute but little to their support.[12]

So ends 'the only extant account of the trials and tribulations of a Poor Black and his family'.[13] Of Gronniosaw's later life, nothing is known.

Phillis Wheatley

The first book by a black woman ever published appeared in London in 1773 and was reprinted many times. It was called *Poems on various subjects, religious and moral*, and it contained 39 poems by a 19-year-old slave living in Boston, Massachusetts. The first black poet of any significance to write in English,[1] Phillis Wheatley had just spent a month in England, partly as a kind of cultural ambassador or involuntary propagandist for the refinement of Boston. In this role, however, she turned out to be something of a boomerang for her pro-slavery sponsors. Though her situation neither equipped nor permitted her to become an abolitionist, she nevertheless became 'a supreme witness to the anti-slavery movement in Britain'.[2]

Wheatley was not of course her own name but that of her Boston mistress, a tailor's wife who in 1761 bought her 'for a trifle' in the local slave-market.[3] Dressed only in a scrap of dirty carpet, the 7-year-old girl – her age was estimated from the shedding of her front teeth – seemed to be suffering from the change of climate but impressed her purchaser by her 'humble and modest demeanor' and 'interesting features'.[4] Before long she was impressing her still more by trying to make letters on the wall with chalk and charcoal.[5] Phillis was segregated from the other household servants and taught to read and write. Within 16 months she was reading the Bible fluently. She learnt Latin and 'was proud of the fact that Terence was at least of African birth'.[6] This child prodigy, whose attainments must have marked her as 'one of the most highly educated young women in Boston'[7] and no doubt gave much satisfaction to the cultivated tailor's wife, was often visited by clergymen 'and other individuals of high standing in society'. But, in spite of the attention paid her, she retained her 'modest, unassuming demeanor'.[8]

She seems to have begun writing poetry at about the age of 13. One of her earliest, and shortest, surviving poems, showing the influence both of missionary propaganda and of Alexander Pope – whose neo-classicism permeates all her later work – was called 'On being brought from AFRICA to AMERICA'.[9]

When Phillis came to England in 1773, in the company of her mistress's son, she was lionized. The Countess of Huntingdon, to whom she had dedicated her first published poem three years before, introduced her to the Earl of Dartmouth and other prominent members of London society. Her visitors included Benjamin Franklin, then agent in Europe of the north American colonies.[10] The lord mayor of London presented her with a valuable edition of Milton's *Paradise Lost*.

When her book was published, soon after her return to Boston, the *London Magazine*'s reviewer found that 'these poems display no astonishing power of genius; but when we consider them as the production of a young untutored African . . . we cannot suppress our admiration of talents so vigorous and lively'.[11] The *Monthly Review* came closer to making a political point. Its reviewer was

> much concerned to find that this ingenious young woman is yet a slave. The people of Boston boast themselves chiefly on their principles of liberty. One such act as the purchase of her freedom would, in our opinion, have done them more honour than hanging a thousand trees with ribbons and emblems.[12]

There were also favourable notices in the *Critical Review*, *Gentleman's Magazine*, *London Chronicle* (reprinted in the *Universal Magazine*), *Scots Magazine*, *Town and Country Magazine*, and *Westminster Magazine*.[13]

Phillis Wheatley is 'easily among the most renowned – and therefore the most variously interpreted – Afro-American poets',[14] and both advocates and adversaries have found in her writing only what they wanted to find. Her work has been overpraised because of her youth, sex, race, and servitude. And it has been undervalued because of this excessive praise. She was not a great poet. All the same, 'some of her poems reveal an exceptional being producing exceptional poetry'.[15] And she displayed 'much more Black consciousness, much more concern for her fellow Blacks, than many readers will admit'.[16] She was well aware of the part black people played in American and European society, and in the popular mind.

Though she adopts the conventional missionary stance of calling Africa 'The land of errors, and *Egyptian* gloom',[17] she often identifies herself as an African and entitles one poem: 'To S.M. a young *African* Painter, on seeing his Works'.[18] Naturally enough, her concern for her fellow-blacks is expressed most strongly in her letters, which, unlike her poems, were not intended for the white reading public.[19]

After her mistress's death in 1774, Phillis Wheatley seems to have made a precarious living hawking her book from door to door and reading selections from her poems to potential lady customers. In 1778 she married John Peters, a free black man whom she had known for five years or more. Though she bore him at least one child, and mothered two others whose origins are not precisely known, it was not a happy marriage. Peters was in and out of jail for debt. Two of Phillis's children died and the third was very sick. America's first black woman poet died in 1784, in a poor boarding-house, 'surrounded by all the emblems of a squalid poverty'.[20] She was hardly more than 30. Her third child survived her by just a few hours.

Ignatius Sancho

The first African prose writer whose work was published in England – his *Letters* appeared in 1782, two years after his death, and proved an immediate best-seller – was born in 1729 on a slave-ship in mid-Atlantic. At Cartagena, on the coast of Colombia, the baby was christened Ignatius. His mother died soon afterwards, and his father killed himself rather than exist as a slave. When the boy was about two his owner brought him to England and gave him to three maiden sisters who lived in Greenwich. These ladies called him Sancho because they fancied that he looked like Don Quixote's squire. Unlike Phillis Wheatley's mistress, they 'judged ignorance the best and only security for obedience' and believed that 'to enlarge the mind of their slave would go near to emancipate his person'. All the same, 'by unwearied application', Ignatius Sancho taught himself to read and write.[1]

The Duke of Montagu, who lived at nearby Blackheath, admired the young man's 'native frankness of manner as yet unbroken by servitude',[2] gave him presents of books, and advised the three sisters to attend to his education. But they were inflexible. What brought matters to a head was a love affair, which would have appeared 'infinitely criminal in the eyes of three Maiden Ladies'.[3]

So Sancho, now 20 years old, ran away and sought refuge with the Montagus. The duke had recently died; the duchess wanted to send the runaway back to Greenwich but he threatened to shoot himself rather than return, so she engaged him as a butler. Now he could freely indulge his passion for reading and cultivate a broad range of talents. He wrote poetry, two stage plays, and a 'Theory of Music', dedicated to the Princess Royal, which was never published and is apparently lost. He emerged also as a minor composer: three small collections of songs, minuets, and other pieces for violin, mandolin, flute, and harpsichord were published anonymously. 'Composed by an African', they are dedicated to members of the Montagu family, which makes their attribution to Sancho reasonably certain. Some of Sancho's music, which Paul Edwards has called 'slight, but elegant, and thoroughly fashionable', was broadcast by the BBC in 1958.[4] Sancho adored the theatre and would spend his last shilling to see Garrick, greatest actor of the age, at Drury Lane. But he was not a clear enough speaker to play Othello and Oroonoko, though it seems he would have liked to. His other passions were for women and gambling; he was cured of the latter weakness when he lost his clothes playing cribbage.

Sancho was soon taken up by London's fashionable literary and artistic circles. Gainsborough painted his portrait in 1768. He became a friend of Garrick. Other friends included the historical painter John Hamilton Mortimer, the sculptor Joseph Nollekens, and the writers Samuel Johnson and Laurence Sterne. Sancho's friendship with Sterne began in 1766, when he wrote to tell the author how much he admired his *Sermons* and *Tristram Shandy*[5] – and to ask for Sterne's help on behalf of the enslaved Africans:

> How very much, good Sir, am I (amongst millions) indebted to you for the character of your amiable Uncle Toby! – I declare I would walk ten miles in the dog-days, to shake hands with the honest Corporal. – Your sermons have touch'd me to the heart . . . Of all my favourite authors not one has drawn a tear in favour of my miserable black brethren – excepting yourself, and the humane author of Sir Geo. Ellison.* – I think you will forgive me; I am sure you will applaud me for beseeching you to give one half hour's attention to slavery, as it is at this day

* i.e. Mrs Sarah Scott, author of *The History of Sir George Ellison* (1766), whose hero's sentiments on the improvement of the conditions of his slaves were said by one reviewer to be 'noble, generous, humane', and deserving 'to be engraven in the heart of every West Indian planter'.[6]

> practised in our West Indies. – That subject handled in your striking manner would ease the yoke (perhaps) of many – but if only of one – gracious God! what a feast to a benevolent heart! and sure I am, you are an epicurean in acts of charity. – You who are universally read, and as universally admired – you could not fail. – Dear Sir, think in me you behold the uplifted hands of thousands of my brother Moors. Grief (you pathetically observe) is eloquent: figure to yourself their attitudes; hear their supplicating addresses! – alas! you cannot refuse.[7]

In reply, Sterne pointed out that, by coincidence, he had been writing 'a tender tale of the sorrows of a friendless poor negro-girl' when Sancho's letter arrived, and added that Sancho's brethren were his also and that he often, looking westward, thought of 'the burthens which our brothers and sisters are *there* carrying'.[8] Ten months later, Sterne was thanking Sancho for getting the Montagu family to subscribe to the ninth and final volume of *Tristram Shandy* and asking him to press his employers to pay their subscriptions since he needed the money.[9] A few weeks later he wrote to Sancho: 'I hope you will not forget your custom of giving me a call at my lodgings next winter.'[10]

Troubled with gout and 'a constitutional corpulence',[11] Sancho left the service of the Montagu family in 1773. By now he was married to Anne, a black woman from the Caribbean who was to bear him six children. Helped by a small legacy and annuity left him by the Duchess of Montagu, Sancho opened a grocery shop in Charles Street, Westminster. Here he was visited by Charles James Fox (for whom he voted in 1780),[12] the Duchess of Queensberry, and Nollekens. The latter took him, as a present, a cast of his bust of Sterne; the visit is described by John Thomas Smith, keeper of prints and drawings in the British Museum:

> As we pushed the wicket door, a little tinkling bell, the usual appendage to such shops, announced its opening: we drank tea with Sancho and his black lady, who was seated, when we entered, in the corner of the shop, chopping sugar, surrounded by her little 'Sanchonets'. Sancho, knowing Mr. Nollekens to be a loyal man, said to him, 'I am sure you will be pleased to hear that Lord George Gordon is taken, and that a party of the guards is now escorting him in an old ramshackled coach to the Tower.' Nollekens said not a word,

> and poor Sancho either did not know, or not recollect, that he was addressing a Papist.[13]

Sancho had, in fact, been an eyewitness of the 1780 Gordon riots, of which he totally disapproved – though some black people took part, one of whom, Charlotte Gardener, was afterwards hanged on Tower Hill for helping to tear down a publican's house.[14] Sancho called the rioters 'the maddest people – that the maddest times were ever plagued with', referred ironically to 'the worse than Negro barbarity of the populace', and gave in one of his letters a vivid running commentary on the scene:

> There is at this present moment at least a hundred thousand poor, miserable, ragged rabble, from twelve to sixty years of age, with blue cockades in their hats – besides half as many women and children – all parading the streets – the bridge – the park – ready for any and every mischief. – Gracious God! what's the matter now? I was obliged to leave off – the shouts of the mob – the horrid clashing of swords – and the clutter of a multitude in swiftest motion – drew me to the door – when every one in the street was employed in shutting up shop. – It is now just five o'clock – . . . This instant about two thousand liberty boys are swearing and swaggering by with large sticks – . . . Thank heaven, it rains; may it increase, so as to send these deluded wretches safe to their homes, their families, and wives! . . .
>
> Postscript,
>
> The Sardinian ambassador offered 500 guineas to the rabble, to save a painting of our Saviour from the flames, and 1000 guineas not to destroy an exceeding fine organ: the gentry told him, they would burn him if they could get at him, and destroyed the picture and organ directly. – I am not sorry I was born in Afric.[15]

Six months after writing this account, Sancho died in his shop. His *Letters*, published two years later with the express intention of proving 'that an untutored African may possess abilities equal to an European',[16] attracted over 1,200 subscribers, more than any publication since the *Spectator* of Steele and Addison 70 years before.[17] The first edition sold so quickly that the *Monthly Review* could not get hold of a review copy and had to wait for the second edition in the following year. ('Let it no longer be said,' concluded the reviewer, 'by half-informed philosophers, and superficial investigators of human nature, that *Nēgers*, as they are vulgarly called, are inferior to any white nation in mental abilities.')[18] Sancho's widow, who carried on the grocery business after his death, is said to have received over £500 from the book's sales.[19] Sancho's son William, after working for a time in the library of the botanist Sir Joseph Banks, turned bookseller, in his father's old shop, and published the fifth edition of the *Letters* in 1803.[20]

Though Sancho's literary style owes an obvious debt to Sterne, he never forgets that he is an African. He signs two letters to the press 'Africanus', sends 'Blackamoor greetings', refers to 'my brother Negroes' and 'my poor black brethren'.[21] Now and again he laughs at himself as 'a poor Blacky grocer', 'only a poor, thick-lipped son of Afric', 'a fat old fellow', and 'a man of a convexity of belly exceeding Falstaff – and a black face into the bargain'.[22] He describes himself as 'a coal-black, jolly African, who wishes health and peace to every religion and country throughout the ample range of God's creation!'[23] Nor is his good humour ruffled when he and his family are subjected to rudeness or racist insults. After a visit to the Vauxhall pleasure-gardens he records: 'We went by water – had a coach home – were gazed at – followed &c. &c. – but not much abused.'[24] Of a later excursion he writes in salty vein:

> I shall take no notice of the tricking fraudulent behaviour of the driver of the stage – *as how* he wanted to palm a bad shilling upon us – and *as how* they stopped us in the town, and most generously insulted us – and *as how* they took up – a fat old man – his wife *fat* too – and child – and after keeping us half an hour in sweet converse of the – of the *blasting* kind – how that the fat woman waxed wrath with her plump master, for his being serene – and how that he caught choler at her friction, tongue-wise – how he ventured his head out of the coach-door, and swore liberally – whilst his —— in direct line with poor S——n's nose – entertained him with *sound* and sweetest of exhalations. – I shall say nothing of being two hours almost on our journey – neither do I remark that S——n turned sick before we left G——, nor that the child p—— upon his legs: – in short it was near nine before we got into Charles Street.
>
> Sir, the pleasures of the day made us more than amends – for the nonsense that followed.[25]

How far can Sancho, butler turned shopkeeper, with artistic

tastes and literary talents and friends, be said to have been 'assimilated' into eighteenth-century English society? Brought to England at the age of two, he grew up as a black Englishman. His cultural models, in literature and music alike, were English, not African. But a black Englishman, even one with the broad talents, white friends, and endless patience and good humour of a Sancho, was not an easy thing to be in the eighteenth century. Sancho himself knew all too well that he was not, and could never be, truly at home in England. 'I am only a lodger – and hardly that', he wrote.[26] He was aware that few Englishmen possessed 'charity enough to admit dark faces into the fellowship of Christians'.[27] In his *Letters* at least, the pervading racial prejudice of the country he has grown up in rarely makes him bitter. But he does note wryly that 'to the English, from Othello to Sancho the big – we are either foolish – or mulish – all – all without a single exception'.[28]

Ottobah Cugoano

Quobna Ottobah Cugoano – his middle name, by which he is usually known, means 'twin'[1] – was born about the year 1757, near the Fante village of Agimaque or Ajumako, on the coast of what is today Ghana. When he was about 13 he was kidnapped by 'several great ruffians'[2] and, amid the rattling of chains, the crack of whips, and the groans and cries of his fellow-captives, was put on board a ship that carried him to Grenada. After nine or ten months in the slave-gang there, and a further year or so at different places in the West Indies, he was brought to England by his owner at the end of 1772 and set free.[3] Advised to get himself baptized in order not to be sold into slavery again, he took the name John Steuart. Somewhat later he entered the service of Richard Cosway, principal painter to the Prince of Wales, and before long had emerged as one of the leaders and spokesmen of London's black community.

In 1786 Cugoano played a key part in the rescue of Henry Demane, a black man who had been kidnapped and was being shipped out to the West Indies. Cugoano and another community leader, William Green, reported the kidnapping to the white abolitionist Granville Sharp, who got a writ of habeas corpus and rescued Demane at the very last minute, just as the ship was weighing anchor.[4]

In the following year Cugoano published a powerful contribution to the campaign for abolition of the slave trade, his *Thoughts and sentiments on the evil and wicked traffic of the slavery and commerce of the human species.* This book, 'one of the earliest expressions of African thought to reach a European audience',[5] seems to have been written with the help of Cugoano's fellow-African and fellow-author Olaudah Equiano.[6] Systematically and trenchantly, Cugoano and his collaborator demolished the arguments in defence of slavery: that Africans thought it no crime to sell their own wives and children; that slavery had divine sanction; that Africans were, by nature and complexion, peculiarly suited to slavery; that black slaves in the Caribbean were better off than the European poor. On the contrary, the slaves were bought and sold and dealt with as their capricious owners thought fit, 'even in torturing and tearing them to pieces, and wearing them out with hard labour, hunger and oppression'.[7] But Cugoano went further than mere denunciation of slavery, the slave trade, and their defenders. He declared – and he was the first writer in English to do so – that enslaved blacks had not only the moral right but the moral duty to resist:

> If any man should buy another man . . . and compel him to his service and slavery without any agreement of that man to serve him, the enslaver is a robber, and a defrauder of that man every day. Wherefore it is as much the duty of a man who is robbed in that manner to get out of the hands of his enslaver, as it is for any honest community of men to get out of the hands of rogues and villains.[8]

No less boldly, Cugoano held 'every man in Great-Britain responsible, in some degree' for the slavery and oppression of Africans – 'unless he speedily riseth up with abhorrence of it in his own judgment, and, to avert evil, declare himself against it'.[9] Men of eminence and power – nobles and senators, clergymen, and every man in office and authority – must incur a double load of guilt: 'not only that burden of guilt in the oppression of the African strangers, but also in that of an impending danger and ruin to their own country'.[10] It was evident that the British legislature encouraged the trade and shared in the infamous profits:

> Is it not strange to think, that they who ought to be considered as the most learned and civilized people in the world, that they should carry on a traffic of the most barbarous cruelty and injustice, and that many . . . are become so dissolute as to think slavery, robbery and murder no crime?

Since the British had acquired 'a greater share in that iniquitous commerce than all the rest together', they ought to set an example by immediately abolishing the slave trade and emancipating the slaves:

> I would propose that a total abolition of slavery should be made and proclaimed; and that an universal emancipation of slaves should begin from the date thereof . . . And . . . I would propose, that a fleet of some ships of war should be immediately sent to the coast of Africa, and particularly where the slave trade is carried on, with faithful men to direct that none should be brought from the coast of Africa without their own consent and the approbation of their friends, and to intercept all merchant ships that were bringing them away.[11]

Within just over 20 years this proposal to send a fleet to suppress the slave trade was being adopted;[12] but almost another half-century of bondage lay ahead for the slaves.

Cugoano buttressed his moral, humanitarian argument with a practical, economic one. Black labour in the sugar islands would be more productive when voluntary than when compulsory; the only people who would lose anything by emancipation would be the slave-owners. And if Africans were dealt with in a friendly manner, a fruitful trade could develop which 'would soon bring more revenue in a righteous way to the British nation, than ten times its share in all the profits that slavery can produce'.[13]

Two years before the French revolution, four years before the uprising of black slaves in Haiti, and almost 200 years before decolonization, Cugoano ventured an audacious prophecy, couched in solemn and mystical terms but no less impressive for that:

> History affords us many examples of severe retaliations, revolutions and dreadful overthrows; and of many crying under the heavy yoke of subjection and oppression, seeking for deliverance . . . Yet, O Africa! yet, poor slave! *The day of thy watchmen cometh, and thy visitation* draweth nigh . . . *In that day thy walls of* deliverance *are to be built, in that day shall the decree of* slavery *be far removed.*
>
> What revolution the end of that predominant evil of slavery and oppression may produce, whether the wise and considerate [i.e. prudent] will surrender and give it up, and make restitution for the injuries that they have already done, as far as they can; or whether the force of their wickedness, and the iniquity of their power, will lead them on until some

> universal calamity burst forth against the abandoned carriers of it on, and against the criminal nations in confederacy with them, is not for me to determine? But this must appear evident, that for any man to carry on a traffic in the merchandize of slaves, and to keep them in slavery; or for any nation to oppress, extirpate and destroy others; that these are crimes of the greatest magnitude, and a most daring violation of the laws and commandments of the Most High, and which, at last, will be evidenced in the destruction and overthrow of all the transgressors. And nothing else can be expected for such violations of taking away the natural rights and liberties of men, but that those who are the doers of it will meet with some awful visitation and righteous judgment of God, and in such a manner as it cannot be thought that his just vengeance for their iniquity will be the less tremendous because his judgments are long delayed.[14]

Cugoano sent copies of *Thoughts and sentiments* to King George III, the Prince of Wales, and the prominent politician Edmund Burke. There is no evidence that any of the three read it or that it had any influence on them if they did. The royal family stood solidly against abolition of the slave trade. The Duke of Clarence, who later came to the throne as William IV, would bitterly attack the abolitionists in a speech to the Lords in 1793, calling them 'either fanatics or hypocrites, and in one of those classes he ranked Mr Wilberforce'. He was forced to apologize to Wilberforce,[15] who 11 years later found it 'truly humiliating to see, in the House of Lords, four of the Royal Family come down to vote against the poor, helpless, friendless Slaves'.[16] George III once asked mockingly at a levee: 'How go on your black clients, Mr. Wilberforce?'[17] As for Burke, his attitude to abolition was dictated, as F.O. Shyllon has pointed out, by political expediency alone.[18] After mature consideration he abandoned the attempt to regulate and, ultimately, suppress the slave trade – 'from the conviction that the strength of the West Indian body would defeat the utmost effort of his powerful party, and cover them with ruinous unpopularity'.[19]

In a postscript to a shorter version of *Thoughts and sentiments*, published in 1791,[20] Cugoano announced his intention of opening a school, mainly for '*all such of his* Complexion *as are desirous of being acquainted with the Knowledge of the Christian Religion and the* Laws *of* Civilization'.[21] We do not know whether he succeeded in opening this school – nor what became of him after 1791, except for a glimpse we catch in a tribute by the Polish patriot Scipione Piattoli, who seems to have been in London between 1800 and 1803. According to a not always reliable source, Piattoli knew Cugoano well, reported that he was married to an Englishwoman, and praised 'his piety, his mild character and modesty, his integrity and talents'.[22]

Ottobah Cugoano was the first published African critic of the transatlantic slave trade and the first African to demand publicly the total abolition of the trade and the freeing of the slaves – a position which scarcely any white abolitionist had taken by 1787. His 'insight into the nature of European–North American hegemony and its dialectical consequences'[23] brilliantly foreshadows what has been called 'the delayed boomerang from the time of slavery'.[24] For, through history's sly irony, the classical triangle of the slave trade was also the geographical pattern whereby the ideas pioneered by Cugoano and his friend Olaudah Equiano became, in the shape of Pan-Africanism, a force for enlightenment and liberation.[25] To Equiano's contribution we now turn.

Olaudah Equiano

The first political leader of Britain's black community was an Igbo, born in eastern Nigeria – probably near Onitsha – about the year 1745. His first name, Olaudah, means 'fortunate' or, possibly, 'having a loud voice and well spoken'. His surname, Equiano, means 'when they speak others listen' or, alternatively, 'if they wish, I shall stay'.[1] Olaudah Equiano was the youngest son of a large family, seven of whom survived infancy. His father was one of the province's elders, who met to decide disputes and punish crimes. Olaudah was his mother's favourite. When he was about 11 he and his only sister were kidnapped by slave-traders. After a journey to the coast lasting six or seven months, during which he was separated from his sister and temporarily reunited with her, he was transported to the West Indies. On the voyage he was brutally flogged for refusing food; saw a white seaman flogged to death and the corpse tossed overboard like so much meat; and experienced the other horrors of the middle passage.

After a fortnight or so in Barbados Equiano was shipped to Virginia and put to work weeding grass and gathering stones, an occupation varied by a few hours spent fanning the plantation-owner, whose black cook prepared his food with an iron muzzle locked over her mouth to prevent her eating any of it. A British naval lieutenant called Michael Pascal soon bought the lad for £30 or £40, renamed him Gustavus Vassa (or Vasa), and cuffed him till he answered to his new name. On the ship that brought him to England with his new master, Equiano made his first white friend: an American, four or five years older than himself, called Richard Baker.

> Soon after I went on board he shewed me a great deal of partiality and attention, and in return I grew extremely fond of him. We at length became inseparable . . . Although this dear youth had many slaves of his own, yet he and I have gone through many sufferings together on shipboard; and we have many nights lain in each other's bosoms when we were in great distress. Thus such a friendship was cemented between us as we cherished till his death . . . I lost at once a kind interpreter, an agreeable companion, and a faithful friend; who, at the age of fifteen, discovered a mind superior to prejudice; and who was not ashamed to notice, to associate with, and to be the friend and instructor of one who was ignorant, a stranger, of a different complexion, and a slave![2]

Equiano was about 12 when he arrived in England, early in the year 1757. Amazed to see snow for the first time, he was hardly less amazed to see the white people eating with unwashed hands; and 'I likewise could not help remarking the particular slenderness of their women, which I did not at first like; and I thought they were not so modest and shamefaced as the African women'.[3] In London, he stayed with two sisters called Guerin, relatives of his master: 'very amiable ladies, who took much notice and great care of me'.[4] They taught him to read, sent him to school, and had him baptized. He served Pascal during Wolfe's Canadian campaign and with Boscawen in the Mediterranean, acting as gunpowder-carrier under heavy fire during one fierce battle against the French fleet. Then, without warning, he was sold to Captain James Doran, commander of the *Charming Sally*.

> In a little time I was sent for into the cabin. When I came there Captain Doran asked me if I knew him; I answered that I did not. 'Then', said he, 'you are now my slave.' I told him my master could not sell me to him, nor to any one else. 'Why', said he, 'did not your master buy you?' I confessed he did. 'But I have served him', said I, 'many years, and he has taken all my wages and prize-money, for I only got one sixpence during the war; besides this I have been baptized; and by the laws of the land no man has a right to sell me:' . . . They both then said

> that those people who told me so were not my friends; but I replied – it was very extraordinary that other people did not know the law as well as they. Upon this Captain Doran said I talked too much English; and if I did not behave myself well, and be quiet, he had a method on board to make me. I was too well convinced of his power over me to doubt what he said; and my former sufferings in the slave-ship presenting themselves to my mind, the recollection of them made me shudder. However, before I retired I told them that as I could not get any right among men here I hoped I should hereafter in Heaven; and I immediately left the cabin, filled with resentment and sorrow.[5]

Equiano's new master took him to Montserrat and sold him to that island's leading merchant, a Quaker called Robert King, whose property he remained from 1763 to 1766. During those years, by dint of petty trading and hard saving, he managed to accumulate the price of his freedom: £40. For a time he went on working for his master as a free man. In 1767 he returned to England, where he was apprenticed to a hairdresser. Then he travelled widely: to Turkey, Italy, Portugal, Jamaica, and the Arctic, where the ship he was on and a companion ship, trying to find a passage to India, were trapped in the ice for 11 days. Returning to Britain once more, he started his anti-slavery activities when he tried to prevent the transportation of a black sea-cook, John Annis, who had been freed by his master on the island of St Kitts. The master now wanted Annis back and had caused him to be kidnapped. Equiano got advice from the abolitionist Granville Sharp, who had been active on behalf of kidnapped runaway slaves since 1765. But the lawyer whom Equiano engaged on Annis's behalf proved useless, 'and when the poor man arrived at St. Kitts, he was, according to custom, staked to the ground with four pins through a cord, two on his wrists, and two on his ancles, was cut and flogged most unmercifully, and afterwards loaded cruelly with irons about his neck'.[6] Returning to the Caribbean, Equiano was himself badly treated. A sloop-owner named Hughes tried to enslave him and strung him up with ropes for several hours, but he managed to escape in a canoe.

In 1777 Equiano came back to Britain and worked as a servant again. One of his employers, who had spent a long time on the African coast, suggested that he go there as a christian missionary; but the bishop of London, 'from certain scruples of delicacy', refused to ordain him.[7] After nearly losing his life in a Shropshire coal-mine and serving as a steward on one voyage to New York and two to Philadelphia, Equiano was in November 1786 appointed commissary of provisions and stores for the black poor going to Sierra Leone.

The Sierra Leone 'resettlement' scheme had been put up by an eccentric botanist called Henry Smeathman, and soon had enthusiastic government backing. It was designed to get rid of several hundred of the destitute black people in London by shipping them out to West Africa. The story will be told in a later chapter; our concern here is with the part Equiano played. At first he was reluctant to go with the settlers, largely 'on the account of the slave dealers, as I would certainly oppose their traffic in the human species by every means in my power'.[8] But he let himself be overpersuaded, and within days he had permission to take a ton of gunpowder on board one of the three ships. Clearly he meant business. But he soon found out that the government agent, Joseph Irwin, was guilty of 'flagrant abuse':

> Government had ordered to be provided all necessaries . . . for 750 persons; however, not being able to muster more than 426, I was ordered to send the superfluous slops [i.e. clothes and bedding], &c. to the king's stores at Portsmouth; but, when I demanded them for that purpose from the agent, it appeared they had never been brought [*sic*], though paid for by the government. But that was not all, government were not the only objects of peculation [i.e. embezzlement]; these poor people suffered infinitely more; their accommodations were most wretched; many of them wanted beds, and many more cloathing and other necessaries . . .
>
> I could not silently suffer government to be thus cheated, and my countrymen plundered and oppressed, and even left destitute of the necessaries for almost their existence. I therefore informed the Commissioners of the Navy of the agent's proceeding; but my dismission was soon after procured, by means of a gentleman in the city, whom the agent, conscious of his peculation, had deceived by letter.[9]

A naval officer to whom Equiano appealed for support agreed that Irwin had done nothing to indicate that he had the would-be settlers' welfare 'the least at heart'. On the other hand this officer, apparently irritated by a black person's daring to take a stand on principles, called Equiano 'turbulent, & discontented', accused him of 'taking every means to actuate the minds of the Blacks to discord', and criticized his 'spirit of sedition'.[10] The Navy Board stood up for Equiano all the same:

> In all the transactions the Commissary has had with this Board he has acted with great propriety and been very regular in his information but having from the beginning expressed his Suspicions of M^{r}. Irwins intention in supplying Tea Sugar and other Necessaries allowed for the use of the Women and Children on their Passage and having complained from time to time of his conduct in this particular we are not surprized at the disagreement that has taken place between them.[11]

But Equiano's adversary was white, so his dismissal was inevitable. His worst crime seems to have been 'his anxiety to see that justice was done to his own people'.[12] He defended himself, unavailingly, in a statement in the *Public Advertiser*.[13] And, as he and Cugoano had feared, the Sierra Leone scheme turned out an unqualified disaster.

Equiano's active participation in the growing movement for abolition of the slave trade was, by contrast, much more successful, though he did not live to see the triumph of his cause. He emerged, in his forties, as a capable and energetic publicist: a fluent writer and speaker, a campaigner prepared to travel wherever he was invited to present the abolitionist case. His friends and associates in the movement included, not only middle-class abolitionists like Granville Sharp, who chaired the largely Quaker Society for the Abolition of the Slave Trade that was launched in May 1787, but also a young Scottish shoemaker called Thomas Hardy, who was chief founder and first secretary of the London Corresponding Society, strongest of Britain's radical working-class organizations in the 1790s.

From 1787 on, abolitionism was a major – indeed, a central – tenet of the emergent radical movement, and Hardy was one of the first to state clearly that black freedom and white were two sides of one coin. He wrote to a Sheffield clergyman in 1792:

> Hearing from Gustavus Vassa that you are a zealous friend for the Abolition of that accursed traffick denominated the Slave Trade I inferred from that that you was a friend to freedom on the broad basis of the Rights of Man for I am pretty perswaded that no Man who is an advocate from principle for liberty for a Black Man but will strenuously promote and support the rights of a White Man & vice versa.[14]

Equiano not only helped Hardy by passing on names and addresses of useful contacts – abolitionists in the provinces whom he had met on his speaking tours – but joined the London Corresponding Society. Writing to Hardy from Edinburgh in May 1792, he sent his 'best Respect to my fellow members of your society', adding: 'I hope they do yet increase.' (For the full text of this letter, see appendix A, pp. 403–4.) While staying in Hardy's Covent Garden house two months earlier Equiano had been, by Hardy's account, 'now writing memoirs of his life' – which evidently meant working on the sixth edition of his autobiography and trumpet-blast against slavery: *The Interesting Narrative of the Life of Olaudah Equiano, or Gustavus Vassa, the African*.[15] (Writing to Hardy from Chesham in April 1792, his wife Lydia reported that her acquaintances there were 'very fond of vassa book', adding: 'Give my respects to him and I wish him a good jorney to Scotland.')[16]

First published in 1789, Equiano's book was both 'a uniquely detailed account of an African's movement out of slavery'[17] and the most important single literary contribution to the campaign for abolition. For the first time the case for abolition, presented by a black writer in a popular form, reached a wide reading public. It was, for instance, the last secular book read by Wesley before his death.[18] And it was highly effective in rousing public opinion. 'We entertain no doubt of the general authenticity of this very intelligent African's interesting story', wrote the *Monthly Review*, adding: 'The narrative wears an honest face: and we have conceived a good opinion of the man . . . His publication . . . seems calculated to increase the odium that hath been excited against the West-India planters.'[19] The *General Magazine* agreed. Condemning 'a traffic disgraceful to humanity, and which has fixed a stain on the legislature of Britain, which nothing but its abolition can remove', the reviewer declared:

> The narrative appears to be written with much truth and simplicity . . . The reader, unless perchance he is either a West-India planter or Liverpool merchant, will find his humanity often severely wounded by the shameless barbarity practised towards the author's hapless countrymen in our colonies . . . That so unjust, so iniquitous, a commerce may be abolished, is our ardent wish.[20]

In its author's lifetime the *Interesting Narrative* went through eight British editions; six more followed in the 22 years after his death. But even before this well-aimed blow at the plantocracy, Equiano had won widespread recognition as principal spokesman of Britain's black community. It was Equiano who in 1783 had called Granville Sharp's attention to the mass murder of 132 black slaves thrown alive into the sea from the decks of the Liverpool slaver *Zong*.[21] (For the *Zong* case, see pp. 127–9 below.) From then on the two men kept in close touch and undoubtedly co-ordinated their plans.

But Equiano was not merely, as we should call it today, a liaison officer between the black community and the white abolitionists. He was one of the acknowledged political leaders of his fellow-blacks. He was not by any means the only leader, in that period, whose name has come down to us. Ottobah Cugoano was, as we have seen, a close colleague and co-thinker. Others were Yahne Aelane (English name Joseph Sanders), Boughwa Gegansmel or Broughwar Jugensmel (both forms were printed; English name Jasper Goree); Cojoh Ammere (English name George Williams), Thomas Cooper, William Green, George Robert Mandeville, and Bernard Elliot Griffiths – all co-signatories with Equiano and Cugoano of a letter from nine 'Sons of Africa', published in the *Diary* newspaper in 1789, declaring that 'thanks to God the nation at large is awakened to a sense of our sufferings, except the Oran Otang philosophers' (i.e. the racist pro-slavery pamphleteers).[22] Other 'Sons of Africa' who signed public statements at various times in 1787–8 were Daniel Christopher, John Christopher, James Forster, John Scot, Jorge Dent, Thomas Oxford, James Bailey, James Frazer, Thomas Carlisle, William Stevens, Joseph Almaze, John Adams, George Wallace, and Thomas Jones.[23] It was no doubt these leaders, or some of them, who went with Equiano to Westminster to listen to debates and the examination of witnesses when Sir William Dolben's Bill to regulate the slave trade was passing through Parliament – against every procedural obstacle the West India lobby could devise. Equiano was constantly consulted by Dolben and was received by both the Speaker of the House of Commons and the prime minister. There could have been no clearer indication that a wind of change was beginning to blow.

The name of 'Gustavus Vassa the African' was now a familiar one to readers of the *Public Advertiser*, one of London's most widely circulated newspapers, items in which were often copied by the provincial press. For the *Public Advertiser* Equiano wrote a review of two pro-slavery pamphlets by the racist James Tobin of Nevis. It was a capable piece of polemical journalism: pointed, reasonable, and securely anchored in personal experience. 'Can any man less ferocious than a tiger or a wolf attempt to justify the cruelties inflicted on the negroes in the West Indies?' Equiano demanded. Tobin had tried to make his English readers frightened of 'the rapid increase of a dark and contaminated breed' in England. Equiano met him head on. Some of the wealthiest planters, he pointed out, had fathered children on their black slaves, and were responsible for infanticide, abortion, 'and a thousand other horrid enormities'. But why should people who loved each other not marry? 'Why not establish intermarriages at home, and in our Colonies? and encourage open, free, and generous love, upon Nature's own wide and extensive plan, subservient only to moral rectitude, without distinction of the colour of a skin?'[24]

For the same newspaper, and equally trenchantly, Equiano reviewed Gordon Turnbull's *Apology for Negro Slavery* (1786), a pamphlet which bore the hopeful sub-title : *The West-India Planters Vindicated from the Charge of Inhumanity*. Equiano cast his review in the form of an open letter to Turnbull:

> To kidnap our fellow creatures, however they may differ in complexion, to degrade them into beasts of burthen, to deny them every right but those, and scarcely those we allow to a horse, to keep them in perpetual servitude, is a crime as unjustifiable as cruel; but to avow and to defend this infamous traffic required the ability and the modesty of you and Mr. Tobin . . . Can any man be a Christian who asserts that one part of the human race were ordained to be in perpetual bondage to another?[25]

In a letter to Lord Hawkesbury, president of the Council for Trade and Plantations, later reprinted in the *Public Advertiser*, we see Equiano shrewdly appealing to capitalist self-interest. He urged, as Cugoano had done, the benefits of trading with Africa in normal commodities instead of human beings:

> A commercial intercourse with Africa opens an inexhaustible source of wealth to the manufacturing interests of Great-Britain.
>
> The abolition of Slavery, so diabolical, will give a most rapid extension to manufactures . . .
>
> The manufacturers of this country must and will, in the nature and reason of things, have a full and constant employ by supplying the African markets . . .
>
> It lays open an endless field of commerce to the British manufacturer and merchant adventurer.[26]

But Equiano was not satisfied with writing letters to the press and book reviews. After his *Interesting Narrative* was published he travelled the country addressing anti-slavery meetings. His speaking tours promoted sales of his book and won new adherents to the abolitionist cause. In 1789 he visited Birmingham 'and increased the indignation of the friends of the slave by the circulation of his narrative'. To the Birmingham people who had given him hospitality and a hearing, and many of whom had bought copies of his book, he wrote this charming letter of thanks:

> I beg you to suffer me thus publicly to express my grateful acknowledgments for their Favours and for the Fellow-feeling they have discovered for my very poor and much oppressed countrymen; these Acts of Kindness and Hospitality have filled me with a longing desire to see these worthy Friends on my own Estate in Africa, where the richest Produce of it should be devoted to their Entertainment; they should there partake of the luxuriant Pine-apples and the well-flavoured virgin Palm Wine, and to heighten the Bliss, I would burn a certain kind of Tree, that would afford us a Light as clear and brilliant as the Virtues of my Guests.[27]

In the following year Equiano spoke in Manchester, Nottingham, Sheffield, and Cambridge. In 1791 he spent eight and a half months touring Ireland, where he sold 1,900 copies of the *Interesting Narrative*, was everywhere 'exceedingly well treated, by persons of all ranks', and 'found the people extremely hospitable, particularly in Belfast'.[28]

The only brief lull in this activity came when Equiano married, on 7 April 1792, Susan Cullen, daughter of James and Ann Cullen of Ely. The marriage was solemnized at Soham church in Cambridgeshire, five miles south-east of Ely. A brief report in the *Gentleman's Magazine* described the bridegroom as 'well known in England as the champion and advocate for procuring a suppression of the slave-trade'.[29] There were two daughters of the marriage, Anna Maria and Johanna. The former died, at the age of four, on 21 July 1797, and there is a memorial inscription to her at Chesterton parish church in north Cambridgeshire.[30]

After a ten-day honeymoon, Equiano pressed on with his speaking engagements, visiting Scotland, Durham, Stockton, and Hull. The year 1793 found him in Bath and Devizes. One practical result of these meetings was to swell the subscription lists of successive editions of the *Interesting Narrative.* The sixth edition (1793) lists 487 subscribers in England (259 of them in Hull alone), 68 in Ireland, and 158 in Scotland. Interestingly, these subscribers included

'William, the son of Ignatius Sancho'.[31] But a still more important effect was to mobilize public antagonism to the slave trade. Equiano wrote to a Nottingham clergyman in 1792:

> I Trust that my going about has been of much use to the Cause of the Abolition of the accu[r]sed Slave Trade – a Gentleman of the Committee . . . has said that I am more use to the Cause than half the People in the Country – I wish to God, I could be so.[32]

As the Belfast abolitionist Thomas Digges put it, Equiano was 'a principal instrument in bringing about the motion for a repeal of the Slave-act'.[33]

Given the strength and determination of the West India lobby, it was inevitable that Equiano should at some stage be the victim of an attack on his integrity. The attack, when it came, was ludicrous and easily refuted. A poisonous paragraph in the *Oracle* newspaper, in 1792, alleged that he was not an African at all, but a native of Santa Cruz, a Danish-held island in the Lesser Antilles. Two days later this slander was reprinted in the *Star*.[34] Equiano was away from London, on a speaking tour. His friends demanded an apology, but none seems to have been printed – though the *Star*'s editor was forced to admit, in a private letter, that the story must have been invented by the enemies of abolition, 'for the purpose of weakening the force of the evidence brought against that trade; for, I believe, if they could, they would stifle the evidence altogether'.[35] Equiano nailed the lie in the next edition of his *Interesting Narrative*. 'It is only needful for me', he pointed out, 'to appeal to those numerous and respectable persons of character who knew me when I first arrived in England, and could speak no language but that of Africa.'[36]

Olaudah Equiano died in London on 31 March 1797, aged about 52. His friend Granville Sharp went to see him on his death-bed; Equiano had lost his voice and could only whisper.

Fourteen years later, when Sharp's niece asked her uncle what sort of a man Equiano had been, he replied: 'A sober, honest man.'[37] So far as it goes, this is an accurate epitaph; but it needs to be supplemented. Equiano was, for his time, exceptionally widely travelled. Experience had made him wise. He had a shrewd grasp of the political realities of his day. He had a fluent pen, a persuasive tongue, and absolute integrity. Abolition of the slave trade was the next link in the chain by which his community could haul themselves out of degradation to dignity. Equiano concentrated single-mindedly on securing this next link. He put his gifts and energy wholly at the service of his community in their struggle against slavery. He made an outstanding contribution to that struggle. He has never lost his voice.[38]

6. Slavery and the law

The legal pendulum

In 1569, 'one *Cartwright* brought a Slave from *Russia*, and would scourge him, for which he was questioned; and it was resolved, That *England* was too pure an Air for Slaves to breathe in'.[1] But was it?

Whatever Elizabeth I's judges had ruled, black slaves were soon being brought to this country in such numbers that it was only a matter of time before their status would be tested in the courts. The first reported case concerning black slaves came before the Court of King's Bench in 1677. *Butts* v. *Penny* was an action for trover – in other words, an action to recover the value of goods wrongfully detained. The 'goods' in question were ten Africans, probably in America (one account says '10 Negroes and a half', for of two tenants – i.e. possessors – in common one might 'bring an action . . . for half a negro'). The court decided that since black people were usually bought and sold among merchants they ranked as merchandise, and that since they were also infidels 'there might be a Property in them sufficient to maintain *Trover*'.[2]

No doubt this judgment, with its reference to infidels, greatly encouraged the widespread belief that baptism would set a slave free, so that the English, as a lord chief justice was later to observe, 'took infinite pains . . . to prevent their slaves being made Christians'.[3] This popular belief must have been strengthened also by the case of *Gelly* v. *Cleve* in 1694, when it was decided 'that *trover* will lie for a *Negro* boy; for they are heathens, and therefore a man may have property in them, and that the court . . . will take notice that they are heathens'.[4]

Although a lay writer had asserted in 1691 that 'a forein Slave brought over into England is, upon Landing, *ipso facto* [by the fact itself] free from Slavery, though not from ordinary Service',[5] in 1700 a Kent man wrote in his will of a black slave: 'I take [him] to be in the nature and quality of my goods and chattels.'[6] In 1706, however, Lord Chief Justice Holt ruled that trover would not lie for a black person, because the common law took no notice of blacks' being different from other people.[7] In another case of probably the same year, Holt was the first to utter the maxim 'That as soon as a Negro comes into England, he becomes free', adding: 'One may be a Villein in England, but not a Slave.'[8] (Villeins were a class of serfs in the feudal system, either entirely subject to a lord (villeins in gross) or attached to a manor (villeins regardant).)

Slave-owners went on bringing their black slaves into England all the same, but by 1729 they were so worried by the law's lack of clarity regarding their property rights that the West India lobby submitted a petition to the attorney-general, Sir Philip Yorke, and the solicitor-general, Charles Talbot. It was presented to those learned gentlemen 'in *Lincoln's Inn Hall*, after dinner . . . on the earnest solicitation of many merchants' and 'British planters'.[9] The law officers' ruling was brief, categorical, and very welcome to the West India lobby:

> We are of opinion, that a slave, by coming from the West Indies, either with or without his master, to Great Britain or Ireland, doth not become free; and that his master's property or right in him is not thereby determined [i.e. ended] or varied; and baptism doth not bestow freedom on him, nor make any alteration in his temporal condition in these kingdoms. We are also of opinion, that the master may legally compel him to return to the plantations.[10]

Twenty years later this opinion was reaffirmed by Yorke, who had meantime become Lord Chancellor Hardwicke, in these words:

> I have no doubt but trover will lie for a Negro slave; it [*sic*] is as much property as any other thing . . . The reason said at the bar to have been given by Lord Chief Justice HOLT . . . as the cause of his doubt, *viz*. That the moment a slave sets foot in *England* he becomes free, has no weight with it, nor can any reason be found, why they should not be equally so when they set foot in *Jamaica*, or any other *English* plantation . . . There was once a doubt, whether, if they were christened, they would not become free by that act, and there were precautions taken in the Colonies to prevent their being baptised, till the opinion of Lord TALBOT and myself . . . was taken on that point. We were both of opinion, that it did not at all alter their state. There were formerly villains or slaves in *England*, . . . and

> although tenures are taken away, there are no laws that have destroyed servitude absolutely.[11]

It remained, however, the popular view that '*Black Slaves*, brought into *England*, and baptized, are free from Slavery, though not from common Service: that is, they are free from being bought and sold.'[12] And in 1762 the legal pendulum swung that way again when Lord Chancellor Henley declared that 'as soon as a man sets foot on English ground he is free', adding: 'A negro may maintain an action against his master for ill usage, and may have a *Habeas Corpus* if restrained of his liberty.'[13]

Granville Sharp challenges the slave-owners

Granville Sharp was an obscure and slightly eccentric clerk in the Ordnance Department and his brother William was a Mincing Lane surgeon who gave free medical advice to the poor. One morning in 1765, as Sharp was leaving his brother's house, he noticed a black youth, about 16 or 17 years old, queueing up with the other sick people. His head was badly swollen, he was almost blind, and he was so weak and lame that he could hardly walk. He looked so desperately ill that Sharp felt he should not have to wait his turn. The brothers interviewed him together. He told them that his name was Jonathan Strong and that a lawyer and planter called David Lisle had brought him from Barbados as a slave, had beaten him savagely with a pistol till he was nearly dead, and had then thrown him into the street as useless.

William Sharp arranged for Jonathan to go into St Bartholomew's hospital. His injuries were so severe that it was four months before he was well enough to be discharged. Meantime the Sharps gave him clothes and shoes, and when he left hospital they paid for his lodgings and gave him money for food until they found him a job as errand boy to a surgeon in Fenchurch Street. Two years went by, during which Jonathan turned into a strong and good-looking young man.

And then one day his former master caught sight of him in the street, followed him home to see where he was living – and sold him to a Jamaica planter called James Kerr. The price, £30, was not to be paid until Jonathan was securely on board a ship ready to sail for Jamaica.[1] Lisle then engaged two professional slave-hunters, who lured the young man from his employer's house and handed him over to Lisle. He was locked up in a stinking jail until sailing time.

Jonathan had been baptized, believed that this had set him free, and sent to his two godfathers for help. They went to the prison but were not allowed to see him. So Jonathan wrote an imploring letter to Granville Sharp, who went to the prison next day. The door-keeper denied that he had any prisoner by the name of Jonathan Strong. Sharp insisted on seeing the keeper of the prison and, after much argument, was at last allowed to see Jonathan. He lost no time in applying to the magistrates for the youth's release. The case came up at the Mansion House before the lord mayor, who said 'the lad had not stolen any thing, and was not guilty of any offence, and was therefore at liberty to go away'.[2]

No sooner had the lord mayor set Jonathan free than the captain of the ship which was to have carried him to Jamaica grasped him by the arm – in open court and in the lord mayor's presence – and said he would secure him as Mr Kerr's property. Sharp warned the captain that he would charge him with assault if he presumed to take Jonathan. Sharp's account continues: 'The Captain thereupon withdrew his hand, and all parties retired from the presence of the Lord Mayor, and Jonathan Strong departed also, in the sight of all, in full liberty, nobody daring afterwards to touch him.'[3]

Within a few days Granville Sharp was served with a writ issued by Kerr alleging trespass and claiming £200 damages for being deprived of his property. As for Lisle, he challenged Sharp to a duel, demanding '*gentlemanlike satisfaction*, because I procured the liberty of his slave'. Sharp's dignified reply was that as Lisle had studied the law for so many years, 'he should want no satisfaction that the law could give him'.[4]

But what was the law, in fact? Sharp's solicitors were, as he put it, 'intimidated' by the Yorke and Talbot ruling of 1729.[5] They told their client that this opinion was decisive; that the case could not be defended; that it must be settled on whatever terms could be obtained. But Sharp was a Durham man and there was a core of granite in him. The incident at the Mansion House had made a deep impression on him, and he was not the kind of person to give way to bullies. Never in his life had he opened a law book. But he was ready to do the necessary homework and determined to put up the best fight he could. He told his lawyers that he would defend himself. He bought, not just a book, but an entire law library, then sat up night after night, combing through the indexes and poring over the leading cases. And he came to the conclusion that Yorke and Talbot, however eminent, had been wrong and that slavery was not sanctioned by the law of England. Since the case against him was *sub judice* he could not yet publish his findings in printed form. But he circulated among lawyers more than 20 manuscript copies of a document which soon had the desired effect: 'it intimidated the Plaintiffs' lawyers from proceeding in their action'.[6] In fact Kerr was non-suited for failing to proceed with his case and was ordered to pay treble costs.

This was victory, but only by default. Kerr was rash enough to launch a second action, but failed to proceed with that one either. Lisle tried softer methods, using

> a great variety of . . . arguments to persuade G.S. to deliver up the Negro, but he was answered by G.S. in general to this effect; that he did not detain the Negro, who was at liberty, and had been twice lawfully discharged by the Civil Magistrate, and therefore, that he (G.S.) could have no more rights to deliver him up, than he (Lisle) had to take him.[7]

So the Strong case petered out. Jonathan never quite recovered from the beating Lisle had inflicted on him, and died five years later at the age of 25.

Sharp was far from content with the partial victory he had won on behalf of black slaves in Britain. So he began a double-edged campaign. He sought a definitive legal ruling that it was unlawful to kidnap black slaves in England and ship them to the plantations. With the Lisle–Kerr action against him out of the way, Sharp could now publish his refutation of Yorke and Talbot: *A Representation of the Injustice and Dangerous Tendency of Tolerating Slavery; or of Admitting the Least Claim of Private Property in the Persons of Men, in England* (1769). It was a *tour de force* of legal and humanitarian argument, declaring that 'a toleration of Slavery is, in effect, a toleration of inhumanity'; citing the opinion of 'that excellent lawyer Lord Chief Justice Holt . . . that "*as soon as a Negro comes into England, he becomes free*" '; challenging lawyers who supported civil liberties to oppose publicly 'all doctrines which may tend to the introduction of the West India slavery'; advising the 'West Indian gentleman' who wanted to bring black servants to England to free them first; and warning the English people that when 'the *uncivilized customs*' which disgraced English colonies became so familiar in England, as to be permitted with impunity, 'we ourselves must insensibly degenerate to the same degree of baseness'.[8] One of the critical letters that Sharp received in response to this book was from a gentleman who said that while its arguments 'appear to be very reasonable and just', should black people be acquainted with the opinion of Lord Chief Justice Holt 'it might be attended with bad consequences to America and in particular to the sugar colonies'.[9]

So much for one cutting edge of Sharp's campaign. The other edge was a practical one: a steady effort, using such machinery as the law provided, to rescue kidnapped slaves. Without hesitation, Sharp did whatever needed to be done whenever such a case was brought to his notice – as many were, once word got around of his stand on Jonathan Strong's behalf. Indeed, he began proceedings in one such case even while the Lisle–Kerr action against him was pending.

John Hylas, born in Barbados, belonged to a woman who had brought him to England in 1754. In that year another Barbados-born slave, called Mary, had been brought to England by her owners, whose name was Newton. John and Mary met and in 1758, with their owners' consent, they were married. John Hylas was then set free and the couple lived happily as man and wife for eight years. But in 1766 Mary was kidnapped on behalf of her former owners and transported to the West Indies to be sold. John Hylas complained to Sharp, who helped him take legal action against the Newtons. The black plaintiff was awarded a shilling nominal damages, and Newton was ordered to bring Mary back by the first ship or within six months, whichever was earlier. Sharp's sense of triumph was tempered by his awareness that, under the Habeas Corpus Act, John Hylas was 'as much entitled to £500 damages at the least, besides treble costs . . . as the first lawyer of the kingdom would be, if he should lose his wife in the same manner'.[10] But John Hylas was black. One of Newton's counsel had expressed the hope that the case might at last decide the difficult question of the status of black people in England. Sharp commented tartly:

> He could not mean, I think, that he wished it to be determined in favour of the oppressed, because that is sufficiently determined already, as well as by the common law and custom of England, which is always favourable to liberty and the freedom of man . . . So that really there is not any difficulty at all in the question, notwithstanding that I have [heard] some very grave and learned lawyers affirm to the contrary, to my great astonishment and mortification. But none of those gentlemen I speak of have yet made it appear that there is anything so commendable, or worthy of imitation, in the West-India slavery, that it deserves to be admitted into this kingdom. And therefore I hope they will no longer persist in defending

so bad a cause, lest they should bring upon themselves also the charges of inhumanity.[11]

In his manuscript 'Remarks on the Case of John Hylas and his Wife Mary', preserved in York Minster Library, Sharp commented that 'West Indian masters, are so tenacious of this kind of property'.[12] This was amply confirmed by the next kidnapping case he took up, that of Thomas Lewis. One dark night in 1770 this former slave was suddenly and brutally seized by his ex-master, Robert Stapylton, and two watermen hired for the job. After a struggle they dragged him to a boat on the Thames, tied his legs with a cord, and tried to gag him with a stick. They rowed him to a ship bound for Jamaica and put him on board, to be sold as a slave. Fortunately his cries were heard by some servants who knew him. When they ran to help him the kidnappers claimed to be seizing Lewis on the lord mayor's orders. Next morning the servants reported the incident to their mistress, who took the news to Sharp and offered to meet the cost of having the kidnappers brought to justice.

Sharp rushed to get a warrant for Lewis's return. But by the time the warrant reached Gravesend the ship had been cleared. The captain refused to hand Lewis over, and sailed for the Downs. Next day Sharp applied to the lord mayor and to three judges in turn before he succeeded in getting a writ of habeas corpus. The ship had been held up by contrary winds but in two or three hours would have been out of sight. The officer who served the writ on the captain saw Lewis, in tears, chained to the mainmast. The captain was furious, 'but knowing the serious consequences of resisting the law of the land, he gave up his prisoner, whom the officer carried safe, but now crying for joy, to the shore'.[13]

Sharp lost no time in taking criminal proceedings on Lewis's behalf against the three kidnappers. Stapylton claimed at the preliminary hearing that Lewis belonged to him and that he had merely been taking possession of his own property. With the idea of minimizing his lady supporter's expenses, Sharp unwisely suggested a compromise. He offered to drop the action if the defendant apologized and promised not to do it again. This offer was 'haughtily rejected',[14] and Stapylton took the case to the King's Bench in order to maximize his opponents' expenses. It was heard by Lord Chief Justice Mansfield, in 1771. The day before it opened Stapylton made another, audacious, but unsuccessful attempt to kidnap Lewis, this time with the aid of a press-gang. No doubt he expected the case to go against him – as it did in the sense that he lost his slave, the jury finding that there was no evidence of Lewis's being his property. But there was to be no clarification yet of the legal status of black slaves in England. Lord Mansfield, himself a slave-owner in a small way,[15] was clearly most reluctant to come to a decision. Lewis's counsel argued 'that our laws admit no such property'. But Mansfield replied:

> There are a great many opinions given upon it; I am aware of many of them; but perhaps it is much better that it should never be discussed or settled. I don't know what the consequences may be, if the masters were to lose their property by accidentally bringing their slaves to England. I hope it never will be finally discussed; for I would have all the masters think them free, and all Negroes think they were not, because then they would both behave better.[16]

To Sharp's disgust, though motions for judgment on Stapylton were made in four successive legal terms, the lord chief justice could not be prevailed on to give judgment. Sharp protested privately, in words of white-hot anger, that this displayed

> open contempt of the principle of the Constitution . . . preferring private to public advantage, pecuniary or sordid property, as that of a master in a horse or dog, to inestimable Liberty, and abusing a noble statute intended for the freedom of injured subjects from imprisonment, to render it on the contrary, an instrument of oppression for delivering up poor innocent men into absolute unlimited slavery, dragging them up like horses or dogs to a private individual as mere property.[17]

Sharp was now virtually obsessed with the need to get a decisive ruling. His next opportunity came a few months later, when a black man named James Somerset was kidnapped and put in irons on board a ship bound for Jamaica.

The Somerset case

When Granville Sharp circulated that memorandum on his researches into the law concerning slavery, the great legal authority Sir William Blackstone, author of *Commentaries on the Laws of England* (1765–9), warned him that it would be 'up-hill work in the

Court of King's Bench'.[1] Sharp was now finding out for himself the truth of Blackstone's words.* Soon after the Thomas Lewis case he rescued three black slaves in quick succession. Each time, however, the judge concerned carefully avoided a decision on the principle involved: whether a black slave could lawfully be shipped back from England to the plantations against his or her will – or, in other words, whether everyone in the country, irrespective of colour, was entitled to personal liberty unless forfeited by the laws of England. Yet, in spite of Mansfield's 'hope' that 'it never will be finally discussed', the judicature could not evade the matter for ever. And Sharp was going to go on pushing until it was settled.

James Somerset was the property of a Boston, Massachusetts, Customs official, Charles Stewart, who brought him to England.[5] After two years he escaped. He was recaptured on 26 November 1771, and two days later Mansfield granted a writ of habeas corpus ordering John Knowles, captain of the Jamaica-bound ship he was imprisoned on, to produce him before the court. When this was done Mansfield postponed the hearing to the following January, and bound Somerset to appear. When proceedings were resumed Knowles's 'return', or reply to the writ, was read, stating that Somerset was Stewart's slave and property and outlining the circumstances of his escape and recapture. The lord chief justice then adjourned proceedings for a fortnight.

They resumed with speeches on Somerset's behalf by two of the five advocates appearing for him, William 'Bull' Davy and John Glynn. Davy's argument was essentially 'that no man at this day *is*, or *can be*, a Slave in England'. Toleration of slavery in the colonies was merely local, and wholly dependent on colonial law. The Court of King's Bench was bound to apply the law of England. The laws of Virginia had no more authority in this country than those of

* Blackstone himself added considerably to the difficulties of Sharp's 'up-hill work' by changing the statement on slavery in the first chapter of his *Commentaries* between the first (1765) and second (1766) editions of Book I – to make it conform to the Yorke–Talbot ruling. In the first edition the relevant passage read: 'A slave or a negro, the moment he lands in England, falls under the protection of the laws, and with regard to all natural rights becomes *eo instanti* [at that moment] a freeman.'[2] In the second edition this became: 'A slave or a negro, the moment he lands in England, falls under the protection of the laws, and so far becomes a freeman; though the master's right to his service may probably still continue.'[3] (This formulation was repeated in the third edition (1768); in the fourth (1770) and subsequent editions '*possibly*' was substituted for 'probably'.) Lord Mansfield was Blackstone's mentor and patron, and there can be no doubt whatever that this change was made at Mansfield's behest.[4]

Japan. Everyone coming into this country immediately became subject to its laws and entitled to their protection. Quoting the 1569 ruling 'That *England* was too pure an Air for Slaves to breathe in', Davy commented:

> I hope, my Lord, the air does not blow worse since. But, unless there is a change of air, I hope they will never breathe here; for that is my assertion, – the moment they put their foot on English ground, that moment they become free. They are subject to the laws . . . of this country, and so are their masters, thank God![6]

After hearing Glynn's argument – that slavery was merely local, and all places, except where the slave came from, must be a refuge – the lord chief justice adjourned the case for another three months.

At the resumed hearing, on 9 May, James Mansfield (no relation to the lord chief justice) argued that Somerset had been perfectly entitled to abscond, because the notion of perpetual service to a master by a slave was an idea unenforceable at English law. 'Where', he demanded, ' . . . is the mighty magic of the air of the West Indies, [that] by transplanting them for a while *there*, . . . they should become our absolute property *here*?'[7] The alteration which had been attempted in the laws of England, by the introduction of a new species of slavery, was so prodigious and important that an express enactment by the legislature was necessary – 'but I hope such a kind of slavery will never find its way into England'.[8]

When the court sat again on 14 May a young advocate called Francis Hargrave, who had written to Sharp offering his services, made his reputation with his first speech in any court. He argued that the law of England would not permit any man to enslave himself by contract. The utmost the law allowed was a contract to serve for life, and there was no case law affirming the lawfulness even of that. The legislature had not extended to England its permission of slavery in America; 'and not having done so, how can this Court be warranted to make such an extension?'[9] The last advocate on Somerset's behalf, Alleyne, warned that if the case went in favour of the slave-owners, 'the horrid cruelties, scarce credible in recital, perpetrated in America, might, by the allowance of slaves amongst us, be introduced here'.[10]

Stewart's case was opened by William Wallace, who said it would be unjust to divest him of his rightful property simply because he sailed, in pursuit of his lawful business, from one country to another. If the court rejected the slave-owners' right to their property in England, great inconvenience would be caused. There were so many blacks in English ports that many thousands of pounds would be lost to the owners by setting them free. Asked by Lord Mansfield whether he supported the proposition that the laws of the plantations relating to slaves were binding in Great Britain and Ireland, Wallace submitted that they must be received in England without cavil; but the lord chief justice rejected this view. In reply to another question, Wallace revealed that Stewart was backed by the West Indian merchants in general, who were going to pay his expenses.[11]

A week later, Stewart's other advocate, John Dunning, addressed the court. 'It is my misfortune', he admitted at the start, 'to address an audience, much the greater part of which, I apprehend, wish to find me in the wrong.'[12] It was a greater misfortune for him that, as most of his hearers knew, he had argued eloquently in the recent case of Thomas Lewis that slavery was contrary to the laws of England. Now, however, the burden of his argument was convenience and expediency. It would be dangerous and inexpedient to free the many blacks in England; and the relation, based on contract, of master and servant was in the universal interest of society and must therefore be maintained everywhere:

> It would be a great surprize, and some inconvenience, if a foreigner bringing over a servant, as soon as he got hither, must take care of his carriage, his horse, and himself in whatever method he might have the luck to invent. He must find his way to London on foot. He tells his servant, Do this; the servant replies, Before I do it, I think fit to inform you, Sir, the first step on this happy land sets all men on a perfect level; you are just as much obliged to obey my commands. Thus, neither superior, or inferior, both go without their dinner. We should find singular comfort, on entering the limits of a foreign country, to be thus at once devested of all attendance and all accommodation.[13]

The Royal African Company, Dunning continued, had a right from the Crown to buy slaves in Africa and sell them in the American plantations. Such slaves were as much the planters' property as any other article of their personal estate. The aggregate value of black slaves in England alone amounted to £800,000 sterling. It would be inexpedient to declare this valuable merchandise free. The change of place did not alter the property; it only exempted from 'that cruel usage they received in foreign parts, but no further'.[14]

Replying, William Davy said Dunning seemed to have discovered that the air of England had been gradually purifying since Elizabeth's reign, since he found it changed a slave into a servant – 'though unhappily he does not think it of efficacy enough to prevent that pestilent disease reviving, the instant the poor man is obliged to quit . . . this happy country'.[15]

When Davy sat down, the 'up-hill work' seemed almost done. But the lord chief justice said he was neither inclined nor prepared to decide straight away on the question 'whether the colony slave-laws be binding here, or if there be any established usage or positive law in this country that sufficiently countenances the coercion here contended for'. He went on:

> Almost insurmountable embarrassments assail us on either side. On one hand we are assured, that there are no less than 15,000 slaves now in England, who will procure their liberty, should the law decide in their favour, and whose loss to the proprietary, estimated at a moderate computation, will amount to no less a sum than 700,000l. [i.e. £700,000]* On the other, should the coercion on the colony slave-laws be found binding to the extent it has been argued, it must imply consequences altogether foreign to the object of our present enquiry. These are the obstructions that militate against an immediate decision . . . If Mr. Stewart consents to emancipate his slave, there is an end of the matter; if, on the contrary, he shall insist on demanding a final judgment, we shall not fail to give it faithfully, however irksome and inconvenient.[17]

Having thrown out this well-nigh desperate hint, Mansfield postponed judgment for a further month. The hint, meanwhile, was ignored. F.O. Shyllon suggests four reasons for Mansfield's vacillation. He lacked moral firmness. He respected property rights. He was reluctant to have the highest legal opinion overturned by the efforts of an obscure layman. Not least, he owed his meteoric rise at the bar to 'the patronage of Talbot and Yorke' – the very lawyers whose opinion, if Somerset won the case, would be overturned.[18]

At last however, on 22 June 1772, the long-awaited judgment was

* Another version of this speech (not a contemporary one) includes the sentence: 'The setting 14,000 or 15,000 men at once loose by a solemn opinion, is very disagreeable in the effects it threatens.'[16]

delivered, in a speech that the *Morning Chronicle* called 'as guarded, cautious, and concise, as it could possibly be drawn up'.[19] Mansfield said the slave Somerset had been put on board the ship by force and detained in secure custody there, to be carried out of the kingdom and sold. He went on:

> So high an act of dominion must derive its authority, if any such it has, from the law of the kingdom *where* executed. A foreigner cannot be imprisoned *here* on the authority of any law existing in his own country. The power of a master over his servant is different in all countries, more or less limited or extensive, the exercise of it therefore must always be regulated by the laws of the place where exercised. The state of slavery is of such a nature, that it is incapable of being now introduced by courts of justice upon mere reasoning, or inferences from any principles natural or political; it must take its rise from *positive law*; the origin of it can in no country or age be traced back to any other source. Immemorial usage preserves the memory of *positive law* long after all traces of the occasion, reason, authority, and time of its introduction, are lost, and in A CASE SO ODIOUS AS THE CONDITION OF SLAVES MUST BE TAKEN STRICTLY. (*Tracing the subject to natural principles, the claim of slavery never can be supported.*) THE POWER CLAIMED BY THIS RETURN WAS NEVER IN USE HERE: (or *acknowledged by the law.*) No master ever was allowed here to take a slave by force to be sold abroad because he deserted from his service, or for any other reason whatever; WE CANNOT SAY, *the cause set forth by this return* IS ALLOWED OR APPROVED OF BY THE LAWS OF THIS KINGDOM, and therefore the man must be discharged.[20]

The delegates from the black community present in court bowed to the bench, then joyfully grasped each other's hands; and those waiting outside the court cheered when the news reached them. 'Here at last', writes Shyllon, 'was the confirmation and admission of all that Granville Sharp had stood for and contended. And the heavens did not fall.'[21]

Even at the time, the Mansfield judgment was misunderstood by some people who thought it meant the emancipation of black slaves in Britain. This misunderstanding has been perpetuated by several generations of lawyers and historians, who ought to have known better.[22] And it still gets copied from book to book. All that Mansfield said was that a master could not by force compel a slave to go out of England. Black slavery still existed here. Long after the Somerset case, advertisements for the sale of black slaves continued to appear in English newspapers. And there were many slave-owners who defied the law by kidnapping escaped slaves and shipping them to the plantations. Less than a year after Mansfield delivered his judgment, a black slave who had run away from his master was kidnapped and put on board a ship in the Thames – and shot himself through the head.[23] This was the incident that led Thomas Day to write his poem *The Dying Negro* (1773). The writer Hannah More witnessed the seizure, in Bristol in 1790, of a black woman who had run away because she did not want to return to the West Indies. The public crier offered a guinea to anyone who hunted her down, and at length 'the poor trembling wretch was dragged out from a hole in the top of a house, where she had hid herself, and forced on board ship'.[24] In 1792 a Bristol citizen sold a black woman for £80 in Jamaican currency – and to Jamaica she was shipped, and someone who saw her put on board the ship said that 'her tears flowed down her face like a shower of rain'.[25]

Slavery and the Scottish law

Scotland was not bound by the Mansfield judgment or by any other decision of the English courts. Black slavery was first considered by the Scottish courts in 1757. One Robert Sheddan bought a black slave in Virginia and took him to Scotland to be taught a trade. Having been baptized, the slave claimed his liberty. But he died during the hearing of the case, so no decision was reached.[1]

Twenty years later, the case of *Knight* v. *Wedderburn* resulted in an explicit judicial condemnation of black slavery – 'the first opinion of that nature delivered by any court in the island'.[2] John Wedderburn had bought the 12- or 13-year-old Joseph Knight in Jamaica and brought him to Scotland as a personal servant. Knight married, then left Wedderburn and declared himself free. Wedderburn had him arrested, and the justices of the peace found 'the petitioner entitled to Knight's services, and that he must continue as before'. Knight then appealed to the sheriff of Perthshire, who ruled 'that the state of slavery is not recognized by the laws of this kingdom' and that Jamaican regulations concerning slaves did not apply to Scotland. Accordingly, he 'repelled the defender's claim to a perpetual service'. Wedderburn appealed to the Court of Session, Scotland's highest tribunal, where the arguments ran much as in the Somerset case south of the border six years before. The Somerset case was, in fact, often cited during the hearing. The court held, on 15 January 1778, that

> The dominion assumed over this Negro, under the law of Jamaica, being unjust, could not be supported in this country to any extent; That, therefore, the defender had no right to the Negro's service for any space of time, nor to send him out of the country against his consent . . . The judgments of the sheriff were approved of.[3]

The four dissenting judges included Lord Monboddo, whose black slave Gory is referred to in Boswell's *Life of Samuel Johnson*,[4] and whose eccentric views on men's tails and other matters we shall be glancing at in the next chapter.

Mass murder on the high seas

The West India interest in Britain sharply opposed Mansfield's judgment in the Somerset case. Not only did they ignore it in practice, as we have seen. They tried to have it overturned by Act of Parliament. They evaded it by binding their slaves as apprentices when they brought them to this country. And they pushed, harder than ever, the argument that plantation slavery was essential to British prosperity.[1] At the same time there was mounting black resistance to slavery and increasing support for the movement to abolish the slave trade. Both resistance and abolitionism were strengthened by the case of the slaver *Zong*, which shocked public opinion more deeply than any other single incident of its kind throughout the eighteenth century.[2]

The *Zong*, owned by the Liverpool banker and slave-trader William Gregson and his partners, sailed from São Tomé, an island off the coast of what is now Gabon, on 6 September 1781. The ship was bound for Jamaica with a crew of 17 and a cargo of about 470 slaves. By 29 November seven of the crew and over 60 of the slaves were dead, and many of the other slaves were sick and unlikely to live much longer. The master of the vessel, Luke Collingwood, told his officers that if the sick slaves died a natural death the ship's owners would have to bear the loss (and Collingwood himself would have had to bear a share of it). If, however, the slaves were thrown alive into the sea, on the pretext that the ship's safety demanded it, the underwriters must stand the loss. Such, indeed, was the law.

The mate, James Kelsal, opposed Collingwood's plan, but was told that 'it would not be so cruel to throw the poor sick wretches into the sea, as to suffer them to linger out a few days under the disorders with which they were afflicted'. The captain personally picked out 133 slaves and ordered the crew to throw them overboard. This was done in batches. Fifty-four were thrown into the sea that day and 43 the next; one of the second batch managed to grasp a rope, climbed back into the ship undetected, and survived. On the third day the remaining 36 put up a fight, so they were shackled before being drowned. The last ten victims succeeded in pulling away from their captors and chose to die as heroes. They jumped over the side.[3]

The owners claimed from the insurers the full value of these murdered slaves, on the ground that scarcity of water had made it essential to dispose of them in order to save the crew and the ship. In fact, on 29 November the ship had 200 gallons of water, which had not been rationed. According to the mate's deposition, Africans were still being thrown overboard even after a heavy fall of rain. The ship arrived in Jamaica on 22 December with 420 gallons of water to spare. The underwriters refused to honour the Gregsons' claim, even when the court ordered them to pay £30 for each murdered slave.

Someone who attended the hearing, and shuddered at what he heard, wrote an anonymous letter to the *Morning Chronicle*, and this alerted Olaudah Equiano to the crime that had been committed. Equiano carried the news to Granville Sharp, who lost no time in launching a vigorous campaign to bring the murderers to justice. Within two days Sharp had the support of the bishops of Chester and Peterborough. Next day he instructed solicitors to start proceedings in the Admiralty Court 'against all persons concerned in throwing into the sea one hundred and thirty slaves'.

Meanwhile the owners, eager for their £3,960, put pressure on the underwriters by asking the Court of King's Bench for a new trial. The solicitor-general himself, John Lee, represented the owners, and he demanded:

> What is all this vast declamation of human people being thrown overboard? The question after all is, Was it voluntary, or an act of necessity? *This is a case of chattels or goods*. It is really so; it is the case of throwing over goods; for to this purpose, and the purpose of the insurance, *they are goods and property: whether right or wrong, we have nothing to do with.*

Lee had evidently got wind of Sharp's intention, for at one point, while he was addressing the judges, he turned round and glared at Sharp, who was attending the hearing, and declared that

> a person was in Court . . . who intended to bring on a criminal prosecution for murder against the parties concerned: '*but*', said he, '*it would be madness: the Blacks were property* . . . If any man of them was allowed to be tried at the Old Bailey for a murder, I cannot help thinking, if that charge of murder was attempted to be sustained, *it would be folly and rashness to a degree of madness*: and so far from the charge of murder lying against these people, *there is not the least imputation – of cruelty, I will not say, but – of impropriety: not in the least*!!!

Sharp afterwards described the solicitor-general as 'the learned advocate for Liverpool iniquity'. The court granted a new trial but, if one did take place, there is no record of it, and we do not know whether Gregson's firm got its money.

Undeterred by the solicitor-general's talk of madness, Sharp now wrote to the Lords Commissioners of the Admiralty, demanding that those of the crew who survived – Collingwood, the captain, had died in the meantime – should be prosecuted for murder. He called their action

> a flagrant offence against God, and against all mankind; which, so far from deserving the favour of a judgment against the insurers, to make good the pecuniary value of the property as of mere goods and chattels, ought to have been examined and punished with the utmost rigour, for the exemplary prevention of such inhuman practices for the future.

Sharp wrote in similar terms to the prime minister. But no notice whatever was taken of either letter, and the murderers were never brought to justice. When Sharp published an account of the *Zong* crime in the press public opinion was stirred, but not enough to be effective. Typical was the reaction of George Gregory, rector of West Ham, who wrote: 'To those who may think that the plea of wanting water was a sufficient justification . . . I will put one plain question – If those persons who suffered had been white men, and not slaves, would they have been thrown overboard?'[4] One is driven to the conclusion that the West India lobby was powerful enough to block a prosecution.

Though those guilty of mass murder went unpunished, Sharp's agitation on the *Zong* case did help to secure the Dolben Act of 1788 regulating the slave trade. London, Liverpool, and Bristol

MPs fought hard against this modest piece of legislation, but it was clear to the more intelligent defenders of the slave trade that some degree of regulation was their only hope. They were losing ground day by day. When a deputation of MPs went to inspect a slaver lying in the Thames, and returned to Westminster sickened and ashamed by what they had seen, it was obvious that the writing was on the wall.

Not until 1796, however, did an English court rule that slaves could not be treated simply as merchandise. This ruling came in a case where a Liverpool slave-merchant tried to recover from the underwriters the value of 128 Africans who had starved to death on an abnormally long voyage. At one point Lord Chief Justice Kenyon pointedly asked whether the captain of the ship had starved to death, and was told that he had not. The merchant lost his case.[5]

The Grace Jones case

Forty-five years after the Somerset case, 20 years after trafficking in slaves by British subjects had been forbidden by law, the case of Grace Jones showed that a slave remained a slave even after she had been brought to England.

In 1822 Mrs Allen of Antigua came to England, accompanied by her domestic slave, Grace Jones.[1] The next year they returned to Antigua together. In 1825 a Customs officer seized Grace as forfeited to the king, on the ground that her exportation to England and reimportation into Antigua contravened the slave laws. Grace, he argued, was a free British subject who had been imported as a slave into Antigua and there unlawfully held in slavery. When this case came before the local Vice-Admiralty Court, the island's attorney-general refused to argue in support of the charge. In 1826 the judge of the Vice-Admiralty Court decreed that Grace be restored to her mistress with costs and damages for her detention. The Customs authorities appealed against this decision, and in 1827 the appeal was heard by Lord Stowell in the High Court of Admiralty.

As Shyllon observes, 'the case of Grace is another and final answer to the boast of Englishmen that the Somerset case made the air in their country incompatible with slavery'.[2] Lord Stowell said he 'should not notice' an advocate's assertion that Grace had told the governor she had gone back to Antigua against her will.[3] Stowell declared categorically:

> She could derive no character of freedom that would entitle

> her to maintain a suit like this (founded upon a claim of permanent freedom) merely by having been in *England*, without manumission . . . This suit, therefore, fails in its foundation: she was not a free person . . . If she depends upon such a freedom, conveyed by a mere residence in *England*, she complains of a violation of right which she possessed no longer than whilst she resided in *England*, but which had totally expired when that residence ceased and she was imported into *Antigua*.[4]

His Lordship frankly expressed concern about 'the public inconvenience that might follow from an established opinion that negroes became totally free in consequence of a voyage to *England*'.[5] And he let fall some observations about slavery and the law. While the law of England certainly discouraged slavery within the British Isles, 'the law uses a very different language and exerts a very different force when it looks to her colonies; for to this trade in those colonies it gives an almost unbounded protection'.[6]

The West Indian press gloated over Stowell's rejection of the appeal. 'Reason and equity', said the *Antigua Free Press*, 'have triumphed over cant and hypocrisy . . . This of course is no more than justice entitled us to.'[7] Jamaica's *Royal Gazette* said the decision

> stamps a value and a consistency upon West-India property, nearly shaken to pieces by injustice and frenzy . . . There will be few remaining in this country who, after perusing his Lordship's speech, will stand up and tell us . . . that the slaves in the West-Indies are not property, and property under the special guarantee of the laws of England . . . It follows that the Colonists have a right to protect that property, and if need be to knock on the head whoever comes forward in the Colonies to wrest it from them, and farther, it calls on the laws of their country to hang those who may forcibly wrest it from them.[8]

Public opinion in Britain was less unanimous and less jubilant. The *New Times* pointed out that Grace Jones had in fact been kidnapped – 'and a criminal indictment may be as legally preferred against those who seduced her to quit England, as if she had been a white native of this island'. Humanity would suffer by Stowell's decision: 'There is flesh and blood on one side, and perishable possessions on the other – the cause of liberty and the cause of gold – God and Mammon. Which is best entitled to consideration?'[9]

Six years later, slavery was abolished in the British Empire, and the black labour force in Britain's Caribbean colonies exchanged their chains for a form of bondage more suited to the new imperialist age that was dawning – and less troublesome to the christian conscience.

Though Grace Jones could be re-enslaved on returning to the West Indies after breathing our pure British air for a few months, slavery had in practice almost entirely disappeared from the British Isles themselves several decades before it was formally abolished in the British Empire. But if, contrary to popular belief, slavery in Britain was not outlawed by Mansfield in 1772, how in fact was it ended? The short answer is that black slaves in Britain voted with their feet. They had always, as we have seen, resisted by running away from their masters and mistresses. Helped and encouraged, and to some extent protected, by the Mansfield decision, they had largely completed this process and freed themselves by the mid-1790s. This gradual self-emancipation is a matter of social rather than legal history; we shall come back to it later. But first, in order to appreciate the magnitude of this achievement by Britain's black community in the eighteenth century, we must trace the rise of the racist ideology whose purpose was to keep black people in their place.

7. The rise of English racism

Race prejudice and racism

Did race prejudice cause slavery? Or was it the other way round? Winthrop D. Jordan, in his monumental study of white American attitudes to black people from 1550 to 1812, argues that prejudice and slavery may well have been equally cause and effect, 'dynamically joining hands to hustle the Negro down the road to complete degradation'.[1] But we must go deeper than that, if we are to understand the rise of English racism as an ideology, the various roles it has played in the past, and the role it is playing today. And first we must distinguish between race prejudice and racism.[2]

Sudden or limited contact between different nations or ethnic groups gives rise, as a rule, to all kinds of popular beliefs. Such beliefs spring from ignorance, fear, and the need to find a plausible explanation for perplexing physical and cultural differences. Specific false beliefs about other nations or other human varieties tend to be corrected, sooner or later, by observation and experience. But race prejudice in general is no less persistent than other oral traditions containing a substantial irrational element. It is specially persistent in communities that are ethnically homogeneous, geographically isolated, technologically backward, or socially conservative, with knowledge and political power concentrated in the hands of an elite. Such communities feel threatened by national or racial differences, and their prejudices serve to reassure them, to minimize their sense of insecurity, to enhance group cohesion. England in the sixteenth and seventeenth centuries was a classic instance of such a community – though its geographical isolation was rapidly being overcome and its technology was about to leap forward. We have already seen how ancient myths about Africa and Africans were widely believed here, and we shall shortly examine further evidence of English race prejudice in that period.

But to assert that their race prejudice, which was considerable, led Englishmen to enter the slave trade – even if we immediately add that slave-trading and slavery perpetuated race prejudice – is to make it harder, not easier, to understand Britain's rise to the position of foremost slave-trading nation in the world. It was their drive for profit that led English merchant capitalists to traffic in Africans. There was big money in it. The theory came later. Once the English slave trade, English sugar-producing plantation slavery, and English manufacturing industry had begun to operate as a trebly profitable interlocking system, the economic basis had been laid for all those ancient scraps of myth and prejudice to be woven into a more or less coherent racist ideology: a mythology of race. Racism is to race prejudice as dogma is to superstition. Race prejudice is relatively scrappy and self-contradictory. It is transmitted largely by word of mouth. Racism is relatively systematic and internally consistent. In time it acquires a pseudo-scientific veneer that glosses over its irrationalities and enables it to claim intellectual respectability. And it is transmitted largely through the printed word.

These distinctions are important, but there is another even more so. The primary functions of race prejudice are cultural and psychological. The primary functions of racism are economic and political. Racism emerged in the oral tradition in Barbados in the seventeenth century, and crystallized in print in Britain in the eighteenth, as the ideology of the plantocracy, the class of sugar-planters and slave-merchants that dominated England's Caribbean colonies. It emerged, above all, as a largely defensive ideology – the weapon of a class whose wealth, way of life, and power were under mounting attack.

Most notorious and influential of eighteenth-century racist writers in Britain was in fact an absentee planter from Jamaica. Edward Long had spent 12 years on that island, where he was judge as well as planter, before he wrote his *History of Jamaica* (1774), a book highly respected both in his own day and long after his death.[3] He justified the degradation of blacks by insisting that in every mental and moral way they were inferior to whites. He summed up the plantocratic ideology of race for consumption in the home country. And his book's pretensions to scientific rigour gave English racism a respectable cover, a spurious authenticity, just as the slave trade and slavery were beginning to trouble public opinion and arouse opposition. As we shall see, the timing of Long's book is significant for British imperial history; it came out just as the British government was taking responsibility for direct rule over a 'native' people, in Bengal. But the really interesting thing about Long's exposition of racism is how essentially unoriginal it was. He relied heavily on previous, deservedly obscure, writings. He copied two key passages practically word for word from his predecessors without scrupling to acknowledge those borrowings. Long's particular contribution was to link the assertion of black inferiority with the defence of slavery more boldly and blatantly and 'scientifically' than anyone had done before. And so, before discussing Long himself, we must examine the components of his attack on black people.

The demonology of race

The very words 'black' and 'white' were heavily charged with meaning long before the English met people whose skins were black. Blackness, in England, traditionally stood for death, mourning, baseness, evil, sin, and danger. It was the colour of bad magic, melancholy, and the nethermost pit of hell. People spoke of black arts, blackmail, and the Black Death. The devil himself was black. So were poison, mourning, sorrow, and forsaken love. When bad people were ostracized, they were blacklisted; when they were punished, their names were entered in a black book; when they were executed, a black flag was hoisted. And the black sheep of the family was, in all probability, a blackguard. White, on the other hand, was the colour of purity, virginity, innocence, good magic, flags of truce, harmless lies, and perfect human beauty.[1]

Spaniards and Portuguese had been invaded and subjected by people at once darker-skinned and more highly civilized than they were. The insular English, whose historical experience had been more limited, found sudden contact with black Africans deeply disturbing. It was a severe cultural shock for them: 'one of the fairest-skinned nations suddenly came face to face with one of the darkest people on earth'. Not merely did the Wolofs and Mandings of Senegambia fail to fit the English ideal; they 'seemed the very picture of perverse negation'.[2]

We all know how much easier it is to slot a new phenomenon into a pre-existing conceptual pigeon-hole than to do the hard work of rethinking one's concepts. And the English happened to have a very old and very convenient pigeon-hole for black Africans. If their skin was black, what else could they be but devils? The Ethiopian as devil can be found in *La Chanson de Roland*, an early version of which is supposed to have been sung by Taillefer at the battle of Hastings. But the idea was much older. The so-called *Epistle of Barnabas*, composed in the second century AD, termed the devil 'The Black One', and in the fourth century St Jerome said: 'Born of the Devil, we are black.'[3] By the early seventeenth century this equation was a commonplace of English literature. One dramatist, John Day, wrote of bad dreams which

> hale me from my sleepe like forked Deuils,
> Midnight, thou Æthiope, Empresse of black soules.[4]

Another, Thomas Heywood, referred to

> a Moor,
> Of all that beares mans shape, likest a devill.[5]

And indeed, those unfortunate people who happened to be visited by the devil often reported that he took the shape of a black man. That had been the distressing experience of St Margaret, Queen of Scotland, in the eleventh century[6] and of St Bridget of Sweden in the fourteenth,[7] and it was still happening in Shakespeare's day. 'A damned soule may and dooth take the shape of a blacke moore', wrote Reginald Scot in his authoritative *Discouerie of witchcraft* (1584).[8] Samuel Harsnet, later to be archbishop of York, told in 1603 of a woman who had seen *'a blacke man standing at the doore, and beckning at her to come away'*; demons in the shape of black men later tempted her to break her neck down the stairs and to cut her throat with a knife.[9] Beliefs such as Harsnet's – whose book Shakespeare raided for the names of the diabolical spirits in *King Lear* – were summed up sardonically by Samuel Butler:

> Some with the Dev'l himself in league grow,
> By's Representative a *Negro*.[10]

So the ground was well tilled for a travel writer like Sir Thomas Herbert, who after visiting parts of Africa in 1627–9 described the inhabitants of that continent as 'fearfull blacke . . . Deuillish Sauages' and 'divels incarnate'.[11] That fitted in splendidly with what many people already knew for a fact; if archbishops and eyewitnesses agreed about it, who could deny it? Small wonder that in Angola, so Herbert assured his readers, there were people so devilish that they actually worshipped the devil – 'in forme of a bloudie Dragon'.[12]

An alternative view, current throughout the Elizabethan and Jacobean periods, was that Africans were not devils but monsters. They often appeared in lists of freaks or undesirables: the 'Amozins', 'Nagars', 'ollive cullord moores', 'Canniballs', 'Hermophrodites', and 'Pigmies' of the lost play *Tamar Cam*,[13] for instance, and the 'beggars/*Gipseys*, and *Iewes*, and *Black-moores*' with whom Ben Jonson's Volpone has coupled to produce his Dwarf, Fool, and Eunuch.[14] And it so happened that the English, hitherto unfamiliar with tailless apes that walked about like human beings, were introduced to the anthropoid apes and to black people at the same time and in the same place, and 'the startlingly human appearance and movements of the "ape" . . . aroused some curious speculations'.[15] These speculations were encouraged by ancient traditions about anthropomorphous monsters. European folklore was full of ape-men and werwolves. When Edward Topsell, later vicar of East Grinstead, published his *Historie of foure-footed beastes* (1607), he included pictures of a baboon and two of those legendary human-like monsters, a 'Satyre' ('a most rare and seldome seene beast') and an 'Ægopithecus' ('an Ape like a Goate'). Each of the three displayed a prominent, and erect, 'genitall member'. Topsell told his readers that apes lusted after women, and insisted that 'Men that haue low and flat Nostrils are Libidinous as Apes that attempt women, and hauing thicke lippes the vpper hanging ouer the neather, they are deemed fooles'.[16] Of course, apes and devils were already linked in the popular imagination, as for instance James VI of Scotland, soon to be James I of England, linked them in his *Daemonologie* (1597).[17] Now Topsell clinched matters by explaining that, very likely, 'Deuils take not any dænomination or shape from Satyres, but rather the Apes themselues from Deuils whome they resemble, for there are many things common to the Satyre-apes and deuilish Satyres'.[18]

These traditions were bound to affect the way in which English people perceived black Africans. As they assimilated new information about Africa and tried to fit it into the steamy mass of ancient folklore, they were predisposed to see a similarity between the human-like beasts of the 'dark' continent and that continent's supposedly beast-like human beings. Richard Jobson retailed this comparison in 1623, attributing it to an unidentified Spaniard.[19] Sir Thomas Herbert was altogether coarser. In 1634 he wrote of Africans: 'Comparing their imitations, speech and visages, I doubt many of them haue no better Predecessors than Monkeys.'[20] He later elaborated this comparison, suggesting that Africans not only resembled apes but copulated with them:

> Their language is rather apishly than articulately founded, with whom 'tis thought they have unnatural mixture . . .

> Having a voice 'twixt humane and beast, makes that supposition to be of more credit, that they have a beastly copulation or conjuncture. So as considering the resemblance they bear with Baboons, which I could observe kept frequent company with the Women, their speech . . . rather agreeing with beasts than men . . . these may be said to be the descent of Satyrs, if any such ever were.[21]

Apes themselves, it was supposed, were the offspring of Africans and some unknown quadruped.[22]

Such bizarre but piquant ideas were not exactly brand-new in Europe. The French lawyer Jean Bodin had asserted in 1566 that 'promiscuous coition of men and animals took place, wherefore the regions of Africa produce for us so many monsters'.[23] But now, supported by the testimony of people who had actually been to Africa, these notions became widespread and extremely persistent in England, and were subscribed to by otherwise intelligent and rational people. Captain Thomas Phillips, though opposed to colour prejudice, repeated a story he had heard that baboons often raped African women;[24] Morgan Godwyn, one of the few who came forward in the seventeenth century to challenge the assertion that Africans were sub-human, nevertheless accepted the story that some Africans had 'too frequent unnatural conjunctions' with apes and baboons ('tho not', he added hastily, 'so as to Unpeople that great Continent');[25] the naval surgeon John Atkins reported that at some places 'the *Negroes* have been suspected of Bestiality' with apes and monkeys.[26] Even the famous eighteenth-century French naturalist Buffon, who at least tried to be scientific, wrote of 'an ape as tall and strong as a man, and as eager for women as for its own females' and referred to 'the violent lust [*appetit véhément*] of male apes for women' and 'the forced or voluntary intermixture of Negresses with apes, the produce of which has entered both species'.[27]

Quite the oddest expression of this idea was to come from the fertile pen of the eighteenth-century Scottish judge Lord Monboddo. In his effort to prove the close relation between human beings and speechless animals, Monboddo was specially fascinated by what he took to be two missing links. He firmly believed that there were humans in the Nicobar Islands who had tails which they waved like cats; and he claimed he could produce legal evidence that there had been a mathematics teacher at Inverness with a tail about six inches long, discovered after his death.[28] When the explorer James Bruce returned to Scotland from Ethiopia and went into Monboddo's courtroom the learned judge sent him a note asking to be *immediately* informed if, in his travels, he had come across any men with tails.[29] So much for one of Monboddo's missing links. The other was the 'Ourang Outang', by which he meant the gorilla, chimpanzee, and probably also baboon, of Africa rather than the orang-utan of Borneo and Sumatra. According to Monboddo, Ourang Outangs were rational human beings that happened to live in a primitive state of nature. They could do everything but talk.[30] The Ourang Outang was 'an animal of the human form, inside as well as outside' – 'a barbarous nation, which has not yet learned the use of speech'. It carried off boys and girls as slaves and kept them for years without harming them. It buried its dead. It played very well on pipes, harps, and other instruments.[31] And an Ourang Outang once served as a cabin-boy.[32] Amid this rigmarole, culled from travellers' tales, the allegation that Ourang Outangs 'carry away young negroe girls and keep them for their pleasure', and almost certainly fathered offspring in that way, was a mere drop in the bucket.[33] Monboddo's aim was to elevate the Ourang Outang, not degrade black people; but it so happened that his evidence for alleged human–simian copulation was travellers' tales from Africa.[34]

Reports of unusual sexual behaviour of any kind have always found an eager and credulous readership, and English people in the seventeenth and eighteenth centuries were only too happy to swallow stories which confirmed their immemorial view of dark-skinned people as lustful beasts. When Shakespeare had Roderigo call Othello's embraces 'the gross clasps of a lascivious Moor'[35] he was drawing on a centuries-old belief. A widely read translation of John Leo Africanus – who was born in Spain and really was a Moor – assured English readers in 1600 that there was 'no nation vnder heauen more prone to venerie' than 'the Negros', who 'haue great swarmes of harlots among them; whereupon a man may easily coniecture their manner of liuing'.[36] And this was 'the most authoritative work on the history of the interior [of Africa] that was to appear in England for more than two centuries'![37] Bodin too had insisted that heat and lust went hand in hand, that 'in Ethiopia . . . the race of men is very keen and lustful'; his authority for this bold generalization was Ptolemy, who lived in the second century AD and who 'reported that on account of southern sensuality Venus chiefly is worshiped in Africa and that the constellation of Scorpion, which pertains to the pudenda, dominates that continent'.[38] Elizabethan literature abounded with lecherous and degenerate black men: 'in

Elizabethan drama before *Othello* there are no Moor figures who are not either foolish or wicked'. Muly Hamet, the 'Negro Moore' in George Peele's *The Battle of Alcazar* (*c.*1588), probably the earliest Moor–villain, in the first full-length treatment of a black character in English drama; Aaron, the 'barbarous Moore' in *Titus Andronicus* (1589–90); Eleazer in *Lust's Dominion* (1599): these characters 'supply the norm of dramatic expectation – of a man whose colour reveals his villainy as (quite literally) of the deepest dye'.[39] And that of course was what gave *Othello* (acted in 1604) its exceptional power, for Shakespeare relied on his audience's knowledge and acceptance of the stereotype in order the more effectively to shatter it.

Outside the theatre, the stereotype remained unshattered, so that Francis Bacon could refer to '*an holy Hermit . . . that desired to see the* Spirit *of Fornication, and there appeared to him, a little foule vgly* Aethiope'.[40] Seventeenth-century travellers' tales strengthened the stereotype by adding spicy details. Andrew Battell of Leigh found the Angolans 'beastly in their liuing, for they haue men in womens apparell, whom they keepe among their wiues'.[41] In Guinea, said another account, the people were 'very lecherous . . . and much addicted to vncleannesse: one man hath as many wiues as hee is able to keepe and maintaine'.[42] Perhaps most piquant of all – though they can't have done much to allay Englishmen's sexual anxieties – were reports that male Africans were all equipped with enormous sex organs. According to Jobson, Manding men were 'furnisht with such members as are after a sort burthensome vnto them';[43] the anonymous author of *The Golden Coast* (1665), remarking on the 'extraordinary greatness' of their 'Members', described African men as 'very lustful and impudent [i.e. shameless] . . . and therefore much troubled with the Pox';[44] while John Ogilby, adapting the writings of the Dutch traveller Olfert Dapper, told his readers that 'most of the *Blacks* upon the *Guinee* Coast' had 'large Propagators'.[45] Nor were African women less sexually aggressive than African men. This was the sort of thing that went on in Guinea:

> If they meet with a Man they immediately strip his lower Parts, and throw themselves upon him, protesting that if he will not gratify their Desires, they will accuse him to their Husbands . . . If they can come to the Place the Man sleeps in, they lay themselves softly down by him, soon wake him, and use all their little Arts to move the darling Passion.[46]

But what else could you expect of savages, of people who lived like animals? This was precisely how West Africans were described in 1555: 'a people of beastly lyvynge, without a God, lawe, religion, or common welth'.[47] How could such people be trusted? According to Sir Thomas Herbert, in 1634, 'black-faced *Africans*, are much addicted to rapine and theeuery'.[48] According to Ogilby, in 1670, it was an 'innate quality' of the inhabitants of 'Negroe-land' to steal anything they could lay their hands on, especially from foreigners.[49] To the Dutchman Willem Bosman a third of a century later – his book was translated into English within a year – black people were 'without exception, Crafty, Villanous and Fraudulent, and very seldom to be trusted . . . they indeed seem to be born and bred Villains'.[50] To John Oldmixon, reporting on Barbados in the same period, 'the Negroes are generally false and treacherous . . . for the most part they are faithless, and Dissemblers'.[51] To Hugh Jones, in 1724, black people were 'naturally of a barbarous and cruel Temper, yet are they kept under by severe Discipline upon Occasion'.[52] To Dr James Houstoun, in 1725, 'their natural Temper is barbarously cruel, selfish, and deceitful', while 'as for their Customs, they exactly resemble their Fellow Creatures and Natives, the Monkeys'.[53] Richard Ligon's was almost a lone voice of dissent. 'I beleive,' he wrote in 1657, 'and I have strong motives to cause me to bee of that perswasion, that there are as honest, faithfull, and conscionable people amongst them, as amongst those of *Europe*, or any other part of the world.'[54] This wholly exceptional statement speaks volumes about the prevailing view.

Some accounts even claimed that hungry Africans were no more to be trusted by their friends than by foreigners. From Sir Thomas Herbert came a picturesque description of how they rather liked having their friends for dinner – and how some even enjoyed being eaten themselves:

> Not satisfied with natures treasures . . . the destruction of men and women neighbouring them, better contenting them, whose dead carkasses they devoure with a vultures appetite; whom if they misse, they serve their friends (so they mis-call them) such scurvy sauce, butchering them, thinking they excuse all in a complement, that they know no rarer way to express true love than in making (not two soules) two bodies one in an inseparable union: yea, some (worne by age, or worme-eaten by the pox) proffer themselves to the shambles, and accordingly are joynted and set to sell upon the stalls.[55]

Africans were not merely devilish, monstrous, ape-like, lustful, treacherous, and given to cannibalism. They were also inherently lazy: 'generally idle and ignorant' (King Charles II's hydrographer);[56] 'Nothing but the utmost Necessity can force them to Labour: They are besides . . . incredibly careless and stupid' (Bosman);[57] 'lazy, careless' (Oldmixon).[58] But this stereotype – which is how slave-owners have seen their slaves throughout history – was hard to sustain when huge numbers of Africans were being worked to death producing sugar for European planters. So it was balanced by, and co-existed quite harmoniously with, a diametrically opposite stereotype: 'They are by Nature cut out for hard Labour and Fatigue' (Hugh Jones).[59]

Black people were also generally described as ugly – though here again there were exceptions, such as the travellers who confessed to finding the young women they saw in Africa aesthetically pleasing and implied that they found them sexually attractive. Richard Ligon was enchanted by the breasts of young African women he saw in Barbados.[60] But William Towerson described the breasts of African women as 'very foule and long, hanging downe low like the vdder of a goate'.[61] A French traveller, in a book translated into English in 1696, said Africans were 'dreadful to look upon' (*haves à voir*): 'It might be properly said, that these Men came out of Hell.'[62] Comparing American 'Indians' with Africans in 1612, colonist William Strachey said the former had 'great bigge Lippes, and wyde mouthes, (yet nothing so vnsightly as the Moores,)'.[63] When Hugh Jones made the same comparison a century later, his perceptions were clearly coloured by the rise of plantation slavery in the intervening years. Blacks, he wrote, 'have uglier Faces and Bodies, and are of a more servile Carriage, and slavish Temper'.[64]

These manifold disabilities of black people became much easier to understand when viewed from a religious point of view, as resulting from God's curse on Ham for looking on his father's nakedness as the old man lay drunk in his tent.[65] In particular, that was how blacks were supposed to have come by their blackness. However strange it may seem to us in the twentieth century to turn to Jewish mythology for an explanation of differences in human pigmentation, the Old Testament was by far the most authoritative place to look, 400 or 500 years ago, for guidance on such problems. Gilbert Génébrard, sixteenth-century Benedictine monk and archbishop of Aix, is often said to have been the first to hold that the ancestor of all Africans, a character by the name of Chus, was made black by the curse on his father Ham.[66] But Génébrard merely copied this notion from a visionary called Guillaume Postel;[67] and it is safe to say that even Postel was probably not the originator of the 'God's curse' as opposed to the 'scorched by the tropical sun' explanation of Africans' blackness. There were of course some tricky aspects to the Postel–Génébrard theory, and a later scholar–monk called Agostino Tornielli did his best to clarify matters. He pointed out that Chus begat Nimrod, who was white, as well as black children. So Ham's wife must have had her mind on something black at the time she conceived Chus or, alternatively, was afflicted with a longing for something black during his gestation. Chus's wife, too, was white and bore both black and white sons to her husband, who very considerately assigned to his dark offspring the hotter and therefore, for them, more comfortable regions of the earth.[68]

The classical English statement of the 'curse of Ham' theory came from the pen of a sea-captain called George Best, who sailed with Martin Frobisher in 1577 in search of the north-west passage. When he came back Best published a book about the expedition in which he explained how, to punish Ham for disobedience, God had willed that

> a sonne shuld be borne, whose name was Chus, who not only it selfe, but all his posteritie after him, should be so blacke & lothsome, that it might remaine a spectacle of disobedience to all the Worlde. And of this blacke & cursed Chus came al these blacke Moores which are in Africa . . .
>
> Thus you see, y[t] the cause of y[e] Ethiopians blacknesse, is the curse & natural infection of bloud.[69]

In 1704 the Englishman Peter Heylyn, historian, theologian, and friend of Archbishop Laud, was being cited as an authority for the theory that Ham's impiety had turned him or his descendants black.[70] But Heylyn was both a late and a half-hearted convert. All he said in the earliest version of his almost unreadable book *Microcosmus* (1621), which grew like a snowball as it rolled through successive editions down the seventeenth century, was that blacks 'doe almost want the vse of reason', were unintelligent, had no arts or sciences, were prone to lust, 'and are for the greater part Idolators'.[71] Six years later he was calling the 'curse of Ham' theory a 'foolish tale'.[72] But after pondering the matter for another 30-odd years, Heylyn was at last persuaded to concede that 'possibly enough the Curse of God on *Cham* and on his posterity . . . hath an influence on it'.[73]

One final, contrasting strand in the tangled skein of prejudice must be identified: the notion of polygenesis, or separate creation of different human varieties. This notion, whose adherents are known as polygenists, brings us to the threshold of pseudo-scientific racism. Polygenists thought, and taught, that black people were in some way intermediate between white people and apes. The theory of polygenesis was canvassed in Isaac La Peyrère's *Præadamitæ* (1655), an English translation of which was soon out as *Men before Adam* (1656),[74] and it turned up in the *Journal des sçavans* in 1684, when François Bernier divided humanity into four 'species', largely on the basis of skin colour, two of these 'species' being Africans – and Lapps, whom he called 'wretched animals'.[75] In 1699 Dr Edward Tyson, physician and authority on the scent-bags of pole-cats, published the results of his dissection of a chimpanzee (which he called an 'orang-outang'). Tyson not only proved that there were anatomical similarities between human beings and apes. He also explained that '*Man* is part a *Brute*, part an *Angel*; and is that *Link* in the *Creation*, that joyns them both together'.[76] Like the German surgeon Johann Meckel's claim in 1757 that black people's blood was black – so black, indeed, that it blackened bandages instead of reddening them[77] – Tyson's work was seized on by writers who held that Africans were a separate species, a link between humans and animals in the 'Great Chain of Being'. (This idea, whereby all inanimate matter, living beings, and supernatural powers were arranged in a hierarchy, with humanity smack in the middle – midway between angels and animals – dates back at least to the ancient Greeks.)[78] After scratching his head in perplexity over what he called 'the distempered skin of Africans', which he found 'extremely difficult to account for', the naval surgeon John Atkins concluded in 1734 'that White and Black must have descended of different Protoplasts [i.e. first human beings]; and that there is no other Way of accounting for it'.[79] A year later he reaffirmed that 'the black and white Race [*sic*] . . . have sprung from different-coloured first Parents' – though he was forced to admit that, from a religious point of view, such a doctrine might be 'a little Heterodox'.[80]

Three notions that have figured in this section were to be specially prominent in racist ideology: the idea that Africans were, in one way or another, closely connected with apes; the idea that people with differently coloured skins had different origins; and the idea that human beings could be graded hierarchically on the basis of skin colour.

It should not be supposed that all English people in the seventeenth and eighteenth centuries were prejudiced against black people.

There were ethnocentric stereotypes other than hostile ones. But they were stereotypes all the same. Immensely popular, for instance, was the idea of the 'noble savage', foreshadowed in the legend of Yarico and Inkle. When that legend made its first appearance in print, in 1657, the lovely Yarico – who saved a christian's life only to be made pregnant and betrayed by him – was not yet an African virgin but a Carib woman in Barbados.[81] Appropriated by anti-slavery writers in the eighteenth century, with the heroine's race suitably changed, this touching tale inspired at least 40 separate works – poems, essays, plays, ballets, and an opera – and was translated into eight languages. The African as 'noble savage' was first portrayed in Aphra Behn's novel *Oroonoko* (*c.*1678), which, adapted by Thomas Southerne, was to be performed on the stage nearly every season for 100 years. In some ways Mrs Behn's 'noble savage' looked more like a European than an African:

> His Face was not of that brown, rusty Black which most of that Nation are, but a perfect Ebony, or polish'd Jett. His Eyes were the most awful [i.e. impressive] that cou'd be seen, and very piercing; the white of 'em being like Snow, as were his Teeth. His Nose was rising and *Roman*, instead of *African*, and flat. His Mouth, the finest shap'd that could be seen; far from those great turn'd Lips which are so natural to the rest of the *Negroes*.[82]

The 'noble savage' crops up in the writings of numerous English and Scottish romantics: Blake, Burns, Coleridge, Cowper, Southey, Wordsworth, and many minor poets and 'forgotten scribblers'.[83] In the hands of lesser writers the 'noble savage' became a stock figure of literary fashion, no less artificially sentimental than the pining slaves that crowd the pages of late eighteenth-century novels, plays, and poems. And just like those grateful Negroes, captive Negroes, dying Negroes, Negroes fettered, Negro's incantations, Negro's prayers, Negro's imprecations, and Negro-mothers' cradle-songs, the stereotype tells us 'more about the white men' – and women – 'who did the writing than about the negroes who did the suffering'.[84]

After all these stereotypes, coarsely hostile or cloyingly sentimental, we badly need a breath of fresh air. It blew rarely. But here is the bluff, common-sense opinion of an English sea-captain, reporting in 1694 on a voyage to Africa and Barbados. Captain Thomas Phillips could not imagine why black people should be despised for their colour, 'being what they cannot help'. And he added: 'I can't think there is any intrinsick value in one colour more than another, nor that white is better than black, only we think so because we are so, and are prone to judge favourably in our own case.'[85]

Plantocracy racism

The oral tradition

'Christianity and the embracing of the Gospel does not make the least difference in civil property', said Thomas Sherlock when speaking about the slave trade in 1727.[1] Sherlock was in turn bishop of Bangor, Salisbury, and London, and he was stating the Church of England's official view. The planters in the West Indies shared the widespread belief that if they let their black slaves be converted to christianity and baptized this would mean setting them free. The Church did its best to reassure the planters on that score; on the issue of slavery it was otherwise totally passive. Dissenting christians were also, with few exceptions, less troubled by the institution of slavery as such than by the planters' opposition to the conversion and baptism of their slaves. In the controversy that developed, the planters argued that black people were not human beings but animals without souls to save. '*What, such as they?*' they cried. '*What, those black Dogs be made Christians? What, shall they be like us?*'[2] And they demanded to know whether ministers of religion would start baptizing horses.[3] Here was the very dawn of English racism, and we find it reflected or reported in 300-year-old religious tracts. These tracts make curious reading today, for most of their authors argue that Africans are human without objecting in the slightest degree to their being slaves.

The earliest tracts of this kind suggest that even before the middle of the seventeenth century race prejudice was crystallizing into an orally transmitted racism that was already leading in practice to cold-blooded killings by members of the dominant race. In 1642 a popular preacher called Thomas Fuller, who served as chaplain to various titled families, published a book called *The Holy State*. His chapter on 'The good Sea-Captain' said that when the latter seized a ship as a prize

> *he most prizeth the mens lives whom he takes*; though some of them may chance to be Negroes or Savages. 'Tis the custome of some to cast them overbord, and there's an end of them: for the dumbe fishes will tell no tales . . . What, is a brother by the half bloud no kinne? a Savage hath God to his father by creation,

> though not the Church to his mother, and God will revenge his innocent bloud. But our Captain counts the image of God neverthelesse his image cut in ebony as if done in ivory, and in the blackest Moores he sees the representation of the King of heaven.[4]

Visiting Barbados in 1671, George Fox, founder of the Society of Friends, was accused of trying to stir up the black slaves by telling them that Christ had died for them, too – though in fact he also 'exhorted them to *Justice, Sobriety, Temperance, Chastity and Piety*, and to be *subject* to their *Masters* and *Governours*'. What he told the island's Quaker slave-owners suggests their prevalent opinion:

> Do not slight them, to wit, the *Ethyopians*, the *Blacks* now, neither any Man or Woman upon the Face of the Earth, in that *Christ* dyed for all, both *Turks*, *Barbarians*, *Tartarians* and *Ethyopians*; he dyed for the *Tawnes* and for the *Blacks*, as well as for you that are called *Whites* . . . You should preach Christ to your *Ethyopians* that are in your Families [*sic*] . . . and be tender of and to them.[5]

The Presbyterian Richard Baxter came still closer to the heart of the matter when he told the planters a few home truths in 1673. To begin with, 'those . . . that keep their *Negro's* and slaves from hearing Gods word, and from becoming Christians . . . declare that their worldly profit is their treasure and their God'. Moreover it was time the planters learnt the difference between human beings and animals. Black slaves, wrote Baxter,

> are reasonable Creatures, as well as you . . . Remember that they have immortal souls, and are equally capable of salvation with your selves . . . How cursed a crime is it to equal *Men* and *Beasts*? Is not this your practice? Do you not buy them and use them meerly to the same end, as you do your *horses*? . . . as if they were baser than you, and made to serve you?[6]

Emergent racism is also reflected in a pamphlet called *Friendly Advice to the Gentlemen-Planters of the East and West Indies* (1684), by the vegetarian and mystic Thomas Tryon. This contained a complaint against slavery put into the mouths of black slaves: 'The Negro's Complaint of their Hard Servitude, and the Cruelties Practised upon them By divers of their Masters professing Christianity in the West-Indian Plantations'. The overseers' racist insults to their helpless victims are quoted. Blacks were 'sold . . . like Beasts to the Merchant' and 'the inconsiderate and unmerciful

Overseers make nothing to Whip and Beat us, and the best words they can afford us, are, *Damn'd Doggs, Black ugly Devils, idle Sons of Ethiopean Whores*, and the like'.[7]

But it was Morgan Godwyn who in 1680 put his finger unerringly on the economic basis and role of plantocracy racism. Grandson of a bishop and son of a canon, Godwyn went out to Virginia, then to Barbados, as a minister of religion. He didn't care for the progress the Quakers had been making in Barbados, and inter-denominational rivalry may have sharpened his attack on the plantocracy. In any case, he showed very clearly that slave-owners and slave-merchants were denying the humanity of black slaves from economic motives. And he said this publicly, giving chapter and verse, in the teeth of the West India lobby's threats to silence him by slander. '*The very worst they can vomit forth*', he retorted, '*will never in the least prejudice me in the opinion and esteem of Good Men.*' Echoing Baxter, he declared that the '*public Agents*' for the West Indies '*know no other* God *but* Money, *nor* Religion *but* Profit'.[8] He was quite prepared 'to undergo . . . the utmost Effects of the Rage and Malice of those incensed *MAMMONISTS* from abroad'.[9]

The object of Godwyn's book *The Negro's & Indians Advocate* (1680) was, in his own words, '*to prove the* Negro's Humanity, *and to shew that neither their* Complexion *nor Bondage, Descent nor Country, can be any impediment thereto*'. He was the first to analyse racism as a class ideology, and even after 300 years neither his analysis nor his language has lost its cutting edge. While in Barbados, he had been told that to teach christianity to blacks and baptize them were unnecessary and destructive to the planters' interest. One person told him 'with no small *Passion* and Vehemency . . . that I might as well Baptize a Puppy'; another, that baptism would do no more good to her black slave 'than to her *black Bitch*'. Baptism of blacks, said the planters, tended 'to no less Mischief than the overthrow of their Estates, and the ruine of their *Lives*, threatning even the utter *Subversion* of the Island'. Even as his book was in the press a Barbadian in London told him '*That* Negro's *were* Beasts, *and had no more Souls than Beasts, and that Religion did not concern them. Adding that they went not to those parts to save Souls, or propagate Religion, but to get Money*' – and Godwyn's printer managed to squeeze in this extra piece of evidence as a let-in note. The heart of the book is the following passage:

> [A] disingenuous and unmanly *Position* hath been formed; and privately (*and as it were in the dark*) handed to and again [i.e. to and fro], which is this, That the *Negro's*, though in their Figure

> they carry some resemblances to Manhood, yet are indeed *no Men* . . . If *Atheism and Irreligion* were the true Parents who gave it Life, surely *Sloth and Avarice* have been no unhandy Instruments and Assistants to midwife it into the World, and to Foster and Nurse it up. Under whose Protection getting abroad, it hath acquired sufficient strength and reputation to support it self; being now able not only to maintain its ground, but to bid defiance to all its *Opposers*; who in truth are found to be but very *few*, and those scarcely *considerable*. The issue whereof is, That as in the *Negroe's all pretence to Religion* is cut off, so their *Owners* are hereby set at Liberty, and freed from those importunate Scruples, which Conscience and better Advice might at any time happen to inject into their unsteadie Minds.[10]

This key passage deserves close study. It tells us five important things about this very early stage of English racism. First of all, racist ideology was created by the planters and slave-merchants out of 'avarice'. Second, it was spread at first in whispers, furtively. Third, by 1680 it had become respectable enough – had gained enough 'strength and reputation' – for its propagators in England to have come into the open (though not yet in print). Fourth, opponents of racism were as yet few and uninfluential. And lastly, one of racism's functions was to justify the planters and merchants in their own eyes as well as in the eyes of the rest of society; Godwyn says it stopped them feeling guilty about what they were doing to their slaves. If this sounds a shade far-fetched, we must bear in mind that in Godwyn's day a lot of people – even sugar-planters – believed that if they sinned they might very well end up frying in hell.

Godwyn's analysis did not end there. He accused the planters and their spokesmen of being prepared to say anything that would safeguard their profits. What they did say wasn't hard to refute. They argued that blacks were not human beings on the slender basis of skin colour:

> Their *Complexion*, . . . being most obvious to the sight, . . . is apt to make no *slight* impressions upon rude [i.e. ignorant] Minds, already prepared to admit of any thing for *Truth* which shall make for Interest . . . And therefore it may not be so improbable . . . that from so poor a *Medium*, our *Negro's* Brutality should be inferred, by such whose affection to so *gainful* a Doctrine, cannot but make the Way smooth and easie to their Conviction.

Even if black skin were a mark of God's curse on Ham, black people were human beings and nothing else. 'The consideration of the shape and figure of our *Negro's* Bodies, their Limbs and Members; their Voice and Countenance, in all things according with other Mens; together with their *Risibility* [i.e. faculty of laughter] and *Discourse* (Man's *peculiar* Faculties) should be a sufficient Conviction.'[11] Godwyn contemptuously dismissed the further argument that the enslavement of blacks had confirmed that they were not human beings: 'If Slavery had that force or power so as to unsoul Men, it must needs follow, that every great Conqueror might at his pleasure, make and unmake Souls.'[12] Yet another racist argument was the alleged stupidity of the blacks – but in fact, Godwyn pointed out, many blacks were 'confessed by their *Owners*, to be extraordinary *Ingenious*, and even to exceed many of the *English*'.[13] And Godwyn concluded that the planter class supported 'that filthy Principle . . . That whatever conduceth to the getting of *Mony*, and carrying on of *Trade*, must certainly be lawful'.[14]

A few years later the 'Hellish Principles' of plantocracy racism were summed up by another of these rather eccentric divines. His name was Francis Brokesby and he was one of those clergymen who refused to take the oath of allegiance to William and Mary in 1690 and was deprived of his benefice. Planters, Brokesby wrote, were teaching 'That *Negroes* are Creatures destitute of Souls, to be ranked among Brute Beasts, and Treated accordingly (as generally they are) and whom Religion (apt only to make Subjects Mutinous) doth no way Concern'. The '*sorry weak Arguments*' used by the Barbados planters were, Brokesby added, '*a clear Indication that their Cause was bad*'.[15]

The eighteenth century

So far we have been examining plantocracy racism as expressed orally and represented in the writings of christians – mostly supporters of slavery – who objected to racism on religious grounds and some of whom were shrewd enough to detect its economic roots and function, honest and brave enough to attack it publicly. Racists did not themselves get into print until the middle of the eighteenth century. And by then the ground had been prepared for them by three eminent thinkers who, each in his own way, helped to make respectable the notion that Africans were intellectually inferior to Europeans.

As early as 1677 Sir William Petty, founder of modern political economy and one of the founders of the Royal Society, in an essay entitled 'The Scale of Creatures', expressed the belief that Europeans differed from Africans not only in colour, hair, shape of nose, lips and cheek-bones, outline of face, and mould of skull: 'They differ also in their Naturall Manners, & in the internall Qualities of their Minds.'[16]

Petty's contemporary John Locke, who happened to have £600 invested in the Royal African Company, not only managed to reconcile a belief in the inalienable rights of man with the view that black slavery was a justifiable institution, but also made a considerable if (as some have it) inadvertent contribution to the view that Africans were in some respects innately inferior to Europeans. Locke's *Essay concerning Human Understanding* (1690), whatever its philosophical merits as the primary classic of systematic empiricism, made it possible to argue that Africans might be human but even so had a level of reason comparable to that of animals.[17] Challenging the Augustinian view that there is something supernatural about human intellectual faculties, Locke emphasized the blank mind's reception of 'sensations' from the outside world, and conceived mental faculties as mechanisms for manipulating sensations. Locke's theory of knowledge paved the way for a mechanistic classification of faculties which, 'by rendering the concept of mental ability less amorphous than previously . . . helped channel much of the debate on the Negro towards the gratifyingly specific question of whether or not he was the mental equal of the white man'.[18] And so the founder of English empiricism and first systematic exponent of liberalism in political theory helped, quite innocently no doubt, to build a plausible foundation for the racist theory of intellectual gradation. Not that Locke was free from race prejudice. 'The Child certainly knows,' he wrote, 'that the *Nurse* that feeds it, is neither the *Cat* it plays with, nor the *Blackmoor* it is afraid of.' And again:

> A Child having framed the *Idea* of a *Man*, it is probable, that his *Idea* is just like that Picture, which the Painter makes of the visible Appearances joyned together; and such a Complication of *Ideas* together in his Understanding, makes up the single complex *Idea* which he calls *Man*, whereof White or Flesh-colour in England being one, the Child can demonstrate to you, that *a Negro is not a Man*, because White-colour was one of the constant simple *Ideas* of the complex *Idea* he calls *Man*: And therefore he can demonstrate by the Principle, *It is impossible for the same Thing to be, and not to be*, that a *Negro is not a Man.*[19]

'Whatever may be the early thoughts of an English child,' dryly comments Léon Poliakov, 'those of Locke betray an unconscious prejudice.'[20]

However embarrassing all this may be for historians of western philosophy, there is worse. Locke's successor, the great empiricist David Hume, came out openly as a racist. White people, he claimed, were naturally superior to all other races. He said this in a footnote added to the 1753 reprint of his essay 'Of National Characters', first published in 1748. Ignoring the mass of evidence that contradicted his prejudices, Hume wrote:

> I am apt to suspect the negroes, and in general all the other species of men (for there are four or five different kinds) to be naturally inferior to the whites. There never was a civilized nation of any other complexion than white, nor even any individual eminent either in action or speculation. No ingenious manufacture amongst them, no arts, no sciences. On the other hand, the most rude and barbarous of the white, such as the ancient GERMANS, the present TARTARS, have still something eminent about them, in their valour, form of government, or some other particular. Such a uniform and constant difference could not happen, in so many countries and ages, if nature had not made an original distinction betwixt these breeds of men. Not to mention our colonies, there are NEGROE slaves dispersed all over Europe, of which none ever discovered any symptoms of ingenuity; tho' low people, without ingenuity, will start up amongst us, and distinguish themselves in every profession. In JAMAICA indeed they talk of one negroe as a man of parts and learning; but 'tis likely he is admired for very slender accomplishments, like a parrot, who speaks a few words plainly.[21]

This passage by the great Scottish philosopher Hume, with its slighting reference to the classical scholar Francis Williams (see p. 421 below), was not the first appearance of racism in print. That honour belongs to the writer of a letter published in the *London Magazine* in 1750. Purporting to summarize Buffon, the author – who chose not to sign his name – described 'the people called Negroes' as 'the most remarkably distinct from the rest of the human species'. After some remarks on the differences between 'Hotentots' and 'Caffers', including differences in the external female genitalia, this writer added his distinctive contribution to the debate by asserting that 'a great difference between Negroes and all other Blacks, both in Africa and the East-Indies, lies in this, that the former smell most abominably when they sweat, whereas the latter have no bad smell even when they are sweating'.[22]

The floodgates were now open, and a lot of muck oozed its way into print over the next few decades. A typical example, worth quoting at length since it is one of Edward Long's two prime sources, is to be found in the *Universal History* (1736–65). Two of this immense compilation's 23 folio volumes contained page after page of lofty abuse of Africans, who 'are now every-where degenerated into a brutish, ignorant, idle, treacherous, thievish, mistrustful, and superstitious people'. Various Greek and Roman authorities were cited for the view that Africans were

> proud, lazy, treacherous, thievish, hot, and addicted to all kinds of lusts, and most ready to promote them in others, as pimps, panders, incestuous, brutish, and savage, cruel and revengeful, devourers of human flesh, and quaffers of human blood, inconstant, base, treacherous, and cowardly; fond of and addicted to all sorts of superstition and witchcraft; and, in a word, to every vice that came in their way, or within their reach . . . It is hardly possible to find in any *African* any quality but what is of the bad kind: they are inhuman, drunkards, deceitful, extremely covetous, and perfidious to the highest degree. We need not add to these their impurities and blasphemies, because in these they outdo all other nations, *Africa* being known to have been ever burning with innumerable impurities; insomuch that one would rather take it for a volcano of the most impure flames, than for a habitation of human creatures . . . St. *Austin*, who was a native of that country, scruples not to confess, that it is as impossible to be an *African* and not lascivious, as it is to be born in *Africa* and not be an African . . .
>
> THUS much shall suffice for the general character of the native *Africans* . . . it is so far from being either unjust or exaggerated, with regard to the far greater part of them, that, in many instances, they deserve, if possible, a much more odious one; they being in many parts so utterly void of all humanity, and even natural affection, that parents will sell their wives and children, and *vice versâ*, for slaves into the *American* colonies . . . even for so small a matter as a gallon or two of brandy . . .

> IF we . . . take a cursory view of their manufactures and mechanic arts . . . we shall find the spirit of indolence running through them all, even the most necessary of them . . .
> IF we look into those few manufactures and handicrafts that are amongst them, we shall find them carried on with the same rude [i.e. ignorant] and tedious stupidity.[23]

Even where the *Universal History* abandoned generalizations in favour of a detailed account of a specific African country, the same invincible prejudice stamped its judgments. Thus the section on Benin insisted that 'IN general the negroes of this country are libidinous, and much addicted to venery'.[24]

One of the earliest openly racist pamphleteers in Britain was William Knox, who had been provost-marshal of the British colony of Georgia from 1757 to 1761. On returning to Britain he was appointed agent for Georgia and east Florida. About the year 1768 he was approached by the archbishop of Canterbury, Thomas Secker, and invited to write, for the edification of the Society for Propagation of the Gospel in Foreign Parts, *Three Tracts respecting the Conversion and Instruction of the Free Indians, and Negroe Slaves in the Colonies*. How completely Knox had soaked up the plantocratic ideology during his years in Georgia is shown by his praise of whipping ('It is no wonder that they are treated like brute beasts . . . If they are incapable of feelling mentally, they will the more frequently be made to feel in their flesh') no less than by his observations on 'the dull stupidity of the Negroe', which 'leaves him without any desire for instruction'. Knox was sure that blacks were intellectually inferior to whites, but not sure why:

> Whether the creator originally formed these black people a little lower than other men, or that they have lost their intellectual powers through disuse . . . I will not assume the province of determining; but certain it is, that a *new Negroe*, (as those lately imported from Africa are called,) is a complete definition of indolent stupidity.

The planters' objection to their black slaves' being taught was simply that 'instruction renders them less fit or less willing to labour' – and, Knox declared, 'experience justifies their opinion'. If black slaves were taught to read they would read literature exhorting them to rebel. And then there would be 'a general insurrection of the Negroes, and the massacre of their owners'.[25] As we shall see,

Knox was not the only plantocracy spokesman who openly expressed fear of the slaves' revolutionary potential.

As might be expected, emergent racism was soon being used to buttress the demand that no more blacks be admitted to Britain and that those already here be expelled. The grounds advanced ranged from concern about unemployment to concern about racial intermarriage.

A writer signing himself 'Anglicanus', in the *London Chronicle* of 1764, characterized the importation of black servants as a 'folly which is becoming too fashionable' and added:

> As they fill the places of so many of our own people, we are by this means depriving so many of them of the means of getting their bread, and thereby decreasing our native population in favour of a race, whose mixture with us is disgraceful, and whose uses cannot be so various and essential as those of white people . . .
>
> To suppose them preferable in the point of service, can by no means be allowed, nor can their tempers recommend them to our superior regard; for it is their general character to be spiteful, sullen, and revengeful . . . They never can be considered as a part of the people, and therefore their introduction into the community can only serve to elbow as many out of it who are genuine subjects, and in every point preferable . . .
>
> It is . . . high time that some remedy be applied for the cure of so great an evil, which may be done by totally prohibiting the importation of any more of them, or by laying such a tax on the doing of it, as may prove an effectual discouragement.[26]

A similarly worded letter in the *Gentleman's Magazine* in the same year complained that blacks would not do servile work more willingly than whites, 'and if put to it, are generally sullen, spiteful, treacherous, and revengeful. It is therefore highly impolitic to introduce them as servants here, where that rigour and severity is impractical which is absolutely necessary to make them useful'.[27] Next year one 'F.Freeman' was bemoaning the abundance of 'Negro and East-India servants' in the kingdom. They were taking jobs from English people, and the 'mixture of their breed with our own' was 'disgraceful'. His proposed remedy was a capitation tax, to be paid by owners and employers of black people. This ought to raise £60,000 a year – and after all, where black people were concerned, 'there can be no just plea for their being put on an equal footing with natives, whose birth-right, as members of the community, entitle [*sic*] them to superior dues'.[28] In 1773 a writer in the *London Chronicle* urged that black people be expelled from Britain and no more allowed in, so as to 'remove the envy of our native servants, who have some reason to complain that the Negroes enjoy all the happiness of ease in domestic life, while many of those starve for want of places'. But two other things worried this writer even more. One was revolution; the other, mixed marriages. There was a danger that enthusiastic advocates of black freedom

> may inspire our Colony Negroes with endeavours to steal away from thence, in order to come into this land of liberty, though it be to starve, in vain hopes of washing the Blackamoor white. If not that effect, they may instil such enthusiastic notions of liberty, as may occasion revolutions in our colonies.

The expulsion of black people and a bar on further entry would somehow diminish this revolutionary danger – and would 'save the natural beauty of Britons from the Morisco tint'. This racist polemic was also published, over the signature 'Britannicus', as the preface to the 1773 edition of *An Essay upon Plantership* by Samuel Martin, agent for Antigua.[29]

Stimulated by the outcome of the Somerset case, and by the unmistakable beginning of a swing of public opinion against the slave trade, these colonial agents were now working overtime. Samuel Estwick, assistant agent for Barbados, energetically pressed the demand for legislation to preserve racial purity by prohibiting the entry of black people into Britain. The son of a Barbados planter, Estwick married the daughter of a governor of Barbados, owned 'very large possessions in the West India islands',[30] became agent for Barbados and paymaster-general, and sat in the House of Commons for 16 years.[31] In his attack on the Mansfield decision, *Considerations on the Negroe Cause* (1772), Estwick urged that a law to keep out black people would 'preserve the race of Britons from stain and contamination'.[32] And in the second edition, published the following year, he elaborated his racist views, contending that blacks were not human beings in the same sense as Englishmen. Among animals there were many kinds, 'each kind having its proper species subordinate thereto'. It was hard to believe that humanity was not also differentiated in that way:

> Does this not seem to break in upon and unlink that great

> chain of Heaven, which in due gradation joins and unites the whole with all its parts? May it not be more perfective of the system to say, that human nature is a class, comprehending an order of beings, of which man is the genus, divided into distinct and separate species of men?[33]

After quoting both Locke and Hume, and providing a thumbnail sketch of African barbarity and inherent moral depravity ('Their barbarity to their children . . . Their cruelty to their aged parents'), Estwick concluded that black people were 'filling up that space in life beyond the bounds of which they are not capable of passing; differing from other men, not in *kind*, but in species'.[34] In short, black people were irredeemably and permanently sub-human. And it followed that the plantocracy of which Estwick was a paid agent was fully entitled to deprive them of freedom and exploit them to the uttermost.

This pamphlet of Estwick's was the second immediate source for Edward Long's racist attack on black people. Born in Cornwall in 1734, Long was the son of a Jamaica planter whose family had been connected with the island since shortly after the English conquest in 1655. He himself went to Jamaica as a young man of 23, married a Beckford heiress, became a man of property, and was appointed justice of the Vice-Admiralty Court. He returned to Britain in 1769 and published his *History of Jamaica* five years later. First however came a sort of trial run for the *History*: a pamphlet called *Candid Reflections Upon the Judgement lately awarded by the Court of King's Bench . . . On what is commonly called the Negroe-Cause* (1772). Candour is not, perhaps, the first term that would spring to mind nowadays for that eloquent passage in which, after describing black people in Britain as 'a dissolute, idle, profligate crew', Long unwittingly revealed his deepest preoccupations:

> The lower class of women in *England*, are remarkably fond of the blacks, for reasons too brutal to mention; they would connect themselves with horses and asses if the laws permitted them. By these ladies they generally have a numerous brood. Thus, in the course of a few generations more, the English blood will become so contaminated with this mixture, and from the chances, the ups and downs of life, this alloy may spread so extensively, as even to reach the middle, and then the higher orders of the people, till the whole nation resembles the *Portuguese* and *Moriscos* in complexion of skin and baseness of mind. This is a venomous and dangerous ulcer, that

> threatens to disperse its malignancy far and wide, until every family catches infection from it.[35]

Long makes plain his political, as well as his sexual and social, anxieties. He observes that if black people acquired the rights of Englishmen they might become MPs or landowners. Such developments would be neither politic, expedient, nor useful. Blacks were incapable of adding anything to the general support and improvement of the kingdom: 'They are neither husbandmen, manufacturers, nor artificers. They have neither strength of constitution, inclination, or skill, to perform the common drudgeries of husbandry in this climate and country.'[36] And Long prefigured both the tone and the subject-matter of twentieth-century racism with his assertion that 'the public good of this kingdom requires that some restraint should be laid on the unnatural increase of *blacks* imported into it'.[37]

Two years later there appeared the three volumes of Long's *History of Jamaica*. It's a sprawling ragbag of a book, with observations of varying degrees of merit on meteorology, climatology, botany, zoology, medicine, history, geography, law, government, and commerce – and a spirited attack on colonial governors, whom Long seems to have hated almost as much as he hated blacks, accusing them of 'artifice, duplicity, haughtiness, violence, rapine, avarice, meanness, rancour, and dishonesty'.[38] But what concerns us is the lengthy section which, containing Long's doctrine of innate black inferiority, may be termed the classic exposition of English racism. We have already identified the two proximate sources which Long lays under contribution without a word of acknowledgment. It is quite clear that he had at his elbow, as he wrote, those volumes of the *Universal History* presenting Africa and Africans in the worst possible light and Estwick's pamphlet, from which he copied virtually word for word the passage about the lowly place of Africans in 'that great chain of Heaven'. We do not have to quote Long at excessive length to display both his venom and his unoriginality.

'For my own part,' he wrote, 'I think there are extremely potent reasons for believing, that the White and the Negroe are two distinct species.' Instead of hair, black people had 'a covering of wool, like the bestial fleece'. Their bodies were infested with black lice. Their 'bestial or fetid smell' was so strong that 'it continues in places where they have been near a quarter of an hour'. They had no plan or system of morality. They were barbarous to their children. Black men had no taste but for women, and eating and drinking to excess; no wish but to be idle. In Africa 'their roads . . . are mere sheep-paths, twice as long as they need be, and almost impassible'. All authors said that blacks were 'the vilest of the human kind'.

> When we reflect on . . . their dissimilarity to the rest of mankind, must we not conclude, that they are a different species of the same *genus*? . . . Nor do [orang-utans] seem at all inferior in the intellectual faculties to many of the Negroe race; with some of whom, it is credible that they have the most intimate connexion and consanguinity. The amorous intercourse between them may be frequent . . . and it is certain, that both races agree perfectly well in lasciviousness of disposition.

In fact, Long went on, the orang-utan had in form a much nearer resemblance to blacks than the latter bore to whites. There was a continuous chain of intellectual gradation, too, from monkeys through varieties of blacks, 'until we mark its utmost limit of perfection in the pure White'. Black people had brutish table-manners, 'eating flesh almost raw by choice, though intolerably putrid and full of meggots'. They tore the meat with their 'talons' and 'chuck it by handfulls down their throats with all the voracity of wild beasts'. They had no notion of shooting birds on the wing, 'nor can they project a straight line, nor lay any substance square with another'. In sexual behaviour (to which enthralling topic Long was drawn back again and again) 'they are libidinous and shameless as monkies, or baboons', and 'the equally hot temperament of their women has given probability to the charge of their admitting these animals frequently to their embrace'. Africa was, in short, the 'parent of every thing that is monstrous in nature'.[39]

What is not plagiarism here is mere trivial prejudice, on the level of planters' dinner-table gossip. And the plagiarism is from sources that, as we have seen, were themselves anything but original. Long's peculiar talent lay in linking a 'scientific'-sounding assertion of black inferiority – he was the first pseudo-scientific racist – with a defence of black slavery that comes across a good deal more plausibly than any previous statement of the slave-owners' case. As a 'scientist', he is beneath contempt but was highly influential; as a pro-slavery propagandist he was rather less influential but, paradoxically, has to be taken rather more seriously. Here is the handy summary of Long's views on black slavery provided by the editor of the 1970 reprint of the *History of Jamaica*; it shows admirably how the racist diatribe fits into, and serves the purpose of, the overall economic argument:

> That the trade in slaves and in goods produced by slaves was immensely profitable, not only to the West Indies, but to Britain itself and that it greatly enriched Englishmen in all walks of life; that West Indian slavery was, on the whole, a mild and benevolent institution and that slaves were better off than the lowest classes in Britain; that negro slavery was inevitable and necessary in certain regions of the world; that the slave trade benefited and helped to civilise Africa; that virtually all the slaves were originally convicted criminals; that in every mental and moral way negroes were absolutely inferior to white men, and that the most constructive thing which could happen to them was to be compelled to work productively.[40]

It is interesting that Long, in his defence of black slavery, omits two of the pro-slavery arguments that were often heard in his day. There is nothing in his book about God's curse on Ham. Long was no friend of orthodox religion, and that argument was evidently not available to him (though in 1789 it was to figure prominently in a pro-slavery pamphlet by the Tobago planter and West India Committee publicist Gilbert Francklyn).[41] Omitted also, from Long's *History*, is the argument that Britain could not give up the slave trade since other European powers would simply fill the gap and mop up the profit. Long had in fact written rhetorically in 1772 that 'a total sacrifice of our *African trade* and *American possessions*' to a 'fantastic idea of *English liberty*' would degrade Britain into 'the tributary province of some potent neighbour'.[42] But the abolitionist movement was only in its infancy in the early 1770s, and Long clearly thought the British about as likely to give up the slave trade and slavery as to give up roast beef and beer. So on this point the *History* is silent.

These omissions make the economic thrust of Long's argument all the more significant. And of course, in one important aspect, he was stating the truth. The slave trade and slavery had indeed proved enormously profitable to Britain and to many rapidly expanding British industries. But what about Long's assertion that slaves in the West Indies were better off than the lowest classes in Britain? That was also true – for the minority who performed household duties on well-run plantations. They lived under perpetual threat of demotion to field work as well as perpetual threat of the lash. But in terms of food, living accommodation, and working conditions their lot was preferable to that of the men, women, and children in small-scale and domestic industry or in the barrack-like factories with their harsh, cruel discipline.[43] Here was the second grain of truth within the big lie. Yet Britain's industrial workers, for all their long hours, drab conditions, miserable wages, and insanitary housing, were incomparably better off than the mass of plantation field slaves. Britain's dark satanic mills were precisely that. But over here the overseers did not flog their workers, or chop arms, legs, hands, fingers, or ears off as a punishment.[44]

'We must not presume', warns David Brion Davis in *The Problem of Slavery in Western Culture* (1966), ' . . . that Edward Long lacked a sympathetic audience, or was totally unrepresentative of his time.'[45] Far from it. He was influential and his opinions were shared by many. In the same year that his *History of Jamaica* appeared, no less a figure than Oliver Goldsmith, author of *The Vicar of Wakefield* (1766), *She Stoops to Conquer* (1774), and other enduring contributions to English literature, described the physical 'deformities' and 'insupportable' smell of black people in terms strikingly similar to Long's. 'This gloomy race of mankind', he wrote in his *History of the Earth*, 'is found to blacken all the southern parts of Africa.' Their minds were 'incapable of strong exertions'. In general, the black race was 'stupid, indolent, and mischievous'.[46] And, again in the same year, a British 'lady of quality' on a visit to Antigua, shocked by the 'dreadful' scars that floggings had left on the slaves' backs, comforted herself with the reflection that 'when one comes to be better acquainted with the nature of the Negroes, the horrour of it must wear off'. For the blacks were 'brutes' whose 'Natures seem made to bear it, and whose sufferings are not attended with shame or pain beyond the present moment'.[47]

It is clear that by the 1770s racism had more than a foothold in Britain. In particular, the spectre of racial intermarriage and 'contamination', incessantly invoked by the West Indians' propagandists, was haunting England. The year after Long's *History* came out, the novelist Charles Johnstone, best known for his scandalous chronicle *Chrysal, or the Adventures of a Guinea* (1760–5), declared in his book *The Pilgrim* that if English people mixed with Jews and blacks 'their progeny will not much longer have reason to value themselves on their beauty, wit, or virtue'.[48] Ten years later James Tobin of Nevis was uttering his warning that 'the great numbers of negroes at present in England, the strange partiality shewn for them by the lower orders of women, and the rapid increase of a dark and contaminated breed, are evils which have long been complained of and call every day more loudly for enquiry and redress'[49] – a statement which, as we saw in chapter 5, was effectively challenged by Olaudah Equiano.[50]

A racist still more virulent – though no more original – than Edward Long was Philip Thicknesse, who had spent some years in the English colony of Georgia and had then gone to Jamaica for a few years' sporadic warfare against the black rebels in the mountains. This experience seems to have bred in him a hatred of black people more violent even than his notorious hatred of men-midwives. He inserted into the second edition (1778) of his book *A Year's Journey through France and Part of Spain* an entire chapter on his pet hate. Black people were

> in every respect, men of a lower order, and so made by the Creator of all things . . . Their face is scarce what we call human, their legs without any inner calf, and their broad, flat foot, and long toes (which they can use as well as we do our fingers) have much the resemblance of the *Orang Outang*, or *Jocko* [i.e. chimpanzee], and other quadrupeds of their own climates. As to their intellects, not one was ever born with solid sense; yet all have a degree of monkey cunning, and even monkey mischief, which often stands them in better stead than sense. They are in nature cruel, to the highest degree . . . The frequent marriages of these men here with white women, and the succession of black, brown, and *whity* brown people, produced by these very unnatural (for unnatural they are) alliances, have been better observed in France, than in this *once* country of greater liberty . . . I laugh when I hear . . . talk of the fidelity of those people. I never yet knew one who was not at bottom a villain . . . They are a bad, gloomy-minded, revengeful people, and in the course of a few centuries they will over-run this country with a race of men of the very worst sort under heaven . . . London abounds with an incredible number of these black men, who have clubs to support those who are out of place, and [in] every country town, nay in almost every village are to be seen a little race of mulattoes, mischievous as monkeys and infinitely more dangerous . . . A mixture of negro blood with the natives of this country is big with great and mighty mischief, and . . . if they are to live

> among us, they ought by some very severe law to be compelled to marry only among themselves, and to have no criminal intercourse whatever with people of other complexions. There is not on earth so mischievous and vicious an animal as a mule, nor in my humble opinion a worse race of men than the negroes of Africa.[51]

This ugly diatribe reads like a souped-up paraphrase of Long, whom Thicknesse had clearly read and who (as Shyllon has suggested) may have been the 'Lover of Blacks' that wrote with such heavy irony in the *World* newspaper three days before Wilberforce was due to move his first Commons motion against the slave trade. The letter contained a leering forecast of what would happen in Britain if the slaves in the West Indies were set free. Having taken over the plantations, they would be able to reside in Britain as 'a new tribe of West-India Planters' and marry the daughters of the nobility: 'The *breed* of the inhabitants would be improved by the *cross* . . . The British Ladies' noses . . . would get a *truss up* . . . It would save the expence of *frizzing their hair*, for their hair would *friz of itself*.' Blacks already in England had in some measure anticipated their future greatness: 'Witness the great and tremendous *tails* they have affixed to their curly pashes [i.e. heads] . . . This degree of vanity . . . may be pardoned, considering the benefit that will arise from this ostensible method of shewing *their parts*; and how much sooner it will attract the notice of the Fair Sex, who are ever partial to *parts* and *abilities*.' One advantage of the '*blending of the two breeds*' would be 'the graceful air that the young bucks, our grandchildren, of the *mixed breed*, will have, in walking in St. James's and Bond-streets; – the *cross* will give them the appearance of a swivel in the backside, or a circuitous motion of the *podex*.'[52]

All this, including the laboured sexual innuendo, is typical of the polemical tone of the period, as is the elegant way that 'Civis', in the *Morning Chronicle*, had of dismissing black literary achievement: 'If I were to allow some share of merit to Gustavus Vasa, Ignatius Sancho, &c. it would not prove equality more, than a pig having been taught to fetch a cord, letters, &c. would shew it not to be a pig, but some other animal'.[53]

By the 1790s the 'taint' of intermarriage had become an obsession with the propagandists of racism. Of course, as Equiano had pointed out, when white planters fathered children on their black slaves, nobody in Britain gave a damn. But when black men married white women a high degree of sexual and social anxiety was expressed. To the merchant John Scattergood, it was 'madness' to admit blacks to the privileges of Europeans 'and treat them as our equals'. If slavery were abolished, 'the Negroes from all parts of the world will flock hither, mix with the natives, spoil the breed of our common people, increase the number of crimes and criminals, and make Britain the sink of all the earth, for mongrels, vagrants, and vagabonds'. Britain would be wise, Scattergood added, to banish black people from her dominions 'while it is yet in her power to hinder their migration hither'.[54] Thomas Atwood, chief judge of Dominica and later of the Bahamas, was another who thought that 'it is too common for the women to form connections with negro men' – in Europe, that is, for such a thing, according to Atwood, was unheard of in the West Indies. No black person could become an artist or scientist:

> There is . . . something so very unaccountable in the genius of all negros, so very different from that of white people in general, that there is not to be produced an instance in the West Indies, of any of them ever arriving to any degree of perfection in the liberal arts or sciences, notwithstanding the greatest pains taken with them.

Atwood claimed unctuously that the treatment the slaves received from their owners 'is, as nearly as can be, that of a parent to his children'. A few pages later he dropped the cant and came out openly in defence of the whip:

> Negros are in general much addicted to drunkenness, thievery, incontinency [i.e. unchastity], and idleness . . . Idleness is so very predominant in negros, and their dislike of labour is so great, that it is very difficult to make them work: it is sometimes absolutely necessary to have recourse to measures that appear cruel, in order to oblige them to labour.[55]

Even Bryan Edwards, a West India merchant who founded a bank at Southampton, became an MP, and is often regarded as the most gentlemanly and civilized of the plantocrat writers, complained of the 'strong and fetid odour' of black people, their 'cowardly, thievish, and sullen disposition', and their 'licentious and dissolute manners'.[56] If this was the gentlemanly and civilized end of the racist spectrum in the 1790s, what, it may be asked, lay at the other end?

The answer can be found in an anonymous pamphlet, *Fugitive Thoughts on the African Slave Trade*, published at Liverpool in 1792. 'Africans being the most lascivious of all human beings,' it said, 'may it not be imagined, that the cries they let forth at being torn from their wives, proceed from the dread that they will never have the opportunity of indulging their passions in the country to which they are embarking?'[57]

Pseudo-scientific racism

By the 1770s racism was firmly established in Britain as 'a principal handmaiden to the slave trade and slavery'.[1] The British slave trade was ended in 1807; slavery, in 1833. Could racism now be dispensed with? By no means. It was too valuable. A new basis and new purpose for it had emerged. It was to become a principal handmaiden to empire. The culminating stage in the rise of English racism was the development of a strident pseudo-scientific mythology of race that would become the most important ingredient in British imperial theory.

This mythology arose in the 1770s, precisely when the British government first had to face the problem of ruling a territory with 'natives' in it. In 1773 the Regulation Act asserted parliamentary control over the East India Company for the first time; Warren Hastings was appointed first governor-general of Bengal and a supreme court was set up in Calcutta. In the following year Edward Long's *History of Jamaica*, the pivotal book in the turn to pseudo-scientific racism, was published. Pure coincidence, of course. But the timing turned out to be crucial for the subsequent history of the British Empire. From the 1770s onwards the empire and the pseudo-scientific racism that served it developed side by side.[2] Even the cosmetic version of the doctrine – the idea of 'imperial trusteeship' for the betterment of 'backward peoples' – took shape in the debates over the abolition of the slave trade in the years before 1807.[3] From the 1840s to the 1940s, Britain's 'native policy' was dominated by racism. The golden age of the British Empire was the golden age of British racism too.

Long's book, furnishing ready-made arguments for the belief that black people were innately inferior to white people, was widely read, and widely accepted, by the scientists of his own time and for some 40 years after his death in 1813. These arguments crop up again and again in the writings of later polygenists of high scientific repute.[4] But Long was not the sole source of pseudo-scientific racism. It was nourished also by a series of theories and 'discoveries' in the biological sciences of the eighteenth century: notably, the infant science of anthropology. This was the great century of classification, and it was the Swedish botanist Carl Linné, generally known as Linnaeus, who laid the basis for the modern classification of plants and animals. He was first to call us *Homo sapiens*, and he arranged us in a hierarchy largely based on skin colour, with whites at the top. In the 1758 edition of his *Systema naturae* he gave thumbnail sketches of, amongst others, European Man and African Man. Here is how these descriptions were translated into English in 1792:

> *H. Europaei.* Of fair complexion, sanguine temperament, and brawny form . . . Of gentle manners, acute in judgment, of quick invention, and governed by fixed laws . . .
> *H. Afri.* Of black complexion, phlegmatic temperament, and relaxed fibre . . . Of crafty, indolent, and careless disposition, and are governed in their actions by caprice. – Anoint the skin with grease.[5]

It was a pupil of Linnaeus who, relating an experiment by the French naturalist Réaumur, in which a rabbit allegedly fertilized a hen to produce chicks covered with fine hair instead of feathers, commented that 'the most frightful conclusion could be drawn from this; . . . one would have reason to think that the Moors had a rather strange origin'.[6] Clearly, all those travellers' tales had become 'thoroughly cemented into Western thought'.[7] The Swiss naturalist Charles Bonnet wrote in 1764 of the 'prodigious number of continued links' between 'the most perfect man' and the ape, and left no doubt in his readers' minds as to the identity of 'the most perfect man': 'Let the flat-faced African, with his black complexion and woolly hair, give place to the European, whose regular features are set off by the whiteness of his complexion and beauty of his head of hair. To the filthiness [*malpropreté*] of a Hottentot, oppose the neatness of a Dutchman.'[8] This brand of 'scientific' thought was reflected in the writings of the British MP and Board of Trade official Soames Jenyns, whose treatise 'On the Chain of Universal Being' also put 'the brutal Hottentot' at the bottom of the scale but preferred Newton at 'the summit' to any Dutchman, however neat.[9]

A major but not always deliberate contribution to pseudo-scientific racism was made in the eighteenth century by pioneering students of the human skull. The 'father of craniology' was a German professor of medicine called Johann Friedrich Blumenbach. Co-founder with Buffon of the science of physical anthropology, Blumenbach disliked the 'Chain of Being', divided humanity first into four and then into five varieties, denied that any of these varieties was inferior to others, and denied that Africans could not acquire learning.[10] A friend of Ignatius Sancho by correspondence, he collected a library of books by black authors.[11] But he also collected human skulls from all over the world, and it was one of these skulls, from the Caucasus in Russia, that led him to suppose that Europeans came from that region, to coin the word 'Caucasian' to describe the white variety of humans, and to prefer this 'most beautiful form of the skull' to the two extremes furthest from it, skulls which he called 'Mongolian' and 'Ethiopian'.[12] Blumenbach's method of studying skulls was to stick them between his feet and examine them from above to see what shape they were. Here he followed Buffon's colleague Louis Daubenton, who had used geometrical projection to measure the position of the head on top of the spinal column and had correlated the angle thus obtained with the amount of will-power in different races.[13]

Blumenbach's method did not satisfy the Dutch comparative anatomist Pieter Camper, whose 'facial angle' – an expression he himself does not seem to have used – was, in a sense, the springboard of modern craniology. Camper was surgeon, obstetrician, authority on medical jurisprudence, artist, and sculptor. His 'facial angle' measured the extent to which the jaw juts out from the rest of the skull. A wide angle was thought to indicate a higher forehead, a bigger brain, more intelligence, and a more beautiful appearance. According to Camper, the angle grew wider as one went from Africans, through Indians, to Europeans. And it was 'amusing', he wrote, to contemplate an arrangement of skulls on a shelf in his cabinet, placed 'in a regular succession' from apes, through Africans, to Europeans. Camper found 'a striking resemblance between the race of Monkies and of Blacks'.[14] (As Jordan points out, if amount of hair had been chosen as the criterion of ranking, Africans would have come out on top, Indians in the middle, and Europeans at the bottom, next to apes: 'When Europeans set about to rank the varieties of men, their decision that the Negro was at the bottom and the white man at the top was not dictated . . . by the facts of human biology.')[15] A similar arrangement of skulls was made by the English physician John Hunter,[16] and the German anatomist Thomas Soemmerring, pupil and friend of Camper, Blumenbach, and Goethe, also tried to prove that Africans' skulls were intermediate between those of Europeans and those of monkeys, and that the African's brain was 'smaller than that of the European'.[17]

Meanwhile the Scottish lawyer, polymath, and 'common sense' polygenist Lord Kames, rival of Lord Monboddo, was pioneering a racist interpretation of society by claiming that ever since the Tower of Babel humanity had been divided into different species, each adapted to a different climate. 'The black colour of negroes, thick lips, flat nose, crisped woolly hair, and rank smell, distinguish them from every other race of men', he wrote – and by 'race', as he made clear, he meant 'species'.[18]

The scene was now set for the influential Manchester physician Charles White to lecture to the Literary and Philosophical Society of that city in 1795, quoting United States President Thomas Jefferson's 'suspicion' that blacks were inferior to whites;[19] quoting lengthy extracts from Soemmerring; quoting Long on black lice; declaring that 'in whatever respect the African differs from the European, the particularity brings him nearer to the ape' and that 'the lowest degree of the human race' resided in Africa; insisting that black people were a different species from whites; stressing that all the same they had souls and that nothing he said was to be taken as a defence of slavery (there is here a sharp break with plantocracy racism); and concluding with this ringing, not to say passionate, declaration of white superiority:

> The white European . . . being most removed from the brute creation, may, on that account, be considered as the most beautiful of the human race. No one will doubt his superiority in intellectual powers; and I believe it will be found that his capacity is naturally superior also to that of every other man. Where shall we find, unless in the European, that nobly arched head, containing such a quantity of brain . . . ? . . . Where that variety of features, and fulness of expression; those long, flowing graceful ringlets; that majestic beard, those rosy cheeks and coral lips? Where that erect posture of the body and noble gait? In what other quarter of the globe shall we find the blush that overspreads the soft features of the beautiful women of Europe, that emblem of modesty, of delicate feelings, and of sense? Where that nice expression of the amiable and softer passions in the countenance; and that general elegance of features and complexion? Where, except on the bosom of the European woman, two such plump and snowy white hemispheres, tipt with vermillion?[20]

With Charles White's lecture, published in 1799 as *Account of the regular gradation in man*, English racism may be said to have come of age. Its later development, throughout the nineteenth century, presents a picture of remarkable diversity and complexity, which there is room here only to summarize. Three facts will help to guide us through this maze of theories.

First, racism was not confined to a handful of cranks. Virtually every scientist and intellectual in nineteenth-century Britain took it for granted that only people with white skin were capable of thinking and governing. Even the distinguished ethnologist James Cowles Prichard, humanitarian and monogenist though he was, insisted on a relation between the 'physical character' of West Africans and their 'moral condition'. The Igbos, 'in the greatest degree remarkable for deformed countenances, projecting jaws, flat foreheads, and for other Negro peculiarities', were 'savage and morally degraded'; the 'most civilized races', on the other hand, like the Mandings, 'have, as far as form is concerned, nearly European countenances and a corresponding configuration of the head'.[21] Scientific thought accepted race superiority and inferiority until well into the twentieth century. Only in the past 30 or 40 years has racism lost intellectual respectability.

Second, amid all the ramifications of contending schools of racist thought, there was total agreement on one essential point:

> Whether the 'inferior races' were to be coddled and protected, exterminated, forced to labor for their 'betters', or made into permanent wards, they were undoubtedly outsiders – a kind of racial proletariat. They were forever barred both individually and collectively from high office in church and state, from important technical posts in law and medicine, and from any important voice in their own affairs . . . They were racially unfitted for 'advanced' British institutions such as representative democracy.[22]

And third, there was an organic connection in nineteenth-century Britain between the attitude the ruling class took to the 'natives' in its colonies and the attitude it took to the poor at home. Though the Chartist movement evaporated after 1848, by the 1860s working people in Britain were once more challenging the political and economic power of those who ruled and employed them. Faced with this challenge, 'the proponents of social inequality slipped all the more readily into racial rhetoric'.[23] 'Lesser breeds' and 'lower orders' had much in common, not least in the threat they presented to law and order:

> The English governing classes in the 1860's regarded the Irish and the non-European 'native' peoples just as they had, quite openly, regarded their own labouring classes for many centuries: as thoroughly undisciplined, with a tendency to revert to bestial behaviour, consequently requiring to be kept in order by force, and by occasional but severe flashes of violence; vicious and sly, incapable of telling the truth, naturally lazy and unwilling to work unless under compulsion.[24]

As V.G. Kiernan puts it, 'discontented native in the colonies, labour agitator in the mills, were the same serpent in alternate disguises. Much of the talk about the barbarism or darkness of the outer world, which it was Europe's mission to rout, was a transmuted fear of the masses at home'.[25]

Bearing these three facts in mind, we can summarize nineteenth-century English racism under the broad headings of phrenology, teleology, evolutionism, anthropology, social darwinism, Anglo-Saxonism, trusteeship, and vulgar racism.[26]

By their bumps ye shall know them

The pseudo-science of phrenology, which told people's characters from the contours of their skulls, served from the start as a prop to racism. Most of the leading phrenologists had large collections of human skulls from all over the world and firmly believed there was a correlation between the shape of the head in different human varieties and their degree of civilization. In 1819 the distinguished surgeon Sir William Lawrence was using phrenology to show that race and culture were connected. 'The Negro structure', he wrote, 'approximates unequivocally to that of the monkey.' Black people

> indulge, almost universally, in disgusting debauchery and sensuality, and display gross selfishness, indifference to the pains and pleasures of others, insensibility to beauty of form, order, and harmony, and an almost entire want of . . . elevated sentiments, manly virtues, and moral feeling . . . The inferiority of the dark to the white races is much more general and strongly marked in the powers of knowledge and reflection, the intellectual faculties . . . than in moral feelings

> and dispositions . . . I deem the moral and intellectual character of the Negro inferior, and decidedly so, to that of the European.[27]

Lawrence's book *Lectures on physiology, zoology, and the Natural History of Man* was denounced – not for its racism, but for views on heredity which anticipated Darwin and were held to endanger society – and he was forced to suppress it.[28]

The Edinburgh lawyer George Combe, chief popularizer of phrenology in Britain, firmly believed it could be applied to the study of race. Africans' skulls, he said, were inferior to those of Europeans. Although they showed a high development of Philoprogenitiveness, Concentrativeness, Veneration, and Hope, they lacked Conscientiousness, Cautiousness, Ideality, and Reflection. Blacks were not unfit for free labour – some as operative mechanics, others as clerks, others as 'mere labourers'.[29]

By the 1820s phrenology was in vogue, and this gave added force to the views of W.F.Edwards, an English anthropologist who lived in France and wrote in French. For Edwards, the form and proportion of the head and face provided the crucial distinction between races.[30] Edwards's racial interpretation of European history 'marked the beginning of a new flowering for pseudo-scientific racism', since, 'if racial interpretations of European history could be made to look "scientific", racial explanations of African culture seemed all the more plausible'.[31]

Phrenology justified empire-building. It told the British that they were ruling over races which, unlike themselves, lacked force of character. According to Combe, before Europeans took civilization to Africa that continent exhibited 'one unbroken scene of moral and intellectual desolation'.[32] The rich phrenologist and physician Robert Verity, an admirer of Lord Kames, predicted that 'the inferior and weaker' races would in due course become extinct and that within 100 years Britain, its wealth, population, and intelligence, would overshadow the whole world and British civilization and language would likewise be dominant. Of all the modern nations, the English had 'a greater and more proportionate admixture of the best races': 'Eminently superior in their cerebral type, and their physical conformation, they join to these advantages the very best combination of temperament.'[33] Here, no doubt, lay the main secret of phrenology's success. The British were already convinced of their high destiny. Phrenology told them why they were lucky and how to remain so.[34]

Blacks as beasts of burden

'The strongest moral force in the literature of his time.' That is how *The Cambridge History of English Literature* describes Thomas Carlyle, author of *Sartor Resartus* (1836) and *The French Revolution* (1837). He 'affirmed without fear', it adds, ' . . . the eternal need for righteousness in the dealings of man with man'.[35] One of Carlyle's less famous works is an *Occasional Discourse on the Nigger Question* (1853), first published under a less insulting title in *Fraser's Magazine* in 1849. From this it emerged that when white men had dealings with black men righteousness gave place to hierarchy. As Carlyle saw it, Africans had been created inferior in order to serve their European masters. Whites were born wiser than blacks, and blacks must obey them: 'That, you may depend on it, my obscure Black friends, is and was always the Law of the World, for you and for all men: To *be* servants, the more foolish of us to the more wise.' Carlyle trounced humanitarians 'sunk in deep froth-oceans of "Benevolence", "Fraternity", "Emancipation-principle", "Christian Philanthropy", and other most amiable-looking, but most baseless . . . jargon' and thereby blinded to black people's innate stupidity and laziness.[36] Though the radical philosopher John Stuart Mill publicly attacked Carlyle for this article, it circulated widely in pamphlet form; after all, 'it matched exactly the opinion of the Colonial Office'.[37] In 1867, Carlyle reaffirmed his position:

> One always rather likes the Nigger; evidently a poor blockhead with good dispositions, with affections, attachments, – with a turn for Nigger Melodies, and the like: – he is the only Savage of all the coloured races that doesn't die out on sight of the White Man; but can actually live beside him, and work and increase and be merry. The Almighty Maker has appointed him to be a Servant.[38]

As for the English, Carlyle saw them as a chosen people, whose special glorious mission was to throw open the world's waste lands – 'Sugar Islands, Spice Islands, Indias, Canadas, – these, by the real decree of Heaven, were ours'. And he was the original discoverer of that idol of later romantic fiction, the Strong Silent Man, his ideal type of Englishman.[39]

Though Carlyle was the most prominent representative of the teleological view of race, he was by no means the only one. Another leading English writer of the period, the novelist Anthony Trollope, thought black people idle, sensuous, and incapable of much sustained intellectual effort. They could 'observe . . . but . . . seldom reason'. On the other hand, they were capable of the hardest physical work, 'and that probably with less bodily pain than men of any other race'.[40] The *Spectator*, quoting the essayist William Rathbone Greg in 1865, put the teleological view in a nutshell: 'The negroes are made on pupose to serve the whites, just as the black ants are made on purpose to serve the red.'[41]

A variant of the teleological view, favoured by the medical profession, held that blacks were capable, whites incapable, of working in the tropics. Since the resources of the tropics had been put there for the whole of humanity to enjoy, they must be exploited by the labour, forced, if need be, of those capable of working there.[42] Extreme supporters of this view went so far as to suggest that emancipation had failed and slavery should be brought back in the West Indies; Disraeli proposed this obliquely in a Commons speech in 1846.[43]

One British colonial administrator who supported the teleological view was the explorer Sir Harry Johnston, who served as commissioner for South Central Africa from 1891 to 1896 and special commissioner for Uganda from 1899 to 1901. He wrote in 1899 that Africans, with few exceptions, were the natural servants of other races: 'The negro in general is a born slave', possessing great physical strength, docility, cheerfulness, a short memory for sorrows and cruelties, gratitude for kindness, and ability to 'toil hard under the hot sun and in the unhealthy climates of the torrid zone'; 'provided he is well fed, he is easily made happy'.[44] The same mythology was expressed in the same period by the respected classical scholar and humanitarian Gilbert Murray, who wrote in 1900:

> There is in the world a hierarchy of races . . . those nations which eat more, claim more, and get higher wages, will direct and rule the others, and the lower work of the world will tend in the long-run to be done by the lower breeds of men. This much we of the ruling colour will no doubt accept as obvious.[45]

The road to extinction

Some white Americans argued in the eighteenth century that the extinction of American 'Indians' was nature's way of making room for a higher race. This evolutionary racism was imported into Britain in the 1830s and was soon dominating discussions about the proper 'native policy' for Australia, Canada, New Zealand, and

South Africa. In 1841 Dr Thomas Arnold, headmaster of Rugby, advanced a racial interpretation of European history. He thought the final stage of history had been reached; races unable to absorb European culture would dwindle away and, in the end, become extinct.[46]

But suppose – just suppose – the dark-skinned races fought back? The outcome of the race struggle might not, after all, be a foregone conclusion. This chilling prospect was a central preoccupation of the Scottish anatomist Dr Robert Knox, 'one of the key figures in the general Western movement towards a dogmatic pseudo-scientific racism'.[47] Knox's career as surgeon had been ruined by his connection with the sordid Burke and Hare body-snatching scandal. He was mobbed and burnt in effigy. He then turned to the 'science' of 'transcendental anatomy', and his popular lectures on this subject were published in 1850 as *The Races of Men*. Here is the key passage, blending racism, belligerence, and dreams of empire in equal measure:

> Look at the Negro, so well known to you, and say, need I describe him? Is he shaped like any white person? Is the anatomy of his frame, of his muscles, or organs like ours? Does he walk like us, think like us, act like us? Not in the least. What an innate hatred the Saxon has for him, and how I have laughed at the mock philanthropy of England! . . . it is a painful topic; and yet this despised race drove the warlike French from St. Domingo [i.e. Haiti], and the issue of a struggle with them in Jamaica might be doubtful. But come it will, and then the courage of the Negro will be tried against England . . . With one thousand white men all the blacks of St. Domingo could be defeated in a single action. This is my opinion of the dark races.
>
> Can the black races become civilized? I should say not . . .
>
> By ascending the Senegal cautiously and rapidly . . . a thousand brave men on horseback might seize and hold Central Africa to the north of the tropic; the Celtic race, will, no doubt, attempt this some day. On the other hand, accident has prepared the way for a speedy occupation of Africa to the south of the equator by the Saxon race, the Anglo-Saxon.

This bold armchair strategist sought to prove that 'race is everything: literature, science, art – in a word, civilization, depends on it'. A generation after Auschwitz, it is hard not to shudder when one reads his gloating vision of the outcome of racial conflict: 'What signify these dark races to us? Who cares particularly for the Negro, or the Hottentot, or the Kaffir? These latter have proved a very troublesome race, and the sooner they are put out of the way the better.' The dark races were simply animals: 'Destined by the nature of their race, to run, like all other animals, a certain limited course of existence, it matters little how their extinction is brought about.'[48]

Like Edward Long 80 years before, Dr Knox was anything but original. He mixed together scraps of various theories put forward in the first half of the nineteenth century and earlier, flavouring this hodge-podge with his own 'wild irrational streak'. He was 'a peculiar example of what a confused, and perhaps dangerous, mind could make of what had often been put forward as precise scholarship'.[49] To Dr Knox, black people were to be hated, feared, fought and, in the end, exterminated. Such a combination of racial arrogance, racial insecurity, and racial mysticism was not peculiar to him, though few matched his hysterical tone. His views were echoed in 1865 by a *Lancet* leader-writer who saw European colonizers as 'military masters lording it over a sort of serf population, and under the continual fear of whose terrible vengeance we must always live'. This writer concluded that 'all schemes of philanthropy and of brotherhood . . . which delude us and take us off our guard, should be at once deprecated'.[50] Dr Knox's fearful doctrine was echoed again in 1876 by the traveller William Hepworth Dixon, who warned of the black threat in his extraordinary book *White Conquest*. The preservation of white values in a racially mixed society was essential, Dixon insisted. 'The surface of the earth', he wrote, 'is passing into Anglo-Saxon hands. If we wish to see order and freedom, science and civilization preserved, we shall give our first thought to what improves the White man's growth and increases the White man's strength.'[51]

Killing blacks no murder

The phrenologists were not the only nineteenth-century 'scientists' fascinated by human skulls. But the Philadelphia physician and palaeontologist Samuel George Morton, who collected 837 of them – his collection, the world's biggest, was called the 'American Golgotha' – was interested in their capacity, not their contours. He spent a lot of time in the 1840s filling his skulls with material that would pack closely – white pepper seeds or shot pellets – and then measuring how much he had poured into each one. All this was far from easy. It was hard to devise a uniform method of closing the openings in the skulls, and hard to decide just when to stop pouring. All the same, convinced that the larger the cranium the greater the intelligence of the skull's former owner, Dr Morton persisted in his attempts to measure 'cranial capacity' and find a relationship between that and race. While confessing that there were probably errors of measurement in his tables, he found that the English skulls in his collection had an average cranial capacity of 96 cubic inches; white Americans and Germans averaged 90; Africans averaged 85, Chinese 82, and Indians 80.[52] Since the skulls in the top three categories were nearly all from whites hanged as felons, 'it would have been just as logical to conclude that a large head indicated criminal tendencies'.[53]

It was 'research' of this calibre on which James Hunt, an expert in the treatment of stammers, based his theory of innate differences between black people and white people. Hunt founded the Anthropological Society of London in 1863, by which time home-grown anthropology, a favourite pursuit of gentlemanly amateurs, had already had much to say on the topic of race. Thomas Hope, expert on architecture, furniture, and interior decoration, had classified orang-utans as human and described West Africans ('the natives of Old Calabar, residing not far from the coast of Guinea') as having

> foreheads and chins almost obliterated; cheeks or rather pouches projecting beyond the nose, wide prominent lipless mouths, armed with long sharp tusks or teeth standing out; eyes almost in contact with each other; bellies that hang down over their thighs; a chest very narrow, arms of prodigious length, thighs extremely short, spider legs void of calves, and splay feet as ill-fitted to stand firm on even ground as those of the neighbouring monkeys.[54]

In 1841, a speaker had assured the British Association for the Advancement of Science that the African variety of man bore anatomically 'a nearer resemblance to the higher Quadrumana [i.e. apes] than to the highest varieties of his own species'.[55]

Hunt's Anthropological Society of London was a breakaway group from the Ethnological Society, founded in 1843, which had offended Hunt and his followers by admitting ladies to its meetings.[56] Within two years the new society had 500 members, mostly medical men, lawyers, journalists, clergymen, and colonial administrators. Vice-president was Richard Burton, who was to be found at the society's meetings 'airing his distaste for negroes, and rejoicing in the rising value of phallic specimens among European collectors'.[57] Rajah Sir James Brooke of Sarawak and Governor Edward Eyre of Jamaica were members, and so were the poet Swinburne and Frederic William Farrar, author of the edifying school story *Eric, or Little by Little* (1858) and afterwards dean of Canterbury.

Hunt's doctrine, as set forth in his annual presidential addresses to the society, was much influenced by Dr Knox, to whose derivative teachings he himself added little that was new. Here is Hunt's own helpful summary of his 'general deductions':

> 1. That there is as good reason for classifying the Negro as a distinct species from the European, as there is for making the ass a distinct species from the zebra: and if, in classification, we take intelligence into consideration, there is a far greater difference between the Negro and European than between the gorilla and chimpanzee. 2. That the analogies are far more numerous between the Negro and the ape, than between the European and the ape. 3. That the Negro is inferior intellectually to the European. 4. That the Negro becomes more humanised when in his natural subordination to the European than under any other circumstances. 5. That the Negro race can only be humanised and civilised by Europeans. 6. That European civilisation is not suited to the Negro's requirements or character.[58]

What is really important here is the political content, which Hunt was later to amplify. As long as Britain possessed an empire, he argued, it was essential to understand the practical importance of race distinctions, because of 'the absolute impossibility of applying the civilisation and laws of one race to another race of man essentially distinct'.[59]

The political role of the Anthropological Society of London, and of its president's brand of racism, became quite clear in 1865 when one of its members, Governor Eyre of Jamaica, reacted to a rebellion of black farmers at Morant Bay with a degree of ruthlessness unusual even in the nineteenth century. He declared martial law and his troops went on a murderous 30-day rampage, killing 439 black people, flogging at least 600 others (some were flogged before being put to death, and some were flogged with a cat among whose lashes were interwoven lengths of piano-wire), dashing out children's brains, ripping open the bellies of pregnant women, and burning over 1,000 homes of suspected rebels.[60] Public opinion in

Britain was polarized, and bitter feelings were aroused on both sides. The Jamaica Committee, called by Thomas Carlyle 'a small loud group . . . of Nigger-Philanthropists, barking furiously in the gutter',[61] was led by John Stuart Mill, Thomas Huxley, and Herbert Spencer, and its supporters included Charles Darwin and Leslie Stephen. At first it sought merely a thorough investigation and Eyre's recall, but after a whitewashing Royal Commission report[62] it demanded the governor's prosecution for murder; at one working-class meeting he was burnt in effigy.[63] On the other side, an Eyre Defence Committee was set up, supported by Carlyle, Ruskin, Dickens, Tennyson, Matthew Arnold, and Charles Kingsley, who thought the governor ought to be given a seat in the House of Lords.[64] They saw him, indeed, as saviour of the West Indies and sought to raise £10,000 for his legal expenses. The Anthropological Society rallied behind its controversial member and drew some sharp political conclusions from the affair. Hunt told the 1866 annual meeting that

> we anthropologists have looked on, with intense admiration, at the conduct of Governor Eyre as that of a man of whom England ought to be (and some day will be) justly proud. The merest novice in the study of race-characteristics ought to know that we English can only successfully rule either Jamaica, New Zealand, the Cape, China, or India, by such men as Governor Eyre.[65]

As a public service, the society invited Commander Bedford Pim, a retired naval officer, to read a paper on 'The Negro and Jamaica'. An audience of upper-class Englishmen heard Pim say that the black man in Africa and the New World was 'little better than a brute, – in mental power a child, in ferocity a tiger, in moral degradation sunk to the lowest depths'. Slavery had rescued 'a decidedly inferior race' from a state of barbarism scarcely human. Pim supported the governor's prompt action and concluded that only through the study of 'anthropological science' could statesmen learn the true art of governing alien races. Of special interest is Pim's comparison between the discontented black people of Jamaica and the lower orders in Britain: 'We do not admit of equality even amongst our own race, . . . and to suppose that two alien races can compose a political unity is simply ridiculous. One section *must* govern the other.' Behind racism lurked the spectre of working-class rebellion in Britain.

Commander Pim's address was greeted with loud cheers and a unanimous vote of thanks, after which speaker after speaker from the floor gave advice on the technique of governing alien races. One advocated killing 'savages' as a 'philanthropic principle': when trouble broke out there might be 'mercy in a massacre'.[66] After almost half a century, the spirit of Peterloo lived on.

Acquitted, as the *Spectator* put it, 'because his error of judgment involves only negro blood',[67] Governor Eyre was retired on a pension.

It is hardly necessary to add that Hunt and the Anthropological Society supported the Confederacy in the American Civil War. And after that war ended they reprinted American material calling for the return of slavery in the south as the only condition under which black people would do any productive work.[68]

Survival of the fairest

Charles Darwin's theory of evolution proved that Europeans were related to Africans and that all human beings were related to apes. Thus it pulled the rug from under the polygenists' feet and made the whole long debate between monogenists and polygenists irrelevant. At the same time darwinism furnished a new rationale for almost all the old beliefs about racial superiority and inferiority. Nineteenth-century sociologists assumed that when they were studying human society they were studying innate racial characteristics at the same time. White skin and 'Anglo-Saxon' civilization were seen as the culmination of the evolutionary process. So the application of Darwin's theories to human society 'had a more pervasive influence in spreading racist assumptions than the comparative anatomy of the anthropologists'.[69]

Social darwinism had been anticipated by Herbert Spencer, a philosopher much influenced by phrenology. It was Spencer, in fact, who coined the phrase 'survival of the fittest'.[70] He pointed out in 1851 that the 'purifying process' by which animals killed off the sick, deformed, and old was at work in human society too, thanks to 'the decrees of a large, far-seeing benevolence'.[71] And when Darwin published his *Origin of Species* eight years later it was Spencer who led the way in systematically applying Darwin's ideas to sociology and ethics.

Spencer had plans to study human psychological development rather as Darwin had studied biological evolution. To understand the minds of 'primitive' races, 'civilized' races should look at the minds of their own children. The minds of 'primitive' races had similar limitations, but their childhood of intellect was permanent. Dominant races overran 'inferior' races because they had a greater 'mental mass', which showed itself in greater energy.[72]

In many ways, however, Spencer was not a typical social darwinian. Other believers in the natural law that the strong must devour the weak went much further in drawing racist conclusions from that law. The economist Walter Bagehot, who wrote *The English Constitution* (1867) and for whom deference to leaders was the essence of parliamentary government, argued that the strongest nations tended to conquer the weaker – 'and in certain marked peculiarities the strongest tend to be the best'.[73] *Social Evolution* (1894) by Benjamin Kidd, a minor civil servant, made its author famous and sold 250,000 copies. It caught the popular imagination with its praise of the 'vigorous and virile' Anglo-Saxon race, in mere contrast with whom the weaker, 'inferior' races tended to die off. Nothing could stay this 'destiny which works itself out irresistibly'.[74] The tropics' rich resources could be developed only 'under the influence of the white man', Kidd added in a later book.[75] 'Feeble races are being wiped off the earth', wrote 'A Biologist' in the *Saturday Review* in 1896.[76] Winwood Reade, best known for *The Martyrdom of Man* (1872), was another who forecast the extermination of the black race. One day 'the cockneys of Timbuctoo' would have tea-gardens in Sahara oases; noblemen, 'building seats in Central Africa, will have their elephant-parks and their hippopotami waters'; and 'young ladies on camp-stools under palm-trees will read with tears "*The Last of the Negroes*" '.[77] Scarcely less bold was John Arthur Roebuck, MP for Sheffield (who made himself unpopular with working men by calling them spendthrifts and wife-beaters). In 1862 he told the Commons that in New Zealand 'the Englishmen would destroy the Maori, and the sooner the Maori was destroyed the better'.[78]

Darwin's cousin Sir Francis Galton, founder of the 'science' of eugenics, believed that 'the average intellectual standard of the negro race is some two grades below our own'. A 'very large' number of black people were 'half-witted'. Other 'inferior populations', too, were congenitally defective; Galton took a specially low view of black Australians and Spaniards.[79] Michael Banton points out that 'the acceptance by a man of Galton's intellect and eminence of the thesis that different races could be distinguished and compared with one another, and his use of a mock statistical technique to this end, must have assisted considerably the propagation of racist theories'.[80] Galton's pupil Karl Pearson, professor at London University and Fellow of the Royal Society, saw colonialism as a means of preparing 'a *reserve of brain and physique*' for times of national crisis: 'Such a reserve can always be formed by filling up with men of our own kith and kin the waste lands of the earth, even at the expense of an inferior race of inhabitants.' From a genetic standpoint, the black race was 'poor stock', and struggle against 'inferior races' was the way to keep a nation up to a high pitch of efficiency:

> History shows . . . one way, and one way only, in which a high state of civilization has been produced, namely, the struggle of race with race, and the survival of the physically and mentally fitter race . . .
>
> This dependence of progress on the survival of the fitter race . . . gives the struggle for existence its redeeming features.

Exterminated 'inferior races', Pearson added, were 'the stepping-stones on which mankind has arisen to the higher intellectual and deeper emotional life of to-day'.[81]

Thus were Darwin's theories distorted and adapted to provide an ideological prop for empire-building – a self-justification for a 'great power' that was expanding aggressively at the expense of 'primitive' and 'inferior' peoples. It should be borne in mind that racial extinction was not just a matter of theory. The black people of Tasmania did not long survive the invasion of their island by the dominant race. They were hunted down without mercy. The last of them died in 1869. And racist ideology justified genocide. Social darwinism taught white people that the Tasmanians were their brothers and sisters. It also taught them that the extermination of those brothers and sisters was an inevitable part of the struggle for existence, in which their own 'superior' race alone was destined to survive.[82]

Britannia rule the world!

By the middle of the nineteenth century the belief in a special Anglo-Saxon tradition of freedom had been turned into a romantic mystique justifying the denial of freedom to other races. Ideas of Teutonic destiny developed by philologists and German nationalists mingled with ideas of inherent white superiority developed by phrenologists and anthropologists to swamp common sense in a flood of racial arrogance. 'The English language, English law, and English institutions seemed ready to dominate the entire world.'[83] To Carlyle, the English had the grand task of conquering half the planet or more.[84] Thomas Arnold, too, stressed the power and destiny of the English race and language, now overrunning the earth.[85] For Macaulay, the British had become the greatest and most highly civilized people that the world had ever seen and the acknowledged leaders of the human race.[86] Sir Edward Bulwer Lytton, colonial secretary, told MPs in 1858 that their common interest was 'to fulfil the mission of the Anglo-Saxon race, in spreading intelligence, freedom, and Christian faith wherever Providence gives us the dominion of the soil'.[87] The Liberal MP Charles Dilke, in his travel book *Greater Britain* (1868) – a title to be purloined by the fascist leader Sir Oswald Mosley in 1932 – painted a rosy picture of the future of the English, 'marching westward to universal rule', 'ever pushing with burning energy towards the setting sun', 'more than a match for the remaining nations of the world, whom in the intelligence of their people and the extent and wealth of their dominions they already considerably surpass'. And Dilke noted complacently that 'the Saxon is the only extirpating race on earth'.[88]

Even these extravaganzas were surpassed by Charles Kingsley, grandson of a Barbados judge and author of *Westward Ho!* (1855) and *The Water Babies* (1863). For 25 years Kingsley extolled the virtues and historical mission of the English. God had fitted the great Teutonic race to rule the world; indeed, 'the welfare of the Teutonic race is the welfare of the world'; and though the German tribes that swept over the Roman Empire had no supreme general on earth, they may have had 'a general in Heaven'.[89] On the other hand, degenerate races, including the American 'Indians', were better dead: 'One tribe exterminated, if need be, to save a whole continent. "Sacrifice of human life?" Prove that it is *human* life. It is beast-life.' The Anglo-Saxons were extending God's kingdom. 'You Malays and Dyaks of Sarawak . . . are enemies to peace . . . you are beasts, all the more dangerous, because you have a semi-human cunning'.[90]

Though he had been taught to box at Cambridge in 1836 by a black prize-fighter (Massa Sutton, for whom see p. 451 below), when Kingsley toured the West Indies in 1869–70 he expressed privately his dislike of black people – 'specially the women'.[91] And when he visited Sligo in 1860 he wrote: 'I am haunted by the human chimpanzees I saw along that hundred miles of horrible country . . . To see white chimpanzees is dreadful; if they were black, one would not feel it so much.'[92] Not only did he defend Governor Eyre, as we have seen; he went out of his way to flatter him as 'so noble, brave and chivalric a man, so undaunted a servant of the Crown, so illustrious as . . . a saviour of society in the West Indies'.[93]

Appropriately enough, Kingsley was appointed chaplain to Queen Victoria in 1859 and regius professor of modern history at Cambridge in the following year. His successor in the latter post, Sir John Seeley, was another convinced Anglo-Saxonist, who saw England's expansion as decreed by 'a Providence which is greater than all statesmanship'.[94]

By the turn of the century English people took it for granted that Europeans were the top race. 'No European can mix with non-Christian races without feeling his moral superiority over them', wrote Sir Francis Younghusband, who was to lead the British invasion of Tibet in 1903–4.[95] And they took it for granted that, among Europeans, the inhabitants of the British Isles 'had achieved the apogee of human existence and were uniquely endowed by the Creator with qualities and attributes lacking in other lesser human beings – be they European, African or Asian'.[96] In particular, the Englishman believed that he had

> a sort of roving commission from above to carry the blessings of good government to all those races of the earth who are either too undeveloped or too effete to provide it for themselves; and that any interference with him in the execution of this commission may justly be resented and resisted by him . . . as a perverse attempt to obstruct the manifest designs of Providence.[97]

That was how an irreverent writer summed it up in 1896. Colonial secretary Joseph Chamberlain had put it even more simply in 1895:

> I believe that the British race is the greatest of governing races the world has ever seen. (Cheers.) I say this not merely as an empty boast, but as proved and shown by the success which we have had in administering vast dominions . . . and I believe there are no limits accordingly to its future.[98]

Much the same thought struck empire-builder Cecil Rhodes as he was wandering across the South African veld: 'As I walked, I looked up at the sky and down at the earth and I said to myself this should be British. And it came to me in that fine, exhilarating air that the British were the best race to rule the world.'[99] As one of his admirers wrote soon after his death, Rhodes was 'the first distinguished British statesman whose Imperialism was that of Race and not that of Empire . . . Mr. Rhodes saw in the English-speaking race the greatest instrument yet evolved for the progress and elevation of mankind.'[100] Or, to quote again Rhodes's own words: 'We are the first race in the world, and . . . the more of the world we inhabit the better it is for the human race . . . Every acre added to our territory means the birth of more of the English race who otherwise would not be brought into existence.'[101] Viscount Milner, who as British administrator in southern Africa was partly responsible for starting the Boer War, was another who saw the British Empire in terms of a mystical mission. 'The British race', he declared, ' . . . stands for something distinctive and priceless in the onward march of humanity.' Deeper, stronger, and more primordial than material ties was 'the bond of common blood'.[102]

The white man's burden

The idea of trusteeship has a long history in Europe, but it did not become central to British imperial policy until the 'scramble for Africa' in the second half of the nineteenth century. Three years after Columbus discovered the New World a Spanish professor of law had first argued that European conquerors should protect the rights of the 'natives' they conquered. Other Spanish jurists, and theologians, developed the idea.[103] In 1775 the British statesman Edmund Burke, in his speech on conciliation with the American colonies in revolt, used the word 'trust' in an ethical sense; and eight years later, in a speech on Fox's East India Bill, he said that the rights or privileges of political dominion were a trust.[104] Moral obligation towards 'backward' races was much discussed during the impeachment and trial (1787–95) of Warren Hastings, and the so-called 'civilizing' of Africa was first discussed in the same period, during the debates on the abolition of the slave trade.[105] But trusteeship was still an ideal, not a guideline. In 1819 Sir Thomas Stamford Raffles, who persuaded the East India Company to acquire Singapore, summed up the ethical view of Britain's civilizing mission:

> Let our minds and policy expand with our empire . . . While we raise those in the scale of civilization over whom . . . our empire is extended, we shall lay the foundations of our dominion on the firm basis of justice and mutual advantage, instead of the uncertain and unsubstantial tenure of force and intrigue.[106]

In the 1837 report of the Commons Aborigines Committee this

doctrine that power exercised over a 'native' race ought to be used ultimately for that race's benefit was asserted with some vigour; the damage already done by treating 'natives' as if they were thieves, robbers, dogs, or kangaroos was deplored; and paternalistic suggestions were made for protecting them, notably by forbidding the sale of strong drink and encouraging christian missionaries.[107] By mid-century, liberal-minded English people accepted Commerce, Colonization, Civilization, and Christianity – in other words, Conversion to western ways – as 'the most effective recipe for the transformation of Africa'.[108]

But in the second half of the century, and especially after 1885, as the European scramble for African territory got under way, the exact purpose of British rule in Africa had to be defined more rigorously. The idea of conversion, which implied merely informal influence, gave way to that of trusteeship, which implied annexation. Two factors in particular made such a strengthening of British imperial policy seem desirable. One was the rivalry of other European powers: Belgium, France, Germany, Italy, and Portugal. The other was the mounting conviction that Africans were inherently incapable of attaining western civilization:

> If it were assumed that the Africans were racially inferior, and yet spiritually equal and capable of receiving the Christian message, the moral duty of the superior race was clear. It was to take up the 'white man's burden' and exercise a trust over the spiritual and material welfare of people whose racial status was equivalent to that of minors.[109]

The trusteeship plank in British imperial policy had two main components. Essentially it was a blend of the missionaries' view that Africans 'represented unregenerate mankind, sinful and unwashed'[110] and the pseudo-scientific arguments for racial superiority. Britain marched across Africa with a clerical boot on one foot and a 'scientific' boot on the other. Since Africans were inferior, said the trusteeship theory, the British who ruled them owed them a special obligation, not unlike the obligation that decent Englishmen owed to women, children, and dumb animals. 'An obligation rests on the controlling Power not only to safeguard the material rights of the natives, but to promote their moral and educational progress': that was how the future Lord Lugard expressed it in his classic defence of British rule in Africa, published in 1922. To this outstandingly able administrator, who had spent some 30 years ruling over Ugandans and Nigerians, black Africans were essentially 'attractive children'. The typical black African was

> a happy, thriftless, excitable person, lacking in self-control, discipline, and foresight, naturally courageous, and naturally courteous and polite, full of personal vanity, with little sense of veracity . . . His thoughts are concentrated on the events and feelings of the moment, and he suffers little from apprehension for the future, or grief for the past . . .
>
> The African negro is not naturally cruel, though his own insensibility to pain, and his disregard for life – whether his own or another's – cause him to appear callous to suffering . . .
>
> He lacks power of organisation, and is conspicuously deficient in the management and control alike of men or of business . . . He is very prone to imitate anything new in dress or custom . . .
>
> In brief, the virtues and the defects of this race-type are those of attractive children . . .
>
> It is extremely difficult . . . to find educated African youths who are by character and temperament suited to posts in which they may rise to positions of high administrative responsibility.[111]

And indeed, for West Africans, the immediate practical result of the turn to trusteeship was the de-Africanization of the government service. The removal of Africans from office and their replacement by Britons confirmed that 'the mass of the Africans were to be the carefully guarded wards of the Empire – . . . permanent wards who were racially incapable of receiving the full measure of Western civilization'.[112]

Another prominent exponent of trusteeship, Sir Charles Eliot, saw Africans as animals rather than as children. Commissioner for East Africa from 1901 to 1904, Sir Charles regarded the African's mind as 'far nearer to the animal world than . . . that of the European' and as exhibiting 'something of the animal's placidity and want of desire to rise beyond the stage he has reached'. The African race would 'greatly improve under a civilised and beneficent rule', but had 'great limitations'.[113] (From Eliot came the interesting admission that 'the average Englishman . . . tolerates a black man who admits his inferiority, and even those who show a good fight and give in; but he cannot tolerate dark colour combined with an intelligence in any way equal to his own'.)[114]

It would be an oversimplification to say that the trusteeship doctrine was merely a cloak for plunder. Even Lugard, however, thought it 'absurd to deny that the initial motive for the penetration of Africa by Western civilisation was . . . the satisfaction of its material necessities'.[115] By the turn of the century, the contrast between imperial policy and imperialist deeds was inescapable. When Joseph Chamberlain went to the Colonial Office in 1895 and opened a new era in British West Africa policy it became clear that Britain 'was at last willing to pursue her interests in Africa to the utmost limits . . . Britain had emerged as the major European aggressor on the African continent'.[116] Under British control before long were over 2,000,000 square miles of African territory with a population of over 40,000,000 black Africans – about a third of the continent's black population. Addressing the British rulers of these 'lesser breeds' now no longer 'without the Law',[117] Rudyard Kipling summed up, in the last year of the nineteenth century, the trusteeship brand of racism:

Take up the White Man's burden –
    Send forth the best ye breed –
Go, bind your sons to exile
    To serve your captives' need;
To wait, in heavy harness,
    On fluttered folk and wild –
Your new-caught, sullen peoples,
    Half devil and half child.[118]

Englishmen, foreigners, and niggers

Hardly any British writers came out openly against racism in the last quarter of the nineteenth century. One who did was the orientalist and philologist Robert Needham Cust. 'The common form description of an African', he wrote in 1883, 'is that he is cruel, dirty, superstitious, selfish, a cannibal, and addicted to fetichism, human sacrifices, sorcery, and slave-dealing, besides being a drunkard, polygamist, a neglector of domestic ties, a liar and a cheat.' And he added: 'How different is the impression gained from an extensive consideration of the whole subject!'[119]

Few bothered to give the subject extensive consideration. And Cust's catalogue reflects pretty faithfully the extent to which racist ideology had soaked into his unreflective countrymen's minds. Not that all educated people were out-and-out rabid racists. But 'the vast majority of the educated public appears to have accepted at least some aspect of the new racial doctrine, if only as a vague feeling that science supported the common xenophobic prejudice'.[120]

Race prejudice was an acceptable subject for a humorous essay. The writer Charles Lamb, confessing himself to be a 'bundle of prejudices', wrote that while he had felt 'yearnings of tenderness' towards some black faces – 'or rather masks' – that had looked kindly on him in casual encounters in the streets, 'I should not like to associate with them – to share my meals and my good-nights with them – because they are black'. Lamb had similar feelings about Jews, Scotsmen, and Quakers, and his account of these feelings was published as one of his *Essays of Elia*.[121] Lamb was no racist. But pseudo-scientific racism both encouraged and fed off the kind of prejudice that afflicted him.

The flood-tide of racism never completely submerged the image of the black as 'man and brother'. Though there is more than a trace of the 'noble savage' in some of the invocations of this image, it was kept alive by three distinct traditions: humanitarian abolitionism; radicalism; and working-class solidarity. Yet the strength of these traditions should not be exaggerated. 'It would be hard to overemphasize the bias of British attitudes in the nineteenth century towards people with dark skins.'[122] Only a minority of any social class, or at any level of education, would have raised strong objections to the 'common form description' as summarized by Cust. Nor would the majority have seriously challenged the more colourful – but totally characteristic – pen portrait drawn by Winwood Reade:

> The typical negro, unrestrained by moral laws, spends his days in sloth, his nights in debauchery. He smokes haschisch till he stupefies his senses, or falls into convulsions; he drinks palm-wine till he brings on a loathsome disease; he abuses children; stabs the poor brute of a woman whose hands keep him from starvation; and makes a trade of his own offspring. He swallows up his youth in premature vice; he lingers through a manhood of disease; and his tardy death is hastened by those who no longer care to find him food.
>
> Such are the 'men and brothers' for whom their friends claim not protection, but equality!
>
> They do not merit to be called our Brothers; but let us call them our Children.[123]

Uneducated whites divided humanity into three 'races'. There were white people born in England, Wales, and Scotland: 'us'. There were white people born elsewhere: Irish people and foreigners. And there were non-Europeans: 'niggers'. This word was applied, not only to persons of African birth or descent, but also to Indians, Maoris, and Polynesians – to anyone, in fact, whose complexion showed that he or she had not been born into the master race.[124]

Unlike the sophisticated varieties of racism, vulgar racism was largely the creation of the press, particularly that part of the press designed for the less educated section of the population. Children's literature too was fairly saturated with racist stereotypes. In the schoolboy literature of E.Harcourt Burrage, for example, people with dark skins are referred to indiscriminately as 'savages'. They are generally treacherous and cruel, and can be kicked, and killed, without compunction.[125] *Boys of England*, 'A Magazine of Sport, Sensation, Fun, and Instruction', started publication in 1866 with a serial story, 'Alone in the Pirates' Lair'. 'Malay scums', Chinese, Japanese, Javans, Papuans, Pintadoes, and Mestizoes, 'most villainous-looking ruffians of every shade of colour', are lumped together as 'yon dingy devils'. A 'gigantic negro' threatens to burn out the eyes of the English hero, a young midshipman named Jack, with red-hot pincers. When Jack fires his pistol, 'a yell, like the scream of a wounded baboon, proclaimed that the negro was hit'.[126] At a higher social level, public school magazines, 'unremitting agents of seduction for an imperial dream of noble service and intoxicating adventure', served as colonial travel brochures, army recruiting advertisements, and farming prospectuses, combining ethnocentrism and chauvinism in 'a powerful instrument of indoctrination' to persuade the sons of the rich to shoulder the white man's burden.[127]

Here, in conclusion, is a summary of how English boys were taught to regard black people, as put into the mouth of a character in one of G.A.Henty's books. Henty was the best-known and most widely read writer of boys' adventure stories in Britain before the First World War. Fifty years after his death in 1902 his books had sold over 25,000,000 copies and were still to be found on the shelves of school libraries. The reader of *By Sheer Pluck: a tale of the Ashanti war* (1884) is told that black people are

> just like children . . . They are always either laughing or quarrelling. They are good-natured and passionate, indolent, but will work hard for a time; clever up to a certain point, densely stupid beyond. The intelligence of an average negro is about equal to that of a European child of ten years old. A few, a very few, go beyond this, but these are exceptions, just as

> Shakespeare was an exception to the ordinary intellect of an Englishman. They are fluent talkers but their ideas are borrowed. They are absolutely without originality, absolutely without inventive power. Living among white men, their imitative faculties enable them to attain a considerable amount of civilization. Left alone to their own devices they retrograde into a state little above their native savagery.[128]

* * *

This chapter is central to this book, because the racism whose rise it outlines has been central to the experience of black people in Britain for the past 200 years. Long after the material conditions that originally gave rise to racist ideology had disappeared, these dead ideas went on gripping the minds of the living. They led to various kinds of racist behaviour on the part of many white people in Britain, including white people in authority. The chapters that follow show how since 1784 black people in Britain have asserted their humanity, dignity, and individuality in the teeth of racist beliefs and practices.

8. Up from slavery

The black poor

'Starvin about the Streets'

Suddenly, in 1784, London's black population was swollen by a stream of mostly penniless refugees from north America. The promise of freedom had lured them to the British side in the American War of Independence (1775–83). The promise was kept. But hundreds of these black 'loyalists', many of them ex-servicemen, exchanged the life of a slave for that of a starving beggar on the London streets.

In 1775, about 15 months before the Declaration of Independence, Virginia's royal governor Lord Dunmore sent a thrill of horror through the rebel colonists by promising to 'arm my own Negroes & receive all others that come to me who I shall declare free'. When he proclaimed martial law a few months later he repeated this promise to all black men able and willing to bear arms. Runaway slaves flocked to him, and before the year was out he had 300 soldiers in his Royal Ethiopian Regiment. Across the front of their uniforms was stitched the incendiary slogan: 'Liberty to Slaves'. This regiment was ravaged by smallpox, but in 1779 the British commander-in-chief, General Sir Henry Clinton the elder, repeated the offer of freedom for slaves who rallied to the royal standard. There was a competition between the two sides, to recruit black people. Neither side treated black recruits well. The British offered freedom only to adult male slaves. They billeted them in segregated camps, put those who fell sick in segregated hospital tents, and gave ex-slaves court-martialled for petty theft anything from 500 to 1,000 lashes. All the same, tens of thousands of black men opted for the British side.

They were used as shock troops: Samuel Burke, one of the 1,500 black soldiers fighting with the British forces in July 1780, was credited with killing ten rebels at Hanging Rock. They were used as cavalry: a black mounted unit was formed in Virginia in 1782.

They were used as guides: a black man called Quamino Dolly led British troops through the swamps to attack Savannah. They were used as spies and couriers and to smuggle messages through the American lines. They were used as labourers: several units of Black Pioneers, with black NCOs, dug trenches, repaired the lines, drained ditches, dragged boats overland, and built dams. Black labourers cleared rubbish off the streets, shovelled cow dung out of the cattle pens, dumped earth on white men's shit in the 'necessary houses'. Before he surrendered Yorktown, the British commander Cornwallis was complaining of a shortage of black labourers, since in his view the heat was 'too great to admit of the soldiers doing it'. Black men were used in many other capacities: as pilots of coastal and river vessels, seamen, canoeists, miners, woodcutters, carpenters, blacksmiths, tailors, foragers, impressers of horses, nurses, servants to officers, servants to common soldiers, waiters, orderlies, drummers, fifers, and recruiters of yet more black men. And when the war ended and the British withdrew, at least 14,000 black men went with them, evacuated from the ports of Savannah, Charleston, and New York. Thousands more escaped overland to Canada. Of those who quit, hundreds came to London.[1]

About some of these we have a few personal details, for the claims that 47 of them made to the British government for compensation for wartime losses are preserved in the Public Record Office, as are the claims of 5,000 white 'loyalists'. The 47 were not typical of the black refugees as a whole; unlike most of their fellows most of the claimants were freemen, not ex-slaves, and some had owned a little property in America. Twelve had served in the British navy and five had been wounded in battle. Benjamin Whitecuff, formerly a small farmer on Long Island, had been a British spy and was credited with having saved the lives of 2,000 troops. The Americans had captured and hanged him, but three minutes after the noose went round his neck he was rescued by British cavalry. Now he was living on a pension of £4 a year, a small dowry from his English wife Sarah, and what he could earn as a saddler and maker of chair bottoms. David King was a shoemaker, earning 2*s.* a day. John Robinson had been a cook on a British warship and was now keeping a cookshop. George Peters was working at a gentleman's house for 18*d.* a day. Samuel Burke, born in Charleston, had served as a brigadier-general's batman and been wounded twice, the second time so badly that he was discharged. Prince Williams, born free in Georgia, had been tricked into slavery and had fled to the British forces. Newton Prince had been a pastry-cook in Boston, where rebels tarred and feathered him after he gave evidence against them in the Boston Massacre trial; when the British left Boston he went with them. Shadrack Furman, a Virginia slave who had given food and information to British troops and had been captured, flogged, and left blind and crippled by the Americans, was making a living playing the fiddle in the London streets. In 1788 he was awarded a pension of £18 a year.[2]

This was the most generous settlement awarded to any of these claimants. For the most part the claims of black 'loyalists' were viewed with sour suspicion by the Commissioners for American Claims, who met in a grand house overlooking Lincoln's Inn Fields. Few white 'loyalists' were denied help. The allowances granted to even the least favoured among them were almost without exception higher than the £18 a year awarded to blind Shadrack Furman. White claimants compensated with lump-sum payments rarely came away with less than £25. Twenty black claimants got lump sums ranging from £5 to £20; the majority got nothing at all. Some ex-servicemen were not even granted the back pay owed them for years of service to the Crown. Many black applicants were told that their claims hardly deserved 'a serious Investigation or a serious Answer', since they had 'gained their Liberty' in the war 'instead of being Sufferers'. They came 'with a very ill grace to ask for the bounty of Government'. One Connecticut man was told that 'he ought to think himself very fortunate in being in a Country where he can never again be reduced to a state of Slavery'. John Provey, born in North Carolina, slave to a lawyer before the war, had served in the Black Pioneers and described himself as 'an entire Stranger in this Country illeterate and unacquainted with the Laws thereof'. He was told how lucky he was to have reached 'a much better Country where he may with Industry get his Bread & where he can never more be a Slave'. Peter Anderson, a Virginia woodcutter who had been press-ganged by one of Dunmore's officers and had escaped and rejoined the British forces after capture by the Americans, told the commissioners that he was completely destitute:

> I endeavour'd to get Work but cannot get Any I am Thirty Nine Years of Age & am ready & Willing to serve His Britanack Majesty While I am Able But I am realy starvin about the Streets, Having Nobody to give me A Morsal of bread & dare not go home to my Own Country again.

At first the commissioners found Anderson's story 'incredible', but when Lord Dunmore vouched for it they changed their tune and forked out £10. Many were denied relief because they could not provide written evidence, or the testimony of knowledgeable witnesses, to back their claims. Those who obtained pensions or grants did so because they had the support of prominent white refugees.[3]

Peter Anderson's case was typical of the black poor as a whole. By mid-1786 there were at the very least 1,144 of them living in London, and most were penniless.[4] Besides ex-servicemen and other black 'loyalists', new arrivals included some Lascars, or East Indian seamen, and it was the plight of the latter that first came to public notice, in March 1785. In a letter to the *Public Advertiser*, 'an old man just arrived from the country' declared himself 'shocked at the number of miserable objects, Lascars, that I see shivering and starving in the streets'. He suggested a charitable subscription to buy clothes and food for 'a race of human beings, who, though different in colour, religion, and country from ourselves, are still our fellow-creatures, and who have been dragged from their warmer and more hospitable climates by our avarice and ambition'.[5] This was probably a tilt at the East India Company, or at certain shipowners, or at both. In that year five Lascars, one named Soubaney, sued a shipowner for wages due to them. Their case was pleaded by the recorder of London, who refused to accept a fee. The court ordered that each of the plaintiffs should be paid the £20 10*s.* that was owing to him.[6] Early in 1786 a 'Committee of Gentlemen' – i.e. bankers, merchants, and MPs – was set up to organize relief for distressed Lascars, and soon extended its activities to help other black people in need. By 11 February the committee knew of about 320 people in need, 35 of whom were from the East Indies. About 100 had served as seamen in the recent war and had come to Britain on warships. Most of the others had been brought from north America or the West Indies 'by various Accidents', and many were seeking work as seamen.[7]

Soon the committee was styling itself 'Committee for the Relief of the Black Poor' and raising money by public appeal. From 24 January it distributed broth, a piece of meat, and a twopenny loaf to 140 people a day, and from 5 February the number thus fed increased to 210 a day. Bread was sent daily to those too sick to leave their homes. For the most serious cases, the committee opened a hospital ('Sickhouse') in Warren Street, and between 40 and 50 were admitted, given medicine – and reported, in July, to be 'in a miserable state'.[8] Clothing was distributed to about 250 people in rags. 'Some have been fitted out, and sent to sea,' said a newspaper report, 'and a place is provided with straw and blankets for such as apply for Lodging.'[9]

By April the committee had given help to 460 people[10] and money was running short. But public opinion was coming to realize that the black 'loyalists' had a watertight moral claim for charity. As a writer in the *Public Advertiser* put it, they

> have served Britain, have fought under her colours, and after having quitted the service of their American masters, depending on the promise of protection held out to them by British Governors and Commanders, are now left to perish by famine and cold, in the sight of that people for whom they have hazarded their lives, and even (many of them) spilt their blood . . . Shall these poor humble assertors of [Britain's] rights be left to the agonies of want and despair, because they are unfriended and unknown?[11]

From mid-April, regular relief in cash was provided for the black poor. The normal rate was 6*d.* a day. The money was handed out at two public houses at opposite ends of London: the White Raven in Mile End and the Yorkshire Stingo in Lisson Green. On 20 April 75 turned up to receive their dole. Three weeks later there were 327 claimants. There was a temporary fall when it was put about that, in future, payment would depend on the recipient's agreeing to be 'resettled' overseas. But in June the handout was given to 364 people, in August to 622, in early September to 736. By the end of September the daily 6*d.* was reaching nearly 1,000 people. Total cost of the relief has been estimated at close on £20,000, of which only £890 came from public subscriptions.[12] The government contributed the rest.

Resettlement – or deportation?

Why did the government contribute the lion's share? Basically, because it was eager to solve the problem of the black poor by dumping them overseas and saw the daily 6*d.* as bait. They were 'indigent, unemployed, despised and forlon', wrote a commentator nine years later, and 'it was necessary they should be sent somewhere, and be no longer suffered to invest [*sic*] the streets of London'.[13] It is only fair to add that, initially, a number of the black poor themselves favoured resettlement, though their own idea seems to have been to go to Nova Scotia, where many other black 'loyalists' had settled and there seemed a reasonable prospect of finding work. What emerged, however, was a scheme to resettle them in Sierra Leone.

This idea was first put forward by the eccentric amateur botanist and elocution teacher Henry Smeathman. Mainly designed to further Smeathman's financial interests, the scheme had the support of two London merchants who saw it as an opportunity to invest in large-scale cotton-growing.[14] Another supporter was Granville Sharp, who jumped at the chance to do some experimental social engineering by furnishing the expedition with an ingenious, elaborate, and naïve code of regulations, curiously foreshadowing utopian socialist blueprints for an ideal society.[15] The black poor themselves were the last to be consulted; their wishes and needs were at the bottom of everyone else's list of priorities.

By May 1786, hard pressed by creditors, Smeathman had managed to persuade both the Treasury and the Committee for the Relief of the Black Poor that his proposal was the only way of removing the 'Burthen' of the black poor 'for ever'.[16] The Treasury agreed to pay him £14 for every black emigrant who went to Sierra Leone, and the committee had a handbill printed telling the black poor that 'no place' was 'so fit and proper' for them as 'the Grain Coast of Africa; where the necessaries of life may be supplied by the force of industry and moderate labour, and life rendered very comfortable'.[17] The black poor themselves were much harder to persuade, largely because the Sierra Leone coast was a notorious slaving area. But in June 1786 Smeathman had control of the relief money, and that no doubt enhanced his powers of persuasion. Still, winning the recipients' confidence was uphill work. Chairman of the committee at that time was Jonas Hanway, philanthropist and pioneer of the umbrella, one of whose more dubious qualifications for the post was his dislike of 'unnatural connections between black persons and white; the disagreeable consequences of which make their appearance but too frequently in our streets'.[18] One day Hanway found a crowd of black people at the Yorkshire Stingo reluctant to go to Africa 'unless they had some Instrument insuring their Liberty'. So he tried oratory. He 'formed them into a Ring and harangued them, appealing to God and the Common Sense of Mankind for the pure and benevolent Intentions of Government'.[19] Despite Hanway's silver tongue, the black poor insisted on a formal agreement between themselves and Smeathman. They would promise to embark when required and Smeathman would guarantee their freedom on arrival, as promised in his pamphlet, *Plan of a settlement to be made near Sierra Leona* (1786).[20] To this the committee agreed. But the contract as drawn up was a palpable trick. Neither the committee nor the British government was bound by it to protect the proposed colony. On the other hand, those who signed it were legally committed to emigrate as promised, since it was drafted as a legal indenture enforceable in the courts. And the committee now started to require that black people sign this agreement as a condition for receiving the daily handout.[21]

Hanway chose eight 'Head Men' or 'Corporals' to act as recruiters of intending settlers. Each undertook to produce a list of a dozen or two people 'for whose Steadiness and good Behaviour they might be respectively answerable'. Of this first group of 'Corporals' – others were appointed later – four were north Americans. James Johnson, aged 31, and Aaron Brookes, aged 25, both born in New Jersey, gave their occupation as 'husbandry'. Johnson had come to Britain as a ship's steward, Brookes as captain's cook on a naval vessel. John William Ramsay (24), born in New York, was a servant who had come over as a ship's steward. John Williams (25), born in Charleston, was a seaman and had come on a naval vessel. Barbados-born William Green (40) was a servant and had come in that capacity. There were two Africans: John Cambridge (40), netmaker and servant, and Charles Stoddard (28), cooper, had both come as servants. The eighth 'Corporal' was a Lascar called John Lemon. Born in Bengal, this 29-year-old hairdresser and cook had come to Britain on a naval vessel. Six of the eight could read, and two of these could write as well.[22] The 'Corporals', who eventually numbered 15, were given an extra 2*s*. a day.[23]

Though these hand-picked men were prepared to trust the scheme, many of their comrades remained sceptical. About 30 refused to accept their sixpences, 'alleging that they wished for time to consider'. And only 130 of the 437 black poor by then drawing the allowance were prepared to give an immediate promise that they would go to Sierra Leone.[24] There were ways of putting pressure on them, however. At the committee's meeting on 7 June it was reported that 'some of the Blacks had been taken up by Beadles and chastised as Vagrants'.[25] As the months went by, this screw was to be turned tighter and tighter.

It is hard to blame the black poor for their doubts and suspicions. After Smeathman's unexpected death from a 'putrid fever' early in July the committee suddenly tried to switch the place of resettlement from Sierra Leone to the Bahamas, where slavery still reigned. Naturally enough this caused the black poor 'considerable uneasiness'. They protested vigorously and said they were 'totally disinclined to go',[26] and the committee, failing to get Treasury support for the switch, now came up with a scheme to carry them to New Brunswick in Canada. Hanway hinted to them that they would be given land, but the Treasury records reveal that the major attraction of New Brunswick was the belief that ex-slaves would make handy servants and labourers for the white 'loyalists' who had recently settled there.[27] In fact the black poor showed 'great reluctance' to go to Canada, and in mid-August the Treasury agreed to the revival of the Sierra Leone scheme, with Smeathman's associate Joseph Irwin now in charge. The Treasury displayed some impatience, urging that the necessary arrangements be made 'with as little Delay as possible'.[28]

On 9 October the committee resolved to give no further money to any black person who had not signed on for resettlement, and it repeated this decision a fortnight later, complaining of the 'want of discipline'.[29] Meanwhile, a black woman and five black men had been arrested and thrown in jail for vagrancy.[30] The committee tried a different kind of pressure by inserting an advertisement in the newspapers telling masters of runaway slaves, and people to whom the black poor owed money, that intending settlers might be viewed at the White Raven at a certain time.[31]

By now the black poor were very worried and suspicious indeed. They made a number of demands to Smeathman's successor, Irwin. Each intending settler must have a 'certificate', as a kind of passport to protect them against the slave-traders of the West African coast. The committee agreed. Printed on parchment, and put up in a twopenny tin box, the document bore the royal arms and certified that the bearer was a '*Freeman* of the Colony of Sierra Leona or The Land of Freedom'.[32] The settlers demanded arms to defend themselves and hunt game. The navy refused to let them have cannon, but they were given 400 guns and a supply of powder, balls, and flints. The settlers also wanted constables' staves, two movable forges, tents, stationery, and extra provisions: 'a little Tea and Sugar for their Women and Children'.[33]

For the voyage, the Navy Commissioners provided first two ships, the *Atlantic* and the *Belisarius*, then a third, the *Vernon*. But 400 of those who had signed on had last-minute doubts and, on the advice of Lord George Gordon (the famous agitator, opponent of the transportation of convicts, and idol of the London 'Mob'), they failed to embark.[34] So the screws were tightened still further. On 6 December the committee's chairman, Samuel Hoare, urged the

Treasury to issue a proclamation threatening black people 'found begging or lurking about the Streets' with action under the Vagrancy Act.[35] A week later – a fortnight before Christmas – the committee asked the public 'to suspend giving alms' to the black poor, 'in order to induce them to comply with the engagement they entered into'.[36] Early in the new year it was reported that London's lord mayor had ordered city marshals and constables

> to take up all the blacks they find begging about the streets, and to bring them before him; or some other magistrate, that they may be sent home, or to the new colony which is going to be established in Africa; near twenty are already taken up, and lodged in the two Comptors [i.e. city prisons].
>
> The conduct of the Lord-Mayor in ordering the blacks who are found begging about the streets to be taken up, is highly commendable, and it is to be hoped will be imitated by the Magistrates of Westminster, Middlesex, Surry, and the other counties. It is however humbly submitted to their judgment, whether instead of mere confinement in a gaol, it would not be preferable to put them to hard labour in Bridewell. The blacks, especially those of the East-Indies, are naturally indolent; nothing but the utmost necessity will make them work; and the very thought of being subjected to that would soon reconcile them to the plan proposed by Government.[37]

Thus wrote the *Public Advertiser.*

Why were the black poor so reluctant to go on board the ships? Some of them had seen the first Australia-bound convict ships being loaded in the Thames alongside the *Atlantic* and the *Belisarius*, and were afraid of being shipped to the new penal colony at Botany Bay; this fear was not lessened by garbled and sensational newspaper reports.[38] But above all, in the words of Ottobah Cugoano, one of the two black leaders who at length came out publicly against the scheme, the 'wiser sort' refused to get involved 'unless they could hear of some better plan . . . for their safety and security'. After all, he asked, 'can it be readily conceived that government would establish a free colony for them nearly on the spot, while it supports its forts and garrisons, to ensnare, merchandize, and to carry others into captivity and slavery'.[39] Here was political opposition to the government's plan for disposing of the black poor. Such opposition struck some people as outrageous, especially when it took the form of a meeting of black people at which they dared to make political demands. When paragraphs appeared in the newspapers, calling on Britain to follow France's example by expelling all black people and banning their entry to this country,[40] a protest meeting of black people was held in Whitechapel. This greatly angered the *Morning Post*, which called for such meetings to be broken up by the police:

> The oppositionists have converted numbers of the *black* poor into zealous *patriots*. They assembled, it seems, in Whitechapel, where they held, what the Indians term a *talk*; the purport of which was, that they had 'heard of an intention of introducing the *arbitrary French laws*, with respect to *black people*, as part of the new French Treaty; and they looked upon the *arts* now practised to inveigle them out of a land of liberty, with the utmost jealousy'. In this instance, as in many others, the lenity of our Government operates to the detriment of the nation. Are we to be told what articles in a treaty should be adopted or rejected, by a crew of reptiles, manifestly only a single link in the great chain of existence above the *monkey*? Should a sooty tribe of Negroes be permitted to arraign, with impunity, the measures of Government? A few constables to disperse their meetings, and a law, prohibiting *blacks* from entering our country, would be the proper mode of treating those creatures, whose intercourse with the inferior orders of our women, is not less a shocking violation of female delicacy, than disgraceful to the state.[41]

Those who did go on board the ships were living, as the months dragged on, in wretched conditions. Many lacked beds; many more lacked clothing and other necessities. We saw earlier that Olaudah Equiano, having reluctantly accepted the post of commissary of provisions and stores, found that Irwin had been pocketing the money given him to buy supplies. Equiano declared that both Irwin and the Revd Patrick Fraser – ordained by the archbishop of Canterbury to serve as missionary to the settlement – had treated the black people concerned, in essence, 'the same as they do in the West Indies'.[42] When the passengers tried to make themselves comfortable they were accused of wasting wood, candles, and water. Before the voyage even began, 50 had died of cold and disease. Others left the ships to avoid 'the prospect of their wretched fate', as Cugoano put it.[43] For one reason or another, nearly one in three of the passengers listed as being on board in November 1786 was absent from the ships when they finally left the Thames on 23

February 1787.[44] One of those who died on the *Belisarius* during the long wait was John Provey, late of the Black Pioneers, whose appeal for help had been rejected, as we have seen, by the Commissioners for American Claims. He and his white wife Ann and their daughter Louisa had each signed the Sierra Leone agreement, and each had been receiving 6*d*. a day. But by February father and daughter were both dead, leaving Ann Provey to go to Africa alone.[45]

Heavy gales drove the three ships and their naval escort into harbour. At Plymouth the sight of black people from these ships 'strolling about' disturbed the local magistrates, who expressed a fear that 'many of these People will be left behind to the great nuisance of the Country'. So the Navy Commissioners told the commander of the naval escort vessel 'to prevent the Blacks from getting ashore', and he did so.[46] It was during this further delay that Equiano was sacked for turbulence and discontent, leaving Irwin in sole charge of the arrangements. While at Plymouth, the *Atlantic* and *Belisarius* were largely resupplied, which tends to confirm Equiano's allegations against Irwin.[47]

The convoy finally left England on 9 April 1787. On board were 350 black settlers, 41 of them women, and 59 white wives (some now widows, of men who had died on board). After a voyage lasting a month, during which about 35 more passengers died, they landed in Sierra Leone. The later history of these settlers is one of disaster piled on disaster. They died like flies. Some were sold to French slave-traders. Incensed by their failure to build him a church and a house, the missionary deserted them. The seeds they had brought from England would not grow in the tropical climate. Caught in the three-way crossfire of a conflict involving an American slave-ship, a British man-of-war, and a local ruler, the settlers were given three days to leave their little town and it was then burnt to the ground. After four years, only 60 were left of the 374 who arrived.

Why did the scheme fail? One recent writer claims that it was 'mainly because the settlers arrived in the wrong season of the year'.[48] Another advances a different explanation:

> The committee and the British government fostered the Sierra Leone settlement not because they were concerned about the welfare of the blacks, but rather because they wanted to rid the nation of what they regarded as a pestilent influence. Throughout its planning for the colony, the committee worried more about speed than about anything else. Crucial questions of supply and organization were left to

> agents who turned out to be incompetent, if not corrupt, and the wishes of the blacks were ascertained only when it was absolutely necessary.[49]

Or, as Cugoano wrote at the time, there was no 'prudent and right plan'. On the contrary, 'they were to be hurried away at all events, come of them after what would'.[50]

There is a strange pendant to the story of the Sierra Leone resettlement scheme. One of the black 'loyalist' refugees that went to Nova Scotia was an ex-slave from North Carolina called Thomas Peters, who had served as a sergeant in the Black Pioneers. Like many others, he was promised land but never got it. After six years of waiting for his land, he decided in 1790, at the age of 52, to go to Britain and complain to the government of the injustice he and many of his fellow-settlers were suffering. This was a brave decision, for an ex-slave travelling alone was at the mercy of any ship's captain who chose to put in at an American port and sell him. Peters reached London in 1791. Granville Sharp and Henry Thornton, chairman of the newly formed Sierra Leone Company, took up his complaint. His old commanding officer gave him an introduction to his old commander-in-chief, General Clinton, who befriended and supported him and spoke to Wilberforce on his behalf. The home secretary, Henry Dundas, ordered the governor of Nova Scotia to investigate and redress the grievances. The directors of the Sierra Leone Company offered the black 'loyalists' in Nova Scotia a new home in Sierra Leone. And Peters returned in triumph to Nova Scotia with the news.

In January 1792 over 1,100 black colonists sailed from Nova Scotia and two months later they arrived in Sierra Leone, where they founded a second settlement, happily more successful, on their predecessors' original site. They called it Freetown, and it is still, after almost 200 years, the capital of Sierra Leone.

Peters was disappointed to find that leadership of the settlement was given, not to him, but to seven 'self-important, and for the most part inefficient and quarrelsome' officials sent out from England to run the colony. Heartbroken, he died less than four months after landing in Africa.[51] 'Without his courage and faith in coming to England', writes Christopher Fyfe, 'no Nova Scotian would have come to Sierra Leone; without the Nova Scotians the Colony would have failed.'[52]

Resistance and self-emancipation

The British government had succeeded in getting rid of 309 black men and 41 black women. They were got rid of to such effect that, within five years of setting sail for Sierra Leone, most of them were dead. But the rest of the black community stayed in Britain. There were at least 10,000 of them. Most were servants. What precisely was their legal and social status?

It was a period of transition. Black slaves in Britain were in the process of freeing themselves, largely by their own efforts but partly with the help of free blacks and sympathetic whites. So much has been shown by Professor Douglas A. Lorimer in an essay which destroys the myth that black slaves in Britain were freed by the courts and the 'rule of law'.

We have already seen that, contrary to general belief, slavery in England was not abolished by Lord Mansfield's decision in the Somerset case of 1772 but persisted after that year. Eighteen years after Mansfield, a black woman was hunted down in the Bristol streets and dragged to the ship that was to take her to the West Indies; and two years later another black woman was sold for £80 in Bristol and shipped to Jamaica. As late as 1822, Thomas Armstrong of Dalston, near Carlisle, bequeathed a slave in his will.[1] Formally, slavery was not ended in this country until the 1833 Act of Parliament freed the slaves throughout the British Empire. But in practical terms the institution of slavery, in Britain itself, largely withered away between the 1740s and the 1790s. And it did so as a result of the slaves' own resistance – which was, to be sure, greatly encouraged from 1772 onwards both by the Mansfield decision and by popular misinterpretation of that decision. The slaves resisted, as so many of their predecessors in the seventeenth century had resisted, by running away. As individuals, over a period of half a century or so, they escaped from bondage. They shook it off, and asserted their dignity as human beings. Individual acts of resistance, multiplied many times over, became self-emancipation: a gradual, cumulative, and irreversible achievement which constituted the first victory of the abolitionist movement in Britain.

Lorimer's argument entails three emphases not made by previous writers on the subject:

First, he introduces the concept of 'slave-servants'. Practically all black slaves in England worked as servants. These servants occupied a position intermediate between chattel slavery and the domestic service of whites. They were bound to their masters' households, much like serfs.

Second, Lorimer stresses the importance of the wage question for the personal autonomy of individual servants both black and white. He shows how the demand for wages posed by black slaves brought into this country helped them attain some degree of independence and enabled them to join in the activities of well-established black communities in larger centres such as London, Bristol, and Liverpool. And this in turn strengthened their will to resist.

In demanding wages, Lorimer adds, slaves were claiming more than mere spending money. Wages certified a free status. No less important, they conferred the right of residence within a parish – a necessary condition under the Poor Law for the payment of parish relief.

Third, while not denying that there existed a social and ideological climate conducive to successful black resistance to slavery, Lorimer shows that the initiative for ending slavery was the slaves' own action in resisting their owners' authority and quitting their households. Credit for this major victory for English liberty belongs therefore, not to the law and the courts – as is claimed by what Lorimer calls 'the mythology giving substance to the ideology of the rule of law' – but to the black slaves themselves. That British air became too pure for slavery was due to brave acts of resistance by individual members of Britain's black community. This initial victory of the abolitionist movement stimulated the assault on the more entrenched slave trade and on plantation slavery in the colonies.[2]

This is a necessarily brief summary of a long-drawn-out process. All available evidence fully supports Lorimer's analysis. In 1764 the *Gentleman's Magazine* complains that black people arriving in England 'cease to consider themselves as slaves, nor will they put up with an inequality of treatment'.[3] In 1768 Fielding the 'Blind Beak' grumbles: '*They no sooner arrive here, than they put themselves on a Footing with other Servants, become intoxicated with Liberty, grow refractory, and either by Persuasion of others, or from their own Inclinations, begin to expect Wages according to their own Opinion of their Merits.*'[4] Forty years later the whole process is already half a generation in the past, so that Clarkson can write, in 1808, that 'we no longer see our public papers polluted by hateful advertisements of the sale of the human species . . . We are no longer distressed by the perusal of impious rewards for bringing back the poor and the helpless into slavery'.[5]

We know, of course, from those very advertisements that black slaves in Britain had been running away right from the beginning. The charge most frequently levelled against black servants was that hey were always ready to desert their masters.[6] West Indians who brought over trusted, long-serving slaves were amazed to find them gone at the first opportunity.[7] Many a faithful retainer, treated for years almost as one of the family, melted swiftly into the 'mob'. What effect did the Mansfield judgment of 1772 have on this process? Clearly it intensified it. Though there was still some illicit kidnapping and shipment to the plantations in the early 1790s – and even, as we shall see, some illicit sales of black children as houseboys in Westmorland early in the nineteenth century – Mansfield had outlawed and so reduced the most serious threat that runaways had to fear: deportation. Thus the social implications of the Somerset case were far wider than its limited legal effect. The ruling did not give runaways absolute protection, but it gave them some. And it could be used to some extent as a lever by those who chose not to run away but to demand, instead, a better deal as employees receiving wages. A former governor of Massachusetts told Mansfield in 1779 that slave-owners who had brought slaves to Britain in recent years 'had, as far as I know, relinquished their property in them, and rather agreed to give them wages, or suffered them to go free'.[8] When, six years later, Granville Sharp's clergyman brother wrote asking for advice on how to protect a runaway black boy from his master's claims, Sharp advised against buying the boy's freedom, since this would implicitly recognize the master's property rights. The servant's desertion from his master's service was in itself, he added, an act of emancipation; the boy should be protected from possible kidnapping.[9] Sharp's role was to prevent slave-owners from using the law to crush the slaves' resistance.

Sharp and other abolitionists themselves used the courts as a weapon against slave-owners seeking to reclaim their property. In practice, since at least the early 1740s, London magistrates had tended to ignore the rulings of higher courts by refusing to recognize black slaves as property at all and setting black petitioners free.[10] After the Somerset case the higher courts, though not invariably liberal, tended to do the same. Mansfield himself ordered the release of two runaway slaves from Virginia who stowed away on a British ship, and he awarded £500 damages to Amissa, a free African seaman sold into slavery by the captain of a Liverpool slaver.[11] By the 1790s the abolitionists' rescue operations were mostly concerned with slaves in transit – locked up in English ports, on or off the ships that had brought them here – and black seamen. Some of the latter had escaped from slavery in the West Indies by stowing away on British ships and then offering to work their passage. Greedier captains would chain them up in the hope of taking them back to the West Indies and reselling them. Abolitionists rescued some of these prisoners by obtaining writs of habeas corpus for their release.[12]

A similar process of resistance and self-emancipation took place in Scotland, as is shown by the case of David Spens. This was the name adopted by the black slave of a West Indian merchant who went to live in the Fife port of Methil. In 1769 this slave was publicly baptized by a local minister, the Revd Dr Harry Spens. His master decided to ship him back to the West Indies and sell him. So David Spens ran away and was given shelter by a farmer in the parish of Wemyss. Local miners and salters – themselves virtually serfs – as well as farmworkers gave generously to aid his defence, and five lawyers took up his case and refused any fees. The merchant died before the case was heard, and David Spens returned to work for the Wemyss farmer and became a popular local figure.[13] The cause of black freedom in Scotland was greatly helped in 1778 by the Court of Session decision in the case of Joseph Knight, which, as we saw in chapter 6, was much more clear-cut than the Mansfield decision in England.

The success of slave resistance led many English people to suppose that their institutions and customs were 'peculiarly antagonistic to slavery' and enabled abolitionists 'to draw a stark contrast between English traditions of liberty and colonial slave practice'.[14] And indeed, a 'libertarian heritage' was '*the* dominant political ideology in the eighteenth century, to which all groups subscribed'.[15] Hence 'the intense popular hatred of the press-gang, the standing army, excise taxes, and other manifestations of intrusive state power'.[16] However paradoxical it may seem to us 200 years later, lower-class culture in eighteenth-century England was 'rebellious in defence of custom'. In E.P.Thompson's words, the 'free-born Englishman' of the lower classes 'took to himself some part of the constitutional rhetoric of his rulers, and defended stubbornly his rights at law and his rights to protest turbulently against military, press-gang or police, alongside his rights to white bread and cheap ale'. The poor displayed 'a generally riotous and unpoliced disposition which astonished foreign visitors'.[17] These riot-prone plebeians, asserting their presence and rights by 'a theater of threat and sedition',[18] were the immediate precursors of the industrial working class. Their belief in, and obstinate defence of, what they saw as their age-old tradition of liberty furnished a social and ideological back-drop favourable to black resistance and self-emancipation. The black slaves in Britain who freed themselves by their own efforts were giving practical expression to the 'libertarian heritage' of the country they found themselves in. And, by winning the anti-slavery movement's first victory, they were making a substantial, though largely forgotten, contribution to that heritage.[19]

Abolitionists and radicals

Abolition of the British slave trade in 1807 was an expression of humanity's slowly awakening conscience. It was the result of a dedicated crusade by the 'Saints', a group of middle- and upper-class christian humanitarians, led by that Great Emancipator William Wilberforce. 'The unwearied, unostentatious, and inglorious crusade of England against slavery', wrote the leading nineteenth-century historian of European morals, 'may probably be regarded as among the three or four perfectly virtuous acts recorded in the history of nations.'[1]

This comfortable and comforting myth was first challenged, early in the present century, by an obscure German economist; since he wrote in German, for an audience of scholars, no notice was taken of his suggestion that the British slave trade may have been abolished for economic and political reasons.[2] The next challenge to the myth came in 1938, from the pen of the great Trinidadian historian, theorist, and activist C.L.R.James, who wrote in his biography of the black statesman Toussaint-Louverture:

> Those who see in abolition the gradually awakening conscience of mankind should spend a few minutes asking themselves why it is man's conscience, which had slept peacefully for so many centuries, should awake just at the time that men began to see the unprofitableness of slavery as a method of production in the West Indian colonies.[3]

To James, abolition was part of a world-wide historical process: a stage in the successive victories of the industrial capitalist class over the landed aristocracy. But James, too, might have been writing in German for all the notice that was taken by historians. They reacted vigorously, however, when another Trinidadian, the late Eric Williams, launched an attack on the myth in 1944, not in an aside, but as the central thesis of his book *Capitalism and Slavery*. In the short term, according to Williams, the Briitish slave trade was abolished in order to curtail overproduction of sugar. Without denying the importance of the humanitarians – 'one of the greatest propaganda movements of all time . . . the spearhead of the onslaught which destroyed the West Indian system and freed the Negro' – Williams, like James, saw abolition in the long term as part of a vast historical process: 'The commercial capitalism of the eighteenth century developed the wealth of Europe by means of slavery and monopoly. But in so doing it helped to create the industrial capitalism of the nineteenth century, which turned round and destroyed the power of commercial capitalism, slavery, and all its works.'[4] Williams's thesis has attracted a large volume of criticism,[5] though even his fiercest critics find it 'difficult . . . to get around the simple fact that no country thought of abolishing the slave trade until its economic value had considerably declined'.[6] As restated in *From Columbus to Castro* (1970), Williams's explanation for the abolition of the Caribbean slave system covers five interlocking sets of factors: economic; political; humanitarian; international and intercolonial; and social.[7] Here is a far more subtle and sophisticated theory than Williams's critics generally credit him with. The controversy, which continues, is beyond the scope of this book; but it ought to be said that the myth which James and Williams were arguing against is still widely believed.

The abolitionist movement was far from being exclusively, or even predominantly, upper- and middle-class. To be sure, it was set in motion by white humanitarians who had the leisure, means, and education to occupy themselves with such matters. Many of the pioneers, on both sides of the Atlantic, were Quakers. It was the Pennsylvania Quaker Anthony Benezet who, by his writings, converted Thomas Clarkson to abolitionism and influenced Granville Sharp and John Wesley, too; Sharp's *Representation of the Injustice and Dangerous Tendency of Tolerating Slavery* appeared in 1769, Wesley's *Thoughts upon Slavery* in 1774. It was Quakers who presented the first substantial anti-slavery petition to Parliament, in 1783. In the same year they formed a special committee on the slave trade, and in the following year they distributed 12,000 free copies of an anti-slavery pamphlet. It was the Quakers' official printer who published, in 1784, *An Essay on the Treatment and Conversion of African Slaves in the British Sugar Colonies* by James Ramsay, an Anglican clergyman who had spent 19 years on St Kitts and whose devastating public opposition to slavery, backed by first-hand knowledge, drew down on his head a vitriolic onslaught from the West India lobby, led by the Nevis planter James Tobin. When the Society for the Abolition of the Slave Trade was formed in 1787, there were nine Quakers on its committee of twelve.

By that year Parliament could no longer ignore the slave trade. Too much was known. Ramsay, meeting William Wilberforce in 1783, had given him an array of facts that prepared him to respond favourably to Pitt's suggestion that Wilberforce should raise the matter in Parliament. Pitt had it in mind to destroy the rise to prosperity of the French colony of St Domingue, or Haiti. The French bought most of their black slaves from British slave-merchants; abolition of the trade would be a crippling blow to them. Wilberforce, with his strict views on religion and morals, was an ideal instrument for Pitt's scheme. Working behind the scenes at first, he initiated a series of Privy Council and select committee inquiries which brought an avalanche of disturbing facts to public attention in the years 1789–91. Sir William Dolben's Bill regulating overcrowding on slave-ships was passed in 1788, but the West India lobby resisted abolition tooth and nail. In April 1791 Wilberforce's first motion to bring in an abolition Bill was defeated in the Commons by 163 votes to 88.

Meanwhile, however, a new and unexpected element had entered the abolitionist movement. In 1788 over 100 petitions had flooded into Parliament, from all over Britain, demanding abolition of the trade.[8] These were not the result of agitation by middle-class humanitarians. They reflected rather the emergence of working-class radicalism. Mass support for abolition was first expressed in Manchester, where it was initiated by two members of the Society for Constitutional Information, founded in 1780 to promote Thomas Paine's doctrine of human rights. The Society was the originator of the wave of radical agitation that was to sweep the country in the 1790s. Its two Manchester leaders, Thomas Cooper and Thomas Walker, surprised and delighted Clarkson, when he visited Manchester in 1787, by telling him of 'the spirit which was then beginning to show itself, among the people of Manchester and of other places, on the subject of the Slave-trade, and which would unquestionably manifest itself further, by breaking out into petitions to parliament for its abolition'.[9] In the event, 10,639 Manchester people signed the petition, which was reprinted in several provincial newspapers as a model for others to copy. Soon they were doing so. A meeting in Nottingham praised Manchester's citizens 'for the Zeal, Activity, and manly Firmness, which they have manifested in this noble cause'.[10] This was the first large-scale use of petitions as a political weapon. Petitioning soon became 'the standard abolitionist approach to Parliament, and it was to remain a dominant feature of radical working class politics until the 1840s'.[11] In 1792 over 500 petitions were sent to Parliament in support of Wilberforce's abolition Bill.[12] When Lydia Hardy, wife of the radical leader Thomas Hardy, wrote to her husband from Chesham in April 1792, her first question was what was happening in Parliament concerning the slave trade – 'for the people are here as much against that as enny ware and there is more people I think hear that drinks tea without suger then there is drinks with'.[13]

The shift in public opinion is shown, above all, by the support for abolitionism even in places that owed a large share of their prosperity to the slave trade. The 1792 petition from Manchester, whose population was somewhat under 75,000, carried over 20,000 signatures.[14] Even Bristol had a petition. It was the spread of radical ideas among working people that had brought about this change.

From the start, opposition to slavery was central to radical beliefs and at the heart of radical agitation. The 'Father of Reform', the respected Major John Cartwright, whose support for American independence had put paid to a brilliant naval career, worked closely with Clarkson, Sharp, and other prominent abolitionists. In 1788 he wrote to his wife: 'Should the West Indian slaves, who but the other day had not the slightest prospect of such an event, find themselves emancipated, who can say that there is no hope of our constitutional rights and liberties being restored?'[15] We have seen that Olaudah Equiano, chief spokesman of Britain's black community, stayed in the house of Thomas Hardy, chief founder of the radical London Corresponding Society; that he joined the society; and that he put Hardy in touch with the provincial abolitionists whom he had met on his speaking tours. When Hardy declared that liberty for blacks and liberty for whites were indivisible, he was expressing more than a theoretical understanding. The unity in struggle of black and white working people found practical expression on the streets of British provincial centres in the 1790s.

This was a feature of the new radical movement that disturbed both the pro-slavery section of the ruling class and its anti-slavery section. Terrified by the French revolution, horrified by the revolution of black slaves on the island of Haiti, the ruling class found the connection between domestic radicalism and abolitionism a fearful portent. Bristol's MP Lord Sheffield actively opposed Wilberforce's 1791 abolition motion and, in the following year, 'reprobated' the abolitionist petitions because they were 'obtained through the medium of associations; to which he had always professed himself an enemy'.[16] Others expressed alarm because many of those signing were working people: poor and ignorant people, 'enthusiastically inclined'.[17] Nothing quite like it had been known before, and it made the upper classes shudder. The very foundations of their privileged existence seemed threatened. One noble earl summed it up like this in 1793:

> The idea of abolishing the slave trade is connected with the levelling system and the rights of man . . . What does the abolition of the slave trade mean more or less in effect, than liberty and equality? What more or less than the rights of man? And what is liberty and equality, and what the rights of man, but the foolish fundamental principles of this new philosophy. If proofs are wanting, look at the colony of St Domingo [i.e. Haiti] and see what the rights of man have done there.[18]

Radicals and abolitionists alike were branded as agents of the French revolution, to the distress of Wilberforce and his supporters. Wilberforce's brother-in-law grumbled that respectable people in Hull and Norfolk connected abolition of the slave trade with 'democratical principles' and therefore would not hear it mentioned; Wilberforce's friends complained of Clarkson's enthusiasm for the French revolution, and Wilberforce asked Lord Muncaster to caution Clarkson against such talk: 'It will be ruin to our cause.'[19] Wilberforce and Clarkson were dubbed 'the JACOBINS of ENGLAND'.[20]

Whereas the Society for the Abolition of the Slave Trade concentrated its efforts on the aim set forth in its title, the radical abolitionists – echoing Ottobah Cugoano, consciously or not – went further. When Sheffield radicals organized their biggest-ever mass meeting in April 1794, attended by thousands of artisan cutlers, a unanimous resolution called for the emancipation of black slaves as well as the ending of the slave trade. The resolution was a fascinating blend of abolitionist humanitarianism, radicalism, and working-class solidarity: precisely the three traditions that were to resist the rising tide of racism throughout the nineteenth century. Slave-merchants and planters were branded as 'unfeeling barbarians'. 'Wishing to be rid of the weight of oppression under which *we* groan,' declared the Yorkshiremen, 'we are induced to compassionate those who groan also.' As 'no Compromise can be made between Freedom and Tyranny', there should be 'a total Emancipation of the Negro Slaves'. Slavery in the West Indies

> is insulting to Human Nature in an age of Reason and Philosophy . . . it tends to open wide the flood gates of

> Patronage, Corruption, and Dependance; inflames and stimulates the sordid passion of Avarice . . . its Abolition will redeem the national honor, too long sullied by the trade of blood . . . will promote the cause of Liberty . . . will avenge peacefully ages of wrongs done to our Negro Brethren.[21]

When John Thelwall of the London Corresponding Society, perhaps the most brilliant of the English radicals of the day and certainly the one most feared by the government, addressed huge meetings in London and the provinces in 1794 and 1795, he directly linked the struggle against slavery with the struggle against a corrupt ruling class at home. 'The seed, the root of the oppression is here; and here the cure must begin', he declared. ' . . . If we would dispense justice to our distant colonies, we must begin by rooting out from the centre the corruption by which that cruelty and injustice is countenanced and defended.'[22] And Thelwall's friend Samuel Taylor Coleridge, then only 22, was bold enough to lecture against the slave trade in Bristol itself, after a day spent reading, or re-reading, the books of Clarkson and Wadström. His lecture, delivered at the Assembly coffee-house on the Quay, showed a grasp of the anomalies in the triangular trade as they were experienced by 'the poor and labouring part of Society' in Britain: 'We export a vast quantity of necessary Tools, Raiment, and defensive Weapons – with great store of provisions – so that . . . the poor with unceasing toil first raise and then are deprived of the comforts which they absolutely want in order to procure Luxuries which they must never hope to enjoy.'[23] To the radicals, writes James Walvin,

> the corrupt political patronage exercised by West Indian wealth provided one of the most telling criticisms of the slave colonies. The corollary was that an end to plantocratic power, based on slavery, would minimize their political leverage in London. Equally, reform of Parliament would undermine the political base that the West Indians needed to defend their economic system.[24]

Government repression, effectively prohibiting public meetings in 1795 and outlawing radical and trade union activities four years later, crippled both radicalism and extra-parliamentary abolitionism. For almost 20 years, working-class political activity was barely smouldering. When such activity did flare up again on a large scale, in 1814, the unpredictable spark was the question of slavery. At the

Congress of Vienna that followed Napoleon's defeat, a proposal was made to renew the rights of French slave-merchants. This roused English working people to fury. Within four weeks some 806 petitions, bearing the signatures of 1,500,000 protesters, were sent to Parliament. As Walvin makes clear, a higher proportion of the population signed these petitions than was to sign even the massive Chartist petition in 1848. In the small West Riding town of Guiseley, for instance, between Leeds and Ilkley, 2,000 signed out of a population of 7,000.[25] Never, wrote Samuel Whitbread, had the country expressed so general a feeling as they had about the slave trade – 'if they had, Parliament would long since have been reformed'.[26]

From then on the grassroots movement for emancipation grew steadily stronger. Between 1826 and 1832 more than 3,500 petitions were submitted to the House of Lords alone. These petitions were 'steeped in the political vernacular of what had once been artisan radicalism'; but now the abolitionists 'assumed that West Indian slaves possessed those rights which, in the 1790s, the popular radicals had claimed for themselves'[27] – and which some Englishmen had been jailed, others transported, others again hanged, for demanding.

Two of the radicals who suffered for their beliefs and activities were black men. William Davidson was hanged and beheaded; Robert Wedderburn, son of a slave, was jailed for two years. Both were born in Jamaica. Both were included – in each case there is a note saying 'Black Man' – in a secret list of 33 'leadeing Reformers' compiled for the home secretary from police reports in October 1819.[28] Both were revolutionary socialists: members of the farthest left of all the radical organizations of the time. These were the followers of Thomas Spence, a poor Newcastle schoolmaster who had been secretary of the London Corresponding Society, had edited radical papers, was several times imprisoned for his radicalism, and was in certain respects ahead of his time. He was a kind of agrarian communist, who held that the poor had had their land stolen from them and were therefore dependent on the rich; his remedy was communal ownership of the land, which would restore the independence of the poor. Spence demanded the right of easy divorce for poor people (the rich already had it). And he addressed some of his writings to working women, an unusual thing to do in those days. At one time his followers called themselves the 'Free and Easy Club', apparently because they met in taverns to talk politics over a pint of beer. In 1812 the club adopted the more formal title of

Society of Spencean Philanthropists (i.e. 'friends of humanity' – the older, wider sense of the word).

Not only were the spenceans the farthest left of the radicals; their group was also the most solidly working-class in composition. Most of its members were 'mechanics and manufacturers' – factory workers and shoemakers, with a sprinkling of discharged soldiers and sailors. Though small in numbers, theirs was the only radical organization to maintain an unbroken continuity throughout the Napoleonic wars. In 1815 it was the only socialist organization in the country, and for a long time it was the most serious, determined, and influential revolutionary trend in London.[29] Spenceans were prominent in the Spa Fields riots of December 1816. Some of them had contacts outside the capital – certainly in Manchester, Stockport, and Bolton, and probably elsewhere.[30] Formally they were organized, rather grandly, into sections and divisions, a structure that seems to have been copied from the old London Corresponding Society – whose last secretary, the brace-maker Thomas Evans, led the spenceans after Spence's death in 1814. But in practice there were splits and quarrels, and various spencean groups were operating independently of each other in the disturbed years 1817–20. One of those groups, as we shall see, was led for a time by Robert Wedderburn. William Davidson was in another group, whose activities against the most repressive regime that Britain has ever known were to end in disaster.

The black radicals

William Davidson

One of the two black men who played a prominent part in the British radical movement during the regency, William Davidson, was hanged with four of his white comrades, Arthur Thistlewood, John Brunt, James Ings, and Richard Tidd, early on the morning of 1 May 1820. It was one of the grimmest scenes ever witnessed by the people of London. The crowd was the largest that had ever turned out for an execution and, in case of a rescue attempt, was split up into small groups separated by contingents of Life Guards. Blackfriars Bridge was guarded by 100 artillerymen and six guns. The five men were hanged on a specially large platform, erected in front of the debtors' door of Newgate jail, where the Old Bailey stands today. Near the drop were five plain coffins, liberally strewn with sawdust to soak up the blood, and a block. Davidson, alone of the five, accepted the holy sacrament and prayed fervently before they hanged him. He called to the crowds: 'God bless you all! Good-bye.' Half an hour later a black-masked 'resurrection man', whose fee was 20 guineas, cut the heads from the bodies with a knife, then held up each head in turn and named each victim thrice as a traitor. The crowds had only murmured before; now they went wild with fury. Some were sick; others fainted. The rest hissed, groaned, shrieked, and shouted: 'Murder!' It was the last public decapitation in England.[1]

A cabinet-maker by trade, with a reputation as an excellent worker, William Davidson was born in Kingston, Jamaica, in 1786. His father was the island's attorney-general, his mother a black woman. Acknowledged and provided for, it seems, by his father, whose second son he was, the boy was educated in Jamaica until he was about 14. Then, against his mother's wishes, he was sent to Edinburgh to complete his education. He may have had some connection with the radical movement in Scotland. He was apprenticed to a Liverpool lawyer, but after three years ran away to sea and was twice impressed into the navy. Discharged, he studied mathematics in Aberdeen for a while but was soon apprenticed to a Lichfield cabinet-maker.

It was in that Staffordshire town that he met and fell deeply in love with a Miss Salt, whom at first he visited without her parents' consent. Her mother was partly won over but her father strongly disapproved, fired a bullet through the young man's hat, and had him arrested on a false charge. When Davidson was released it was the father's turn to be locked up, for shooting at him. He promised Davidson his daughter's hand if he would refuse to prosecute, then asked him to wait until the girl came of age. Sent far away, Miss Salt married another suitor nine months later – and took with her a dowry of £7,000. When he heard this news Davidson tried to poison himself, but was saved by a friend who administered a strong antidote in the nick of time.

Davidson bought himself a house in Birmingham and set up in business there as a cabinet-maker, probably with £1,200 sent from Jamaica by his mother. But his business failed and he made for London, where he become journeyman to a Haymarket cabinet-maker and taught in a Wesleyan Sunday school. He was accused of making passes – that is all it seems to have amounted to – at a lady teacher, or a young lady in his class. Accounts differ. But they agree that, before long, he set up in business for himself once more, at Walworth, and married Mrs Sarah Lane, a poor widow with four sons. They took a cottage at 12 Elliott's Row, near Lord's Old

Cricket Ground in St Marylebone, paying an annual rent of £22. A son called John was born in 1816 and another, Duncan, in 1819. Though government spies later described him as 'a desperate character' and 'a terror to the neighbourhood', Davidson was in fact a popular figure, who invited neighbours to his birthday party and entertained them with wine and radical songs.[2] He was 5ft 10½in. tall, with dark eyes and dark curly hair, strong and 'able looking' and often dressed in a light brown overcoat.[3] His wife and children and step-children loved him very much, and they loved him no less when he was arrested and convicted. While in jail he petitioned the Privy Council to ask that his 3-year-old son be allowed to 'Stop with me Occasionally from one Visit to another of his Mother'.[4] (For a letter from William Davidson to his wife, written while he was in prison awaiting trial, see appendix B, p. 405.)

An avid reader of Thomas Paine,[5] Davidson joined the Marylebone Union Reading Society, formed in 1819 in response to the Peterloo massacre, in which 11 unarmed demonstrators had been killed and 500 injured. Members paid 2*d*. a week and met on Monday evenings to read radical newspapers and discuss political matters. Soon Davidson was holding meetings in his own house, and one informer counted 18 people arriving. Another, who alleged that his dog had been shot by Davidson, told of seeing him and others 'exercising like Soldiers' on Sunday mornings.[6] All over the country, radicals were doing the same. Those who practised drilling acted as stewards at open-air meetings, and at one such meeting, in Smithfield in November 1819, Davidson helped guard the banner from capture by police. It was a black flag with skull and crossbones and the legend: 'Let us die like Men and not be sold like Slaves.'[7]

At some stage a fellow-radical called John Harrison, later to be transported for life for his politics, introduced Davidson to a certain George Edwards, by trade a modeller of statuettes. Edwards, whose brother was a policeman, pretended to be a radical but was in fact a police spy and *agent provocateur*. The movement accepted him with an innocence that seems utterly reckless, for the government's use of informers was by then notorious and it was Edwards who was always urging his fellow-members to desperate acts of violence – meanwhile writing copious reports to his masters on the preparations for a rising. These reports, in crabbed handwriting on long thin strips of paper, show how cunningly he baited his trap. Davidson had great physical strength and courage – just the qualities that Arthur Thistlewood was looking for. Thistlewood was one of London's most influential radical leaders and organizers, who had earned fame and a year's imprisonment by challenging the home secretary, Viscount Sidmouth, to a duel. Thistlewood, like many others, was burning with indignation over the Peterloo massacre. He thirsted for revenge on the Cabinet of tyrants whom he held responsible for this crime – notably the hated Viscount Castlereagh, of whom Shelley wrote that autumn:

> I met Murder on the way –
> He had a mask like Castlereagh.[8]

And Thistlewood, again like many others, was certain that a mass uprising was imminent. The country was seething with unrest. All that was needed, many supposed, was a dramatic signal. By the end of 1819 Thistlewood had gathered round him a group of about 30 poor and determined men who believed that assassination was the only way to dislodge a government of murderous tyrants. Most of them were shoemakers, who still called each other 'Citizen' in the old Jacobin manner. Edwards the police spy was one of Thistlewood's best recruiters. It was he who introduced 'Black Davidson' to the group. Before long Davidson had become secretary of the newly formed shoemakers' trade union,[9] and was chairing meetings of the 'Committee of Thirteen' and 'Executive of Five'.

It was Edwards the police spy who, at these meetings, urged plan after plan for executing the guilty members of the government. One of his schemes was to blow up the House of Commons. But Thistlewood and the others rejected each fresh plan in turn because they did not want the innocent to suffer with the guilty. At length, an announcement planted by the government in the *New Times* gave them, as they supposed, the chance they were waiting for. The Cabinet, it said, would be dining all together at the Grosvenor Square house of Lord Harrowby, Lord President of the Council (for whom Davidson had worked for a time and in whose opinion he was 'a damned seditious fellow').[10] It was decided to kill the ministers as they sat at dinner. This would serve as the signal for an insurrection. Barracks would be set on fire, artillery seized, strategic locations in London occupied, and a prepared proclamation issued to rally the country around a provisional government installed in the Mansion House. Even now, Thistlewood and his supporters were merely agreeing to a plan suggested to them, in every detail, by Edwards.

One account says that it was Edwards who gave Davidson some money to get his blunderbuss out of pawn – though, according to another version, Davidson obtained the necessary 30*s*. from the Society for the Suppression of Mendicity 'under pretence of redeeming his Working tools'. Davidson had in fact been found begging in the street the previous January; he told the society that he had pawned his tools and other property for nearly £50, and had been out of work and had 'not earned one penny for the last 18 weeks'.[11]

At all events, Davidson was appointed by Thistlewood's group to raise money and buy weapons. There was nothing exceptional in this. All over the country, working men were arming; if there were more attacks on radical demonstrations, all the casualties would not be on one side. So Davidson bought 450 muskets and 2,700 rounds of ammunition – and was canny enough to keep none of them in his house, so that when it was searched in the December nothing was found. He was given gunpowder by the Marylebone Union Reading Society, apparently as a gesture of support from some of the many radicals who were not told details of the assassination plan but knew that a rising was on the cards. There is a story that he took seven or eight old files to be sharpened for pike-heads – this sort of activity, too, was widespread all over the country – and that he replied, when asked if they were for turning tools: 'They are for turning men's guts out.'[12] Because he was physically strong and a capable swordsman, it was Davidson who was posted as sentry in the Cato Street loft, just off the Edgware Road, where the group kept their store of home-made grenades, muskets, pistols, cartridges, swords, and pikes.

As they were about to set out for Grosvenor Square, police stormed the loft. Amid shouts of 'Kill the buggers!' Thistlewood stabbed a Bow Street constable to death and escaped, only to be arrested next day at a hide-out known to Edwards. Davidson fired a shot at one intruder and aimed a cutlass blow at the commander of the raiding party, Lieutenant Frederick Fitzclarence of the Coldstream Guards, bastard son of the future King William IV. But he was overpowered and led away, 'damning every Person that would not die in liberty's cause' and singing 'Scots wha hae wi' Wallace bled' until his captors silenced him.[13]

There was no rising in London. Almost simultaneous insurrections were attempted, but fizzled out, in Barnsley, Huddersfield, and Sheffield,[14] and about 60,000 weavers went on spy-fomented strike in Glasgow and Paisley. The Scottish insurgents were defeated in the 'Battle of Bonnymuir' and three men were put to death. Then the movement collapsed.

When Thistlewood, Davidson, and their three companions stood trial for high treason, before the lord chief justice and a series of carefully selected juries,[15] Edwards was not called as a witness. He had been packed off to Guernsey under a false name to protect his hide.[16] Instead, the prosecution relied very largely on the testimony of Robert Adams, a shoemaker who had turned king's evidence. Davidson and Tidd were tried together. Davidson pleaded not guilty and suggested that his colour might go against him, whereupon one of the judges assured him: 'God forbid that the complexion of the accused should enter, for a single moment, into the consideration of the Jury.' Davidson told the court that his house had been practically torn down in the search for incriminating evidence; but none had been found.[17] In his final plea, he complained of a biased trial and an unfair summing up. Then, referring to Magna Charta, he defended the English tradition of resistance to tyranny. It was, he declared, an ancient custom

> with arms to stand and claim their rights as Englishmen; and if every Englishman felt as I do, they would always do that . . . And our history goes on further to say, that when another of their Majesties the Kings of England tried to infringe upon those rights, the people armed, and told him that if he did not give them the privileges of Englishmen, they would compel him by the point of the sword . . . Would you not rather govern a country of spirited men, than cowards? . . . I can die but once in this world, and the only regret left is, that I have a large family of small children, and when I think of that, it unmans me.[18]

The five accused were all sentenced to be hanged, to have their heads severed from their bodies, and to have their bodies divided into four quarters; but this last part of the sentence was remitted by the king.

Though their dream of tyrannicide had failed miserably, the five revolutionaries died bravely. Brought from his cell, Davidson 'ascended the scaffold with a firm step, calm deportment, and undismayed countenance. He bowed to the crowd, but his conduct altogether was equally free from the appearance of terror, and the affectation of indifference.'[19] He said his prayers and clasped the hand of the attendant clergyman. Then the drop fell. The five widows begged the king, in a letter signed by them all, to be allowed to take away 'the mutilated remains of their deceased husbands' for decent burial.[20] But the bodies were buried in quicklime in an underground prison passage.[21]

The radical freethinker Richard Carlile, then in Dorchester jail as a result of his fight for a free press, had suspected Davidson of being an *agent provocateur*. Davidson had offered to spring Carlile from jail; Carlile was more cautious and less trusting than most of his contemporaries and hotly denounced Davidson in his journal *The Republican* soon after the Cato Street group was arrested. It was characteristic of Carlile that, when Davidson was hanged, he not only sent Mrs Davidson £2 and asked others to help her too, but also wrote a public letter of apology:

> Little did I think that villain Edwards was the spy, agent, and instigator of the government, and Mr. Davidson his victim. I now regret my error, and hope that you will pardon it as an error of the head, without any bad motive . . . Be assured that the heroic manner in which your husband and his companions met their fate, will in a few years, perhaps in a few months, stamp their names as patriots, and men who had nothing but their country's weal at heart. I flatter myself as your children grow up, they will find that the fate of their father will rather procure them respect and admiration than its reverse.[22]

Robert Wedderburn

Freedom of the press was not handed to the British people on a plate by enlightened rulers. It was fought for and won by the working-class radicals of the early nineteenth century, a number of whom served prison sentences for publishing opinions, on religious and other matters, which challenged the ideas of the ruling class. In 1817 alone there were 26 prosecutions for seditious and blasphemous libel. But the radicals persisted. One of those imprisoned for freedom of speech was a black radical tailor named Robert Wedderburn, who led a spencean group in London.

Wedderburn was some 25 years older than Davidson, having been born in Jamaica in 1762 or 1763. We know rather less about his life than about Davidson's. But we do know that his mother, Rosanna, was a slave on the estate of Lady Douglas, a distant relative of the Duke of Queensberry, and that his father, James Wedderburn, who came from Inveresk, near Edinburgh, owned large sugar plantations on the island. James Wedderburn had Rosanna bought for him in another planter's name and sold her back to Lady

Douglas when she was five months pregnant, stipulating that the child she bore should be free from birth.[23] That child was Robert Wedderburn. He was cared for by his grandmother, 'Talkee Amy', a Kingston merchant who made a little extra on the side by handling smuggled goods. When Robert was about 11 he had the searing experience of seeing his grandmother flogged by a white man who fancied she had bewitched his uncle's ship, causing it to be captured by the Spaniards: 'He tied up the poor old woman of seventy years, and flogged her to that degree, that she would have died, but for the interference of a neighbour'.[24] Robert also saw his mother flogged, while pregnant, by a certain Dr Boswell, whose friend Captain Parr was notorious for having chained a woman slave to a stake until she starved to death.[25] Forty years later, Robert's blood still boiled when he recalled these scenes, and he wrote in a journal he edited and published:

> My heart glows with revenge, and cannot forgive. Repent ye christians, for flogging my aged grandmother before my face, when she was accused of witchcraft by a silly European. O Boswell, ought not your colour and countrymen to be visited with wrath, for flogging my mother before my face, at the time when she was far advanced in pregnancy. What was her crime? did not you give her leave to visit her aged mother; (she did not acquaint her mistress at her departure,) this was her fault. But it originates in your crime of holding her as a slave.[26]

In 1778, when he was 17, Robert Wedderburn came to Britain. He went to sea, serving first on a warship (where he learnt gunnery) then on a privateer.[27] Later in life he was a jobbing tailor; perhaps his apprenticeship or his time at sea was what he meant by seven years spent 'amongst a set of abandoned reprobates'. One Sunday he heard a Wesleyan preacher at Seven Dials and became intensely interested in ideas, including those of various fringe groups of unorthodox christians: Arminians, Calvinists, and Unitarians. At some stage he was licensed as a Unitarian preacher, which entitled him to put 'Reverend' before his name.[28] About the year 1790 he wrote and published a pamphlet called *Truth, Self-supported; or, A refutation of certain doctrinal errors, generally adopted In the Christian Church*, in which he rejected the doctrine of the Trinity.

When Wedderburn was 51 or 52 he met Thomas Spence. Spence had only nine months left to live, but in that time he clearly had much influence on the Jamaican, who joined the Society of Spencean Philanthropists and became, as he put it nearly 20 years later, 'an attentive and active member'. In March 1817 an Act of Parliament was passed with the aim of suppressing the spenceans, and Wedderburn first came into prominence when their leader Thomas Evans and his 20-year-old son were jailed later that year for 'high treason'. They had dared to advocate in print the expropriation of the landowners, 'than which', as E.P.Thompson remarks, 'a Parliament of landowners could imagine no greater crime'.[29] Wedderburn's first periodical, *The 'Forlorn Hope', or A Call to the Supine, To rouse from Indolence and assert Public Rights*, launched in 1817 'to establish something in the shape of a free Press', carried in its first issue Mrs Evans's appeal for help for her imprisoned husband and son.[30]

The movement, as has been made clear, was plagued by spies and informers. But it is from their reports that we can piece together some picture of Wedderburn's political activities – though naturally such material has to be interpreted with caution. One spy comes up with the news that Wedderburn has been chosen to lead Evans's group after Evans is jailed. Then there is apparently a merger with a spencean group led by the apothecary 'Dr' James Watson, charged but acquitted for his part in the previous year's Spa Fields riots.[31] Another spy takes us into the Mulberry Tree tavern in Long Alley, Moorfields, one of the spenceans' four regular meeting places in London. It is 'Polemic Society' night. The room, which holds 100 people with ease, is 'crowded to Suffocation' with as many as 150, all very poor. The meeting starts at eight in the evening and goes on for five hours. Pamphlets representing various shades of radical opinion are on sale, and 'Wedderburn, a noted Spencean is very active', distributing 'Seditious Pamphlets'. Readings are given from well-known radical writers: William Cobbett, W.T.Sherwin, and Jonathan Wooler. The landlord is sympathetic, looks hard at everyone entering the club-room, and if a stranger comes in signals to the speaker; then 'the subject of Spies is started and violent declarations made as to the Manner they would treat a Spy if discovered'.[32] The spy's state of mind at this moment is not hard to imagine.

When Evans came out of jail the two leaders quarrelled, accusing each other of stealing group property. Evans tried to have Wedderburn charged with felony; Wedderburn alleged that Evans, whom he called 'my apostate son' and 'a Double-Faced Politician', had broken into his house and taken away a stool.[33] This dispute seems to have stimulated Wedderburn to open his own meeting-house, in the shape of a Unitarian chapel in Hopkins Street, Soho, where he and the spencean shoemaker-poet Allen Davenport were reported to be making 'very violent, seditious, and bitterly anti-Christian Spencean speeches'. By the autumn of 1819 up to 200 people were paying 6*d.* a head to attend debates on Monday and Wednesday evenings, besides 'Lectures every Sabbath day on Theology, Morality, Natural Philosophy, and Politics, by a Self-Taught West Indian'.[34] The Sunday audiences were disapprovingly referred to by a spy as 'mostly young Men: who kept their Hats on and applauded any thing that he ridiculed in the Scriptures most violent'.[35] Wedderburn, who described himself as '*The Offspring of an African*', was '*highly gratified*' by the outcome of a debate on whether a slave had the right to kill a master. This question 'was decided in Favor of the Slave without a dissenting Voice, by a numerous and enlightened Assembly, who exultingly expressed their Desire of hearing of another sable Nation freeing itself by the Dagger from the base Tyranny of their Christian Masters'; indeed, '*Several Gentlemen declared their readiness to assist them*'.[36] This led the authorities to prosecute Wedderburn for sedition and blasphemy.[37] He was locked up briefly in Newgate jail until £200 bail was raised for him by means of the following handbill:

> To the Philanthropists Of every Denomination, Are the following Lines addressed, stating the Case of *Robert Wedderburn*, a Prisoner in *Newgate*, – for what he knows not! but £200 Bail is required of him, which he is not able to procure. His Political and Theological Sentiments being well known to the World, through his Exertions at *Hopkins Street*, and other Public Meetings, supersedes the necessity of his giving particulars of those Sentiments; but the Public may rest assured that he is fully persuaded that no Persecutions from the Tyrant, the Bigot, or the Hypocrite will be able to move him from the cause of Truth and Justice.
>
> Should the candid [i.e. impartial] and independent Public think him worthy of their Assistance, Subscriptions will be thankfully received.[38]

A few days later the political climate was transformed by Peterloo, when Manchester factory-owners, merchants, and shopkeepers on horseback – the Yeomanry – brought the class war to the working people of Lancashire with the blades of their sabres. Week after week these events and their implications were discussed at the Hopkins Street chapel. 'Is the slaughter at Manchester Legal or Not?' was the subject on 13 and 15 September, with Wedderburn as main speaker and about 60 in the audience. It was 'unanimously agreed it was an act of Murder, committed by the Magistrates and Yeomen'. A fortnight later, with a fraternal delegate from Manchester present, they debated whether Peterloo was the start of the revolution, and an informer reported Wedderburn as saying:

> I am not such a fool to suppose nor to advise that the poor and half starved part of the Population should meet the regular Army of the Borough mongers in the field because they would have no chance, one party being armed & the other not, but arms are now preparing as fast as the means of paying for them will admit.

The revolution, he added, would give land to the soldiers. On 4 October he called the ministers and prince regent 'bloody Tyrants' and told his hearers: 'Arm & be ready, the day is near at hand.' Two days later: 'We must all learn to use the Gun the Dagger, the Cutlass and the Pistols – We shall then be able to defy all the Yeomanry of England.' Later that month he said the revolution had begun in blood at Manchester and must now end in blood; old as he was – 57 – he was learning his exercise as a soldier and hoped to live to see the revolution victorious. 'It is the Duty of every one to arm . . . But if we cant all get Arms, theirs them Iron railings in front of these Big fellows Houses . . . they will make excellent Pikes used by a strong Arm.' Wedderburn never lost this faith in the imminent overthrow of 'these Bloody Murdering thieves who would rob us of the Shirt from of our Backs'. 'The Poor would be Victorious, should a Civil War Commence', declared one of his handbills.[39]

Yet even in the turbulent aftermath of Peterloo, Wedderburn and his group did not neglect the issue of colonial slavery. A meeting at the chapel in November heard two black West Indian speakers, specially invited by Wedderburn to expose a Wesleyan scheme for sending missionaries to the West Indies. He and his fellow-spenceans saw missionaries as 'vipers' and 'church robbers' whose role was to try to make the slaves submit instead of rebelling, at the same time taking money from them. 'Which is the greater crime', he demanded, 'to preach passive obedience to the Poor Black Slaves . . . or to extort from them at the rate of £18,000 per an[nu]m under the pretence of supporting the Gospel'.[40]

Wedderburn was also busy writing pamphlets, with such titles as *A shove for a heavy-breach'd Christian*, *Crutches for the lame in faith*,

High-heel'd shoes for dwarfs in holiness, and *Cast-iron parsons; or Hints to the public and the legislature, on political economy: clearly proving that the clergy can be entirely dispensed with*. Two of his pamphlets, an open letter to the Chief Rabbi and *A critical, historical and admonitory letter to the . . . Archbishop of Canterbury*, are described by J.M.Robertson, the historian of freethought, as showing 'a happy vein of orderly irony and not a little learning'.[41] But again, not all his writings were on theoretical and religious questions; some were addressed to fellow-Jamaicans still oppressed by slavery, and Wedderburn found ways of getting copies out to Jamaica, where they caused consternation in the planters' assembly.[42]

This was the first revolutionary propaganda sent to the West Indies from Britain, and the content is fascinating. Wedderburn suggests an annual one-hour strike by all the slaves on the island. He advises strongly against petitions for emancipation, 'for it is degrading to human nature to petition your oppressors'. And, whatever happens, they must gain and keep control of the land: 'Take warning by the sufferings of the European poor, and never give up your lands.' Wedderburn was fired by the vision of a simultaneous revolution of the white poor of Europe and the black slaves of the West Indies. He warns the planters: 'Prepare for flight, . . . for the fate of St. Domingo awaits you. Get ready your blood hounds, the allies which you employed against the Maroons.' And he warns the slaves: 'You will have need of all your strength to defend yourself against those men, who are now scheming in Europe against the blacks of St. Domingo.' His own position he makes defiantly plain:

> Oh, ye Africans and relatives now in bondage to the Christians because you are innocent and poor; receive this the only tribute the offspring of an African can give, for which, I may ere long be lodged in a prison . . . ; for it is a crime now in England to speak against oppression . . . I am a West-Indian, a lover of liberty, and would dishonour human nature if I did not shew myself a friend to the liberty of others.[43]

We catch a glimpse of Wedderburn as political leader and tactician when we find him supporting a break with the popular radical orator Henry Hunt. For three years Hunt had been an ally of the spenceans; but it was an alliance based on mutual convenience rather than harmony of principles, and it could not long survive Peterloo. Wedderburn came out against Hunt on the ground that 'his principles of Reform would not suit their purpose, which must be nothing short of a Revolution – and that they had now force enough to carry on their plans independent of the Huntites' – and independently, he added, of the middle-class supporters of the radical MP Sir Francis Burdett.[44] Though some historians make much of Wedderburn's alleged violence and extremism, he was in fact far more cautious and sensible than Thistlewood. He opposed as premature the idea of an insurrection in London in November 1819, and that may have been why his group split. They could not, he argued, count on more than 2,000 people in London, and not all of these were armed; better, therefore, to wait until Parliament roused popular fury by suspending habeas corpus.[45] Wedderburn had contacts among London's Irish community, who assured him that they would join the uprising when it began.[46]

When Wedderburn stood trial the sedition charge was apparently dropped. He was accused of 'blasphemous libel' – a convenient way of muzzling dissenters in an age when political and religious dissent were closely connected, and the charge most likely to obtain a conviction.[47] A parish constable named William Plush testified that he had heard Wedderburn call Moses 'a d——d old liar for saying that he had seen God, when according to Jesus Christ no man had ever seen God'. Moreover, Wedderburn had said that 'as religion is part of the law of the land . . . your fat-gutted parsons, priests, or bishops, would see Jesus Christ d——d, or God Almighty either, rather than give up their twenty or thirty thousand a year, and become poor curates at twenty pounds per annum'.[48] In court Wedderburn defended himself so ably that the lord chief justice had to acknowledge that his defence was 'exceedingly well drawn up'.[49] Wedderburn said to the jury:

> Where, after all, is my crime? – it consists merely in having spoken in the same plain and homely language which Christ and his disciples uniformly used . . . There seems to be a conspiracy against the poor, to keep them in ignorance and superstition; the rich may have as many copies as they like of . . . sceptical writers . . . ; but if I find two most decided contradictions in the bible, I must not in the language of the same book assert that one or the other is a lie . . .
>
> As to my explanation of the doctrines of Christ, I must still maintain it to be particularly faithful. He was like myself, one of the lower order, and a genuine radical reformer. Being poor himself, he knew how to feel for the poor, and despised the rich for the hardness of their hearts. His principles were *purely republican*; he told his followers they were all brethren

> and equals, and inculcated a thorough contempt for all the titles, pomps, and dignities of this world . . .
>
> As NATURE has blest me with a calm and tranquil mind, I shall be far happier in the dungeon to which you may consign me, than my persecutors, on their beds of down.[50]

Found guilty, Wedderburn was sent to join Carlile in Dorchester jail for two years. A contemporary comment pointed out that he had been

> thrust into a solitary dungeon for TWO YEARS, to live upon grey pease, and barley broth, merely because he differed in opinion from the State religion, and had too much honesty, and too little education to wrap his sentiments up in that *cautious*, *decent*, and *guarded* manner which the Solicitor-General said he could tolerate.[51]

Though submerged in the 1820s, the spencean tradition did not die out. In the early 1830s old spenceans were members of the National Union of the Working Classes, and Others; Spence's ideas had much influence on Robert Owen's socialist theories and on the owenite movement; and veteran spenceans were to play an 'important and continuous' role in London Chartism.[52] Of Wedderburn's contribution after he came out of jail, however, disappointingly little is known. In 1824 he published an autobiographical sketch, *The Horrors of Slavery*, in which he declared that he would have gone back to Jamaica had he not been afraid of the planters – 'for such is their hatred of any one having black blood in his veins, and who dares to think and act as a free man, that they would most certainly have trumped up some charge against me, and hung me. With them I should have had no mercy.'[53] He got precious little mercy from the English courts. In 1831, when he was 68, he was serving a sentence of hard labour for his part in an affray outside a brothel.[54] He wrote from the Giltspur Street prison to the reformer Francis Place in reply to an inquiry about Thomas Spence. (For the text of this letter, see appendix C, p. 406.) What became of him when he was released is not known.

The everyday struggle, 1787–1833

It is hardly surprising that, of the black people living in Britain in this period whose names are known, so many were fighters of one sort or another: political activists or prize-fighters. (For the black prize-fighters of the eighteenth and nineteenth centuries, see appendix I, pp. 445–54.) Everyday life was a grim struggle for all poor people in those days. The great majority of the black people who lived in Britain were very poor indeed and had to fight, in one way or another, to survive. Daily experience knocked into black people the art of self-defence, with brains for choice, with fists or other weapons as a last resort. To be a radical or a boxer was merely to apply, at a public level, a lesson transmitted by oral tradition and reinforced on the street every day of one's life.

Whoever did not learn this lesson was liable to become a victim. One such victim, chained to his master's table like a dog, was rescued by the long arm of the African Institution from a house in Long Acre, in the heart of London, in 1814. According to the master, the lad he had chained up and 'otherwise ill treated' was his apprentice, whom he had brought from the West Indies two months before and who had cheated him of money and stolen his wine. No, he could not produce the boy's indentures. No, he had not paid him any wages. He had been going to send him back to the West Indies by the next fleet and had chained him up to stop him running away.[1] Other victims were the black children sold as house-boys in Westmorland early in the nineteenth century. The Liverpool merchant John Bolton would pick out young boys from his slave cargoes and transfer them to Greenodd. A local man would smuggle them up the Leven valley to Windermere, where they were taken to Storrs Hall, which Bolton owned, and sold to the surrounding gentry.[2] Other victims again were the black youths who toiled in the marble quarries at Rigg End, near Dent in the West Riding, in the same period. Rigg End, right up in the fells, was owned by a Liverpool slave-merchant called Sill, who had black servants in his fine new house, not far from the quarries.[3]

Victims of another kind were the Africans, and descendants of Africans, exhibited as freaks for public amusement. Mrs Amelia Lewsam (or Newsham), 'the White Negro Woman', brought from Jamaica in 1754 at the age of about five, was offered for sale as 'the greatest Phænomenon ever known'. The price demanded was 400 guineas, but probably much less was paid. At all events, the little girl was being exhibited a year later at Charing Cross, where people paid a shilling a head to gawp at her. She was described as having 'all the features of an Æthiopian, with a flaxen woolly Head, a Skin and Complexion fair as the Alabaster'. In 1788 she was exhibited again, at Bartholomew Fair.[4] Sixteen-year-old Primrose, 'The Celebrated PIEBALD BOY', born in Jamaica of African parents, was on display in

London's Haymarket in the following year.[5] George Alexander Gratton, 'the beautiful spotted negro boy', was born to an African couple on the island of St Vincent in 1808 and brought to Bristol at the age of 15 months, and was soon being exhibited at 41 Strand (from 11 a.m. to dusk), Bartholomew Fair, and elsewhere. At the theatre of the travelling showman John Richardson 'he stood on the bills between the *Monk and Murderer*, or the *Skeleton Spectre*, and *Love and Liberty*, or *Harlequin in his Glory*'. Though he became Richardson's favourite among his freaks, the child had not long to live. His tombstone, in the churchyard at Marlow, Buckinghamshire, says he died on 3 February 1815, aged 4 years and 9 months.[6]

Most painful of all is the story of Saartjie Baartman, probably a San ('Bushwoman'). Daughter of a cattle-drover, she was brought to Britain in 1810 by a Boer farmer called Hendrik Cezar, who saw commercial possibilities in her large buttocks. Told that she could make her fortune by letting herself be put on public display, and promised repatriation after two years – a promise which was not kept – she was exhibited at 225 Piccadilly as the 'Hottentot Venus'. Spectators were charged 2*s*. a head. The exhibition was, by present-day standards, wholly degrading; and even in regency London there were some who protested. *The Times* said that Saartjie was 'produced like a wild beast, and ordered to move backwards and forwards, and come out and go into her cage, more like a bear in a chain than a human being'. A letter in the *Morning Post* complained that she was exhibited 'like a *prize ox* or a *rattle-snake*'; one in the *Morning Chronicle* reported that, when she seemed tired, her master 'holds up a *stick to her, like the wild beast keepers*, to intimidate her into obedience'. Another visitor 'found her surrounded by many persons, some *females!* One pinched her, another walked round her; one gentleman *poked* her with his cane; and one *lady* employed her parasol to ascertain that all was, as she called it, "*nattral*"'. Not surprisingly, Saartjie was often heard to sigh deeply and seemed anxious and uneasy. Some of those who objected took Cezar to court, but the case was dismissed after Saartjie had been interviewed for three hours, through interpreters (using Dutch) and in the presence of representatives from both sides. The interview established – to the court's satisfaction, at any rate – that she was under no restraint, was happy in England, and was under contract to receive a share of the profits. But it is highly likely that the contract was drawn up in haste and antedated.

Saartjie featured in coarse street ballads and even coarser political cartoons. She was baptized in Manchester on 1 December 1811, under the name Sarah Bartmann, and was reported to have married a black man by whom she had two children. In 1814 she was again exhibited, for 11 hours a day – this time in Paris, where she died on 29 December 1815. Her corpse was treated with still less dignity than her living body. Before dissecting it, the naturalist Cuvier made plaster casts of it and wax moulds of her genitals and anus. A replica of these moulds was presented to the Royal Academy of Medicine ('J'ai l'honneur de présenter à l'Académie', wrote Cuvier, 'les organes génitaux de cette femme'), and Saartjie's skeleton and brain, too, were preserved for posterity and may still be seen, with a plaster cast of her body, in the arrestingly named Musée de l'Homme, in Paris.[7]

There were a good many beggars among London's black population in the early nineteenth century, much as there had been in the mid-1780s. 'In Angel-Gardens and Blue Gate Fields, about twelve beggars, four of them blacks', reported a parliamentary committee in 1815.[8] The Society for the Suppression of Mendicity concerned itself with approximately 400 black beggars in the years 1820 to 1826 inclusive – roughly one in 40 of the beggars who came to its notice in those years.[9] This average of 60 or so black beggars passing through the society's hands each year dropped sharply to four in 1827,[10] in line with a general, though far more gradual, decline in the the size of the black population as a whole, for 'the death rate in London was high and there was little fresh immigration'.[11]

Undoubtedly a great many black beggars managed to slip through the society's net. Its treatment of some of those it did catch gave those it did not excellent reasons for keeping out of its clutches if they could. In 1819 it was responsible for sending a Jamaican to the house of correction for seven days. In 1820 it had another Jamaican, aged 58, imprisoned for six months and 'well flogged'; he had a previous history of begging. And in the same year a young Barbadian, formerly a ship's cook, who had been sleeping rough for several nights, had not eaten for several days, and was taken to the society's office 'in a miserable state', was shunted into a workhouse – probably a worse place to be than a house of correction.[12] Of course this is not the whole story. In 1822 a black man born in New York, who had served in the British navy for many years, was fainting with hunger and nearly naked when he reached the office, and the society did manage to squeeze out of a reluctant Admiralty the £47 due to him as prize money.[13] But to keep out of the hands of this charity, if one possibly could, was simple common sense. A parliamentary committee recommended in 1816 that black beggars should be deported to the West Indies, which could be done 'at no great expense'.[14] Threats of that kind, which spelt slavery, sharpened their wits and toughened them. Cornered, they would put up a desperate struggle, like the beggar who pulled a knife on his persecutors in 1815[15] or the young Haitian whose friends came to his aid when he was grabbed by four of the Mendicity Society's busybodies in Mayfair in 1821:

> J.F. aged 22, a native of St. Domingo, was apprehended in Park-lane, by four of the Society's officers, after a most desperate resistance, during which, the constables were compelled to use their staves, in consequence of five other blacks attempting a rescue . . . The prisoner . . . was handcuffed to the iron railing until a coach was procured. He however, escaped, but was stopped by a Soldier . . . He was . . . brought up at Clerkenwell Sessions, sentenced to be imprisoned for three months, and to be twice flogged during that period.[16]

Most of the beggars 'apprehended' in this way seem to have been transients in the profession. The survival against heavy odds of those who turned professional earned them both the grudging respect of the better-off (in the form of persistent folklore about the immense wealth they were supposed to accumulate)[17] and the ungrudging tribute of London's down-and-outs, who elected the black one-legged violinist Billy Waters 'King of the Beggars' and turned out in force for his funeral in 1823.

Married, with two children, 'Black Billy' had lost a leg in 'his Majesty's service', and was famous for his feathered hat and 'peculiar antics': 'Every child in London knew him.' He and his successor as 'King of the Beggars', a crippled dwarf called Andrew Whiston, together with 'Black Sal' and a dustman known variously as 'Nasty Bob' and 'Dusty Bob', became the four favourite characters in the best stage version of Pierce Egan's *Life in London*.[18] These four are immortalized in the vigorous Cruikshank illustrations to Egan's book, as is another successful black beggar, the one-eyed 'Massa Piebald', whose real name was Charles M'Gee.

Born in Jamaica in 1744, of a father who lived to be 108, M'Gee was a familiar figure on his regular pitch at the bottom of Ludgate Hill, with his white hair tied up behind in a tail. He was said to have bequeathed 'many hundred pounds' to a lady who 'not only gave him a penny or a halfpenny more frequently than any one else, but enhanced the value of the gift by condescending to accompany it with a gracious smile'.[19]

Toby, another well-known black beggar, who lived in Church Lane, St Giles, 'was destitute of toes, had his head bound with a white handkerchief, and bent himself almost double to walk upon two hand-crutches, with which he nearly occupied the width of the pavement'.[20]

One of the best-known black mendicants in London was the merchant seaman turned street singer Joseph Johnson, famous for the model of a sailing ship which he built and carried round on his cap. 'By a bow of thanks, or a supplicatory inclination to a drawing-room window', he could give this model 'the appearance of sea-motion'. A 'Regular Chaunter', Johnson often hitched a lift in a farmer's wagon to such market towns as Romford, St Albans, and Staines, where he would entertain the local people with nautical ditties: *The British Seaman's Praise* and *The Wooden Walls of Old England*.[21]

Were these successful professional beggars victims or fighters? They were fighters who consciously adopted the role of victim and knew how to make it pay. Generally they had something to offer: music, a colourful costume, a gimmick of some sort, if only a witty turn of phrase. 'Black men', said a writer on mendicants in 1817, 'are extremely cunning and often witty.'[22] In every sense, the professional beggars lived on their wits. That was their weapon in the fight to survive.

Their success in this fight contrasts with the hard lot of most of the Lascars in London in the same period – though a few of these Indian seamen, shanghaied, then dumped in a cold and inhospitable foreign land, did manage to join the ranks of the professional beggars. One was reported in 1817 to be making an average of 15*s*. a week – almost certainly an exaggeration – hawking halfpenny ballads round the streets.[23]

Over 1,000 of his countrymen lived in a barracks in Ratcliff Highway, where the East India Company, legally obliged from 1814 to feed, clothe, and shelter them, paid a contractor 1*s*. 6*d*. a day for their board and lodging.[24] It was estimated that at least 130 Lascars had died in Britain in each of the years from 1790 to 1810, and that this death rate doubled in 1813. During the severe winter of 1813–14, by the company's own admission, Lascars at the barracks were dying at the rate of almost two per week and five died in one single bitterly cold day.[25] When company officials heard that some of these men had been complaining of their treatment, they 'resolved to send the grumblers off by the first ship'.[26] There was plenty to grumble about. A parliamentary committee, visiting the barracks without notice, found that they were often overcrowded; that there was neither bedding nor furniture nor fireplace nor proper accommodation for the sick; that the men slept on a plank floor, making do with one blanket apiece.[27] The company publicly admitted that the superintendent and his assistants used to strike the men in their care.[28] Missionaries and magistrates joined in a racist chorus of hate:

> They are the senseless worshippers of dumb idols, or the deluded followers of the licentious doctrines of a false prophet . . . They are enemies to God by wicked words . . . They are practically and abominably wicked . . . They have none, or scarcely any, who will associate with them, but prostitutes, and no house that will receive them, except the public house, and the apartments of the abandoned . . . It is not to be denied that they are extremely depraved.[29]

That was the 'orthodox' christian view of Indian seamen in 1814. Three years later a London magistrate told a parliamentary committee that 'little good can be done by taking away the licences of [public] houses in Shadwell, for this reason, that the population consists entirely of foreign sailors, Lascars, Chinese, Greeks and other dirty filthy people of that description'.[30]

Not every single black person in Britain had to struggle. At the opposite end of the social spectrum from the black beggars and the despised Lascars, a small number of well-to-do black residents and visitors found themselves tolerated by white society, though often in a patronizing, 'tokenist' kind of way. The key to social acceptance was money. In 1805 a black man able to afford fashionable clothes could walk along Oxford Street arm in arm with a well-dressed white woman, unmolested and largely unremarked – except by a surprised and primly disapproving white American visitor.[31] Wealth, however modest, in the hands of a black person lent an exoticism that mere blackness by itself could no longer command. It was now possible, though exceptional, for a black servant to save enough money from his wages to make a will. Take, for example, James Martin. His life was typical of a slave-servant's: kidnapped in Africa, taken to the West Indies, sold to a planter, bought by a British officer who brought him to England. When Martin died at Clifton, near Bristol, in 1813 the event would have attracted no more attention than the deaths of so many of his fellows. But he had some modest savings, and he left half of them to the Church Missionary

Society, the other half to the African Institution, and this combined triumph of thrift and christianity was greatly to the taste of the times.[32]

The question the liberally minded asked themselves was: 'Is he a gentleman?' or 'Is she a lady?' In 1802 'men of colour in the rank of gentlemen' were commented on, as a sign of social change, by the blue-stocking Mrs Hester Piozzi. She also noticed 'a black Lady, cover'd with finery, in the Pit at the Opera, and tawny children playing in the Squares, – the gardens of the Squares, I mean, – with their Nurses'.[33] Clearly falling within the category of black 'gentlemen' were Prince Sanders or Saunders, a New Englander who served as Haiti's agent in London in 1816 and was taken up briefly by the middle-class abolitionists;[34] and Paul Cuffe, a black American sea captain born in Africa. Visiting Liverpool in 1811, four years after abolition of the British slave trade, Cuffe was himself tolerant enough to dine with two former slave-ship captains, who, as he recorded in his journal, treated him 'politely'.[35] The son of a St Lucia judge 'by a dark coloured woman', who had received from his father 'a good plain education at Liverpool', was described in 1831 as 'a young gentleman'.[36]

But tolerance often turned out to be a genteel cloak for racism, in that bland and irresponsible way that later became so familiar to black people looking for a job or for somewhere to live. 'Unfortunately he is a Mulatto, a native of the West Indies, which circumstance, added to a family of nine children, has kept him down in the world – where so dark a complexion is not objected to, he would make a very valuable Schoolmaster': thus a referee's confidential report on an applicant for a teaching post in Bisley, Gloucestershire, in 1815.[37] When members and friends of the African and Asian Society dined at a tavern in 1816, with Wilberforce in the chair, the token Africans and Asians invited to the gathering were separated from the other guests by a screen set across one end of the room.[38]

Black people were tolerated, after a fashion, if they had money, knew their place, and kept it. For black to marry white was, in the eyes of many, not just stepping out of place; it was contrary to nature. In 1804, when he was already moving towards political radicalism, William Cobbett demanded:

> Who, that has any sense or decency, can help being shocked at the familiar intercourse, which has gradually been gaining ground, and which has, at last, got a complete footing between

> the Negroes and the women of England? No black swain need, in this loving country, hang himself in despair. No inquiry is made whether he be a Pagan or a Christian; if he be not a downright cripple, he will, if he be so disposed, always find a woman, not merely to yield to his filthy embraces, that, among the notoriously polluted and abandoned part of the sex, would be less shocking, but to accompany him *to the altar*, to become his wife, to breed English mulattoes, to stamp the mark of Cain upon her family and her country! Amongst white women, this disregard of decency, this defiance of the dictates of nature, this foul, this beastly propensity, is, I say it with sorrow and with shame, *peculiar to the English*.[39]

Though he often wrote erratically as well as with gross prejudice, Cobbett here provides an accurate answer to the question that is often asked: What became of the black people, numbering 10,000 or so, who were living in Britain at the beginning of the nineteenth century? Males among them heavily outnumbered females: and, like Olaudah Equiano and Ukawsaw Gronniosaw and others before them, many of these black men married white women. At the 1816 dinner just referred to, chaired by Wilberforce, 'a black man led in a white woman, with a party-coloured child, the fruit of their mutual loves'.[40] The grandchildren of such unions – the children of the 'English mulattoes' that Cobbett wrote of so scornfully, the children of those 'tawny children' observed by Mrs Piozzi – no longer thought of themselves as constituting a distinct black community. They were part of the British poor. The records of their lives are obscure and scattered, and they have for the most part been forgotten by their descendants. But there must be many thousands of British families who, if they traced their roots back to the eighteenth or early nineteenth century, would find among their ancestors an African or person of African descent.

Let one example of this intermarriage serve for all the rest. We cannot call it typical, for each is in some way or other unique. This one is from Caernarvonshire, and the record spans close on 150 years.

John Ystumllyn, otherwise known as 'Jack Black', was kidnapped on the African coast around the year 1745, when he was about eight years old. According to oral tradition first published in 1888 and 'accepted as authentic' 70 years earlier, he 'spoke no proper language' but eventually acquired two: presumably Welsh and English. He was baptized at either Criccieth or Ynyscynhaiarn church;

learned to write; and was taught gardening. He is described as 'a meticulous and skilful worker', 'adept at mastering almost everything he saw others doing', such as making model boats, wooden spoons, and baskets. He loved flowers and grew them with success. He was 'an active, healthy looking youth and even though his skin was black, the local maidens used to dote on him and would compete for his favours'. The one who won his heart was a maidservant named Margaret, and they were married at Dolgellau church in 1768, with the son of Criccieth's vicar as best man. John was appointed steward at a local big house and took the name Jones. He died in July 1791 and was buried at Ynyscynhaiarn. He and his wife had raised a large family. Ann, their elder daughter, married a Liverpool musican and seller of musical instruments. One of their sons, Richard, became huntsman to Lord Newborough; described as a 'quiet, unassuming man', who used to wear top hat, velvet jacket, and high white collar, he died in 1862 at the age of 92 and was buried at Llandwrong, near Caernarvon, where his descendants were said to be still living in the 1880s.[41]

Does this widespread intermarriage, coupled with the dwindling of black immigration to a trickle, mean that Britain's black community disappeared in the last 60 years of the nineteenth century? Research in Liverpool clearly establishes that there never was a time, throughout the century, when that city did not have black citizens – and that those black citizens were always united by common problems and common interests.[42] There were black people in Cardiff, as we shall see, from the 1870s or earlier. How far a continuity of tradition and struggle was maintained elsewhere is a question that cannot be answered without detailed local inquiry. But if the black community as such shrank in size and importance for 100 years, black people were here to stay. In the next chapter we look at the lives and achievements of some of them.

9. Challenges to empire

The aim of this chapter is to describe the lives and achievements of some of the black people who lived in Britain between about 1830 and 1918. Some were born here; others, born in Africa, the West Indies, the United States, and India, made a permanent home here or stayed for months or years. They were active in politics, medicine, law, business, the theatre, music, dance, sport, journalism, local affairs. They included writers and men of God, orators and entertainers, two editors, a nurse, and a photographer. One, born in Chatham, was transported for life as a working-class rebel. Another, born in Liverpool, became mayor of Battersea. Another, born in Bombay, sat in the British House of Commons for three years as a Liberal MP. Two at least – the American actor Ira Aldridge and the London-born composer Samuel Coleridge-Taylor – were artists of genius. What these people had in common gives this chapter its title. All of them, in one way or another, to some degree or other, challenged empire or – it came to much the same thing – challenged racism. A black person leading any kind of public life in Britain could hardly help doing so. Long before the First World War, Asians living in Britain were active in the cause of Indian freedom from British rule. And, by the turn of the century, Africans and persons of African descent living in Britain had done much to create the political tradition known as Pan-Africanism, whose challenge to imperialism would later inspire freedom movements all over Africa and the Caribbean.

William Cuffay

A little tailor called William Cuffay was one of the leaders and martyrs of the Chartist movement, the first mass political movement of the British working class. His grandfather was an African, sold into slavery on the island of St Kitts, where his father was born a slave. Like Davidson and Wedderburn before him, Cuffay was made to suffer for his political beliefs and activities. In 1848, Europe's year of revolutions, he was put on trial for levying war against Queen

Victoria. At the age of 61 he was transported for life to Van Diemen's Land (now Tasmania), where, after being pardoned in 1856, he spent the rest of his days active in radical causes.

William Cuffay was born in Chatham in 1788.[1] Soon after coming to Britain his father, who had evidently been freed, found work as a cook on a warship. William was brought up in Chatham with his mother and his sister Juliana. As a boy, though 'of a very delicate constitution' – his spine and shin bones were deformed – he 'took a great delight in all manly exercises'.[2] He became a journeyman tailor in his late teens and stayed in that trade all his life. He married three times but left no children.[3]

Though he disapproved of the owenite Grand National Consolidated Trades Union, formed in 1834 on the initiative of the London tailors, and was nearly the last to join the appropriate affiliated lodge, Cuffay came out on strike with his fellow-members. As a result he was sacked from a job he had held for many years, and found it very hard to get work afterwards. That was what took him into politics. In 1839 he joined the great movement in support of the People's Charter drawn up by the cabinet-maker William Lovett with the help of Francis Place, demanding universal male suffrage, annual parliaments, vote by secret ballot, payment of MPs, abolition of property qualifications for MPs, and equal electoral districts. It was a year when 'magistrates trembled and peaceful citizens felt that they were living on a social volcano'[4] – a year when one noble general wrote to his brother: 'It looks as if the falling of an empire was beginning.'[5] Before long Cuffay, the neat, mild-mannered black tailor, 4ft 11in. tall, had emerged as one of the dozen or so most prominent leaders of the Chartist movement in London. Unlike the movement's more celebrated national leaders, these were artisans, for Chartism in the capital was 'a sustained movement which produced its own leaders, stuck to its traditional radicalism yet worked out its own class attitudes'.[6] In the autumn of 1839 Cuffay was helping to set up the Metropolitan Tailors' Charter Association – about 80 joined on the first night[7] – and in 1841 the Westminster Chartists sent him to represent them on the Metropolitan Delegate Council. In February 1842 Cuffay chaired a 'Great Public Meeting of the Tailors', at which a national petition to the Commons was adopted.[8] Later the same year the Metropolitan Delegate Council responded to the arrest of George Julian Harney and other national leaders by appointing Cuffay (as president) and three others to serve as an interim executive 'to supply the place of those whom a tyrannic Government has pounced upon'.[9]

For all his mildness of manner, Cuffay was a left-wing, militant Chartist from the beginning. He was in favour of heckling at meetings of the middle-class Complete Suffrage Movement and Anti-Corn Law League. His militancy earned him recognition in the press of the ruling class. *Punch* lampooned him savagely and *The Times* referred to London's Chartists as 'the Black man and his Party'; as a direct result of this press campaign his wife Mary Ann was sacked from her job as charwoman.[10] In 1844 Cuffay was a member of the Masters and Servants Bill Demonstration Committee, opposing a measure which would have given magistrates power to imprison a neglectful worker for two months merely on his employer's oath. The radical MP Thomas Slingsby Duncombe was chief parliamentary opponent of what he called 'one of the most insidious, oppressive, arbitrary, iniquitous, and tyrannical attempts to oppress the working classes that had ever been made',[11] and Cuffay was the tailors' delegate at meetings to arrange a soirée for Duncombe. A strong supporter of Feargus O'Connor's Chartist land scheme – the idea was to take the unemployed out of the slums and give each family two acres of good arable land – Cuffay moved the resolution at the Chartists' 1845 national convention 'that the Conference now draw up a plan to enable the people to purchase land and place the surplus labourers who subscribe thereto on such land'.[12] In 1846 he was one of London's three delegates to the Birmingham land conference, and he and another London tailor, James Knight, were appointed auditors to the National Land Company, which soon had 600 branches all over the country.[13] In the same year Cuffay served as one of the National Anti-Militia Association's ten directors and was a member of the Democratic Committee for Poland's Regeneration, of which Ernest Jones, friend of Marx and Engels, was president. In 1847 he was on the Central Registration and Election Committee, and in 1848 he was on the management committee for a Metropolitan Democratic Hall.*

For Cuffay, as for so many other working people in western Europe, 1848 was 'the year of decision'.[15] He was one of the three

* William Cuffay was by no means the only black man who played an active part in the London Chartist movement. Two of the leaders of a demonstration in Camberwell on 13 March 1848 were 'men of colour': David Anthony Duffy (or Duffey), a 21-year-old out-of-work seaman, described as 'a determined looking and powerful fellow' and known to the police as a beggar in the Mint, where he was said to go about 'without shirt, shoe, or stocking'; and another seaman, an 'active fellow' called Benjamin Prophitt (or Prophet), known as 'Black Ben', aged 29. Duffy was transported for seven years, Prophitt for fourteen.[14]

London delegates to the Chartists' national convention that met in the April. From the start of the proceedings he made his left-wing position plain. Derby had sent as delegate a sensational journalist and novelist called George Reynolds – he gave his name to what eventually became *Reynolds News* – and Cuffay challenged the middle-class newcomer, demanding to know if he really was a Chartist. Cuffay also at first opposed the granting of credentials to Charles M'Carthy of the Irish Democratic Federation, but the dispute was settled, and M'Carthy admitted, by a sub-committee of which Cuffay was a member. The convention's main task was to prepare a mass meeting on Kennington Common and a procession that was to accompany the Chartist petition, bearing almost two million signatures, to the Commons. When Reynolds moved an amendment declaring 'That in the event of the rejection of the Petition, the Convention should declare its sitting permanent, and should declare the Charter the law of the land', Cuffay said he was opposed to a body declaring itself permanent that represented only a fraction of the people: he was elected by only 2,000 out of the two million inhabitants of London. He moved that the convention should confine itself to presenting the petition, and that a national assembly be called – 'then come what might, it should declare its sittings permanent, and go on, come weal or come woe'.[16] At length the idea of a national assembly was accepted. In a later debate Cuffay told his fellow delegates that 'the men of London were up to the mark, and were eager for the fray'. In a speech sharply critical of the national leadership, he declared that the Irish patriots ('confederates')

> were also in an advanced state of preparation, and if a spark were laid to the train in Ireland, they would not wait for Chartists. A deputation from the two bodies met together on Monday night last, and the result was, that the confederates were ready to march in procession with them under the green flag of Erin (cheers). The trades were also coming out, and amongst the rest the tailors, to which he belonged (a laugh). Well, if they did not get what they wanted before a fortnight, he, for one, was ready to fall; and if the petition was rejected with scorn, he would move at once to form a rifle club (cheers) . . . He did think that their leader Feargus [O'Connor] was not quite up to the mark, and he suspected one or two more of the executive council strongly; and if he found that his suspicions were correct, he would move to have

> them turned out of office (laughter and cheers). The country had no right to despair of the men of London . . . There were only 5,000 soldiers in London.[17]

When a moderate speech was made, Cuffay burst out: 'This clapping of hands is all very fine, but will you fight for it?' There were cries of 'Yes, yes' and cheers.[18]

Appointed chairman of the committee for managing the procession, Cuffay was responsible for making sure that 'everything . . . necessary for conducting an immense procession with order and regularity had been adopted', and suggested that stewards wear tricolour sashes and rosettes. Things had now come to a crisis, he said, and they must be prepared to act with coolness and determination. It was clear that the executive had shrunk from their responsibility. They did not show the spirit they ought. He no longer had any confidence in them, and he hoped the convention would be prepared to take the responsibility out of their hands and lead the people on themselves.[19] At the final meeting, on the morning of the demonstration, Cuffay opposed endless debate. 'The time is now come for work', he insisted. An observer recorded that, as the convention broke up and delegates took their places on the vehicles carrying the petition, Cuffay 'appeared perfectly happy and elated' for the first time since the proceedings opened.[20]

The commissioner of police had declared that the proposed procession was illegal. The queen had been packed off to the Isle of Wight for her safety, and the royal carriages and horses and other valuables had been removed from the palace. Tens of thousands of lawyers, shopkeepers, and government clerks had been enrolled as special constables. All government buildings were prepared for attack: at the Foreign Office, the ground-floor windows were blocked with bound volumes of *The Times*, thought to be thick enough to stop bullets, and the clerks were issued with brand-new service muskets and ball cartridges. The British Museum was provided with 50 muskets and 100 cutlasses. The Bank of England was protected with sandbags. Along the Embankment, 7,000 soldiers were distributed at strategic points. Heavy gun batteries were brought up from Woolwich. The bridges were sealed off and guarded by over 4,000 police. O'Connor was interviewed by the commissioner of police – who said afterwards that he had never seen a man so frightened – and decided to call off the procession.

When the crowd at Kennington Common heard this, many of them were very angry. There were shouts that the petition should have been carried forward until actively opposed by the troops and then withdrawn altogether on the ground that such opposition was unlawful. One of the protesters was Cuffay, who

> spoke in strong language against the dispersal of the meeting, and contended that it would be time enough to evince their fear of the military when they met them face to face! He believed the whole Convention were a set of cowardly humbugs, and he would have nothing more to do with them. He then left the van, and got among the crowd, where he said that O'Connor must have known all this before, and that he ought to have informed them of it, so that they might have conveyed the petition at once to the House of Commons, without crossing the bridges. They had been completely caught in a trap.[21]

Cuffay was elected as one of the commissioners to promote the campaign for the Charter after its rejection by Parliament. As with Davidson and Wedderburn, however, most of our scanty information about his activities comes from police spies, one of whom was actually a member of the seven-strong 'Ulterior Committee' that was planning an uprising in London. Cuffay was certainly a late, and almost certainly a reluctant, member of this body. On 16 August 1848, 11 'luminaries', allegedly plotting to fire certain buildings as a signal for the rising, were arrested at a Bloomsbury tavern, the Orange Tree, near Red Lion Square. Cuffay was arrested later at his lodgings. He had not been a delegate to the committee for more than 12 days, and had not been elected secretary until 13 August.[22] So he was certainly not, as *The Times* called him, 'the very chief of the conspiracy'.[23] Indeed it is claimed that, before the police swooped, he had realized that the plan was premature and hopeless but, from solidarity, had refused to back out.[24] He could have gone underground, but he chose not to: he 'refused to fly, lest it should be said that he abandoned his associates in the hour of peril'.[25]

'CUFFEY', sneered *The Times*, ' . . . is half a "nigger". Some of the others are Irishmen. We doubt if there are half-a-dozen Englishmen in the whole lot.'[26] Cuffay's bearing in court soon wiped the smirk off the face of *The Times*. He pleaded not guilty in a loud voice and objected to being tried by a middle-class jury. 'I demand a fair trial by my peers,' he said, 'according to the principles of Magna Charta.' Then the prospective jurors were challenged, and one, asked if he had ever expressed an opinion as to Cuffay's guilt or innocence, or what ought to be the result of the trial, replied: 'Yes, I have expressed an opinion that they ought all to be hanged.' He was told to retire, 'and after considerable delay a jury was at length formed'. Though counsel for the boot cleaver Thomas Fay and the bootmaker William Lacey – two Chartists who stood in the dock with Cuffay – said his clients were satisfied, Cuffay made it clear that he himself was not. 'I wish it to be understood', he exclaimed, 'that I do object to this jury. They are not my equals – I am only a journeyman mechanic.'[27]

Cuffay's conviction for levying war on the queen was obtained through the evidence of two police spies. One, Thomas Powell, widely known as 'Lying Tom', said in cross-examination that he had told the Chartists how to make grenades: 'I told them that gunpowder must be put into an ink-bottle with an explosive cap, and I dare say I did say that it would be a capital thing to throw among the police if it had some nails in it.'[28] The other spy, George Davis, a second-hand book and furniture dealer from Greenwich and a member of the Chartists' 'Wat Tyler brigade' there, told how he had attended its meetings and 'reported within two hours all that had occurred at each meeting to the inspector of police'. For the past few weeks the people of Greenwich had suspected him of being a spy, and he had lost his trade as a result.[29] The Metropolitan Police had paid Powell £1 per week, Davis a lump sum of £150, and had also bought information from at least two other Chartists.[30]

In his defiant final speech Cuffay denied the court's right to sentence him. He had not been tried by his equals, and the press had tried to smother him with ridicule. He asked neither pity nor mercy; he had expected to be convicted. He pitied the attorney-general – who ought to be called the spymaster-general – for using such base characters to get him convicted. The government could only exist with the support of a regular organized system of police espionage. Cuffay declared his total innocence of the charge: his locality never sent any delegates, and he had nothing to do with the 'luminaries'. He was not anxious for martyrdom, but he felt that he could bear any punishment proudly, even to the scaffold. He was proud to be among the first victims of the Act of Parliament making the new political crime of 'felony' punishable by transportation. Every proposal that was likely to benefit the working classes had been thrown out or set aside in Parliament, but a measure to restrain their liberties had been passed in a few hours. (For the full text of Cuffay's speech from the dock, see appendix D, pp. 407–9.)

Cuffay and his two comrades were sentenced to transportation 'for the term of your natural lives'. 'A severe sentence, but a most just one', commented *The Times*.[31] The radical press praised the tailor's steadfastness and courage. The *Northern Star*, most influential of Chartist newspapers, said:

> The conduct of CUFFAY throughout his trial was that of *a man*. A somewhat singular appearance, certain eccentricities of manner, and a habit of unregulated speech, afforded an opportunity to the 'suckmug' reporters, unprincipled editors, and buffoons of the press to make him the subject of their ridicule. The 'fast men' of the press . . . did their best to smother their victim beneath the weight of their heavy wit . . . In a great measure, CUFFAY owes his destruction to the Press-gang. But his manly and admirable conduct on his trial affords his enemies no opportunity either to sneer at or abuse him . . . His protest from first to last against the mockery of being tried by a jury animated by class-resentments and party-hatred, showed him to be a much better respecter of 'the constitution' than either the Attorney General or the Judges on the bench. CUFFAY's last words should be treasured up by the people.[32]

The author of 'A word in defence of Cuffey' in the *Reasoner* had this to say:

> When hundreds of working men elected this man to audit the accounts of their benefit society, they did so in the full belief of his trustworthiness, and he never gave them reason to repent of their choice.
>
> Cuffey's sobriety and ever active spirit marked him for a very useful man; he cheerfully fulfilled the arduous duties which devolved upon him.

And the *Reasoner* added: 'He was a clever, industrious, honest, sober, and frugal man.'[33] A profile of Cuffay in *Reynolds's Political Instructor* said he was

> loved by his own order, who knew him and appreciated his virtues, ridiculed and denounced by a press that knew him not, and had no sympathy with his class, and banished by a government that feared him . . . Whilst integrity in the midst of poverty, whilst honour in the midst of temptation are

> admired and venerated, so long will the name of William Cuffay, a scion of Afric's oppressed race, be preserved from oblivion.[34]

After a voyage lasting 103 days on the prison ship *Adelaide*, Cuffay landed in Tasmania in November 1849. He was permitted to work at his trade for wages – which he did until the last year of his life – and after much delay his wife was allowed to join him in April 1853.[35] Cuffay was unique among veteran Chartists in exile in that he continued his radical activities after his free pardon on 19 May 1856. In particular, he was active in the successful agitation for the amendment of the colony's Masters and Servants Act. He was described as 'a fluent and an effective speaker', who was 'always popular with the working classes' and who 'took a prominent part in election matters, and went in strongly for the individual rights of working men'. At one of his last public appearances he called his working-class audience 'Fellow-slaves' and told them: 'I'm old, I'm poor, I'm out of work, and I'm in debt, and therefore I have cause to complain.'[36]

In October 1869 Cuffay was admitted to Tasmania's workhouse, the Brickfields invalid depot, in whose sick ward he died in July 1870, aged 82. The superintendent described him as 'a quiet man, and an inveterate reader'. His grave was specially marked 'in case friendly sympathisers should hereafter desire to place a memorial stone on the spot'.[37]

Cuffay makes fleeting appearances in three mid-nineteenth-century works of literature. Thackeray, in 'The Three Christmas Waits' (1848), poked fun at him as 'the bold CUFFEE' and 'A pore old blackymore rogue'.[38] A character in Charles Kingsley's novel *Alton Locke, tailor and poet* (1850) praises Cuffay's 'earnestness'; in the same novel the police spy Powell is described as a 'shameless wretch' and Cuffay is patronizingly called 'the honestest, if not the wisest, speaker' at Kennington Common.[39]

A fuller, more faithful portrait was painted by Cuffay's friend, admirer, and fellow-Chartist Thomas Martin Wheeler, whose semi-autobiographical 'Sunshine and Shadow' was serialized in the *Northern Star* in 1849. Wheeler recalled how, at a Chartist meeting in the early 1840s, he first

> gazed with unfeigned admiration upon the high intellectual forhead and animated features of this diminutive Son of Africa's despised and injured race. Though the son of a West Indian and the grandson of an African slave, he spoke the

> English tongue pure and grammatical, and with a degree of ease and facility which would shame many who boast of the purity of their Saxon or Norman descent. Possessed of attainments superior to the majority of working men, he had filled, with honour, the highest offices of his trade society . . . In the hour of danger no man could be more depended on than William Cuffay – a strict disciplinarian, and a lover of order – he was firm in the discharge of his duty, even to obstinacy; yet in his social circle no man was more polite, good-humoured, and affable, which caused his company to be much admired and earnestly sought for – honoured and respected by all who knew him . . . Yes, Cuffay, should these lines ever meet thine eyes in thy far-distant home, yes, my friend, though thou hast fallen – thou hast fallen with the great and noble of the earth . . . Faint not, mine old companion, the darkness of the present time will but render more intense the glowing light of the future.[40]

Mary Seacole

A challenge to empire of a very different kind was that of Mary Seacole, the Jamaican nurse whose reputation just after the Crimean War (1853–6) rivalled Florence Nightingale's. Mary Seacole's challenge, quite simply, was to have her skills put to proper use in spite of her being black. A born healer and a woman of driving energy, she side-stepped official indifference, hauteur, and prejudice; got herself out to the war front by her own efforts and at her own expense; risked her life to bring comfort to wounded and dying soldiers; and became the first black woman to make her mark in British public life. But while Florence Nightingale was turned into a legend in the service of empire, Mary Seacole was soon relegated to an obscurity from which she has only recently been rescued, by Ziggi Alexander and Audrey Dewjee.[1]

Mary Seacole was born in Kingston around the year 1805. Her father was a Scottish soldier possibly called Grant;[2] her mother, a competent practitioner of Jamaican traditional medicine, kept a boarding-house where she cared for invalid officers and their wives.[3] From early youth, Mary had 'a yearning for medical knowledge and practice'; at first she practised on her doll and on cats and dogs, but in due course she was helping her mother look after the invalid officers.[4] She soaked up knowledge from her mother, soon gaining a reputation as 'a skilful nurse and doctress'.[5]

Both before and after her marriage to Horatio Seacole, who died young, she travelled widely. There were two trips to Britain, where London street-urchins jeered at her. In 1851, during the California gold rush, she joined her brother Edward in Panama, where she opened an hotel. Soon she had saved her first cholera patient and had gained valuable knowledge from a post-mortem examination of an orphan baby that had died of this disease – which she herself contracted and recovered from. A white American who toasted her, as 'Aunty Seacole', for her work in the cholera epidemic, ventured to suggest that she be bleached in order to make her 'as acceptable in any company as she deserves to be'. Mary Seacole replied stingingly:

> I must say that I don't altogether appreciate your friend's kind wishes with respect to my complexion. If it had been as dark as any nigger's, I should have been just as happy and as useful, and as much respected by those whose respect I value; and as to his offer of bleaching me, I should, even if it were practicable, decline it without any thanks. As to the society which the process might gain me admission into, all I can say is, that, judging from the specimens I have met with here and elsewhere, I don't think that I shall lose much by being excluded from it. So, gentlemen, I drink to you and the general reformation of American manners.[6]

When she returned to Jamaica in 1853 her house was filled with victims of the yellow-fever epidemic. One man died in her arms, and the medical authorities asked her to provide nurses for the stricken soldiers.[7] The following autumn found her in London, where news was beginning to come through of the collapse of the British army's nursing system in the Crimea and the agonies, heightened by gross mismanagement, of the sick and wounded. Feeling that her skills and experience could and should be put to good use, Mary Seacole applied in turn to the War Office, the army medical department, the quartermaster-general's department, and the secretary for war. She produced fine testimonials and pointed out that she already knew many of the officers and soldiers in the regiments concerned, having nursed them when they were stationed in Jamaica.

But authority closed ranks against this plump, middle-aged West Indian lady in her flamboyant red or yellow dress and blue straw bonnet from which flowed a length of scarlet ribbon. She was turned away by everybody – including one of Florence Nightingale's assistants, in whose face she read 'the fact, that had there been a vacancy, I should not have been chosen to fill it'. Was it possible, she asked herself, 'that American prejudices against colour had some root here? Did these ladies shrink from accepting my aid because my blood flowed beneath a somewhat duskier skin than theirs?'[8] And, in her disappointment, Mary Seacole wept in the street.

A distant relative, a man called Day, was going to Balaklava on business. They came to an agreement to launch a firm called Seacole and Day, and to open, as a joint enterprise, a store and an hotel near the British camp in the Crimea. So, taking with her a large stock of medicines and home comforts, Mary Seacole, at the age of 50, went out to the battle zone as a sutler – i.e. one who follows an army and sells provisions to the troops. Skill, experience, and personality together made her the right woman in the right place at the right time.

Hardly had she landed at Balaklava when a party of sick and wounded arrived on the wharf. Here was work for her to do:

> So strong was the old impulse within me, that I waited for no permission, but seeing a poor infantryman stretched upon a pallet, groaning heavily, I ran up to him at once, and eased the stiff dressings. Lightly my practised fingers ran over the familiar work, and well was I rewarded when the poor fellow's groans subsided into a restless uneasy mutter . . . He had been hit in the forehead, and I think his sight was gone. I stooped down, and raised some tea to his baked lips . . . Then his hand touched mine, and rested there, and I heard him mutter indistinctly, as though the discovery had arrested his wandering senses –
>
> 'Ha! this is surely a woman's hand.' . . .
>
> He continued to hold my hand in his feeble grasp, and whisper 'God bless you, *woman* – whoever you are, God bless you!' – over and over again.[9]

Mary Seacole's British Hotel opened its doors in the early summer of 1855 at Spring Hill near Kadikoi, 'a small town of huts'[10] between Balaklava and the besieged city of Sevastopol. It was built from floating wreckage, for virtually all the trees in the area had long since been cut down. Soon almost the entire British army knew of 'Mother Seacole's', where 'you might get everything . . . from an anchor down to a needle'.[11] The soldiers were her 'sons' and she was their 'mother'. At the sound of a new arrival, she would come to the door, crying: 'Who is my new son?' That was how she greeted the head chef of London's Reform Club, Alexis Soyer, who revolutionized army cooking methods during his visit to the Crimea. He describes her as 'an old dame of jovial appearance, but a few shades darker than the white lily'.[12]

A lieutenant in the 63rd (West Suffolk) regiment wrote in his memoirs:

> She was a wonderful woman . . . All the men swore by her, and in case of any malady would seek her advice and use her herbal medicines, in preference to reporting themselves to their own doctors. That she did effect some cures is beyond doubt, and her never failing presence among the wounded after a battle and assisting them made her beloved by the rank and file of the whole army.[13]

Another account of her 'store-dispensary-hospital' claims that

> She had the secret of a recipe for cholera and dysentery; and liberally dispensed the specific, alike to those who could pay and those who could not. It was bestowed with an amount of personal kindness which, though not an item of the original prescription, she evidently deemed essential to the cure, and innumerable sufferers had cause to be grateful.[14]

Though some of the army doctors, despite her saving them a lot of work, may well have looked on her as 'a cunning and resourceful quack',[15] others were less bigoted. The assistant surgeon of the 90th Light Infantry saw her on the Balaklava landing-stage, serving hot tea to the wounded as, numb with cold in a temperature well below freezing-point and exhausted by the long journey from the front, they waited to be lifted into the boats:

> She did not spare herself . . . In rain and snow, in storm and tempest, day after day she was at her self-chosen post, with her stove and kettle, in any shelter she could find, brewing tea for all who wanted it, and they were many. Sometimes more than 200 sick would be embarked in one day, but Mrs. Seacole was always equal to the occasion.[16]

Mary Seacole was generally up and busy by daybreak, serving breakfast to off-duty troops, caring for the sick and wounded able to make their own way to her hut, visiting the military hospital with books and papers, mending torn uniforms. Rats and thieves gave her much trouble: she lost over 20 horses, 4 mules, 80 goats, and numerous sheep, pigs, and poultry. Frequently she was under fire, and she was so overweight that she found it easier to take cover than to rise to her feet again when the danger had passed:

> Those around would cry out, 'Lie down, mother, lie down!' and with very undignified and unladylike haste I had to embrace the earth, and remain there until the same voices would laughingly assure me that the danger was over, or one more thoughtful than the rest, would come to give me a helping hand, and hope that the old lady was neither hit nor frightened.[17]

It was W.H.Russell, the first modern war correspondent – and the last war correspondent to be free from military censorship – who made Mary Seacole famous in Britain. This 'kind and successful physician', he wrote in a dispatch dated 14 September 1855, 'doctors and cures all manner of men with extraordinary success. She is always in attendance near the battle-field to aid the wounded, and has earned many a poor fellow's blessings'.[18] He added later:

> I have seen her go down under fire with her little store of creature comforts for our wounded men, and a more tender or skilful hand about a wound or a broken limb could not be found among our best surgeons. I saw her at the assaults on the Redan, at the Battle of the Tchernaya, at the fall of Sebastopol, laden . . . with wine, bandages and food for the wounded or the prisoners. Her hands, too, performed the last offices for some of the noblest of our slain. Her hut was surrounded every morning by the rough navvies and Land Transport men, who had a faith in her proficiency in the healing art, which she justified by many cures and by removing obstinate cases of diarrhœa, dysentery, and similar camp maladies.[19]

She was, as she had vowed to be, the first woman to enter Sevastopol when it fell. But the end of the war left the firm of Seacole and Day with expensive and now unsalable stores on their hands. They were forced into bankruptcy, and Mary Seacole returned to England, 'ruined in fortune and injured in health' to live at 1 Tavistock Street, Covent Garden.[20] There was talk of her setting up a provision store at Aldershot, but this scheme evidently fell through, for a letter in *The Times* was soon demanding:

> Where are the Crimeans? Have a few months erased from their memories those many acts of comforting kindness which made the name of the old mother venerated throughout the camp? While the benevolent deeds of Florence Nightingale are being handed down to posterity . . . are the humbler actions of Mrs. Seacole to be entirely forgotten . . . ?[21]

Punch published an appeal on her behalf, entitled 'A stir for Seacole':

> That berry-brown face, with a kind heart's trace
> Impressed in each wrinkle sly
> Was a sight to behold, though the snow-clouds rolled
> Across that iron sky.
>
> The cold without gave a zest, no doubt,
> To the welcome warmth within:
> But her smile, good old soul, lent heat to the coal,
> And power to the pannikin.
>
> No store she set by the epaulette,
> Be it worsted or gold-lace;
> For K.C.B., or plain private SMITH
> She still had one pleasant face . . .
>
> The sick and sorry can tell the story
> Of her nursing and dosing deeds.
> Regimental M.D. never worked as she
> In helping sick men's needs . . .
>
> And now the good soul is 'in the hole',
> What red-coat in all the land,
> But to set her upon her legs again
> Will not lend a willing hand?[22]

Lord Rokeby, who had commanded a British division in the Crimea, joined with Lord George Paget, another Crimea commander, and others to arrange for her benefit a gigantic four-day musical festival at the Royal Surrey Gardens in Kennington. There were almost 1,000 performers, including nine military bands and an orchestra, and Mary Seacole sat between Rokeby and Paget in the front of the centre gallery. At the end of both parts of the programme her name was 'shouted by a thousand voices' and 'the genial old lady rose from her place and smiled benignantly on the assembled multitude, amid a tremendous and continued cheering'. 'Never', wrote a reporter, 'did woman seem happier.'[23] Unfortunately, though the admission charge was quintupled for the first performance, the festival raised only £228. At an official dinner in honour of the Guards, Mary Seacole was 'cheered, and chaired, . . . by the adoring soldiers', receiving, it is claimed, 'the reception that Florence Nightingale would have had, had she not studiously avoided it'.[24] In 1857 Mary Seacole published her autobiography, an outstandingly vivid piece of writing: the 'as-told-to' narrative is so skilfully edited that her voice, personality, and individual turn of phrase shine through on page after page. *Wonderful adventures of Mrs. Seacole in many lands* is prefaced by a further tribute from the pen of W.H.Russell: 'I trust that England will not forget one who nursed her sick, who sought out her wounded to aid and succour them, and who performed the last offices for some of her illustrious dead.'[25]

England did, of course, forget Mary Seacole very quickly. Prince Victor of Hohenlohe-Langenburg (afterwards known as Count Gleichen), sculptor and nephew of Queen Victoria, did a bust of her. She was awarded a Crimean medal, and one officer who had known her in the Crimea saw her wearing it in London some years later: 'The medal first attracted my eye . . . Of course I stopped her, and we had a short talk together about Crimean times.'[26] But the last 25 years of her life were passed in obscurity. Not, however, in penury, for when she died on 14 May 1881, she left over £2,500. Some money and a diamond ring went to Count Gleichen, and her 'best set of pearl ornaments' was left to his eldest daughter. Rokeby and his daughter were also remembered.[27] *The Times* had room for a curt obituary: 'She was present at many battles, and at the risk of her life often carried the wounded off the field.'[28]

Mary Seacole was buried, by her own wish, in the Roman Catholic section of Kensal Green cemetery. In 1973 her grave was reconsecrated and the headstone was restored.

Ira Aldridge

'The first to show that a black man could scale any heights in theatrical art reached by a white man – and recreate with equal artistry the greatest characters in world drama': that is how Herbert Marshall and Mildred Stock sum up the subject of their trail-blazing biography, *Ira Aldridge: The Negro Tragedian* (1958). They add:

> He did this alone, without the aid of any social or political organizations . . ., without any subsidies or scholarships, on his own two feet, with his own skill, versatility and talent.
>
> He did this in a white world, and showed that if a white can blacken his skin to represent Othello, then a black man can whiten his skin to represent Lear, Macbeth, or Shylock with equal artistry.

Aldridge, his biographers conclude, was 'a pioneer in laying the foundations of that still-to-come theatre of the human race'.[1]

Ira Aldridge was born in New York on 24 July 1807. His father, a clerk and lay preacher who became a minister, intended him for the church and sent him to New York's African Free School, where many future leaders of the American abolitionist movement were educated. But young Ira was attracted to the theatre, at a time when Edmund Kean and other prominent British actors were playing in New York and when the city's free black community had just launched its own African Theatre. Inspired above all by the black American actor James Hewlett, Aldridge made his début as Rolla in *Pizarro*, a Sheridan adaptation of August von Kotzebue's *Die Spanier in Peru*. But the only way for a serious and ambitious young black actor to succeed was to emigrate. Accordingly, when he was 17 or 18, Aldridge worked his passage to Liverpool as a ship's steward.

His first known British performance was at the Royal Coburg (afterwards the Old Vic) on 10 October 1825, as Oroonoko in *The Revolt of Surinam, or A Slave's Revenge*, an adaptation of Thomas Southerne's popular play based on Aphra Behn's novel. The playbill announced him as 'a *Man of Colour*' – 'the theatre's trump card for novelty appeal'.[2] It was common practice for an aspirant actor to use an assumed name similar to that of a famous star, and Aldridge was billed as 'MR. KEENE, Tragedian of Colour'; by 1831 he was 'F.W. Keene Aldridge, the African Roscius'[3] (Quintus Roscius Gallus (d. 62 BC) was the most famous Roman actor of his day); the 'Keene' was dropped by 1833.[4] His first performance had a mixed reception. *The Times* distinguished itself by saying that it was utterly impossible for him to pronounce English properly 'owing to the shape of his lips';[5] the *Globe*, on the other hand, found his enunciation 'distinct and sonorous' and praised several 'impressive' touches.[6] Purely on account of Aldridge's colour, the press was largely hostile. Since this hostility prevented Aldridge from establishing himself in London he went to the provinces – first marrying, only six weeks after they met, Margaret Gill, a young 'English lady of respectability and superior accomplishments'.[7]

The next six years or so were Aldridge's apprentice years. He was learning and experimenting. Some ideas, like having Othello go into a swoon, did not come off and were discarded. It was a gruelling training. In 1827 alone he appeared in Sheffield, Halifax, Manchester, Newcastle, Edinburgh, Lancaster, Liverpool, and Sunderland, singing to his own guitar as well as acting.[8] In 1829 he played in Belfast with Edmund Kean's son Charles, and in Hull with the outstanding shakespearian actor Samuel Phelps. Reviews, steadily more favourable, show his dedication to dramatic realism and hard work. His Othello, as seen in Scarborough in 1831, inspired a critical pamphlet describing him as 'certainly an actor of genius'.[9] At Kendal, in the previous year, he had played a white character for the first time, in an adaptation of a Scott novel; at Hull, in 1832, he tried out several other white roles, including Shylock, Macbeth, and Richard III, using white make-up, a wig, and possibly a beard. There were successful tours of Ireland and Scotland in 1833.

The evidence painstakingly assembled by Marshall and Stock shows that, at the age of 26, with only eight years' professional experience behind him, Aldridge was in 1833 the victim of a sustained London press campaign motivated by naked racism. He was the butt of 'damning criticism and insults', of 'devastating remarks' and 'ridicule'.[10] Indeed, when he went back to London to play Othello at the Covent Garden theatre, the press did all it could to destroy him. To take just one example from many, the *Athenæum* thought it 'impossible that Mr. Aldridge should fully comprehend the meaning and force of even the words he utters' and protested 'in the name of propriety and decency' against 'an interesting actress and lady-like girl, like Miss Ellen Tree' being 'pawed about' on the stage by a black man.[11] As Marshall and Stock point out, London was the centre of the pro-slavery lobby, then fighting its final rearguard action against the abolition of slavery in the British colonies:

> Their attacks on Aldridge grew more virulent as their position grew indefensible, and the appearance of a Negro playing the finest roles in all drama on the boards of Covent Garden was

itself a damning negation, as Aldridge well knew, of their arguments and 'theories' about the so-called inferior races. So the challenge was not that of actor *versus* actor. It was much more. Aldridge stood upon the stage . . . as the lone protagonist of his oppressed and vilified people.[12]

The theatre's French lessee bowed to the racist storm by cutting short Aldridge's engagement. When, soon afterwards, Aldridge made 11 appearances at the Surrey Theatre, the press campaign against 'the unseemly nigger'[13] went on, in what was clearly an attempt to inflame the public against him. There was nothing the London papers would not stoop to, including the publication of false reports of the actor's death.

His response to these 'scurrilous scribblings'[14] was to stick to his guns. Ouside London, he continued to win respect; a Hull paper said his Othello 'was such as can be equalled by very few actors of the present day'.[15] And professionals of the highest calibre, such as Eliza O'Neill and Maria Malibran, praised his work. In the provinces, he played to crowded houses. Yet the West End stage boycotted him for years: it was 1848 before he again appeared, briefly, at the Surrey. Fed up with 'the endless round of provincial tours, with its heartaches, hardships, and frustrations',[16] and with his failure to break into the West End, Aldridge decided to seek recognition on the Continent. On 14 July 1852, he and his family sailed from England.

On those first two Continental tours Aldridge played in Brussels, Cologne, Frankfurt-on-Main, Basle, Leipzig, Berlin, Dresden, Hamburg, Prague, Vienna, Budapest, Danzig, Munich, and Cracow. And he returned to London so loaded with honours that the West End stage could no longer exclude him – though it never welcomed him with anything like the enthusiasm shown abroad. Having become the Chevalier Ira Aldridge, Knight of Saxony, he was at last, in 1858, deemed worthy to act at the Lyceum. Then came an invitation to give 12 performances at St Petersburg's Imperial Theatre, receiving the equivalent of £60 for each performance – about as much as a Russian actor earned for four months' work – and being provided with accommodation and an equipage at government expense. In fact he played on 31 nights, 21 of which were devoted to *Othello*. He was lionized. Though he was playing in English with a German company, the controlled passion of his performances stirred Russian audiences as they had never been stirred before. Théophile Gautier, the French poet and novelist, saw him act in St Petersburg and testified to the 'stupendous effect' he produced.[17] One Russian critic said that the evenings on which he saw Aldridge's Othello, Lear, Shylock, and Macbeth 'were undoubtedly the best that I have ever spent in the theatre'.[18] 'After Aldridge', wrote another, 'it is impossible to see Othello performed by a white actor, be it Garrick himself.'[19]

After another tour of the British provinces in 1859–60, Aldridge went to Russia again. This time he gave 14 performances in Moscow and made several lengthy tours of the provinces in the years 1861–6, visiting many places where no foreign actor had set foot before. He was on tour when he died, in the Polish town of Lodz, on 7 August 1867, at the age of 59. The whole town turned out to mourn the passing of an artist of world stature.

Ira Aldridge left a widow – his second wife, Amanda Pauline von Brandt, a Swedish opera singer – and three young children: Luranah, Ira Frederick, and Amanda (another daughter, Rachel, was born four months after his death and died in infancy). Ira Frederick, talented pianist and composer, died in 1886. Luranah became a professional singer; she died in 1932. Amanda, singer, teacher, and (under the name 'Montague Ring') composer, gave elocution lessons to the young Paul Robeson in 1930 when he was preparing for his first appearance as Othello in London. She died in 1956, on the day before her ninetieth birthday.

Samuel Coleridge-Taylor

He called himself an Anglo-African and fought against race prejudice all his short life. His was the biggest contribution yet made by a black person to British concert music. He tried to do with black traditional music – in terms of integrating it into concert music – what his contemporaries Dvořák and Grieg were doing with Czech and Norwegian traditional music. From his pen, and his heart, flowed a stream of compositions dedicated to this aim: *African Romances* (op. 17, 1897), *African Suite* (op. 35, 1898), *Overture to the Song of Hiawatha* (op. 30, no. 3, 1899), *Ethiopia Saluting the Colours* (op. 51, 1902), *Four African Dances* (op. 58, 1902), *Six Sorrow Songs* (op. 57, 1904), *Twenty-four Negro Melodies* (op. 59, no. 1, 1904), *Symphonic Variations on an African Air* (op. 63, 1906), and *The Bamboula* (op. 75, 1910). The first performance of his *Hiawatha's Wedding Feast* (op. 30, no. 1, 1898) was described by the principal of the Royal College of Music as 'one of the most remarkable events in modern English musical history',[1] and this cantata for tenor solo, chorus, and orchestra was soon widely acclaimed on both sides of the Atlantic.

And yet, for all their interest, colour, vigour, and originality, the works of Britain's Anglo-African composer are now out of fashion. Little of his music is available in printed form; still less, on records. Performances are quite rare. Though he became a 'leader and shining light' to the black cultural renaissance in the United States,[2] Samuel Coleridge-Taylor is today all but forgotten in the country of his birth.

He was born at 15 Theobalds Road, Holborn, on 15 August 1875. His father, Daniel Peter Hughes Taylor, came to Britain from Sierra Leone in the late 1860s, studied medicine, qualified as Member of the Royal College of Surgeons, practised in Croydon, went back to Africa, was appointed coroner of The Gambia in 1894, and died in Banjul (now Bathurst) in 1904. Recent research by Jeffrey P. Green strongly suggests that Alice Holmans, the Englishwoman who married Daniel Taylor and brought up his son, was not the boy's real mother.[3] Samuel was named after the poet; the hyphen came later.

The romantic story has often been told of how the 6-year-old Samuel's musical gifts were discovered by a Croydon violin teacher who saw him playing marbles in the street, clutching a tiny violin in one hand and some marbles in the other. In 1890, at the age of 15, he entered the Royal College of Music as a violin student. His musical education was paid for, according to one account, by a Croydon choirmaster, who felt that an offer by a local firm of piano manufacturers to apprentice the boy to the tuning trade was not suited to his exceptional gifts, and who turned a deaf ear to busybodies' claims that black children showed early promise that never came to anything. The RCM principal, Sir George Grove, 'hesitated over Coleridge-Taylor's colour' before admitting him, apparently because he was afraid the other students might object.[4] Once at least the painfully shy and sensitive young man had the epithet 'nigger' hurled at him by a fellow-student. His professor, Charles Villiers Stanford, overheard and told him he had more music in his little finger than his abuser had in his whole body.[5] He had dropped his violin studies after two years, switching to composition under Stanford, whom he revered. An admirer of Brahms, Stanford challenged his pupil to write a clarinet quintet without showing Brahms's influence. Reading the manuscript, he exclaimed: 'You've done it, my boy!' When this early work was revived in 1973 the *New York Times* critic called it 'something of an eye-opener . . . an assured piece of writing in the post-Romantic tradition, sweetly melodic without being cloying, sometimes with a powerful thrust and beautifully written for the five players'.[6]

In 1896 an important influence came into Coleridge-Taylor's life when he met the American poet Paul Laurence Dunbar, son of a former slave. Visiting London to give public readings of his works, Dunbar made friends with the composer, three years his junior. Coleridge-Taylor set some of Dunbar's poems to music (*African Romances*) and in 1897 the two men gave joint public performances in London. Another black American whom Coleridge-Taylor met, a year or two later, was Frederick J. Loudin, former director of the Fisk Jubilee Singers, the choir that had introduced Afro-American spirituals to British audiences in 1873 (see pp. 440–1 below).

By 1898 Elgar, then Britain's leading living composer, was describing Coleridge-Taylor as 'far and away the cleverest fellow amongst the young men' and recommending his *Ballade in A minor* (op. 33, 1898) to the Three Choirs Festival.[7] Coleridge-Taylor conducted it himself, and its warm reception was a turning-point in his career. A few weeks later came the triumphant first performance of *Hiawatha's Wedding Feast*, which captivated the public and established him as one of Britain's outstanding young composers. Sir Arthur Sullivan, who was present, wrote in his diary that night: 'Much impressed by the lad's genius. He is a *composer* – not a music-maker. The music is fresh and original . . . his scoring is brilliant and full of colour – at times luscious, rich and sensual.'[8]

Though *Hiawatha* was the most popular English choral-orchestral work from 1898 to 1912, and brought its publishers immense profits, the composer reaped little reward from it. In 1904 Stanford wrote to Elgar, who thought that music publishers were 'considerate': 'If by accident you saw the accounts of Messrs Novello concerning Hiawatha, it might open your eyes a little.'[9] Coleridge-Taylor told a friend: 'If I had retained my rights in the *Hiawatha* music I should have been a rich man. I only received a small sum for it.'[10] According to one source, the first royalty payment for *Hiawatha* totalled three farthings, and this was delivered in an unstamped envelope for which a twopenny fee was charged.[11] In order to live, Coleridge-Taylor had to shoulder a formidable load of teaching, conducting, and adjudicating. From 1903 to his death in 1912, he was professor of composition at Trinity College of Music, London, and held various other teaching posts. He was conductor of the Handel Society, the Rochester Choral Society, and the Stock Exchange Orchestral and Choral Society, and was regularly engaged to conduct provincial orchestras. In the role of adjudicator he was a familiar figure at Eisteddfodau.

In 1904, 1906, and 1910 he visited the USA. The first of these visits was by invitation of an all-black choral society, the 160-strong Samuel Coleridge-Taylor Society of Washington, DC, which had been formed in 1901 with the chief aim of bringing the composer to Washington to conduct a festival of his works. At a time when it was still extremely hard, if not impossible, for talented black Americans to fulfil their cultural aspirations, a large number saw him as a champion. As part of his preparation for the visit, Coleridge-Taylor read *The Souls of Black Folk* (1903) by the militant black American leader W.E.B.DuBois, finding it one of the best books he had ever read.[12] His hosts feared that he might become the target of racist insults during his visit. He replied:

> As for the prejudice, I am well prepared for it. Surely that which you and many others have lived in for so many years will not quite kill me . . .
>
> I am a great believer in my race, and I never lose an opportunity of letting my white friends here know it. Please don't make any arrangements to wrap me in cotton-wool.[13]

In the event, the 1904 visit was an unqualified triumph. In Washington, thousands of black people turned out to greet their hero and hundreds visited him to pay their respects. The critics praised both his music and his skill as conductor. The audiences gave him tumultuous ovations. He met the famous black educator Booker T. Washington (though he agreed with DuBois that Washington was not militant enough). President Theodore Roosevelt invited him to the White House. In 1906 he repeated his success, with concerts in New York, Boston, and other cities.[14] In 1910 he conducted his own works at a musical festival in Norfolk, Connecticut, and received, once again, a reception that he himself called 'royal', adding: 'I never in my life have known anything like it.'[15]

His reception in America was certainly very different from his everyday experience in his native country. His daughter tells of the great pain caused him by the coarse insults of Croydon street lads: 'When he saw them approaching along the street he held my hand more tightly, gripping it until it almost hurt.'[16] He was evidently gripping her hand to stop himself retaliating. Once, at least, he had had enough and, when a 'big lad' shouted 'Blackie', seized the offender by the scruff of the neck and beat him with his walking-stick.[17] But the prejudice he met was not confined to street boys.

His white wife Jessie – she had been a fellow-student at the RCM, and they were married in 1899 despite her parents' objection to a 'mixed marriage' – recalled some instances in her 1943 *Memory Sketch*. There were the two 'silk-hatted "toffs"' who insulted the couple as they passed them in the street. There was the lady who, when the composer was taking a bow at a performance of *Six Sorrow Songs*, loudly exclaimed to her companion: 'What a killing little Nigger!' And there was the Church of England canon who, a guest at tea, leaned forward, gazed at the composer, and remarked: 'It really is surprising: you eat like we do, dress like we do, and talk as we do.'[18]

Not long before Coleridge-Taylor's death he read a local newspaper report of a barrister's crudely racist address to a debating society in Purley. He protested vigorously:

> Doubtless the 'Purley Circle' is working up for a lynching in the near future . . .
>
> It is amazing that grown-up, and presumably educated people, can listen to such primitive and ignorant nonsense-mongers, who are men without vision, utterly incapable of penetrating beneath the surface of things . . .
>
> There is an appalling amount of ignorance amongst English people regarding the Negro and his doings . . .
>
> Personally, I consider myself the equal of any white man who ever lived, and no one could change me in that respect; on the other hand, no man reverences worth more than I, irrespective of colour and creed. May I further remind the lecturer that really great people always see the best in others; it is the little man who looks for the worst – and finds it . . .
>
> It was an arrogant 'little' white man who dared to say to the great Dumas, 'and I hear you actually have negro blood in you!' 'Yes', said the witty writer; 'My father was a Mulatto, his father a Negro, and his father a monkey. My ancestry begins where yours ends!'
>
> Somehow I always manage to remember that wonderful answer when I meet a certain type of white man (a type, thank goodness! as far removed from the best as the Poles from each other) and the remembrance makes me feel quite happy – wickedly happy, in fact![19]

Coleridge-Taylor's 'racial solidarity', as it has been termed,[20] was never so warmly displayed as when black visitors called unexpectedly at his house. One such visitor, a shabby-looking man shouldering a stick with a bundle tied up in a brightly coloured handkerchief, asked the composer to hear him sing – and turned out to have a fine voice, the result being an introduction to a London concert agent, with a subsequent platform appearance.[21]

Strangely neglected in most accounts of Coleridge-Taylor's life is his consistent support for the Pan-African movement (whose rise is described in a later section of this chapter). He took charge of the musical side of the programme at the Pan-African Conference held at Westminster Town Hall in July 1900, and was elected to the executive committee of the Pan-African Association.[22] Twelve years later, when Dusé Mohamed Ali succeeded in launching the *African Times and Orient Review* in London, Coleridge-Taylor wrote shrewdly in the first issue:

> There is, of course, a large section of the British people interested in the coloured races; but it is, generally speaking, a commercial interest only. Some of these may possibly be interested in the aims and desires of the coloured peoples; but, taking them on a whole, I fancy one accomplished fact carries far more weight than a thousand aims and desires, regrettable though it may be . . .
>
> Therefore, it is imperative that this venture be heartily supported by the coloured people themselves, so that it shall be absolutely independent of the whites as regards circulation. Such independence will probably speak to the average Britisher far more than anything else, and will ultimately arouse his attention and interest – even to his support.[23]

Two months after these words were printed, the first black composer to win world fame and recognition died of double pneumonia at the tragically early age of 37. 'There will be thousands', wrote Sir Hubert Parry, principal of the RCM, 'who will feel a sense of saddening loss when . . . they miss the arresting face in which gentleness, humour, and modesty were so strangely combined with authoritative decision when matters of art were in question.'[24] Among those thousands were the black people living in Britain. One of the wreaths at the composer's funeral was in the shape of a map of Africa. It came 'From the Sons and Daughters of West Africa at present residing in England'.[25]

Samuel Coleridge-Taylor left two children. Hiawatha (born 1900) became a conductor, notably of his father's music. Avril (born

Gwendolyn, 1903) had a distinguished career in her own right as composer and conductor.

Challenges from Asia

We have seen that Asians were among the black pageant performers in seventeenth-century London; that Asians were among the black servants in this country in the eighteenth century; that Indian seamen, known as Lascars, were among London's black poor in the 1780s; and that a small shifting population of Lascars were a shamefully ill-treated group in this country in the early part of the nineteenth century. In the 1850s Indian seamen, during their stay in Britain, were still enduring appalling conditions. They were 'herded like cattle', six or eight to a single room without bedding, chairs, or tables. Those who fell ill lay in hospitals or workhouses 'in a most desolate condition', unable to communicate their needs across the language barrier. In the winter of 1856–7 eight Indian seamen died of cold and hunger in the London streets, and the coroner said that, in the past few years, he had held 40 such inquests.[1]

The treatment these seamen met with in Britain had evidently given them 'the very reverse of a favourable impression of the Christian religion'. So a group of philanthropists around the Revd Henry Venn, secretary of the Church Missionary Society, opened a 'Strangers' Home for Asiatics, Africans, and South Sea Islanders' in West India Dock Road, Limehouse, with room for 150 people. It was opened in 1857, barely a month after the start of India's first War of Independence – the brutally suppressed 'Mutiny'.

Joseph Salter, who spent much of his time trying to convert them to christianity, claimed that around this time as many as 2,000 Lascars had been visiting Britain every year. But this seems an exaggerated figure in the light of Salter's account of a missionary tour he made in 1869 'in search of the wandering Asiatic'. In Glasgow, Sterling, Leith, Edinburgh, Sunderland, Durham, Hull, Liverpool, Manchester, Birmingham, Bath, Bristol, Southampton, Portsmouth, the Isle of Wight, and Brighton, he met and spoke to a total of 81 Indians. Eighteen of them were in Liverpool and 14 in Manchester; in Birmingham he found three lodging-houses for Asians.[2]

The first Asian in Britain to engage in any kind of political activity was Raja Rammohan Roy, who was here from 1830 to 1833. Poet, philosopher, reformer, and journalist, he was the first Brahman to visit London, where he became a friend of the English radical Jeremy Bentham. During his stay Roy submitted to the parliamentary committee on Indian affairs a memorandum which was 'the first authentic statement of Indian views placed before the British authorities by an eminent Indian'. Both Roy and Dwarkanath Tagore, who visited Britain in 1842 – he was grandfather of the great Bengali poet – 'felt the need of carrying on propaganda in England on behalf of India, and made permanent arrangements for this work'.[3] Roy's English friend the Revd William Adam helped to form a British India Society in 1839 ('for bettering the conditions of our fellow-subjects – the Natives of British India') and edited its journal, the *British Indian Advocate* (1841–2).[4]

A 'small band of Indians' in the nineteenth century 'made England their centre of activity for the political advancement of India by awakening the consciousness of the British people to their sense of duty towards India and appealing to their democratic instincts and liberal principles'.[5] The most distinguished of them was Dadabhai Naoroji, the first Asian elected to the House of Commons.

Son of a Parsee priest, Naoroji was born in Bombay in 1825 and, at the age of 29, became the first Indian professor of mathematics and natural philosophy. He came to Britain in 1855 as a partner in the first Indian business house in this country, and was appointed professor of Gujerati at University College, London. In 1859 he set up in business on his own account and began to agitate against the discriminatory system of recruitment to the Indian civil service. From then on, Naoroji 'seldom missed an opportunity of voicing the grievances of Indians', becoming indeed 'an unofficial ambassador for India in England'.[6]

In 1865 he helped form the London Indian Society and served as its president. Its object was to bring English people and Indians together at social gatherings and exchange views on subjects connected with India. Two other organizations Naoroji helped to found were the London Zoroastrian Association (1861), dedicated to the welfare of Parsees living in Britain, and the East India Association (1866), which was eventually taken over by Anglo-Indians opposed to Naoroji's aim of 'India for the Indians'.[7]

After unsuccessfully contesting Holborn in the 1886 general election, Naoroji became famous overnight when the prime minister, Lord Salisbury, declared in a speech that 'however great the progress of mankind has been, and however far we have advanced in overcoming prejudices, I doubt if we have yet got to that point of view where a British constituency would elect a black man'.[8] 'Those two words – BLACK MAN – simply kicked Dadabhai into fame', writes his biographer. 'The name of the hitherto little-known Indian . . . was within twenty-four hours on the lips of everyone throughout the United Kingdom!'[9] Salisbury's opponents took him literally; and since Naoroji was conspicuously pale-complexioned, the prime minister was regarded as having committed a colossal gaffe. The National Liberal Club gave a banquet in Naoroji's honour 'to mark their disapproval of Lord Salisbury's intolerant language',[10] and for long he was known as 'Salisbury's black man'. Despite frantic efforts to stir up race prejudice – the Tories put it about that he was a fire-worshipper – Naoroji was elected Liberal MP for Central Finsbury in 1892. His majority of three earned him the punning nickname 'Narrow Majority'. He lost the seat three years later and was heavily defeated when he stood in North Lambeth in 1907.

But for Naoroji election to the British Parliament had been 'only a means to an end; the welfare of India was his daily thought'.[11] And for him the welfare of India was synonymous with that of the Indian National Congress, which he called 'the child of the British rule'.[12] He was its president in 1886, 1893, and 1906, and it was on his urging that a British committee of the Congress was formed in 1889. He campaigned long and hard, with pen and voice, to tell the British people about the wrongs being done to India in their name.

He did not altogether lack for allies. One of his close friends was the British socialist pioneer H.M.Hyndman, who wrote to him in 1884: 'I always told you . . . that little could be done for India unless we had a revolution here . . . There is no hope for you unless we move here and your movement helps our movement.'[13] Hyndman got to know Naoroji after casually picking up a copy of his pamphlet *Poverty of India* (1878) and noticing that the statistics it contained were just what he needed to clinch the argument of an article he had written on 'The Bankruptcy of India'.[14] Hyndman's book of the same name, published eight years later, was the first attempt by a British writer to show the connection between political tyranny and economic exploitation in the British Empire. At the time of Queen Victoria's diamond jubilee Naoroji and Hyndman collaborated in an 'Anti-Famine' agitation, and Hyndman spoke of a 'British-made famine' in India.[15] Whether or not Hyndman's influence had anything to do with it, Naoroji was moving steadily to the left year by year and his denunciation of British imperialism because steadily sharper. In 1904 he was an honoured guest at the

International Socialist Congress in Amsterdam. He spoke of the drain of India's wealth and her people's poverty. Hope of a remedy, he went on,

> rests in the hands of the working classes. Working men constitute the immense majority of the people of India, and they appeal to the workmen of the whole world, and ask for their help and sympathy. Let them condemn the wrongs done in India. We constantly denounce barbarities. What does barbarity mean? Does it not mean that, when a savage knocks down a weaker man and robs him, an act of barbarism has been perpetrated? The same applies to nations, and this is the way in which the British Government is treating India. This must end . . . The remedy is in the hands of the British people. They must compel their Government to fulfil the promises that have been made to India. The remedy is to give India self-government.[16]

Without opposition, the congress carried a resolution branding Britain with 'the mark of shame for its treatment of India'.[17]

India's first great statesman – and the economist 'who laid the foundation of an Indian school of economic thinking'[18] – died in Bombay at the age of 91. Highest reward of his life, Naoroji had said, was the title 'Grand Old Man of India'.[19]

Co-founder with Naoroji of the London Indian Society was the lawyer Womesh Chandra Bonnerjee. Born in 1844 in the Kidderpore district of Calcutta, Bonnerjee came to Britain in 1864 to study law. He was elected a Fellow of the Royal Geological Society, and was called to the bar in 1868 (a few months after Monmohon Ghose, the first Indian to be called to the English bar). Bonnerjee went home to practise in the Calcutta high court, served as first president of the Indian National Congress when it was formed in 1885, and led its first deputation to Britain. In 1889 Bonnerjee helped to organize the British Committee of the Indian National Congress, one of whose aims was 'to rouse the English working classes to a sense of the duties which England owes to India'; this committee published a journal, *India* (1890–1921) 'to popularise Indian thoughts and aspirations in England'. Bonnerjee twice stood for Parliament, unsuccessfully, as a Liberal, settled permanently in Britain in 1902, and died in 1906.[20]

Bonnerjee was a moderate, as was Sir Mancherjee Merwanjee Bhownagree, who sat as Conservative MP for Bethnal Green North-East from 1895 to 1906.[21] But from the middle of the nineteenth century onwards the political history of Indian students and intellectuals in Britain is one of gradual but steady radicalization. This is clear from Naoroji's own political evolution; it is equally clear when we compare four pioneers of the Indian National Congress who each spent some time in Britain as students – Surendranath Banerjea, Romesh Chunder Dutt, Ananda Mohan Bose, and Lal Mohan Ghosh – with their successors who were students here in the first decade of the twentieth century.

Banerjea and Dutt, both born in Calcutta in 1848, came to Britain together in 1868 to take the Indian civil service examinations. Banerjea went back to India in 1871, was dismissed from his post as assistant magistrate on a technicality, and was in Britain again in 1874–5 to make an unsuccessful appeal to the India Office. Two years later he founded the Indian Association, precursor of the Indian National Congress; his 1877–8 speaking tour of India, described as a triumphal progress, marked the dawn of the modern nationalist movement there. A superb orator, Banerjea was twice president of the Congress and for 20 years remained one of its principal leaders. But he led the moderate wing out of the Congress in 1918, accepted a ministry and a knighthood, and retired from politics after a crushing electoral defeat. He died in 1925.[22]

R.C.Dutt, after a career in the Indian civil service, was in 1897 appointed lecturer in Indian history at London University. He served as president of the Indian National Congress in 1899. Besides historical and other novels, he wrote works, still consulted today, on economics, economic history, and the ancient civilization of India. He died in 1909.[23]

A.M.Bose was born in the Bengal village of Jaisiddhi in 1847. An outstandingly brilliant student, he came to Britain in 1870 to read higher mathematics at Cambridge, where he distinguished himself by becoming the first Indian Wrangler (i.e. he was placed first class in the mathematical tripos). Later he was called to the bar. In 1872 he formed an Indian Society in London to 'foster the spirit of nationalism among the Indian residents in Britain', and afterwards co-operated with Banerjea in launching the Indian Association. Bose died in 1906.[24]

Lal Mohan Ghosh, born in Krishnanagar in 1849, was in Britain from 1869 to 1873, qualified as a barrister, and visited Britain again in 1879–80 and 1883 to agitate for reform in India. In 1883 and 1886 he stood as a Liberal Party candidate in Deptford but was defeated. He was elected president of the Indian National Congress in 1903 and died in 1909.[25]

So much for the moderates. By the turn of the century, the bulk of Indian students and intellectuals in Britain accepted the need for an armed struggle against British occupation. For a time the central figure here was Shyamaji Krishnavarma, founder in 1905 of *The Indian Sociologist*, a monthly journal, published first in London then in Paris, which had much influence on Indian opinion. Born into a poor family in the Kathiawar peninsula in 1857, Krishnavarma first came to Britain in 1879 to read Sanskrit at Balliol, law in the Inner Temple. He took his BA, was called to the bar, and went back to India in 1885. He began to advocate 'complete non-co-operation with the foreigner in maintaining his domination over India',[26] and in 1897 left India to avoid arrest. In London he would show sympathetic visitors 'a mass of papers which revealed . . . the tyranny of the British Government cloaked under an astute semblance of justice'.[27] As the government's dislike of him grew, so did his popularity among young Indians. He gave 10,000 rupees to send back to India a succession of 'political missionaries': young men who had come to Britain for their education and had developed into dedicated revolutionaries. He gathered round him in London a group of such young men, and on 18 February 1905 they launched the Indian Home Rule Society.

> No systematic attempt has ever been made [Krishnavarma wrote] to enlighten the British public with regard to the grievances, demands and aspirations of the people of India. It will be our duty and privilege to plead the cause of India and its unrepresented millions before the bar of public opinion in Great Britain and Ireland.[28]

The Indian Home Rule Society had the support of Hyndman, who formally opened its headquarters, India House, at 65 Cromwell Avenue, Highgate, on 1 July 1905.[29] India House served both as a hostel for Indian students in London and a centre for their political education. They learned, among other things, how to make bombs. An apologist for British rule was to describe the Indian Home Rule Society in 1910 as 'the most dangerous organization outside India'.[30] *The Indian Sociologist*, subtitled 'an organ of freedom, and of political, social, and religious reform', stood for absolute freedom from British control, advocated extreme passive resistance, and supported active resistance in so far as civil liberties were repressed by the British authorities. Under the impact of the Russian revolution of 1905, Krishnavarma told his supporters: 'It seems that any agitation in India now, must be carried on secretly and that the only methods which can bring the English Government to its senses are the Russian methods vigorously and incessantly applied until the English relax their tyranny and are driven out of the country.'[31]

Increasingly anxious about the rise of nationalist feeling among Indian students in Britain, the British authorities called a meeting of them, chaired by Lord Lamington, a former governor of Bombay. Feelings ran high, especially when Sir William Lee-Warner, formerly a secretary in the India Office's political and secret departments, called one of the young Indians present, Kunjabihari Bhattacharyya, a 'dirty nigger', whereupon another young Indian, Vasudeo Bhattacharyya, punched him in the face, an offence for which he was afterwards fined.[32]

At least two of the revolutionaries around Krishnavarma gave up their studies to become full-time workers in the freedom movement. One was a brilliant young man called Pandurang Mahadev Bapat, later famous throughout India as Senapati Bapat. Born into a poor Brahman family at Parner, Maharashtra, in 1880, he came to Edinburgh in 1904 to study mechanical engineering. Deprived of his scholarship for writing a pamphlet demanding home rule for India, he went back to India in 1908, spent five years underground, and was imprisoned by the British five times – on the last two occasions for a total of 14 years. In 1955 he played a leading part in the liberation of Goa from Portuguese rule.[33]

Another of Krishnavarma's ardent supporters was Lala Hardyal. Born in Delhi in 1884, he came to Britain in 1905 to read modern history at Oxford. But, having decided that 'no Indian who really loves his country ought to compromise his principle and barter his rectitude for any favour whatever at the hands of alien oppressive rulers of India', he gave up his scholarship to become a full-time revolutionary and went back to India in 1908. He was later active in the United States in the cause of Indian freedom.[34]

The outstanding member of this group of young Indian nationalists in Britain in the first decade of the present century was Vinayak Damodar Savarkar (Veer Savarkar), who was to play a significant part in every subsequent phase of the Indian freedom struggle. He was born in 1883 in the village of Bhagur, near Nasik in Maharashtra, and at the age of 16 he formed a political organization aiming at complete independence. Its slogan was 'instruction and insurrection'. In 1906 Savarkar came to London, where he founded the Free India Society with the aim of recruiting Indian students to the revolutionary movement.

In May of the following year Indian students in Britain honoured the fiftieth anniversary of the War of Independence by wearing badges commemorating the martyrs. There were scuffles when British jingoists tried to tear these badges off, and a vehement press campaign was launched against Krishnavarma, who prudently left London for Paris. He died in Geneva in 1930.[35] After Krishnavarma left London, Savarkar took over the management of India House. One of the visitors there was an English boy of 16, David Garnett, who was deeply impressed by Savarkar's personal magnetism. In his memoirs *The Golden Echo* (1953), Garnett has this description of him:

> He was small, slight in build, with very broad cheekbones, a delicate aquiline nose, a sensitive, refined mouth and an extremely pale skin . . . His was the most sensitive face in the room and yet the most powerful . . . There was an intensity of faith in the man and a curious single-minded recklessness which were deeply attractive to me.

The only member of the group whom Garnett disliked turned out to be a police informer.[36] Not, however, a very effective one, since he failed to prevent the assassination of Sir William Curzon Wyllie, the man whose task at the India Office was to keep watch on the political views and activities of Indian students in Britain.

In 1909 an Indian student named Madan Lal Dhingra – born in the Punjab about the year 1887, he had come to Britain when he was about 18 – went to the annual meeting of the National Indian Association at the Imperial Institute, and shot Wyllie dead with a Colt revolver. The police found on Dhingra a written statement which they confiscated and whose existence they denied. But Savarkar had another copy and, when Dhingra was sentenced to death, asked David Garnett to try to get it published. Garnett took it to Robert Lynd of the *Daily News* and it was published, much to the annoyance of the police, on the morning of the execution:

> I attempted to shed English blood as an humble revenge for the inhuman hangings and deportations of patriotic Indian youths . . .
>
> I believe that a nation held down by foreign bayonet is in a perpetual state of war. Since open battle is rendered impossible to a disarmed race I attacked by surprise . . .
>
> As a Hindoo I felt that wrong to my country is an insult to God.[37]

The police closed down India House. Savarkar fled to France but returned several months later and was arrested. After an unsuccessful rescue attempt by Indian and Irish revolutionaries he was sent to India for trial. Near Marseilles he escaped from the ship through a porthole but was recaptured. Sentenced to two consecutive transportations for life, he spent ten years in jail on the Andaman Islands. Deprived of pen and paper, he scratched his poems on the walls of his cell with thorns and pebbles, and learnt by heart more than 10,000 lines of his poetry till they reached his people through the mouths of returning fellow-exiles. He had been a living legend for many years when he died in 1966[38]

Three other prominent Indian nationalist visitors to Britain remain to be mentioned: Gokhale, Pal, and Tilak. The first represents the 'moderate', the other two the 'extremist', wing of the Congress.

Regarded by some as 'a discerning liberal', by others as 'a faint-hearted "Moderate"', Gopal Krishna Gokhale made in all seven visits to Britain – 'political pilgrimages' to put India's case before the British public – in the years 1897–1914. Born in 1866 in a village in the Ratnagiri district of Maharashtra, south of Bombay, he first came to give evidence before the Welby Commission on the administration of India's expenditure. In 1905 he came as a representative of the Congress and, amongst other meetings, spoke to the National Liberal Club – on 'England's Duty to India' and the 'Awakening of India' – and to the Fabian Society. He told the Fabians that the way India was administered was 'unworthy of free England', being based largely on 'confidential police reports, . . . and on hostility towards the educated classes'. The next year Gokhale was back, speaking to Indian students at Cambridge and Oxford. In 1908 he was here again; there was another, brief, visit in 1912; his last visits, in 1913 and 1914, were as a member of the Public Services Commission, appointed 'to consider the claims of Indians to higher and more extensive employment in the public service connected with the civil administration of the country'. Gokhale never lost his faith in British justice, fair play, and rule of law. But when he died in 1915 it was clear to many Indians that more than faith was needed.[39]

Whereas Gokhale's main British support came from the Liberal Party, the 'extremists' Bipin Chandra Pal and Bal Gangadhar Tilak found their natural allies in Britain on the left. First and most pugnacious of their left-wing allies was Keir Hardie. During his visit to

India in 1907 he spent some days touring the villages near Poona with Tilak as his guide, and his eyes were opened to the true character of British imperialism. (Thus a 'vivid memory which stayed with [Keir Hardie] was of the close watch kept on him in Poona by the C.I.D.; it so enraged him that he publicly threatened to expose these "un-British" methods on his return to England'.)[40] So when the great nationalist orator Pal came to this country in 1908 it was natural for Hardie to welcome and befriend him. It was not Pal's first visit. Born in 1858, in the Sylhet district of what is now Bangladesh, Pal had studied theology in Britain in 1898, and was in fact one of the first of the nationalist-minded students to throw up his scholarship in favour of full-time political activity. In March 1910 Pal was a guest at the annual conference of the Independent Labour Party. After a resolution was carried urging that the Indian people be granted the rights of lawful association and freedom of speech, Pal was 'received with great enthusiasm by the delegates'. He spoke very briefly, saying he was grateful to the conference for having accepted the resolution, 'although he did not suppose that their protest would put wisdom into the brains of the government. Nothing would do that except the extremity of circumstances'.[41] In the following year Pal went back to India, where he died in 1932.

Tilak was a later and, in terms of success as a lobbyist, a more effective visitor. Leaving aside Pal's reception by the ILP, Tilak was the first Indian leader to approach the British people, not through drawing-room gatherings, but through working-class organizations and newspapers. During his 1918–19 visit he was to be seen at the Labour Party conference and the Trades Union Congress. The Labour movement gave him platforms all over the country, and Lansbury's *Daily Herald* published several of his articles and strongly supported the demand for Indian home rule.[42] Known as 'the Father of Indian unrest', Tilak was born in Ratnagiri in 1856. In 1897 he was sentenced to 18 months in jail for sedition. Between 1908 and 1914 he was imprisoned in the Mandalay jail in Burma, having been transported on a charge of 'bringing into hatred and contempt and exciting disloyalty and feelings of enmity towards His Majesty and the Government established by Law in British India'. When Tilak's wife died in 1912 Keir Hardie tried to get the sentence remitted, but the authorities were implacable. Tilak came to Britain in 1918, not primarily as a propagandist, but to fight an unsuccessful libel action against Sir Valentine Chirol, a former foreign editor of *The Times*. His visit has been called 'the first serious attempt on the part of India to enlighten the British people about Indian affairs and make them realize that the administration of India was carried on in their name, and that therefore they were responsible for the poverty, disease and illiteracy of the country'.[43]

During his stay he made friends with George Lansbury, Ramsay MacDonald, Sidney Webb, and Bernard Shaw; and only then did India become one of the main planks in the Labour Party's programme. An illuminating aspect of the visit was the 'sharp eye' kept on Tilak by Scotland Yard – though the policemen who spied on him 'never made their presence felt',[44] which must have disappointed Tilak a little since he used to say that 'he always liked to have a talk with the secret police because from his talks with them he read the mind of the Government'.[45] The confidential reports on Tilak show that the police spies invariably found sinister motives for everything he did and said; but most of the reports were 'mere gossip or unfounded speculation, by which the writers hoped to please their superiors'.[46] Tilak died in 1920, soon after his return to India.

We have surveyed the rise of one of the two anti-imperialist political traditions that developed among black people living in Britain while Britain held their countries in bondage. The Asian anti-imperialist tradition was also represented in this country between the First and Second World Wars, as will appear. We turn now to the corresponding tradition created, largely in Britain, by Africans and people of African descent.

The rise of Pan-Africanism

Pan-Africanism, one of the major political traditions of the twentieth century, was largely created by black people living in Britain. In 1787 Ottobah Cugoano published in London his *Thoughts and sentiments on the evil and wicked traffic of the slavery and commerce of the human species.* In that seminal book, at the very dawn of the abolitionist movement, an African writer not only demanded freedom for the slaves but also forecast 'universal calamity' for the 'criminal nations' that profited from their enslavement. Two years later, Cugoano's friend Olaudah Equiano published in London his *Interesting Narrative.* These two writers together anticipated many of the leading ideas of Pan-Africanism: racial solidarity and self-awareness; Africa for the Africans; opposition to racial discrimination; emancipation from white supremacy and domination. With their work begins the prehistory of Pan-Africanism – or, in other words, the history of 'proto-Pan-Africanism'.[1]

Of the forerunners and creators of Pan-Africanism, some were born in Britain, others visited this country for varying periods. Why was Britain the womb of the movement? Chiefly because it was the centre of a fast-expanding empire. It was here that Africans, West Indians, Afro-Americans, and Anglo-Africans could most conveniently meet, exchange ideas, create networks of contacts. And, when the time was ripe to organize, it was here that they could most easily launch a movement that challenged the whole imperialist system.[2]

At the turn of the century the British Empire was so powerful that it seemed to its rulers as if the sun would never set on it. But the first Pan-African Conference, held in London in 1900, gave notice to the white imperialists who ruled over millions of Africans and West Indians that their minority rule could not last for ever. And within two generations decolonization was no longer a dream, but a fact.

Delany, Blyden, and Horton

The most important north American 'proto-Pan-Africanist' was the Pittsburgh-born, Harvard-trained physician Martin Robison Delany, explorer, soldier, orator, novelist, abolitionist, radical, and black nationalist, who spent the last eight months of 1860 in Britain. He was to be the first black soldier commissioned with field rank by President Lincoln – at 53 he became a major in the 104th Regiment of United States Colored Troops. And he was one of the first to use a form of the slogan, 'Africa for the African'.

A pioneer of the 'Back to Africa' dream, Delany anticipated also many of the more realistic tenets of Pan-Africanism. He was dedicated to black self-regeneration and the redemption of Africa. He held that the only way for black people to overcome the destructive effects of white racism was to assert a separate course of action for themselves. Afro-Americans, to whom his main message was directed, must see themselves as a distinct group in the United States whose cultural heritage was African, not European. They must recognize and appreciate the achievements, cultural stability, and humanism of ancient African civilizations. And they must work for racial solidarity with black people elsewhere in the world.[3]

Delany, who had just led an expedition into equatorial Africa, came to Britain as a delegate to the fourth International Statistical Congress. A distinguished participant in the congress, and the president of one of its sections, was the elderly Lord Brougham, former lord chancellor and an uncompromising enemy of slavery. On the platform on the opening day, among the assembled dignitaries from some 20 countries, sat George Mifflin Dallas, United States minister in London. After an inaugural address by Prince Albert, Lord Brougham electrified the delegates by remarking: 'I hope my friend Mr. Dallas will forgive me reminding him that there is a negro present, a member of the Congress.' There was 'loud laughter and vociferous cheering', after which Delany stood up in the body of the hall and said quietly: 'I pray your Royal Highness will allow me to thank his Lordship, who is always a most unflinching friend of the negro, for the observation he has made, and I assure your Royal Highness and his Lordship that I am a man.' 'This novel and unexpected incident', wrote *The Times*, 'elicited a round of cheering very extraordinary for an assemblage of sedate statisticians.'

One of the two white American delegates, Georgia-born Judge Augustus Baldwin Longstreet, reacted by walking out of the congress, writing a long, angry letter to the *Morning Chronicle*, and reporting to his government that Brougham's action was 'an assault upon our country, a wanton indignity offered to our minister, and a pointed insult offered to me'. But Dallas himself, who could hardly believe his ears, sat tight and said nothing; he wrote in his diary that night: 'It was a premeditated contrivance to provoke me into some unseemly altercation with the coloured personage . . . Is not the government answerable for this insult? Or must it be regarded as purely the personal indecency of Lord Brougham?' Was Brougham, he wondered, 'on this question of slavery, deranged?' White Americans in London told him they wished he had 'knocked the old blackguard down'.

Delany was a focus of attention during the five further days the congress was in session, and on the last of them there was 'great applause' when he made a short speech of thanks:

> I should be insensible, indeed, if I should permit this Congress to adjourn without expressing my gratitude for the cordial manner in which I have been received . . . I am not foolish enough to suppose that it was from any individual merit of mine, but it was that outburst of expression of sympathy for my race . . . whom I represent, and who have gone the road of that singular Providence of degradation, that all other races in some time of the world's history have gone, but from which, thank God, they are now fast being regenerated. I again tender

> my most sincere thanks and heartfelt greetings to those distinguished gentlemen with whom I have been privileged to associate, and by whom I have been received on terms of the most perfect equality.

Delany was asked to read a paper to the Royal Geographical Society on his African expedition, and he spent seven months addressing crowded anti-slavery meetings in England and Scotland.[4]

During Delany's stay in Britain he and his colleague and fellow-explorer Robert Campbell, a Jamaican science teacher, were approached by the English philanthropist Dr Thomas Hodgkin, who had helped to found the British and Foreign Aborigines' Protection Society in 1837. Hodgkin now had it in mind to form an 'African Association' to foster African economic, social, and political development and combat racism and colonialism. He had discussed this project in 1859 in correspondence with Thomas Hughes, a member of the Cape Coast municipal council in West Africa, with the caveat that he did not wish to stir Africans to 'wild revolutionary or democratic struggles'. All that materialized while Delany was in Britain was an African Aid Society, which published a journal called *African Times* and saw Africans and Afro-Americans as objects of philanthropy rather than agents in their own struggles. But on 7 November 1861, the 'Native African Association and their Friends' met in Hodgkin's house. Besides British abolitionists, the 12 people who attended included an R.Campbell – probably but not certainly Delany's Jamaican colleague – and the Haitian chargé d'affaires. The meeting discussed plans for collaboration between British abolitionists, Africans, Afro-Americans, and Haitians. These plans seem to have come to nothing; but the ideas later to be called Pan-Africanism were clearly in the air.[5]

Such ideas were to be put forward in 13 books by Edward Wilmot Blyden, who served as Liberian commissioner to Britain in 1861–2 and, after six visits to Britain, as Liberian ambassador here in 1877–8 and 1892, and as envoy extraordinary to London and Paris in 1905. Born in 1832 of free parents on the Danish-held island of St Thomas, and refused admission to an American university because of his colour, Blyden was 'the most articulate and brilliant vindicator' of black interests in the nineteenth century. His aim was to create among black people pride, confidence, and cultural identity, and he has been called 'the most important historical progenitor of Pan-Africanism'.[6]

But his proto-Pan-Africanism was not unflawed. He romanticized Africa, believed that the 'African personality' was not cut out for political or scientific achievement, and, towards the end of his life, praised European missionaries, including the openly racist ones, and welcomed European colonialism as a vehicle of progress for Africa.[7] There was in fact an irrational element in his outlook, exemplified by his deep hatred of people of mixed race, which may have been what led him to boycott the Pan-African Conference in 1900.[8]

If Blyden prefigures one of the two main contrasting trends within Pan-Africanism – the mystical concept of *Négritude* – his friend James Africanus Beale Horton, whose pride in his race was no less intense but was securely grounded in a rational outlook, gave early expression to the other. Like Blyden, Horton called for independent action by Africans; unlike Blyden, he called on Africans to master Europe's advanced technology. Like Blyden, he stood for racial equality; unlike Blyden, he did not suppose that races were unchanging and complementary, but believed that all races shared the ability to draw from the storehouse of human achievements.[9]

Born near Freetown, Sierra Leone, in 1835, the son of an Igbo snatched from a slave-ship, Horton spent five years at King's College, London, and became a Member of the Royal College of Surgeons in 1858. In the following year he graduated from Edinburgh University as MD and was commissioned in the British army for service in West Africa, with the rank of staff assistant surgeon. One of the first African doctors trained in Europe and one of the first African regular officers, he retired after 20 years with the rank of lieutenant-general. He wrote four medical and three political books. His major book, *West African Countries and Peoples* (1868), was the first call for self-government by a West African author. It had two aims: 'to prove the capability of the African for possessing a real political government and national independence'; and to develop among the different nationalities of West Africa 'a true political science'.[10]

The heart of this book – as its sub-title 'A Vindication of the African Race' suggests – is its trenchant attack on pseudo-scientific racism. Horton's demonstration that 'the African people is a permanent and enduring people'[11] has been termed his greatest contribution to emerging Pan-Africanism. But we should not forget his defence of the African historical past; his 'practical and far-seeing'[12] scheme for a West African university, with special emphasis on the teaching of science and the education of females; his detailed blueprint for West African independence; his call for the industrialization of Africa; his interest (shared with Blyden) in the construction of railways in West Africa; his creation of West Africa's first bank.[13] He was one of the foremost pioneers of the national liberation movement in both Ghana and Nigeria.[14] Above all, he was a pioneer of practical Pan-Africanism: 'representative rather than exceptional: a figure within a broad movement . . . of Pan-African economic and social modernization'.[15] He was only 48 when he died in 1883. Until recently he was largely forgotten. But, in George Shepperson's phrase, he was 'the father of modern African political thought',[16] and his optimism, his faith in the rising generation, have a clear message for our own day.

Celestine Edwards

Another long-forgotten forerunner of Pan-Africanism was Samuel Jules Celestine Edwards. He was the youngest of nine children of a poor French-speaking couple on the Caribbean island of Dominica, where he was born on 28 December 1858 (or possibly 1859). When he was about 12 he stowed away on a French ship and became a seaman, a temperance advocate, a strongly anti-freethought christian, and a staunch upholder of human rights and brotherhood. Sometime in the 1870s he settled in Britain, plunged into activity in the temperance movement in Edinburgh, and spoke on the movement's behalf elsewhere in Scotland. About the year 1880 he moved to Sunderland. Then he went to live in London's East End, earning a living as a casual building worker and soon gaining a reputation as a public speaker in Victoria Park. His lectures on temperance and religion often contained references to black people's problems and future. He told a Newcastle audience:

> My ancestors proudly trod the sands of the African continent; but from their home and friends were dragged into the slave mart and sold to the planters of the West Indies . . . The very thought that my race should have been so grievously wronged is almost more than I can bear . . . Of the condition of my people today I but tarry to say that by diligence, thought, and care they have given the lie to many a false prophet who, prior to their Emancipation, sought to convince the world that the black man was in all respects unfit for freedom . . . Their position . . . today is one over which I proudly rejoice. To their future I look with confidence.[17]

In a lecture in Hackney, on 16 September 1886, he had this to say of racism: 'It is a sad and terrible thing to see nigh a whole generation of men and women comparing those whose skins are black to baboons and the like.'[18]

Despite long hours of physical toil, Celestine Edwards found time to write penny pamphlets on religious questions and a biography of Walter Hawkins, a former slave who had become bishop of a Canadian church; to study at King's College, London, where his fellow-students of theology held him in 'high esteem and great love',[19] and where he took a theological degree in 1891; to embark on the study of medicine; and to accept the editorship of two magazines, thus becoming Britain's first black editor. *Lux*, 'a weekly Christian Evidence Newspaper', appeared from 1892 to 1895. *Fraternity*, published from 1893 to 1897, was the monthly organ of the Society for the Recognition of the Brotherhood of Man, of which Celestine Edwards was executive secretary[20] and which numbered Quaker humanitarians among its members. These two journals are prototypes of what Ian Duffield has called 'the religious mode of the Pan-African struggle for vindicating the dignity and humanity of black people'. *Fraternity* especially, with its declaration of war on racism, 'was a large step towards the production in Britain of a politically committed Pan-African press'.[21]

In an impassioned protest against the imminent British seizure of Uganda, Celestine Edwards wrote in a *Lux* editorial at the end of 1892:

> As long as such unrighteous deeds as cold-blooded murders are permitted under the British flag, as long as avarice and cupidity prompt the actions of a missionary nation, . . . so long we shall protest against public money being spent in the interest of land-grabbers . . .
>
> The injustice under which [the black man] is smarting will come home to his oppressors' children's children . . . He will surprise and disappoint those who never dreamt that the quiet, happy-go-lucky black would turn like the worm upon those who wronged him . . . If the British nation stole no more, they have stolen enough and have sufficient responsibility at home and abroad to occupy her maternal attention for the next hundred years. If the British nation has not murdered enough, no nation on God's earth has.[22]

Two months later he was warning that 'the British Empire will come to grief unless it changes its method of dealing with aboriginal races'. Denouncing the cunning, lies, 'abominable greed', and injustice of European colonizers, he prophesied:

> The day is coming when Africans will speak for themselves . . . The day is breaking, and . . . the despised African, whose only crime is his colour, will yet give an account of himself . . . We think it no crime for Africans to look with suspicion upon the European, who has stolen a part of [their] country, and deluged it with rum and powder, under the cover of civilisation.[23]

Celestine Edwards worked himself to death. Advised by Sir Andrew Clark of the London Hospital, where he had enrolled as a medical student, to lay aside all study and to travel if possible, he chose to combine travel and work by undertaking a punishing lecture tour. In Bristol, on 3 July 1893, he spoke on 'Lynch Law, or American Atrocities'; a week later 1,200 people heard him speak in London on the same subject; a month later he was in Liverpool speaking on 'Blacks and Whites in America'; in September, after a visit to Plymouth, there were meetings in Aberdeen, Edinburgh, Glasgow, and Liverpool again. In November he thought nothing of travelling from Ashton-under-Lyne to London, lecturing the same night, returning north to Huddersfield next day and lecturing there at night.[24] He started travelling by night mail so as to cram in still more speaking engagements. After spending the winter on the south coast he was stumping the country again when spring came. Before he fell ill he had been a commanding figure on the platform, hardly more than an inch short of six feet tall, with a joyous laugh that people remembered him by, 'full of life, full of energy, full of boyish enthusiasm; his eyes flashing as no English eyes can, and his big, brawny frame glowing with health'. Now a colleague heard him coughing half the night in the next-door hotel bedroom.[25] In a desperate effort to get better he sailed for Dominica. Two months later, on 25 July 1894, he died there, in his brother's arms. The Christian Evidence movement mourned a 'beloved chief, friend, and illustrious champion'.[26] One obituarist wrote: 'He was proud of his colour and his people. He lived not for himself.'[27]

Sylvester Williams and the African Association

That the threads of emergent Pan-Africanism were at last drawn together, and a Pan-African conference convened in London in July

1900, was due above all to the work and vision of yet another long-neglected pioneer: the Trinidadian Henry Sylvester Williams. He was born on 19 February 1869, in the village of Arouca, about ten miles east of Port of Spain, and was the eldest of five children of a Barbadian wheelwright who had settled in Trinidad. An able student, he qualified as a schoolteacher at the early age of 17 and was put in charge of a school a year later. But teachers were poorly paid in Trinidad, and Williams went to New York at the age of 22. After two years in the United States he entered Dalhousie University, Halifax, Nova Scotia, in 1893, to study law. Three years later he came to London, enrolling at King's College and making ends meet by lecturing for the Church of England Temperance Society and the National Thrift Society. In 1897 he joined three other Trinidadian law students at Gray's Inn. While reading for the bar he met and fell in love with an Englishwoman slightly older than himself: Agnes Powell, daughter of a Royal Marines officer who fiercely opposed the match. The couple were married in 1898 and their first child, Henry Francis Sylvester, was born in the following year.

Besides lecturing on Trinidad – he denounced crown colony rule as a 'heartless system . . . a synonym for racial contempt'[28] – Williams led a deputation of Trinidadians living in London to meet MPs, becoming the first person of African descent to speak under the House of Commons roof. Of more lasting importance was his initiative in founding the African Association in 1897. Its aims, in the year of Queen Victoria's diamond jubilee, were:

> To encourage a feeling of unity to facilitate friendly intercourse among Africans in general; to promote and protect the interests of all subjects claiming African descent, wholly or in part, in British Colonies and other places, especially in Africa, by circulating accurate information on all subjects affecting their rights and privileges as subjects of the British Empire, by direct appeals to the Imperial and Local Governments.[29]

Williams was the association's secretary. Its president was the Revd Henry Mason Joseph, an Antiguan, and its treasurer was Mrs E.V.Kinloch, an African woman from Natal married to a Scotsman. She campaigned with Williams against the maltreatment of black people in South Africa and went back home in 1898.* At a meeting of members and friends on 11 January 1898, Williams said the association wanted to be as representative as possible, 'so that its information shall be direct and first hand from the various parts of the Empire', and suggested that branch societies should be encouraged in the colonies and protectorates.[31] 'This promising society . . . appears to be making steady progress', wrote the journal of the Aborigines' Protection Society in March 1898. 'Frequent meetings of its increasing number of members are held, at which information is exchanged on important questions affecting the welfare of Africans, not only on their own continent, but also in the West Indies and elsewhere.'[32] The association, in fact, acted as an African and West Indian lobby. In March 1898 it sent the colonial secretary, Joseph Chamberlain, a memorial 'on the distress in the West Indies',[33] and seven months later it petitioned him asking for the interests of Africans to be safeguarded in the new Rhodesian constitution.[34]

The Pan-African Conference (1900) and after

Even before the African Association was formed, Williams had conceived the idea of a world conference of black people, and in 1898 a call for such a conference was issued. On 19 March an association meeting decided to issue a circular, signed by Williams and Henry Joseph, announcing a conference in two years' time 'in order to take steps to influence public opinion on existing proceedings and conditions affecting the welfare of the Natives in the various parts of the Empire, viz., SOUTH AFRICA, WEST AFRICA and the B[ritish]. WEST INDIES'.[35] After discussions with leaders of black opinion, in London on other business (including Bishop James T. Holly, an old colleague of Delany; Bishop James Johnson, a friend of Blyden; and the American educator Booker T. Washington), the scope of the proposed conference was broadened to cover 'the treatment of native races under European and American rule', and specifically

* Vice-president of the African Association was the Sierra Leonean T.J.Thompson; assistant secretary was the Trinidadian A.C.Durham. Other leading members were Durham's brothers Ernest and Frederick, both barristers; Antiguan Frederick Ellis Bass, a graduate of Mehorry Medical College, Nashville, Tennessee; the Revd C.W.Farquhar, Antiguan schoolmaster ordained a deacon in the Church of England; Richard E. Phipps, Trinidadian law student; and Dr Ernest Jones Hayford, elder brother of the prominent Gold Coast lawyer, author, and nationalist J.E.Casely Hayford.[30]

those in South Africa, West Africa, the West Indies, and the United States.[36]

The term 'Pan-African' seems to have been first used in 1899, though it is not clear who first used it.[37] By April 1900 the Pan-African Conference committee had adopted the motto 'Light and Liberty'. This committee included Williams as general secretary; Joseph as chairman; the Revd Thomas L. Johnson, a West African, as vice-chairman; and the Trinidadian law student Richard E. Phipps as secretary for the West Indies.

Williams told a gathering of delegates at the Reform Club on 6 July that the conference would be 'the first occasion upon which black men would assemble in England to speak for themselves and endeavour to influence public opinion in their favour'. The conference, he added, would consider the position of black people in South Africa and must see to it that their interests were not overlooked in any settlement of the Boer War.[38] It was in reports of this meeting that the British press first used the term 'Pan-African'.[39] At a meeting of the African Association a week before the conference an engrossed memorial was presented to Bishop James Johnson, who was about to leave for Lagos. In this document the association held that it was time for black people to develop their own talent and energy. The position of Africans, 'either at home or under the flags of the known powers', was not reassuring. Their efforts should be directed to the education of the young so as to bring forth the 'prolific possibilities of the race'. Aware of the distortions of history as presented by white writers, and of the need to redress the balance, the association believed that black people should develop 'our own chroniclers' and set up 'our own libraries and organizations'.[40]

The plenary sessions of the conference were held in Westminster Town Hall on 23, 24, and 25 July 1900. Never before, said Williams afterwards, had black people 'assailed London with a conference'.[41] There were about 37 delegates and about ten other participants and observers.[42] The chair was taken by the most distinguished participant, Bishop Alexander Walters, a leader of the African Methodist Episcopal Zion Church in the United States and president of the National Afro-American Council. The vice-chairmen were representatives of independent African states: Frederick Johnson, former attorney-general of Liberia, and the Haitian Benito Sylvain, aide-de-camp to the Ethiopian emperor. Also on the platform was Mrs Jane Rose Roberts, elderly widow of Liberia's first president.

In his opening address on 'The Trials and Tribulations of the Coloured Race in America', Bishop Walters said that for the first time in history black people had gathered from all parts of the globe to discuss and improve the condition of their race, to assert their rights and organize so that they might take an equal place among nations. The first paper, read by C.W.French of St Kitts, on 'Conditions Favouring a High Standard of African Humanity', demanded that black people be recognized as human beings enjoying equal rights with white people. Miss Anna H. Jones from Kansas, in a paper on 'The Preservation of Race Equality', said it was important to preserve the identity of the black race and develop its artistic talents. In his speech of welcome the bishop of London, Mandell Creighton,[43] obliquely criticized the ruling ideas of the epoch by referring to 'the benefits of self-government' which Britain must confer on 'other races . . . as soon as possible'.

Sylvain's paper that evening, on 'The Necessary Concord to be Established between Native Races and European Colonists', pulled no punches in its attack on colonialism. It had been right, he said, to choose the metropolis of the British Empire as their meeting-place, for the British people were responsible for the anti-liberal reaction that had characterized colonial policy over the preceding 15 years, and the British government had tolerated the most frightful deeds of the colonizing companies. Before many years had passed, however, every colonial power would have to recognize the rights of the indigenous peoples. These peoples must no longer be considered as serfs. No human power could halt Africans' social and political development. A Latin teacher from Washington, Mrs Anna J. Cooper, brought the first day's proceedings to a close with a paper on 'The Negro Problem in America'.

Next day the Liberian Frederick Johnson opened a discussion on 'The Progress of Our People in the light of Current History'. John E. Quinlan from St Lucia said British capitalists seemed determined to enslave black people again, especially in South Africa; William Meyer, Trinidadian medical student at Edinburgh University and one of the two delegates from the Afro-West Indian Literary Society there, attacked pseudo-scientific racism for 'trying to prove that negroes were worthless and depraved persons who had no right to live'; and Richard Phipps complained of discrimination against black people in the Trinidadian civil service: they got the worst jobs and were passed over in promotion. D.E.Tobias, an American, led a discussion on 'Africa, the Sphinx of History, in the Light of Unsolved Problems'. Dr W.E.B. DuBois said the fact that black people could nowhere maximize their potential was not merely an injustice and hindrance to them but hindered human evolution. The Revd Henry Smith, who lived in London, forecast a grand and glorious future for Africans and warned against letting differences in the various shades of colour of black people interfere with their progress – they should all work together.

On the last day Bishop Walters thanked the liberal and philanthropic elements in Britain and America who had stood up for black people in their countries, and George James Christian from Dominica led a discussion on the subject: 'Organized Plunder *v.* Human Progress Has Made Our Race its Battlefield'. In the past, he said, Africans had been kidnapped from their land, and in South Africa and Rhodesia slavery was being revived in the form of forced labour. Closing the discussion, Bishop Walters said their object was to secure moral, political, and civil rights for black people. They had the force of numbers on their side. The conference was just the beginning of the work, and it meant that black people throughout the world would organize for their own betterment.[44]

Then the conference turned to some practical tasks. The African Association was merged into a new Pan-African Association. Bishop Walters was president; the Revd Henry B. Brown, a Canadian, vice-president; Williams, general secretary; Dr R.J.Colenso, son of Bishop Colenso of Natal, treasurer; Sylvain, general delegate for Africa. Two of those elected to the new association's executive committee were Samuel Coleridge-Taylor the composer and Frederick J. Loudin, former director of the Fisk Jubilee Singers (see pp. 440–1 below). A third, John Richard Archer, was later mayor of Battersea; we shall come back to him presently. The other three were Henry Francis Downing, a former member of the United States consular service; Mrs Cooper, the Washington teacher; and an Englishwoman, Mrs Jane Cobden Unwin, wife of the publisher T. Fisher Unwin. Officers of several overseas branches were appointed, and the conference defined the new association's aims thus:

1. To secure to Africans throughout the world true civil and political rights.
2. To meliorate the conditions of our brothers on the continent of Africa, America and other parts of the world.
3. To promote efforts to secure effective legislation and encourage our people in educational, industrial and commercial enterprise.

4. To foster the production of writing and statistics relating to our people everywhere.
5. To raise funds for forwarding these purposes.

The conference unanimously adopted an 'Address to the Nations of the World', to be sent to the heads of those states in which people of African descent were living. Signed by Walters, Williams, DuBois, and the Revd Henry B. Brown, this document contained the lapidary phrase, 'The problem of the Twentieth Century is the problem of the colour-line', which DuBois was to use three years later in his book *The Souls of Black Folk*. 'Let not the cloak of Christian missionary enterprise', the address declared, 'be allowed in the future, as so often in the past, to hide the ruthless economic exploitation and political downfall of less developed nations, whose chief fault has been reliance on the plighted troth of the Christian Church.' Demanding an end to colour and race prejudice, the address called on Britain in particular to give, 'as soon as practicable, the rights of responsible government to the black colonies of Africa and the West Indies'. (Four years earlier, colonial secretary Joseph Chamberlain had written privately that black people in the West Indies were 'totally unfit for representative institutions'.)[45]

A petition was sent to Queen Victoria on the situation of black people in South Africa and Rhodesia, drawing attention to forced labour, the indenture system whereby black men, women, and children were placed in legalized bondage to white colonists, the pass system, and various kinds of segregation. To this petition the colonial secretary at length sent a bland reply, promising that her Majesty's government would not 'overlook the interests and welfare of the native races'.[46]

The conference was reported in the leading London newspapers. The *Westminster Gazette* observed that it 'marks the initiation of a remarkable movement in history: the negro is at last awake to the potentialities of his future', and quoted Williams's words to a reporter:

> I felt that it was time some effort was made to have us recognised as a people, and so enable us to take our position in the world. We were being legislated for without our sanction – without a voice in the laws that were made to govern us. My idea of bringing about some alteration in this respect was confined in the first place to the British Colonies, but the scheme developed into a Pan-African one. Our object now is to secure throughout the world the same facilities and

> privileges for the black as the white man enjoys . . . There is an attempt in the world to-day to re-enslave the negro race. Especially is this the case in South Africa. We feel that we must bring our whole forces together to prevent that.[47]

The press coverage contained little comment, except in W.T.Stead's *Review of Reviews*. Stead, one of the few journalists of the day who could rise above the prevailing jingoism and imperial arrogance, called the 'Address to the Nations of the World' 'a sign of the times of which we shall all do well to take note'.[48]

Those who gave financial help to the conference included the most distinguished figure in Britain's small Indian community: the ex-MP Dadabhai Naoroji. According to Williams's biographer Owen Mathurin, Naoroji 'saw some affinity between his work for the Indian people and what Williams was trying to do for Africans at home and abroad', and Naoroji's work in and out of Parliament had 'inspired Williams to seek to do the same for his own people'.[49] Naoroji's support for the 1900 Pan-African Conference is the earliest recorded instance of Afro–Asian solidarity in Britain – of practical help from the Asian community to their brothers and sisters of African descent here.

After the conference Williams went to Jamaica, Trinidad, and the United States to set up branches of the Pan-African Association. He was abroad for more than half of 1901, and while he was away there was some manoeuvring against him. It seems to have been led by the treasurer, Dr R.J.Colenso, who dissolved the organization on the pretext of lack of funds. When Williams came back to London he tried to revive it, but the momentum was spent. All the same, Williams did manage to launch a journal called *The Pan-African* in October 1901. It was designed to spread information 'concerning the interests of the African and his descendants in the British Empire' and to be 'the mouthpiece of the millions of Africans and their descendants'. Declaring that 'little or nothing is known of the educated British Negro', the editorial in the first issue expressed the conviction 'that no other but a Negro can represent the Negro', adding that 'the times demand the presence of that Negro to serve the deserving cause of a people the most despised and ill-used today'.[50] A woolly message of support from the Labour leader Keir Hardie claimed that 'apart from a few interested parties of the South African millionaire type, the wrongs done to your people under British rule are more due to ignorance than to any desire to act unjustly' and advised 'temperate yet strenuous action' to redress those wrongs.[51] *The Pan-African* was short-lived; probably only one issue appeared.

The Pan-African Association's rapid decline is not hard to understand. As Mathurin points out, 'organizations formed by colonials in a metropolitan capital tend to fluctuate in strength and activity with the ebb and flow of residents'.[52] Williams claimed in 1901 that the association had 50 working members – there were 150 white sympathizers, admitted to honorary membership only[53] – but few of the 50 black members were permanent residents and most were students. Nor could Williams devote his entire time to the organization. He resumed his legal studies, was called to the bar in June 1902 and became probably the first barrister of African descent to practise in Britain.[54] He went to South Africa a few months later to defend black people in the courts, in the teeth of bitter prejudice and boycott by the Cape Law Society.[55] When he came back to Britain in 1905 he continued to work on behalf of black South Africans. In the following year he became the only black member of the committee of the League of Universal Brotherhood and Native Races Association. Little is known about this body except that its motto was 'United to Aid', its symbol was a black hand and a white hand clasped in greeting, and its vice-president was the Revd F.B.Meyer, head of the Free Church Council.[56]

In November 1906 Williams, who had joined the Fabian Society, became one of the first two persons of African descent to be elected to public office in Britain when he won a seat on Marylebone borough council as a 'Progressive' (i.e. Liberal-Labour) candidate, polling 701 votes in the Church Street ward. After visiting Liberia in 1908 – the British consul sent home three confidential dispatches in two weeks denouncing him – Williams suddenly decided, for unknown reasons, to go back to Trinidad with his family. He was building a successful legal practice there when he fell ill towards the end of 1910. On 26 March 1911 he died in hospital.[57] His fifth child was born five days later.

Dusé Mohamed Ali

The ideas of Pan-Africanism inspired the activities of another vivid but, again, little-remembered personality in this country: Dusé Mohamed Ali.

His origins are something of a mystery. He claimed to be the son of an Egyptian officer and his Sudanese wife. He was born, he said, in 1866 or 1867, was sent to Britain as a boy of nine or ten to be educated, and never returned to Egypt after his father was killed in battle in 1882. Various doubts have been cast on this story and Ian Duffield, examining the evidence, draws attention to the fact that Ali had not even a smattering of Arabic. On the other hand, Duffield emphasizes that Ali never wavered in his claim to be of Egypto–Sudanese parentage 'even when it caused him great inconvenience (as when it allowed the British authorities to register him as technically an enemy alien during the First World War)'; that Egyptians in London seem never to have challenged his claim 'and even accepted him as, for some purposes, a leader of their community'; and, above all, that 'he was undoubtedly black, and identified with other blacks'.[58] Between 1883 and 1921 he lived mainly in Britain, earning his bread mostly as a penny-a-line journalist and ill-paid touring actor. He was often desperately poor. In 1909–11 he was a fairly regular contributor to A.R.Orage's *New Age*. In 1911 he published a hastily written anti-imperialist book, *In the Land of the Pharaohs*, 21 passages in which were lifted without acknowledgment from writings by Theodore Rothstein, Wilfrid Scawen Blunt, and the Earl of Cromer.[59] But to many of his readers the plagiarism mattered little or not at all. Ali was defending black rights and forecasting the downfall of the British Empire, and his book had a lasting impact in the United States and West Africa.

Ali's chief contribution to the Pan-African movement, and to the struggle against imperialism and racism, was the *African Times and Orient Review*. He launched this magazine in July 1912, in partnership with the Sierra Leonean businessman and journalist John Eldred Taylor,[60] and kept it alive, with certain gaps, until the end of 1920. This was the first political journal produced by and for black people ever published in Britain. It was in a sense a by-product of the Universal Races Congress that had been held in London the previous year. Attended by DuBois, Gandhi – then leader of the Indian minority in South Africa – and several African representatives, this gathering was emphatically 'not a Pan-African event but rather a well-meant sentimental attempt to contribute towards a better relationship between the various races by means of personal contact and scholarly discussion'.[61] Where the congress had been sentimental, the *African Times and Orient Review* was militant. The congress had clearly demonstrated the need, wrote Ali in the frst issue, for 'a Pan-Oriental, Pan-African journal at the seat of the British Empire which would lay the aims, desires, and intentions of the Black, Brown, and Yellow Races – within and without the Empire – at the throne of Cæsar'. For 'the voices of millions of Britain's enlightened dark races are never heard'. Their capacity was underrated. They were victims of 'systematic injustice'. And the first issue gave a shameful example of this injustice when it described the public flogging, at Zaria in northern Nigeria the previous February, of two African railway clerks named Taylor and Hall, who had failed to prostrate themselves before a third-class British Resident named Laing. (The public flogging of Africans in the nude, women as well as men, on the orders of British administrators in Africa was 'so common' in the early twentieth century that 'only the more flagrant examples . . . attracted much attention'.)[62]

'A Word to our Brothers' in the same issue told black people plainly: 'Your day is coming. Your place in the Sun has been and will come again . . . The future of Africa, the future of India, will not be decided in the Chanceries of Europe, but upon the hills of India and the plains of Africa.'[63] And when the First World War began Ali did not mince his words (though, once Britain entered the war, prudence clearly prevented his being so outspoken again). He wrote in the issue dated 4 August 1914: 'All the combatants, the conquerors and the conquered alike, will be exhausted by the struggle, and will require years for their recovery, and during that time much may be done. Watch and wait! It may be that the non-European races will profit by European disaster.'[64]

As Duffield points out, the quality of the *African Times and Orient Review* was consistently high. It built up an international circulation; it was read by black intellectuals in Africa, north America, and the West Indies; it preached Afro-Asian solidarity. Not least, the paper 'received the backhanded tribute of being disliked and rather feared by the Colonial Office, the Foreign Office and the India Office'.[65] Geiss justly calls it 'a mine of information' which 'diligently unearthed abuses of colonial rule in the British colonies and passed on information to Labour M.P.s who asked embarrassing questions in the House of Commons'.[66]

One of the contributors to Ali's journal was a young Jamaican called Marcus Garvey, later to become the first black leader to inspire millions of Afro-Americans with pride in their race. Another who made his literary début in the *African Times and Orient Review* was the Ghanaian philosopher, lawyer, and nationalist Kobina Sekyi (William Essuman-Gwira Sekyi), then a 20-year-old student, who graduated from London University with honours in philosophy in 1914 and was called to the bar five years later. Garvey and Sekyi were two of the many black visitors to London who made Ali's tiny Fleet Street office their 'general meeting place and informal headquarters'.[67]

In 1921 Dusé Mohamed Ali went to the United States, where he lived for the next ten years. In 1931 he settled in Nigeria, where he launched the *Comet*, a weekly news magazine which came to play an important part in the nationalist movement (and, in 1937–8, serialized his autobiography). He died in Lagos in 1945.

John Richard Archer and the African Progress Union

The first person of African descent to hold civic office in Britain. The first British-born black councillor, alderman, and mayor. The first black person to become an election agent for a constituency Labour Party. The first British-born black person to represent his country at an international conference abroad. John Richard Archer's list of 'firsts' is impressive indeed. 'A significant force in both the Pan-Africanist and Battersea labour movements for over a quarter of a century',[68] he saw no conflict between these two spheres of activity. Nor, it seems, did his colleagues in either. He was a byword in Battersea for diligence in the performance of municipal duties; the list of public offices he held is huge; but when he died the leader of the local Labour Party singled out also for praise his ardent work 'for the benefit of the coloured races'.[69]

He was born on 8 June 1863, in a tiny house in Blake Street, Liverpool, a few minutes' walk from Lime Street. Richard Archer, his father, was a ship's steward who hailed from Barbados; Mary Theresa, his mother, whose maiden name was Burns, was Irish. Almost nothing is known of his early life A nervous breakdown in his youth obliged him to give up the study of medicine. He claimed to have gone round the world three times – presumably as a seaman – and he may have lived for a time in north America and the West Indies. He was in his late twenties when he and his wife, a black Canadian, arrived in Battersea and set up house at 55 Brynmaer Road, at the south end of Battersea Park. Archer earned his living as a photographer, with a studio in Battersea Park Road; he seems to have been a successful one, for his work won many prizes. He started to read for the bar, but political activity took precedence over his studies, which he at length abandoned.

In those days Battersea was London's most radical borough. It was the base for such pioneers as John Burns and Tom Mann, Charlotte Despard and Mary Gray. Its council opposed the Boer War as imperialist and criticized the lavish expenditure over the crowning of Edward VII. A supporter of Burns, who was Battersea's MP from 1892 to 1918, Archer was first elected to the borough council in November 1906, as one of the six councillors for the

Latchmere ward, where he topped the poll with 1,051 votes. He lost his seat in 1909 but was re-elected three years later. On 10 November 1913, when he was elected mayor of Battersea by 40 votes to 39 in a contest with a West End tailor, the borough had a population of 167,000 and the council's annual income from rates was just over £400,000.

For a couple of weeks before the election the prospect of one of its boroughs having a black mayor gave 'a thrill to novelty-loving London', as one paper put it.[70] The *Daily Mail*, not knowing or not caring that Archer was a Liverpudlian, referred to his 'keen contest with an Englishman'.[71] The *Daily Chronicle* seemed surprised to find that Archer's 'well-dressed and well-groomed appearance' was 'that of a busy and prosperous business man'.[72] There was opposition from proto-fascists like the anonymous 'True Progressive' who wrote in a local paper: 'It is not meet that the white man should be governed and controlled by a man of colour. It has always been that the white man ruled and it must always be so. If not, good-bye to the prestige of Great Britain.'[73] Archer's supporters said he was 'a most useful public man, and a man of whom Battersea has reason to be proud'; he was 'a clever speaker' and 'a man of strong intellect'.[74] There was much excitement at the council meeting and a large crowd waited outside to hear the result.[75] The newly elected mayor told the council: 'You have made history to-night . . . Battersea has done many things in the past, but the greatest thing it has done is to show that it has no racial prejudice, and that it recognises a man for the work he has done.'[76]

Archer received letters of congratulation from leading members of the black community in the United States, and his mayoralty was featured in DuBois's journal *The Crisis*, with photographs of Archer and Mrs Archer in their robes of office. *The Crisis* told its readers that Archer 'fears no man, and brooks no insult because of the race to which he is proud to belong'. Archer wrote to an American friend:

> Last week I attended a great function at the Guildhall when the twenty-eight London mayors were present with the lord mayor. It filled my heart with joy to walk in the procession of mayors in that old historic building – the first time that one of our race has done so as mayor.[77]

Like most of his Progressive fellow-councillors, Archer moved to the left in his political views during the First World War, and when he defended his Latchmere ward seat in 1919 he did so as a Labour candidate. Once again he topped the poll. In December of that year he helped in the election campaign of Charlotte Despard, radical, socialist, feminist, and pre-war suffragette.[78] Three years later he gave up his council seat so that he could concentrate on winning back for Labour the constituency of North Battersea, lost to a Coalition Liberal in the 'khaki election' of 1919. He now became election agent for Shapurji Saklatvala, a Parsee and a member of both Communist Party and Labour Party in those days when dual membership was still possible. Through skilful negotiation Archer succeeded in having Saklatvala adopted as North Battersea's Labour candidate. He did so by persuading Battersea Trades Council, the sponsoring body, to pledge its support for the Labour Party constitution and to withdraw opposition to the MP's membership of the Parliamentary Labour Party. This compromise made Saklatvala the only communist candidate, in the general elections of 1922, 1923, and 1924, not to have a Labour Party opponent; as we shall see, he sat as Labour MP in 1922–3, lost his seat in the 1923 election, and regained it in 1924, sitting as a communist MP until 1929. But Archer, who had become an alderman in 1925, found it impossible after the General Strike to co-operate with an increasingly Moscow-dominated Communist Party, and he gave up his business to become secretary of Battersea Labour Party and agent for the candidate who in 1929 won North Battersea back for Labour.

Archer returned to the council in 1931. He topped the poll in the Nine Elms ward and became deputy Labour leader on the council. When he died suddenly in the following July, colleagues looked back on an extraordinary record of service to the local community. At various times he served on the health, works, finance, and valuation committees of the council, the committee responsible for baths and wash-houses, and those concerned with unemployment, health, and tuberculosis care. His record of attendance at both committee and full council meetings was outstanding.[79] He was a governor of Battersea Polytechnic, president of Nine Elms Swimming Club, chairman of the Whitley Staff Committee, and a trustee of the borough charities. He served on Wandsworth Board of Guardians, and it was said that there never was a case in which he did not try to get more generous treatment for the applicant: 'The poor had no better friend.'[80] He was active in securing a minimum wage of 32*s.* a week for council workers and 30*s.* for those employed by the Board of Guardians.

Amid all these everyday tasks, Archer's devotion to the cause of Pan-Africanism was no less consistent. When the African Progress

Union was formed in London in 1918 he was chosen as president, and he held the post for three years. Members, mostly students but with a sprinkling of business people, came 'from various parts of Africa, the West Indies, British Guiana, Honduras and America'. The Union's aims were 'to promote the general welfare of Africans and Afro-Peoples'; to set up a social and residential club in London as a 'home from home'; to spread 'knowledge of the history and achievements of Africans and Afro-Peoples past and present'; and to create and maintain 'a public sentiment in favour of brotherhood in its broadest sense'.[81] The Union 'saw itself as a Pan-Negro club linking Afro-Americans with other African peoples'.[82] Dusé Mohamed Ali was a foundation member. So were the Gold Coast merchant Robert Broadhurst, a man in his sixties who became the Union's secretary; and Edmund Fitzgerald Fredericks from British Guiana, who later became a member of the Georgetown legislative council and chaired the colony's Negro Progress Convention.

Another foundation member of the African Progress Union was John Alcindor, a Trinidadian physician practising in London. Born in Port of Spain in 1873, Alcindor made his home in Britain after graduating from the University of Edinburgh medical school in 1899 with first-class honours in three subjects. He was one of the two delegates from Edinburgh's Afro-West Indian Literary Society to the Pan-African Conference in 1900. From 1907 until his death in 1924 he was one of the borough of Paddington's four district medical officers – and as recently as 1981 he was still remembered with respect by old people in Paddington when Jeffrey P. Green interviewed them. Known as 'the black doctor of Paddington', Alcindor gave free medical treatment to those too poor to pay. His family recall how, more than once, he came home, took his dinner, and left the house with it, remarking: 'My patient needs feeding, not doctoring.' In 1911 he married Minnie Martin, a white Londoner; two of their three sons are living. In 1921 Alcindor succeeded Archer as president of the African Progress Union, and in the same year, as we shall see in chapter 10, he played a prominent part in the second Pan-African Congress.[83]

Other leading supporters of the African Progress Union included John Alexander Barbour-James from British Guiana, whose house in Acton was a meeting-place for black visitors to Britain; Barbour-James's daughter Muriel; E.P. Bruyning, another Guyanan; Felix Hercules from Trinidad (for whom see pp. 313–16 below); the Trinidadians Audrey Jeffers, Sylvia Acham-Chen, and Alphonso Luke; Alfred Adderley from the Bahamas; Kwaminah F. Tandoh from the Gold Coast; and John Eldred Taylor, the businessman and journalist from Sierra Leone who had helped Dusé Mohamed Ali launch the *African Times and Orient Review* in 1912 and was now proprietor of the *African Telegraph*, also published in London.[84]

In 1919 Archer went to Paris as British delegate to the first Pan-African Congress. At the second Pan-African Congress, in London in 1921, he chaired a session on colonial freedom, called on the British government to heed the colonial people's growing political demands, and introduced Saklatvala, who made a declaration of solidarity, on behalf of the Indian national movement, with the 'Coloured World'.[85]

But Archer's most important single contribution as a Pan-Africanist was a remarkable speech he made at the African Progress Union's inaugural meeting a few weeks after the end of the First World War. (For the full text of this speech, see appendix E, pp. 410–16.) It was remarkable alike for its simplicity and its militancy:

> The people in this country are sadly ignorant with reference to the darker races, and our object is to show to them that we have given up the idea of becoming hewers of wood and drawers of water, that we claim our rightful place within this Empire. That if we are good enough to be brought to fight the wars of the country we are good enough to receive the benefits of the country. One of the objects of this association is to demand – not ask, demand; it will be 'demand' all the time that I am your President. I am not asking for anything, I am out demanding.[86]

And the room rang with cheers.

Black workers and soldiers

John Richard Archer was speaking on behalf of a black community that had been transformed by the war. It had grown in numbers; it had grown in self-confidence; above all, its expectations had grown.

Before the war, black students and Pan-African activists had been a relatively fortunate minority within the community. The majority of black people in Britain in the late nineteenth and early twentieth centuries lived very hard lives indeed. The largest group, in terms of occupation, were seamen. Dumped from tramp steamers or attracted by the prospect of casual work, black seamen had begun to find a berth in Cardiff by the 1870s, when the south

Wales coalfield was growing rapidly and Cardiff, Newport, and Barry were beginning to flourish as coal ports.[1] By 1881 Cardiff had a big enough floating population of black seamen for a Sailors' Rest to be instituted for them.[2] Thirty years later, Cardiff was second only to London in the proportion of its population that was foreign-born, and about 700 of these were Africans and West Indians.[3] Laid off in Cardiff, Newport, Barry, London, Liverpool, Hull, Tyneside, or Glasgow, black seamen found it hard to get another ship, harder still to find work ashore. Most white seamen rejected them as shipmates; white dockers, too, refused to work alongside them. Having spent the small sums they had been paid off with, having pawned any spare clothes and other belongings, destitute seamen tramped from port to port, desperate for work. Their quest was endless and almost hopeless. Help from compatriots and parish hand-outs kept them from starving; but they often went hungry. From time to time the Colonial Office would repatriate unemployed seamen, but in the case of West Indians the authorities in the islands they came from often refused to let them go back.

At length this state of affairs led to a parliamentary inquiry. The Committee on Distressed Colonial and Indian Subjects reported in 1910. One witness told the committee that about three in five of the distressed blacks were seafaring men; another, that as many as 50 distressed West Indians came to his notice in London every year; a third, that 'men of their own race domiciled in London are often kind to them'. About a quarter of the destitute black people were said to be 'student adventurers'. There were also a number of people brought to Britain as servants ('butlers and nurses' from the West Indies), who had left their employers because of bad treatment, much as their eighteenth-century predecessors had done. One witness warned the committee that 'the desperate Indians of the student type not infrequently lend themselves as tools in the hands of the dangerous agitators settled in this country as well as on the continent'. Someone from the Colonial Office's West African Department said the Africans who called there for help were 'generally wasters . . . probably people who would not stay in the workhouse, but simply go out into the streets to sponge upon anybody they can.' And he added: 'It might be a useful thing to have some compulsory power of repatriating people like that.'[4]

The outbreak of war in 1914 brought dramatic changes for black workers in Britain. Now there was well-paid work for them to do. Their help was needed for the war effort. Black labourers were made welcome in the munition and chemical factories. Black seamen, replacing men needed by the navy, were made welcome in the merchant service. By the end of the war there were about 20,000 black people in Britain.[5]

But there was change of another kind. Black men were also needed as cannon-fodder. 'If we are good enough to fight the wars of this country' was Archer's phrase in 1918. And they had been. Although the War Office decided to confine the 3rd and 4th battalions of the West India Regiment to ammunition-carrying and labour services in France – 'black Bermudans and West Indians were never allowed to be actively engaged in the fighting on the western front'[6] – troops from the West Indies and Africa fought bravely and well in many other theatres of war, including campaigns against German forces in Africa, just as Indian troops fought bravely and well in France and elsewhere.[7]

In 1917 the *Daily Mirror* published pictures of the Gold Coast Regiment's black machine-gunners, who had 'shown marked ability . . . in fights against the Huns'.[8] In the same year an entire book, published in London, was devoted to black soldiers' contribution to the British war effort. Written by the former colonial administrator Sir Harry Johnston, friend of Rhodes and Stanley, it was called *The Black Man's Part in the War*. It told how commanders had praised black troops for their 'pluck, gallantry and devotion', and for the tenacity with which they stood up to heavy machine-gun fire. It even had a chapter, honeyed with promises, on what the British Empire must do for the 'dark races' after the war.[9] Just as the war took a huge toll of black seamen – from Cardiff alone, 1,000 were killed at sea, and another 400, rescued after their ships were sunk, went back to the port to die of the effects of exposure[10] – so a large number of black soldiers were wounded, crippled for life, or killed in battle. The British West Indies Regiment alone (not to be confused with the West India Regiment), whose rank and file were almost entirely black troops, lost 185 killed or died of wounds and 1,071 who died of sickness; a further 697 were wounded.[11]

Many wounded and crippled black soldiers were brought back to Britain for treatment in military hospitals. Many were decorated as heroes. Sixteen members of the West African Frontier Force (whose white officers customarily referred to their rank and file as 'the Apes')[12] and the King's African Rifles were awarded the DCM.[13] The British West Indies Regiment had 5 DSOs, 9 MCs, 2 MBEs, 8 DCMs, 37 MMs, and 49 Mentions in Dispatches.[14] Many black soldiers were demobilized in Britain. So, by the end of the war, Britain's black population was not only bigger than ever before but also included a proportion of seasoned fighting men, trained to defend themselves against attack. Soon they would have to.

A few weeks before the end of the First World War, about 2,000 wounded soldiers were patients in the Belmont Road Military Auxiliary Hospital, Liverpool. About 50 of them were black men. Most of these were in the British West Indies Regiment, and most had one or both feet blown off. Relations between black and white patients were good – until some newcomers arrived. These were white soldiers who had served in South Africa. When the newcomers started taunting the black soldiers there was a fight in which a sledgehammer was flung at a group of black men, two of whom were legless. When black soldiers were taunted in the concert-room, two decided to leave and, as they were hobbling out on their crutches, a white soldier called: 'Make room for the swine to pass.' The concert-room was then put out of bounds to black troops. A rumour went round that the ban had been lifted, and a legless black sergeant called John Demerette, known as 'Demetrius', crawled towards the guard with the intention of asking if the rumour were true. The guard seized him and threw him into a cell. His shouts brought ten crippled black soldiers to his aid. The cry went round, 'The niggers are fighting the guard.' Between 400 and 500 white soldiers went into battle against 50 black soldiers, attacking them with crutches and sticks and throwing pots, pans, and kettles at them. A white nurse, knocked down in the mêlée, went into shock and later died of pneumonia. Some of the white soldiers, to their credit, defended their black comrades as best they could. A contemporary report said:

> Some of the British Tommies who had fought side by side with these coloured soldiers in the trenches . . . took sides with the coloured soldiers . . . When the Provost Marshal arrived on the scene with a number of military police to restore order, there were many white soldiers seen standing over crippled black limbless soldiers, and protecting them with their sticks and crutches from the furious onslaught of the other white soldiers until order was restored.[15]

London newspapers blamed the black soldiers for the rioting, but a War Office inquiry found otherwise.[16]

10. Under attack

Racism as riot: 1919

Lynch mobs in Liverpool and Cardiff

When armistice was signalled on 11 November 1918, the war-time boom for black labour fizzled out as quickly as it had begun. Once again shipping companies chose to sign on white foreign seamen rather than black British seamen. The National Sailors' and Firemen's Union and National Union of Ships' Stewards, Cooks, Butchers and Bakers, the two forerunners of the National Union of Seamen, were implacably opposed to the employment of black seamen when white crews were available. Seven weeks after the end of the war William P. Samuels from British Guiana, a seaman stranded in Cardiff, wrote to the Colonial Office:

> We kindly beg to appeal to you for justice. We are seafaring men that has served this Country faithfully in her past difficulties either in the services of His Britanic Majesty or in Merchantile Marine. The Places of our birth are surely British Possessions or Protectorates and here in Great Britain which is the Capital of the British Empire we are badly treated by the British People. We do not want any favour all we want is fair play. Every morning we go down to shipping offices to find our selves work so as to make an honest bread and are bluntly refused on account of our colour. Whereas, foreigners of all nationality get the preference. This is not only in Cardiff but throughout the United Kingdom. What is the British Motto? are we not men and brothers whom Christ died for? . . . Why take such filthy advantages of men who have done you no wrong? . . . Is it Because we have no one to fight our cause? Why treat us as mere brute? Is it because we are mere dogs which neither Bark nor bite? No sir, we are men, men that gives the British Empire little or no trouble . . . We kindly ask to step before foreigners on any British Ship.[1]

By the following spring over 130 black British seamen were on the beach in Glasgow, and hundreds more elsewhere.[2] It was these men who were cheated when the Ministry of Labour's Employment Department sent secret instructions to labour exchange managers that unemployed black seamen of British nationality should be left in ignorance of their rights: 'The majority of these are eligible for out-of-work donation, but they have apparently not realised this, and it is not considered desirable to take any further steps to acquaint them of the position.'[3]

The first of the so-called race riots in British ports took place on Tyneside. Arab and Somali seamen are said to have settled in South Shields in the 1860s, and there were some West African and West Indian seamen in North Shields before the First World War. The war increased the area's black population fourfold.[4] In February 1919 some Arab seamen, all British subjects, having just paid £2 each to clear their union books, which had to be up to date before they could ship out, were then refused work. An official of the stewards' and cooks' union, J.B.Fye, incited a crowd of foreign white seamen against them; he was later convicted of using language likely to cause a breach of the peace. Fye hit one of the Arabs, who hit him back. The crowd chased the Arabs to Holborn, the district of South Shields where they lived. Here they were joined by some compatriots armed with revolvers, who fired warning shots over the heads of the attackers. The Arabs then turned the tables by chasing the crowd back to the shipping office, wrecking it pretty thoroughly, and beating up Fye and another union official. Army and navy patrols were called in and 12 Arabs were arrested. At Durham assizes, where the judge expressed some sympathy for them, three were acquitted, 12 were sentenced to three months', and two to one month's, hard labour.[5]

Demobilization had increased Liverpool's black population to a figure variously estimated at 2,000 and 5,000, of whom a large proportion was out of work. In one week alone, in the spring of 1919, about 120 black workers employed for years in the big Liverpool sugar refineries and oilcake mills were sacked because white workers now refused to work with them. Unemployed black workers, living on credit from day to day, were being turned out of their lodgings.[6]

On 13 May the secretary of the Liverpool Ethiopian Association, the merchant D.T.Aleifasakure Toummavah, went to see the lord mayor. He told him that between 500 and 600 black men, mostly discharged British soldiers and sailors, were out of work and stranded in the area and anxious to go home. Some were 'practically starving, work having been refused to them on account of their colour'. He suggested that the Colonial Office repatriate them and give each man a bounty of £5, since most had pawned their clothes to buy food. Some, he added, 'have been wounded, and lost limbs and eyes fighting for the Empire'. The mayor also received a deputation claiming to represent 5,000 jobless white ex-servicemen and complaining of the presence of black workers in the city competing for jobs. 'Only the other night', the lord mayor told the Colonial Office, 'there was a fight between the two races, and matters are not likely to improve in this direction as the position develops and probably grows worse.'[7] (Initial reaction of one official at the Colonial Office to the £5 bounty suggestion was that 'the Lord Mayor should be given a hint that if Liverpool wants to get rid of men on these terms it is up to that city to find the £5'.)[8] Liverpool police did little to lessen the tension when, in the same month, they fought a battle with black men alleged to be running an illegal gaming house.[9]

By the second half of May black men peacefully walking the Liverpool streets were being 'attacked again and again'.[10] On 4 June two Scandinavians stabbed a West Indian, John Johnson, when he refused to give them a cigarette. Johnson was severely wounded in the face, and the news spread quickly. Next evening eight of his friends went to the pub the Scandinavians used, threw beer over a group of them, then attacked them with sticks, knives, razors, and pieces of iron taken from lamp-posts, knocking unconscious a policeman who tried to stop them. Five Scandinavians were taken to hospital, but only one was detained.

In an effort to arrest those involved, police raided boarding-houses used by black seamen. The seamen defended themselves, one with a poker, others with revolvers, knives, and razors. One policeman was shot in the mouth, another in the neck, a third was slashed on face and neck, and a fourth had his wrist broken. At one of the raided houses, 18 Upper Pitt Street, lived Charles Wotten, a 24-year-old ship's fireman, variously described as a Bermudan and a Trinidadian, who had been discharged from the navy in the previous March. Wotten ran from the house, closely pursued by two policemen – and by a crowd of between 200 and 300 hurling missiles. The police caught him at the edge of Queen's Dock, but the lynch mob tore him from them and threw him into the water. Shouting 'Let him drown!', they pelted him with stones as he swam around. Soon he died, and his corpse was dragged from the dock. No arrests were made.[11]

For the next few days an anti-black reign of terror raged in Liverpool. On 8 June three West Africans were stabbed in the street. On 9 and 10 June mobs of youths and young men in 'well organised' gangs, their total strength varying from 2,000 to 10,000, roamed the streets 'savagely attacking, beating and stabbing every negro they could find'.[12] So said a confidential police report to the Colonial Office, which was naturally anxious about possible repercussions in the West Indies. 'Whenever a negro was seen he was chased, and if caught, severely beaten', reported *The Times*. When they were able to make a stand, in their own dwellings, black people did so, defending themselves as best they could. Hunted down in the streets as individuals all they could do was flee from their pursuers – some of whom took their belts off and lashed their quarries' heads and shoulders with the buckle ends as they fled. 'Quite inoffensive' people were attacked in the streets, including an ex-serviceman who held three decorations for war service. A black man 'holding a good position on one of the Liverpool liners' was dragged from a car, beaten up, and robbed of £175. On the evening of 10 June Toxteth Park was reported to be 'in a wild state of excitement, thousands of people filling the thoroughfares'.[13]

Hysteria grew as house after house occupied by black people was wrecked, looted, and set on fire. In Jackson Street, a crowd of 2,000 wrecked a lodging-house, breaking up chairs to use the legs as bludgeons. A boarding-house on the corner of Chester and Dexter Streets had its windows and doors smashed with sticks and stones, the coping-stones and rails in front of the house torn down. The Elder Dempster shipping line's hostel for black seamen, accommodating between 300 and 400, was wrecked. The David Lewis hostel for black ratings was attacked and its windows were smashed. A house in Stanhope Street was set on fire. In Mill Street, the furniture was carried from a house, piled up outside, and set on fire; then the house itself went up in flames. In Beaufort Street the mob tore down a house's shutters for battering-rams, smashed doors and windows to splinters, dragged out furniture and bedding and made a bonfire of them. Houses in Parliament Street and Chester Street were wrecked. Five white youths were seen on a roof, stripping off the slates and throwing them down on the occupants' heads.

'There is a feeling of terror among the coloured people of the city', reported a local newspaper. All night long until sunrise, it added, 'black men could be seen in companies hastening along unfrequented thoroughfares to the nearest police station'. Seventy people who left their homes to shelter in the Ethiopian Hall, the

Ethiopian Association's social club, were transferred to the Cheapside bridewell in police vans for their protection. By 10 June, 700 men, women, and children had taken refuge in the bridewells and more were arriving hourly. Others sought sanctuary in fire stations.[14]

At the height of the rioting, the *Liverpool Courier* poured oil on the flames with a feature article headed 'Where East Meets West' and an editorial headed 'Black and White'. The former told how, on a visit to St James Place,

> You glimpse black figures beneath the gas lamps, and somehow you think of pimps, and bullies, and women, and birds of ill-omen generally, as now and again you notice a certain watchful callousness that seems to hint of nefarious trades and drunkenness in dark rooms . . .
>
> Behind the smashed glass of the upstairs rooms negroes hide in the darkness, protected from violence by a cordon of police. An ambulance goes past, and the howl of the mob dies away on a delighted note when the word goes about that 'another bloomin' nigger has been laid out'.

The editorial, demanding 'the stern punishment of black scoundrels', was more inflammatory still:

> One of the chief reasons of popular anger behind the present disturbances lies in the fact that the average negro is nearer the animal than is the average white man, and that there are women in Liverpool who have no self-respect . . . The white man . . . regards [the black man] as part child, part animal, and part savage . . .
>
> It is quite true that many of the blacks in Liverpool are of a low type, that they insult and threaten respectable women in the street, and that they are invariably unpleasant and provocative.[15]

An 'experienced' police officer took a slightly different view. Attributing much of the trouble to outsiders, he told the *Manchester Guardian*: 'The people here understand the negroes . . . They know that most of them are only big children who when they get money like to make a show . . . The negroes would not have been touched but for their relations with white women. This has caused the entire trouble.'[16]

It was left to a local magistrate to say that it was the white mobs which were 'making the name of Liverpool an abomination and disgrace to the rest of the country'.[17]

That was not however the feeling in south Wales, which was experiencing at the same time 'one of the most vicious outbreaks of racial violence that has yet occurred in Britain'. During a week of anti-black rioting, three men were killed and dozens injured, and the damage caused to property cost Cardiff council over £3,000 to repair. The rioting 'left a scar on the race relations of the city which took more than a generation to heal'.[18]

The trouble began in Newport. On 6 June 1919 a crowd collected when a black man was alleged to have made an offensive remark to a white woman. One account said he put his arm round her and was attacked by a soldier. There was a fight in which many people were hurt, crowds started smashing the windows of black people's homes, and the occupants defended themselves with pokers and staves and fired warning shots over their assailants' heads. Two houses in George Street were wrecked and ransacked by a mob of several thousands that smashed every window, tore out the window-frames, threw bedding and furniture, including a 'valuable piano', into a nearby railway siding, and set fire to them. In Dolphin Street, Chinese laundries and a Greek-owned lodging-house were wrecked, as were black people's houses in Ruperra Street and a restaurant in Commercial Road owned by a black man named Delgrada. Twenty black and two white men were arrested. Plain-clothes and mounted police were drafted into the town, but it took a baton charge to disperse crowds making fresh attacks on George Street boarding-houses. 'We are all one in Newport and mean to clear these niggers out', one rioter told a reporter. The scene in Newport, said the *South Wales Argus*, looked like the aftermath of an air raid: 'Windows are smashed, furniture in the front rooms has been wrecked, blood-stains are visible.'[19]

On 11 June, at Cadoxton near Barry, a 30-year-old demobilized white soldier named Frederick Henry Longman, a dock labourer by trade, accosted a 45-year-old seaman from the French West Indies named Charles Emanuel with the words 'Why don't you go into your own street?' then punched him on the forehead. Three other white men joined in, one of whom began hitting Emanuel on the back with a poker. Emanuel took out a clasp-knife and stabbed Longman, killing him instantly. Emanuel was chased by a large crowd and arrested with the knife still in his hand; he was later found guilty of manslaughter and sent to prison for five years. After his arrest crowds gathered outside the police station, smashed the windows of black people's homes, and 'paraded the streets of Cadoxton looking for coloured men' until the early hours of the morning. Next day, though extra police had been drafted in, there were attempts to wreck black people's homes.[20]

Cardiff's black population had increased from about 700 on the eve of the war to about 3,000 in April 1919. About 1,200 of these were unemployed seamen. There were at least as many demobilized white soldiers in the city, most of them unskilled. On 11 June a brake containing black men and their white wives, returning from an excursion, attracted a large and hostile crowd. Soon a crowd of whites and a crowd of blacks were lined up on opposite sides of Canal Parade bridge. A reporter saw 'a howling mob of young fellows and girls facing the blacks at about 100 yards distance'. With shouts of 'Come on and set about them!' the whites made a rush from the north side throwing stones, whereupon revolver shots came from the black crowd and a white soldier was wounded in the thigh. The whites pressed forward in an attempt to reach Bute Town, the narrow cluster of streets between the Glamorganshire Canal and the Taff Vale Railway where a large number of Cardiff's black citizens had their homes, but police managed to stop most of them.

The chief constable's report, issued a month later, blamed whites for the original incident. 'If the crowd had overpowered the police and got through', he wrote, 'the result would have been disastrous, as the black population would probably have fought with desperation and inflicted great loss of life.'

Some attackers did get into Bute Street, where they smashed the doors and windows of Arab-owned lodging-houses with sticks – one shop front was 'smashed to matchwood' – and where a woman was arrested for flourishing a razor and 'vowing vengeance on "niggers" '. A house in Homfray Street was set on fire and gutted, and in Caroline Street a white man died after his throat was cut – by a black man, it was alleged, though no eyewitness ever came forward, no black man was found in the vicinity, and no one was ever charged with the crime. A house owned by black people at the corner of Morgan Street and Adam Street was ransacked. Police broke into a house in Hope Street and dragged out a black man with blood streaming from his head: 'He was greeted by a howl from the crowd, and several kicks and punches were aimed at him.' A second soon appeared, 'in much the same condition as his compatriot'. Last to be brought out was 'a white girl, whose mouth was bleeding'. A black man called Norman Roberts was admitted to hospital with a severe knife wound in the abdomen. The disturbances went on until around midnight.[21]

This was only the prelude to a much more determined and organized attack on Cardiff's black community over the next few days. The whole of the city's police force was concentrated in the cordoned-off area that *The Times* called 'nigger town'; a company of the Welsh Regiment was secretly drafted into Cardiff and held in readiness; and the stipendiary magistrate was preparing to read the Riot Act. Contemporary reports make it clear that 'Colonial soldiers' (i.e. Australians) armed with rifles placed themselves at the head of the lynch mobs. 'The methods adopted by the soldiers', said one report, 'were those of active service, and the men, after firing from the prone position upon the blacks, crawled back to safety.' Some of these riflemen were in khaki or blue uniforms, others in mufti with medal ribbons. The *Western Mail* gave a vivid account of an attack on the former Princess Royal hotel in Millicent Street:

> Several Colonial soldiers present constituted themselves the ringleaders of the besieging party, which was largely made up of discharged soldiers . . .
>
> The door of the house was attacked and it was quickly burst in. Men crowded into the narrow hall and began to ascend the stairs . . .
>
> A revolver shot rang out, and with it the exclamation, 'My God, I am hit!' Five other shots quickly followed.

The attackers dropped flat on their faces, crawling back and telling those behind to do the same. They held up a table as a shield, and the defenders backed to the wall of the room. 'Once at close quarters, each of the surviving attackers took his man, and soon desperate struggles were in progress around the room.' Meanwhile 'others of the raiding party were . . . busily engaged in ransacking the premises. Kit-bags containing clothing were hastily abstracted, and there were willing "receivers" outside.' After it had been looted the house was set on fire. It was in Millicent Street that 40-year-old John Donovan, wearing his Mons ribbon, was shot through the heart by a cornered Arab.[22]

Ibrahim Ismaa'il, a Somali seaman and poet who was living in Cardiff at this time, refers to the Millicent Street fighting in his remarkable autobiography, completed in 1928 and recently discovered by Dr Richard Pankhurst. A Warsangeli, from the eastern part of what was then the British Somaliland protectorate, Ismaa'il was between 18 and 23 years old and worked as a ship's fireman. He and some companions had only just come to Cardiff:

> Shortly after our arrival the black people in Cardiff were attacked by crowds of white people . . .
>
> A Warsangeli named 'Abdi Langara had a boarding house in Millicent Street, right in the European part of the town. It is there that I used to have my dinner every day. 'Abdi acted as a sort of agent for the Warsangeli, who left their money with him when they went to sea, and also had their letters sent to his place. As soon as the fight started, all the Warsangeli who were in Cardiff went to Millicent Street to defend 'Abdi's house in case it was attacked. But to me and to my best friend – who has since died in Mecca – they said : 'You are too young to come, and you have never faced difficulties of this kind.' We insisted, for we could not bear to stay away when our brothers were in danger of being killed, but our plea was of no avail . . . So we went to the Somali boarding house of Haadzi 'Aali and there we waited, ready for an attack, as we expected that a crowd of white people might break in at any moment.
>
> In Millicent Street, the fight started at about 7:30 p.m. and lasted a fairly long time. Seven or eight Warsangeli defended the house and most of them got badly wounded. Some of the white people also received wounds. In the end, the whites took possession of the first floor, soaked it with paraffin oil and set it alight. The Somalis managed to keep up the fight until the police arrived. One of them was left for dead in the front room and was later carried to the hospital where he recovered; some escaped through a neighbouring house and came to tell us the story of what had happened, the others gave themselves up to the police, and we did not see them for a long time.[23]

Crowds led by soldiers were surging from street to street wherever the cry of 'blacks' went up. One victim had a crowd of about 1,000 after him. The newspaper accounts are eloquent: 'Always "the black man" was their quarry, and whenever one was rooted out by the police . . . the mob rushed upon him, and he got away with difficulty' – amid cries of 'Kill him!' A black man spotted near the Wharf bridge was

> first insulted and then attacked by three whites, one of whom blew a whistle. This seemed to be an expected signal, because hundreds of persons rushed up from the neighbouring streets,

> including many women and girls, who had sticks and stones, and flung them at the unfortunate coloured man as they chased him along the street.

Two men dragged out of their Bute Street house 'fought desperately with frying pans and pokers'. A Somali priest, Hadji Mahomet, was prepared to face the mob, but his white wife pleaded with him to hide so he clambered up a drainpipe, hid on the roof, 'and with true Eastern stoicism watched his residence being reduced to a skeleton'. A Malayan boarding-house in Bute Terrace was wrecked and the occupants, fleeing to the roof, were pelted with stones. In Homfray Street an Arab named Ali Abdul fired a revolver at his assailants; when he was arrested there were shouts of 'Now we've got him!' and 'Lynch him!' (Charged later with attempted murder, he 'had some difficulty in walking into court owing to an injured leg, and he also bore evidence on his forehead of having received injuries'.) An Arab 'caught and maltreated' in Tredegar Street lay unconscious for a long time.

One whom the lynch mob did succeed in killing, a young Arab named Mahommed Abdullah, died in hospital of a fractured skull after being savagely beaten in an attack on an Arab restaurant and boarding-house, used chiefly by Somalis, at 264 Bute Street. The mob charged down the street, threw stones into the building from both sides, and smashed the windows. Shots were fired from upstairs. The mob surged in, and police arrived soon afterwards. The inquest on Abdullah could not decide whether he had been hit on the head with a chair leg or a police truncheon. Hundreds of black people attended his funeral. Murder charges against six white men were dropped for lack of evidence.[24]

Some former members of the British West Indies Regiment were daring enough to go about the streets with their uniforms on, which afforded them some protection. But not much. One black ex-serviceman, described in a local paper as 'a well-set-up young fellow', 'proved to be a brave man, and in perfect English appealed to the crowd not to molest him, but this did not prevent him receiving several blows' before police escorted him away.[25]

For the most part however, in the words of the *Western Mail*, 'the efforts of the police were confined to keeping the white men from damaging property'. Property being more important than people, the community under siege had two choices. They could leave the city; or they could turn their ghetto into a fortress. A few did leave, on the afternoon of 13 June: a sad little procession of seamen with kit-bags on their backs and sticks in their hands, escorted by police and followed by jeering crowds.[26] The majority chose to stay and, if need be, fight.

As crowds gathered again that evening in St Mary Street, Custom House Street, The Hayes, and the top end of Bute Road, the black citizens of Loudoun Square, Maria Street, Sophia Street, and Angelina Street 'established quietly determined means of self-protection'.[27] They posted sentries, loaded their guns, and left no one in doubt of their mood, as a *South Wales News* reporter who got through the police cordon testified:

> The coloured men, while calm and collected, were well prepared for any attack, and had the mob from the city broken through the police cordon there would have been bloodshed on a big scale, and the attacking force would have suffered heavily . . . Hundreds of negroes were collected, but these were very peaceful, and were amicably discussing the situation among themselves. Nevertheless, they were in a determined mood, and ready to defend 'our quarter of the city' at all costs. They had posted sentries at each entrance to give notice of the approach of any hostile crowd . . . An old resident of Loudoun-square told me that he and his wife had watched the negroes loading revolvers. They made no secret of it . . . As my informant put it, 'There is enough arms and ammunition among them to stock an arsenal.' Long-term black residents said: 'It will be hell let loose . . . if the mob comes into our streets . . . If we are unprotected from hooligan rioters who can blame us for trying to protect ourselves?'[28]

An outstanding leader of Cardiff's black community had emerged in the shape of Dr Rufus Leicester Fennell. A West Indian medically trained in the United States, he had survived 314 days of trench warfare and had been wounded three times while serving in Mesopotamia, where he had attended thousands of British troops. Lacking British medical qualifications, he had been practising as a dentist in Pontypridd. When the rioting started in Cardiff he went there. Neil Evans, interviewing old people in Cardiff a few years ago, found that Fennell was remembered for his courage and intelligence: 'During the riots he was said to have walked boldly into the centre of the town, despite warnings of the possible dire consequences of this action.'[29] Aged 31, about six feet tall, well dressed and highly articulate, Fennell acted as the community's spokesman in negotiations with the authorities; pressed the claims of those who wanted to be repatriated; told reporters 'that it is absolutely necessary to grip the evil, and not to play with it'; and told one of several protest meetings held at the docks by West Indians, Somalis, Arabs, Egyptians, and 'Portuguese subjects' that it was their duty to stay within the law, but 'if they did not protect their homes after remaining within the law they would be cowards, not men'.[30]

By mid-September 600 black men had been repatriated.[31] But not everyone involved wanted to be, and part of Cardiff's black population indignantly rejected the offer. What the chief constable, in a confidential report to Scotland Yard, called the 'militant section' insisted on their right as British subjects to get fair treatment and stay in the United Kingdom. And some of the militants, the chief constable added, 'expressed their willingness to be repatriated but openly stated that it would only be for the object of creating racial feeling against members of the white race domiciled in their country'.[32]

Two hundred of those who did want to be repatriated – Egyptians, Somalis, and Arabs – were sent to Plymouth by train, and Fennell went with them. It may have been Fennell who told the weekly paper *John Bull* how shamefully they were treated. They were penniless, but the tiny gratuity promised them was never paid. They were hungry, but were given nothing to eat on the journey. And when they went on board ship the staff were all off duty, the captain was asleep, and there was no food at all for them. 'These coloured Britons had all done first-class war work', commented *John Bull*, 'yet they were treated worse than repatriated enemy aliens.'[33]

Soon afterwards Fennell was in London, complaining to MPs and the Home Office about the flaws in the repatriation process. Some had been sent home before they were paid compensation for losses suffered in the riots; others, before receiving the back pay due to them. Fennell accused the Cardiff police of prejudice against black people and asked that police cease to supervise the departures.[34] But the officials were unsympathetic. Soon after leaving the Home Office Fennell found himself under arrest on a trumped-up fraud charge. After being kept in custody in London for a while he came up in court in Cardiff on 22 July, accused of obtaining £2 by false pretences from Ahmed Ben Ahmed Demary, a boarding-house master. Fennell's solicitor told the court that there was 'a great deal at the back of the case' and that 'certain men were anxious to keep the accused in prison because of the way he had watched the interests of the coloured men'. The magistrate dismissed the charge.[35]

London was not spared sporadic outbreaks of anti-black – and anti-Chinese – rioting. On 16 April there was a 'serious riot' in Cable Street, Stepney. Shots were fired, a violent street fight took place, and several black seamen were injured.[36] On 29 May a seaman named William Samuel, described by a Colonial Office civil servant as 'a burly negro, with an aggressive manner', wrote from the Sailors' Home in St Anne Street, Limehouse, to the colonial secretary, complaining of attacks on black men in the London streets: 'a sargeant of police said to us last night, why; We want you niggers out of our country this is a white man's country and not yours.'[37] That same evening large crowds gathered outside the Strangers' Home in West India Dock Road, cat-calling and insulting every black person who appeared and trying to force their way in. There were similar scenes outside lodging-houses used by black seamen. Outside the St Anne Street sailors' hostel 29-year-old John Martin, a Jamaican on four weeks' leave from the Royal Navy, was seized by the head from behind, knocked down by men armed with sticks, and kicked in the mouth. Alleged to have fired a revolver towards the crowd, Martin was arrested with injuries to head and face, and charged with wounding a ship's fireman. He was found not guilty.[38] On 16 June a coffee-shop in Cable Street used by black people was stormed by a crowd that seized one of the customers and beat him.[39] Next day there were disturbances in Poplar, where a gang attacked a house occupied by a Chinese family, cleared out the furniture, stacked it in the middle of the street, and set fire to it, causing a 'huge blaze' that gutted the house.[40]

During that hot summer of 1919 black people in Britain were not only being attacked physically, in their homes and in the streets. They were attacked also with the pen by those who excused the aggressors by blaming their victims. The *Manchester Guardian*, for instance, blamed black people for daring to defend themselves against lynch mobs: 'The quiet, apparently inoffensive, nigger becomes a demon when armed with revolver or razor.'[41] Above all, black men were blamed, as that Liverpool policeman had blamed them, for associating with white women. This explanation for the riots was advanced by a former British colonial administrator, Sir Ralph Williams, who had served in Bechuanaland and Barbados and had been governor of the Windward Islands in 1906–9. His recreation was 'ceaseless travelling to far-away countries',[42] and when the riots reached their climax he wrote a letter to *The Times* summing up what he had learnt on his travels:

> To almost every white man and woman who has lived a life among coloured races, intimate association between black or coloured men and white women is a thing of horror . . . It is an instinctive certainty that sexual relations between white women and coloured men revolt our very nature . . . What blame . . . to those white men who, seeing these conditions and loathing them, resort to violence? . . .
>
> We cannot forcibly repatriate British subjects of good character, but we can take such steps as will prevent the employment of an unusually large number of men of colour in our great shipping centres.[43]

Five days later *The Times* printed a stinging reply, drawing attention to the existence of hundreds of thousands of persons of mixed race in South Africa and the West Indies, where 'young girls of 13 and 14 years of age are used to gratify the base lust of white seducers'. These girls were left with children of mixed race on their hands 'to mourn the "honour" of the civilized white man'. The writer went on:

> I do not believe that any excuse can be made for white men who take the law into their own hands because they say they believe that the association between the men of my race and white women is degrading.
>
> Sir Ralph Williams and those who think like him should remember that writing in this way gives a stimulus to these racial riots and can only have one ultimate result, the downfall of the British Empire . . .
>
> If Sir Ralph Williams thinks that the problem can be solved by sending every black or coloured unit forthwith back to his own country, then we should be compelled to see that every white man is sent back to England from Africa and from the West India islands in order that the honour of our sisters and daughters there may be kept intact.[44]

The writer of this letter was Felix Eugene Michael Hercules, for a brief but key period one of the inspirers and leaders of the national liberation movement in the British West Indies.

Felix Hercules and the lessons of 1919

To understand the anti-black riots in Britain – and the black community's response – we have to see them in the context of social unrest both in Britain and in Britain's Caribbean colonies. The end of the First World War ushered in 'the most troublous and stormy age of profound social crisis ever known by this country and that overwhelming majority of its people who toil to live'.[45] In 1919 a strikers' demonstration in Glasgow was attacked by police and its leaders were mercilessly beaten; miners and railway and transport workers were in highly militant mood; there was a lightning police strike; there were mutinies in army camps and depots, and thousands of Army Service Corps men commandeered lorries and poured into London to lay their grievances before the government.

The divisive role of racism in Liverpool and Cardiff that year is obvious. White workers in bitter economic competition with black workers were mobilized into lynch mobs led by armed groups. This was very far from the revolution that Britain's rulers feared and Glasgow's strike leaders admitted afterwards they should have been aiming for. But the social unrest of 1919 was not limited to the heart of the British Empire – and that was what gave Hercules' reply to Williams considerably more political bite than either, perhaps, could have realized when it was printed. A 'rising tide of colour' was bringing 'serious race riots in the United States, constitutional agitation in India, and economic and political unrest in several British African colonies, in South Africa, and the Belgian Congo . . . It was believed that this new race-consciousness was a direct result of the Great War'.[46] Events in Liverpool and Cardiff could not but stimulate the growth of black consciousness in Britain's colonies. In particular, they 'hastened the growth of anti-colonialism in the British West Indies'.[47]

In a memorandum on 'Repatriation of Coloured Men', the colonial secretary, Lord Milner, pointed out that many of the black men attacked in the riots had served in the army, navy, and merchant service during the war and bitterly resented the ingratitude shown in the attacks. He feared the effect their return to the colonies would have on attitudes to white minorities there.[48] His fears were soon justified.

By mid-July some of the Trinidadians who had experienced the Cardiff riots were back home, and within days of their return there was fighting in the streets against sailors from HMS *Dartmouth*. Four months later the Trinidad workers' fury erupted in a dock strike that brought British colonialism to its knees within days, when the governor persuaded the shipping agents to grant the strikers' demand for a 25 per cent wage increase.[49] Soldiers demobilized from the British West Indies Regiment began an insurrection in Belize in July, and people were heard shouting: 'This is our country and we want to get the white man out. The white man has no right here.'[50] In the same month five or six seamen from HMS *Constance* were wounded in hand-to-hand fighting in Kingston, Jamaica, and the captain landed an armed party to put down the outbreak – which Jamaica's acting governor attributed to 'the treatment which had been received by coloured sailors at Cardiff and Liverpool'.[51] Another repercussion of the British riots was a mutiny in the September on board the SS *Ocra*, carrying black seamen for repatriation and military prisoners.[52] Protests about the British riots from such groups as the St Kitts Universal Benevolent Association also caused concern at the Colonial Office.[53]

By the October of that year the upsurge of black consciousness in the West Indies, the growing labour troubles there, and the start of the national liberation struggle had so alarmed the British government that it sent the State Department a confidential report on 'Unrest among the Negroes', a copy of which came to light in the United States National Archives in the 1960s. Britain's rulers feared that black radicalism in the USA might infect, and inflame, their black subjects in the Caribbean. They were pretty scared of Marcus Garvey's militant paper, the *Negro World*. And the activities of Felix Hercules also caused them much concern.[54]

Born in Venezuela in 1888, Felix Eugene Michael Hercules grew up in Trinidad, where his father was a civil servant. While still at school he launched the colony's first Young Men's Coloured Association. He graduated from Queen's Royal College, taught at a college in San Fernando, married, and fathered several children. During the First World War he came to Britain and took a BA degree at London University. Towards the end of 1918 the Sierra Leonean businessman and journalist John Eldred Taylor offered him the editorship of the *African Telegraph*, published in London.* He also became general secretary of the Society of Peoples of African Origin and associate secretary of the African Progress Union.

* Taylor, earlier an associate of Dusé Mohamed Ali, was soon to be ordered to pay £400 libel damages to Captain Joseph Fitzpatrick, a British colonial official whom he had accused of ordering the flogging of two women in Nigeria. The captain's legal costs were secretly paid by the British government.[55] The jury added a rider that 'if the flogging is still practised in Northern Nigeria the proper authorities should take steps to stop it'.[56]

Scotland Yard's director of intelligence, Sir Basil Thomson, an eager consumer of police spies' gossip, was soon speculating about alleged disharmony between Hercules and the Union's elderly secretary, Robert Broadhurst.[57] (The Society and the Union were merged in July 1919, the new organization being called the Society of African Peoples,[58] but the amalgamation seems to have been short-lived.)

Towards the end of June 1919 Hercules began a tour of the West Indies, with the dual aim of investigating conditions and recruiting for the Society of Peoples of African Origin. He spent two months in Jamaica and a few weeks in Trinidad, then went to British Guiana. Three months later he tried to get back into Trinidad, but the governor would not let him land. In the West Indies as in Britain, police kept close watch on him and reported every word he said. 'He is a very learned man', said one police report.[59] But they could not pin anything on him. There is an air of frustration about Sir Basil Thomson's comment in December 1919: 'Though Hercules is careful what he says in public, in private he is inciting the negroes to take matters into their own hands.'[60] Eleven days later Major-General Sir Newton James Moore, MP, former premier of Western Australia, was assuring the Commons that Hercules' activities had 'a great deal to do with the unrest in the West Indies'.[61]

After 1920 we lose sight of Hercules; but early in 1921, in an intelligence summary of economic and social conditions in the West Indies, Rear-Admiral Sir Allan Everett reported that 'agitators of the Hercules and Marcus Garvey type, who thunder against white rule and preach the doctrine of self determination in countries where blacks greatly preponderate, are growing factors to be reckoned with as regards potential unrest'.[62]

Hercules' published statements make it clear that he 'thundered' in the Pan-Africanist tradition. He told readers of the *African Telegraph* that he had originally been an internationalist. But 'England, with its barriers and its prejudices, its caste system . . . Western civilisation with . . . its deification of Money and Force where one hoped to find Christ, these things it is that have driven me to the refuge of my own people'. Yet he still believed, he added, 'that the day will surely come when men of every nationality and of every race will look back of colour . . . and see clearly the brotherhood in man'.[63] Toasting 'The African Race' at the African Progress Union's inaugural dinner in 1918, he declared: 'I believe in the destiny of the Race to which we have the honour to belong.'[64] When he spoke in Jamaica in 1919 on 'Unity of the Coloured Race', stressing the need for race pride and consciousness, and for co-operation among the black people of Africa, the West Indies, and the United States, he was not reported in the island's press, 'on a hint from Government'. His telegrams were scrutinized and he himself was 'carefully watched.'[65]

Hercules showed his mettle and his political acumen above all in his reaction to the anti-black riots in Britain. He was not a member of the deputation, led by Archer as president of the African Progress Union, that went to see Liverpool's deputy lord mayor on 16 June 1919. (The deputation also included the Gold Coast merchant Alfred S. Cann and the Revd E.A.Egesa-Osora, chaplain to the African Hostel and pastor to Liverpool's black community.)[66] But Hercules was one of the speakers at a protest meeting in Hyde Park, convened by the Society of Peoples of African Origin. And, as the society's general secretary, he wrote to the colonial secretary asking whether the government intended 'to take adequate measures for the protection of British subjects in this country' and calling for an inquiry – which never took place – into the death of Charles Wotten. His letter went on:

> Hundreds of Africans and West Indians have for years been living as law-abiding citizens in Liverpool, at Cardiff and in other large towns, some of them have married British Women and settled down, and the records of the Police will show, even better than we can profess to, what has been the incidence of law-breaking amongst them.
>
> My Society has, however, learned with horror and regret that large numbers of Africans and West Indians who came here either as seamen or in a military capacity to help the Mother Country during a critical period have been 'signed off' and left stranded at various ports.[67]

Lord Milner's bland reply promised that black British seamen, and black men from the colonies who had served in the Forces during the war, would be granted a resettlement allowance of £5 and a voyage allowance, provided that they applied within two months.[68]

For Hercules, as for the entire black community in Britain, the final straw came a month after the riots, when it was decided not to allow any black troops to take part in London's victory celebrations: the much-trumpeted Peace March on 19 July 1919. In an *African*

Telegraph editorial written on the eve of his departure for the West Indies, Hercules put into words what every black person in the country was feeling about British ingratitude, injury, and insult – and went on to draw the necessary political conclusions:

> Every ounce of strength was put into the struggle by the black man . . . He fought with the white man to save the white man's home . . . and the war was won . . . Black men all the world over are asking to-day: What have we got? What are we going to get out of it all? The answer, in effect, comes clear, convincing, and conclusive: '*Get back to your kennel, you damned dog of a nigger!*' . . .
>
> Residences of black men were demolished; black men were pounded in the streets, drowned, butchered in cold blood and terribly maltreated and maimed, with the Imperial Cabinet looking on without a clear statement of policy on the subject. No black troops were allowed to take part in the Peace March . . .
>
> The supineness of the Imperial Government during the race riots drives home the fact they approve of them, that they are in line with Imperial policy.[69]

Four years after the riots of 1919 they had been expunged from white memories. The author of an article on 'Britain's Negro Problem' in the *Atlantic Review* could assure his American readers that 'up to the present time, Great Britain has been spared the odium of race riots'.[70] Black memories, however, were not so conveniently short. For Britain's black community, 1919 illuminated reality like a flash of lightning. The lessons of the riots were etched into the consciousness of an entire generation. Through the 1920s, 1930s, and 1940s black people in Britain, struggling against the hidden and open attacks on them that went by the name of 'colour bar', knew very well what their fate would be if they failed to struggle. All they had to sustain them in this struggle against racism was a pride and militancy that owed much to the work of 'agitators' like Felix Hercules.

Claude McKay and the 'Horror on the Rhine'

Racist propaganda attacks on black people were not the prerogative of right-wingers. One such attack came in 1920 from the pen of the prominent left-winger E.D.Morel, secretary and part-founder of the Union of Democratic Control and editor of its journal *Foreign*

Affairs. Morel, whose father was French and whose real name was Georges Edmond Pierre Achille Morel-de-Ville, had founded the Congo Reform Association in 1904 and was 'more than any other individual . . . responsible for terminating King Leopold's infamous regime in the Congo'.[1] A member of the Independent Labour Party and later a Labour MP, Morel was 'the most powerful driving force in the U.D.C.' and suffered 'agonies of sympathy with his beloved black man'.[2] These agonies, exquisite though they may have been, did not stop his attacking the object of his affections as an oversexed, syphilitic rapist. The attack was made in the *Daily Herald*, then Britain's leading left-wing daily and, with a circulation of 329,000, 'probably at the height of its power'.[3]

Morel was protesting against France's use of black troops in occupied Germany. His article was printed under front-page banner headlines that proclaimed: 'BLACK SCOURGE IN EUROPE: Sexual Horror Let Loose by France on the Rhine'.

According to Morel, France was 'thrusting her black savages . . . into the heart of Germany'. 'Primitive African barbarians', spreaders of syphilis, had become a 'terror and a horror unimaginable' to the German countryside and an 'abominable outrage upon womanhood'. The 'barely restrainable bestiality of the black troops' had led to many rapes, a particularly serious problem since Africans were 'the most developed sexually of any' race and 'for well-known physiological reasons, the raping of a white women by a negro is nearly always accompanied by serious injury and not infrequently has fatal results'. The corpses of young women had been found under manure heaps. German local authorities were forced to provide brothels for these oversexed blacks – otherwise 'German women, girls, "and boys" would pay the penalty'. And the *Herald* warned that whereas today, with British connivance, the French were using black troops against the Germans, tomorrow they might use African mercenaries against white workers elsewhere.[4]

Morel repeated and elaborated his attack in a pamphlet called *The Horror on the Rhine*, in which he claimed that black troops '*must be satisfied upon the bodies of white women*'.[5] The first two editions each sold out in less than a month, and by April 1921 eight editions had appeared. A free copy was presented to every delegate attending the 1920 Trades Union Congress and, according to one of Morel's colleagues, it left delegates with 'a feeling of physical and spiritual revulsion'.[6] Sober journals joined in the chorus. *The Commonweal* referred to 'a horde of Senegalese savages' and 'the lust of a black soldiery',[7] *The Nation* to 'these savages', 'black terrorists', and the 'horrible excesses' of African troops.[8] The *Contemporary Review* complained about the 'sexual excesses of these Africans'.[9] At least one public protest meeting was staged. To Morel, as to 'most of the British intellectual world of 1920, the African was an inferior and he was viewed not as a real person but as a "native" – a stereotype. There is no evidence that Morel actually knew a single Negro except on a master–servant level'. Moreover 'the British left were part of a . . . milieu in which a cutting analysis and scathing criticism of . . . imperialism (including attacks on the colour bar in the colonies) did not exclude racialist attitudes'.[10]

Morel's campaign did not go unanswered. The person who came forward to challenge him was the young Jamaican poet, novelist, and socialist Claude McKay, who lived in London from the end of 1919 to the beginning of 1921. The first black socialist to write for a British periodical – Britain's first black reporter, in fact – McKay was the youngest son of hard-working and relatively prosperous peasants. He was born in 1890. Two years in the United States had taught him 'how completely his race was being exploited',[11] and he had won sudden fame for his sonnet 'If We Must Die', written for Max Eastman's magazine *The Liberator* under the impact of the 1919 anti-black riots in the United States. A few days after Morel's article appeared in the *Daily Herald* the editor, George Lansbury, received an indignant letter from McKay. Lansbury sent it back with the excuse that it was too long for publication and the assurance that he personally was not prejudiced against black people. So McKay published his letter in a revolutionary socialist paper with a much smaller circulation than the *Herald*: the *Workers' Dreadnought*, run by Sylvia Pankhurst, who had led the left wing of the women's suffrage movement before the war.

'Why', asked McKay, 'all this obscene, maniacal outburst about the sex vitality of black men in a proletarian paper?' Black men were no more oversexed than white men; when the latter went among coloured races they did not take their women with them – hence the children of mixed race in the West Indies. If black troops had syphilis, they had been contaminated by the white world. As for German women, they were selling themselves to anyone because of their economic plight. McKay added:

> I do not protest because I happen to be a negro . . . I write because I feel that the ultimate result of your propaganda will be further strife and blood-spilling between the whites and the many members of my race, boycotted economically and

> socially, who have been dumped down on the English docks since the ending of the European War.[12]

'Maybe I was not civilized enough', McKay commented ironically 17 years later, 'to understand why the sex of the black race should be put on exhibition to persuade the English people to decide which white gang should control the coal and iron of the Ruhr'.[13]

For McKay, Britain had been a spiritual homeland. He left it totally disenchanted, as his autobiography, *A Long Way from Home* (1937), makes clear. When a collection of his poems, *Spring in New Hampshire*, was published in London in 1920 the *Spectator* reviewer wrote:

> Perhaps the ordinary reader's first impulse in realizing that the book is by an American negro is to inquire into its good taste. Not until we are satisfied that his work does not overstep the barriers which a not quite explicable but deep instinct in us is ever alive to maintain can we judge it with genuine fairness.[14]

Even Bernard Shaw, the person McKay had most wanted to meet in London, saw fit to ask him why he had not become a boxer instead of a poet. McKay reflected later that he did not think he could have survived 'the ordeal of more than a year's residence in London' if he had not belonged to two clubs, each with overwhelmingly foreign membership.[15] One, in a Drury Lane basement, was a club for black soldiers, provided for them by the British government (according to a letter McKay wrote to Trotsky in 1922) and patronized by troops from all parts of Africa and America.

> They had all been disillusioned with the European war, because they kept on having frightful clashes with English and American soldiers, besides the fact that the authorities treated them completely differently from the white soldiers. They were deeply aroused by the propaganda of the policy of 'Back to Africa' which came from New York. In place of their former pride because they were wearing khaki uniforms put on for 'the defense of civilization', they had become disillusioned, had begun to look at things critically, and were imbued with race consciousness.
>
> I was working at that time in London in a communist group. Our group provided the club of Negro soldiers with revolutionary newspapers and literature, which had nothing in

> common with the daily papers that are steeped in race prejudice. Moreover, we invited some of the more sophisticated soldiers to lectures at the socialist club.[16]

The socialist club, otherwise known as the International Club, had premises in East Road, Shoreditch, and McKay described it as 'full of excitement, with its dogmatists and doctrinaires of radical left ideas: Socialists, Communists, anarchists, syndicalists, one-big-unionists and trade unionists, soap-boxers, poetasters, scribblers, editors of little radical sheets'.[17] Here McKay met a cross-section of the far left: Walton Newbold and Shapurji Saklatvala, soon to be communist MPs; A.J.Cook, the miners' leader; Guy Aldred, the anarchist editor; Arthur MacManus and William Gallacher, the Clydeside strike leaders. Here Polish, Russian, and German Jews rubbed shoulders with Czech, Italian, and Irish nationalists.

With very few exceptions, McKay's experience of the English convinced him that prejudice against black people had become 'almost congenital among them'.[18] From the lowest to the highest, he found, the English could not think of a black man as being anything but an entertainer, a boxer, a Baptist preacher, or a menial.[19] One exception was Sylvia Pankhurst, who 'was always jabbing her hat pin into the hides of the smug and slack labor leaders'[20] and who, after printing his letter in reply to Morel, invited McKay to do some reporting for the *Workers' Dreadnought*. While he was active in Sylvia Pankhurst's tiny Workers' Socialist Federation he did his share of 'standing on street corners and selling red literature in London',[21] and narrowly escaped involvement when police raided the *Dreadnought* office. The paper had carried a pseudonymous article about unrest in the navy, written by a young sailor called David Springhall (who was dismissed from the navy, became a Communist Party organizer, and was to be convicted in 1943 of spying for the Russians).[22] When the police came, McKay had the original:

> Quickly I folded it and stuck it in my sock. Going down, I met a detective coming up. They had turned Pankhurst's office upside down and descended to the press-room, without finding what they were looking for.
>
> 'And what are you?' the detective asked.
>
> 'Nothing, Sir', I said, with a big black grin. Chuckling, he let me pass. (I learned afterwards that he was the ace of Scotland Yard.) I walked out of that building and into another, and entering a water closet I tore up the original article,

> dropped it in, and pulled the chain. When I got home to the Bow Road that evening I found another detective waiting for me. He was very polite and I was more so. With alacrity I showed him all my papers, but he found nothing but lyrics.[23]

Sylvia Pankhurst was sentenced to six months' imprisonment for the offending issue of the *Workers' Dreadnought*.

As a communist reporter, McKay did not always see eye to eye with his editor. During a strike of sawmill workers he found out that non-union men employed in a sawmill owned by none other than George Lansbury were scabbing. But Sylvia Pankhurst refused to print this scoop because she owed Lansbury £20 and had borrowed newsprint from the *Daily Herald*. Yet when McKay covered the 1920 Trades Union Congress and gave the Scottish miners' leader Bob Smillie a favourable write-up she was angry at his uncritical attitude to a labour leader.[24]

McKay went back to the United States to become a leading light in the Harlem Renaissance, the race-conscious poetry, prose, and song of a new generation of black writers to whom his fourth volume of verse, *Harlem Shadows* (1922), was a powerful stimulus. He visited Russia in 1922–3 and spoke on the 'Negro question' at the Comintern's fourth congress, but later broke with communism and turned to Catholicism. He wrote several novels, in two of which – *Home to Harlem* (1928) and *Banjo* (1929) – there are references to the anti-black riots in Britain.[25] He died in Chicago in 1948, and was posthumously honoured by his native Jamaica.

Defence and counter-attack

Pan-African congresses in the 1920s

Unlike the Pan-African Conference of 1900, the first Pan-African Congress did not meet in London. Organized by W.E.B.DuBois, the American champion of black rights, it was held in Paris on 19, 20, and 21 February 1919. There were 57 delegates, including Africans abroad, representing 15 countries. J.R.Archer and the Guyanan E.F.Fredericks were present. But the British Caribbean colonies were not represented, which may help to explain why the congress's demands were so moderate. It petitioned the peace conference then meeting in Paris to administer the former German territories in Africa as a condominium on behalf of the Africans who lived there; and it demanded that Africans be allowed to take part in governing their countries 'as fast as their development permits' until, in the fullness of time, 'Africa is ruled by consent of the Africans'.[1]

Two years later the second Pan-African Congress went much further. It met in several sessions, in London, Brussels, and Paris. Preceded by discussions with Beatrice Webb, Leonard Woolf, and other Labour Party notables interested in international affairs, the London sessions were held at the Central Hall, Westminster, on 27 and 29 August 1921. There were 113 delegates. Three veterans of the 1900 Pan-African Conference took the chair in turn: DuBois; Dr John Alcindor, now president of the African Progress Union; and his predecessor in that post, J.R.Archer, who, as we have seen, introduced the Indian revolutionary Shapurji Saklatvala to the congress. Coleridge-Taylor's widow was present, as was the American singer Roland Hayes.

Alcindor started the proceedings with a plea for 'restraint and circumspection' in the discussions. The public conscience was waking up to the fact that all was not well with Africa and the Africans. It was the delegates' duty to speed up that awakening and galvanize it into activity by means of wise propaganda. They should fight for their cause with all their might, but always with clean weapons. Other speakers at the London sessions included the Ghanaian W.F.Hutchison, who had worked on Dusé Mohamed Ali's *African Times and Orient Review*; John Eldred Taylor; and Albert Marryshow from Grenada, who vigorously attacked the domination of that colony by an all-powerful British governor and added that some black workers in Grenada, with wives and children, were paid as little as a halfpenny a day; this was an impossible situation, for which British capitalism must take a large share of the blame.

The historian J. Ayodele Langley has called the London portion of the 1921 Pan-African Congress 'perhaps the most radical' of all the 1920s congresses: 'Most of the speakers openly criticized aspects of colonial policy and of life in America, and the resolutions . . . were soberly presented but remarkably outspoken in their condemnation of imperialism and racism.' Unanimously adopted was a document afterwards known as the *Declaration to the World* or the *London Manifesto*, which demanded 'the recognition of civilised men as civilised despite their race and colour' and upheld 'the ancient common ownership of the Land and its natural fruits and defence against the unrestrained greed of invested capital'. There was forthright criticism of British colonial rule:

England, with all her *Pax Britannica*, her courts of justice,

> established commerce, and a certain apparent recognition of Native law and customs, has nevertheless systematically fostered ignorance among the Natives, has enslaved them, and is still enslaving some of them, has usually declined even to try to train black and brown men in real self-government, to recognize civilized black folk as civilized, or to grant to coloured Colonies those rights of self-government which it freely gives to white men.

The basic maladjustment in the distribution of wealth, claimed the *Declaration*, lay in 'the outrageously unjust distribution of world income between the dominant and suppressed peoples'.

At the Brussels sessions the radical tone of this document greatly alarmed Blaise Diagne, who had chaired the 1919 congress and who represented Senegal in the French Chamber of Deputies. He called the phrase about land ownership 'Bolshevist' and refused to put the *Declaration* to the vote. Instead he declared carried a milk-and-water compromise text calling for joint efforts by blacks and whites to develop Africa – despite the protests of the English-speaking delegates who constituted the majority of the congress and had not voted in favour of this text. Diagne was soon to abandon Pan-Africanism. The Paris sessions of the 1921 congress were, however, as outspoken in their condemnation of colonialism as the London sessions had been, and the resolutions adopted in Paris were much on the lines of those adopted in London.[2]

The third congress met in London and Lisbon. The London sessions were held at Denison House, Vauxhall Bridge Road, on 7 and 8 November 1923. Thirteen countries were represented, including the Gold Coast, Nigeria, and Sierra Leone; but French-speaking African groups, having sent delegates to London, decided at the last minute to withdraw – 'a sudden and unexpected defection', DuBois called it. Other speakers included Dr Alcindor and Harold Laski of the London School of Economics, who gave a critical analysis of the hypocritical mandates system, whereby Germany's former colonies in Africa were governed as 'a sacred trust of civilization'. H.G.Wells, Gilbert Murray, Sir Sydney Olivier, former governor of Jamaica, and the historian R.H.Tawney attended as guests.

In terms of attendance and enthusiasm this third congress, convened, as DuBois put it, 'without proper notice or preparation', was markedly less successful than its predecessors. It demanded on behalf of peoples of African descent 'a voice in their own Government', 'the right of access to the land and its resources', and 'the development of Africa for the benefit of Africans, and not merely for the profit of Europeans'. 'Home rule and responsible government' were demanded for British West Africa and the British West Indies. For Kenya, Rhodesia, and South Africa, the Congress demanded 'the abolition of the pretension of a white minority to dominate a black majority, and even to prevent their appeal to the civilized world'. There was a call for suppression of lynching and mob law in the United States. The congress summed up its demands thus: 'We ask in all the world that black folk be treated as men. We can see no other road to Peace and Progress.' These demands were endorsed at the Lisbon sessions on 1 and 2 December, attended by delegates from 11 countries, seven of them Portuguese colonies.[3]

Ladipo Solanke and the West African Students' Union

The first African students' union in Britain 'of more than local scope'[4] was formed in March 1917. Its first president was E.S. Beoku Betts, Fellow of the Royal Anthropological Institute. Born in Sierra Leone in 1895, he came to London in 1914 and joined the Middle Temple, was called to the bar in June 1917, and went back to West Africa four months later. The Union's other officers in that year were the Ghanaians K.A.Keisah (secretary), T.Mensah-Annan (assistant secretary), and S.F. Edduh Atakora (treasurer), and the Sierra Leonean C. Awooner Renner (financial secretary).[5] Initially the organization was called the African Students' Union of Great Britain and Ireland, but the name was changed to Union for Students of African Descent when a number of West Indian students joined. It had 25 members in 1921 and 120 in 1924.[6]

There was also a Gold Coast Students' Union in the early 1920s, and in 1924 a Nigerian Progress Union was formed, largely through the efforts of a Yoruba law student named Ladipo Solanke, who came to Britain in 1922 and was called to the bar in 1926. Solanke was outraged by the wholly degrading way in which Africans were presented as curiosities at the British Empire Exhibition staged at Wembley in 1924 and felt 'personally involved in every discrimination experienced by other West African students in London'.[7] He set his heart on building an organization that could speak for all West African students in Britain.

Such an organization was formed on 7 August 1925, at a meeting attended by 21 law students who afterwards became famous in West Africa as judges, magistrates, barristers, and politicians. It was called the West African Students' Union, and for the next quarter of a century it provided a social and political centre for its members, articulating their criticisms of British colonial rule and the discrimination they suffered in Britain, and reflecting their aspirations for West Africa's future. Not least, it functioned as a training ground for leaders of the West African nationalist movement.

In 1928 the Union moved into a house put at its disposal for a year by Marcus Garvey. When the lease expired it sent Solanke on two fund-raising tours of West Africa. He came back from his three years' mission with about £1,500. Another result of his work in West Africa was the creation of WASU branches, known as 'fraternities', in the four British colonies. In this way the Union became one of the channels through which West African intellectuals expressed their views and exchanged ideas. And when national liberation movements developed in West Africa 'it was often ex-members of the Union who became their leaders'.[8]

Soon after Solanke's return to Britain WASU obtained a house in Camden Road, London, for use as a centre and hostel, and this was opened in January 1933. But the funds brought back by Solanke were only enough to cover a few months' expenses, even when eked out with contributions sent from West Africa. When WASU approached the Colonial Office for help, conditions were imposed which would have brought the hostel under government control. So WASU, already suspicious of Colonial Office attempts to keep all colonial students under close surveillance,[9] rejected this offer, whereupon the Colonial Office opened its own hostel for colonial students. WASU accused the government of seeking 'a plan whereby it might exercise the same control over those studying in England' as it did over its subjects in the colonies. And it called on 'all Africans, students or otherwise, to wash their hands of this scheme . . . which would destroy their individuality'.[10]

Relations with the Colonial Office improved when WASU demonstrated that, with the backing of relatively prosperous black well-wishers, it could be self-supporting. Paul Robeson, for instance, became a patron and gave financial help. In 1938 WASU moved into new headquarters in Camden Square which was 'not only a social centre but also a hive of intellectual and political activity' and 'a market-place of ideas'.[11]

Influenced by such events as the Italian attack on Ethiopia, WASU took an increasingly anti-imperialist position in the 1930s. During the Second World War a WASU Parliamentary Committee was formed which met twice a month with MPs interested in African problems; with the co-operation of the Fabian Society's Colonial Bureau this committee became 'a channel for bringing African grievances before Parliament'.[12] WASU's 1942 conference on West African problems demanded immediate self-government and independence within five years of the end of the war,[13] and the Union played an active part in the fifth Pan-African Congress, held in Manchester in 1945 (see pp. 347–51 below).

The historical significance of Ladipo Solanke, who died in London in 1958, and of the West African Students' Union is summed up by James S. Coleman: 'Solanke and WASU influenced a critical segment of a whole generation, from which many of Nigeria's most militant post-World War II leaders emerged. From a historical standpoint Solanke was an outstanding figure in the nationalist awakening in Nigeria.'[14]

Dr Harold Moody and the League of Coloured Peoples

Unlike most of those African students in Britain between the wars, Harold Moody was 'not . . . a transient . . . , perfecting his skills prior to returning home to the anti-imperial struggle, but . . . one who had made the commitment to a lifetime's residence in England and as such was primarily concerned with the welfare of his people in an alien land'.[15] And for the last 16 years of his life he led the first effective black pressure group in this country, the League of Coloured Peoples.

Harold Arundel Moody was born in Kingston, Jamaica, on 8 October 1882, the eldest child of a prosperous retail chemist and strict Congregationalist. Young Harold came to London in 1904 to study medicine at King's College. He was totally unprepared for the colour bar in Edwardian London. He found it hard to get lodgings; after winning many prizes and qualifying in 1910 he was denied a hospital house appointment because the matron 'refused to have a coloured doctor working at the hospital'; though the best-qualified applicant, he was rejected for the post of medical officer to Camberwell Board of Guardians since 'the poor people would not have "a nigger to attend them"'.[16] In February 1913 he started his own practice in Peckham and, though his first week's earnings came to no more than £1, he made a success of it. Later that year he married the English nurse whom he had met and courted as a medical student. It was to be a life-long happy marriage.

An impressive public speaker who took enormous pains over each lecture – he would pray before the meeting and offer his manuscript to God – Moody was elected to the chair of the Colonial Missionary Society's board of directors in 1921 and president of the London Christian Endeavour Federation ten years later. In these and other religious and philanthropic bodies he had wide and valuable contacts. Increasingly he found himself using these contacts to give practical help to the stream of black people who came to him in distress, having experienced at first hand some specially degrading or humiliating or frustrating aspect of the colour bar. Worst of all, they found it hard to get lodgings, almost impossible to get work. Moody had trudged down the same road, and no one appealed to him in vain.

He carried the battle into the enemy's camp. Careful to hide his anger, he would confront employers and plead powerfully on behalf of those victimized because their skins were not the right colour. Before long other relatively successful middle-class black people joined him in this battle – professional people who shared both his anger at the handicaps imposed on their brothers and sisters and his determination to give them practical help. Little by little, the work took on the dimensions of a crusade. At last the time was ripe to form an organization. With the help and encouragement of Dr Charles Wesley, an Afro-American history professor visiting Britain, the League of Coloured Peoples was born at a meeting in the Central YMCA, Tottenham Court Road, London, on 13 March 1931. One of the League's foundation members, Stella Thomas, was called to the bar in 1933 and became the first woman barrister, and later the first woman magistrate, in West Africa. Members of the original executive included Dr Belfield Clark from Barbados; Sgt George Roberts from Trinidad; Samson Morris from Grenada; Robert Adams from British Guiana; and the Communist Party member Desmond Buckle from the Gold Coast. From the League's inauguration until his death in 1947 Moody served as its president: 'the League was his life and . . . he was the life of the League'.[17]

At first the League had four aims, printed in each issue of its quarterly journal *The Keys*: 'To promote and protect the Social, Educational, Economic and Political Interests of its members'; 'To interest members in the Welfare of Coloured Peoples in all parts of the World'; 'To improve relations between the Races'; and 'To co-operate and affiliate with organizations sympathetic to Coloured People'.[18] In 1937 a fifth aim was added: 'To render such financial assistance to coloured people in distress as lies within our capacity'.[19]

A balanced view of the League of Coloured Peoples and its

achievements must take into account the criticisms levelled at it by the younger, more militant generation of black activists in London in the 1930s. As early as March 1932 the *Negro Worker*, an English-language marxist periodical published first in Hamburg, later in Copenhagen, later still in Paris, and mainly distributed by black seamen, appealed to black students in London 'to break with the sycophantic leadership of Dr. Harold Moody, a typical "Uncle Tom", whose coat strings are so tied up with the Colonial Office that he is out to have every self-respecting Negro kow-towing before his arrogant imperialist masters'.[20] Moody was attacked (with justice) for not accepting Asians as League members and (with somewhat less force, since the Gold Coast students also broke ranks) for failing to support WASU in its boycott of the students' hostel opened by the Colonial Office.

But the League was not, and never pretended to be, a radical campaigning organization – although, as will be seen later, it made strenuous efforts in the mid-1930s on behalf of the shamefully mistreated black seamen of Cardiff, and became steadily more active and effective politically, especially after the start of the Second World War. Its nature is well summed up by one of the closest students of its history: 'social club, housing bureau, pressure group, investigative agency and employment agency' – in short, 'Humanitarianism, Pan-African Style'.[21] And, despite the various national, class, and political cleavages and rivalries that frustrated Moody's efforts for unity, and despite his League's small membership – 262 in 1936, of whom 178 were in Cardiff, 34 were in Liverpool, and 99 were white[22] – it 'eventually became a powerful advocate and exerted some influence on public affairs'.[23] Some of the fiercest contemporary critics of Moody and the League have since paid tribute to their achievements. In his fascinating memoirs, *Pan-Africanism from Within* (1973), the Guyanan Ras Makonnen, who lived in Britain from 1937 to 1956, acknowledges that the League 'had quite a hold over the loyalties of the blacks who had settled in Britain'. The militants' relationship with it was 'one of convenience. We recognized it as a powerful organization amongst the liberals . . . Our only hesitation was that it tended to divert from a more radical line.'[24] And the Trinidadian C.L.R.James acknowledges that Dr Moody's efforts – lobbying of MPs, letters in the press – 'mattered because there were too few black people around, and here was somebody who wasn't an insignificant person, who was a well-established medical practitioner'.[25]

Looking back after 50 years, one cannot doubt that there was plenty of scope both for Moody's kind of struggle and for the more aggressive political assertion of black people's rights favoured by his critics. And in practice, as is wholly consistent with the Pan-Africanist tradition, there was often a high degree of co-operation between Moody and the radicals. James, for instance, served on the League's executive for a time and contributed to *The Keys*;[26] a resolution on the Scottsboro case* passed by a League meeting in 1933 was proposed by the Barbadian Arnold Ward, who chaired the left-wing Negro Welfare Association and was a frequent contributor to the *Negro Worker*;[27] and another Barbadian leader of the Negro Welfare Association, Peter Blackman, was editor of *The Keys* in 1938–9 and wrote some of its most powerful and far-sighted editorials. Blackman had come to Britain, early in the decade, to study theology. His first posting was to West Africa, and when he found racist attitudes within the Church of England establishment he left the church and turned to marxism. On the eve of the Second World War, in his last editorial before the *The Keys* ceased publication, he wrote of the isolation of the British people from the peoples of the empire, 'to whom they remain alien in thought and for all matters of practical politics'. The British people were 'ignorant of what obtains in the Empire'; did not realize how much their fortunes were bound up with those of the millions in the colonies controlled in their name from Downing Street; and must in their own interests dissociate themselves from 'those forces which shape the policy of Greater Britain, and which by their control of the strength of Empire can hamper or deflect any movement for peace and progress in the world'.[28]

In fact, from Mussolini's 1935 attack on Ethiopia onwards, despite the 'ideological and philosophical differences' that separated the League of Coloured Peoples from other black organizations in Britain, 'a series of issues provided them with a common

* Nine black men were charged with the rape of two white women on a goods train in Alabama. The first trial, held locally in 1931, resulted in death sentences for eight of the men. After a campaign by liberals and radicals who held that the verdict was the result of race prejudice, the US Supreme Court declared that the defendants' right to counsel had been infringed. Although one of the women recanted, one of the accused was again sentenced to death and the case again came before the Supreme Court, which in 1935 ordered a retrial since the defendants' constitutional rights had been violated by the illegal exclusion of blacks from jury service. Four of the defendants were later convicted, receiving sentences equivalent to life imprisonment, and rape charges against the other five defendants were dropped.

ground for either joint or parallel action'.[29] One such issue, of burning importance to every West Indian in Britain, was the working-class struggle in the Caribbean that culminated in the Trinidad oilfield riots of June 1937 and the strikes in Jamaica in the following summer. Writing in *The Keys*, the brilliant young economist from St Lucia, W. Arthur Lewis, flayed the pro-employers report of the commission of inquiry into the Trinidad disturbances.[30] On the Jamaican strikes – during which police and troops attacked the strikers and 11 people were killed and many wounded – Moody had three letters published in *The Times* in a fortnight.[31] He presided at a protest meeting in the Memorial Hall, Farringdon Street; the speakers included Blackman and Lewis, and a radical resolution was carried, demanding for the British West Indies redistribution of the land, universal free education, 'the same civil liberties as are enjoyed by the people of Britain, including universal adult suffrage', and 'Federation of the West Indies with complete self-government'.[32] It was to a great extent as a result of League pressure that the government appointed a royal commission, under the chairmanship of the future colonial secretary Lord Moyne (Walter Edward Guinness), to investigate social and economic conditions in the West Indies. The League of Coloured Peoples, the Negro Welfare Association, and the radical International African Service Bureau (see pp. 345–6 below) submitted a joint memorandum to this commission.[33]

After the war started, collaboration between the League and the radicals continued on the vexed question of the colour bar in the British armed forces and, in particular, the question of commissions for black servicemen and women. Following private and public representations by Moody, the Colonial Office declared on 19 October 1939 that 'British subjects from the colonies and British protected persons in this country, including those who are not of European descent, are now eligible for emergency commissions in His Majesty's Forces'.[34] 'We are thankful for this,' wrote Moody, 'but we are not satisfied. We do not want it only for the duration of the war. We want it for all time. If the principle is accepted now, surely it must be acceptable all the time.'[35] Moody's own family took immediate advantage of the concession. His children Arundel, Ronald, Garth, Harold, and Christine all received army or RAF commissions, the latter two as doctors, and Arundel and Harold both rose to the rank of major. And their father shouldered his full share of civil defence work in Peckham, was called to the New Cross rocket explosion in which nearly 200 were killed and hundreds were injured, and often worked night and day amid the falling bombs.[36]*

Moody's fatherly care extended to all the children born into Britain's black community. Each year he took coachloads of them on a summer outing to Epsom; each year he gave them a Christmas party. And the welfare of the black children among the evacuees at the start of the war caused him as much anxiety as it did their own parents. An item in the League's *News Letter* for November 1939, sent by a correspondent in Blackpool, is eloquent:

> Among a large party of children which came to our district were two little coloured boys. Nobody wanted them. House after house refused to have them. Finally a very poor old lady of 70 years volunteered to care for them. She gave them a good supper, bathed them and put them to bed. As she folded their clothes she discovered two letters addressed to the person who adopted them. Each letter contained a five pound note.[38]

Moody found time to reprove the BBC when one of its announcers, speaking about some records, used the word 'nigger'. The last public use of this word, by Prime Minister Baldwin in the late 1920s, had aroused some comment, and educated white people were beginning to avoid it. 'This', wrote Moody with his usual precision, 'is one of the unfortunate relics of the days of slavery, vexatious to present day Africans and West Indians, and an evidence of incivility on the part of its user.' In those Reithian times the BBC took only two days to make honourable amends:

> I find that our announcer was at fault. The point raised in your

* Many other black people served in the blitz, as air-raid wardens, auxiliary firefighters, stretcher-bearers, first-aid workers, and helpers with mobile canteens. In St Pancras ARP were the Jamaicans Sam Blake and Granville ('Chick') Alexander, a first-aid worker; the Trinidadians E.Gonzalez and Singh; the Sierra Leoneans Charles Allen and A.K.Lewis, a law student; Laryea from the Gold Coast; the Nigerians Ote Johnson and A.Kester; and the Liberian S.Shannon. The Indian V. K. Krishna Menon (for whom see pp. 353–5 below) and D.E.Headley, a mining engineer from British Guiana, were St Pancras air-raid wardens, and the South African E.Mahlohella was driver to a stretcher party in the borough. The Trinidadian G.A.Roberts was a leading auxiliary in the New Cross AFS. The Sierra Leonean Billy Williams was an air-raid warden in St Marylebone, and the Nigerian Ita Ekpeyon was a senior air-raid warden in the same borough. The Jamaican boxer 'Buzz' Barton was a first-aid worker. Alderman D.A.Miller, son of a Sierra Leonean, was a senior air-raid warden in Plymouth, one of Britain's worst-blitzed cities.[37]

> letter is fully appreciated, and is one which the B.B.C. is at pains to keep constantly in mind. It was unfortunately overlooked on this occasion, and a reminder on the subject is being given to all announcers.
>
> I hope that your Committee will accept the B.B.C.'s apology for this slip, which is sincerely regretted.[39]

The war, in Roderick J. Macdonald's words, gave 'a fresh relevance and sense of mission to the League'.[40] Membership and revenues increased rapidly. The increased support was partly due to the entry into British factories of skilled workers recruited in the West Indies. They were followed to Britain by large numbers of black troops, first from the West Indies, then from the United States. And the humiliating fall of Singapore brought 'a newfound receptivity'[41] to the League's message.

By 1943 the League of Coloured Peoples had reached the peak of its influence as a pressure group. After a long, hard fight it had persuaded the Colonial Office to modify its recruitment regulations – but only in part. When the League published the entire correspondence that passed betwen Moody and the colonial secretary, Lord Moyne, on this issue, Arthur Lewis added a tart postscript:

> On the one hand it is denied that there ever has been any barrier to the appointment of coloured people, while on the other it is admitted that advertisements have been published stating that applicants must be of pure European descent. It is admitted that the regulations might well be 'simplified so as to make their meaning clearer' to those who think that prohibitions against non-Europeans mean what they say, yet the Secretary of State sees no reason why the new regulations should not continue to divide British subjects into (a) those of European descent and (b) those who are not. We are accustomed to some hypocrisy in official circles, but this correspondence, we submit, is a masterpiece. Discussion between the public and its servants should not be conducted as if it were a boxing performance . . .
>
> Whatever may be said of the French, in their Empire a man may rise to the highest posts merited by his intelligence; the appointment of a Negro Governor is taken as a matter of course. In the British Empire there can be no Negro Governor because the maintenance of white prestige is considered to be an essential pillar of the imperial regime, and Negroes are not

> allowed, except when it cannot be helped, into administrative posts of distinction and responsibility.[42]

Deputy Prime Minister Attlee gave a public assurance to a group of West African students that 'we fight this war . . . for all peoples' and that 'I look for an ever-increasing measure of self-government in Africa' – an assurance promptly contradicted by Churchill as prime minister.[43] Moody then used what has been called a 'double-barrelled strategy', combining 'an appeal to the Liberal-humanitarian sacred sanctions' with 'the spectre of Communist influence on the colonies if reforms were not made'.[44] And inch by inch, grudgingly, lumberingly, the Colonial Office began its slow retreat. It set up, for one thing, an advisory committee on the welfare of 'Empire Colonials'; as a member of this committee Moody was partly responsible for the opening of hostels ('Colonial Centres') in different parts of the country.

The League's twelfth annual general meeting, in March 1943, was held in Liverpool. The 39 delegates from 12 UK centres, hailing from 13 different countries, were officially welcomed by the lord mayor, and the League staged a public meeting attended by over 500 people and addressed by the bishop of Liverpool, on the theme of 'A Charter for Colonial Freedom'. The situation in Liverpool had been causing Moody much concern. Fighting had broken out at a dance hall where a white American forcibly separated a Jamaican technician from his white dancing partner, then pulled a dagger on him. After this incident, black patrons were barred from the hall.[45] These technicians, Moody pointed out, were volunteers who had come at tremendous sacrifice to help Britain's war effort. Liverpool's large resident black population had been treated between the wars as outcasts, had been despised and looked down on.[46] To hold the League's conference in that city was a gesture of solidarity both with them and with the West Indian technicians in the area.

In July 1944 the League organized a three-day conference in London to draw up a 'Charter for Coloured Peoples' that in many ways foreshadowed the resolutions of the fifth Pan-African Congress held in Manchester in the following year. Arthur Creech Jones, soon to be the Labour government's colonial secretary, helped in the drafting of this charter, which demanded 'full self-government' for colonial peoples 'at the earliest possible opportunity' and insisted that: 'The same economic, educational, legal and political rights shall be enjoyed by all persons, male and female, whatever their colour. All discrimination in employment, in places of public entertainment and refreshment, or in other public places, shall be illegal and shall be punished.'[47]

Moody was a sick man when he came back from a strenuous five-month visit to the West Indies and the United States in the winter of 1946–7. He died on 24 April 1947, ten days after his return. The league he founded survived him by four years.

Precise and lucid in his writings and speeches, passionate in his emotions but controlled in their expression, tireless in his devotion to his life's work, Moody was thought too cautious, patient, and conservative by the younger generation of radicals. He did not share their conviction that the gale of black rebellion in the colonies would soon blow away the old order. In many ways, events after his death proved them right and him wrong. For all that, he was nobody's 'Uncle Tom'; in his own way, he struck blow after well-aimed blow in the struggle against racism.

The Pan-Africanist radicals

Who were the leaders of this younger generation of black radicals, and what did they achieve? We look first at the careers of five remarkable men who, in Britain and elsewhere, did much to bring about the end of colonialism in Africa and the West Indies: George Padmore, C.L.R.James, Ras Makonnen, Jomo Kenyatta, and I.T.A.Wallace-Johnson.

Malcolm Ivan Meredith Nurse, later known as George Padmore, was born in Arouca, Trinidad, in 1902 or 1903. His father was a schoolteacher and his grandfather was a Barbadian small farmer who had been born a slave. He always claimed to be a nephew of Henry Sylvester Williams. After working as a reporter he went to the United States in 1924 to study sociology and political science. He joined the Communist Party and wrote for the New York *Daily Worker* under the cover name George Padmore, which he had adopted by 1928. In 1929 he went to Moscow, where, despite his lack of Russian, he became a token member of the local soviet and, much more important, was appointed head of the Negro Bureau of the Red International of Labour Unions (Profintern) and helped to organize the first International Conference of Negro Workers (1930). In his first year as an official of the International Trade Union Committee of Negro Workers he wrote six pamphlets; based in Hamburg in 1931 as editor of the *Negro Worker*, he is said to have had about 4,000 contacts in various colonial countries.

But in August 1933 the Communist International, seeking no doubt to improve relations between the Soviet Union and France, suddenly dissolved the International Trade Union Committee of Negro Workers. Padmore immediately resigned in disgust from all his positions and was expelled from the Comintern as a 'petty-bourgeois nationalist' a few months later. He told his nephew afterwards how he had been sent a series of directives from Moscow instructing him to stop attacking French imperialism, then British imperialism, then American imperialism, till he was left with the Japanese – and, as he observed with some asperity, they were not the ones that had their boots across the black man's neck.

In 1935 Padmore settled in London, making a living by private teaching and journalism. He often wrote for the Independent Labour Party's weekly, the *New Leader*, and for other independent, non-stalinist, left-wing publications: *Controversy*, *Left*, *Socialist Leader*, and *Tribune*. In 1936 he published *How Britain Rules Africa*, a detailed and outspoken indictment; *Africa and World Peace* followed in 1937. Though Padmore never joined the ILP he became its colonial expert, collaborating closely with Fenner Brockway and with Reginald Reynolds of the No More War Movement.

Padmore's political and intellectual heritage, training, and experience, and the use he made of them, are summed up by Imanuel Geiss:

> His career extended to all the terminal points of the classical 'triangle' of Pan-Africanism . . . The memory of his direct descent from slavery was combined with a middle-class education and studies at Afro-American universities; his temporary proximity to Garveyism was combined with work for the Communist party on a national as well as an international level, in both the trade-union and the purely political arena. [He had] great veneration for Blyden . . . and . . . respect for Du Bois . . . He established a link with the francophone wing of Pan-Africanism. In England he came into contact with the humanitarian liberal and socialist element of the British left . . .
>
> With his dynamism and his insistence on intellectual precision and political action he exerted a strong influence upon the young African and Afro-West Indian intelligentsia between 1935 and 1958 – by the strength of his personality, and by means of articles and several books, lectures,

> contributions to discussions and a wide circle of personal contacts . . .
>
> With his wholly modern rational approach he came closest to the trend of which Horton is the . . . representative in Pan-Africanism and in African nationalism.[48]

Padmore, who died in 1959, was Kwame Nkrumah's personal representative in London during the struggle for Ghanaian independence and spent his last two years as Nkrumah's personal political adviser on Pan-African questions in Ghana. He was 'the originator of the movement to achieve the political independence of the African countries and people of African descent. That is why he is increasingly known as the Father of African Emancipation.'[49] This was written of him by his lifelong friend and fellow-radical C.L.R.James, to whose life we now turn.

In her hilarious novel *Comrade O Comrade* (1947), Ethel Mannin portrays 'an eminent Trotskyist' – 'an extremely handsome young Negro' who comes to tea accompanied by two white friends. They 'arrived punctually at four and they left punctually at five'; and in those 60 minutes their hostess utters exactly 12 words. For the 'eminent Trotskyist', pausing only to sip his tea, soliloquizes non-stop on political matters in his 'dark rich beautiful voice', 'one fine hand beating in another as he emphasised his points'.[50]

This caricature of Cyril Lionel Robert James in his, and the century's, thirties is as good a way as any to begin a sketch of a man whose stature simply bursts any category a writer tries to squeeze him into. 'What an extraordinary man he is!' wrote E.P.Thompson on James's eightieth birthday:

> It is not a question of whether one agrees with everything he has said or done; but everything has had the mark of originality, of his own flexible, sensitive and deeply cultured intelligence. That intelligence has always been matched by a warm and outgoing personality. He has always conveyed, not a rigid doctrine, but a delight and curiosity in all the manifestations of life. I'm afraid that American theorists will not understand this, but the clue to everything lies in his proper appreciation of the game of cricket.[51]

In truth, one can no more catch and label the essence of C.L.R.James than one can cage a cloud. But here are the bare facts from which some idea can be gained of this uncommon man and his life's work.

He was born in Tunapuna, near Port of Spain, in 1901, the son of a schoolteacher, the grandson, on one side, of a pan-boiler on a sugar estate, on the other, of an engine-driver. At the age of six he was reading Shakespeare. A boyhood friend of George Padmore, he won a scholarship to Trinidad's main government secondary school. In the 1920s he taught at the same school, played club cricket, and began writing – fiction, a history of West Indian cricket, and a biography of the Trinidadian labour leader Captain Arthur Andrew Cipriani. James came to Britain in March 1932 at the suggestion of the cricketer Learie Constantine, with whom he stayed for a while in Nelson, Lancashire. He made a living by reporting cricket matches for the *Manchester Guardian* and the *Glasgow Herald*, joined the Independent Labour Party, chaired its Finchley branch, wrote for the *New Leader* and *Controversy*, refused to join the Communist Party, left the ILP with a marxist group that took the name Revolutionary Socialist League, edited its paper *Fight*, wrote a play on the life of the Haitian revolutionary Toussaint-Louverture, himself acted in it, alongside Paul Robeson, at the Westminster Theatre, wrote an account of a West Indies childhood in the form of a novel (*Minty Alley*, 1936), wrote a classic study of the Haitian revolution (*The Black Jacobins*, 1936), wrote a classic history of 'the rise and fall of the Communist International' (*World Revolution 1917–1936*, 1937) which, in its publisher's words, became 'a kind of Bible of Trotskyism'[52] and was shamelessly plundered by a succession of lesser experts, translated into English Boris Souvarine's massive *Staline*, and was one of the two British delegates to the founding conference of the Fourth International in 1938. All this before his fortieth birthday.

In October 1938 James went to lecture in the United States and stayed there illegally for 15 years, an active participant in the working-class movement. In his writings he extended and enriched the versatile pattern begun in London. It was he who, long before 'black power' was ever heard of, 'pioneered the idea of an autonomous black movement which would be socialist but not subject to control by the leaderships of white-majority parties and trade unions'.[53] His *Notes on Dialectics* (1948) was the most 'hegelian' – and most original and creative – contribution to marxist philosophy since Lenin's *Philosophical Notebooks*. His *State Capitalism and World Revolution* (1950) completed his break with 'orthodox' trotskyism. *Facing Reality* (1958) drew lessons from both the workers' councils that sprang up in the 1956 Hungarian revolution and the rank-and-file workers' movements in Britain and the United States. *Beyond a Boundary* (1963) is partly a classic book on cricket, partly a kind of autobiography. *Nkrumah and the Ghana Revolution* (1977) records 'a sequence of political responses to an extreme political situation, the African situation, as it has developed during the last thirty years'.[54] In his ninth decade, James has been belatedly discovered by the media.

Such are the bare facts, or enough of them to place C.L.R.James in his time. But they are inadequate to explain the fertilizing and inspiring effect this scholar-revolutionary's thought and life have had, especially on the younger generation of activists that has emerged since the end of the 1960s. James's achievement, it is said, 'staggers the mind simply in the recounting of it'. Merely in the six and a half years he spent in Britain in the 1930s – the period of his life that chiefly concerns us – he 'added significantly to the emancipation and understanding of the human condition'.[55]

If James was a wizard with words and ideas, another Pan-Africanist radical active in Britain in the 1930s – and 1940s – was a financial wizard, a fund-raiser extraordinary. He was born George Thomas Nathaniel Griffith in the small British Guiana village of Buxton at the beginning of the century. As he became more deeply involved in the Ethiopian cause following the Italian invasion he took the name Ras Tefari Makonnen, and it was under the name Ras Makonnen that his autobiography, *Pan-Africanism from Within*, was published in 1973. After staying in the United States from 1927 to 1934, latterly studying agriculture and animal husbandry at Cornell University, he spent a couple of years in Copenhagen. He was expelled from Denmark when he not only found out that the Danish government was manufacturing mustard gas but was incautious enough to publish his discovery. Early in 1937 he settled in Britain. He shared a flat with George Padmore, plunged into daily political activity, and moved to Manchester in 1939. He lectured for the Co-operative Union, read history at Manchester University, and showed his resource and financial skill by starting a chain of restaurants. First there was the Ethiopian Teashop, then a bigger and better place called the Cosmopolitan. Renovated at a cost of about £3,000, this became a social centre for the many black American troops stationed within reach of Manchester. A third restaurant, the Orient, a club called the Forum, and a place called the Belle Etoile followed.

Besides providing a much-needed social base for Afro-Americans, West Indians, and Africans in the black-out gloom of wartime Lancashire, Makonnen's restaurants provided also the funds for political activity, and in the first place for 'a whole range of defence operations for blacks at home and abroad'.[56] These operations included the largely successful defence of 120 black seamen charged with mutiny, and the wholly successful legal defence of Donald Gerald Newton Beard, a Jamaican in the RAF who, after a street fight in which one of the attackers was stabbed, was charged with murder. Makonnen raised the money to bring over the renowned Jamaican barrister Norman Manley:

> The man was so methodical. The first person he wanted to see was the meteorologist to know what had been the snowfall on that particular night and what had been the visibility. Finally when he got to court, he made asses of the police; on the one hand he showed that they really believed all niggers looked alike; yet individual police were claiming that they had identified Beard at a distance of forty yards. That night the visibility had of course been less than ten yards. Well, the judge had to stop the case.[57]

As we shall see, Makonnen's profits were also used to organize the fifth and by far the most important Pan-African Congress, held in Manchester in 1945 – and to finance a publishing house, a bookshop, and a monthly journal.

Makonnen, like Padmore, was close to Nkrumah, and he went to settle in Ghana shortly before independence in 1957. After Nkrumah's overthrow he was imprisoned for several months, was freed when Jomo Kenyatta intervened on his behalf, and went to live in Kenya, whose citizen he became in 1969.

Kenya's president was an old friend of Makonnen. Kenyatta, in fact, had been another of the Pan-Africanist radicals active in Britain in the 1930s, and Makonnen later described him as 'much more obviously marked for leadership than many of the others in England at that time'.[58] Born into a Kikuyu peasant family about the year 1897, Jomo Kenyatta was educated at a mission school. He joined the Young Kikuyu Association in 1922, became an official of the Kikuyu Central Association in 1925, took up full-time political work three years later, and came to London in March 1929 armed with a petition signed by 30 members of the association asking for the release of its chairman and listing Kikuyu grievances. Kenya's governor, Sir Edward Grigg, who was in London at the time, saw Kenyatta and reacted to his visitor by 'putting the police Special Branch on to . . . [him] and circulating their report'.[59] The police spies asserted that Kenyatta was 'a representative of the "Universal Negro Improvement Association"' who had 'come to this country to obtain justice for people of his race in Kenya'. While in London he had been in the company of 'prominent Communists' – Shapurji Saklatvala was one of them – and of the secretary of the British section of the League against Imperialism.[60] He also got in touch with Fenner Brockway and Kingsley Martin (soon to become editor of the *New Statesman*), went to Russia for a brief visit and, when he came back, gave an interview to the communist *Sunday Worker* and wrote two articles for the new-born *Daily Worker*.[61] More influential, perhaps, was a carefully argued letter to *The Times* and the *Manchester Guardian* outlining the objects of the Kikuyu Central Association and correctly forecasting a 'dangerous explosion' if local views were repressed by legislative measures.[62] Kenyatta went back to Kenya in September 1930 to find that a song in praise of him had been banned by the governor as seditious.[63]

Kenyatta's second stay in Europe lasted much longer: from 1931 to 1946. He came first to London then, under George Padmore's auspices, made a second visit to Moscow in the winter of 1932–3. Back in London, he studied anthropology under the celebrated Malinowski and lived a life of extreme poverty. Often he was so poor that he went hungry until the mail from Kenya came; then he could sell the stamps and buy a penny bun. He picked up a little money by acting as one of the 250 black extras in Alexander Korda's *Sanders of the River*, thus beginning a deep friendship with Paul Robeson, who starred in the film. Meanwhile he was working on his book *Facing Mount Kenya* (1938): studies in Kikuyu life and customs based on the papers he had written for Malinowski's seminars, and the first inside account of an African community by an anthropologist who had been born into it and brought up in it.

Kenyatta's activities in the Pan-Africanist movement in Britain in the second half of the 1930s inevitably led the Colonial Office to reopen their files on him. The new dossier was entitled 'Jomo Kenyatta: Libellous statements made to the Workers' Educational Association', and it noted that he was making 'mischievous allegations' about British rule in Kenya: 'The difficulty is, however, that he is spreading his poison by word of mouth at relatively obscure meetings (organised by a perfectly reputable organisation)'.[64] During the Second World War Kenyatta worked on a

Sussex farm, helped with the preparations for the Manchester Congress, and wrote a pamphlet called *Kenya: The Land of Conflict* (1945), which stated plainly: 'There is not one of the boasted blessings of white civilization which has yet been made generally available to the Kenya Africans.'[65] In 1946 he went back to Kenya. His subsequent career during and after the 'Mau Mau' crisis – his arrest, trial, and long, cruel imprisonment, followed by his triumphant emergence as president of independent Kenya: all this belongs to a different, and tolerably well-known, history.

Padmore, James, Makonnen, and Kenyatta are all, indeed, fairly well known. There was another Pan-Africanist radical in Britain in the 1930s who is much less so. Admittedly, his stay here was brief: from March 1937 to April 1938. Yet I.T.A.Wallace-Johnson was highly influential. He was the only one of the five with direct experience of the West African trade union movement. In 1931 he organized the first trade union in Nigeria; and in 1938–9 he organized no fewer than eight trade unions in his native Sierra Leone, a feat which greatly alarmed that colony's British rulers. In fact he did more 'to introduce Marxist ideas and mass-oriented politics to West Africa than any other person in the years between the two world wars', and 'became a major force in colonial politics in English-speaking West Africa, both hated and feared by British colonial authorities'.[66]

Isaac Theophilus Akuna Wallace-Johnson was born of poor parents in Wilberforce village, near Freetown, in 1894 or 1895. His father was a small farmer, his mother a fishmonger. He entered government service at the age of 18 as an outdoor officer in the Sierra Leone Customs, and was dismissed when he brought his fellow-workers out on strike for better pay. During the First World War he served as army records clerk in the Cameroons, east Africa, and the Middle East. Demobilized in 1920, he became chief clerk in the Freetown waterworks department, and was sacked for organizing his colleagues to demand higher pay and better working conditions. For the next five years he roamed the world as a seaman.

In 1930 he represented Sierra Leonean railwaymen at the first International Conference of Negro Workers in Hamburg, and in the following year he visited Moscow. An associate editor of the *Negro Worker*, he edited the Nigerian *Daily Telegraph* until he was deported from Nigeria for trade union activities. In the Gold Coast, he founded the West African Youth League and wrote for the *Gold Coast Spectator* and the *African Morning Post*. In 1934, when a tunnel collapsed in the Prestea mines, killing 41 men, he disguised himself as a miner and went down the mines to gather first-hand information. In 1936 he was arrested, along with his friend Nnamdi Azikiwe ('Zik'), later to be Nigeria's first president, and charged with seditious libel for an article in the *African Morning Post* expressing his reaction to the Italian invasion of Ethiopia:

> I believe the European has a God in whom he believes and whom he is representing in his churches all over Africa. He believes in the god whose name is spelt *Deceit*. He believes in the god whose law is 'Ye strong, you must weaken the weak.' Ye 'Civilised' Europeans, you must 'civilise' the 'barbarous' Africans with machine guns. Ye 'Christian' Europeans, you must 'Christianise' the 'pagan' Africans with bombs, poison gases, etc.[67]

Fined £50 by the Gold Coast Supreme Court, Wallace-Johnson appealed finally to the Judicial Committee of the Privy Council, which disagreed with the sedition charge but upheld the conviction on the ground that under the Gold Coast criminal code such an attack on religion reflected adversely on the colony's government.

While in Britain for the hearing of this appeal Wallace-Johnson worked closely with Padmore, James, Makonnen, and Kenyatta. With them he helped to found the International African Service Bureau, becoming its general secretary and editing its bulletin *Africa and the World*. This soon developed into the *African Sentinel*, 2,000 copies of which, containing an article by Kenyatta, were seized from Wallace-Johnson by the Freetown Customs when he went back to Sierra Leone in April 1938. 'It is most undesirable', the governor wrote to the colonial secretary, 'that such nonsense should be circulated among the population of Sierra Leone.'[68]

Within a year of his return Wallace-Johnson had formed the highly successful Sierra Leone branch of the West African Youth League, had launched its newspaper, the *African Standard*, and had succeeded over and over again in making the government look silly – notably by publishing accurate details of the governor's confidential and secret dispatches, both to the Colonial Office and to his subordinates. One dispatch declared that an African workman and his wife could subsist on 15*s*. a month, and that there was little difficulty in getting labour at about 9*d*. per day.[69] It was hardly surprising that the Youth League candidates swept the board in the November 1938 municipal elections in Freetown. (One Youth League candidate, Constance Agatha Cummings-John, became the first woman to hold elective office in British West Africa.) It was even less surprising that Wallace-Johnson was arrested, detained, charged with criminal libel (for an article on the death of an African who had been tied to a post and flogged by order of a British district commissioner), sentenced to a year's imprisonment, and finally exiled. Released from detention in 1944, he represented Sierra Leone at the World Trade Union Congress in London in February 1945 and helped organize the Manchester Congress later that year. Killed in a car accident in Ghana in May 1965, Wallace-Johnson was buried in Freetown. His funeral attracted the greatest crowd of mourners in Sierra Leone's history. His old friend Ras Makonnen spoke movingly at the graveside.[70]

These five men made up a powerful team. Even without James and Wallace-Johnson, Britain still had, from 1938 on, a Pan-Africanist centre linked by a thousand threads to the anti-imperialist mass movement in Africa and the West Indies. And this is the really significant difference between these radicals and Harold Moody. It was not that they were on the left and he was on the right. His self-appointed task was to save his people in Britain, so far as he could, from suffering from the tree's poisoned fruit; theirs was to chop the tree down. And they and the millions of Africans and West Indians they spoke for did what they set out to do. They won independence. The conventional political spectrum is not very helpful here. More important than 'left' and 'right' labels – and clearly Moody cannot be placed anywhere on the British political spectrum – is that none of the black activists in Britain during the 1930s and 1940s let himself be used by white politicians. Even when they joined a white political organization they did so to further the cause of black freedom. Some of them found out the hard way that the Communist International could not be trusted, since in the interests of Soviet foreign policy it could dissolve overnight a black organization it had itself created. The black activists in Britain certainly found white allies and helpers. But they took good care to keep control of their own organizations. So that the MPs, for instance, who asked questions about colonial matters in the Commons were being skilfully fed material and guided by this 'small' – but, in the long run, both influential and successful – 'group of West Indian and African intellectuals and agitators'.[71]

This, then, was the group that in 1936 began 'to formulate a new ideology of colonial liberation designed to challenge existing ideological systems, including Communism'.[72] And the chief stimulus was the Italian invasion of Ethiopia, which touched a highly sensitive nerve. Ethiopia and Liberia were, in the whole of Africa, the only territories not under European control. A young Ghanaian on his way to study in the United States – his name was Kwame Nkrumah – suddenly saw in London a newspaper placard announcing 'MUSSOLINI INVADES ETHIOPIA' and felt

> almost as if the whole of London had suddenly declared war on me personally. For the next few minutes I could do nothing but glare at each impassive face wondering if those people could possibly realise the wickedness of colonialism, and praying that the day might come when I could play my part in bringing about the downfall of such a system.[73]

Africans and people of African descent now saw, if they had not seen it before, that 'black men had no rights which white men felt bound to respect if they stood in the way of their imperialist interests'.[74] Not only did Britain and France fail to respond to Ethiopia's appeal to the League of Nations; they cynically sold oil to the fascist dictator whose troops were gassing defenceless Ethiopians. In *The Keys*, C.L.R.James rammed home the implications:

> Africans and people of African descent, especially those who have been poisoned by British Imperialist education, needed a lesson. They have got it. Every succeeding day shows exactly the real motives which move Imperialism in its contact with Africa, shows the incredible savagery and duplicity of European Imperialism in its quest for markets and raw materials. Let the lesson sink in deep.[75]

In 1934 black radicals in London had formed an *ad hoc* committee to help two delegates from the Gold Coast, S.R.Wood and Tufuhin Moore, who had come to protest against certain laws – one of which gave the government power to confiscate literature deemed seditious – and to demand constitutional reform in the colony.[76] (The Colonial Office granted the delegates an interview but conceded none of their demands. When it was pointed out in the Commons that the delegates had been in Britain for almost two years without receiving a sympathetic hearing from the government, the colonial secretary, J.H.Thomas, remarked: 'African gentlemen being in this country for 21 months only indicates what a good country it is.')[77] Early in 1935 Arnold Ward, who chaired the Negro Welfare Association, was suggesting 'a permanent secretariat of Negroes in London to represent colonial interests and to co-ordinate opposition in the Empire.'[78] When Mussolini's troops marched, the *ad hoc* committee was revived as the International

African Friends of Abyssinia, whose main purpose was to arouse the British public's sympathy and support for the victim of fascist aggression and 'to assist by all means in their power in the maintenance of the Territorial integrity and political independence of Abyssinia'.[79] When the defeated emperor Haile Selassie came to London in 1936 the IAFA organized a reception for him at Waterloo station. James chaired the IAFA; its secretary was Kenyatta, who wrote an article for the communist *Labour Monthly* entitled 'Hands off Abyssinia!', declaring that 'to support Ethiopia is to fight Fascism';[80] its treasurer was Mrs Amy Ashwood Garvey, former wife of Marcus Garvey. Padmore, Sam Manning from Trinidad, and Mohamed Said from Somaliland were on the executive committee, and other officials were two respected senior members of Britain's black community: Albert Marryshow from Grenada, who had spoken at the 1921 Pan-African Congress, and Dr Peter McDonald Milliard, president of the Negro Welfare Association in Manchester. Born in British Guiana in 1882, Milliard graduated MD from Howard University in 1910, practised among the West Indian emigrant workers in Panama for many years, helped them to form a trade union, obtained his British MD from Edinburgh University in 1923, and settled in Manchester. Described by Padmore as 'a man of considerable charm and striking presence', Milliard was 'a life-long democrat and socialist' and 'a passionate internationalist'.[81]

In March 1937 the IAFA was replaced by the International African Service Bureau, with Wallace-Johnson as general secretary, Padmore in the chair, James as editorial director, and Makonnen as treasurer and fund-raiser. The executive committee included Chris Jones (otherwise Chris Braithwaite), leader of the Colonial Seamen's Union, and Africans from the Gold Coast, Nigeria, Sierra Leone, South Africa, and French West Africa. Though it had several white patrons, including the future Labour colonial secretary Arthur Creech Jones, Nancy Cunard, Victor Gollancz, Sylvia Pankhurst, D.N.Pritt, and Dorothy Woodman, the Bureau insisted that it owed 'no affiliation or allegiance to any political party, organization or group in Europe'. Its members saw Pan-Africanism as 'an independent political expression of Negro aspirations for complete national independence from white domination – Capitalist or Communist'.[82] As Makonnen put it many years later, 'We were simply not prepared to compromise, we were not going to have any European leadership'.[83] One of the Bureau's chief functions was 'to help enlighten public opinion . . . as to the true conditions in the various colonies',[84] and it did so by producing and distributing literature and sending speakers on the colonial question to Labour Party and trade union branches, co-operative guilds, and the like.

When Wallace-Johnson went back to Sierra Leone the *African Sentinel* was succeeded by a monthly journal called *International African Opinion*, edited by James, sold at IASB meetings in Hyde Park, and 'sent everywhere to every address we could find'.[85] The new journal's motto was 'Educate, Co-operate, Emancipate: Neutral in nothing affecting the African Peoples'. It was to be a journal for activists, not a literary paper giving advice from ivory towers; and it sought, not to dominate other black organizations, but to co-ordinate and centralize their activities so as 'to bring them into closer fraternal relation'.[86] In his memoirs, Makonnen tells how the IASB co-operated with, amongst others, 'the most radical caucus of the Sinhalese students' and with 'a little group around the Burmese students attached to the London School of Economics'.[87]

When war broke out in 1939 the IASB was necessarily much less active for some years. There were disagreements over financial matters which led to a breakaway by Wallace-Johnson's successor as general secretary, the Nigerian Edward Sigismund (otherwise Babalola Wilkey), who launched a small organization called the Negro Cultural Association. The chief interest of this development lies in the close watch kept on both organizations by Scotland Yard's Special Branch. This reported that the new body was being infiltrated by the Communist Party, which was said to be planning an anti-colonial conference, carefully packed so that the communists could 'damp down the notorious Trotskyite tendencies of many colonials'. The Special Branch observed, however, that the communist Sigismund was unlikely to carry much weight and that 'the policy of the International African Service Bureau will remain in the hands of the Trotskyist, George Padmore'.[88]

Towards the end of 1944 the IASB joined with a number of other black organizations in Britain, and with representatives in Britain of various colonial organizations, to form a 'loose umbrella association'[89] called the Pan-African Federation. Support came from the Negro Welfare Centre, Negro Association (Manchester), Coloured Workers' Association (London), Coloured People's Association (Edinburgh), United Committee of Coloured and Colonial People's Association (Cardiff), African Union (Glasgow University), Association of Students of African Descent (Dublin), Kikuyu Central Association, African Progressive Association (London), Sierra Leone section of the West African Youth League, and Friends of

African Freedom Society (Gold Coast).[90] Milliard was president of the federation; J.E.Taylor of Liverpool was treasurer; and Makonnen was general secretary. The new grouping had four objects:

1. To promote the well-being and unity of African peoples and peoples of African descent throughout the world.
2. To demand self-determination and independence of African peoples, and other subject races from the domination of powers claiming sovereignty and trusteeship over them.
3. To secure equality of civil rights for African peoples and the total abolition of all forms of racial discrimination.
4. To strive to co-operate between African peoples and others who share our aspirations.[91]

It was a piece of luck for the Pan-Africanist movement to have a man like Makonnen in Manchester when that city became a magnet for black American servicemen stationed in the north of England. His restaurants were a brilliant stroke, and the black GIs came in droves.[92] This success enabled the movement to set up a publishing company, issue a stream of pamphlets on specific colonial problems, launch a monthly periodical, *Pan-Africa* (described as a journal of African life, history and thought, and soon declared a seditious publication and banned by several colonial governments), open a bookshop – and organize the most important and influential of all the Pan-African congresses, which issued, from Manchester, some 20 weeks after VE Day, a clarion call for colonial freedom.

The Manchester Congress (1945)

Why Manchester? First, because Makonnen had established himself in business there, knew the lord mayor, and had good contacts inside the local Labour Party, of which he was a member. All this made it easier to book halls and find accommodation for delegates. Second, 'Manchester had become quite a point of contact with the coloured proletariat in Britain, and we had made a name for ourselves in fighting various areas of discrimination'; the congress was 'not only concerned with international issues' but also 'a protest against increasing discrimination in Britain'. And, third,

> you could say that we coloured people had a right there, because of the age-old connections between cotton, slavery and the building up of cities in England . . . Manchester gave us an important opportunity to express and expose the

> contradictions, the fallacies and the pretensions that were at the very centre of the empire.[93]

Why 1945? Unlike the DuBoisian congresses of the 1920s, Manchester was not an isolated event but 'a natural outgrowth of a ferment of pan-African activity',[94] of an upsurge of black consciousness stimulated by the Second World War. In a letter to DuBois, written just after the end of the war, Padmore described the militant mood of black people from the colonies whom he was meeting in Britain:

> Living under alien rule, their first manifestation of political consciousness naturally assumes the form of national liberation, self-determination, self-government – call it what you may. They want to be able to rule their own country, free from the fetters of alien domination. On this all are agreed, from even the most conservative to the most radical elements . . . This does not mean that there are no individual Negroes who subscribe to political philosophies . . . But these are more in the nature of personal idiosyncracies than practical politics. In brief, even those who call themselves Communists are nationalist.[95]

The Manchester Congress was timed to coincide with the second conference of the newly formed World Federation of Trade Unions, held in Paris in September and October 1945; and it was preceded by an Anti-Colonial Peoples' Conference held in London on 10 June 1945. The latter was organized jointly by the Pan-African Federation, WASU, the Federation of Indian Organizations in Britain, the Ceylon Students' Association, and the Burma Association, and it called for an end to imperialism; the application of the Atlantic Charter to the colonies; the formation of a World Colonial Council, with representatives from the colonies, to formulate policy, supervise elections, and generally oversee the devolution of imperial control; an end to the colour bar everywhere; and guarantees that Italian- and Japanese-controlled territories would not revert to colonial status.[96]

Though French-speaking African and Caribbean colonies were unrepresented, the Manchester gathering was in most other respects far and away the most representative of all the Pan-African congresses. There were 90 delegates and 11 fraternal delegates and observers. Twenty delegates represented 15 organizations in West Africa; 6 represented organizations in east Africa and South Africa;

33 represented the West Indies; and 35 represented various organizations in Britain, including WASU. There were fraternal delegates or observers from, amongst other bodies, the Somali Society and the Federation of Indian Organizations in Britain. DuBois, now 77, had made a personal appeal to Truman to get a passport at short notice and had flown over from New York to preside over 'the coming of age of his political child'.[97] Kenyatta and Wallace-Johnson were prominent among the delegates. The Nyasaland African Congress was represented by Dr Hastings K. Banda, first student from that colony to graduate in medicine, first president of the Liverpool branch of the League of Coloured Peoples, and afterwards first president of Malawi. The young South African writer Peter Abrahams, whose novel *A Wreath for Udomo* (1956) would paint a rather one-sided picture of Padmore and his group, was one of two delegates from the African National Congress; he also represented the IASB, along with Mrs Garvey, Makonnen, Nkrumah, and Padmore. Other delegates later to be prominent included three Nigerians: Obafemi Awolowo, a future finance minister; H.O.Davies, a future federal minister; and Ja-Ja Wachuku, a future foreign minister. Assembled in Chorlton Town Hall, in fact, was 'the future political leadership of British territories in Africa around 1960'.[98]

More important than the big names, however, was what Padmore called the 'plebeian character' of the gathering. By contrast with the DuBoisian congresses of the 1920s, which had 'centred around a small intellectual *élite*', Manchester was an expression of 'a mass movement intimately identified with the under-privileged sections of the coloured colonial populations'.[99] 'As compared with the bourgeois notabilities, ministers and academics who attended earlier Pan-African meetings', writes Geiss, 'one can now sense a turn towards the masses.'[100] Many trade unions were represented, including the Gold Coast railwaymen's union, the Sierra Leone teachers' union, the Trinidad oilfield workers' union, and the St Lucia seamen's and waterfront workers' union. And, for the first time, political parties were represented: the National Council of Nigeria and the Cameroons, founded the year before by Dusé Mohamed Ali, Azikiwe, and the veteran nationalist Herbert Macaulay; the Grenada Labour Party; the People's National Party of Jamaica; the West Indies National Party of Trinidad; and the Trinidad Labour Party.

Significantly, the whole of the first day's proceedings of such an internationally strong and representative gathering – representative, at any rate, of British-held colonial territories – was devoted to 'The

Colour Problem in Britain'. The discussion was opened by the Ghanaian Eddie Duplan, who represented the Negro Welfare Centre in Liverpool, where he was working with black seamen; between the wars, he said, most black workers in Britain had lived below the subsistence level. He was supported by a fellow-Ghanaian, E.A.Aki-Emi (Coloured Workers' Association) and by A.E.Moselle from Cardiff, 'an area which had the largest coloured population in Great Britain'. Intermarriage had created a community of coloured youths, said Moselle; they found it hard to get work, the labour exchange was not at all anxious to place them, and it had been strongly suggested that – though born in Britain, with mothers and grandparents here – they should be got rid of. Peter Abrahams spoke of the injustices suffered at the hands of the police by black people in London's East End. For instance, when black men and white men were arrested for gambling together, 'the white men were dismissed and advised not to associate with coloured men, the latter being sentenced to fines or terms of imprisonment'. Miss Alma La Badie, representing the Universal Negro Improvement Association of Jamaica, raised the problem of unwanted babies fathered by black American troops stationed in Britain and abandoned by their mothers.

Later sessions discussed 'Imperialism in North and West Africa', 'Oppression in South Africa', 'The East African Picture' (Kenyatta led this discussion), 'Ethiopia and the Black Republics', and 'The Problem in the Caribbean'. The multiple oppression of black women was raised by Mrs Garvey, who declared: 'Very much has been written and spoken of the Negro, but for some reason very little has been said about the black woman. She has been shunted into the social background to be a child-bearer.'

Among the large number of resolutions carried was one on 'Coloured Seamen in Great Britain' and one on the 'Colour Bar Problem in Great Britain', demanding that discrimination on account of race, creed, or colour be made a criminal offence. The essence of the congress resolutions was summed up in two brief, militant statements. 'The Challenge to the Colonial Powers', proclaiming the need for force, as a last resort, in the struggle for freedom, declared:

> We are determined to be free . . .
>
> We are unwilling to starve any longer while doing the world's drudgery, in order to support by our poverty and ignorance a false aristocracy and a discredited Imperialism.

> We condemn the monopoly of capital and the rule of private wealth and industry for private profit alone . . . We shall complain, appeal and arraign. We will make the world listen to the facts of our condition. We will fight in every way we can for freedom, democracy and social betterment.

The 'Declaration to the Colonial Workers, Farmers and Intellectuals', drafted by Nkrumah, called on colonial workers to be in the front of the battle against imperialism, assured them that 'your weapons – the Strike and the Boycott – are invincible', and called on 'the educated Colonials' to play their part in organizing the masses.[101]

Though all but ignored by the British press, the Manchester Congress was, in Geiss's words, 'a landmark . . . in the history . . . of decolonization', for it 'served as the pace-maker of decolonization in Africa and in the British West Indies', and the strategy proclaimed was 'put into effect with surprising ease'.[102] And the chief reason for this, Makonnen suggests, is that the leaders were closely tied to those they led[103] – however much that may have ceased to be true for some of them once power had been won.

The Asian radicals

Two Indian revolutionaries who lived in Britain between the wars were active in British politics as well as contributing to the upsurge of Indian national consciousness. They were Shapurji Saklatvala and V.K. Krishna Menon.

Born into a Parsee family in the state of Bombay in 1874, Shapurji Saklatvala came to Britain for medical treatment at the age of 31 and stayed here for the rest of his life. A liberal when he arrived, he moved steadily to the left, joining the Independent Labour Party's Central London branch in 1910. Six years later he formed the Workers' Welfare League of India in London, which at first worked among Indian seamen but soon extended its scope to cover the working conditions of all Indians in Britain. In 1921 it became the agent in Britain of the All-India Trade Union Congress, and it was seen by British Intelligence as 'the first foreign agency to introduce Bolshevik principles into the trade-union movement in India'.[104] After the Russian revolution of 1917 Saklatvala became an active member of the ILP's marxist wing and, with people like Emile Burns, Helen Crawfurd, R. Palme Dutt, and J.T. Walton Newbold, strongly supported affiliation to the Communist International. When their affiliation motion was turned down by 521 votes to 97 at the ILP's March 1921 conference, Saklatvala was one of the 200 or so who left the ILP to join the newly formed Communist Party of Great Britain.

Saklatvala contested North Battersea in the 1922 general election as a Labour Party candidate after negotiations in which, as we have already seen, J.R.Archer played a leading part. The precise terms on which the Labour Party executive agreed to endorse his candidature were stated thus at the party's 1922 annual conference:

> The candidate should appear before the constituency with the designation of 'Labour Candidate' only, independent of all other political parties, and, if elected should join the Parliamentary Labour Party; that at the General Election he should, in his election address and in his campaign give prominence to the issues as defined by the National Executive from the general Party programme; that if elected he should act in harmony with the Constitution and Standing Orders of the Party.[105]

Saklatvala was elected with a majority of 2,000 but lost the seat in the 1923 election. In 1924 communists were barred from standing as Labour candidates and excluded from Labour Party membership, and in that year's general election Saklatvala contested North Battersea as a communist. He won back the seat with the support of the local Labour Party and held it until 1929.

Saklatvala's militancy and outspokenness brought him constantly into the news. In 1921 his house was searched by the police. In 1925, when he was appointed a member of the British delegation to the Inter-Parliamentary Union Congress in Washington, the American authorities revoked his visa. He was the first person in Britain to be arrested during the 1926 General Strike: he was charged with sedition for a May Day speech in Hyde Park urging soldiers not to fire on workers. Refusing to be bound over – 'In circumstances such as those existing today', he told the court, 'I shall refuse to be silenced except by *force majeure*' – he spent two months in Wormwood Scrubs. On his way to a meeting of the League against Imperialism in 1929 he was arrested by the Belgian police and sent back to Britain.

Both inside and outside the House of Commons Saklatvala was a fervent opponent of imperialism and champion of colonial liberation. He said in his first speech:

> No Britisher would for a moment tolerate a constitution for Great Britain if it were written outside of Great Britain by people who are not British. In a similar way the constitutions for Ireland and India and Egypt and Mesopotamia should be constitutions written by the men of those countries, in those countries, without interference from outside.[106]

In 1927 Saklatvala spent three months in India, addressing huge audiences and advocating trade union and peasant organization. After this visit, which was a personal triumph, India was crossed off the list of countries his passport was valid for – and the ban was not lifted when the Labour Party returned to office in 1929.

Though a disciplined communist Saklatvala was no blind follower of the party line, and is said to have been 'single-minded' where his own views or, indeed, interests were concerned. He died in 1936, survived by his English wife Sarah and their three sons and two daughters.[107]

Vengalil Krishnan Krishna Menon was born in 1896 on India's Malabar coast, in what is now Kerala. His mother was an accomplished Sanskrit scholar and musician; his father, a successful small-town lawyer. In 1918 he took his BA degree at the Presidency College, Madras, where he created a stir by hoisting on the college flagpole the red and green flag of Mrs Annie Besant's Home Rule League. He spent five years at Adyar College – which Mrs Besant had founded – studying, teaching Indian history, and working on the weekly *New India*. In 1924 Mrs Besant helped him come to Britain; the idea was that he should stay for six months, attend an educational conference, and acquire a law degree. He was to stay for close on a quarter of a century.

After teaching history for a year at a school in Letchworth, Krishna Menon studied political science for two years under Harold Laski at the London School of Economics, and in 1927 took a first-class BSc in economics. Seven years later he was called to the bar, but his work as a barrister was always subordinated to his political activity. Almost single-handed he revitalized the Commonwealth of India League – founded in 1912, by Mrs Besant, as the Home Rule for India British Auxiliary – and was elected its joint secretary in 1928. Within two years most of the old guard had dropped out, Krishna Menon and his fellow-radicals had won their fight against support for dominion status for India, and the league was calling itself the India League. Its object now was to support India's claim for self-rule (*swaraj*).

Right through the 1930s Krishna Menon 'was reading, writing, thinking, dreaming India' – and, still more to the point, was talking about India, mostly to British working-class audiences. He talked with a thrilling combination of knowledge and passion. 'You could almost hear the pounding of his heart', said one person who heard him speak.[108] He would travel 300 miles to speak to a handful of people. No meeting was too small, no venue too remote. It was his willingness to speak to a humble group of Unitarians in an obscure Walthamstow church hall 'that awakened Reginald Sorensen, MP, to the moral significance of India's cause'.[109] Gradually Krishna Menon drew into the league's work a long list of left-wing publicists. Stafford Cripps, Palme Dutt, J.B.S.Haldane, Monica Whately, and Ellen Wilkinson were among the league's speakers; Bertrand Russell was in the chair; Fenner Brockway, A.A.Purcell, George Hicks, H.N.Brailsford, and J.F.Horrabin supported in various ways. One of the league's biggest propaganda blows against British rule in India was the fact-finding mission it sent to India in 1932. The members were Whately, Wilkinson, and the former Labour MP Leonard W. Matters; Krishna Menon went with them as secretary. The mission spent 83 days in India, interviewing Indians of every class, caste, and shade of opinion – though they were not allowed to see the nationalist leaders who were in jail – and when they came back published a devastating 534-page report, *Condition of India*. This was banned in India; according to the British chief of intelligence there, 'very many of the allegations are or may be true'.[110] This report was 'perhaps the greatest single contribution made by the India League towards a proper appreciation of the Indian case by the British people',[111] and it shook the British public.

Back from this mission, Krishna Menon plunged into his work for India with redoubled vigour and dedication. He ate very little (and never ate meat), slept very little, neither smoked nor drank, remained a bachelor, and lived in one room in the utmost austerity. He was regarded with something approaching awe by his fellow-members of South-West St Pancras Labour Party. Though he found time to help Allen Lane launch the Penguin imprint and was the first editor of the Pelican series, he was a legend in St Pancras for the conscientious way he performed his duties as a borough councillor. He served for 14 years, increasing his majority at each successive election. He chaired the libraries committee and launched the local arts and civic council. In the blitz he was one of the borough's air-raid wardens, wearing a helmet but spurning the uniform. He was on duty every night of the blitz: the first to arrive, the last to leave. He seemed totally without fear; once at the Conway Hall he carried on with his speech while the bombs dropped and all but a dozen of the audience left the hall for the shelters. In January 1941 he resigned from the Labour Party when the national executive withdrew its endorsement of his parliamentary candidature in Dundee on the ground that his 'first loyalty' appeared to be to India. He was often called a communist. But his attitude to the Communist Party was dictated solely by its support for the Indian freedom struggle, and he rejoined the Labour Party towards the end of the war.

Having played an important part in the negotiations leading to independence, he was appointed India's first high commissioner in the United Kingdom. The appointment was not to Attlee's taste, but Nehru – one of Krishna Menon's few close friends – insisted, and Krishna Menon held the post from 1947 to 1952. He showed the same unworldly austerity and probity that had marked his life in St Pancras in the 1930s. For the sake of India's prestige much had to be spent on the trimmings of the High Commission's offices. But Krishna Menon lived with his usual extreme simplicity in one back room of India House, subsisting, it was said, on tea and biscuits. He was at his desk by half past seven each morning; normally he worked until two the next morning. He never drew any salary, and often found himself without any money in his pockets. And when his niece, a student at Oxford, visited him he would not let her stay at his official residence but put her up at the YWCA. With this fastidious disdain for the perks of office there went, however, a degree of arrogance and irascibility that made many people dislike him. He was a man apart.

Krishna Menon's career did not end triumphantly. After leading India's delegation to the United Nations, and playing a large part in the Suez negotiations in 1956, he served India as defence minister from 1957 to 1962. He came in for much of the blame for India's humiliation in the 1962 war with China, and resigned his post. After living in virtual retirement he died in 1974. The *Times* obituary called him 'a lone wolf' – a 'remarkable but unlikable man who worked untiringly all his life for his country, yet never received a nation's gratitude'.[112]

Racism as colour bar

The racism that poisoned the everyday lives of black people in Britain between the end of the First World War and the end of the Second characteristically did so in the form of what was called 'colour bar'. In industry the colour bar was virtually total. Only in the early forties, when their labour was needed for the war effort, could black workers get jobs in British factories; and even then there was often resistance from employers and white employees alike. The colour bar also meant 'the refusal of lodgings, refusal of service in cafés, refusal of admittance to dance halls, etc., shrugs, nods, whispers, comments, etc., in public, in the street, in trams and in buses': that was how Kenneth Little summed it up in 1943.[1] From numerous examples that could be given, four are here selected to show, not only how the colour bar operated in Britain in those years, but also how black people fought back against these racist attacks on their humanity.

The Cardiff seamen

In 1921 there were about 250 West African seamen stranded in British ports. They were living 'in a state of semi-starvation' in Cardiff, Liverpool, Glasgow, and London's East End, since 'the unions . . . will not allow a coloured man to sign on for a ship while there is a white applicant for the job'.[2] The effects of discrimination became particularly harsh after the slump began in 1929. Tramp shipping was hard hit. Shipowners were given government help in the form of a subsidy, and it was made a condition of payment that only British labour might be employed on subsidized ships. Since black seamen registered as aliens were precluded from employment on subsidized ships, hundreds were thus deprived of any chance whatever of work.

By 1935 there were an estimated 3,000 non-European seamen in Cardiff, about two-thirds of whom were Africans or persons of African descent, the rest being mostly Arabs, Lascars and Malays.[3] The local police, high-handedly and quite illegally, placed their own interpretation on the Aliens Order 1920 and the Special Restriction (Coloured Alien Seamen) Order 1925. In the eyes of the police, these measures automatically made every black seaman in Cardiff an alien, regardless of any documentary evidence a man might produce to prove that he was British. When a black seaman produced a British passport the police would confiscate it without giving any receipt. If a seaman refused to hand over his passport he would be threatened with arrest and imprisonment. The shipping companies, in cahoots with the police, often refused to give black seamen the pay due to them at the end of a voyage until they presented an alien's certificate of registration.

This state of affairs led Cardiff's black seamen to form the Coloured Colonial Seamen's Union and send one of their leaders, Harry O'Connell, to London to seek help from the League of Coloured Peoples. In April 1935 two investigators from the League, George W. Brown and P. Cecil Lewis, spent a week in Cardiff interviewing over 200 seamen and others. They wrote in *The Keys*:

> We found a canvas crowded with strange figures: shipowners, aldermen, police, trade unionists, pulling from various angles a net which has entangled people from all over the British Empire. We lived in a compact community of West Indians, West Africans, Arabs, Malays, Somalis, men from Singapore, East Africa and every land where the Union Jack has planted itself; a settled, orderly community, trying with desperate success to keep respectable homes under depressing conditions . . . We met men as British as any Englishman, forced by fraud to register as aliens, after living here since the war; charges and counter-charges; misleading newspaper reports; men in authority bellowing 'repatriation'; muttered resentments against British children called 'half-castes'; and, dominating everything, an imminent danger that deliberate trickery would mean for these men and their families expulsion from British shipping and ultimately from Britain.[4]

The report of Brown and Lewis established that, in Cardiff, all black men were classified as aliens in spite of indisputable evidence of British nationality. This included men with honourable records of military service. One had fought in the battle of Jutland; two had joined the army in the West Indies and served in campaigns in Africa; two had medals for good conduct and long service; three had been torpedoed and had been awarded compensation for their injuries. All these were now registered as aliens. Nineteen men had resided in Britain for more than ten years – three of them for 30 years or more, and one of these three, a man of 60, had lived in this country for 37 years. All these men had been issued with alien cards. In short, 'a studied and deliberate policy had been instituted to deprive them of their nationality and the privileges attached thereto'.[5]

As soon as he had the facts in his possession Harold Moody got in touch with the Board of Trade's unemployment branch and the Unemployment Assistance Board, himself visited Cardiff, and enlisted the aid of Cardiff's MP, who raised the matter in the Commons. Moody also confronted officials of the National Union of Seamen and the head of the Shipping Subsidy, and sent a devastating memorandum to the British Shipping Federation. As a result of these efforts a large number of Cardiff's black seamen had their British nationality restored to them.[6]

But the investigation brought something else to light, too: the shameful conditions in which Cardiff's black community was condemned to live.

> Discrimination, social or economic, has limited the social contacts of these people, has segregated them from the more salubrious quarters of the town; has interfered seriously with the possibilities of the Coloured children, particularly the girls, from obtaining virtually any but the lowest-paid occupations; has led to African families paying higher rents . . . than White families of similar social status.[7]

These rents, be it noted, were paid for dwellings described by an observer in 1937 as

> slums . . . the houses are either not well built or are in bad repair . . . The dock area lies low and is damp . . . Five or six families may share a six roomed house, with a common staircase, one lavatory in bad repair and one tap which may even be outside . . . Rooms are often small . . . ventilation is rarely good, and sometimes the walls are verminous.

Those living in such slums for the most part put their children's needs above their own. The same observer added: 'It is noteworthy that children of coloured men almost always appear well fed and are warmly dressed in spite of poverty.'[8]

Yet these children, when they left school, could *never* find work in a factory or an office, no matter what their qualifications.[9]

Jim Crow in England

Black American servicemen started to arrive in Britain in the spring of 1942. By the late summer there were over 10,000 here – at one point, there would be more than ten times as many – and their proximity had aroused strong anxieties in the breast of Mrs Annie Gertrude May, wife of the Revd Frederick May, vicar of Worle, near Weston super Mare. Mrs May called the women of the village together and gave them a little talk in which she suggested the following code of behaviour:

1. If a local woman keeps a shop and a coloured soldier enters she must serve him, but she must do it as quickly as possible and indicate that she does not desire him to come there again.
2. If she is in a cinema and notices a coloured soldier next to her, she moves to another seat immediately.
3. If she is walking on the pavement and a coloured soldier is coming towards her, she crosses to the other pavement.
4. If she is in a shop and a coloured soldier enters, she leaves as soon as she has made her purchases or before that if she is in a queue.
5. White women, of course, must have no relationship with coloured troops.
6. On no account must coloured troops be invited into the homes of white women.

'The vast majority of people here', commented the *Sunday Pictorial*, to which Mrs May's little talk had been leaked, 'have nothing but repugnance for the narrow-minded, uninformed prejudices expressed by the vicar's wife. There is – and will be – no persecution of coloured people in Britain.'[10]

And yet black American troops were finding their reception in Britain a strange mixture of genuine welcome and genuine discrimination – the latter often instigated (indeed, insisted on) by white American troops. The American army was in those days a Jim Crow army, segregated on racial grounds, 'and it became clear when the first black troops began to arrive . . . that this policy was to be rigidly applied overseas'.[11] It became equally clear that the British government was in a quandary. On the one hand, there were many British people who did not and would not accept the American view; on the other hand, the British government did not want to offend its ally. And in fact the government 'never squarely faced up to the problem until its hand was forced, and equivocated throughout the war'.[12]

In September 1942 the Labour MP Tom Driberg caused Churchill great embarrassment by asking him in the Commons

> whether he is aware that an unfortunate result of the presence here of American Forces has been the introduction in some parts of Britain of discrimination against negro troops; and whether he will make friendly representations to the American military authorities asking them to instruct their men that the colour bar is not a custom in this country and that its non-observance by British troops or civilians should be regarded with equanimity.

'The Question is certainly unfortunate', replied Churchill. 'I am hopeful that without any action on my part the points of view of all concerned will be mutually understood and respected.' There was no reply when the communist MP William Gallacher said he had received a letter from a number of servicemen 'informing me that an officer has given them a lecture advising them on the necessity for discrimination in connection with negroes who are in London'.[13]

A few days later a letter from the manager of an Oxford snack bar was published in *The Times*. A black American soldier had come in and 'very diffidently presented me with an open letter from his commanding officer explaining that "Pte. —— is a soldier in the U.S. Army, and it is necessary that he sometimes has a meal, which he has, on occasions, found difficult to obtain. I would be grateful if you would look after him."' The manager went on:

> Naturally, we 'looked after' him to the best of our ability, but I could not help feeling ashamed that in a country where even stray dogs are 'looked after' by special societies a citizen of the world, who is fighting the world's battle for freedom and equality, should have found it necessary to place himself in this humiliating position. Had there been the slightest objection from other customers I should not have had the slightest hesitation in asking them all to leave.[14]

After consulting senior American officers in his area, the major-general responsible for administration in Southern Command issued to district commanders and regional commissioners a set of 'Notes on Relations with Coloured Troops', a document which a recent writer had described, mildly enough, as a 'monument to white arrogance':[15]

> While there are many coloured men of high mentality and cultural distinction, the generality are of a simple mental outlook. They work hard when they have no money and when

> they have money prefer to do nothing until it is gone. In short they have not the white man's ability to think and act to a plan. Their spiritual outlook is well known and their songs give the clue to their nature. They respond to sympathetic treatment. They are natural psychologists in that they can size up a white man's character and can take advantage of a weakness. Too much freedom, too wide associations with white men tend to make them lose their heads and have on occasions led to civil strife. This occurred after the last war due to too free treatment and associations which they had experienced in France.

Advice was given to British troops on the need to take account of this 'mental outlook', to 'conform to the American attitude', and to avoid making 'intimate friends' with black troops.[16] This document, issued without War Office authority, was appended to a memorandum prepared for the Cabinet in September 1942 by Sir James Grigg, secretary of state for war. Largely supported by the Foreign Office, Grigg was proposing to follow the lines of this document and let British officers instruct those under their command, including the women in the ATS, to adopt towards black American soldiers the attitude of the United States army authorities.

The Cabinet discussed the matter at great length and, if Sir Alexander Cadogan's eyewitness account is to be believed, rather incoherently. Ministers generally agreed that 'it was desirable that the people of this country should avoid becoming too friendly with coloured troops' – though the colonial secretary Viscount Cranborne (afterwards Marquess of Salisbury) was not too happy about this, no doubt because of possible repercussions in the colonies. He instanced the case of a black official at the Colonial Office who was now barred from his usual lunch-time restaurant because it was patronized by American officers. 'That's all right;' retorted Churchill, 'if he takes his banjo with him they'll think he's one of the band!'[17] All the Cabinet members were now talking at once, but at length it was decided that Grigg and two leaders of the Labour Party, Sir Stafford Cripps and Herbert Morrison, should prepare confidential guidelines for the services and also approve a suitable article for *Current Affairs*, published by the Army Bureau of Current Affairs. The draft was shown to Eisenhower and endorsed by the Cabinet a week later, and the British press was asked not to refer to the existence of the instructions and not to draw attention to the *Current Affairs* article when it appeared.[18]

Published early in December 1942, the article told members of the services that 'the average American attitude' must be respected: the Americans had to 'exercise a certain measure of control to prevent the mixture of blood which would, at the present stage, benefit neither side'. If the black American was 'brought into close social contact with English home life or with English women, the situation is so new and unexpected that he may not understand it. Such contacts are not frequently made in his home country and thus great care should be exercised over here'.[19]

By now there were about 8,000 West Indian troops in Britain, most of them flight mechanics, and they too were falling foul of white American racists. As early as March 1942 two white US marines attacked a West Indian serviceman in a London street. White American soldiers started ordering black British people out of at least one London dance-hall. Dr A. Tuboku Metzer, a West African on the house staff of St Andrew's Hospital, Billericay, was insulted by two American military policemen in a Brentwood hotel. Before long Colonel P.B.Rogers of the London Command was telling the Commanding General of the Services of Supply for the European theatre of war that 'in London the negro British nationals are rightly incensed. They undoubtedly have been cursed, made to get off the sidewalk, leave eating places and separated from their white wives in public by American soldiers'.[20]* A Jamaican called George Roberts, one of the 345 skilled technicians who had come to help the British war effort – he was working as an electrician in a Liverpool factory – had volunteered for the Home Guard and, wearing his Home Guard uniform, found himself refused entry to the Grafton dance-hall in October 1943 on account of his colour. He resigned from the Home Guard, was fined £5 for failing to perform Home Guard duties, and had the fine reduced to a nominal farthing by the recorder of Liverpool.[22]

These West Indian servicemen and skilled workers were hurt and disillusioned by the colour bar they found in Britain. For some, the last straw came when WAAFs – members of the Women's Auxiliary Air Force – told them they had been ordered not to be seen with black troops 'because of the Americans'; four WAAFs, it was

* When some of the black American troops joined a London club run by black people and wrote on their application forms that certain British towns were out of bounds to them, Colonel Rogers warned the American authorities that the club was 'a hotbed of colour-consciousness .... They are stirring up the coloured American soldiers'.[21]

alleged, were posted for refusing to obey this order.[23] A Barbadian in the RAF complained in the *Manchester Guardian* of the 'silent, subtle and obviously racial prejudice and indecent display of superiority from people of British nationality'.[24] What particularly upset many West Indians was that, while the racial discrimination practised in the American army was open and admitted, the colour bar they experienced in Britain was often hypocritically masked by a show of welcome. A Jamaican socialist called Lancelot O.A. DaCosta wrote from an RAF hospital to the League of Coloured Peoples complaining that the British authorities had done nothing about the 'gross insults' meted out to black volunteers in the services. 'I hate this country and these English people', he added, 'and I am not an hypocrite to disguise my feelings as they do, in pretending that they welcome you here.'[25] Soon after the war ended the weekly *John Bull* summed up what DaCosta and many like him had experienced during their stay:

> Colonial troops came to this country to help us win the war. But they are bitter because the colour bar still exists in Britain. They are shunned at service camps, banned from hotels and called intruders. . . .
>
> At one R.A.F. station, just before a detachment of West Indian airmen was due to arrive, all the W.A.A.F.s were called together and told that, though they were to be polite to the coloured Colonials, they were on no account to 'fraternise'.
>
> There was to be no sharing a table with them in the N.A.A.F.I. or sitting beside them in the camp cinema. The West Indians were, in fact, to be treated as pariahs in the community of the camp. Yet these men had come of their own accord 5,000 miles to a strange land and an unfriendly climate to help us in the war.
>
> Rudeness to Colonial Service girls in this country is surprisingly common . . .
>
> A West Indian girl in the A.T.S. was refused a new issue of shoes by her officer, who added: 'At home you don't wear shoes anyway.' An Army Officer to a West Indian A.T.S.: 'If I can't get white women I'll something well do without.' . . .
>
> Colour prejudice . . . still persists in the hearts and minds of many of the people of Britain, and it may increase again as war memories fade.[26]

The case of Amelia King

Amelia E.King was a young black woman from a Stepney family that had been in Britain for three generations. Her father was in the merchant navy, her brother in the royal navy. But when, in 1943, she volunteered for service with the Women's Land Army she was rejected by its Essex county committee because she was black. Apparently some farmers had objected to her and some of the local people on whom she might have been billeted had objected, too.

The matter was raised in the Commons, where the minister of agriculture said: 'Careful inquiry has been made into the possibility of finding employment and a billet for Miss King, but when it became apparent that this was likely to prove extremely difficult, she was advised to volunteer for other war work where her services could be more speedily utilised.' One MP told the minister that 'the world listens to matters of this kind, which affect the integrity of the British people', but the minister made no reply.[27]

A Mass Observation poll found that 'even those who did not entirely believe in colour equality were against this particular case of colour prejudice which was regarded as detrimental to the war effort'.[28]

The Constantine case

Before 1944 it was common for London's West End hotels to refuse accommodation to black people. In 1941 one such hotel had turned away Sir Hari Singh Gour on account of his colour. A distinguished jurist, poet, and novelist, he was vice-president of Delhi and Nagpur universities, deputy president of the Indian Legislative Assembly, a member of the Simon Commission's Indian Committee, and a Fellow of the Royal Society of Literature. Two years later the same thing happened to the Trinidadian Learie Constantine, one of the world's most distinguished cricketers. Constantine sued the hotel and won his case. As C.L.R.James put it, he revolted 'against the revolting contrast between his first-class status as a cricketer and his third-class status as a man'.[29] His legal victory was a turning-point in the struggle against one of the most pernicious and humiliating forms of colour bar in Britain.

Learie Nicholas Constantine was born in Trinidad in 1902. His father, an overseer on a cocoa estate, was a keen cricketer. At the age of three Learie would be seen outside his home, bat in hand, asking passers-by to bowl to him. His performance in three first-class matches having won him a place on the West Indies team, he first came to Britain in 1923. As batsman, so powerful were his strokes, he was likened to a blacksmith. He was a devastating fast bowler. His fielding was near-perfect: he 'gave the impression of climbing an invisible ladder to get the ball'[30] and the great Bradman ranked him 'a marvellous fieldsman, no matter where he was stationed'.[31] His performance at Lord's in 1928 – he took 100 wickets and made 1,000 runs – led to an invitation, which he accepted, to turn professional and join the Nelson team in the Lancashire League. With his wife Norma – their baby daughter Gloria joined them later – he settled in two-room 'digs' in the cotton town of Nelson. Black people were a novelty in the area, and at first the Constantines had to endure rudeness, anonymous letters, and much curiosity. But they stuck it out, winning respect, admiration, and friendship. James, their lodger for a while, helped Constantine write his first book, *Cricket and I* (1933). And during Constantine's nine years with the Nelson team it won the League championship seven times.

In 1942 Constantine, now working in a solicitor's office, was asked by the Ministry of Labour to become a temporary civil servant in its welfare department, with responsibility for the West Indian technicians who had come to Merseyside factories. It was an inspired choice: 'his organisational ability, personal prestige , experience of Lancashire and racial background made him the ideal person to deal with the absorption of West Indians into the Merseyside industrial and social scene.'[32] He had problems with both trade unions and employers; solving them called for both tact and cunning:

> Some firms either flatly refused to take on coloured men, or put endless delays in their way hoping to make them seek work elsewhere. I used to get the Ministry to press those firms for most urgent deliveries of orders, and then they found that they must take some coloured workers or get none of any kind. With urgent work to be done, they were forced to give way.[33]

In the summer of 1943 Constantine was given four days' special leave to captain the West Indies team against England at Lord's. The person who telephoned the Imperial Hotel, Russell Square, on his and his family's behalf asked if there were any objection to them on account of their colour and was told there was not. Two rooms were reserved for the Constantines and their daughter and a deposit of £2 was paid. But when the family arrived it was made clear that they were not welcome. The manager said: 'You may stop tonight;

you cannot stop any longer.' Constantine's chief at the Ministry of Labour arrived and was told: 'We are not going to have all these niggers in our hotel. He can stop the night, but if he does not go tomorrow morning his luggage will be put outside and his door locked.' Asked why, the manageress replied: 'Because of the Americans.' She added, in an indignant tone: 'Apparently there are three more niggers to come.' 'I happen to be one of the niggers', said a friend of Constantine's, to which she replied: 'Well, you don't look like one.' The man from the Ministry pointed out that Constantine was a civil servant and a British subject, and the manageress replied: 'He is a nigger.' So the family went to another hotel, and Constantine brought an action against the Imperial for breach of contract.

The case was heard by Mr Justice Birkett, who said he accepted without hesitation the evidence of the plaintiff and his witnesses and rejected that given by the defendants. The manageress had been 'a lamentable figure in the witness-box'. When she could be heard she was vague and incoherent, and he was satisfied that, on the material points, she was not speaking the truth. She was grossly insulting in her reference to Constantine, and her evidence was unworthy of credence. From the outset she made it clear that the plaintiff could not stay in the hotel, and used the word 'niggers' and was very offensive. She declined to receive him, and would not listen to reason. In the witness-box, the judge went on, Constantine bore himself with modesty and dignity, dealt with all questions with intelligence and truth, was not concerned to be vindictive or malicious, but was obviously affected by the indignity and humiliation which had been put on him and had occasioned him so much distress and inconvenience, which he naturally resented. Constantine was awarded token damages of £5.[34]

Though Birkett's decision was clear-cut, it should not be supposed that the colour bar in British hotels and restaurants was swept away overnight. In 1946, two Sikh VCs were refused admission to a West End restaurant because of their colour.[35] In 1948 Tom Boatin, a West African lecturer at London University, was refused service by Rules Restaurant in Maiden Lane. The Ministry of Food intervened, and the management was forced to apologize.[36]

Constantine became a popular broadcaster, was awarded the MBE in 1945, was called to the Trinidad bar in 1955, and served from 1961 to 1964 as high commissioner for Trinidad and Tobago. He was knighted in 1962 and was created a life peer – Baron Constantine of Maraval and Nelson – in 1969. He died two years later.

In his book *Colour Bar* (1954) Constantine summed up his experience of Britain and the British in two sentences:

> Almost the entire population of Britain really expect the coloured man to live in an inferior area . . . devoted to coloured people . . . Most British people would be quite unwilling for a black man to enter their homes, nor would they wish to work with one as a colleague, nor to stand shoulder to shoulder with one at a factory bench.[37]

Such was the state of affairs in 1954. By then, black people had been coming to Britain for six years to help solve the country's peacetime economic problems by their labour, just as their countrymen had helped Britain in two world wars. The new stage in the development of Britain's black communities that opened in 1948 is the subject of the next chapter. The present one ends, as it began, with anti-black riots in Liverpool.

Racism as riot: 1948

By 1948 there were about 8,000 black people in Liverpool, most of whom had come to Britain during the war to help the war effort. About 30 per cent of the adults were seafarers; another 10 per cent had shore jobs; the rest were chronically unemployed as a result of the colour bar.[1]

The immediate background to the anti-black riots of 1948 was a determined effort by the National Union of Seamen, since the end of the war, to keep black seamen off British ships. Addressing the union's 1948 annual conference, its assistant general secretary made it clear that Liverpool and other British ports were to be 'no go' areas for black seafarers. 'In quite a few instances', he said, 'we have been successful in changing ships from coloured to white, and in many instances in persuading masters and engineers that white men should be carried in preference to coloured.' And 'committees have been set up in the main ports to vet all coloured entrants to the country who claim to be seamen.'[2]

There was little that black people could do to defend themselves against this attack on their livelihood. When they dared to defend themselves against the physical attacks that NUS policy could not but stimulate and encourage, the Liverpool police retaliated with what one commentator has called 'a singular lack of discrimination'. Except, of course, racial discrimination: 'The police took action which they thought would bring the disturbances to a close as quickly as possible – which, in their view, meant removing the coloured minority, rather than attempting to arrest the body of irresponsible whites involved.'[3] In fact about 60 blacks and about 10 whites were arrested – and most of the latter were subsequently acquitted. Police raided a seamen's hostel and a dance-hall, and attacked the black people they found there. Black people were even beaten in their own homes. The police raided a club used by black seamen, batoning many on the head and forcing those they hauled out to run the gauntlet between two lines of police, who kicked their victims as well as belabouring them with truncheons. And they threw a frail Jamaican boy of 15 downstairs so that his head was split open and needed stitches.

The fighting began early in August when a white crowd between 200 and 300 strong gathered outside an Indian restaurant in Park Lane. They set on a West African when he came out, then threw bricks and stones through the windows, damaging tables and chairs. The police were sent for, but took half an hour to arrive. There were skirmishes throughout the South End district.

Next day a crowd estimated at 2,000 attacked Colsea House, a hostel for black seamen in Upper Stanhope Street, and threw bricks through the window. The seamen barricaded themselves in. When the police came they forced their way into the hostel and arrested some of the defenders. One of the few white men to appear later in court had been kicking and hammering at the door of Colsea House and shouting: 'Come out, you black ——.' He was foolish enough also to kick a policeman in the stomach, and for that he was arrested and sentenced to three months' imprisonment.

On the third day the black community got wind of a plan to attack and vandalize a club known as Wilkie's, in Upper Parliament Street. They made ready for the threatened attack by pushing crates of bottles near to the club windows and arming themselves with stones, swords, daggers, iron coshes, and axes. At first they were content with a display of strength and a warning: a black radio mechanic was later said in court to have been brandishing a carving knife and shouting: 'Do not come over to this side of the street!' White men were seen charging a group of black men and shouting: 'Come and fight!' At least one such white group, spoiling for a fight, 'sensibly took to their heels and ran away because they were hopelessly outnumbered'.

Liverpool's chief constable had declared that 'all the resources of the police service in the city will, so far as it is possible, be brought to bear to stamp out once and for all this disorder'. But it was clear to every black person in Liverpool that what the police were really interested in was 'stamping out' black people's capacity to defend themselves. When a large force of police now approached the besieged club, a black defender shouted: 'Why don't the police come and get the white —— who are going to break up the club?' But the police advanced, and it became clear that they meant to force their way into the club as they had forced their way into the hostel. A volley of hundreds of bottles and stones thrown from the windows halted their advance for a time. But when the defenders ran out of ammunition the police burst their way in, breaking down doors, hitting out right and left with their truncheons, and throwing people down the stairs. Inside and outside the club, they brought their resources to bear. One police witness later admitted hitting a black seaman on the head with his baton; another admitted batoning three black men.

Police witnesses for the most part simply said they did not know how the accused came by their injuries. A young man called Hermon McKay had a bruise on his upper lip as big as a hen's egg, a black eye, and bruises on shoulder and knee. 'It would not be due to a little baton practice, would it?' his defending solicitor asked a police witness. 'Plain clothes officers do not carry batons', was the reply. Doctors who examined the accused men in Walton jail testified to their injuries, and independent witnesses testified that they had seen police badly knocking black men about. A white woman who saw police beating up black men 'unmercifully', and was unwise enough to protest about it, got arrested for her pains; the police tried to destroy her credibility by alleging in court that she had looked as if she had been 'smoking dope', and she was fined £2 for 'disorderly behaviour'.[4]

Police in search of particular men now went on the rampage, breaking into people's houses and beating them up – and demanding sometimes to know where they 'got the money to buy the beautiful furniture'. A great many other allegations of 'unlawful and vicious behaviour on the part of the police' were made in the *News Letter* of the League of Coloured Peoples. It was alleged, for instance, that the police had planted weapons on black people. A 15-year-old Jamaican told how police had pushed a penknife into his pocket. He had been dragged from his room, beaten up, thrown downstairs, and wounded so badly in the head that he needed stitches. While he was in a cell at the police station the police were breaking bottles which were later produced in court as having been taken from some of the arrested men. Another of the accused told how a police sergeant looked through the peep-hole in his cell door and said to a fellow-officer: 'That one there looks vicious enough; we'll say he had the knife.' His colleague thought the other prisoner looked 'the more vicious of the two' and would 'do nicely'. White women involved were 'called by unprintable epithets' and warned not to give evidence.[5]

An account by Mrs Betty Spice, a former member of the research staff at Liverpool University's Department of Social Sciences, usefully supplements the rather deadpan press reports of the court hearings. She attended the trial of six black men who were acquitted. She found the police witnesses

> rather unintelligent and certainly uneasy while giving evidence . . . The police case was rather thin and though they had all evidently been well-rehearsed, several slips were made, and each constable was mauled in turn by the defending solicitor . . . [Police witnesses] 'could not say' how the defendants had received injuries described in picturesque detail by the defence . . . All four constables gave identically inaccurate descriptions of the clothing worn by some of the defendants at the time of their arrest.

The defendants, on the other hand,

> were so convincing in the witness stand and so unshakeable in their evidence that the four policemen . . . were put to shame.
>
> All six men gave an excellent account of themselves . . . All told their tales with a quiet confidence which the prosecution found difficult to shake.
>
> There can be no doubt that these men were handled roughly by the police . . . Violent treatment had been given. Although the arrests were made two weeks before, one defendant still had a badly swollen face, and one boy – a slight, rather delicate lad of 15 – had a scar on the back of his head which we could see quite plainly from several yards away . . . there were several stitches in the scalp.
>
> He looked rather frail . . . He seemed intelligent and mature far beyond his age . . . He pointed out the policeman who had knocked him about and this gentleman certainly became scarlet in the neck and rather shamefaced at this stage. The boy came from Jamaica quite recently.[6]

In other trials, Peter Dick (24), a Nigerian sailor, was sentenced to three months' imprisonment; another sailor, John Edward Duncan (41), got two months; Hogan Bassey (32) and Charles Brooks (39), a Jamaican factory worker, each went down for one month. But the League of Coloured Peoples noted as 'an odd and somewhat significant' feature that, despite the seriousness of some of the charges, most black defendants were merely fined between £3 and £5.[7] Some cases – against students who had been arrested while studying in their rooms – were dismissed. Two black women – Rene Martis (24), a pianist, and Ruth Mann (35), a factory worker – were charged with obstructing the police and found not guilty. At the end of the hearings one of the magistrates, Alderman W.A. Robinson, said the police had behaved admirably and deserved great credit.[8]

The leaders of Liverpool's black community, 'desirous of bringing an end to the disturbances and restoring harmonious relations between the racial groups', called a meeting at Stanley House, the black community centre, and invited the police to send a representative. Liverpool's first-assistant chief constable told his black audience: 'There isn't any colour question in Liverpool at this moment. I know a great deal about your particular position . . . I am responsible for law and order, and I am going to get it.' Also at the meeting was Ras Makonnen, who, on behalf of the Pan-African Federation, demanded a full and impartial investigation into the outbreaks; full compensation to black people for injuries to themselves and damage to their property; and the prosecution of those responsible for the outrages.[9]

Somalis and Arabs in Liverpool, though untouched by the violence, declared their solidarity with the rest of the black community and gave money to the fund that was raised to meet the defence costs. A Somali spokesman was quoted as saying: 'This is as much our business as the West Africans or anyone else. If it can happen to them it can happen to us.'[10]

Present in this overture were *all* the themes that the next generation of black people in Britain were to know so well in their daily relations with the police. The next generation were the sons and daughters of those who had just seen racism in action on the Liverpool streets – and of the settlers who had just begun to arrive in Britain.

11. The settlers

The post-war immigration

On 22 June 1948, the author of this book, then a young reporter on a national newspaper, went to Tilbury to see 492 Jamaicans come ashore from the *Empire Windrush* and to interview some of them. His account of their arrival was headlined: 'Five Hundred Pairs of Willing Hands'.[1] Three weeks later his follow-up article, 'The Men from Jamaica are Settling Down', reported that '76 have gone to work in foundries, 15 on the railways, 15 as labourers, 15 as farm workers, and ten as electricians. The others have gone into a wide variety of jobs, including clerical work in the Post Office, coach-building and plumbing.'[2]

The British economy, short of labour, needed these willing hands. The door stood open. To the London *Evening Standard* some of the *Empire Windrush* passengers – those who had served here during the Second World War – were making a return to 'the Motherland', and its account of their arrival was headlined: 'WELCOME HOME'.[3] Officialdom, at both government and local levels, moved swiftly to make the Jamaicans feel welcome and find them accommodation and work. Jobs were found immediately for 202 skilled men; the others did not have to wait long.

For five years, despite the demand for their services, there was only a trickle of West Indian workers into Britain. In October 1948 the *Orbita* brought 180 to Liverpool, and three months later 39 Jamaicans, 15 of them women, arrived at Liverpool in the *Reina del Pacifico*. Next summer the *Georgic* brought 253 West Indians to Britain, 45 of them women. A few hundred came in 1950, about 1,000 in 1951, about 2,000 in 1952 and again in 1953. Larger numbers arrived in the next four years, including many wives and children of men who had settled here: 24,000 in 1954; 26,000 in 1956; 22,000 in 1957; 16,000 in 1958. Ten years after the *Empire Windrush* there were in Britain about 125,000 West Indians who had come over since the end of the war.

British industry gladly absorbed them. In some industries the demand for labour was so great that members of the reserve army of black workers were actively recruited in their home countries. In April 1956 London Transport began recruiting staff in Barbados, and within 12 years a total of 3,787 Barbadians had been taken on. They were lent their fares to Britain, and the loans were repaid gradually from their wages. Even this number was not enough, and in 1966 London Transport would begin to recruit in Trinidad and Jamaica too. The British Hotels and Restaurants Association recruited skilled workers in Barbados. And a Tory health minister by the name of Enoch Powell welcomed West Indian nurses to Britain. Willing black hands drove tube trains, collected bus fares, emptied hospital patients' bed-pans.

From the early 1950s, Britain's other black community – the hitherto tiny community of settlers from the Indian sub-continent – also began to grow as rural workers from India and Pakistan came to work in Britain, again with official encouragement. By the end of 1958 there were in this country about 55,000 Indians and Pakistanis.

All these West Indians and Asians were British citizens. The 1948 Nationality Act had granted United Kingdom citizenship to citizens of Britain's colonies and former colonies. Their British passports gave them the right to come to Britain and stay here for the rest of their lives.

In their own countries there were strong incentives to take advantage of their right to settle in Britain. In the Indian sub-continent, millions had found themselves adrift without homes and jobs when Pakistan and India went their separate ways after independence. Emigration to Britain offered the prospect of a new life unthreatened by flood, famine, or the miserable poverty that was their countries' chief legacy from imperial rule. In the British West Indies, the cost of living had almost doubled during the war. There was large-scale unemployment, and those without work were desperate. There was no relief of any kind: no dole; no children's allowances; no social security at all. 'No one knows exactly how the jobless live', wrote Joyce Egginton in 1957. She added: 'It is not surprising that thousands have left the West Indies. The surprising thing is that so many have stayed.'[4] In Jamaica, hurricane damage in 1951 piled on fresh sufferings and hardships. The Caribbean had a long tradition of migration – to other islands, to central America, to the United States – in search of work; but in 1952 the US McCarran-Walter Act restricted immigration into the United States from many areas, including the West Indies. It was to Britain, therefore, that young men and young women came to get away from high unemployment, low wages, and chronic lack of opportunity. The 'Motherland' offered them a gleam of hope.

The great majority of the West Indian settlers were in their twenties. And they had plenty to offer Britain. Most white people in this country believed – and many still suppose – that the bulk of them were unskilled manual workers. But that is not so. Of the men who came here, a mere 13 per cent had no skills; of the women, only 5 per cent. In fact, one in four of the men, and half of the women, were non-manual workers. And almost half the men (46 per cent) and over a quarter of the women (27 per cent) were skilled manual workers. Yet the newcomers found themselves in most cases having to settle for a lower job status than they had enjoyed at home. This indeed was their first big disappointment. For, by and large, the jobs they were offered were those the local white people did not want: sweeping the streets, general labouring, night-shift work. In the late 1950s, more than half the male West Indians in London had lower-status jobs than their skill and experience fitted them for.

Disappointment and disillusionment of many kinds were the everyday experience of the 1950s settlers. It cannot be denied that the West Indians, in particular, had totally unrealistic expectations. The anti-imperialist tradition notwithstanding, their ideas about Britain were largely derived from a colonial education system in which Britain was revered as the 'mother country'. They 'took their British citizenship seriously, and many regarded themselves not as strangers, but as kinds of Englishmen. Everything taught in school . . . encouraged this belief.'[5] What they found here dismayed and shocked them.

Though half of Britain's white population had never even met a black person – and among those who had the acquaintance had mostly been casual – prejudice against black people was widespread. More than two-thirds of Britain's white population, in fact, held a low opinion of black people or disapproved of them. They saw them as heathens who practised head-hunting, cannibalism, infanticide, polygamy, and 'black magic'. They saw them as uncivilized, backward people, inherently inferior to Europeans, living in primitive mud huts 'in the bush', wearing few clothes, eating strange foods, and suffering from unpleasant diseases. They saw them as ignorant and illiterate, speaking strange languages, and lacking proper education. They believed that black men had stronger sexual urges than white men, were less inhibited, and could give greater satisfaction to their sexual partners. Half of this prejudiced two-thirds were, to be sure, only 'mildly' prejudiced. The other half were extremely so. This deeply prejudiced third of the white population strongly resisted the idea of having any contact or communication with black people; objected vehemently to mixed marriages; would not have black people in their homes as guests or lodgers; would not work with them in factory or office; and generally felt that black people should not be allowed in Britain at all.[6] To the prejudiced and ignorant majority it seemed 'strange and out-of-place' merely to see black people in the centres of large industrial cities in Britain.[7] In short, as Ruth Glass and Harold Pollins wrote in 1960,

> coloured people are feared as competitive intruders; they are thought of as promoters of crime and carriers of disease; they are resented when they are poor; they are envied when they are resourceful and thrifty. They are looked down upon; they are patronised; occasionally they are treated just like everyone else.[8]

Every encounter with white people was a fresh hazard. Typical was the experience of Wallace Collins, a Jamaican who came to Britain in 1954 at the age of 22. On his first Saturday night in London he was abused by 'a big fellow with side-burns', who shouted 'You blacks, you niggers, why don't you go back to the jungle?' then lunged at him with a knife.[9] Verbal abuse and physical violence were, on the whole, easier to deal with than the strange hypocrisy which excused discrimination on the ground that somebody else – usually, in the case of people who had rooms for rent, the neighbours – might object. A character in A.G.Bennett's *Because They Know Not* (1959) spoke for tens of thousands who, at first sickened by such hypocrisy, found in their sense of humour a reliable strategy for coping with it:

> Since I come 'ere I never met a single English person who 'ad any colour prejudice. Once, I walked the whole length of a street looking a room, and everyone told me that he or she 'ad no prejudice against coloured people. It was the neighbour who was stupid. If we could only find the 'neighbour' we could solve the entire problem. But to find 'im is the trouble! Neighbours are the worst people to live beside in this country.[10]

From many points of view the first-generation Asian settlers had a still harder time of it. Most of them knew little or no English, and culturally there was less common ground between them and the white people of Britain than between the latter and the West Indian settlers. Dr Bhikhu Parekh has summed up their plight:

> The first generation Asian immigrant in Britain . . . was not used to the mores and practices of an industrialised society. His presence was resented, and he suffered racialist insults and indignities. He was denied a decent house and a job commensurate with his abilities. He was often not promoted to a higher position . . .
>
> The Asian immigrants are predictably frightened and bewildered. They are haunted by a sense of impending tragedy.[11]

In many industries white trade unionists resisted the employment of black workers, or insisted on a 'quota' system limiting them to a token handful, generally about 5 per cent. Often there was 'an understanding with managements that the hallowed rule of "last in, first out" shall not apply to whites when coloured immigrants are employed, and that coloured workers shall not be promoted over white'.[12] In 1955 Wolverhampton bus workers banned overtime 'as a protest against the increasing number of coloured workers employed'. The Transport and General Workers' Union insisted that no more than 52 of the city's 900 bus workers should be black. A branch secretary said they were not operating a colour bar, but 'don't intend to have the platform staff made up to its full strength by coloured people only'.[13] West Bromwich bus workers staged one-day strikes in 1955 against the employment of a solitary Indian conductor, and a TGWU official said: 'I do not think there is any racial antagonism behind this.'[14] The Bristol Omnibus Company refused to take on black bus crews until a boycott of its buses by black people forced a change of policy.[15] So far as the craft unions were concerned, a Jamaican clerical worker summed up the situation like this: '*Union*: "Get a job and we will give you membership." *Employer*: "Join the union and you will get a job." '[16]

Throughout this ten-year laissez-faire period the government, and almost everybody else in the country, viewed the plight of the black settlers with utter complacency. In the summer of 1958, in the space of a few weeks, events in Nottingham and north Kensington dealt a death-blow to that complacency.[17]

Racism as riot: 1958

In August 1958 Nottingham, where about 2,500 West Indians and about 600 Asians were living, experienced a short outbreak of anti-black rioting. The disturbances were in part whipped up by media sensationalism. For 18 months there had been a series of attacks on individual black people in the Nottingham streets, and such attacks were becoming more frequent. On the evening of Saturday 23 August, there was fighting for 90 minutes between blacks and whites in the St Ann's Well Road area, north of the city centre. Police claimed that this was 'a reprisal by coloured people for previous incidents recently when some of their number were attacked by white men'. A black miner, leaving a cinema with his wife, was mobbed by whites shouting: 'Go back to your own country.' A white woman was quoted as saying: 'The coloured men should be banned from the pubs.' Others demanded that black people in Nottingham should be subjected to a curfew.

Immediately, as if they had been waiting for the signal, the two Nottingham MPs – one Tory, the other Labour – raised the cry that no more black people should be allowed to enter the country and that new deportation laws should be passed. The *Manchester Guardian* found it 'deplorable' that the MPs should have 'reacted as though the entire onus rested on the coloured community', and Trevor Huddleston said the proposed restrictive legislation would show that Britain 'positively desires a colour-bar'.

Within a day or two, 35 reporters had descended on Nottingham, and their sensational second- and third-hand accounts of the fighting made St Ann's Well Road a magnet for would-be anti-black rioters the following weekend. On the evening of Saturday 30 August thousands of white people were on the streets, shouting: 'Let's get the blacks.' But black people stayed off the streets. 'At one time', according to a local newspaper, 'it appeared as though a determined effort was being made to storm Robin Hood-chase, the home of many coloured people.' A crowd surrounded a car with three black people in it, shouting 'Let's lynch them' and 'Let's get at them', hammering on the windows and trying to overturn the car until the driver accelerated and managed to get clear. In the absence of other black victims, a television camera operator – so it was alleged by Nottingham's chief constable – persuaded a gang of white youths to stage a mock battle. He set off a magnesium flare, which caused much excitement. Twenty-four people were arrested in the course of this all-white 'race riot'; five were jailed for three months. A few days later windows of black people's houses were smashed with bricks and a West Indian was taken to a Nottingham hospital with a stab wound in his back. The local Labour Party declared that black people had been made the scapegoats, and Edward Scobie reported that Nottingham's black community felt the police were 'biased and not fair in their dealings with coloured people'. By mid-September an enterprising bus company was offering coach tours to see 'the terror spots of Nottingham'.[1]

The anti-black riots in London in 1958, also encouraged to some extent by sensational journalism, were more protracted and more serious than those in Nottingham. There was nothing new about such attacks. Four years earlier, in Camden Town, black people had defended themselves against white attackers whose weapons included a petrol bomb thrown into a house occupied by a West Indian family. Stimulated by fascist propaganda urging that black people be driven out of Britain, racist attacks were by 1958 a commonplace of black life in London. On weekend evenings in particular, gangs of 'teddy boys' cruised the streets looking for West Indians, Africans, or Asians. As the *Manchester Guardian* put it, 'they chose streets where only an occasional black person was seen, and then attacked in the ratio of six to one'. The police generally took little notice of these attacks, whose frequency and violence steadily increased. In July, five white youths attacked and wrecked a black-owned café in Askew Road, Shepherd's Bush. It was 'just like an earthquake', said the owner. The youths were later conditionally discharged and ordered each to pay £40 compensation.

In north Kensington and the districts around – an area conveniently if inaccurately called 'Notting Hill' by the press – black and white working-class families lived in squalid, overcrowded slums. Black and white tenants alike were exploited, bullied, and harassed by racketeering slum landlords. Few landlords were willing to let to black families. One that was, the notorious Rachman, who owned 147 properties in the area, sent strong-arm men and fierce dogs to intimidate any tenant who dared to appeal to the rent tribunal. Police gave these tenants little or no protection. The fascists blamed black people exclusively for the overcrowding and other bad conditions that afflicted everyone who lived in north Kensington.

On 17 August a white crowd smashed the windows of a house occupied by black people in Stowe Road, Shepherd's Bush. A few days later a black man was savagely attacked in a north Kensington pub by white men who battered him with metal dustbin lids and jabbed him with broken milk bottles. Over a wide area, gangs of white teenagers armed with iron bars, sticks, and knives went, as they put it, 'nigger-hunting'. In one evening's systematic and pitiless pursuit of isolated black victims, six West Indians were badly injured. Nine white youths were later sentenced to four years' imprisonment by a judge who said it was everyone's right, regardless of skin colour, 'to walk through our streets with their heads erect and free from fear', adding that the teddy-boys' exploits had 'filled the whole nation with horror, indignation and disgust'. Yet those who had incited them went free.

By the end of August brawls, disturbances, and racist attacks were a daily, and nightly, feature of life in north Kensington. A Jamaican was shot in the leg. Petrol bombs were thrown into black people's homes, including the homes of pregnant women. Such attacks were often preceded by a threatening letter or a shouted warning: 'We're going to raid you tonight if you don't clear out.' Crowds hundreds strong shouted abuse at black people. A young African student, a stranger to the area, emerged from an Underground station to find himself chased by a hostile crowd shouting 'Lynch him!' He took refuge in a greengrocer's shop whose proprietor gave him sanctuary by locking and bolting the door and defying the mob. Sensational press reports generated extra excitement. Thousands of outsiders, not all of them merely sightseers, swarmed into the borough. So trivial an incident as the collision of two prams, one pushed by a black mother, the other by a white mother, drew an expectant crowd. The *Manchester Guardian* reported that 'some of the West Indians, who always come here with such high hopes, are so downcast that they are talking seriously about accepting the last humiliation and getting a ship home'. A West Indian was quoted as saying: 'A black man's treated worse than a dog here. They watch you wherever you go. You daren't go out in the evening – it's a prison, this country.'

Not all the West Indians were so depressed. The militants organized to defend their homes and their clubs. Militants in 'The Grove', the decaying 'royal' borough's black ghetto, reasoning that attack was the best form of defence, made a pre-emptive strike against a local fascist headquarters and a club where white men were known to be planning racist attacks. Some lobbed petrol bombs in at the back of each building while others waited in ambush at the front. A number of fascists were put out of action for one night at least.

The climax came at the beginning of September. After an open-air fascist meeting a crowd of hundreds of white youths surged through the area 'in an excited state', shouting 'Let's get the niggers' and 'Give 'em to us and we'll string 'em up', smashing windows, and knocking down all who stood in their way. Mervyn Jones reported that the fascists were using the Kensington Park hotel as their rallying centre: 'The gangs certainly have a plan of campaign . . . I saw obvious messengers on fast motor-cycles. Gangs arrive in cars from other parts of London.' One young man told him: 'We're going to scare hell out of the niggers.' The *Manchester Guardian* told how cars driven by 'respectably dressed' older men had tried to run black people down in the streets.

Police, already hostile to black people in north Kensington, had offered no effective opposition to either the fascists or their teenage dupes. Ordered by their masters to keep the streets clear of crowds, they showed themselves especially diligent in breaking up groups of two or three black people on the streets. When Norman Manley, chief minister of Jamaica, toured the area on foot, and stopped to note down the name and address of a black man he spoke with, police brusquely told him to move on.

Attacks on black people spread to Kensal Green, north Paddington, and Harlesden, and were reported from as far afield as Southall, Hornsey, Islington, Hackney, and Stepney. By mid-September the situation in north Kensington had returned to normal – or, rather, to what passed as a 'normal' incidence of racist violence. Eight months later, in May 1959, a West Indian carpenter named Kelso Cochrane was stabbed to death in a north Kensington street. His murderer was never found.[2]

Outside London, an identical pattern emerged in virtually every area of black settlement: cowardly hit-and-run attacks on individuals or houses, with an occasional eruption of mob violence like the Middlesbrough riot of August 1961, when thousands of whites, chanting 'Let's get a wog', smashed the windows of black people's houses and set a café on fire while the terrified Pakistani family that owned it took refuge in cupboards.[3]

Amid the rising chorus of demands for immigration control, the voice of reason could still be heard. Labour Party chairman Tom Driberg told the Trades Union Congress:

> People talk about a colour problem arising in Britain. How can there be a colour problem here? Even after all the immigration of the past few years, there are only 190,000 coloured people in our population of over 50 million – that is, only four out of every 1,000. The real problem is not black skins, but white prejudice.[4]

Quoting a black American leader who had said that the United

States had 'no Negro problem' but 'a white problem', *Tribune* observed: 'That is true of Britain. It is prejudice, and the surrender to prejudice, that we have to fight.'[5]

Within ten years the fight had been lost, the surrender ignominiously accomplished. Racism had not merely become respectable. Enshrined in a series of 'overtly racist' immigration laws,[6] it had become official.

Surrender to racism

Between 1958 and 1968 black settlers in Britain watched the racist tail wag the parliamentary dog. It was a sustained triumph of expediency over principle. Fearful of being outflanked by fascists and each other, fearful of losing votes and seats, Tory and Labour politicians progressively accommodated themselves to racism. Driberg, it seemed, had somehow got it wrong. The problem was not white racism, but the black presence; the fewer black people there were in this country the better it would be for 'race relations'. This 'common sense' belief was the dogma on which the entire debate was based. It was rarely challenged; and when it was few white people were prepared to listen. So there was a continuum of opinion, from the fascists (who fixed the acceptable maximum at zero) to Roy Hattersley (who said in 1965, 'Without limitation, integration is impossible').[1] The legislators made one surrender after another. Step by step, racism was institutionalized, legitimized, and nationalized. That which had been unthinkable in 1958 was by 1968 the law of the land.

As sop after sop was thrown to racism, attacks on black people, far from diminishing, mounted from year to year. But the worst violence of all, since it affected every black settler without exception, was their relegation as 'immigrants' to the permanent status of second-class citizens. This was brought about in 1962, in the following way.

Soon after the 1959 general election a group of Tory MPs from the Birmingham area had launched a systematic campaign for the introduction of immigration controls. A lobbying organization, the Birmingham Immigration Control Association, was set up. The first Commonwealth Immigrants Bill, described by the Labour leader Hugh Gaitskell as 'miserable, shameful, shabby',[2] became law in 1962. This measure restricted the admission of Commonwealth settlers to those who had been issued with employment vouchers. Here was 'the decisive political turning point in contemporary British race relations'.[3] Blackness was officially equated with second-class citizenship, with the status of undesirable immigrant. Serious inroads were made into the civil rights of British citizens whose passports had been issued outside the UK. They were now subject to entry control. They were now liable to the double jeopardy of deportation if convicted of an offence within five years of arrival. And the separation of families by law had now become possible in certain circumstances. E.R.Braithwaite, author of *To Sir, with Love*, summed up in 1967 what it felt like to be a second-class citizen:

> In spite of my years of residence in Britain, any service I might render the community in times of war or peace, any contribution I might make or wish to make, or any feeling of identity I might entertain towards Britain and the British, I – like all other colored persons in Britain – am considered an 'immigrant'. Although this term indicates that we have secured entry into Britain, it describes a continuing condition in which we have no real hope of ever enjoying the desired transition to full responsible citizenship.[4]

It's the first step that counts. The 1962 Act was a piece of discriminatory legislation whose 'obvious intention' was to reduce the total annual inflow of black people into Britain.[5] Its 'unstated and unrecognized assumption' was that black people were the source of the problem. From this assumption everything else flowed and would flow – including, as Stuart Hall has pointed out with justified acerbity, all those liberal television programmes on the 'problems' of 'race relations' every word and image in which are 'impregnated with unconscious racism' since they are 'precisely predicated on racist premisses'.[6]

Two years after the 1962 Act there came the next turning-point in the evolution of English racism. Peter Griffiths, Tory candidate for Smethwick in the 1964 general election, fought on an openly racist platform: the ending of immigration and the repatriation of 'the coloureds'. His slogan was: 'If you want a nigger neighbour vote Labour.' Though Labour won the general election, Griffiths defeated a Labour minister and won Smethwick. Here, in Hall's words, was 'the first moment when racism is appropriated into the official policy and programme of a major political party and legitimated as the basis of an electoral appeal'; here was 'the beginning of racism as an element in the official politics of British populism – racism in a structured and "legitimate" form'.[7]

Though Prime Minister Harold Wilson called Griffiths a 'parliamentary leper',[8] victorious Labour was not going to let itself be outflanked. 'Shedding its temporarily assumed concern for the restoration of those civil rights lost in 1962',[9] the Labour government issued in August 1965 a White Paper on Immigration from the Commonwealth. This document accepted, indeed assumed, that the essence of the problem was numbers. It therefore 'placed considerable emphasis on the desirability of defining new and restricted terms on which newcomers could reside here and bring their families to this country'.[10] Immigration controls were tightened. Stringent restrictions were imposed on the entry of black people into Britain. No more than 8,500 employment vouchers a year would henceforth be issued – and these, as it turned out, were largely restricted to skilled workers and professional people. This was a system which, as A.Sivanandan says, 'took discrimination out of the market place and gave it the sanction of the state' – a system which 'made racism respectable and clinical by institutionalising it'.[11]

Labour had, of course, to appear to be slamming the door in a more civilized fashion than the Tories, and a year later the Race Relations Act outlawed 'incitement to racial hatred'. This measure, 'a half-hearted affair which merely forbade discrimination in "places of public resort" and, by default, encouraged discrimination in everything else: housing, employment, etc. ,[12] was spectacularly inaugurated in the prosecution of the Trinidadian Michael X (Michael de Freitas), founder in 1965 of the Racial Adjustment Action Society, for an allegedly inflammatory speech. 'Equally off-target and ineffectual' were two statutory bodies set up by Labour: the National Committee for Commonwealth Immigrants (headed by the archbishop of Canterbury, no less) and the Race Relations Board. 'To ordinary blacks', writes Sivanandan, 'these structures were irrelevant: liaison and conciliation seemed to define them as a people apart who somehow needed to be fitted into the mainstream of British society – when all they were seeking was the same rights as other citizens.'[13]

In 1968 yet another piece of nakedly discriminatory legislation, the Commonwealth Immigrants Act 1968, was steamrollered through Parliament in three days of emergency debate, with the sole purpose of restricting the entry into Britain of Kenyan Asians holding British passports. The British government was thereby enabled to break a solemn pledge by disclaiming responsibility for certain of its citizens merely because of the colour of their skin. A special clause in the Act, of course, gave ex-colonials with white skins the continued right of free entry.

> So for the first time Britain's politicians were forced to admit that there was a racial basis to their policy. They could no longer hide behind the front of general limitations from the Commonwealth for economic and social reasons. Thus Britain's coloured population lost any fond illusions or lingering doubts they might have had about British Government policy. They saw through all the sham and pretence, and they lost confidence in any efforts being made to promote racial harmony and understanding.[14]

Such a dishonourable measure did not go through, even in three days, without some opposition. Peter Mahon, MP, called it 'a deplorable concession to racialism'. Andrew Faulds, MP, said: 'This Measure makes racialism respectable, and the situation in which it is presented makes its discriminatory nature even clearer . . . This Bill panders to the racialist Lobby; it goes along with its arguments . . . That a Socialist Government should be responsible fills me with shame and despair.' Ben Whitaker, MP, said: 'This is a miserable Measure . . . I believe that Britain will become a lesser nation if it is passed . . . It is not the immigrants who are the problem. The problem is the prejudice which certain people in this country attempt to arouse.'[15]

These dissenting voices went unheeded and the Bill was rushed into law. The haste was at least partly due to the intervention of Enoch Powell. Shortly before the 1968 Bill became law, Powell had made his bid for leadership of Britain's racists. At Walsall in February he had demanded, not only a virtual embargo on the entry of Kenyan Asians, but also a virtual end to the voucher system. Soon after the Bill became law Powell returned to his vomit. His rabble-rousing speech at Birmingham in April, with its images of foaming blood, and shit pushed through letter-boxes, and overcrowded maternity wards, and impending national disaster – soon to be followed by unaffectionate and icily calculated references to 'grinning piccaninnies' – mobilized and inspired popular racism all over the country. Dockers and Smithfield porters downed tools and marched to the House of Commons in his support. In the aftermath of Smethwick, a Jamaican had been shot and killed; a black schoolboy in north Kensington had been almost killed by a white gang armed with iron bars, axes, and bottles; and crosses had been burnt outside black people's homes in Leamington Spa, Rugby, Coventry, Ilford, Plaistow, and Cricklewood.[16] In the aftermath of Powell, the terror campaign mounted once more. In many areas, Asians and West Indians now went in daily fear of their lives.

But the surrender to racism was not yet complete. Still to come was the Immigration Act of 1971, clearly reflecting three years of unremitting agitation by Powell, who was now calling for a 'Ministry of Repatriation'. The new Act, which came into force in 1973, virtually ended all primary immigration. The only black people now permitted to enter Britain were those who, under a kind of contract-labour system, were allowed to come to do a specific job for a limited period: no longer than 12 months in the first instance. Enormous power was put in the hands of police and immigration officers: they could arrest suspected illegal immigrants without a warrant. At the home secretary's discretion, an immigrant worker could be deported if that was thought to be 'conducive to the public good'. Entry of dependants was further restricted. Every help would be given to immigrants who wished to be repatriated.

The black communities were now condemned by law to every kind of abuse, to harassment, detention without trial, separation of families, 'fishing raids' – to all manner of personal indignities, humiliations, and sufferings, from the vaginal examination of women to find out if they were virgins to the mocking laughter of British officials when an 11-year-old girl burst into tears on being told that she could not have an entry certificate to join her mother, sisters, and brothers in Britain.[17]

And again, as always, the legislative endorsement of racism, far from improving 'race relations', encouraged the fascists to step up their attacks.

But black people could defend themselves, and had been doing so, in ways that white society found both unforgivable and totally forgettable. Sivanandan, in his essays, has rescued from oblivion these struggles of a black working class at bay. One area of self-defence in the 1960s was the factories, where black newcomers were invariably shunted into the most menial, dirty, dangerous, and ill-paid jobs. Yet they struggled valiantly against two kinds of discrimination: that of employers determined, if they accepted black workers at all, to keep their pay and conditions inferior to those of white workers; that of trade unions, and trade unionists, who failed to support their strikes or actively opposed them. Black strikers in the 1960s were mainly Asians, whose only support came from their local organizations and local communities: 'The temples gave free food to the strikers, the grocers limitless credit, the landlords waived the rent.'[18] Sivanandan charts with pride these struggles that went largely unreported in the white press and struck no echoing sparks of solidarity in the white trade union movement: at Rockware Glass, Southall, in 1965; at Courtauld's Red Scar Mill, Preston, in the same year, against a management decision to force black workers to operate more machines for less pay than white workers got; at the Woolf Rubber Company, again in 1965; at the Coneygre Foundry, Tipton, in 1967; at the Midland Motor Cylinder Company, and the Newby Foundry, West Bromwich, in 1968.*

Sivanandan records also another aspect of black self-defence:

> On the same day as the dockers and porters marched [in support of Powell], representatives from over fifty organisations . . . came together at Leamington Spa to form a national body, the Black People's Alliance (BPA), 'a militant front for Black Consciousness and against racialism' . . .
>
> From Powell's speech and BPA, but nurtured in the Black Power movement, sprang a host of militant black organisations all over the country, with their own newspapers and journals, taking up local, national and international issues.[19]

Throughout the 1970s, as the settlers' children – the 'second generation' – strove to make sense of the situation they found themselves born into, it was precisely this consciousness, with its rich tradition of militancy, resistance, and struggle, to which they would increasingly turn for guidance. And it was there they would find their strength.

* For the black working-class struggles of the 1970s, including the Grunwick strike and other militant activity by Asian women workers, see Sivanandan's *A Different Hunger* (1982) and Ron Ramdin's forthcoming history of the black working class in Britain.

12. The new generation

Born at a disadvantage

By the mid-1970s, two out of every five black people in Britain were born here. What has it been like to be born black in Britain in the second half of the twentieth century? Many white people complacently assume that black people born, brought up, and educated in Britain receive equal treatment to white British people in every respect. They are mistaken. In the key areas of employment, housing, and education, those born in Britain of Asian and West Indian parents face – as their parents have faced since arriving here – 'a very substantial amount of unfair discrimination'.[1]

The nature and extent of this discrimination were described at length in four Political and Economic Planning reports published in 1974–6 and usefully summarized in David J. Smith's *Racial Disadvantage in Britain* (1977). It should perhaps be pointed out that these reports were neither superficial in treatment nor propagandist in tone. They were based on the most thorough and searching interviews with a total of 3,292 Asians and West Indians, as well as other inquiries. And their conclusions were set forth in the coldly objective language of the statistician and the scholar. The plain fact is that the two million black people in Britain's population of 57,000,000 'show up in highly disproportionate terms in all unfavourable social statistics'.[2]

Black people find it much harder to get work than white people, and employers' discrimination against them 'is based mainly on colour prejudice'. Moreover 'it is quite clear . . . that, in most cases where an Asian or West Indian job applicant is rejected because of unfair discrimination', he or she 'is not told the real reason' for this rejection. Such discrimination operates more strongly against applicants for unskilled jobs than applicants for skilled ones.[3] But black people who do succeed in finding work tend to be given jobs well below the level of their qualifications and experience; many of these are jobs in marginal and service industries, with low wages, unattractive conditions, and no prospects. It is hardly surprising that the younger generation have tended to refuse, when available, the kinds of low-status jobs that their parents were shunted into.

The present economic crisis has borne most heavily on young black workers. Between 1973 and 1976 the unemployment rate went up twice as steeply for black people as it did for the population as a whole.[4] To find work, if you are a black school-leaver, you have to be more than talented: you have to be lucky. The mass of black youth, like a growing number of their white contemporaries, 'know, viscerally, that there will be no work for them, ever, no call for their labour . . . They are not the unemployed, but the never employed.'[5] This is how David J. Smith summarizes racial disadvantage in employment:

> The minority groups are more vulnerable to unemployment than whites; they are concentrated within the lower job levels in a way that cannot be explained by lower academic or job qualifications; within broad categories of jobs they have lower earnings than whites, particularly at the higher end of the job scale; they tend to shiftwork, which is generally thought to be undesirable, but shiftwork premiums do not raise their earnings above those of whites, because the jobs are intrinsically badly paid; they are concentrated within certain plants, and they have to make about twice as many applications as whites before finding a job.[6]

When it comes to housing, black people in Britain are again substantially worse off than white people. To be sure, the once ubiquitous 'no coloured' tag is no longer seen in landlords' advertisements; but black people are still far more likely than white people to suffer overcrowding and the lack of various housing amenities that even the poorest whites tend to take for granted. The PEP reports show that in south-eastern England black households were five times as likely as white households to be occupying shared dwellings; elsewhere the disproportion was still more glaring. Compared with white households, four times as many Asian and three times as many West Indian households were living at a density of two or more persons per bedroom. Or, to put it another way, almost 40 per cent of black people, compared with only 11 per cent of white people, were overcrowded. Over half of the Pakistanis in Britain, compared with some 17 per cent of white people, had neither their own bath, nor their own hot water, nor their own inside lavatory.[7] The long-term effects of such conditions on children's health and welfare, and the problems thereby caused for mothers – especially mothers of babies and young children – scarcely need emphasis. Nor can it be claimed that this pattern of racial disadvantage in housing has changed since the PEP surveys were conducted.

And what of the black child when she reaches the age of five and goes to school? From the start, writes Sivanandan,

> West Indian children were consistently and right through the schooling system treated as uneducable and as having 'unrealistic aspirations' together with a low IQ. Consequently, they were 'banded' into classes for backward children or dumped in ESN (educationally subnormal) schools and forgotten. The fight against categorisation of their children as under-achieving, and therefore fit only to be an under-class, begun in Haringey (London) in the 1960s . . . spread to other areas and became incorporated in the programmes of black political organisations.[8]

An American scholar, David L. Kirp, has shown that children of West Indian parents are three to four times as likely as white children to be classed as educationally subnormal; that proportionately few black children continue their studies beyond secondary school; that the Department of Education and Science has pursued, on issues of race and schooling, a policy of 'inexplicitness'; that black voices have seldom been heard in discussions on the proper place of race in educational policy. Above all, 'there is a marked and growing recognition on the part of minority organizations' that black children 'are getting a "raw deal" in the schools'.[9] According to Michael Marland, the chief problem that black children face in British schools is not hostility, open or hidden, on the part of those who teach them, but 'a well-meaning low expectation':

> At its worst this approach can be summed up in the 'steel bands and basketball' approach of some teachers to their black children of West Indian origin, expecting little by way of learning, but passing such failures off as inevitable for children who 'have got so much rhythm'! This is disenabling and belittling.[10]

Much of the discrimination experienced by black pupils stems, indeed, from a prejudice that is not merely unverbalized but unconscious. An east London 15-year-old told of a reading teacher who let her white pupils read aloud for long periods but stopped each of her black pupils after a short time:

> That woman never knew she was doing it, man. You would have asked her, maybe she'd tell you she treats us all the same but for some reason the white kids just do better than the black kids. Can't tell you why that is, but they do. Maybe it's their home life, you know. That woman never once saw what she was doing, and I'm not sure the white kids did either. But the black kids did.[11]

This chapter began with the question: what is it like to be born black in Britain? The answer, until just now, has taken the form of impersonal facts and figures. We have been outside looking in. But hidden behind those statistics there are individual human beings. Let's consult another of them. His name is Chris Mullard, and his answer to our question was published as *Black Britain*. This was no dry statistical survey, but a passionate human document. It was, however, honest, realistic, and clear-sighted:

> We are different from our parents in many ways. The only home we know is Britain . . . All the statutory and voluntary white agencies have now adopted the white race experts' label – 'second generation immigrants' – for black Britons. By the use of such labelling devices the vicious circle of racial discrimination becomes institutionalized and perpetuated. Merely because of the colour of their skin, black children become second-class citizens, doomed to a life of ostracism, exploitation, difference . . .
>
> We will not put up with racist behaviour. Rather than acquiesce we will react. Through our understanding of the British way of life we will be better equipped than our parents to organize constructive rebellion . . .
>
> We are now heading towards a complete breakdown in communication between white and black society. This process began in the early sixties and gathered momentum . . . with the emergence of Powellism and the country's expressed wish to tighten up controls and ostracize (and possibly later on repatriate) black immigrants and Black Britons alike. We cannot help but feel that white society is knifing us in the back . . . Most of us have withdrawn our co-operation from the official agencies and have organized resistance to race

> relations policy and the meddling of whites in our affairs. This resistance has been passive in the tradition of civil disobedience . . . But as the breakdown in communication becomes more and more absolute, passive resistance could give way to more violent forms of behaviour.
>
> This could happen in the next decade when the majority of black people living in Britain will be like me – Black British . . . Unless steps are taken immediately, we shall be filled with more hatred and bitterness than our black American brothers. Enoch Powell has predicted race riots in this country by 1986. For completely different reasons I see violent expressions of our position in and disgust with white society some years before then.[12]

These sombre and prescient words were published *in 1973*, just as Mullard's generation was beginning to emerge in the vanguard of black struggle in Britain. Similar analyses and warnings could be found in the black press of the period. And it was clear that the most troubled and potentially explosive area was the relation between black people, especially young people, and the police. 'Police relations with the black communities', wrote Mullard, 'will never be improved while the police are seen by blacks as the agents of a white racist society, while blacks are not treated as fully fledged members of British Society and accorded the same rights, equalities, and opportunities.'[13]

Police against black people

Little notice was taken outside the black communities of accusations that, in their attitude and behaviour towards black people, the police were not so impartial as they claimed to be.

When the British West Indian Association complained in 1963 that police brutality against black people had been on the increase since the passing of the Commonwealth Immigrants Act in the previous year, there was no great stir. Following a spate of anti-black operations by the Brixton police, who called what they were doing 'nigger-hunting', Joseph A. Hunte's report to the West Indian Standing Conference on police brutality was published in 1966 as *Nigger-hunting in England?* But there was little public reaction. In 1970 and 1971 the police 'task force' in Liverpool became 'a hated and dreaded unit as stories of their seizures, beatings up and plantings went the rounds'. Community relations, in Derek Humphry's words, 'were strained to near breaking point' and 'observers close to the scene were surprised that the city got through the summer [of 1971] without rioting'.[1] But that was in Liverpool's forgotten inner city, and few people elsewhere either heard or wanted to hear of such tensions.

In 1971, at Leeds assizes, a police sergeant named Kenneth Kitching was sentenced to 27 months' imprisonment, and a former police inspector named Geoffrey Ellerker to three years' imprisonment, for assaulting a Nigerian vagrant, David Oluwale. On the judge's direction, they were acquitted of manslaughter charges. Again there was little commotion, perhaps because the evidence in the case was so revolting that few cared to dwell on it. Oluwale's battered body had been found floating in a river, and witnesses told the court how the two police officers had ruthlessly kicked the tramp, how Sergeant Kitching had pissed on him as he lay in a shop doorway, how the two guardians of law and order had dumped him in the countryside outside Leeds.[2]

In 1972 a select parliamentary committee on relations between black people and the police was surprised to receive from the West Indian Standing Conference a memorandum that sought to expose what was going on and to warn of the consequences if police racism were allowed to continue unchecked. Their surprise, amounting to disbelief, was manifested in the chairman's first remark to Clifford Lynch, public relations officer of the WISC, who attended as a witness: 'The memorandum which you have submitted to us does present a case almost akin to civil war between the West Indians and the police.'[3]

Hardly anybody outside the black communities was prepared to listen, let alone believe. Magistrates and judges, with negligible exceptions, believed police witnesses and disbelieved black witnesses; they displayed open partiality towards the police, 'with little regard for the course of justice'.[4] Nor was much attention paid when the sociologist Maureen Cain, in her book *Society and the Policeman's Role* (1973), showed how racism had become a key component of policemen's occupational culture. She found that policemen generally believed that 'niggers', or 'nigs', were 'in the main . . . pimps and layabouts, living off what we pay in taxes'. At a police station where she did some of her field work, over an hour was spent in trying to find the address of a party an American air force officer wanted to go to, but a homeless black man was turned away three times in one night without any advice as to where he could find somewhere to stay. Black people were 'by definition permanently in the area of suspicion'. One police officer reminisced to her:

> There was this enormous negro and we kept batting him over the head with our sticks and he didn't even seem to feel it . . . I hit him hard where it hurts most and in the stomach and as I went past – just happened to knock against him with my foot, and he went down like a light . . . We had to take him [to court] for assault on police or we could never have accounted for all those knocks.

After all, black people were 'different, separate, incomprehensible. There was, therefore, no good reason for not being violent if the occasion arose.'[5]

In 1979 a further, comprehensive, account of police–black relations also fell on largely deaf ears. This was the evidence submitted by the Institute of Race Relations to the Royal Commission on Criminal Procedure, published under the title *Police against Black People.* It was largely based on evidence from lawyers' case files, legal and advisory centres, black self-help groups, and personal interviews. The police, it was claimed, no longer merely reflected or reinforced popular morality: 'they re-create it – through stereotyping the black section of society as muggers and criminals and illegal immigrants'. Criminal procedure was being used to harass a whole community. The police refused to protect a community under constant attack from sections of the white population; and black people's efforts to defend themselves gave rise to police reprisals.

These allegations were scrupulously documented, with evidence of police overmanning of black events (e.g. the 1976 Notting Hill Carnival); the harassment of black people in their meeting-places (e.g. raids on black youth clubs); police concentration on predominantly black localities all over Britain; the use of the Special Patrol Group and the Illegal Immigration Intelligence Unit to harass black people; police refusal to give black people any protection against racial violence, unwillingness to prosecute attackers, misguided advice to victims, hostility to complainants, and treatment of victims as if they were the aggressors; bias in police evidence; the treatment of black self-protection against racial violence as if it were criminal activity; the arbitrary arrest of black people; the use of unnecessary violence in arresting black people; the harassment of juveniles; the arrest of black people merely for asserting their rights; the harassment of witnesses to police malpractices; repeated arrests of individuals on frivolous grounds; the entry of black homes and premises at will; and, inside police stations, the flouting of Judge's Rules, the use of brutality and intimidation, the forcing of confessions, the medical neglect of detained suspects, and the use of pressure or force to obtain photographs and fingerprints.[6] To the black communities the police had become, in effect, an army of occupation charged with the task of keeping black people in their place.

It was this political aspect of police–black relations which came to dominate discussions of the problem within the embattled black communities, and helped to shape their response. We have been witnessing a large-scale attempt at 'social control', with black political activists the central focus of police interest and attack. This was clear by 1970, when the Special Branch, Britain's political police, 'started to harass the political activists in the black community in a systematic way'.[7] When a demonstration took place in August of that year against repeated police raids on the Mangrove restaurant in north Kensington, a meeting-place of black radicals, the police unhesitatingly picked out the organizers and arrested them. And when the home secretary called for a report on black political activity, the *Guardian* revealed: 'He will have a complete dossier within 48 hours. The Special Branch has had the movement under observation for more than a year . . . Police now regard Black Power as, at least, worthy of extremely tight surveillance.'[8] In the event, the 'Mangrove 9' were acquitted at the Old Bailey in 1971, having skilfully used their rights to challenge jurors – and, as Ian McDonald has pointed out, it was largely because of these acquittals that the defence rights they used so vigorously were subsequently 'modernized' out of existence.[9] Further attacks on black political activists followed – attacks that were scrupulously documented, case by case, in the columns of *Race Today*, launched by a collective of black activists. For instance, the 'Oval 4' – members of a south London black organization known as the Fasimbas – were pounced on by plain-clothes detectives at the Oval tube station, beaten up inside the police station, forced to sign confessions, found guilty of attempted theft and of assault on the police, and sentenced, the youngest to Borstal, the others to two years' imprisonment each.[10] There has indeed been, as the British Black Panthers warned in October 1970, a deliberate campaign 'to "pick off" Black militants' and to 'intimidate, harass and imprison black people prepared to go out on the streets and demonstrate'.[11]

Unfortunately for the police, black political organization is too flexible and resilient to be easily monitored. This indeed is one of the fatal weaknesses at the heart of the ' "crisis management" which has operated since the early seventies' and has chosen 'the option of control and containment of forms of black resistance against racial domination'.[12] The police have almost entirely failed to find informers within the black communities.[13] They have failed to drive a wedge between black youth and their parents. They have failed to 'pick off' activists in any significant numbers. On the other hand, their own activities have hugely contributed to the 'mass politicization of youth cultures', so that 'the resistance and oppositional symbols provided by Afro-Caribbean political culture' have become 'central reference-points for the struggles of other young people'.[14] After an entire decade of police harassment, aimed at suppressing black resistance, black and white youth together, in the summer of 1981, set Britain's inner cities ablaze.

Resistance and rebellion

To those blind to what had been happening all through the 1970s, and deaf to the many protests and warnings, the 1981 events came as a severe shock. Those in shock included government and MPs. Their mood, wrote the *Guardian* on 7 July 1981, 'was overwhelmingly one of bafflement . . . Suddenly, forces appear to have been unleashed which nobody knows how to control.' And next day: 'The ruling class in Britain has lost its competence and its confidence.'[1] 'Riot', being a four-letter word, is excellent for headlines; but its use to describe what were in fact uprisings by entire inner-city populations, black and white together, served to obscure the true nature and causes of these events.

Right through the 1970s, Britain's black communities had been under attack from fascists and police. They had been forced to defend themselves, since nobody else could or would defend them. The rebellion of black youth in the inner cities was the logical and, as is now clear, inevitable response to racist attacks. It was the culmination of years of harassment. Its message was simply: 'We have had enough.'

Between 1976 and 1981, 31 black people in Britain had been murdered by racists. They included Gurdip Singh Chaggar, aged 18, stabbed to death in Southall by a gang of white youths; Altab Ali and Ishaque Ali, murdered in Brick Lane; Michael Ferreira, murdered in Hackney; Akhtar Ali Baig, murdered in Newham; Mohammad Arif and Malcolm Chambers, murdered in Swindon; Sewa Singh Sunder, murdered in Windsor; Fenton Ogbogbo, murdered in south London; Famous Mgutshini, a Zimbabwean student, stabbed to death outside Liverpool Street station; a young boy in Manchester, stabbed to death by a motorist at whose car he had idly flicked an apple core. Besides the knife, the racists also used fire: by 1981, arson attacks on black people's homes had become commonplace. In Chapeltown, Leeds, a disabled Sikh woman was burnt to death when a petrol bomb was thrown into her house. In Leamington Spa, an elderly Asian woman died after racists poured petrol over her and set fire to her sari. In Walthamstow, Mrs Parveen Khan and her three children were burnt to death when petrol was poured through their letter-box and set alight at three in the morning. And for every black person murdered, scores of others were attacked, beaten, kicked unconscious.

> Black places of worship, black shops, black centres are targets for brutal attack, vandalism and fascist daubings. Nor is there safety inside the house – bricks may be thrown through windows and burning petrol-soaked rags pushed through letter-boxes. Day in, day out black people, young and old, men and women, are subjected to abuse and assault. Yet, by and large, this violence, even arson and murder, goes unreported, except at the local level – and not always then.[2]

And in almost every case, in the teeth of the evidence, the police denied that there had been, that there could have been, any racist motive. Sometimes they went further, by arresting the victims and letting the attackers go free. That was what happened in the notorious case of the Virk brothers, in April 1977.

These four Asians, repairing their car outside their east London house, were attacked by a gang of white youths. One brother went to call the police; the others defended themselves as best they could. When the police arrived, it was the Virk brothers who found themselves under arrest. Their attackers were not arrested. The judge accepted the police witnesses' evidence; said it was 'irrelevant' for the defence to speak of race prejudice; and reprimanded the defence for asking whether the attackers were members of the National Front.

> When judges unquestioningly accept police versions of events, turn a blind eye to the racial dimensions of a case and even accuse black defendants of introducing racial issues where there are none, justice is not only not done, but is no longer seen to be done.

> In the face of such a massive onslaught from the fascists, the police, the politicians, the press, the judges and the law, the black community must perforce defend itself.[3]

But when second-class citizens dared to defend themselves, the police turned out in overwhelming numbers in an effort to crush their resistance and give the fascists the freedom of the streets. That was what happened in Southall on 23 April 1979. To protect a handful of National Front supporters, 2,756 police, including paramilitary Special Patrol Group units, horses, dogs, vans, and a helicopter, poured into the area. The police violently broke up a crowd of 5,000 protesters, drove their vans into the crowd, bludgeoned people at random as they scattered and ran, vandalized the premises of Peoples Unite, a black meeting centre, arrested 342 people, injured hundreds – and beat Blair Peach to death with unauthorized weapons. 'If you keep off the streets in London and behave yourselves, you won't have the SPG to worry about', were the reassuring words of the Metropolitan Police Commissioner afterwards.

By now officials in the health service and the employment, education, housing, and welfare services were more and more insisting that before black citizens could be given their rights, they must produce their passports and submit to identity checks:

> Since, in British thinking, all black people are immigrants and some of them are illegal, the only thing to do is suspect the lot. What this means in practice is that black people may be called on at any time to prove their right to be in Britain . . . The new Nationality Act . . . embodies, regularises and codifies the discriminatory essence of all the Immigration Acts from 1962 to 1971. It becomes the discriminatory mechanism par excellence. In sum, what we are left with is an Immigration Act masquerading as a Nationality Act; an Immigration Act which, because of that masquerade, has jurisdiction not only over the right of black people to enter Britain, but over the rights of black people resident in Britain.[4]

But here is a future prime minister explaining it all on television: 'People are really rather afraid that this country might be rather swamped by people with a different culture.' Decoded, this means 'people with a different colour'. She goes on: 'The British character has done so much for democracy, for law, and done so much throughout the world, that if there is any fear that it might be swamped, people are going to react and be rather hostile to those coming in.'[5]

Meeting-places are essential for democracy, and any 'law' that stamps them out is oppressive and unjust. In April 1980, after years of harassing Bristol's black community, police raided one of the few meeting-places black youth had left to them. The resistance was tougher than they had bargained for, and they withdrew after two hours' fighting. In fact, they ran away, and for four hours St Pauls was a 'no go' area. Bristol became a symbol of resistance.

In January 1981, 13 young black people perished in a fire at a house in Deptford, an area where other black homes had been attacked and a black community centre had been burnt down. As usual, police discounted the possibility of a racial motive; but the entire community, not just the anguished parents, were convinced that the fire had been started by fascists.

Three months later some 15,000 black people, in the most remarkable demonstration ever mounted by Britain's black communities, marched the ten miles from Deptford to central London. They demanded justice for black people and an end to racist murders. They protested against police conduct of the Deptford inquiry. And, as they marched through Fleet Street, they protested against media indifference to the mass murder.

Another month, and police in Brixton launched 'Swamp 81'. This was merely the first local part of a London-wide exercise known as 'Operation Star', which many black people saw as a police reply to the Deptford march. Brixton was now well and truly 'swamped by people with a different culture' – 120 plain-clothes policemen, who in six days stopped 943 people in the street and arrested 118 of them. 'It was', said the head of the local CID, 'a resounding success.'[6] They beat up a man outside a local school, and a parent who tried to remonstrate with them was hit on the head with a truncheon and arrested for obstruction. On 10 April a crowd rescued a black youth from a police car, then stood up to police reinforcements and forced them to withdraw.

Next day, Brixton exploded. In July, the rebellion spread to Southall after an attack on an Asian woman by people from outside the area. The uprising in the Toxteth district of Liverpool lasted four days: young workers, white and black, fought and defeated the police under the leadership of black Liverpudlians described by the local chief constable as 'the product of liaisons between white prostitutes and African sailors'.[7] Under that leadership they succeeded in burning down 150 buildings, including some of symbolic significance, putting 781 policemen out of action, and holding the area until the police returned with CS gas, which they fired at people with cartridges intended for use against walls.

Back to the television screen came Margaret Thatcher. 'Nothing', she said, 'can justify, nothing can excuse and no one can condone the appalling violence we have seen.' Within hours, the rebellion had spread to Manchester, where 1,000 youths, black and white, besieged Moss Side police station. Then it hit Handsworth in Birmingham, Chapeltown in Leeds, Bolton, Luton, Leicester, Nottingham, Birkenhead, Hackney, Wood Green, Walthamstow, Hull, High Wycombe, Southampton, Halifax, Bedford, Gloucester, Sheffield, Coventry, Portsmouth, Bristol, Edinburgh, Reading, Huddersfield, Blackburn, Preston, Ellesmere Port, Chester, Stoke, Shrewsbury, Wolverhampton, Newcastle, Knaresborough, Derby, Stockport, Maidstone, Aldershot, and dozens of other places, black and white youth together against the police. 'Copycat riots'? Some cats – and some claws!

With remarkable historical symmetry, this burst of youthful rage began, and proved to be most powerful and sustained, in the very cities which had once been this country's chief slave ports: Bristol, London, and Liverpool. There, if anywhere, the persistent bullying of black people was bound, sooner or later, to provoke rebellion. The size and scope and ferocity of the rebellion astonished everyone, including the youth themselves. They learnt that, tactically, they could defeat the police; that, strategically, they could hold them to a draw. The police learnt how far, in future, they could goad. On both sides of the barricades many other lessons are no doubt still being digested. Those who at present rule this country, and for whom control of Britain's black communities has been a major consideration in the turn to 'hard' policing, would be ill-advised to underestimate the intelligence, determination, and proud traditions of those they desire to control. And if, as has been suggested, 'traces of black life have been removed from the British past to ensure that blacks are not part of the British future',[8] the present book is offered as a modest contribution to setting the record straight.

Appendixes

Appendix A. Letter from Olaudah Equiano to Thomas Hardy, 1792

Edingburg May 28th. – 1792

D^{r}. Sir, &c. &c.

With Respect I take this oppertunity to acquaint you (by M^{r}. Ford – an acquantance of mine who is to go to Day for London) that I am in health – hope that you & Wife is well – I have sold books at Glasgow & Paisley, & came here on the 10th. ult. I hope next month to go to Dunde, Perth, & Aberdeen. – Sir, I am sorry to tell you that some Rascal or Rascals have asserted in the news parpers viz. Oracle of the 25th. of april, & the Star. 27th. – that I am a native of a Danish Island, Santa Cruz, in the W^{t}. Indias. The assertion has hurted the sale of my Books – I have now the aforesaid Oracle & will be much obliged to you to get me the Star, & take Care of it till you see or hear from me – Pray ask M^{r}. & M^{rs}. Peters who Lodged in the next Room to me, if they have found a Little Round Gold Breast Buckel, or broach, sett in, or with fine stones – if they have, I will pay them well for it. – & if they have found it pray write to me on that account Directly. & if tis not found you need not write on that account* (& the Direction is to me, to be left at the Post Office here.) My best Respect to my fellow members of your society. I hope they do yet increase. I do not hear in this place that there is any such societys – I think M^{r}. Alex^{r}. Mathews in Glasgow told me that there was (or is) some there – Sir. on Thursday the 24th. Inst. – I was in the General assembely of the Church of Scotland, now Convened, & they agreed unanimously on a petition, or an address to the House of Lords to abolish the Slave Trade – & on which account I gave them an address of thanks in two news papers which is well Rece^{d}. I find the Scotchmen is not Like the Irish – or English – nor yet in their Houses – which is to High – Especially here. But thanks to God the Gospel is Plantifully preached here – & the Churches, or Karks is well filled – I hope the good Lord will enable me to hear & to profit, & to hold out to the end – & keep me from all such Rascals as I have met with in London – M^{r}. Lewis wrote me a Letter within 12 Days after I Left you & acquaint^{d}. me of that Villain who owed me above 200£ – Dying on the 17th. of April – & that is all the Comfort I got from him since – & now I am again obliged to slave on more than before if possible – as I have a Wife.

May God ever keep you & me from atachment to this evil World, & the

* it was wreped up in a bit of paper.

things of it – I think I shall be happy when time is no more with me, as I am Resolved ever to Look to Jesus Christ – & submit to his Preordainations.

Dr. Sir, – I am with Christian Love to you & Wife – &c.

Gustavus Vassa
The African

P.S. – pray get me the Gentlemens. Magazine for April 1792 & take Care of it for me.

Source: PRO TS 24/12/2.

Note: the issue of the *Gentleman's Magazine* referred to in the postscript contained a report of Equiano's marriage to Susan Cullen seven weeks before this letter was written; see p. 110 above.

Appendix B. Letter from William Davidson to Sarah Davidson, 1820

My dear Sarah, – According to the promise your entreaties caused me to make to you concerning matters of counsel, &c. I have sent you here the order I received last night – an order for application to either of the several justices therein mentioned, whereby an order will be granted to the applicant for the free admission of counsel, solicitors, &c. But I would rather, for my part, use such an order for you and my dear children, in preference to counsel, &c.; and would now retain my integrity of not having any, only as it is the first time you ever ask the favour of being dictator, and, as in such considerations, I did grant you that request, I will not now fall from such a promise, to one whose sole interest & young family entirely depends on the result of this trial. Therefore you can be advised how you are to act; for my own part I am careless about it, as I am determined to maintain my integrity as a man against all the swarms of false witnesses; and I hope you will never be persuaded, or suffer the public to be led away with a belief, that I am fallen from that spirit maintained from my youth up, and had so long been in possession of the ancient name of Davidson (Aberdeen's boast), and is now become fables. Death's countenance is familiar to me. I have had him in view fifteen times, and surely he cannot now be terrible. Keep up that noble spirit for the sake of your children, and depend that even in death, it will be maintained, by your ever affectionate husband,

Wm. Davidson

Mrs. Sarah Davidson, 12, Elliott-row, Lord's Old Cricket Ground, St. Mary-le-bone, New Road

Source: *Observer*, no. 1520 (7 May 1820), [3].

Appendix C. Letter from Robert Wedderburn to Francis Place, 1831

Sir

The Works of M^{r}. Spence I lent and lost, has to the Bust, Edwards inform me that M^{r}. Galloway gave him the orders to make about fiveteen for particular persons, it appears to me that M^{r}. Galloway will be able to give you information, and young M^{r}. Evans (M^{r}. G's nephew) was very familiar with M^{r}. Spence, and no doubt will assist you, I was not acquainted with M^{r}. Spence for more than nine Months before his death. If you want information of the fundamental principals of M^{r}. Spence's plan, and how he came to conceive it, I can give it from Memory has I was an attentive and active member of the Spencian society after his Death, but you must allow me a fortnight or three Weeks to commit it to paper, has I am convicted to labour I cannot attend to it only at Evening

I remain
Your's respectfully
Robert Wedderburn

Giltspur S^{t}. prison – March 22nd. 1831

Source: British Library Add. MS. 27,808 (Place Papers, vol. XX), fol. 322.

Appendix D. William Cuffay's speech from the dock, 1848

My lords, I say you ought not to sentence me, first, because although this has been a long and important trial, it has not been a fair trial, and my request was not complied with to have a jury of my equals. But the jury as it is I have no fault to find with; I daresay they have acted conscientiously. The next reason that I ought not to be sentenced is on account of the great prejudice that has been raised against me in particular, for months past. Everybody that hears me is convinced that almost the whole press of this country, and even other countries, has been raising a prejudice against me. I have been taunted by the press, and it has tried to smother me with ridicule, and it has done everything in its power to crush me. I crave no pity. I ask no mercy.

The prisoner Fry [i.e. Thomas Fay] (*with violence*): Nor I.

The prisoner Cuffey: Keep yourself cool, my boy. You will never get through your troubles if you do not. The press has strongly excited the middle class against me; therefore I did not expect anything else except the verdict of guilty, right or wrong; and instead of my being pitied I pity the *Attorney-General* and the Government that they could descend to such means as to raise up a conspiracy against me by infamous and base characters. I should have said 'The *Spy Master-General*', for that is the fact. The present Government is now supported by a regular organized system of espionage which is a disgrace to this great and boasted free country. The locality to which I belong never approved of any violence of this sort and never sent any delegates to any such meetings, and that you will find proved in the trials of my fellow prisoners who have not yet been tried. They sent no delegates, and consequently there were no luminaries nor firebrands sent to Orange Street from that locality. That is another reason why I should not be sentenced; that will be hereafter proved. Then I have to complain of the Whig manœuvres of keeping the spy *Davis* back to the last moment after he had had an opportunity of reading the evidence in the newspaper and seeing what was deposed to, and then coming here with a statement written out by the inspectors of police against me and filling up all the discrepancies in the evidence of the principal spy, that miscreant with so many *aliases*, *Powell* being his proper name, it seems. He had never proved I was a delegate. He had never proved I was elected on the Ulterior Committee, and he did not state that I went out on Tuesday evening with the Ulterior Committee and proposed the place and scheme of the intended outbreak. But then comes *Davis*, after he had had an opportunity of reading in the papers the evidence that *Powell* had given, to say the time when I was elected, as he states, secretary. He states I went out with the Ulterior Committee and returned with them. All this I deny. It is most gross, perilous, and degrading to any Government to resort to such means, and, if my letters had been read, it would have been proved that my life had been threatened months ago, and that would easily account for my having a small pocket-pistol at home loaded. I was also threatened with assassination, and therefore I considered I had a right, and indeed every Englishman has a right, according to the old statute, to have arms, and he was liable to punishment, as your lordship is aware, for not practising the use of those arms. At the same time I am aware that there was an Act passed in the time of George the Third for punishing people for assembling to drill and practise the use of arms, but I also know that the statute to which I have alluded had never been rescinded. I did attempt to pass a pistol to my wife, because I knew what would be made of it, but it was for self-defence I kept it. And it has been stated by your lordship to-day that it was very important that these spies should go about with a brace of pistols loaded, because their lives were in danger. Certainly I cannot conceive it is any crime therefore in me to have a small pocket pistol at home. There has been an accusation made against me likewise as to my name being mentioned in one of the books found at *Lacy's* about the subscription, about the Victim fund towards defraying my expenses at this trial. It is mentioned, but it is never proved in that book; nothing of the sort, my lord. That is all I need say at present, except that this is no more than what I have expected for some time. As I certainly have been an important character in the Chartist movement, I laid myself out for something of this sort from the first. I know that a great many men of good moral character are now suffering in prison only for advocating the cause of the Charter; but, however, I do not despair of its being carried out yet. There may be many victims. I am not anxious for martyrdom, but I feel that, after what I have gone through this week, I have the fortitude to endure any punishment your lordship can inflict upon me. I know my cause is good, and I have a self-approving conscience that will bear me up against anything, and that would bear me up even to the scaffold; therefore I think I can endure any punishment proudly. I feel no disgrace at being called a felon. As to that Act, which your lordship has called attention to, which was passed by the legislature in the most hurried manner without time for due consideration, I am almost one of the first victims after glorious *Mitchel* to fall under that Act.* Any Act that has been brought forward for the good of the country has been delayed and great time has been lost in attending to it, and indeed most of them have been thrown aside or put

* Found guilty of felony by a shamelessly packed jury, John Mitchel, founder of the *United Irishman* and a leading advocate of co-operation between Irish patriots and Chartists, had been sentenced to transportation for 14 years on 27 May 1848.

off to the next session; but anything to abridge the rights of the working classes can be passed in a few hours. I have done, my lords.

Source: *Reports of State Trials*, n.s. VII, ed. John E.P. Wallis (1896), cols. 478–80. Shorter reports will be found in *The Times*, no. 19,983 (2 October 1848), 7, and R.G. Gammage, *The History of the Chartist Movement* (1854), 364, reprinted in the revised edition (1894), 340.

Appendix E. J.R. Archer's presidential address to the inaugural meeting of the African Progress Union, 1918

I greatly dislike bringing coals to Newcastle, and in addressing you to-night, as one born in England, I fear that is what I am doing, but I take courage from the fact I will not accept second place with any here for love of my race. I am, and always will be, a race-man. That feeling was born in me when quite a little boy in my natal city, Liverpool. A famous company of American Negroes were playing that soul-stirring Negro tragedy *Uncle Tom's Cabin*. I saw the play, and from that moment the seeds of resentment were planted within me that have resulted in making me the race-man I am. Too long, much too long, has the Negro race suffered. 'Mislike me not for my complexion, the shadowed livery of the burnished sun.' Why should he suffer because of that shadowed livery? As the Prince of Morocco pleaded to Portia, so the Negroes of to-day plead. I raise my voice to-night against that plea having to be made in future. We are living in stirring times. We have seen the end of the greatest war in the annals of history, a war that marks an epoch in the history of our race. Side by side with the British Army, for the first time, our compatriots from Africa, America, and the West Indies have been fighting on the fields of France and Flanders against a foreign foe. A war, we have been repeatedly told, for the self-determination of small nations and the freedom of the world from the despotism of German rule. The truth of that statement will be proved by the way they deal in America with Afro-Americans, in France with their Negro subjects, in Belgium with their Congo subjects, and in Great Britain with India, Africa and the West Indies. We shall be told the old, old story. Africa is not ready; the time is not ripe; they are not sufficiently advanced. According to some critics the Negroes will only be ready when the Angel Gabriel sounds his trumpet. I do not know when that great day will come, but I am hoping it is far distant, because we are inaugurating to-night an association which I trust to be the parent of a large number of similar institutions, whose sole reason for existence will be the progress of our African race.

I have said according to some people the African is not ready. Upon whom, then, can the blame be placed more equitably than the white race? What have they done, what are they doing, to rectify the great wrong inflicted upon our forbears? The children of the white race to-day owe a great debt still to the children of the darker race. We are hearing a great deal about indemnities on the one hand, reparation on the other, that the Peace Conference is going to demand from Germany. I venture to submit to each delegate to the Conference this proposition: 'Keep your minds on the patent fact that Negroes have been associated with you in bringing about the possibility of this great conference of the nations who are so desirous for the world's freedom.'

I suggest by way of instalment they put down a motion for the better treatment of the coloured races under their rule, greater facilities for their educational advancement in part payment of the debt they owe to them. It is rather significant to me that India is the only country of the darker race which will be directly represented. One of the greatest blots upon the escutcheon of the white race is their enslavement of our people in America and the West Indies. The discovery and colonisation of America were primarily for greed, and this dominant principle was illustrated in different stages of the growth and development of the country. Spain, which in the sixteenth century was not only a world-wide Power, but one of the greatest of modern times, bore a very important part in the conquest and settlement of the New World. It was mainly her merchantmen that ploughed the Main, her capital and the patronage of her sovereigns that led. The Dutch and the English followed in the rear. Settlements in North America and the West Indies were made by her sons early in the sixteenth century, but it was one hundred years after, at Jamestown, Virginia, in 1607, that the English made the first permanent settlement within the continental limits of the United States of America.

In the early voyages it was not at all remarkable that Negroes were found as sailors, though slaves. It is well authenticated that among the survivors of the Coronado expedition was Estevan, a Negro, who was guide to Friar Narcoz in 1539 in the search for the Seven Cities of Cibola. The celebrated anthropologist, in *The Human Species*, strongly intimates that Africa had its share in the peopling and the settlement of some sections of South America. The exception but proves the rule that the Negro came to the New World as a slave. He was stolen from or bought on the West Coast of Africa, to add to the wealth of America by his toil as bondman and labourer. Large numbers of Negroes were imported by the Portuguese, but I am more concerned with what England had to do with this traffic in human beings.

The English gentleman Sir John Hawkins made three trips to America from the West Coast of Africa between 1563 and 1567, taking with him several hundreds of the Natives, whom he sold as slaves. Queen Elizabeth became a partner in this nefarious traffic. So elated was she at its profits that she knighted him, and he most happily selected for his crest a Negro head and bust, with arms pinioned. It was a lucrative business, and though it at first shocked the sensibilities of Christian nations and rulers, they soon reconciled themselves, not only to the traffic, but introduced the servitude as part of the economic system of their dependencies in America. That it became a fixture after its introduction in these Colonies was due to the prerogative of the Home Government rather than to the importunities of the Colonists – especially because it was a source of revenue to the Crown.

Hence I say we who were born under British rule and are of the Negro race here still need reparation to be made to us. We are the ones to show resentment, if it should be shown. We, the offspring of those islands, are the ones to bear malice, if it should be borne. How have we shown this resentment? How have we borne this malice? Look in France and Flanders, and we get the answer. When England was in dire need, African, American and West Indian Negroes forgot injustice, forgot wrongs, forgot insults, and hastened to the nation's call. How have they been requited?

We come from an ancient race. We have a history to be proud of. Before Romulus founded Rome, before Homer sang, when Greece was in its infancy, and the world quite young, 'Hoary Meroe' was the chief city of the Negroes along the Nile. Its private and public buildings, its markets and public squares, its colossal walls and stupendous gates, its gorgeous chariots and alert footmen, its inventive genius and ripe scholarship, made it the cradle of civilisation and the mother of art. It was the queenly city of Ethiopia – for it was founded by colonies of Negroes. Through its open gates long and ceaseless caravans laden with gold, silver, ivory, frankincense and palm-oil poured the riches of Africa into the capacious lap of the city. The learning of this people, embalmed in immortal hieroglyphic, flowed down the Nile and like spray spread over the Delta of that time-honoured stream, on by the beautiful and venerable city of Thebes – the city of a hundred gates, another monument to Negro genius and civilisation, and more ancient than the cities of the Delta. Greece and Rome stood transfixed before the ancient glory of Ethiopia! Homeric mythology borrowed its essence from Negro hieroglyphics. Egypt borrowed her light from the venerable Negroes up the Nile. Greece went to school to the Egyptians, and Rome turned to Greece for law and the science of warfare. England dug down into Rome's centuries to establish a Government and maintain it. Thus the flow of civilisation has been from the East, the place of light, to the West; from the Orient to the Occident.

Some writers have striven to prove that the Egyptians and Ethiopians are quite a different people from the Negro, but Jeremiah the prophet asks: 'Can the Ethiopian change his skin or the leopard his spots?' The Prophet was as thoroughly aware that the Ethiopian was black as that the leopard had spots. We have in addition to this testimony the evidence of Herodotus, Homer, Josephus, Eusebius, Strabo, and others, and I am content to accept their evidence. Here is our ancient past. We have no need to be ashamed of it.

Our modern record we can also proudly speak about, since freedom came to Africa's sons. What have we achieved, in spite of prejudice, in the realms of science, literature and art! The race can proudly point to Daniel A. Payne, eminent as a pioneer educator, first President of a Negro college and Bishop of the African Methodist Episcopal Church; Henry Highland Garnet, the orator become Minister and Consul-General to Liberia; Dr. Alexander Crummell, D.D., scholar and brilliant conversationalist; the great Frederick Douglass (cheers), who visited this country and became the friend of Cobden, Bright, Brougham, O'Connell, Disraeli, Peel; Paul Laurence Dunbar, the poet, who also visited this city in 1897; Booker T. Washington (cheers), the first Negro to receive the distinction of Master of Arts from Harvard University; Mrs. Fanny Jackson Coppin, the first coloured woman to graduate from a recognised college in the United States of America, who visited the country in 1888 to attend a missionary congress, and so eloquently did she plead the cause that the Duke of Somerset arose and commended her in glowing terms for her eloquence, and the cause that she so ably represented; Henry Osawa Tanner, the famous artist whose paintings can be seen in the Paris Salon; Ida B. Wells, whom I met here when she was rousing the people to the highest pitch of indignation against the lynching of Negroes – these are a few of the names of Afro-Americans we are all proud of. I could go on giving evidence of our race's progress, but time will not permit. I shall therefore conclude this portion of my address with three names of eminent men of our race, one from Africa, one from the West Indies and one from England.

In 1864 the most important event in the life of a great African took place in Canterbury Cathedral, when Samuel Crowther was consecrated first Bishop of the Niger (cheers). Remembering, as doubtless many did, the touching history of his childhood and early struggles as a slave, the crowded congregation must have been moved to tears as this African humbly knelt in God's glorious house to receive the seals of the high office of Shepherd of His earthly fold. The West Indies have given us that master of erudition, Edward Wilmot Blyden. As linguistic scholar, Dr. Blyden ranked deservedly high. He possessed a working knowledge of the French, German, Italian and Spanish among modern languages, and of Hebrew, Greek and Latin among the classics. It has been said of him: 'The life and work of the late Edward Wilmot Blyden, D.D., have attracted the attention of Europeans and Africans as one of the most conspicuous expressions and manifestations of the belief that a man of unmixed African ancestry possesses the mental capacity, the intellectual and imaginative power, of acquiring and assimilating alike the literary culture of the ancient civilisation of the Greeks, the Romans and the Hebrews; and of the modern civilisations of the Anglo-Saxons, the Latins and the Arabs. He must be regarded as one of the first-fruits of a maturing literary harvest which in the fulness of time will be ingathered, and which will thus reveal to all mankind the view-point, the outlook and the ideals of the Westernised Africans of America and the West Indies; and also of the Westernised Africans of the Continent of Africa who have lived throughout all of their generations in Africa, governed and surrounded mainly by Pagan and Mahommedan religious influences and by African laws and institutions.' Lastly, those of us who were born here can point to Samuel Coleridge Taylor, the great composer. His *Hiawatha* proved him to be in the front rank of musical composers, and will for ever live; in his early death the race lost a great man, and I a personal friend.

It is now my pleasure and duty to pay tribute, very briefly, as time will not permit, to some of the great and noble men and women of the white race who have stood firmly for African progress. My hero in American history is John Brown, who gave his life for the freedom of the slaves. This is part of John Brown's last speech at his trial: 'This court acknowledges, I suppose, the validity of the Law of God. I see a book kissed here which I suppose to be the Bible, or at least the New Testament. That teaches me that all things whatsoever I would that men should do unto me I should do even so to them. It teaches me further to remember them that are in bonds, as bound with them. I endeavour to act up to that instruction. I say I am yet too young to understand that God is any respecter of persons. I believe that to have interfered, as I have done, as I have always freely admitted I have done, in behalf of this despised poor, was not wrong but right. Now, if it is deemed necessary that I should forfeit my life for the furtherances of the end of justice, and mingle my blood further with the blood of my children and with the blood of millions in this slave country, where rights are disregarded by wicked, cruel and unjust enactments, I submit; so let it be done.'

England is rich in names of grand, fearless and noble men and women who have stood out boldly in the Negro's cause. The chief merit unquestionably belongs to Granville Sharp. He was encouraged by none of the world's huzzas when he entered upon his work. He stood alone, opposed to the opinion of the ablest lawyers and the most rooted prejudices of the times; and alone he fought out, by his single exertions, and at his individual expense, the most memorable battle for the constitution of this country and the liberties of British subjects of which modern times afford a record. It was Granville Sharp who secured the judgment from Lord Chief Justice Mansfield in the test case of James Somerset, the slave, whether he could be held as a slave in England. Lord Mansfield declared that the claim of slavery can never be supported; that the power claimed never was in use in England; therefore the man James Somerset must be discharged – and so firmly established the glorious axiom that as soon as any slave sets his foot on English ground that moment he becomes free. He lighted the torch which kindled other minds, and it was handed on until the illumination became complete.

Another honoured name for Negro rights is Bishop Colenso, who gave the major portion of his life to the uplifting of his cause, assisted by his daughter in Africa, and we are honoured in having members of his family here to-night. Little did I think when a boy, struggling with Colenso's *Arithmetic*, I should live to become the friend and associate of his sons. To the memory of the late M.P., Frank Colenso, I pay my tribute. He was imbued with his father's love for the Negro, and fought for him to the day of his death. He was my guide and helped me through many thorny paths and I cherish the fact that he numbered me among his friends. We also have with us to-night Mr. and Mrs. Fisher Unwin, and again I can speak from personal experience that their hearts are in sympathy with our cause. There are many, many others that I could mention, but I must conclude with a few words about the objects of our African Progress Union. But they are not forgotten, and the thanks of this African Progress Union will be accorded them.

Now about the objects of the African Progress Union. The objects are to promote the general welfare of Africans and Afro-peoples, through such agencies as may be deemed best; to establish in London, England, a place as 'home from home' where the members of the association may meet for social recreation and intellectual improvement, where movements may be promoted for the common welfare, and where members may receive and entertain their friends, under the regulations of the board of management; to spread by means of papers to be read and addresses to be given from time to time, and by means of a magazine or other publications, a knowledge of the history and achievements of Africans and Afro-peoples past and present; and to promote the general advancement of African peoples.

A very necessary thing. The people in this country are sadly ignorant with reference to the darker races, and our object is to show to them that we have given up the idea of becoming hewers of wood and drawers of water, that we claim our rightful place within this Empire. (Cheers.) That if we are good enough to be brought to fight the wars of the country we are good enough to receive the benefits of the country. (Renewed cheers.) One of the objects of this association is to demand – not ask, demand; it will be 'demand' all the time that I am your President. I am not asking for anything, I am out demanding, because I have been speaking all through this election, and we have been telling people that what we want to do is to give advancement for the poorer people, that children of the poor shall have an opportunity of going from the school to the college; and we demand the same right for Africa. (Cheers.) The last is 'To create and maintain a public sentiment in favour of brotherhood in its broadest sense'. Now I do like that. I do not know who it was that suggested this, but I do like 'brotherhood in its broadest sense'. In America they had a brotherhood, and they used to say that God had made of one blood all nations of the earth to dwell. They preached it all right, but preaching it and practising it was a different thing. (Laughter.) There happened to be a man who fell in love; he was a coloured man, and he fell in love with a white girl, and she fell in love with him. He said: 'Well, what do you think your brother will say?' He had already heard the brother preach a sermon on 'God hath made of one blood all nations', and she said: 'Well, I do not know but we will go and ask him', and they went, and he said: 'Certainly not.' (Laughter.) Said the coloured man: 'I heard you in the pulpit last Sunday, "God hath made of one blood all nations on the earth to dwell".' 'Yes,' he said, 'and I will do so next Sunday; I do not object to you being my brother in Christ, but I object to your being my brother-in-law.' (Laughter.) Well, that is not the sort of brotherhood we want here; we want a brotherhood that will extend itself right out to the nations of the world, and when that is extended they will find that the darker peoples, because of what they have suffered and because of their future, that fleecy locks and black complexions cannot forfeit a nation's claims; skins may differ, but affection dwells in black and white the same. (Cheers.)

Source: *West Africa*, II/101 (4 January 1919), 840, 842.

Appendix F. Birmingham, the metal industries, and the slave trade

Birmingham and its slave guns

At the end of the seventeenth century, the best place in England to have large quantities of cheap guns, cutlery, brass rods, and brass rings made to order was Birmingham, which had been described in 1610 as 'full of inhabitants and resounding with hammers and anvils, for the most of them are Smiths'.[1] The Birmingham manufacturers took swift advantage of the opening of the African trade in 1698, 'and their exports of all sorts increased enormously'.[2] The first order for flint-lock muskets to be exported to Africa was in fact executed at Birmingham in 1698.[3] Soon the hammers and anvils were resounding more than ever. By 1707 the gunmakers, cutlers, and other manufacturers of wrought iron in Birmingham were petitioning the House of Commons, 'setting forth, that since the Act . . . for laying open the trade to *Africa*, the Manufactories [i.e. manufactures] of wrought Iron, of all Sorts, have been made, and exported, by several Traders in greater Quantities, than was ever known before: And praying, the said Trade may not be monopolized to any Persons in a joint Stock'.[4] There were similar petitions in 1708 and 1710.[5]

From 1713 onwards, when British slave-merchants had the privilege of supplying Africans to Spain's American colonies, the 'slave gun . . . rapidly became the most numerous and important product of the Birmingham gun trade'.[6] The steady demand for slaves and guns created 'a mass market capable of supporting what was for that time a large labour force',[7] and 'the business was one of the supports of the town's prosperity'.[8] By 1766 Birmingham was sending over 100,000 guns a year to the African coast; Lord Shelburne's estimate in that year was 150,000; the annual average between 1796 and 1805 was 161,531.[9] In 1788 the Lords of Trade were informed that between 4,000 and 5,000 persons in Birmingham were employed in making guns for the African trade.[10] Despite the abolition of the British slave trade in 1807, Birmingham's exports of guns to Africa did not begin to decline until after the middle of the nineteenth century.[11] In 1907 it was estimated, by authors who 'seem generally reliable in their arithmetic',[12] that a total of 20,000,000 Birmingham guns had gone to Africa.[13]

Trade guns for the African market were made by sub-contractors working by hand, the gunmakers often being mere assemblers.[14] Surplus or rejected military parts were sometimes used, but the guns are said to have been generally a poor type of musket with a long barrel of low-quality iron and a beechwood stock, known colloquially as 'park palings'.[15] According to Shelburne, some of these were sold 'for five and sixpence apiece, but what is shocking to humanity, above half of them from the manner they are finished in, are sure to burst in the first hand that fires them'.[16] Forty years later a writer claimed that such guns, made in Birmingham at 7*s.* 6*d.* each and bartered for human flesh and blood, were formidable in appearance but in fact harmless and innocent 'except to the luckless wight who should load and fire them'.[17] Recent research suggests however that 'a large proportion of the firearms were very much better than the contemporary observers would want us to believe'; all the same, 'it . . . seems that the quality of firearms exported from England to the African coast deteriorated somewhat in the second half of the eighteenth century'.[18]

One Birmingham gunmaking firm, Farmer and Galton (afterwards Galton & Son), not only supplied guns to British, French, Portuguese, and other European slave-dealers, but also itself dealt directly in slaves. On one occasion '£54,000 of slaves were handled in America'.[19] Besides other evidence on the connection with the slave trade, the Galton Papers contain a careful estimate of the 'Expenses attending the Ship *Perseverance* on a Voyage from Liverpool to Africa, thence to the West Indies, and from the West Indies, back to England', with a cargo of goods and 527 slaves from whose sale £6,430 'nett gain' was expected.[20] In 1795 Samuel Galton was formally disowned by the Society of Friends, not for trading in slaves but for 'fabricating and selling instruments of war'. But he 'entirely disregarded the disownment and went on attending the meetings until his death in 1832'.[21] On 17 June 1806, Galton and some other Birmingham gunmakers complained to the Board of Ordnance that owing to the abolition of the slave trade 'they were shut from the Market at which they had been enabled to dispose of the Barrels which were rejected by the Ordnance', and the Board agreed to a price increase.[22] Greatly enriched by the double trade in guns and slaves, the Galtons became bankers. Samuel Galton left £300,000 to provide £4,000 a year for each of his three surviving sons, 'who were thus able to live comfortably without engaging in further business pursuits'.[23]

The copper and brass industries and the slave trade

The output of the British copper industry grew from less than 1,000 tons in 1712 to almost 7,000 tons a year at the close of the eighteenth century.[24] By 1750 the Swansea area was producing 50 per cent of British-made copper, and 50 years later 90 per cent of the copper ores smelted in Britain were smelted at Swansea.[25] Indeed 'it is no exaggeration to say that the growth of Swansea as a metallurgical centre is founded upon copper'.[26] And at least three of the Swansea area's copper works were of outstanding importance for the slave trade:

1. The Forest works at Morriston, built in 1717. This was owned by Morris, Lockwood, and Co., which in 1745 had a capital of £20,000. In 1768 rods and manillas were being manufactured there for use in the slave trade.[27]

2. The White Rock works at Landore, founded in 1737 by Joseph Percevall and owned by Freeman and Co. from 1764. This had 26 furnaces with a weekly output of about 50 tons. In 1744 one department was wholly engaged in the manufacture of copper rods and manillas for use in the slave trade.[28]

3. The Penclawdd works, owned in 1788 by the Anglesey Mines, in 1792 by the Cheadle Brass Wire Co. In the late 1780s the entire output of this establishment was used to buy slaves in Africa.[29]

Starting from small beginnings in 1719, the Cheadle Co., primarily concerned with brass, at length became 'one of the most important, if not the most important, of the brass and copper concerns of the eighteenth century'. It made manillas for the slave trade at Warrington and Greenfield, Flintshire, as well as Swansea, and in 1790 its rolling mills were greatly extended to equip them for the manufacture of 'Guinea rods'.[30]

A rival firm was Charles Roe & Co. of Macclesfield, which set up a smelting works in Liverpool in 1767 and supplied copper and brass goods to slave-merchants.[31] In fact the development of the Lancashire copper and brass industry 'was instrumental in enabling Liverpool to gain a competitive edge in the African trade'.[32] As early as 1726 copper was listed, with cloth and pewter, as a Lancashire industry influenced by the growth of the Liverpool slave trade.[33]

Liverpool was an active centre for the copper sheathing of slave-ships, a procedure which, though costly, reduced the dangers of fouling and worm-eaten timbers and improved the ships' sailing speed and their speed under attack. The slave trade was the first British merchant trade to adopt this invention, which greatly boosted the demand for copper. By 1786, 124 British slave-ships were copper-sheathed, and by the early years of the nineteenth century the practice was virtually universal in the trade.[34] The industrialist who made copper sheathing for ships 'both practicable and safe' was Thomas Williams of Llanidan, Britain's leading copper and brass manufacturer. His copper concerns had a total capital of £800,000 – about half of the national capital invested in the trade – and he controlled one-fifth of British smelting. In 1788 he pleaded before both Houses of Parliament against interference with the slave trade, on the ground that he and his partners had over £70,000 invested in works at Holywell in Flint, Penclawdd in Glamorgan, and Temple Mills in Berkshire, whose produce was entirely destined for the African market; and that they had in hand goods to the value of at least £15,000 'for which there was no other vent than the African market'.[35]

The initial development of the copper and brass industries of the Greenfield valley, 18 miles west of Chester, resulted from the growth of the slave trade. By the end of the eighteenth century the valley had six sites with copper and brass works on them, and there were between 30 and 40 small ships engaged in carrying their products to Liverpool, where they were transferred to slavers for shipment to Africa.[36]

The demands of the slave trade also put the Bristol brass industry on its feet. As early as 1713 copper was listed as a Bristol industry dependent on the African trade.[37] William Champion & Co., established in 1746 – the name was changed to Warmley Co. in 1761 – owned what was probably Britain's most up-to-date and efficient brass works. In 1767 the company's sales stock on hand, totalling £94,000, included 'Guinea manillas' and 'Guinea rods' made of copper and 'Guinea kettles' and 'Guinea neptunes' (shallow dishes for the evaporation of salt) made of brass. Though these were 'produced for barter in Africa as part of the Bristol slave-trade system', in later years the full name was 'carefully avoided'.[38]

Appendix G. Eighteenth-century biographies

Francis Williams

Francis Williams was the subject of a kind of social experiment by the Duke of Montagu, who wanted to find out 'whether, by proper cultivation, and a regular course of tuition at school and the university, a Negroe might not be found as capable of literature as a white person'.[1] So Francis, born in Jamaica of free black parents about the year 1700, was sent to England as a young boy. He studied classics at a grammar school and mathematics at Cambridge University. When he went back to Jamaica, the duke tried to have him appointed to the governor's council, but the governor, Edward Trelawney, found him unacceptable. Francis Williams then ran a school in Spanish Town for several years.

It was his practice to welcome each new governor with a Latin ode, and one of these is printed, translated, and criticized in Edward Long's *History of Jamaica* (1774).[2] Replying to Long's racist criticism, the abolitionist James Ramsay pointed out: 'Though his verses bear no great marks of genius, yet, there have been bred at the same university an hundred white masters of arts, and many doctors, who could not improve them.'[3]

Ayuba Suleiman Diallo

Born about 1701, Ayuba Suleiman Diallo – known in England as Job ben Solomon – was the son of a Moslem high priest (*alfa*) of Bondou, a Fula principality several days' journey to the north-west of the river Gambia. Ayuba's father often sent him to sell domestic slaves, and once he had travelled for five weeks in the direction of Egypt in search of trade. But early in 1731 he was unlucky. On a slave-selling expedition to Cower (now Kau-Ur), chief trading centre on the Gambia, he had the misfortune to be captured, with his interpreter, by a band of Mandings who shaved their captives' heads and sold them to an English captain called Pyke. When the dismayed Ayuba pointed out that only a few days earlier he himself had been trying to sell two boys to the captain – with whom he had failed to strike a bargain – Pyke agreed to ransom both Ayuba and the interpreter at the price of two slaves each. Ayuba sent his father a message, but the ship set sail for Maryland before a reply was received.

Soon after being landed Ayuba was sold for £45 to a tobacco-planter called Alexander Tolsey, who unwisely dispensed with the customary 'seasoning' and set him immediately to the toil of tobacco-making. But when he saw that his new acquisition was growing weaker day by day Tolsey transferred him to the less arduous task of tending the cattle. A devout Moslem, Ayuba withdrew periodically to pray. His devotions were interrupted by a white boy who, amused by the prayers and the ritual of abasement, mocked him and threw soil in his face. At length Ayuba ran away. He had not got far before he was captured by people who 'by his affable Carriage, and the easy Composure of his Countenance, . . . could perceive he was no common Slave'.[4] An old slave was found who understood the Fula language, interpreted for Ayuba, and possibly exaggerated his rank and importance. At all events, Tolsey now made sure that Ayuba had privacy for his prayers and even let him write in Arabic to his father, asking for help. The letter came into the hands of the philanthropist James Oglethorpe, then deputy governor of the Royal African Company, who sent it to the professor of Arabic at Oxford University and was so impressed by the translation that he decided to have Ayuba set free. He paid the necessary £45, and Ayuba duly arrived in England in 1733 as a guest of the Royal African Company.

While the company undoubtedly showed 'foresight as much as altruism'[5] in treating Ayuba decently – they had the idea that he might be of great use to them if they could get him back to Africa – it is equally true that he made a very favourable impression in England. He was tall: 5ft 10in. He was handsome: 'His Countenance was exceeding pleasant, yet grave and composed.'[6] And he was clever: he had learnt the Koran by heart before he was 15, could write it out from memory, and did so three times during his stay in England, without once referring to the text. He was soon enthralling the local gentry of Cheshunt in Hertfordshire, and the London merchants who had their country houses there, with the tale of his adventures and accounts of life and customs in his homeland. He was taken up by the group of scholars and virtuosi around Sir Hans Sloane, the famous naturalist and collector, for whom he translated several Arabic inscriptions. He was elected an honorary member of the Gentlemen's Society of Spalding, first and most distinguished of provincial antiquarians' societies. And, at his own request, he was presented to the king and queen, receiving from the latter the gracious present of a gold watch. For this auspicious occasion Ayuba was decked out, not in the European clothes he normally wore in England, but in an African gown and turban of rich silk, tailored to his own design. There is a well-known portrait of him in such a gown, with the Koran hanging from a cord round his neck.

But Ayuba's social position was much more significant, in determining the sort of reception he was given in England, than his personal appearance or talents. He came from the class of West African merchants and slave-dealers who had much more in common with English merchants, gentry, and nobility than with the slaves they conspired to buy and sell. It was natural enough that people of equivalent social class to his in England should, once their visitor's status was made plain to them, have displayed not merely 'a romantic interest in his rank and fate'[7] but also a shrewd hope that he might be a useful lever in extending their trade.

A certificate of freedom, 'handsomely engrossed' and authenticated with the Royal African Company's seal, was formally handed over to him, and in 1734, loaded with presents worth £500, he was shipped back to West Africa. He found that his father had died; that his country had been devastated by war; and that his wife had married another man.

> Notwithstanding the Joy he had to see his Friends, he wept grievously for his Father's Death, and the Misfortunes of his Country. He forgave his Wife, and the Man that had taken her; *For*, says he, . . . *she could not help thinking I was dead, for I was gone to a Land from which no* Pholey [i.e. Fula] *ever yet returned; therefore she is not to be blamed, nor yet the Man neither.*[8]

It would be pleasant to relate that, having experienced the middle passage and slavery, Ayuba suffered a change of heart, gave up the trade, and sought to end it. On the contrary, no sooner did he set foot in Africa again than he sold some of the presents he had brought with him and bought a woman slave and two horses with the proceeds.[9] He seems to have kept in touch with British slave-traders on the Gambia until his death in 1773.[10]

William Ansah

A few years after Ayuba Suleiman Diallo was sold into slavery another high-born African had the same unfortunate experience; and he too came to England for a time when he was freed. His name was William Ansah. He was a son of John Corantee, ruler of the Fante town of Anomabo in what is now Ghana. His half-brother had been sent to France to attract French trade; he was graciously received by Louis XV and returned in style on a French ship. William had picked up some English and his father decided to send him to England, again as a sort of commercial traveller, by way of the West Indies. But when William reached Barbados he was sold into slavery. Fighting broke out soon afterwards between the English and the French in West Africa, and Corantee, though he headed the pro-English Fantes at Cape Coast, now refused to help the English unless his son was freed. He proposed that another son, Frederick, should fetch William from Barbados and take him to England, and this proposal was accepted. William was thus 'happily restored to Liberty, and to his former good Opinion of the Candour [i.e. kindliness] of the *British* Nation'.[11]

William Ansah and his brother received much attention during their stay in England in 1736. They were given some education by the Revd Mr Territ of the Temple, and William's 'sweet and amiable Temper' earned him the nickname 'Cupid' from his English friends.[12] On their return to Africa, Frederick served as interpreter to the Revd Thomas Thompson, missionary of the Society for the Propagation of the Gospel.[13] A pamphlet about William Ansah, entitled *The Royal African: or, Memoirs of the Young Prince of Annamaboe* was published in London around the year 1750, and his portrait was published, beside that of Ayuba Suleiman Diallo, in the *Gentleman's Magazine*.[14]

Francis Barber

Francis Barber was born in Jamaica about the year 1735 and was brought to England at the age of 15 or so by a plantation-owner who was father of one of Samuel Johnson's closest friends. For a year he attended a village school at Barton, a small Yorkshire village about half-way between Darlington and Richmond. Then he entered the service of his owner's son, who sent him as valet to Johnson in April 1752, a fortnight after the death of Johnson's wife. Two years later the plantation-owner died, leaving 'to Francis Barber, a negroe whom I brought from Jamaica aforesaid into England, his freedom and twelve pounds in money'.[15]

Francis was still a very young man. So it is hardly surprising that he ran off 'and served an apothecary in Cheapside' – still, however, paying Johnson an occasional visit.[16] He soon went back, but in 1758 – to the horror of Johnson, who thought of ships as peculiarly nasty prisons – he ran away to sea and spent two years on HMS *Stag*, protecting English fishermen in the North Sea. Smollett wrote on Johnson's behalf to Wilkes, who numbered two Lords of the Admiralty among his friends, and the young man was at length discharged, apparently no worse for the experience.[17]

Johnson was clearly very fond of Francis Barber. As his housekeeper never tired of reminding him in later years whenever she had occasion to complain about Francis, Johnson laid out £300 in fees to have him educated at Bishop's Stortford grammar school from 1767 to 1772.[18] Two of Johnson's letters to Francis while he was attending this school have been preserved, and in one of them he wrote:

> I am very well satisfied with your progress, if you can really perform the exercises which you are set . . .
>
> Let me know what English books you read for your entertainment. You can never be wise unless you love reading.
>
> Do not imagine that I shall forget or forsake you; for if, when I examine you, I find that you have not lost your time, you shall want no encouragement from
>
> Yours affectionately,
>
> SAM. JOHNSON.[19]

When Barber left school Johnson came to rely on him more and more, not merely as valet and butler, but also as secretary. Barber arranged trips, received documents, and made sure that Johnson kept his dinner engagements punctually: 'I am going to dine with Mr. Dyot, and Frank tells sternly, that it is past two o'clock.'[20] He answered the door, waited at table, and attended on his master's person. When Boswell called, Johnson 'roared, "Frank, a clean shirt", and was very soon drest'.[21] Or he cried out from his bed, 'Frank, go and get coffee, and let us breakfast *in splendour*'.[22] But, in general, Johnson disliked being waited on. Barber told an interviewer nine years after Johnson's death that 'as master, he required very small attention: Francis brought and took away his plate at table, and purchased the provisions for the same. But if Francis offered to buckle the shoe, &c. "No, Francis, time enough yet! When I can do it no longer, then you may." '[23] When Johnson's beloved cat, Hodge, grew so old that he could digest nothing but oysters, Johnson would go out and buy them himself rather than send Barber, 'saying that it was not good to employ human beings in the service of animals'.[24] Master and servant often knelt in prayer together.

In his youth, Francis Barber had a reputation for success with women. When a circle of ladies laughed to hear this, Johnson insisted that 'Frank has carried the empire of Cupid further than most men', adding that, on their return from a trip to Lincolnshire, 'I found that a female haymaker had followed him to London for love'.[25] Some time before September 1776 Barber married an Englishwoman called Elizabeth ('Betsy') – her maiden name is unknown but she is described as 'eminently pretty'[26] – of whom he was said to be jealous and who bore him two sons and two daughters. About seven years after the marriage Johnson took into his household Mrs Barber and the two children she had borne by then, 'and made them a part of his family' in what Sir John Hawkins, a biographer of Johnson who was spitefully hostile to Barber, sneered at as 'the excess of indiscriminating benevolence'.[27]

Johnson died in 1784, leaving Barber a handsome annuity of £70, making him residuary legatee, and giving him, a day or two before his death, a gold watch that Sir John Hawkins, who was one of the executors, tried unsuccessfully to purloin. Barber and his family then settled in Lichfield, Staffordshire, as Johnson had advised – Lichfield being out of reach of metropolitan temptations. Boswell, with whom Barber had always been on good terms, wrote to him in 1787, soon after the publication of Hawkins's *Life of Johnson*, pointing out that it slandered Johnson and the Barbers, and asking Francis to help him force Hawkins to hand over Johnson's papers, which were legally Barber's property and which Hawkins was reluctant to yield up to a rival biographer. Barber was very willing to help and did so – and took the opportunity to touch Boswell, successfully, for a loan.

An extreme Methodist was later to observe sourly that the Barbers were 'improvident, strove to make a figure in the world, lived above their means, and dissipated their property'.[28] It is true that Francis Barber did not handle money wisely, and in 1788 he was asking Dr Percy, bishop of Dromore, for an advance of £50 on the repayment of a loan Johnson had made to Percy ten years before. Barber's wife and elder daughter had been ill, and

> I should not have troubled your Lordship, but as Christmas is drawing near and it is customary for apothecaries and other Tradespeople to bring in their accounts, some of which I have already received, and much larger than I ever Expected – I have it not in my power, *without the assistance of your Lordship*, to discharge the same with my Quarterly annuity, except I leave myself destitute of money.[29]

The bishop complied, but Barber had later to sell Johnson's gold watch and other keepsakes.

An interview with Francis Barber that appeared in the *Gentleman's Magazine* in 1793 described him as

> low of stature, marked with the small-pox, has lost his teeth; appears aged and infirm; clean and neat, but his cloaths the worse for wear; a green coat; his late master's cloaths all worn out. He spends his time in fishing, cultivating a few potatoes, and a little reading . . .
>
> Mr. Barber appears modest and humble, but to have associated with company superior to his rank in life.[30]

About three years later the Barbers moved to Burntwood, a few miles from Lichfield, and Francis taught at the village school there. He had not much longer to live. He died in Stafford infirmary, early in 1801, after 'a painful operation'.[31] Nine years later his widow and one of her daughters were still living in Lichfield, where they kept a school. A writer described Mrs Barber as a 'poor, though sensible and well-informed, woman' who had been forced to part with many Johnson relics.[32] She was 60 when she died in April 1816.[33] Her son Samuel, born in 1785 or 1786 and obviously named after Johnson, became a Primitive Methodist preacher in Staffordshire; he died in 1828, leaving a wife and six children.[34]

Philip Quaque

The first African to be ordained as a priest in the Church of England was Philip Quaque, son of the Cape Coast ruler (*caboceer*) Birempon Cudjo. Philip's Fante name was probably Kwaku, which means 'born on Wednesday'. In 1754, at the age of 13, he was sent to England with two other boys, Thomas Caboro and William Cudjo, to be educated at London charity schools at the expense of the Society for the Propagation of the Gospel. On arrival the three were placed in the care of an Islington schoolmaster. After seven weeks they were examined by the Society's committee: 'One of them repeated the Lord's prayer and the Apostles Creed, and the other two answered well to the questions put to them.'[35] The committee recommended that the schoolmaster be paid £15 a year for each boy's instruction, boarding, and clothing.

Thomas died of tuberculosis in 1758. The next year Philip and William (who died in 1764) were baptized at Islington parish church and placed in the charge of the Revd John Moore, curate and lecturer at St Sepulchre's, Holborn, for further religious instruction. Moore had taught John Acqua and George Sackee when they were in England from 1753 to 1755.[36]

In 1765 Philip Quaque was twice ordained: first as deacon, by the bishop of Exeter in the St James's Palace chapel royal; two months later as priest, by the bishop of London in the same chapel. According to a press report, his 'devout behaviour' at the first ordainment 'attracted the notice of the whole congregation'.[37] A few weeks after the second one, his tutor Moore married him to an Englishwoman, Catherine Blunt. And a fortnight after that, at a meeting attended by the archbishop of Canterbury and the bishops of Winchester and London, he was appointed 'Missionary, Catechist and Schoolmaster to the Negroes on the Gold Coast in Africa', at a salary of £50 a year.[38] In February 1766 Philip and Catherine Quaque arrived at Cape Coast Castle, where Philip was to spend the next 50 years, broken only by a brief visit to England in 1784–5, to arrange for his children's education.

Moore had assured the secretary of the Society for the Propagation of the Gospel that Philip had 'rewarded my labours by improving in every branch of knowledge necessary to the station for which he was designed, and it is to be hoped will prove a worthy missionary'.[39] Through no fault of Philip's, his mission did not turn out very successfully. Helped later by his son – who in turn was educated by Moore in England – he ran a small school for African children; there were never more than 16 pupils. Philip had lost his fluency in the Fante language; in any case, the society had little confidence in vernacular preaching, believing that English was 'the heaven-sent medium of religion and civilisation'.[40] He was discouraged by the British authorities' indifference to his ministry. One of the governors he served under openly ridiculed religion; and a Mr Cohouac refused to obey another governor's summons to be present at divine service at half past eleven, stating that he did not choose 'to attend to hear any blackman whatever'.[41] Philip Quaque must have been a disappointed man when he died, aged 75, in 1816.

John Nemgbana

One of the first Africans from Sierra Leone to be educated in England was John Frederick, eldest son of Nemgbana or Naimbana, regent (styled king) of the Temne. Born between 1762 and 1767, and perhaps partly of Manding origin,[42] John came to England in 1791 and was soon afterwards baptized Henry Granville as a token of respect for his benefactors and godfathers Henry Thornton, chairman of the Sierra Leone Company, and Granville Sharp. John travelled to England with Alexander Falconbridge, whom the company had sent to Sierra Leone to re-establish its settlement there. Supervised by two clergymen in succession, John's education was based on intensive study of the Bible and a little Hebrew.

He was a keen student, learning in 18 months to read English fluently and write a letter with ease. But he was inclined to be quick-tempered. When someone in his hearing 'asserted something very degrading to the general character of Africans, he broke out into violent and vindictive language'. Reminded of his christian duty to forgive his enemies, he rose from his seat with much emotion and declared: 'If a man takes away the character of the people of my country, I can never forgive him.'[43] When an MP proposed the gradual abolition of the slave trade, John observed that 'he should have his carriage drawn by asses, for they go very gradually'.[44]

John's virtues and industry were celebrated in a tract variously entitled *The African Prince* and *The Black Prince*; on the cover of one edition he is shown spurning an improper book.[45] He greatly looked forward to preaching the gospel to his countrymen, but was taken ill on the homeward voyage – on a ship optimistically called *The Naimbanna* – and died a few hours after landing at Freetown. 'Thus terminated the days of this amiable and enlightened African, from whose exertions, if he had lived, the [Sierra Leone] Company might have expected the most important and extensive services.'[46]

George Polgreen Bridgtower

If Beethoven hadn't fallen out with George Polgreen Bridgtower – over a girl, it is said – his 'Kreutzer' sonata (op. 47) would certainly have been known as the 'Bridgtower' sonata.[47] Beethoven wrote it for Bridgtower, scribbling on a rough score this jocular dedication: 'Mulatto sonata composed for the mulatto Brishdauer, the great mulatto idiot and composer' (*Sonata mulattica composta per il mulatto Brishdauer, gran pazzo e compositore mulattico*).[48] And it was Bridgtower who, in Vienna in 1803, with the composer at the piano, gave the sonata's first performance.

George's father, Friedrich Augustus Bridgtower, identified himself as a Barbadian in a Dresden visitors' book in 1796:[49] it has been suggested that his name, otherwise unknown (and often spelt Bridgetower) was derived from the Barbados place-name Bridgetown.[50] He seems to have come to Europe in the 1770s; by 1780 he was living in eastern Austria, where he served as personal page (*Kammerpage*) and valet (*Kammerdiener*) to Prince Miklós Esterházy at his summer palace of Kis Marton (Eisenstadt), where Haydn lived for many years.[51] He had married a woman, probably of Austro-German ancestry, who bore him two sons. George, the elder, was born in 1779.[52] His birthplace is generally stated to be Biala, a small town in east Poland, north-east of Lublin.

From his earliest youth George Polgreen Bridgtower showed extraordinary musical gifts, and there is a strong possibility that he was taught by Haydn.[53] He made his professional début in Paris at the age of nine, on 11 April 1789, playing a violin concerto by the fashionable Italian violinist and composer Giovanni Giornovichi.* A few months later, brought to England by his father, he was entertaining the king and queen at Windsor. A courtier described him as

> a most prepossessing lad . . . and a fine violin player Both father and son pleased greatly. The one for his talent and modest bearing, the other for his fascinating manner, elegance, expertness in all languages, beauty of person, and taste in dress . . . The young performer played to perfection, with a clear, good tone, spirit, pathos, and good taste.[55]

Soon there were highly successful concerts in London, Bath (at least four public recitals in December 1789), and Bristol. But Bridgtower senior, despite his fascinating manner, his gaudy, flowing Turkish robes, and his self-conferred title of 'The African Prince', did not please for long. He was accused of treating his son badly and squandering the money the young performer earned. In judging this accusation we should not forget that Friedrich Augustus 'supervised his son's musical training during the early years and brought him to England', and then 'utilized his charm and talent to open the hearts and purse strings of English audiences to his ten-year-old prodigy'.[56] Eventually the Prince of Wales, who was himself a cellist and had taken a liking to George, told Friedrich Augustus to 'leave the kingdom immediately' and, on 5 January 1791, paid him £25 to do so.[57]

From then on, the boy was under the protection of the prince, who appointed tutors for him and engaged eminent musicians to teach him musical theory. By the age of 12 George Bridgtower was recognized by London's music-lovers as a respected member of the artistic community. A recent writer calculates that between 1789 and 1799 he performed in about 50 publicized concerts as soloist or principal violinist in professionally trained orchestras, such as those at the Covent Garden, Drury Lane, and Haymarket theatres. Bridgtower's career, she adds,

> intertwined with the lives of so many musicians who were residents or visitors to London in the 1790s that a detailed chronicle of his life when it is finally written will fill in many gaps in our present knowledge of English concert life during the late eighteenth century and will illuminate the role that a black prodigy played in it.[58]

For 14 years the young Bridgtower held the post of first violinist in the Prince of Wales's private band, which divided its time between Carlton House in London and the Brighton Pavilion. In 1802 he was given leave of absence for a concert tour in Germany and Austria. He visited his mother in Dresden and, in Vienna in April and May 1803, made friends with Beethoven, ten years his senior. In a letter of introduction to a noble-

* On a visit to London in 1790, Giornovichi was accompanied by the 'Creole' violinist, composer, and swordsman Joseph Boulogne, chevalier de Saint-Georges, whose mother was a black woman from Guadeloupe, and who gave exhibition fencing matches before the Prince of Wales and other notables.[54]

man, Beethoven described him as 'a very able virtuoso and an absolute master of his instrument'.[59] At the first performance of what came to be known as the 'Kreutzer' sonata, Bridgtower had the formidable task of playing one movement from the composer's scarcely legible manuscript, completed too late for a fair copy to be made.[60] He was bold enough to alter a brief passage in the first movement, making the violin echo a preceding piano flourish, whereupon Beethoven jumped up and hugged him, exclaiming: 'Once more, my dear fellow!'[61] Apparently, when Beethoven quarrelled with Bridgtower and changed the original dedication, he had not even met Rodolphe Kreutzer.

Beethoven's high opinion of Bridgtower's talent was widely shared. Thus Samuel Wesley, who performed with him for several years, ranked him 'with the very first Masters of the Violin' and was specially delighted by his flawless rendering, from memory, of Bach's works for unaccompanied violin. 'It was', he wrote, 'a rich Treat.'[62]

George Bridgtower's younger brother, whose name is thought to have been Friedrich, was also a musician. He made a living playing the cello in Dresden, and came to London in 1805 to perform at a benefit concert for his brother in the Hanover Square rooms.[63]

George Bridgtower took the degree of Bachelor of Music at Cambridge on 28 June 1811, and the anthem he composed as an examination exercise was performed there.[64] His published compositions are slight: a set of studies for the piano and a ballad called 'Henry'. In later life he seems to have spent much time abroad. He was in Rome in 1825 and 1827, 'evidently moving in aristocratic circles'.[65] The organist and composer Vincent Novello wrote to him in 1843, signing himself 'your much obliged old pupil and professional admirer'.[66] Bridgtower died at Peckham on 20 February 1860, in humble circumstances.[67]

Joseph Emidy

The 'exquisite violinist'[68] Joseph Emidy (also spelt Emidee and Emedy) was born in Guinea. Sold to Portuguese slave-traders, he was taken to Brazil and later went with his owner to Lisbon, where he played second violin in the opera-house. In the summer of 1795 he was kidnapped, violin and all, by British seamen on the instructions of Sir Edward Pellew (afterwards Admiral Viscount Exmouth), commander of the *Indefatigable*, who wanted a good fiddler to entertain his frigate's crew with jigs, reels, and hornpipes, admired Emidy's energetic playing, and coolly decided to have him 'impressed'. The young musician was for several years not allowed to go ashore, lest he escape. He was the only black man on board, and had to take his meals alone. Finally, in 1799, when Pellew was moved to another ship, Emidy was put ashore at Falmouth, where he spent the rest of his life.

Here he made a living by music, first playing the violin at parties, 'which he did to a degree of perfection never before heard in Cornwall',[69] then teaching, and playing first violin at concerts. He became leader of the Falmouth Harmonic Society and wrote many chamber works and symphonies, which were played at local concerts and much admired. About the year 1807 his pupil James Silk Buckingham, whom he taught to play piano and flute – he also taught violin, cello, and clarinet – took several of Emidy's compositions to London and showed them to the impresario Johann Peter Salomon, who suggested that Emidy be invited to give a public performance in London. But it came to nothing, since London musicians 'thought his colour would be so much against him, that there would be a great risk of failure'. So they took up a subscription for him instead, sending him 'a handsome sum' and letters praising his compositions.[70]

On 16 September 1802, Emidy married Jenefer Hutchins, 'a young white woman of a respectable tradesman's family',[71] by whom he had at least five children.[72] The second child, Thomas, born in 1805, was a musician like his father: *The Royal Cornwall & Devon Artillery Quadrilles*, 'composed & arranged for the Piano Forte by Thos. Emidy (of Truro)' were published in 1854.[73]

Appendix H. Visitors, 1832–1919

American abolitionists and fugitive slaves

In the 30 years leading up to the American Civil War a procession of Afro-Americans came to Britain to plead the cause of their enslaved brothers and sisters. The value of their work became clear when the war broke out and north and south competed for British support.

The procession began in 1832, when the Baptist clergyman Nathaniel Paul arrived in Britain to raise funds for the Wilberforce Colony: 32 families from Cincinnati who had settled in Ontario. He addressed the Commons committee that was considering the Bill to free the slaves in the West Indies; spoke to audiences averaging between 2,000 and 3,000; and toured northern England and Scotland in company with John Scobie, afterwards secretary of the British and Foreign Anti-Slavery Society.[1]

Three years later Moses Roper came to Britain. Son of a North Carolina slave by her master – who sold Moses because the boy looked too much like him – he obtained some education and religious instruction in this country and in 1837 published *A Narrative of the adventures and escape of Moses Roper from American Slavery*, one of the earliest, and not the least gripping, of many such accounts that circulated widely in Britain. Like Olaudah Equiano before him, Roper sold his book at his meetings. He claimed in 1844 to have sold 25,000 copies, plus 5,000 in Welsh translation, at meetings in over 2,000 places. He married a Bristol woman and appealed to the Anti-Slavery Society for funds to go to the Cape of Good Hope to grow cotton. He was reported to be in Britain in 1854, but it is not known what became of him.[2]

In 1836 Robert Purvis, one of the three black men who helped to found the American Anti-Slavery Society in 1833, came to Britain to do some lobbying. The Irish patriot Daniel O'Connell, when Purvis was presented to him at the House of Commons, thought he was a white American and refused to shake hands with him. Told by John Scobie who Purvis was, O'Connell greeted him warmly, explaining that he never took an American's hand without first knowing where he stood on slavery.[3]

The first prominent black American abolitionist to visit Britain, Charles Lenox Remond, came in 1840 as delegate to the World's Anti-Slavery Convention, stayed for 19 months, and was warmly welcomed everywhere he lectured. He had 'a good voice, a pleasing countenance', and 'a prompt intelligence', and was said to 'captivate and carry away an audience by the very force of his eloquence', even though his standard speech ran to two hours. Remond did not, in fact, take his seat at the convention. When it voted to exclude women delegates he protested by joining the unseated American women delegates in the gallery. He took back to the United States in December 1841 a 'Great Irish Address', signed by Daniel O'Connell and 60,000 other Irishmen, urging their countrymen in America to treat black people as friends and make common cause with the abolitionists.[4]

Next to arrive was the runaway slave Frederick Douglass, the nineteenth century's most distinguished black American, who took the British Isles by storm in 1845–7. Douglass teamed up with the Chartist leader Henry Vincent and specifically called himself a Chartist. For 20 months he held great audiences spellbound for anything up to three hours at a time; at the end of each lecture people would crowd forward to shake his hand. In one month (March 1847) he gave an address every night, including Sundays. Another who followed Equiano's example, he sold at his meetings autographed copies of his *Narrative of the Life of Frederick Douglass*; over 13,000 copies of five editions were sold in 1846–7. Douglass was a powerful and outspoken orator. In Scotland, where he spent three months, he attacked the Free Church's willingness to accept 'blood-stained' money for its development fund from slaveholding congregations in the southern states. 'Send back that money!' he cried in Arbroath, calling on his audience to give three cheers in those words. They did so, and soon the slogan was being chalked on fences and pavements all over Scotland. At a world temperance conference in London Douglass exposed the racism of the US temperance movement, and the American delegates were furious. In 1859–60, on the eve of the Civil War, he spent a further five months in Britain, giving a fillip to popular British support for the north.[5]

Another fugitive slave who made good use of both the written and the spoken word was William Wells Brown, 12,000 copies of whose *Narrative* were sold in Britain in 1850. Born in Kentucky around the year 1814, Brown came to Europe in 1849 to attend an international peace congress organized in Paris by pacifist groups and stayed for five years – mostly in Britain, where he travelled about 12,000 miles and spoke at over 1,000 meetings. He took the chair at a meeting of fugitive American slaves held in London on 1 August 1851 and attended also by black West Indians, by prominent British abolitionists, and by Tennyson, the newly appointed poet laureate. It was Brown who drafted the 'Appeal to the People of Great Britain and the World' which this meeting adopted unanimously. And during his stay in Europe he published in London the first of four versions of his *Clotel; or, The President's Daughter: A Narrative of Slave Life in the United States* (1853), usually considered the first novel written by a black American.[6]

The Revd James W.C.Pennington, who had escaped from slavery in Maryland and was one of the most scholarly clergymen of the century, had first visited Britain in 1843. On a repeat visit in 1849–50 he travelled up and down Scotland as a lecturer on behalf of the Glasgow Female Anti-Slavery Society and aroused great sympathy.[7] In May 1851 he was one of four black American guests at a soirée given by the Anti-Slavery Society. The others were the Revd Alexander Crummell (an Episcopalian priest who was sent to Queen's College, Cambridge, by British abolitionists in 1849, took his BA in 1853, preached to Anglican congregations, contributed a refutation of the 'Ham's curse' theory to the *Christian Observer*, went to Liberia to teach theology, and in 1873 returned to America, where he died in 1898);[8] the Revd Josiah Henson (who claimed to be the original of Harriet Beecher Stowe's Uncle Tom and was a guest of the queen when he visited Britain again in 1876–7);[9] and the Revd Henry Highland Garnet (who was grandson of a Manding dignitary, was one of the most radical anti-slavery lecturers, spent two years (1850–2) in Britain, and pledged himself to work to unify the struggles of slaves and poor whites).[10]

John Brown, who arrived in Liverpool in 1850, had been inspired to escape from slavery by John Glasgow, a British seaman born of free parents in Demerara and married to a Lancashire woman. Glasgow had been seized in Savannah and was enslaved on a Georgia plantation. When Brown reached Britain he worked for a builder in Heywood, Lancashire, for a time, but 'found that there is prejudice against colour in England, in some classes', so turned to anti-slavery lecturing.[11]

In 1853 the Revd Samuel Ringgold Ward and William G.Allen came to Britain. Ward, yet another runaway slave, described as 'the ablest thinker on his legs before the American people', was sent by the Anti-Slavery Society of Canada. When he checked in at his London hotel six white Americans left in protest. Before he had been in this country a month he had spoken 'on the platforms of the Bible, Tract, Sunday School, Missionary, Temperance, and Peace, as well as the Anti-Slavery, Societies'. In 1855 he published his autobiography.[12]

Allen, teacher and editor of the *National Watchman*, had fallen in love with one of his white students, and she with him. After a threat to tar and feather him, the couple fled to New York and were married before sailing to Britain, where they spent the rest of their lives. Allen published a vivid account of his experiences. His British friends bought control of an Islington school and installed him as head – 'the first instance in this country', according to the *Anti-Slavery Reporter*, 'of an educational establishment being under the direction of a man of colour'.[13]

Another romantic story was that of William and Ellen Craft. They escaped from the south by a simple but nerve-racking stratagem: Ellen posed as a white man, William as 'his' slave. In Britain, they were befriended by Harriet Martineau and Lady Byron, and William distinguished himself at the 1863 meeting of the British Association by challenging the racist remarks of James Hunt, president of the Anthropological Society of London.[14]

One of the most impressive of all these champions of abolition was the brilliant orator Sarah Parker Remond, sister of Charles Lenox Remond. This intelligent and well-educated advocate of freedom gripped her audiences, not by an emotional or sentimental recital of the horrors of slavery, but by 'clear elucidation of just principles'. Her aim was 'to extend the active sympathy of the whole British nation towards the cause of abolitionism in America'. She worked here, under the auspices of various anti-slavery societies, from 1859 to 1867. At Warrington, in March 1859, her address was signed by the mayor, the rector of the parish, the local MP, and 3,522 inhabitants of all ranks and classes.[15]

The outbreak of the Civil War brought yet more black publicists to Britain to seek support for their cause. 'There is no end to the colored here', wrote the Boston clergyman and orator John Sella Martin when he reached London in October 1861; soon he had so moved his audiences with the story of his sister Caroline and her two children that they had donated the amount needed to buy the freedom of these three slaves from the Georgia clergyman whose son was the children's father.[16] The next year the most newsworthy visitor was William Andrew Jackson, a coachman who had escaped from servitude to Jefferson Davis, president of the Confederacy. Jackson spoke to over 3,000 children at Sunday schools in Staffordshire, then visited Manchester, Sheffield, the west of England, south Wales, and Derbyshire.[17]

Other black Americans who visited Britain in this period, not as anti-slavery publicists, included the Revd Jeremiah Asher, a Baptist preacher who toured Britain and raised £500 for his church;[18] Francis Fedric, a fugitive slave who married an Englishwoman and ran a lodging-house in Manchester;[19] Henry Watson, another fugitive slave, who wrote an account of his adventures;[20] and Linda Brent, an ex-slave who worked as servant to an English family in America and spent ten months in Britain as a nursemaid.[21]

Lastly, here is a moving glimpse of an unnamed fugitive slave who appears briefly in William Wells Brown's *Three years in Europe* (1852). It was a foggy day, and Brown had just given a halfpenny to a beggar boy near Temple Bar when he saw a fellow-black standing close to a lamp-post:

> He eyed me attentively as I passed him, and seemed anxious to speak. When I had got some distance from him I looked back, and his eyes were still upon me. No longer able to resist the temptation to speak with him, I returned, and commencing conversation with him, learned a little of his history, which was as follows. He had, he said, escaped from slavery in Maryland, and reached New York; but not feeling himself secure there, he had, through the kindness of the captain of an English ship, made his way to Liverpool; and not being able to get employment there, he had come up to London. Here he had met with no better success; and having been employed in the growing of tobacco, and being unaccustomed to any other work, he could not get

> to labour in England . . . He informed me that he had not a single penny, and that he had nothing to eat that day. By this man's story, I was moved to tears; and going to a neighbouring shop, I took from my purse my last shilling, changed it, and gave this poor brother fugitive one-half. The poor man burst into tears as I placed the sixpence in his hand, and said – 'You are the first friend I have met in London'.[22]

Students

In an hour's walk through central London, William Wells Brown wrote in 1852, one might meet half a dozen black people who were attending various colleges in the metropolis: 'These are all signs of progress in the cause of the sons of Africa.'[23] Of the many African and West Indian students who came to Britain in the nineteenth century, a large number were sponsored by missionaries and philanthropists. Thus 23 West Africans visited Britain between 1840 and 1883 under the auspices of the Church Missionary Society, some for missionary training or higher education.[24] Other black students were sent by their parents or otherwise funded privately. Before the 1870s most attended Scottish universities or the University of London; but an increasing number went to Oxford or Cambridge when religious qualifications for entrance to those universities were removed. Some black students were educated at medical schools and Inns of Court.

Even in the eighteenth century, as we have seen, it was not uncommon for young Africans to be sent to Britain for their education. These visitors were mostly the offspring of well-to-do West Africans, as was a successor of theirs in the 1830s. Thomas Jenkins, said to be son of a king on the Guinea coast, was left stranded in Hawick when his benefactor died. He found work as cowherd and handy-man, meanwhile studying hard until he was qualified to apply for a job as schoolteacher. Though only 20, he was the best-qualified applicant. But he was turned down because he was black – whereupon the Duke of Buccleuch provided him with his own school and a stipend. After attending Edinburgh University for a time Jackson went to Mauritius as missionary to the slaves.[25]

John Thorpe, son of a Sierra Leone trader and mason, was the first Sierra Leonean to enter a university institution in Britain. He came to the newly founded University College, London, in 1832 to study physics and law. He returned to Sierra Leone to practise law, came back to Britain in 1846, entered the Inner Temple and was called to the bar in 1850. He died in Britain about 1860. Thorpe was first in the long line of Sierra Leone barristers.[26] Two young girls from Sierra Leone were brought to England in 1848 to be trained as schoolteachers; one of them, Mary Smart, died in Reading in the following year.[27]

An early Nigerian student in Britain was the Revd Joseph Wright, who had been enslaved in the 1820s, sold to the Portuguese, freed by a British cruiser, and taken to Sierra Leone. He was trained in England for two years by the Wesleyan Methodist Missionary Society and returned to Sierra

Leone as assistant missionary in 1844. Four years later he was one of the first two Africans ordained as full ministers in Sierra Leone's Wesleyan Church.[28]

Most notable of the Africans educated in Britain in the nineteenth century were the Sierra Leonean James Africanus Beale Horton (see pp. 276–7 above) and the Ghanaian patriot and statesman John Mensah Sarbah. The latter came to Britain in 1880, at the age of 16, to attend Taunton School, Somerset; entered Lincoln's Inn in 1884; and three years later became the first person from the Gold Coast to qualify as a barrister. He wrote major studies of Fante traditional laws and national constitution, and in 1897 was a founder of the Gold Coast Aborigines' Rights Protection Society.[29]

Among the many other African students who visited Britain was Samuel Lewis. Born in Freetown in 1843, the son of Egba slaves rescued from a slave-ship, he came to Britain in 1866, entered University College, London, and was called to the bar in 1871. Appointed acting chief justice of Sierra Leone in 1886, he was knighted in 1896, the first African to be honoured in that way. It was his reward for his 'declared policy of supporting government measures not contrary to his principles with constructive criticism, rather than oppose them . . . as an unthinking partisan'.[30] To honour thus a representative of West Africa's privileged minority and supporter of British imperial expansion was one way of meeting the growing challenge to Britain's newly acquired colonial empire.

Sir Samuel Lewis was the first African knight, but not the first black man to be honoured by Queen Victoria. That was a Jamaican, Edward Jordan, who was made a Companion of the Bath in 1861. He was a rebel in his youth: he helped to launch a radical journal called *The Watchman* and, in 1830, was tried for 'treason' and acquitted. He became the colony's prime minister in 1854 and mayor of Kingston in 1859.[31] Jordan was not educated in Britain, but a number of his fellow-Jamaicans were. One of these was Richard Hill, son of a Lincolnshire-born merchant by a Jamaican black woman. Hill spent his school days in England and, on returning to Jamaica, promised his dying father that he would 'devote his energies to the cause of freedom'. He came to Britain again in 1826 to present to the Commons a petition from the black people of Jamaica demanding civil rights. From 1832 he served as a stipendiary magistrate in Jamaica. He was a naturalist: a species of bird is named after him, as are two fishes and four molluscs. His published writings include *Lights and Shadows of Jamaica History* (1859), *The Picaroons* (1869), and many contributions to learned journals.[32] Another Jamaican, Peter Moncrieffe, was educated at Oxford, married an Englishwoman, and became a judge in Jamaica's Supreme Court, retiring in 1854.[33] And Alexander Heslop, who took his BA at Queen's College, Oxford, in 1835 and married an Englishwoman, became a member of the Jamaican legislative council and the colony's attorney-general.[34] He was described as 'a sound lawyer, a good classical scholar and a true philanthropist'.[35]

Two of the earliest students in Britain from other parts of the West Indies were Lambert Mackenzie, 'of pure African descent, and the son of poor labouring parents in Berbice' (later part of British Guiana), who attended a missionary college in Canterbury and was the first black West Indian to be ordained in the Church of England;[36] and Dr Christopher James Davis from Barbados, who studied medicine at Aberdeen, served as house physician at St Bartholomew's, went to France to help the starving and fever-stricken peasants in the Franco–Prussian War, and died of smallpox at the age of 31. 'He had accomplished a noble work,' said an obituary, 'and earned the gratitude of hundreds who owe their lives to his self-sacrifice.'[37]

In 1913 it was estimated that there were usually about 70 African students in London, mostly from the Gold Coast, Nigeria, and Sierra Leone, and 'a good proportion of West Indians'.[38] There seems to be no reliable estimate of the number in the provinces at that date. Nor is much known about their organizations, all of which seem to have been of purely local scope until 1917.

The Afro-West Indian Literary Society of Edinburgh University sent two Trinidadians as delegates to the Pan-African Conference in London in 1900: William Meyer and John Alcindor (for whom see p. 293 above). In 1906 Liverpool University had a students' club known as the Ethiopian Progressive Association.[39] Two years later Pinley Ka Isaka Seme, a Zulu, organized an African students' club at Jesus College, Oxford, and wrote to Booker T. Washington: 'Here are to be found the future leaders of African nations . . . these men will, in due season, return each to a community that eagerly awaits him and perhaps influence its public opinion.'[40] Seme was later one of the founders of the African National Congress.

What was life like for these black students in Britain around the turn of the century, when imperialism and racism were at their zenith? Part of the answer can be found in the writings of a Jamaican who eventually settled in London: Theophilus Edward Samuel Scholes. He studied medicine in London and Edinburgh, training as a missionary physician, spent five years in the Congo, came back to Britain, and was associated with the African Training Institute, Colwyn Bay, for a time. (Founded by the missionary William Hughes in 1889–90, this college had 18 students from all over West and central Africa in 1899, combining education as missionaries with practical training as artisans. There was also at least one American student, from Charleston, South Carolina.)[41] Scholes went to Nigeria, returned to Britain in the late 1890s, and wrote three far-sighted critical studies of British imperialism and racism: *The British Empire and Alliances* (1899); *Chamberlain and Chamberlainism* (1903), under the pen-name 'Bartholomew Smith'; and the two-volume *Glimpses of the Ages* (1905–6).

The last of these books takes the reader into a leading London hospital, where a West Indian, already qualified as a doctor of medicine in the United States and now seeking a British qualification, is treated with icy rudeness by his white fellow-students, who elbow him aside when he arrives early to witness an important operation and who say in his hearing: 'What is he doing here?' Black students at 'a great northern university' are hooted at and insulted; the students' magazine calls for their expulsion; their lives are made all but intolerable by the white students' 'calculated and systematic bearishness and boorishness'. Nor can a black person even walk the streets of central London without affront:

> Recently, three white men, of gentlemanly appearance, . . . going in the opposite direction to that of a coloured man who was returning home at about eleven p.m. along one of the fashionable thoroughfares in London, one of the company . . . called the attention of his comrades to the presence of the coloured man, and then said: 'Look at that thing' . . . This laceration of the feelings of coloured people, which has now become a practice in England, is due partly to the fact that Englishmen, having adopted the notion that they are superior to coloured men, have found rudeness and incivility to be the best supports of the imposure.[42]

On the eve of the First World War black graduates were not admitted to the newly formed London University Club, and black barristers were excluded from the messes of the northern and south-eastern circuits.[43] In 1913 a conference sponsored by the African Society and the Anti-Slavery and Aborigines' Protection Society was held in the Westminster Palace Hotel to consider ways of giving a more sympathetic reception to African students coming to London. About 40 African students were present, one of whom, W.F.Hutchison from the Gold Coast, said 'the African arriving in London felt himself in a great desert, and, as a great many of his countrymen knew, they were often treated in a manner which went to their hearts'.[44] The conference set up a small committee that petitioned the Colonial Office to give financial help for an African students' club, but such help was twice refused, in 1913 and 1914.[45]

A West African Student Christian Union, with Oladipo Lahanmi as secretary, was formed in 1916; three years later the West African and West Indian Christian Union had the Trinidadian Audrey Jeffers as secretary. An African Students' Union of Great Britain and Ireland, later renamed the Union for Students of African Descent, was formed in 1917 (see p. 324 above) and had some Afro-Caribbean students amongst its members. Another black students' organization in London was The Coterie of Friends, formed in the spring of 1919 by four people; Harold Piper, a Montserrat-born member of the Pharmaceutical Society; Randall H.Lockhart, a law student from Martinique; Felix Hiram ('Harry') Leekham, a Trinidadian medical student at St Mary's hospital, Paddington; and Edmund Thornton Jenkins, from Charleston, South Carolina, who studied and taught at the Royal Academy of Music. The only West African member of The Coterie was Manyo Plange from the Gold Coast. In August 1919 The Coterie arranged an international gathering in London, attended by delegations from South Africa (led by the pioneer nationalist Sol T.Plaatge) and Guinea.[46]

American singers and dancers

We turn now to a different kind of visitor: performers who gave British audiences their first taste of Afro-American spirituals, dance music, and dancing.

In 1873, when the Fisk Jubilee Singers toured Britain for the first time, 'Negro spirituals', now so familiar, were completely unknown on this side of the Atlantic. In a world without gramophone, radio, and television, travellers alone had access to such music. And both the songs and the way they were sung had a powerful impact on everyone in Britain who heard them, from the 'simple Highland girl' who said of the singing, 'It filled my whole heart!'[47] to the baffled music critic of *The Times* who wrote: 'Though the music is the offspring of wholly untutored minds, and, therefore, may grate upon the disciplined ear, it possesses a peculiar charm.'[48]

This choir, the first to introduce black spirituals to white audiences in the United States, had been organized in 1871 to raise $20,000 for the newly established Fisk University, for black students, in Nashville, Tennessee. In less than three years they had raised five times as much. And their first fund-raising trip abroad was to Britain. Though the choir's membership changed over the years, the group that landed here in the spring of 1873 consisted of seven young women and four young men, almost all emancipated slaves. Average age of the nine whose ages are known was 20.

Their first performance was at a private concert, attended by nobility, MPs, leading clergymen, editors, and other people of influence, invited by the Earl of Shaftesbury. Their fame spread quickly, and soon they were singing for Queen Victoria, who 'listened with manifest pleasure'.[49] After three crowded months in London they went to Scotland, toured England and south Wales, and by the time of their farewell concert in London's Exeter Hall had raised nearly £10,000. There were further visits to Britain in 1875 and 1884; altogether the choir raised £30,000 in this country.

Two of the original group stayed in Britain after the 1873 tour. Edmund Watkins studied music in London; Isaac P. Dickerson went to Edinburgh to study theology and started evangelistic work in France in 1878;[50] both were still in Europe in 1902.[51] A third, Thomas Rutling, after seven and a half years with the Jubilee Singers, stayed in Europe to study modern languages and music. He spent 12 years on the Continent, returning to Britain about the year 1890. From 1905 to 1910 he was living in Dragon Avenue, Harrogate, where he taught singing; and around the latter year he wrote for publication a short autobiography.[52] Frederick J. Loudin, who joined the choir in 1875 – he became their director, and later settled in

Britain – attended the first Pan-African Conference in London in 1900, as did his wife, and was elected to the executive committee of the Pan-African Association.[53]

Some of the Fisk Jubilee Singers' songs passed quickly into the everyday British musical repertory. They brought us, for instance, *Swing Low, Sweet Chariot*, *Deep River*, *Steal Away*, and *Nobody Knows the Trouble I See*. Their spirituals soon entered songbooks and hymnals 'and became a regular and popular part of chapel music'.[54] What did their singing sound like? A rough idea can be gained by listening to a recording of *Roll, Jordan, Roll* made by a later Fisk group, the Fisk Jubilee Quartet, about the year 1913 (and re-issued on a long-playing disc in 1962).[55] The singing is sombre, majestic, and – compared with the authentic spirituals sung by black Americans for themselves – highly polished for concert performance to white audiences. Yet something of the essence of the vernacular tradition remains: the flattened leading note on the third 'Roll', for example, later familiar as one of the so-called 'blue notes'.

Londoners, as we have seen, had attended 'black hops' in the 1780s and had flocked to St James's Park, in the same decade, to hear black military bandsmen. In the 1870s they found a 'peculiar charm' in black religious singing. And they were gradually becoming familiar with Afro-American secular songs and dances. Some 40 years before the advent of the Fisk Jubilee Singers, this had begun in a small way – but, for the most part, in a distorted way. Since 1833, British audiences had been used to 'blackface' entertainers who blacked their faces with burnt cork and sang minstrel songs. This caricature of black Americans, and of their music, had a long-lasting vogue.[56]

But there were also some early glimpses of genuine black American musicians and dancers. In 1838 the Afro-American violinist, bugler, horn-player, conductor, and composer Frank Johnson toured Britain with his woodwind and percussion band. At a command performance for the new queen in Buckingham Palace, Johnson was given a silver bugle.[57] Outside the vernacular tradition was the soprano Elizabeth Taylor Greenfield, born a slave in Natchez, Mississippi, who sang for Queen Victoria at Buckingham Palace during a tour of Britain in 1853–4. Known as the 'Black Swan', she was the most famous black concert artist of her day.[58] Ira Aldridge included minstrel songs in his very varied musical repertory.[59]

In 1848, British audiences saw, and marvelled at, their first Afro-American dancer. William Henry Lane, known as 'Master Juba', the most famous dancer of his day and one of the few black dancers in the early minstrel shows, delighted the crowds at London's Vauxhall Gardens and later performed in Liverpool. He was billed everywhere as 'Boz's Juba', and it is virtually certain that he was indeed the brilliant dancer whom Dickens had described in his *American Notes* six years before as 'a lively young negro, . . . the greatest dancer known':

> Single shuffle, double shuffle, cut and cross-cut: snapping his fingers, rolling his eyes, turning in his knees, presenting the backs of his legs

> in front, spinning about on his toes and heels like nothing but the man's fingers on the tambourine; dancing with two left legs, two right legs, two wooden legs, two wire legs, two spring legs – all sorts of legs and no legs.[60]

Contemporary descriptions of Lane's performances in Britain are strikingly similar to Dickens's. The *Illustrated London News* has Lane tying his legs into knots, flinging them about recklessly, making his feet 'twinkle until you lose sight of them altogether in his energy', and producing 'marvellous harmonies' on the tambourine: 'We almost question whether, upon a great emergency, he could not play a fugue upon it.'[61] 'The style as well as the execution is unlike anything ever seen in this country', reports another critic. 'The manner in which he beats time with his feet, and the extraordinary command he possesses over them, can only be believed by those who have been present at his exhibition.'[62] Lane's dancing was often compared to a musical instrument: 'He dances demisemi, semi, and quavers, as well as the slower steps.'[63] Lane is said to have died in London in 1852, but not before he had exerted a lasting influence on English clowns, whose imitations of some of his more spectacular steps became a permanent part of their tradition.[64]

A black American group called the Southern Troupe of Sable Harmonists were playing at the Dublin Music Hall in 1852; though not a 'blackface' group, they probably sang songs akin to those of the minstrels. At any rate, they claimed that they faithfully portrayed 'the peculiarities of the Ethiopian Race, which cannot be delineated by any of their imitators who use cork to black, and they wish it to be distinctly understood that individually or collectively, they challenge the world'.[65] Black minstrelsy proper, which sprang up in the United States in the mid-1850s, first crossed the Atlantic in 1866 in the shape of Sam Hague's Georgia Minstrel Troupe. This group of 26 singers and dancers, former slaves from a Georgia plantation, in a company managed by an English clog dancer, gave their first performance at the Theatre Royal, Liverpool, on 9 July 1866, and later played at the Old Philharmonic Theatre, Islington.[66] There were two comedians, Aaron Banks and Abe Cox; the latter sang a song called *Hen Convention*, with farmyard imitations. Most of the performers, however, were not professionals but ordinary plantation workers, whose only stage wardrobe was 'the identical garments worn in the plantation';[67] and, on the whole, British audiences 'found the music and theatrics of the visitors from Georgia less entertaining than the performances of the professionals who blackened themselves for their stage appearances'.[68]

Far more successful were Haverly's Colored Minstrels, 65 strong, whose elaborate and highly romanticized portrayal of plantation life opened at Her Majesty's Theatre in 1881. There were 20 dancers, a banjo orchestra, and 8 players of bones and 8 of tambourines – 16 musicians who sat in two rows on the stage and made 'a most picturesque display in unison'. The singers included the bass Richard Little and the 'heart-breaking' tenor Wallace

King. Principal comedian was Billy Kersands, highest-paid black minstrel star and expert dancer of the 'buck and wing' and of a dance later known as the 'soft shoe', but then called the 'Essence of Old Virginia'. Derived from the 'shuffle', this graceful and elegant step was the first popular dance borrowed by professionals from the Afro-American vernacular tradition, and when Kersands did it before Queen Victoria 'he had her laughing heartily over it'. His other specialities were dancing with a cup and saucer and reciting a monologue with his mouth full of billiard balls.[69] Two more of this show's talented dancers were the Bohee brothers, James and George, who danced the 'soft shoe' and played the banjo at the same time. *The Times* wrote of Haverly's Colored Minstrels: 'There can be no doubt of the spontaneity of the outbursts of sound, or of the enjoyment with which the performers take part in the dances and frolics of the evening. The heartiness of their fun seems to communicate itself to the audience.'[70]

When the Haverly troupe went home, after touring the provinces, they left behind the prolific Afro-American composer James Bland, who had sung his own song, *Oh dem Golden Slippers*, as part of the show. Bland also composed *Carry Me Back to Old Virginny* and about 700 other songs. Discarding the 'blackface' make-up he had worn as a minstrel, he toured Britain and the Continent for two decades as a singer-banjoist, becoming the 'idol of the Music Halls' and returning to America in the early 1900s.[71]

Close on the heels of the Haverly troupe came Callender's Colored Minstrels, who opened at the Holborn Amphitheatre in April 1884, later transferring to the Standard Theatre, Shoreditch. With them were three virtuoso banjoists: Horace Weston (who was also a composer) and the Bohee brothers. This time the brothers stayed in Britain, 'for several years were an attraction on the halls with their smart and novel entertainment' and 'were greatly in demand in London at society functions and private entertainments'. James Bohee is said to have given banjo lessons to the future King Edward VII (perhaps for this reason, the banjo was the favourite amateur instrument among the British aristocracy up to the early nineties, when it was replaced by the mandolin). George Bohee was the first to sing *A Boy's Best Friend is his Mother* in this country.[72]

In the 1890s a wave of Afro-American performers toured British music-halls. Bishop and Vale, 'negro comedians and acrobatic dancers'; 'Texarkansas', a 'female sand dancer'; Dan Leeson, dancer; Henry Blackburn, dancer and comedian; 'Sir' Isaac de St Vincent, 'eccentric dancer' and 'champion bones and tambourine player': these, as well as several black American comedians, a 'musical ventriloquist', and a juggler, were billed at such British music-halls as Peckham Theatre of Varieties in 1897.[73]

But English people not only watched these dances: they also imitated them. The cakewalk was being danced in London before 1903. What made it all the rage – the first in a long line of Afro-American dances that captured fashionable London – was the all-black musical *In Dahomey*, which opened at the Shaftesbury Theatre on 16 May 1903. It featured the outstanding comedy dance team of Bert Williams and George Walker, with the latter's wife Aida Overton Walker, Hattie McIntosh, and Lottie Williams. The lyrics were by Paul Laurence Dunbar, the libretto by Jesse A. Shipp, and the catchy music by Will Marion Cook, whose *Clorindy – the Origin of the Cakewalk* had caused a sensation on Broadway in 1898.

For the first month the show's success was only moderate. And then the company received a royal command for a performance at Buckingham Palace, as part of the ninth birthday celebrations of the future King Edward VIII. A Buckingham Palace appearance spelt success for *In Dahomey*. Night after night the theatre was full; the show ran for 250 performances. *In Dahomey* was the rage of London, and by early October the *Era* could report that 'the ubiquitous "cake-walk" is at the height of its popularity'. After London, *In Dahomey* toured the provinces and Scotland, and the cakewalk's triumph was complete.[74]

Appendix I. Prize-fighters, 1791–1902

Joe Leashley

The first black boxer in Britain of whom any record has been preserved was Joe Leashley, a 14-stone African who defeated Tom Treadway at Marylebone Fields on 13 June 1791. He showed 'great activity, skill, and game [i.e. pluck]; pourtraying a knowledge of the art, superior to most amateurs'. He knocked out his opponent cleanly and decisively after 35 minutes. In 1796 he fought and defeated a boxer known as Stewey the Breakman.[1]

Bill Richmond and Young Richmond

Born near New York in 1763, the son of Georgia-born slaves, Bill Richmond was the first black boxer to gain international recognition. He came to Britain at the age of 14 as servant to a British general who later became Duke of Northumberland, and who sent him to school in Yorkshire and then apprenticed him to a cabinet-maker in York. Richmond taught himself to box in a series of fights with soldiers. Though only 10st. 12lb. against his opponent's 14st., he thrashed a knife-grinder who had insulted him, and who was notorious as 'the terror of Sheffield', in a fight lasting 25 minutes. A 13st. blacksmith who was rash enough to add injury to insult by kicking Richmond soon had cause to regret it. And a York brothel-keeper, who called him a 'black devil' as he was walking out with a white girl, and insulted the girl too, soon received 'a complete *milling*' from Richmond's fists.

After moving to London Richmond found a way of putting this early training to practical use. He became a prize-fighter, and was soon a famous one. In 1805 he had two victories – he beat a Jewish boxer called Youssop in six rounds at Blackheath and a coachman called Jack Holmes, known in the ring as 'Tom Tough', in 26 at Kilburn – but lost to the future English heavyweight champion, the redoubtable Tom Cribb, in a 90-minute contest at Hailsham. Richmond hadn't trained properly, and this defeat taught him a lesson. He didn't fight again in public for three years; then, when he felt he was ready, he faced and beat Jack Carter at Epsom Downs. It is said that after winning this fight Richmond leapt over the ropes and grabbed a man in the crowd who had been shouting that he had '*a white feather in his tail*'. Having lost to George Maddox at Wimbledon Common, Richmond fought a return match at Reculver in 1809 for 100 guineas – and won, after 52 punishing rounds.

Richmond married a woman with enough money to enable him to keep a fashionable public house, the Horse and Dolphin near Leicester Square. Though he was a well-known and popular figure, customers taunted him sometimes on account of his colour. He usually handled such people so calmly that he was 'considered good tempered, and placid, even to a degree that could not be expected'. But once at least he took more than he could endure and taught a 'young ruffian' a lesson. Besides the pub he ran a boxing academy where he gave less painful lessons to hundreds of pupils, including the essayist William Hazlitt. And he sometimes gave exhibition bouts at London theatres.

When Richmond was 50 he was said to look 15 years younger. This was attributed to his 'temperate mode of living'; many retired boxers in that period drank to excess. He was described as intelligent, communicative, humorous, and an excellent cricketer. He died in his house near the Haymarket on 28 December 1829.

Bill Richmond's son, always referred to as Young Richmond, was 'only a featherweight, but he was nimble and could box like a master'. Trained by his father, he had powerful muscles and 'took to boxing like a duck to water'. But after losing his first two fights, to Jack Adams and Byng Stocks, he decided that if he could not repeat his father's success he had no right to carry his father's name into the ring any longer. So he retired from the sport – but sometimes helped to train amateurs.[2]

Tom Molineaux

Bill Richmond's fellow-American and protégé Tom Molineaux would have been heavyweight champion of England but was robbed of the title by a trick. Born in 1784 and reared in Virginia, he was the son of America's first black pugilist, Zachary Molineaux, and slave to a rich playboy who staked $100,000 that the young man would beat another slave in a boxing match. Tom was promised $500 and his freedom if he won the fight. Trained, it is said, by a Bristol sailor – though one imagines that his father must have given him some idea of how to handle himself – he saved his master from ruin and gained his freedom. In 1803, working his passage as deckhand, he came to England 'an entire stranger, destitute of friends or money'. But Bill Richmond gave him a warm welcome. As soon as he realized the young man's capabilities he began nursing him for a fight with Tom Cribb. Having made short work of two opponents chosen by Cribb, Molineaux was judged worthy to meet the champion himself.

The big fight took place at Copthorne, near East Grinstead, in December 1810. The weather was atrocious: intensely cold, with driving rain. In those days boxers hammered each other with bare fists for round after round, and several wrestling holds and falls were used which are now against the rules. The fight between Molineaux and Cribb went to 39 rounds. By the nineteenth it was impossible to distinguish the fighters by their faces, so dreadfully had both been battered. In that round Molineaux held Cribb in such a way that he could neither hit his opponent nor fall. While the seconds were debating whether to separate the two men, about 200 spectators rushed the ring and one of Molineaux's fingers was broken in the scrimmage. All the same, though shivering violently from the cold, he seemed to be doing better than Cribb, and in the twenty-third round, when odds of four to one were being laid on Molineaux, Sir Thomas Price, veteran member of the 'Fancy', shouted: 'Now, Tom, now; for God's sake don't let the nigger win. Remember the honour of Old England. Go for him; go for him!' The key round was the twenty-eighth. Cribb could not rise from his second's knee at the beginning of this round, and it looked as if the fight was over. Sure that he had won, Molineaux hopped up and down in the middle of the ring. Suddenly Cribb's second shouted that Molineaux was hiding lead bullets in his fists. By the time this charge had been proved false Cribb was able to get up and 'mill on the retreat', dodging his opponent's blows. Then Molineaux had a piece of bad luck. His head hit one of the stakes and he lay on the stage half-stunned. In the thirty-second round the two men were staggering against each other as if drunk, and they fell without exchanging a blow. Seven rounds later the challenger had had enough. But within three days he sent Cribb this letter:

> Sir, – My friends think, that had the weather on last Tuesday, the day upon which I contended with you, not been so unfavourable, I should have won the battle; I therefore challenge you to a second meeting, at any time within two months, for such sum as those gentlemen who placed confidence in me may be pleased to arrange.
>
> As it is possible this letter may meet the public eye, I cannot omit the opportunity of expressing a confident hope, that the circumstances of my being a different colour to that of a people amongst whom I have sought protection will not in any way operate to my prejudice.

The return match, arrangements for which were made at Richmond's pub, took place in the following year at Thistleton Gap, where Leicestershire, Lincolnshire, and Rutland – as they then were – met. Attended by a record crowd of at least 15,000, a quarter of them nobility and gentry from the countryside around, it was one of the great sporting events of the nineteenth century. According to *The Times*, 'the Black's prowess' was regarded by Cribb's supporters 'with a jealousy which excited considerable national prejudice against him'. It was 'a most obstinate and sanguinary combat, the equal to which record can scarcely furnish'. Molineaux never recovered from a suspected low blow to the body, in the sixth round, which badly winded him. In the ninth his jaw was broken, and in the eleventh he was knocked out. Despite the jealousy and 'national prejudice', the ballad-makers paid tribute to his courage:

A brave man is Molineux, from America he came,
And boldly tried to enter with Crib the lists of fame.

The Black stripp'd, and appeared of a giant-like strength,
Large in bone, large in muscle and with arms a cruel length;
With his skin as black as ebony and Crib as white as snow,
They shook hands like good fellows, then to it they did go.

* * * * * *

The Black's strength forsook him, he'd not a chance to win;
He fought like a brave fellow, but was forc'd to give in.
Ye swells, ye flash, ye milling coves, who this hard fight [did] see,
Let us drink to these heroes, come join along with me,
A bumper to brave Crib, boys, to the Black a bumper too,
Tho' beat, he proved a man my boys, what more could a man do.

After his jaw mended, Molineaux went on to meet and beat Jack Carter in 1813 and Bill Fuller in 1814. But in 1815 he lost to George Cooper, who had been trained by Bill Richmond. It was his last prize-fight. He ended his days in Ireland, where he went with a group of boxers to give exhibition fights. He died penniless in 1821, at the early age of 34. For the last few months of his life he was taken care of by the black bandsmen of the 77th Regiment, then stationed in Galway. He great-great-nephew John Henry Lewis was to become light-heavyweight champion of the world in 1935.[3]

Sam Robinson

Another of Bill Richmond's many pupils was the Afro-American Sam Robinson. Born in New York in 1778, he was a docker at 13, then a cabin-boy and steward. When he was 20 he settled in London as servant to a Westminster family. From 1800 to 1815 he was often in demand as a sparring partner to various boxers, and Richmond, who thought highly of him, trained and encouraged him. In 1816 he won three of his first four important fights: he beat Tom Crockery, Alf Butcher, and a black boxer called Stevenson, about whom little is known; he lost to Jack Carter. In the same year, at Doncaster, he fought another black American, Harry Sutton (see below). Sutton's first punch hurt him so badly that he went down and groaned. His second claimed the fight on a foul, but the referee refused to allow this. After 25 rounds Robinson gave in. Two months later he knocked out the Yorkshireman Tom Taylor at Ferrybridge in 19 minutes. But he was no match for George Cooper, who beat him in 12 minutes, at Costerton, near Edinburgh, with a series of ripping upper cuts.

It was almost two years before Robinson went back to the ring, and he did so in curious circumstances. He had married a white girl with whom a young man called Alexander Fangill was also in love. Fangill wanted to take revenge with his fists and challenged Robinson to a prize-fight at short notice. Robinson insisted on a month's training, and knocked Fangill out after a bloody 40 rounds. Nothing is known of Robinson's later life.[4]

Harry Sutton

The black American who beat Sam Robinson in 1816 had been a deckhand on ships plying between his native Baltimore and Liverpool. Then young Harry Sutton settled in Deptford, where he worked as a corn-porter and learnt to box by defending himself against tough local dockers who resented his presence among them. In 1816 he went to see the fight between Robinson and Stevenson, and was offered a purse if he would fight another black spectator, there and then. This hastily arranged contest lasted only three rounds and, encouraged by his success, Sutton met Robinson and, as we have seen, beat him. He went on to beat Ned Painter in 1817 but was carried from the ring in a return match. Two years later he beat the black boxer Massa Kendrick (see below) in a 12-round fight. He brought his sporting career to a close with a sparring tour of Lancashire and Ireland, accompanied by Jack Carter. Sutton was described as

> a master with the mauleys, a giant in height, being more than 6 foot and knew all the tricks in the art of milling. He possessed first rate weight, had longer arms than any one in the prize ring, was game of the first quality [i.e. very plucky], showed great activity, did not dissipate in his mode of life, and . . . possessed prodigious strength.[5]

Massa Kendrick

Born on the island of St Kitts in 1798, Massa Kendrick came to England about the year 1811. He is described as quarrelsome and courageous. He provoked Bill Richmond into a fist-fight in the street and tried to do the same with Molineaux. His most famous fight, with George Cooper in Westminster, was arranged on the spur of the moment and lasted 69 rounds before Kendrick admitted defeat. Cooper refused a return match on the ground that beating Kendrick would not add to his reputation. Kendrick beat Dick Acton in 1822. His defeats were attributed to his failure to train properly. He retired from the ring in 1826 and died at the age of 46.[6]

Minor prize-fighters of the 1820s and 1830s

Four black prize-fighters of whom little is known were active in Britain in the 1820s and early 1830s. Jemmy Johnson, said to have been trained by

Bill Richmond, beat Waterman Smith (1820), Harris Tod (1823), Bishop Harris (1824), and Jewin, 'a Navigator' (1824), and lost to C. Smith (1823) and perhaps to Nixon (1823), though the black contestant in this last match may have been a different Johnson.[7] A black boxer known as Sambo was beaten by Deaf Burke in 1828.[8] Another called Morgan beat Fleming (or Flemming) in a single round in 1829.[9] 'Black Joe' lost to Miles Hatting in a fight near Manchester in 1832.[10]

James Wharton

Perhaps the greatest, and certainly the most successful, of the black boxers in Britain in the first half of the nineteenth century was James Wharton, otherwise known as 'Young Molineaux', 'The Morocco Prince', and 'Jemmy the Black'. He fought nine prize-fights and did not lose one of them – though one ended in a draw after four hours' slogging. Wharton was born in Morocco on 3 March 1813. He is said to have been 'half-Nubian', which must mean that one of his parents was a black African. He came to London in 1820, worked as a cabin-boy on ships plying to India, and learnt to box on these voyages. He was tutored by a prominent 1820s boxer, Jem Burn, who saw in him another potential Richmond or Molineaux.

Wharton's first public appearance was at Whetstone in 1833. It was a tough fight and much blood was spilt, but the 20-year-old black fighter was declared the winner after 54 minutes. Two boxers named Wilsden and Evans (alias the 'Herefordshire Pippin') were easier to defeat; and even Bill Fisher, a formidable Liverpool man, succumbed to Wharton after 49 rounds.

The toughest battle of Wharton's career – one of the longest fights in the annals of boxing – took place in Staffordshire on 9 February 1836, when he met Tom Britton of Liverpool. In their determination not to let their man lose, Britton's supporters did everything but climb into the ring and fight:

> They chased Dick Curtis, Wharton's chief second, out of the ring, and thereafter made certain that no one would take his place. The ropes were cut, the stakes were trampled down, Wharton was repeatedly threatened and time and again sticks were whistling around the Negro's head. That was how the Liverpool idol was enabled to remain so long and get a draw.

The fight went to 200 rounds, lasting four hours and four minutes.

Wharton now found it hard to get a British fighter to face him and was about to leave the country when a fight was arranged with Harry Preston of Birmingham, known as 'Young Cribb'. It lasted an hour. Wharton followed this victory with two wins against the Tyneside collier William Renwick: the first, in Staffordshire in 1837, ended with a knock-out in the eighty-sixth round; in the return match, at Shap Fells, Westmorland, two years later, Renwick gave in after 65 rounds. Wharton's last and most brilliant fight was in 1840, when he beat the Birmingham boxer Hammer Lane in 53 rounds of hard fighting. After Wharton retired undefeated he formed a close friendship with Lane, and they toured together giving exhibition bouts. Then Wharton married, taught boxing, and eventually settled in Liverpool. He died on 25 April 1856. The boxing historian Nat Fleischer writes of him:

> There was not in his day a more clever or craftier fighter . . . His science, both in attack and defense, was perfect. In ring generalship there was no fighter of his era to equal him. No matter how tough the fighting, he always held something in reserve. He possessed both cunning and courage, the latter being his greatest asset. He knew no fear and was willing at all times to face any man.[11]

Massa Sutton

Thomas Welsh, better known as Massa Sutton or Sambo Sutton, was the welterweight who taught Charles Kingsley to box at Cambridge. He came to Britain from the United States about the year 1832 and was soon famous as the licensed jester of British boxing. He would stand on his head and wave his feet in the air and could dance and sing for hours at a time. 'To these accomplishments', wrote a sporting paper, 'he adds great bodily strength, a tremendous reach, a powerful blow and can take it until doom's day.' Sutton's first big fight was in 1839, when he was beaten by Jemmy Shaw at Seven Dials. Soon afterwards he was unlucky enough to lose his right eye, but did not retire from the ring. In 1844, at Twyford, he knocked out John Sears after 45 minutes. In the thirty-fourth round of his fight with Billy Jordan in 1845, Sutton slipped and, as he was falling, took a heavy blow to the face. The crowd broke into the ring and threatened the referee for awarding the fight to Jordan. Sutton won the return match, but was badly beaten in his last big fight, a bloody contest with Alec Keene in 1848.[12]

John Perry

John Perry turned up in London in 1845, seeking help from Johnny Broome, a former British lightweight champion. He had walked from Birmingham in the hope of persuading someone to back him in the prize-ring. He was born of African parents in Annapolis, Nova Scotia. His father had served on a British man-of-war, and he himself had done the same for four years. Discharged, he had earned a precarious living with his fists. Broome gave him a helping hand, and in 1846 Perry faced his first professional opponent, Bill Burton. Perry

> made a handsome appearance with his six feet one and

> one-half inches and 212 pounds, an unusually husky fighter for his time. His frame was symmetrical and the muscles made him look like a Hercules. His legs were proportioned to his size and he had powerful arms and splendid shoulders that indicated tremendous hitting power . . .
>
> Perry's style of milling was pretty to watch. Poised on his toes, he danced around his man, jabbed with consistency and accuracy and delivered his punches cleanly. He was perfection so far as science was concerned.

Although hopelessly outclassed, Burton refused to give in. Perry was clearly reluctant to hurt his opponent, but finally knocked him out.

Perry's career in Britain came to an abrupt end a few months later when he was arrested as accomplice to a group of American forgers and transported for life to New South Wales. Freed on ticket of leave after three years, he resumed his boxing career and took the Australian heavyweight championship from George Hough in 1849. That was his last important fight. He stayed in Australia, where he trained several famous boxers.[13]

Jemmy Robinson

Born a slave in Virginia, Jemmy Robinson worked his passage to Liverpool in 1840. He was 17, weighed 126lb., and stood 5ft 7in. In quick succession, sponsored by a promoter called Young Norley, he beat Jemmy Evans, Johnny Peach, Charles Mallett, and Enoch Horridge, the Salford 'Pocket Hercules'. At 21, Robinson was recognized as the best and cleverest boxer of his weight in Europe. But he fell victim to the cholera epidemic of 1849 and died within 36 hours. 'His splendid manners and general good conduct had made him a likeable fellow and his death shocked an army of friends. Had he been able to continue he undoubtedly would have gone down in ring history as one of the greatest colored fighters of all time.'[14]

Bob Travers

The real name of Bob Travers, 'the Black Wonder', was Charles Jones. The son of a slave, he was born in Norfolk, Virginia, on 30 May 1836, and was brought to England as a boy. In his teens he worked in a crockery factory, then toured the British fair-grounds in boxing booths. Travers, his professional name, was borrowed from his father's master. He won his first prize-fight in 1854 and over the next ten years made more appearances in the ring than any other boxer of the time. He was 5ft 6in. tall, weighed about 140lb., and was famous for his staying power. When Joe Cobley, 'The Elastic Potboy', beat him in 1856, the fight went to 110 rounds and lasted almost three and a half hours. Cobley's ribs were broken and his stomach badly injured, but Travers conceded defeat when he could no longer see. By 1860 Travers had won 32 of his 44 fights. In that year he lost to a Norwich publican in a 57-round fight that ended in a riot. After his defeat by Patsy Reardon in 1862, *Bell's Life in London* commented

> Although Travers has had the mortification to be defeated, yet no man ever in the Ring acquitted himself in a manner that redounded more to his honour; for, with that heroic determination which has ever been so conspicuous in him throughout his career, he fought with the most unyielding pluck and desperate resolution.

Travers retired from the ring in 1864.[15]

Bob Smith

Born in Washington, DC, on 11 March 1840, Bob Smith came to Britain on a tramp steamer, landed at Liverpool, and made his home there. In bare-knuckle fights, he had held his own against the toughest members of the crew, and the captain offered to back him against any fighter in the prize-ring. A dockside tough known as the 'Liverpool Greyhound' heard of Smith's skill and, by way of challenge, openly insulted him in a seamen's pub. The captain insisted on a fight according to the rules of the sport instead of an impromptu match. The 'Greyhound' lasted just three rounds and Smith's victory made him very popular. He beat the American heavyweight champion, Tom Allen, near Liverpool in 1864 in a 50-round fight lasting two hours and 49 minutes. Allen trained hard for the return match in the following year, but yielded to Smith's punishing body-blows after 29 rounds. Smith, who weighed only 10½st. and was 5ft 10in. tall, retired from the ring in 1866.[16]

Bobby Dobbs

Lightweight and welterweight, Bobby Dobbs fought in the ring more than a thousand times between the ages of 16 and 60. He was born a slave at Knoxville, Tennessee, on 27 December 1858, picked cotton till he was 15, embarked on a prize-fighting career, and came to England in 1898 for a match with Dick Burge. A bookmaker offered him £100 in cash if he would agree to lose the match in the fourth round – and, just to be on the safe side, made it part of the deal that he should drink a large dose of a strong purgative beforehand. Dobbs pretended to agree, found a willing substitute – an acquaintance who resembled him closely enough to fool the bookmaker, badly needed the money, and had no fear of the purgative – and went on to win the fight in eight rounds. Before returning to the United States he knocked out two leading British pugilists: Pat MacDonald and Jerry Driscoll.

Dobbs, who stood 5ft 8½in. and weighed 9st. 9lb., came to Britain again in 1902 and made his home here for eight years. During that period he took part in 42 prize-fights and won 25 of them. He ran boxing schools in Berlin and Budapest for a time. His last officially recorded fight was in Berlin in 1910, when he knocked out Dick Green in the sixteenth round. After the First World War he worked as a trainer in Philadelphia and Charleston, where he died on 2 December 1930.[17]

Notes

Authors' names and book titles are taken from the title-pages of the works referred to, and the spelling of the originals has been followed. Details supplied from other sources are enclosed in square brackets. Unless otherwise indicated, place of publication is London. The following abbreviations have been used:

ALHTS	*Accounts of the Lord High Treasurer of Scotland*
BSB	F.O. Shyllon, *Black Slaves in Britain* (Oxford University Press for Institute of Race Relations, 1974)
CSP	*Calendar of State Papers*
DNB	*Dictionary of National Biography*
HCSP	*House of Commons Sessional Papers*
OED	*Oxford English Dictionary*
PRO	Public Record Office

Preface

1. See, e.g., Ernest Kaiser, 'Recent literature on black liberation struggles and the ghetto crisis (A Bibliographical Survey)', *Science & Society*, XXXIII (1969), 175; and cf. Neville Maxwell, *The Power of Negro Action* (Neville Maxwell, [1966]), 15.
2. See, e.g., Earl E. Thorpe, *The Central Theme of Black History* (Westport, Conn., Greenwood Press, 1979 reprint), 154–5.
3. Cf. Benjamin A. Quarles, 'Black History's Diversified Clientele', in *Africa and the Afro-American Experience: Eight Essays*, ed. Lorraine A. Williams (Washington, DC, Howard University Press, 1977), 176–82: 'Black history . . . is no longer a matter of limited concern. Whites need to know black history . . . For whites it furnishes a new version of American history, one that especially challenges our national sense of smugness and self-righteousness.'

1. 'Those kinde of people'

Africans in Britannia

1. *Notitia Dignitatum*, ed. Otto Seeck (Berlin, Weidmann, 1876), Occ. xl. 47, p. 212; David J. Breeze and Brian Dobson, *Hadrian's Wall* (Allen Lane, 1976), 208, 246, 257, [258].
2. Eric Birley, 'The Beaumont Inscription, the Notitia Dignitatum, and the Garrison of Hadrian's Wall', *Transactions of the Cumberland & Westmorland Antiquarian & Archæological Society*, n.s. XXXIX (1939), 191–4; R.G.Collingwood and R.P.Wright, *The Roman Inscriptions of Britain*, I, *Inscriptions on Stone* (Oxford, Clarendon Press, 1965), no. 2042, p. 626. I owe these references to Paul Edwards, 'Africans in Britain before 1560' (paper presented to the International Conference on the History of Blacks in Britain, London, 28–30 September 1981).
3. *Scriptores Historiae Augustae*, ed. Ernest Hohl (Leipzig, B.G.Teubner, 1965), 154–5. I am grateful to N.P.Tanburn for help with the translation of this passage. The validity of the *Historia Augusta* is closely examined in Sir Ronald Syme, *Ammianus and the Historia Augusta* (Oxford, Clarendon Press, 1968), and his *Historia Augusta Papers* (Oxford, Clarendon Press, 1983) sees it as 'fictional history'. Nevertheless (as Edwards points out) Anthony Birley, *Septimius Severus: The African Emperor* (Eyre & Spottiswoode, 1971), 265–6, is inclined to accept this story.
4. See G.L.Cheesman, *The Auxilia of the Roman Imperial Army* (Oxford, Clarendon Press, 1914), 96: 'Africa in particular sent *praefecti* from its many flourishing towns to almost every frontier during the latter half of the second century, and the accession of the African Septimius Severus at its close possibly gave his fellow countrymen a specially favoured position in the succeeding period.'
5. Roger Warwick, 'The Skeletal Remains', in Leslie P. Wenham, *The*

Romano-British Cemetery at Trentholme Drive, York (Ministry of Public Buildings and Works Archaeological Reports no. 5, HMSO, 1968), 157: 'Several of the Trentholme men show limb proportions close to those of negroid people . . . These findings raise a most interesting question; were there negroid people amongst those buried at Trentholme? . . . The evidence is . . . disappointingly neutral. Only one skull with pronouncedly negro characters was found, and this was not associated with the rest of its skeleton.'

Africans in Scotland

1. *Annals of Ireland: Three Fragments, copied from ancient sources by Dubhaltach Mac Firbisigh*, ed. John O'Donovan (Dublin, Irish Archæological and Celtic Society, 1860), 162, 163.
2. P.Edwards, 'Africans in Britain before 1560' (1981), 2.
3. James Kinsley, ed., in *The Poems of William Dunbar* (Oxford, Clarendon Press, 1979), 308. There were African slaves in Spain from the eighth century but their numbers do not appear to have grown appreciably until the eleventh and twelfth; see Charles Verlinden, *L'Esclavage dans l'Europe médiévale*, I, *Péninsule ibérique – France* (Brugge, 'De Tempel', 1955), 225–6, and Hans Werner Debrunner, *Presence and Prestige: Africans in Europe: A History of Africans in Europe before 1918* (Basel, Basler Afrika Bibliographien, 1979), 17. For black slaves in thirteenth-century Spain, see Robert I. Burns, 'Christian-Islamic Confrontation in the West: The Thirteenth-Century Dream of Conversion', *American Historical Review*, LXXVI (1971), [1413]–1431, reproducing miniatures from the *Cántigas*, or 'Songs in Praise of St Mary'; for black slaves in fourteenth-century Seville, see Ruth Pike, 'Sevillian Society in the Sixteenth Century: Slaves and Freedmen', *Hispanic American Historical Review*, XLVII (1967), 345; I am grateful to Professor J.S.Cumins for these references. The demand for black slaves in Europe had grown to such proportions by the fourteenth century that a special caravan route was created from the Sudan across the Sahara to the Barka peninsula in Cyrenaica; see Charles Verlinden, *Les Origines de la civilisation atlantique: De la Renaissance à l'Âge des Lumières* (Neuchâtel, Éditions de la Baconnière, 1966), 175, or Charles Verlinden, *The Beginnings of Modern Colonization*, trans. Yvonne Freccero (Ithaca, Cornell University Press, 1970), 29. For free black communities in Seville, Valencia, Granada, Cadiz, and Jaen from the fifteenth century, see Eileen E. McGrath Grubb, 'Attitudes towards Black Africans in Imperial Spain', *Legon Journal of the Humanities*, I (1974), 68–90. A fifteenth-century Italian silhouette of a black woman slave, in the Galleria Estense, Modena, is reproduced in Margaret Aston, *The Fifteenth Century: The Prospect of Europe* (Thames & Hudson, 1968), 60.
4. John Pinkerton, *The History of Scotland from the Accession of the House*

of Stuart to that of Mary (C.Dilly, 1797), 60–1. Besides Africans, a musk cat and a 'Portugall hors' with a red tail were brought back to Edinburgh (*ALHTS*, II. 465, 468).

5. *ALHTS*, II. 427, 477, 458, 461–2.
6. *ALHTS*, III. 108, 115, 132, 206, 330, 377, 388, 182. When two black friars ('the blak More freris') visited Scotland in 1508 the king helped defray their expenses and bought clothes for them (*ALHTS*, IV. 62, 112, 139, 178, 191).
7. *ALHTS*, II. 469.
8. *The Poems of William Dunbar*, ed. Kinsley, 196.
9. *ALHTS*, III. pp. xlix, 256, 258, 259.
10. *The Great Tournament Roll of Westminster: A Collotype Reproduction of the Manuscript*, ed. Sydney Anglo (Oxford, Clarendon Press, 1968), 32 n. 1.
11. Robert Lindesay of Pitscottie, *The Historie and Cronicles of Scotland*, ed. Æ.J.G.Mackay (Edinburgh, Scottish Text Society, 1899–1911), I. 243. See also Marc de Vulson, sieur de la Colombière, *La Science héroïque* (Paris, Sebastien & Gabriel Cramoisy, 1644), 453–8.
12. *The Poems of William Dunbar*, ed. Kinsley, 106. Sir James Balfour Paul, editor of the third volume of *ALHTS*, though delicately not mentioning this line in Dunbar's poem, is plainly nonplussed by the king's choice of a black woman to be jousted for at the tournament: 'That he . . . should set up an absolute negress . . . as the one whose excellencies were to be defended at the sword's point, seems well-nigh incredible . . . The tourney [was] an institution which, notwithstanding all his magnificence, he did much to bring into disrepute from his fantastic elevation of a negress to a position which in the palmy days of chivalry had only been held by the fairest and noblest in the land' (*ALHTS*, III. pp. xlvii–xlix, lii).
13. Lindesay of Pitscottie, I. 244.
14. *ALHTS*, IV. 401.
15. *ALHTS*, IV. 232, 404, 434, 324, 436.
16. *ALHTS*, IV. 428.
17. *ALHTS*, IV. 338.
18. *ALHTS*, V. 328.
19. *Accounts of the Treasurer of Scotland*, XII. 97, 181.
20. *A true reportarie of the most triumphant, and royal accomplishment of the Baptisme of the most Excellent, right High, and mightie Prince, Frederik Henry* ([Edinburgh], R.Walde-graue, [1594]), sigs. C3r–C4r.

Africans in England

1. *The Great Tournament Roll of Westminster*, ed. S.Anglo (1968), 85 n. 2.
2. Sydney Anglo, 'The Court Festivals of Henry VII: a Study Based upon the Account Books of John Heron, Treasurer of the Chamber', *Bulletin of the John Rylands Library*, XLIII (1960–1), 42.
3. *The Great Tournament Roll of Westminster*, ed. Anglo, pl. iii, membrane

4; pl. xviii, membrane 28. I am grateful to Ziggi Alexander, and to P.L.Gwynn-Jones of the College of Arms, for help in identifying these portraits.

4. *The Decades of the newe worlde or west India* [ed. Richard Eden] (William Powell, 1555), fol. 359v; cf. Richard Hakluyt, *The Principal Navigations Voyages Traffiques & Discoveries of the English Nation* (Glasgow, James MacLehose & Sons, 1903–5), VI. 176; *Europeans in West Africa, 1450–1560*, ed. John W. Blake (Hakluyt Society, 1942), II. 346.

5. Eldred Jones, *Othello's Countrymen: The African in English Renaissance Drama* (Oxford University Press, 1965), 12; Eldred D. Jones, *The Elizabethan Image of Africa* ([Charlottesville], University Press of Virginia, 1971), 16. Noël Deerr, *The History of Sugar* (Chapman & Hall, 1949–50), II. 268, says they were 'kidnapped', but this is clearly incorrect. F.O.Shyllon (*BSB*, 2) calls them 'not slaves, but linguisters'. Perhaps they were domestic slaves whom an African ruler had lent to the English traders?

6. Richard Hakluyt, *The Principall Navigations, Voiages and Discoveries of the English nation, made by Sea or ouer Land* (George Bishop & Ralph Newberie, 1589), 114, 107, 115; cf. Hakluyt (1903–5), VI. 217, 200, 218–19; *Europeans in West Africa*, ed. Blake, II. 398, 381, 399.

7. Hakluyt (1589), 86–7; cf. Hakluyt (1903–5), VI. 149–50; *Europeans in West Africa*, ed. Blake, II. 318.

8. *A Summarie of the Antiquities, and wonders of the Worlde* (Thomas Hacket, [1566]), sigs. B3v–B4v. This was a translation of Pierre de Changy, *Sommaire des Singularitez de Pline* (Paris, R.Breton, 1559). Much the same legends appear in *The Decades of the newe worlde* [ed. Eden], fols. 335v–356v; cf. Hakluyt (1903–5), VI. 167–9; *Europeans in West Africa*, ed. Blake, II. 338–40. Cf. also *Othello*, seventh Arden edition, ed. M.R.Ridley (Methuen & Co. Ltd, 1958), I. iii. 144–5: 'The Anthropophagi, and men whose heads / Do grow beneath their shoulders.'

9. [William Waterman], *The Fardle of facions: conteining the aunciente maners, customes, and Lawes, of the peoples enhabiting the two partes of the earth, called Affrike and Asie* (Jhon Kingstone & Henry Sutton, 1555), sigs. F8v–G2r. This was a translation of books 1 and 2 of Johan Boemus, *Omnium gentium mores* (Augsburg, S.Grimm & M.Wirsung, 1520).

10. Jones, *Elizabethan Image*, 7.

11. Winthrop D. Jordan, *White over Black: American Attitudes Towards the Negro, 1550–1812* (Chapel Hill, University of North Carolina Press, 1968), 158–9.

12. The gold alone is said to have been easily worth £20,000 in the currency of the time; see James A. Williamson, *Maritime Enterprise 1485–1558* (Oxford, Clarendon Press, 1913), 287. See also Alice M. Kleist, 'The English African Trade under the Tudors', *Transactions of* *the Historical Society of Ghana*, III (1957), 140: 'The cargo . . . was the greatest haul [yet] recorded by any single expedition.'

13. *The Decades of the newe worlde* [ed. Eden], fol. 354v; cf. Hakluyt (1903–5), VI. 165; *Europeans in West Africa*, ed. Blake, II. 335–6.

14. C.M.MacInnes, *England and Slavery* (Bristol, Arrowsmith, 1934), 18.

15. Captain George Berkley, *The Naval History of Britain, from the Earliest Periods of which there are Accounts in History, to The Conclusion of the Year M.DCC.LVI.* [ed. John Hill] (T.Osborne & J.Shipton, etc., 1756), 292.

16. George Francis Dow, *Slave Ships and Slaving* (Salem, Mass., Marine Research Society, 1927), 21; Tom Glasgow Jnr, 'List of Ships in the Royal Navy from 1539 to 1588 – the Navy from its Infancy to the Defeat of the Spanish Armada', *Mariner's Mirror*, LVI (1970), 302.

17. Mary W.S. Hawkins, *Plymouth Armada Heroes: The Hawkins Family* (Plymouth, William Brendon & Son, 1888), 66; the coat of arms and crest are reproduced on p. 67. 'Sir John Hawkins's crest', in Nigel File and Chris Power, *Black Settlers in Britain, 1555–1958* (Heinemann Educational Books, 1981), 5, is a modern drawing.

18. When William Bragge claimed £6,875 from the East India Company for, amongst other items, 'thirteen negroes or Indian people, six women, seaven men and boyes'; see W.Pinkerton, 'Cats, Dogs, and Negroes as Articles of Commerce', *Notes and Queries*, 3rd ser. II (1862), 345–6. This is evidently a reference to Asian, not African, slaves.

19. Revd J.F.Chanter, 'On Certain Documents Relating to the History of Lynton and Countisbury', *Report and Transactions of the Devonshire Association for the Advancement of Science, Literature, and Art*, XXXVIII (1906), 240. It is sometimes asserted, as by James Walvin, *Black and White: The Negro and English Society 1555–1945* (Allen Lane, 1973), 7, that Edward Stanley, third Earl of Derby, employed black servants in the 1560s. This assertion is based on two of the earl's household regulations, dated 12 February 1568: 'No Slaves nor boyes shall sitt in the Hall but in place therefore to be appoynted convenyent' and 'The Yeman of Horses and Gromes of the Stable shall not suffre anie boyes or Slaves to abyde about the Stables nor lie in theym nor in any place aboute theym'; see William ffarington, *The Derby Household Books*, ed. Revd F.R.Raines (Stanley Papers, pt 2, Chetham Society, XXXI, 1853), 9. Alexander Savine, 'Bondmen under the Tudors', *Transactions of the Royal Historical Society*, n.s. XVII (1903), 250, calls this 'a very strange passage' and asks: 'May we suppose that Lord Derby had coloured people in his household?' According to C.S.L.Davies, 'Slavery and Protector Somerset: the Vagrancy Act of 1547', *Economic History Review*, 2nd ser. XIX (1966), 548 n. 3, 'Savine's suggestion . . . that they were Negroes seems the most likely'. But an editorial note by Raines in ffarington, 94–5, explains that these 'Slaves' were simply 'the villeins regardant of the manor' and adds: 'The manumission of these slaves was effected soon after the Reformation'. A 'barbaryen' named Lambert Waterson, who 'goeth to his parishe church', is recorded as living in St Giles in the Fields in 1568 (*Returns of Aliens Dwelling in the City and Suburbs of London from the Reign of Henry VIII to that of James I*, pt III, ed. R.E.G. and Ernest Kirk (Publications of the Huguenot Society of London, X, Aberdeen, 1907), 407), but his ethnic origin is not stated; James Walvin's assertion, in *The Black Presence: a documentary history of the Negro in England, 1555–1860* (Orbach & Chambers, 1971), 13, that some blacks 'actively participated in their local churches' by the end of the sixteenth century, seems to be based only on this doubtful reference.

20. *The Register of Baptisms, Marriages & Burials of the Parish of St. Andrews Plymouth Co. Devon A.D. 1581–1618 with Baptisms 1619–1633*, ed. M.C.S.Cruwys (Exeter, Devon & Cornwall Record Society, 1954), 57.

21. *Returns of Aliens*, pt III, ed. Kirk, 28, 54, 55; cf. W.E.Miller, 'Negroes in Elizabethan London', *Notes and Queries*, CCVI (1961), 138, noting 'the possibility that the writer was observing a distinction between the masculine and feminine forms of the word *Negro*'. Though no such distinction is recorded in *OED*, the feminine form *Negra* was used by Thomas Jordan in 1671; see p. 27 above. Walvin, *Black and White*, 8, asserts that 'a group of Negroes built their own house in London in 1597, contrary to building regulations'. This, if true, would indeed be remarkable, but it was in fact not 'a group of Negroes' but a man by the name of Negoose against whom the attorney-general informed for a breach of the building regulations; see John Hawarde, *Les Reportes de Cases in Camera Stellata 1593 to 1609*, ed. William Paley Baildon (Alfred Morrison, 1894), 79. The name is miscopied as 'Negroose' in the source cited by Walvin: E.M.Leonard, *The Early History of English Poor Relief* (Cambridge, University Press, 1900), 297n.

22. *CSP, Domestic Ser. 1595–1597*, 381.

23. See p. 473, notes 42 and 43, below.

24. *CSP, Domestic Ser. 1598–1601*, 199.

25. G.B.Harrison, *Shakespeare at Work 1592–1603* (Routledge, 1933), 311, 310; *Gesta Grayorum: or, The History of the High and mighty Prince, Henry, Prince of Purpoole* (W.Canning, 1688), 12.

26. Lord Chamberlain's Book, v. 34, p. 240, as quoted by Charlotte Carmichael Stopes, 'Elizabeth's Fools and Dwarfs', *Athenæum*, no. 4477 (16 August 1913), 160, and in her *Shakespeare's Environment* (G.Bell & Sons Ltd, 1914), 271.

27. A.C.Sewter, 'Queen Elizabeth at Kenilworth', *Burlington Magazine*, LXXVI (1940), 75. The entire panel is reproduced, in monochrome, as the frontispiece and the relevant detail as pl. ii(b). I am grateful to George F. Rehin for this reference. For doubts about the location of this scene, see H.M.Hake, ' "Queen Elizabeth at Kenilworth" ', *Burlington Magazine*, LXXVI (1940), 166, and Allardyce Nicoll, *The World of Harlequin: A Critical Study of the Commedia dell'Arte* (Cambridge, University Press, 1963), 225.

28. *Ben Jonson*, ed. C.H.Herford and Percy Simpson (Oxford, Clarendon Press, 1925–52), II. 265. The fashion continued after Elizabeth's death. Explaining the plot of his *Masque of Blackness* (1604–5), written for James I's queen, Anne, Ben Jonson says of the masquers: 'it was her Maiesties will, to haue them *Black-mores* at first'; see *The Workes of Beniamin Jonson* (Will Stansby, 1616), 893.

Queen Elizabeth's response

1. Cf. W.D.Jordan, *White over Black* (1968), 7–8, and see p. 135 above.
2. *Acts of the Privy Council of England*, n.s. XXVI, 1596–7, pp. 16–17.
3. *Acts of the Privy Council of England*, n.s. XXVI. 20–1.
4. Cecil Papers, 91/15, as quoted by E.D.Jones, *The Elizabethan Image of Africa* (1971), 20–1, and reproduced in facsimile, Jones, *Elizabethan Image*, 18–19, E.Jones, *Othello's Countrymen* (1965), pl. 5, and N.File and C.Power, *Black Settlers in Britain* (1981), 7. There is a summary of the proclamation in *Calendar of the Manuscripts of the Most Hon. Marquis of Salisbury*, XI (Dublin, HMSO, 1906), 569. The transcription in *Tudor Royal Proclamations*, ed. P.L.Hughes and J.F.Larkin (New Haven, Yale University Press, 1964–9), III. 221–2, contains several errors.

A Khoi-khoin in England

1. H.W.Debrunner, *Presence and Prestige* (1979), 58.
2. Edward Terry, *A Voyage to East-India* (J.Martin & J.Allestrye, 1655), 20–1; Major R.Raven-Hart, *Before van Riebeeck: Callers at South Africa from 1488 to 1652* (Cape Town, C.Struick (Pty) Ltd, 1967), 83.
3. Debrunner, 58.

2. 'Necessary Implements'

Sugar and slavery

1. C. Anne Wilson, *Food & Drink in Britain from the Stone Age to recent times* (Constable, 1973), 303.
2. Richard B. Sheridan, *Sugar and Slavery: An Economic History of the British West Indies 1623–1775* (Baltimore, Md, Johns Hopkins University Press, 1973), 25, 21.
3. *CSP, Colonial Ser. America and West Indies, 1677–1680*, 573.
4. Pinney Papers, Business Letter-books, 1764, as quoted by C.M.MacInnes, 'The Slave Trade', in *The Trade Winds: A Study of British Overseas Trade during the French Wars 1793–1815*, ed. C. Northcote Parkinson (Allen & Unwin, 1948), 257. See also Frank

Wesley Pitman, *The Development of the British West Indies 1700–1763* (Yale Historical Publications, Studies, IV, New Haven, Yale University Press, 1917), 62: 'It is very probable that the production of sugar would not have taken place as soon as it did if slavery had not existed to furnish a sufficiently large and continuous body of labor.'

5. See Richard Pares, *A West-India Fortune* (Longmans, Green & Co., 1950).
6. *Report of The Lords of the Committee of Council appointed for the Consideration of all Matters relating to Trade and Foreign Plantations* (1789), pt iv, Appendix to N° 1. A considerable part of this table is omitted from the reprint (*HCSP of the Eighteenth Century*, LXX (George III: Report of the Lords of Trade on the Slave Trade 1789, pt 2), 183), to which however subsequent references are given. See also James E. Merritt, 'The Trials and Tribulations of the late 18th century West African Slave Trade merchant', *Middlesex Polytechnic History Journal*, [no. 1] (June 1980), 113.
7. Attempts to show that in the eighteenth century the transport of manufactured goods to Africa, slaves to the West Indies, and sugar to England by the same ships was exceptional, and that the triangular trade was feasible only in the early stages of Caribbean economic development, are refuted by Walter E. Minchinton, 'The Triangular Trade Revisited', in *The Uncommon Market: Essays in the Economic History of the Atlantic Slave Trade*, ed. Henry A. Gemery and Jan S. Hogendorn (New York, Academic Press, 1979), 331–52 (see expecially p. 352: 'If the carriage of freight-earning cargoes on the three legs of a venture, one leg of which was devoted to the transport of slaves across the Atlantic, constituted a triangular trade, then the English slave trade in the eighteenth century was such a trade'). The traditional view of the triangular trade is also defended ('the classical triangular trade was still quite normal in the eighteenth century') by A.G.Hopkins, *An Economic History of West Africa* (Longman, 1973), 99, though he adds that 'the transportation of slaves and sugar cannot be understood simply in terms of the triangular trade alone'.
8. British Library Add. MS. 38,416 (Liverpool Papers, CCXXVII), fol. 26v.
9. [Adam Anderson], *An Historical and Chronological Deduction of the Origin of Commerce, From the Earliest Accounts to the present Time* (A.Millar etc., 1764), II. 379.
10. Alfred P. Wadsworth and Julia de Lacy Mann, *The Cotton Trade and Industrial Lancashire 1600–1780* (Publications of the University of Manchester, Economic History Ser. vii, Manchester University Press, 1931), 118–19, 151, 153–4, 425; D.C.Coleman, *Industry in Tudor and Stuart England* (Macmillan, 1975), 32.
11. Wadsworth and Mann, 146; C.R.Fay, *English Economic History mainly since 1700* (Cambridge, W. Heffer & Sons Ltd, 1940), 140. See also: [John Ogden], *A Description of Manchester* [1783] (reprinted,

Manchester, John Heywood, [1860]), 49; George W. Daniels, *The Early English Cotton Industry with some unpublished letters of Samuel Crompton* (Publications of the University of Manchester, Historical Ser. xxxvi, Manchester University Press, 1920), 29 n. 3, 60. For Liverpool's cloth exports (and, of Indian textiles, re-exports) to Africa in 1770, including large quantities of sailcloth, see William Enfield, *An Essay towards the History of Leverpool* (Warrington, 1773), 84–5.

12. *HCSP of the Eighteenth Century*, LXX. 195.
13. *An Historical Geography of England before A.D. 1800*, ed. H.C.Darby (Cambridge, University Press, 1951), 495.
14. It is beyond the scope of this book to enter into the controversy on the view advanced by Eric Williams, in his *Capitalism and Slavery* (Chapel Hill, University of North Carolina Press, 1944), that the profits from the triangular trade became a major factor in the accumulation of British capital, and that this accumulation was a major and probably, at times, decisive contribution to the process of industrialization. As Basil Davidson remarks (*Black Mother: Africa and the Atlantic Slave Trade*, revised edition (Harmondsworth, Penguin Books, 1980), 83), 'in spite of much largely irrelevant controversy, it is a view that has not been overturned'. See also Richard B. Sheridan, 'The Plantation Revolution and the Industrial Revolution, 1625–1775', *Caribbean Studies*, IX/3 (October 1969), [5]: 'An adequate analysis of the Industrial Revolution involves a consideration of not just a single economy but of a whole trading area of economic interactions within which one national economy, Great Britain, managed to take the lead . . . The Atlantic was the most dynamic trading area, and . . ., outside the metropolis, the most important element in the growth of this area in the century or more prior to 1776 was the slave-plantation, particularly of the cane sugar variety in the islands of the Caribbean Sea.'
15. John Lord, *Capital and Steam-Power: 1750–1800* (P.S.King & Son, 1923), 113 ('It was with the money gained from the West Indian trade that capital was eventually found to finance Watt'); Erich Roll, *An Early Experiment in Industrial Organization, being a history of the firm of Boulton & Watt, 1775–1805* (Longmans, Green, 1930), 101.
16. Capital for south Wales industry was obtained in the eighteenth century partly from 'Bristol and London merchants, much of whose wealth had originally been derived from the slave trade'; see D.J.Davies, *The Economic History of South Wales prior to 1800* (Cardiff, University of Wales Press Board, 1933), 101. In 1765 Anthony Bacon was granted a contract to furnish 'seasoned, able and working negroes' to the government in the islands of Grenada, the Grenadines, Tobago, St Vincent, and Dominica; in 1768–76 a total of almost £67,000 was paid to Bacon and his partner Lewis Chauvet under this heading; Bacon took a 99-year lease on 4,000 acres of virgin mineral land around the then hamlet of Merthyr Tydfil for an

annual rent of £100 (some sources say £200), developed iron-foundries and coal-mines there which were known colloquially as 'Bacon's Mineral Kingdom', made the Cyfarthfa ironworks into 'the largest munition works yet established on the coalfield', and accumulated 'a splendid fortune'; see Benj. Heath Malkin, *The Scenery, Antiquities, and Biography, of South Wales* (T.N.Longman & O.Rees, 1804), 174–6; Harry Scrivenor, *A Comprehensive History of the Iron Trade* (Smith, Elder & Co., 1841), 121–2; Samuel Smiles, *Industrial Biography: Iron Workers and Tool Makers* (John Murray, 1863), 130; Charles Wilkins, *The History of Merthyr Tydfil* (Merthyr Tydfil, Harry Wood Southey, 1867), 144ff.; Robert L. Galloway, *Annals of Coal Mining and the Coal Trade* (Colliery Guardian Co., 1898), 360; John Lloyd, *The Early History of the Old South Wales Iron Works (1760 to 1840)* (Bedford Press, 1906), [48]–63, [72]–77, 156–60; T.S.Ashton and Joseph Sykes, *The Coal Industry of the Eighteenth Century* (Publications of the University of Manchester, Economic History Ser. v, Manchester University Press, 1929), 191; L.B.Namier, 'Anthony Bacon, M.P., an Eighteenth-Century Merchant', *Journal of Economic and Business History*, II (1929–30), 25, 39ff.; J.H.Clapham, *The Early Railway Age* (An Economic History of Modern Britain, [I], second edition, Cambridge University Press, 1950), 187–8; A.H.John, *The Industrial Development of South Wales 1750–1850: An Essay* (Cardiff, University of Wales Press, 1950), 99; John P.Addis, *The Crawshay Dynasty: A Study in Industrial Organisation and Development, 1765–1867* (Cardiff, University of Wales Press, 1957), 1–2. Bacon was MP for Aylesbury, 1764–84, paying five guineas a head for his votes; for a brief biography see Sir Lewis Namier and John Brooke, *The House of Commons 1754–1790* (HMSO, 1964), II. 35–6. Thomas Harris, a Bristol slave-merchant with interests in the sugar industry, was a partner in the New Willey furnace and in 1768 bought an interest in the Dowlais ironworks, neighbour and rival to Cyfarthfa and by 1815 the third largest in Merthyr Tydfil; see Alan Birch, *The Economic History of the British Iron and Steel Industry 1784–1879* (Frank Cass & Co. Ltd, 1967), 67, and D.W.Thoms, 'The Mills Family: London Sugar Merchants of the Eighteenth Century', *Business History*, XI (1969), 10.

17. Capital for the Thorncliffe ironworks at Chapeltown, producing iron rails for the south Yorkshire colliery wagon-ways, came partly from a bequest by 'a wealthy West Indian merchant of Sheffield'; see Thomas Southcliffe Ashton, *Iron and Steel in the Industrial Revolution* (Manchester, University Press, 1924), 156–7.

18. Richard Pennant, first Baron Penrhyn, inherited the largest estate in Jamaica, succeeded through marriage to estates in Caernarvon in 1785, devoted his plantation profits to the development of the Penrhyn slate quarries (where he paid a shilling a day to workmen producing roofing slates), built roads, and constructed the harbour of

Port Penrhyn (formerly Abercegin), near Bangor, in 1790; see Elias Owen, 'The Penrhyn Slate Quarry', *Red Dragon*, VII (1885), [318]–339; A.H.Dodd, *The Industrial Revolution in North Wales* (Cardiff, University of Wales Press Board, 1933), 37, 91, 125, 204–8, 214; R.B.Sheridan, 'The Wealth of Jamaica in the Eighteenth Century', *Economic History Review*, 2nd ser. XVIII (1965), 307–8; Michael Craton, *Sinews of Empire: A Short History of British Slavery* (Temple Smith, 1974), 153; Jean Lindsay, *A History of the North Wales Slate Industry* (Newton Abbot, David & Charles, 1974), 40ff. Pennant was MP for Petersfield (1761–7) and Liverpool (1767–80 and 1784–90) and chairman of the West India Committee; for a brief biography see Namier and Brooke, III. 262.

19. For the connections of the Liverpool West India interest (General Isaac Gascoyne, John Gladstone, John Moss) with the building of the Liverpool and Manchester Railway, see John Francis, *A History of the English Railway; its social relations and revelations: 1820–1845* (Longman, Brown, Green & Longmans, 1851), I. 122, 123; Frederick S.Williams, *Our Iron Roads: their history, construction, and social influences* (Ingram, Cooke, & Co., 1852), 323, 337; W.F.Crick and J.E.Wadsworth, *A Hundred Years of Joint Stock Banking* (Hodder & Stoughton, 1936), 144–5; Robert E.Carlson, *The Liverpool & Manchester Railway Project 1821–1831* (Newton Abbot, David & Charles, 1969), 47–8.

20. For the connections of the Bristol West India interest (Robert Bright etc.) with the building of the Great Western Railway, see John Latimer, *The Annals of Bristol in the Nineteenth Century* (Bristol, W.& F. Morgan, 1887), 189.

21. N.Deerr, *The History of Sugar* (1949–50), II. 290.

22. J.F.Rees, *A Survey of Economic Development with special reference to Great Britain* (Sir Isaac Pitman & Sons, Ltd, 1933), 143.

23. *CSP, Colonial Ser. America and West Indies, 1661–1668*, 167. In 1676 Sir Jonathan Atkins, governor of Barbados, told the Lords of Trade that '3 blacks work better & cheaper than 1 white man'; see A.P.Thornton, 'The Organization of the Slave Trade in the English West Indies, 1660–1685', *William and Mary Quarterly*, XII (1955), 400.

24. [Edward Littleton], *The Groans of the Plantations: or A True Account of their Grievous and Extreme Sufferings By the Heavy Impositions upon Sugar, And other Hardships* (M.Clark, 1689), 7.

25. [Charles Davenant], *Discourses on the Publick Revenues, and on the Trade of England* (James Knapton, 1698), II. 255–7. Twenty years later the secretary to the Customs copied the last two sentences almost word for word; see [William Wood], *A Survey of Trade* (W.Hinchliffe, 1718), 179, 191.

26. [Joshua Gee], *The Trade and Navigation of Great-Britain Considered* (Sam. Buckley, 1729), 25, 126.

27. [Malachy Postlethwayt], *The African Trade, the Great Pillar and Support of the British Plantation Trade in America* (J.Robinson, 1745), 34.
28. [Malachy Postlethwayt], *The National and Private Advantages of the African Trade Considered* (John & Paul Knapton, 1746), 2. Cf. also Malachy Postlethwayt, *Considerations On the Revival of the Royal-British-Assiento; between His Catholick-Majesty, And the Honourable The South-Sea Company* (John & Paul Knapton, 1749), 43 ('it is certain the best Branch of the *African*-Trade is that of *Negroes*'); Malachy Postlethwayt, *The Importance of the African Expedition Considered* (M.Cooper, 1758), p. ii ('The trade of *Africa*, as well to the *French* as the *English*, is the great foundation of their American commerce and navigation, as that alone supplies both nations with negroe-labourers to cultivate their West India colonies.').
29. *A Treatise upon the Trade from Great-Britain to Africa, Humbly recommended to the attention of Government*, by an African Merchant (R.Baldwin, 1772), 4. J.F.Rees, 'The Phases of British Commercial Policy in the Eighteenth Century', *Economica*, V (1925), 143, attributes this quotation to Postlethwayt, but gives no reference.
30. Patrick Richardson, *Empire & Slavery* (Longmans, 1968), 12.
31. [Edward Long], *The History of Jamaica: or, General Survey of the antient and modern state of that island* (T.Lowndes, 1774), I. 378; Pitman, 11–13, 30–41, 104; Sheridan, *Sugar and Slavery*, 59. See also K.G.Davies, 'The Origins of the Commission System in the West India Trade', *Transactions of the Royal Historical Society*, 5th ser. II (1952), 91: 'Many . . . retained family ties with England. Almost, it seems, as soon as the "frontier phase" in a West Indian colony's history was ended and the estate put on a working footing, the planter and his family began to aspire to the pleasures of civilized life "at home".'
32. *Parliamentary History of England*, XIX (1777–8), col. 1316.
33. Lillian M.Penson, 'The London West India Interest in the Eighteenth Century', *English Historical Review*, XXXVI (1921), 374.
34. And 'a curious complaint on this score is to be found in the West India Committee archives'; see Lowell Joseph Ragatz, *The Old Plantation System in the British Caribbean* (Bryan Edwards Press, [1925]), 37 and n. 57, reprinted in his *The Fall of the Planter Class in the British Caribbean, 1763–1833: a study in social and economic history* (New York, Century Co., 1928), 50 and n. 5. See also Lowell Joseph Ragatz, 'Absentee Landlordism in the British Caribbean, 1750–1833', *Agricultural History*, V (1931), 10–11.
35. [Tobias Smollett], *The Expedition of Humphry Clinker* (W.Johnston, 1771), I. 70–1. See also William Cobbett, *Rural Rides in the Counties of Surrey*, etc. (William Cobbett, 1830), 522: 'CHELTENHAM . . . is what they call a "*watering-place*"; that is to say, a place, to which East India plunderers, West India floggers, English tax-gorgers, together

with gluttons, drunkards, and debauchees of all descriptions, *female* as well as male, resort, at the suggestion of silently laughing quacks, in the hope of getting rid of the bodily consequences of their manifold sins and iniquities. When I enter a place like this, I always feel disposed to squeeze up my nose with my fingers.'

36. [Trelawney Wentworth], *The West India Sketch Book* (Whittaker & Co., 1834), II. 70n.

37. [John Fothergill], *Considerations Relative to the North American Colonies* (Henry Kent, 1765), 41–2.

38. [Davenant], II. 203 ('There are Grounds to believe, that for these last 20 Years, the *West-Indies* have sent us back annually, about 300 Persons, of their Offspring, with this Advantage, that the Fathers went out Poor, and the Children came home Rich'); [Long], I. 510–11; *Caribbeana, being Miscellaneous Papers relating to the History, Genealogy, Topography, and Antiquities of the British West Indies*, ed. Vere Langford Oliver (Mitchell Hughes & Clarke, 1910–19), I. 55; Ragatz, *Old Plantation System*, 15; Ragatz, *Fall of the Planter Class*, 22; Ragatz, 'Absentee Landlordism in the British Caribbean', 9–10; Pares, 76.

39. Entertainingly described by Richard S.Dunn, *Sugar and Slaves: the rise of the planter class in the English West Indies, 1624–1713* (Jonathan Cape, 1973), 268–9, 279–80, 285–6.

40. For 'privilege Negroes', see: John Latimer, *The Annals of Bristol in the Eighteenth Century* ([Bristol], for the author, 1893), 146 and 144 (the captain and mate of the *Dispatch*, sailing from Bristol in 1725, were each allowed to buy two slaves on his own account); F.C.Prideaux Nash, 'Extracts from a Slaver's Log', *Mariner's Mirror*, VI (1920), 8 (the inventory of the goods of John Chapman, first mate of the *Daniel and Henry* of Exeter, who died during a slaving voyage in 1700, included '1 man slave' and '1 girl ditto', both 'marked J.C.'; these and '19 small ellophant teeth' were 'goods for private trading'); W.E.Minchinton, 'The Voyage of the Snow *Africa*', *Mariner's Mirror*, XXXVII (1951), 192; Bradbury B.Parkinson, 'A Slaver's Accounts', *Accounting Research*, II (1951), 144–50; Ralph Davis, *The Rise of the English Shipping Industry In the Seventeenth and Eighteenth Centuries* (Macmillan & Co. Ltd, 1962), 148–9.

41. A.P.Kup, 'Instructions to the Royal African Company's factor at Bunce, 1702', *Sierra Leone Studies*, n.s. no. 5 (December 1955), 52.

42. *Africa Remembered: Narratives by West Africans from the Era of the Slave Trade*, ed. Philip D.Curtin (Madison, University of Wisconsin Press, 1967), 14.

Chattels and status symbols

1. Richard Iobson, *The Golden Trade: or, A discouery of the Riuer Gambra, and the Golden Trade of the Aethiopians* (Nicholas Bourne, 1623), 88–9.

2. N.Deerr, *The History of Sugar* (1949–50), II. 267.
3. James A.Williamson, *The Caribbee Islands under the Proprietary Patents* (Oxford University Press, 1926), 31.
4. *CSP, Colonial Ser. 1547–1660*, 114; Elizabeth Donnan, *Documents Illustrative of the History of the Slave Trade to America* (Washington, DC, Carnegie Institution of Washington, 1930–5), I. 84.
5. *CSP, Domestic Ser. 1637*, 533–4; *CSP, Colonial Ser. 1547–1660*, 259–60; William Robert Scott, *The Constitution and Finance of English, Scottish and Irish Joint-Stock Companies to 1720* (Cambridge, University Press, 1910–12), II. 15; Donnan, I. 84.
6. J.H.Parry, *The Age of Reconnaissance* (Weidenfeld & Nicolson, 1963), 266.
7. *The Several Declarations of the Company of Royal Adventurers of England trading into Africa* (1667), 8. For the text of the Royal Adventurers' charter, see *Select Charters of Trading Companies A.D. 1530–1707*, ed. Cecil T.Carr (Publications of the Selden Society, XXVIII, Bernard Quaritch, 1913), 177–81. George Frederick Zook, *The Company of Royal Adventurers Trading into Africa* (Lancaster, Pa, New Era Printing Co., 1919) is a useful brief account.
8. *The Several Declarations*, 11–12; Donnan, I. 169–72; K.G.Davies, *The Royal African Company* (Longmans, Green, 1957), 41; Charles Wilson, *England's Apprenticeship 1603–1763* (Longmans, 1965), 173. For the Royal African Company, see also D.A.G.Waddell, 'Queen Anne's Government and the Slave Trade', *Caribbean Quarterly*, VI (1960), 7–10.
9. Donnan, I. 126, 128. For the Guinea Company, see: *CSP, Colonial Ser. 1547–1660*, 20, 153; *CSP, Domestic Ser. 1631–1633*, 186; *Select Charters of Trading Companies*, ed. Carr, p. xliv (with the text of the 1618 charter at pp. 99–106); Scott, II. 11–15; Donnan, I. 78–81; Davies, 39–40.
10. Donnan, I. 129, 130.
11. *Diary of Samuel Pepys*, ed. Robert Latham and William Matthews, III (G.Bell & Sons Ltd, 1970), 95. This entry is dated 30 May 1662.
12. *CSP, Domestic Ser. November 1667 to September 1668*, 59.
13. Davies, 300.
14. Contrary to the assertion of Anthony J.Barker, *The African Link: British Attitudes to the Negro in the Era of the Atlantic Slave Trade, 1550–1807* (Frank Cass, 1978), 29, such advertisements began to appear long before the 1680s.
15. *Mercurius Politicus comprising The sum of Foreign Intelligence with the Affairs now to foot in the Three Nations of England, Scotland, & Ireland*, no. 582 (4–11 August 1659), 654.
16. *The London Gazette*, no. 2185 (25–28 October 1686).
17. *The London Gazette*, no. 2270 (18–22 August 1687).
18. *The London Gazette*, no. 2564 (5–9 June 1690).
19. e.g. in *The London Gazette*, no. 2114 (18–22 February 1685 [1686]),

two guineas reward was offered for the return of a spaniel bitch; no. 2120 (11–15 March 1685 [1686]), three guineas was offered for the return of a black mare; no. 2326 (1–5 March 1687 [1688]), £4 was offered for the return of a spaniel dog; no. 2328 (8–12 March 1687 [1688]), four guineas was offered for the return of a dapple grey gelding.

20. But see p. 228 above and pp. 526–7 n. 3 below.

21. *The London Gazette*, no. 2122 (18–22 March 1685 [1686]).

22. *The London Gazette*, no. 2309 (2–5 January 1687 [1688]).

23. *The London Gazette*, no. 2433 (4–7 March 1688 [1689]).

24. *The London Gazette*, no. 2605 (27–30 October 1690).

25. *The London Gazette*, no. 2661 (11–14 May 1691).

26. 'Black Slaves in England', *Chambers's Journal*, [5th ser.] VIII (1891), [65].

27. John Dryden, 'Prologue to *The Prophetess*', in *The Poems and Fables of John Dryden*, ed. James Kinsley (Oxford University Press, 1970), 440.

28. [Colley] Cibber, *The Double Gallant: or, the Sick Lady's Cure*, second edition (Bernard Lintott, [*c.* 1715]), 28.

29. *The London Gazette*, no. 2122 (18–22 March 1685 [1686]).

30. *The London Gazette*, no. 2150 (24–28 June 1686).

31. *The London Gazette*, no. 2176 (23–27 September 1686).

32. *The London Gazette*, no. 2203 (27–30 December 1686).

33. *The London Gazette*, no. 2270 (18–22 August 1687).

34. *The London Gazette*, no. 2279 (19–22 September 1687). This is one of the rare advertisements that state where the slave was brought from. On arriving in England, Peter would have been about nine years old.

35. *The London Gazette*, no. 2631 (26–29 January 1690 [1691]). Slaves were normally branded on breast or shoulder; children of slaves were branded at the age of three; see also p. 53 above and pp. 495–6 n. 35 below.

36. *Memoirs of Sir John Reresby*, ed. Andrew Browning (Glasgow, Jackson, Son & Co., 1936), 108.

37. Middlesex Sessions Book 472, February 1690, p. 41, as summarized in W.J.Hardy, *Middlesex County Records: Calendar of the Sessions Books 1689 to 1709* (Sir Richard Nicholson, 1905), 6.

38. *Moneys Received and Paid for Secret Services of Charles II. and James II. from 30th March, 1679, to 25th December, 1688*, ed. John Yonge Akerman (Camden Society, LII, 1851), 58.

39. *Diary of Samuel Pepys*, ed. Latham and Matthews, IX (G.Bell & Sons Ltd, 1976), 510. This entry is dated 5 April 1669.

40. Cf. J.Jean Hecht, *Continental and Colonial Servants in Eighteenth Century England* (Smith College Studies in History, XL, Northampton, Mass., 1954), 40, illustrating this usage by quoting from a letter written by Horace Walpole in 1752: visiting Mrs George Boscawen, he had found 'a black boy at the door – Lord thinks I, this can't be Mrs Boscawen's – however, Pompey let me up' (*Horace Walpole's Correspondence with George Montagu*, i, ed. W.S.Lewis and Ralph S.Brown, Jr, The Yale Edition of Horace Walpole's Correspondence, IX (Oxford University Press, 1941), 141). Steele used 'Pompey' as the signature to a satirical letter in *The Tatler*, no. 245 (31 October–2 November 1710): 'I Am a Black-moor Boy, and have, by my Lady's Order, been christened by the Chaplain. The good Man has gone further with me, and told me a great deal of good News; as, that I am as good as my Lady her self as I am a Christian, and many other Things: But for all this, the Parrot who came over with me from our Country is as much esteemed by her as I am. Besides this, the Shock-Dog [i.e. rough-haired dog] has a Collar that cost almost as much as mine. I desire also to know, whether now I am a Christian, I am obliged to dress like a *Turk*, and wear a Turbant.'

41. [Charlotte Mary Yonge], *History of Christian Names* (Parker, Son, & Bourn, 1863), I. 323.
42. V.Sackville-West, *Knole and the Sackvilles* (Heinemann, 1922), 191. He appears as 'John Morockoe, *a Blackamoor*', under the heading 'Kitchen and Scullery', in a list of the Earl of Dorset's household and family, 1613–24; see George C.Williamson, *Lady Anne Clifford, Countess of Dorset, Pembroke & Montgomery, 1590–1676: her Life, Letters and Work* (Kendal, Titus Wilson, 1922), 478; cf. also *The Diary of the Lady Anne Clifford*, ed. V. Sackville-West (Heinemann, 1923), p. lxi.
43. 'Grace Robinson, a *Blackamoor*' appears in the Earl of Dorset's 1613–24 household list under the heading 'The Laundry-maids' Table'; see Williamson, 478, and cf. also *The Diary of the Lady Anne Clifford*, ed. Sackville-West, p. lxi.
44. *A Conference, On the Doctrine of Transubstantiation, between His Grace the Duke of Buckingham, and Father Fitzgerald, an Irish Jesuit* (Ferd. Burleigh & A.Dod, 1714), 11–13.
45. *Diary of Samuel Pepys*, ed. Latham and Matthews, VI (G.Bell & Sons Ltd, 1972), 215. This entry is dated 7 September 1665. I am grateful to Deirdre Toomey for this reference.
46. G.Bernard Wood, 'A Negro Trail in the North of England', *Country Life Annual*, 1967, p. 42.
47. The Mignard portrait is reproduced in colour in Colin Nicolson, *Strangers to England: Immigration to England 1100–1952* (Wayland Publishers, 1974), [62], in monochrome in *History Today*, XXVII (1977), 45, and XXXI/[9] (September 1981), 37. For the Kneller portraits, see J. Douglas Stewart, *Sir Godfrey Kneller* (G.Bell & Sons, 1971), 71, 72, 28.
48. *CSP, Domestic Ser. 1627–1628*, 521.
49. See the advertisement in *The London Gazette*, no. 1996 (1–5 January

1684 [1685]), referring to 'a Negro about 16 years of age' who had run away from Sir Phineas Pet 'at the Navy Office'.

50. *The London Gazette*, no. 5343 (2–5 July 1715).

Pageant performers

1. *A Calendar of Dramatic Records in the Books of the Livery Companies of London 1485–1640*, ed. Jean Robertson and D.J.Gordon (Malone Society Collections, III, 1954), pp. xvii, 5, 6, 27; Sheila Williams, 'The Lord Mayor's Show in Tudor and Stuart Times', *The Guildhall Miscellany*, 1/10 (September 1959), 5, 6. In 1519 the Skinners' Company paid 2*d.* each to ten boy 'morens' (*A Calendar*, ed. Robertson and Gordon, pp. xvii, 4). There is a contemporary account of the Midsummer Show by Lodovico Spinelli, secretary to the Venetian ambassador in England, who took the King of the Moors to represent Pluto and his attendants goaded by men and naked boys, 'dyed black like devils'. The King was seated on a serpent that spat fire when he brandished his sword; in front of him were an ox, a lion, and some serpents (*CSP and Manuscripts . . . in the archives and collections of Venice*, III. 136–7). Norwich too had a taste for the exotic: an image of a naked 'morien' on top of a pavilion was a prominent feature of the inauguration of its mayor in 1556 (Robert Withington, *English Pageantry: an Historical Outline* (Cambridge, Mass., Harvard University Press, 1918–20), II. 16).
2. *A Calendar*, ed. Robertson and Gordon, pp. 38, xxv, 81; [George Peele], *The Device of the Pageant borne before Woolstone Dixi Lord Maior of the Citie of London* (Edward Allde, 1585), sig. A2r, reprinted in *The Harleian Miscellany*, X, ed. Thomas Park (White & Cochrane, etc., 1813), 381.
3. The Midsummer Show was 'the principal root of the mayorial pageantry' (Williams, 4).
4. Thomas Middleton, *The Triumphs of Truth: A Solemnity vnparalleld for Cost, Art, and Magnificence* (Nicholas Okes, 1613), sigs. B4v–C1v.
5. A[nthony]. M[unday]., *Chrysanaleia: The Golden Fishing: Or, Honour of Fishmongers* (George Purslowe, 1616), sig. B1v. The contemporary illustration, which shows the 'tributarie Kings' on foot, in feathered coronets and gilt armour, four carrying javelins, five carrying ingots of precious metal, is reproduced in Anthony Munday, *The Fishmongers' Pageant, on Lord Mayor's Day, 1616*, ed. John Gough Nichols (Worshipful Company of Fishmongers, 1844), pl. [3].
6. John Webster, *Monuments of Honour* (Nicholas Okes, 1624), as reprinted in *The Complete Works of John Webster*, ed. F.L.Lucas (Chatto & Windus, 1927), III. 323.
7. Thomas Dekker, *London Tempe, or, The Feild of Happines* (Nicholas Okes, 1629). sig. B2r; cf. *A Calendar*, ed. Robertson and Gordon, 118: 'The third Shewe is an Estridge cutt out of Timb[er] to life

biting a horse Shoe. On this bird rides an Indian boy holding in one hand a longe Tobacco pipe and in t'other a darte.'

8. The contemporary sketch, by Abram Booth, secretary to the Netherlands East India Company delegation which was in England in 1629, is reproduced in *A Calendar of Dramatic Records of the London Clothworkers' Company*, ed. Jean Robertson (Malone Society Collections, V, 1959 [1960]), facing p. [2].
9. J[ohn]. B[ulteel]., *Londons Triumph: or, The Solemn and Magnificent reception of of* [sic] *that Honourable Gentleman, Robert Tichburn, Lord Major* (N.Brook, 1656), 12.
10. John Tatham, *Londons Triumphs, celebrated The Nine and twentieth day of this present Month of October, 1657* (J.Bell, 1657), sig. B2r.
11. J[ohn]. Tatham, *Londons Tryumph, presented by Industry and Honour* (Thomas Mabb, 1658), 9.
12. John Tatham, *Londinum* [sic] *Triumphans: Londons Triumphs Celebrated* (W.G., 1663), 5.
13. Tho. Jordan, *London's Resurrection to Joy and Triumph Expressed in Sundry Shews, Shapes, Scenes, Speeches, and Songs in Parts* (Henry Brome, 1671), 3–4, 20. For an earlier use of the feminine form *Negra*, unrecorded in *OED*, see p. 9 above.
14. Tho. Jordan, *London Triumphant: or, The City in Jollity and Splendour: expressed In various Pageants, Shapes, Scenes, Speeches and Songs* (Nath. Brook & John Playford, 1672), 3–4, 6, 8–9, 11.
15. I have argued this in detail in a paper on 'Black Pageant Performers and Musicians in Britain before 1800', presented to the International Conference on the History of Blacks in Britain, London, 28–30 September 1981.
16. Tho. Jordan, *London in its Splendor: consisting of Triumphant Pageants* (Nath. Brook & John Playford, 1673), 7, 9, 11–12.
17. Tho. Jordan, *The Goldsmiths Jubile: or, Londons Triumphs: containing, A Description of the several Pageants* (John Playford, 1674), 8.
18. Tho. Jordan, *The Triumphs of London: Performed on Friday, Octob. 29. 1675* (John Playford, 1675), 13.
19. Tho. Jordan, *The Triumphs of London: performed On Tuesday, October XXIX. 1678* (John Playford, 1678), 3, 7.
20. Tho. Jordan, *London in Luster: projecting Many bright Beams of Triumph: disposed into Several Representations of Scenes and Pageants* (John Playford, 1679), 13.
21. Tho. Jordan, *London's Glory, or, the Lord Mayor's Show: Containing an Illustrious Description of the several triumphant pageants* (John & Henry Playford, 1680), 8.
22. Tho. Jordan, *London's Joy, or, the Lord Mayor's Show: triumphantly Exhibited in Various Representations, Scenes, and splendid Ornaments, with divers pertinent Figures and Movements* (John & Henry Playford, 1681), 5, 13–14.

23. M[atthew]. Taubman, *London's Triumph, or the Goldsmiths Jubilee* (J.Leake, 1687), 5.
24. E[lkanah]. S[ettle]., *The Triumphs of London, Performed on Thursday, Octob. 29. 1691* (Abel Roper, 1691), 9.
25. E[lkanah]. S[ettle]., *The Triumphs of London: Performed on Saturday, Octob. 29. 1692* (Randal Taylor, 1692), 3. There were also 'two Tawny-Moors richly adorned', on griffins (p. 5).
26. E[lkanah]. S[ettle]., *The Triumphs of London: Performed on Monday, Octob. 30th. 1693* (Benjamin Johnson, 1693), 14–15.
27. E[lkanah]. S[ettle]., *The Triumphs of London: Performed on Tuesday, Octob. 29. 1695* (Richard Baldwin, 1695), 14.
28. [Elkanah Settle], *The Triumphs of London For the Inauguration of the Right Honourable Sir Charles Duncombe, Knight: Lord Mayor of the City of London* (A.Baldwin, 1708), 3, 5, pl. [3]; cf. Withington, II. 86.
29. [Edward Ward], *The London Spy*, pt x (August 1699), 13, 14.
30. Bryant Lillywhite, *London Signs* (Allen & Unwin, 1962), 44–6, 53, 41–3; Jacob Larwood and John Camden Hotten, *English Inn Signs* (Chatto & Windus, 1951), 252–3.
31. *A Reply of Sir George Downing Knight and Baronet, Envoy Extraordinary from His Majesty of Great-Britain, &c. to the Remarks of the Deputies of the Estates-General, upon his Memorial Of December 20. 1664. Old Stile* (1665), 42–3, 44.
32. *The Character of a Town Misse* (W.L., 1675), 7.
33. *Register of Baptisms . . . of the Parish of St. Andrews Plymouth*, ed. M.C.S. Cruwys (1954), 587 (Elizabeth, daughter of 'Angell, *a Blackmoore*', baptized in 1633, the reputed father being a Fleming); *Bedfordshire Parish Registers*, ed. F.G. Emmison, VIII (Bedford, County Record Office, 1934), 18 ('Robart the blake more servant to Sr Gorge Blundell' baptized at Cardington, 1662); *Bedfordshire Parish Registers*, ed. Emmison, III (1931), 40 (George, son of 'Adkins, a blackimore', baptized at Woburn, 1682); John Kennedy, *A History of the Parish of Leyton, Essex* (Leyton, Phelps Brothers, 1894), 116 (a 'blakeomore' baptized, 1667), 117 (a 'Black mayd' baptized, 1696); *The Registers of St Bees, Cumberland*, trans. H.B.Stout (Parish Register Section of Cumberland and Westmorland Antiquarian and Archæological Society, 1968), I. 137, II. 131 (Jane, 'a Negro servant of Mr George Gale' of Whitehaven, baptized January 1700 and buried the following month). I owe these references to J.Walvin, *Black and White* (1973), 14–15.
34. Walvin, *Black and White*, 11.
35. Henry T.Weyman, 'The Members of Parliament for Bishops Castle', *Transactions of the Shropshire Archæological and Natural History Society*, 2nd ser. X (1898), 53, citing Shelve parish register. I owe this reference to Walvin, *Black and White*, 11.
36. *The Records of a Church of Christ in Bristol, 1640–1687*, ed. Roger Hayden (Bristol Record Society, XXVII, 1974), 9, 101–2.

37. *Records of a Church of Christ*, ed. Hayden, 9, 189.
38. John Latimer, *The Annals of Bristol in the Seventeenth Century* (Bristol, William George's Sons, 1900), 344. 'There was a Dorothy Smith in membership [of the Church of Christ] at Broadmead during these years, but the connection cannot be clearly established' (*Records of a Church of Christ*, ed. Hayden, 10).
39. R.J.Mitchell and M.D.R.Leys, *A History of the English People* (Longmans, Green & Co., 1950), 526. Unfortunately the location of this tradition is not stated.

3. Britain's slave ports

A profitable business

1. C.M.MacInnes, *Bristol and the Slave Trade* (Bristol branch of the Historical Association, 1963), 7.
2. For the use of this metaphor in relation to Bristol, see J.F.Nicholls and John Taylor, *Bristol Past and Present* (Bristol, J.W.Arrowsmith, 1881–2), III. 165: ' "There is not", writes a local annalist in the reign of Queen Anne, "a brick in the city but what is cemented with the blood of a slave. Sumptuous mansions, luxurious living, liveried menials, were the produce of the wealth made from the sufferings and groans of the slaves bought and sold by the Bristol merchants. From the first cargo of human flesh sent to Ireland until the abolishing of the abhorrent traffic, they traded largely in the living commodity. In their child-like simplicity they could not feel the iniquity of the merchandise, but they could feel it lucrative; advancing it as a reason for certain privileges." ' This is clearly a reference to the Bristol traffic in English slaves, for which see p. 38 above and p. 482 n. 2 below. No source is given, and I have not succeeded in tracing the 'local annalist'. The earliest use in print of the metaphor in relation to Liverpool seems to be by J[ohn]. Corry, *The History of Lancashire* (Geo. B.Whittaker, 1825), II. 690: 'Several of the principal streets of the town may be said to have been marked out by the chains, and the walls of the houses cemented by the blood[,] of Africans!' It appears in a more familiar form as an anecdote told of the actor George Frederick Cooke (1756–1812), who 'was not famous for his sobriety, and one night, being hissed for his usual sin, he rushed forward to the lights, and most unceremoniously told the audience that "he was not there to be insulted by a set of wretches, every brick in whose infernal town was cemented by an African's blood!" This was a home-thrust for our grandfathers' ([James Aspinall], *Liverpool a few Years since: by an Old Stager* (Whittaker & Co., 1852), 152).
3. James Evan Baillie, as quoted by C.M.MacInnes, *A Gateway of Empire* (Bristol, Arrowsmith, 1939), 370.

4. Walter Minchinton, *The Port of Bristol in the Eighteenth Century* (Bristol branch of the Historical Association, 1962), 1–2: 'The eighteenth century was Bristol's golden age . . . Rum, slaves, tobacco and sugar were the main ingredients of Bristol's prosperity.'
5. Paul G.E.Clemens, 'The Rise of Liverpool, 1665–1750', *Economic History Review*, 2nd ser. XXIX (1976), 211; T.W.Freeman, H.B.Rodgers, and R.H.Kinvig, *Lancashire, Cheshire and the Isle of Man* (Nelson, 1966), 46. See also P.Richardson, *Empire & Slavery* (1968), 21: 'Liverpool evolved from a mere village to a great port on the strength of the [slave] trade alone.'
6. Ramsay Muir, *A History of Liverpool* (Williams & Norgate, 1907), 194, 195. See also Paul Mantoux, *The Industrial Revolution in the eighteenth century: an outline of the beginnings of the modern factory system in England* (Jonathan Cape, 1961), 107: 'We do not only know when, but how the fortune of Liverpool was made. Above all it was by its connection with the colonies – or plantations as they were then called; by the import of colonial produce such as sugar, coffee and cotton, and above all, by the slave trade which, since the *asiento* treaty, had become one of the most lucrative sources of revenue to British ship-owners.'
7. *Population in History: Essays in Historical Demography*, ed. D.V.Glass and D.E.C.Eversley (Edward Arnold, 1965), 192 n. 27; *A New Historical Geography of England*, ed. H.C.Darby (Cambridge University Press, 1973), 459; *The Social Survey of Merseyside*, ed. D. Caradog Jones (Liverpool University Press, 1934), I. 42.
8. John Latimer, *The History of the Society of Merchant Venturers of the City of Bristol: with some Account of the Anterior Merchants' Guilds* (Bristol, J.W.Arrowsmith, 1903), 179; C.M.MacInnes, *England and Slavery* (1934), 27; G.D.Ramsay, *English Overseas Trade during the Centuries of Emergence: Studies in some modern origins of the English-speaking world* (Macmillan & Co. Ltd, 1957), 148; MacInnes, *Bristol and the Slave Trade*, 8; Frank Walker, *The Bristol Region* (Nelson, 1972), 190.
9. C. Northcote Parkinson, *The Rise of the Port of Liverpool* (Liverpool University Press, 1952), 89, 94. Bristol Customs officers in the late seventeenth century were notoriously corrupt. Large-scale evasion of tobacco duty by Bristol merchants, with the connivance of Customs officers, was brought to light in 1691; £2,772 was recovered for the king and three officers were fined a total of £500. See *Calendar of Treasury Books*, IX. ii.426, 430; iii.900, 909, 936, 1148, 1155; iv.1493; v.1938; or the brief account in *Bristol and its Environs: Historical Descriptive & Scientific* (Houlston & Sons, 1875), 48.
10. *Calendar of Treasury Books*, VIII.iv.1891–2, 1049; *Merchants and Merchandise in Seventeenth-Century Bristol*, ed. Patrick McGrath (Bristol Record Society, XIX, 1955), p. xxii.
11. K.G.Davies, *The Royal African Company* (1957), 126.
12. 9 & 10 William III c. 26, reproduced in E.Donnan, *Documents*

Illustrative of the History of the Slave Trade to America (1930–5), I. 421–9; cf. Davies, 134.

13. John Cary, *An Essay on the State of England In Relation to its Trade, Its Poor, and its Taxes, For Carrying on the present war against France* (Bristoll, for the Author, 1695), 74–5.
14. R.B.Sheridan, *Sugar and Slavery* (1973), 249.
15. Donnan, II. pp. xxxv, 151–2; Charles Wells, *Historic Bristol* (Bristol, T.D.Taylor, Sons, & Hawkins, 1902), 94. For earlier English involvement in the Spanish trade see Donnan, I. 107–21.
16. Robert Paul Thomas and Richard Nelson Bean, 'The Fishers of Men: the Profits of the Slave Trade', *Journal of Economic History*, XXXIV (1974), 886 n. 5; Seymour Drescher, *Econocide: British Slavery in the Era of Abolition* (Pittsburgh, Pa, University of Pittsburgh Press, 1977), 30 ('The British share of the trade rose sharply at the end of the eighteenth century and was maintained through 1805, reaching a peak or near peak just before abolition. Britain remained the premier carrier of slaves to the end, accounting for over half the world total between 1791 and 1806').
17. James Ramsay, 'Memorial on the Supplying of the Navy with Seamen', as quoted by E.Williams, *Capitalism and Slavery*, third impression (André Deutsch, 1972), 34.
18. W.Enfield, *An Essay towards the History of Leverpool* (1773), 67; [James Wallace], *A General and Descriptive History of the Ancient and Present State, of the Town of Liverpool . . . together with a circumstantial account of the true causes of its extensive African trade* (Liverpool, R.Phillips, 1795), 187n., 212n., 254; J[ohn]. Aiken, *A Description of the Country from thirty to forty miles round Manchester* (John Stockdale, 1795), 369; [John Corry], *The History of Liverpool from the Earliest Authenticated Period down to the Present Time* (Liverpool, William Robinson, 1810), 79, 104–5, 111, 265; Edward Baines, *History, Directory, and Gazetteer, of the County Palatine of Lancaster* (Liverpool, Wm. Wales & Co., 1824–5), I. 162 (see also I. 188:'This trade had scarcely any existence here till the year 1723'); Corry, *History of Lancashire*, II. 690; Henry Smithers, *Liverpool, its Commerce, Statistics, and Institutions; with a history of the Cotton Trade* (Liverpool, Thomas Kaye, 1825), 104, 106; Thomas Baines, *History of the Commerce and Town of Liverpool, and of the Rise of Manufacturing Industry in the Adjoining Counties* (Longman, Brown, Green & Longmans, 1852), 694, giving the date of the first sailing as 1708, as does Eric Williams, 'The Golden Age of the Slave System in Britain', *Journal of Negro History*, XXV (1940), 67; Richard Brooke, *Liverpool as it was during the last Quarter of the Eighteenth Century* (Liverpool, J.Mawdsley & Son, 1853), 234; Thomas Baines and William Fairbairn, *Lancashire and Cheshire Past and Present* (William Mackenzie, [1868–9]), II. 70; J.A.Picton, *Memorials of Liverpool Historical and Topographical including a History of the Dock Estate* (Longmans, Green, 1873 [1872]), I. 122;

Edward Baines, *The History of the County Palatinate and Duchy of Lancaster*, revised edition, ed. James Croston (Manchester, John Heywood, 1888 [1886]–93), V. 131, 190; Gomer Williams, *History of the Liverpool Privateers and Letters of Marque, with an Account of the Liverpool Slave Trade* (William Heinemann, 1897), 467–8, 469; Muir, 191; L.J.Ragatz, *The Old Plantation System in the British Caribbean* [1925], 62; G.F.Dow, *Slave Ships and Slaving* (1927), 91; L.J.Ragatz, *The Fall of the Planter Class in the British Caribbean* (1928), 83; E.Williams, *Capitalism and Slavery*, 34; Philip D. Curtin, *The Atlantic Slave Trade: A Census* (University of Wisconsin Press, 1969), 147; Eric Williams, *From Columbus to Castro: The History of the Caribbean 1492–1969* (André Deutsch, 1970), 149. An interesting exception is Sir William B. Forwood, 'The Trade and Commerce of Liverpool', in *Handbook to Liverpool and the Neighbourhood*, ed. W.A.Herdman (Liverpool, British Association, 1896), dating the first voyage 1703.

19. Parkinson, 88, 89–90; Stanley Dumbell, 'The Beginnings of the Liverpool Cotton Trade', *Economic Journal*, XXXIV (1924), 279; Norris Papers, II. 179, as quoted by A.P.Wadsworth and J. de L.Mann, *The Cotton Trade and Industrial Lancashire 1600–1780* (1931), 72 n. 4. The merchants' letter to the master of the *Blessing* is transcribed in R.Davis, *The Rise of the English Shipping Industry in the Seventeenth and Eighteenth Centuries* (1962), 295–7; see also George Chandler, *Liverpool Shipping: a short history* (Phoenix House, 1960), 168. Sir Richard Norris was MP for Liverpool, 1695–1701.

20. Parkinson, 94.

21. Palatinate of Lancashire Chancery records, as quoted by Wadsworth and Mann, 228. A brigantine was a two-masted ship with the mainmast of a schooner and the foremast of a brig.

22. Parkinson, 89.

23. Muir, 192; MacInnes, *Gateway*, 190; Walker, 190.

24. *The Liverpool Memorandum-Book; or, Gentleman's, Merchant's and Tradesman's Daily Pocket-Journal For the Year M,DCC,LIII* (Liverpool, R.Williamson, [1752]); John Newton, *Thoughts upon the African Slave-Trade* (J.Buckland & J.Johnson, 1788), 33–4 ('The Slaves lie in two rows, one above the other, on each side of the ship, close to each other, like books upon a shelf. I have known them so close, that the shelf would not, easily, contain one more'); Herbert S. Klein, *The Middle Passage: Comparative Studies in the Atlantic Slave Trade* (Princeton, New Jersey, Princeton University Press, 1978), 229.

25. Enfield, 67, 68; MacInnes, *Gateway*, 191 (giving slightly different figures for Liverpool in 1771).

26. Herbert S. Klein, 'The English Slave Trade to Jamaica, 1782–1808'. *Economic History Review*, 2nd ser. XXXI (1978), 42, 43.

27. [Wallace], 238–9. F.E.Sanderson, 'Liverpool and the Slave Trade: a Guide to Sources', *Transactions of the Historic Society of Lancashire and Cheshire*, CXXIV (1972), 155, comments: 'We may doubt the accuracy of this claim, for the extent of the European slave trade was very imperfectly known; but certainly this was the one trade in which Liverpool merchants surpassed those of any other port in the kingdom or elsewhere.'

28. M.Craton, *Sinews of Empire* (1974), 119.

29. J.Latimer, *The Annals of Bristol in the Eighteenth Century* (1893), 144–5. Curtin, 133–4, gives the average loading rate for the whole British slave trade in 1771 as 248 slaves per ship.

30. Richard Pares, *Merchants and Planters* (*Economic History Review* Suppl. 4, Cambridge University Press, 1960), 82 n. 6. Ragatz (*Old Plantation System*, 65, and *Fall of the Planter Class*, 87) says it was one in four, but cf. J. Harry Bennett, Jr, *Bondsmen and Bishops: Slavery and Apprenticeship on the Codrington Plantations of Barbados, 1710–1838* (University of California Publications in History, LXII, Berkeley and Los Angeles, University of California Press, 1958), 58: 'West Indian writers varied in placing the loss of new Negroes at from one-third to one-half the number imported.'

31. [Wallace], 216–17n.; Ragatz, *Old Plantation System*, 62; Ragatz, *Fall of the Planter Class*, 83; E.Williams, 'The Golden Age of the Slave System in Britain', 68.

32. [Wallace], 216n.; G.Williams, *History of the Liverpool Privateers*, 471.

33. [Wallace], 229.

34. Francis E.Hyde, 'The Growth of Liverpool's Trade, 1700–1950', in *A Scientific Survey of Merseyside*, ed. Wilfred Smith (Liverpool University Press, 1953), 153; Wadsworth and Mann, 228.

35. Roger Anstey, *The Atlantic Slave Trade and British Abolition 1760–1810* (Macmillan, 1975), 46, 47; David Richardson, 'Profitability in the Bristol-Liverpool Slave Trade', *Revue française d'histoire d'outre-mer*, LXII/226–227 (1975), 301–8, reprinted in *La Traite des noirs par l'Atlantique* (Paris, Société française d'histoire d'outre-mer, 1976), 301–8. Roger Anstey, 'The Volume and Profitability of the British Slave Trade, 1761–1807', in *Race and Slavery in the Western Hemisphere: Quantitative Studies*, ed. Stanley L. Engerman and Eugene D. Genovese (Princeton University Press, 1975), 19, [20], argues that the average annual rate of profit in the British slave trade, between 1761 and 1807, was 9·5 per cent.

36. Anstey, *Atlantic Slave Trade*, 403.

37. Francis E.Hyde, Bradbury B.Parkinson, and Sheila Marriner, 'The Nature and Profitability of the Liverpool Slave Trade', *Economic History Review*, 2nd ser. V (1952–3), 369; Hyde, 'The Growth of Liverpool's Trade', 153; S.G.Checkland, 'Finance for the West Indies, 1780–1815', *Economic History Review*, 2nd ser. X (1957–8), 461–9; R.B.Sheridan, 'The Commercial and Financial Organization of the British Slave Trade, 1750–1807', *Economic History Review*, 2nd ser. XI (1958–9), 252–3; J.E.Merritt, 'The Triangular Trade', *Business History*, III (1960–1), [1]–7; Sanderson, 'Liverpool and the

Slave Trade', 160; Anstey, *Atlantic Slave Trade*, 35–6, 42–3, 45; Richardson, 'Profitability in the Bristol-Liverpool Slave Trade', 307; Clemens, 'The Rise of Liverpool', 221 ('Accepting bills of exchange gave the ship captain flexibility, for he could return directly to Africa – and occasionally did so – or could sail to Maryland, Virginia, or South Carolina with credit and rum; but ship captains also accepted notes because they had difficulty selling an entire cargo of slaves in one port or in a short period of time, and found the risk of the note more palatable than delay'); B.K.Drake, 'Continuity and Flexibility in Liverpool's Trade with Africa and the Caribbean', *Business History*, XVIII (1976), [85]–97; B.L.Anderson, 'The Lancashire bill system and its Liverpool practitioners: The case of a slave merchant', in *Trade and transport: Essays in economic history in honour of T.S.Willan*, ed. W.H. Chaloner and Barrie M. Ratcliffe (Manchester University Press, 1977), [59]–97. But 'only in times of scarcity, like the [seventeen-]nineties, did large numbers of Liverpool slave ships return in ballast or light freight' (Drescher, 32).

38. Klein, 'The English Slave Trade to Jamaica', 42.

39. D.W.Thoms, 'The Mills Family: London Sugar Merchants of the Eighteenth Century', *Business History*, XI (1969), 10; A.G.Hopkins, *An Economic History of West Africa* (1973), 95–6.

40. Wadsworth and Mann, 149, 156–7, 231, 233, 244–7, 444–5; Sheridan, *Sugar and Slavery*, 478. For Samuel Touchet's relation with Francis Baring, see p. 489 n. 18 below; for a brief biography of Samuel Touchet see Sir L.Namier and J.Brooke, *The House of Commons 1754–1790* (1964), III. 533–6.

41. Mabel Nembhard, 'Hibbert of Jamaica', *Caribbeana*, ed. V.L.Oliver (1910–19), IV. 193–202, 258–65, 324–30, 342–9; Wadsworth and Mann, 231; Sheridan, 'The Commercial and Financial Organization of the British Slave Trade', 255; Sheridan, *Sugar and Slavery*, 478. For George Hibbert, MP, see p. 49 above and p. 491 n. 39 below.

The slave-merchants of Bristol and Liverpool

1. Roger North, *The Life of the Right Honourable Francis North, Baron of Guilford* [ed. Montagu North] (John Whiston, 1742), 121.

2. According to William of Malmesbury's 'Vita Wulfstani' (*c.* 1124–43) the traffic in slaves was already 'a very ancient custom' at Bristol in the eleventh century. See *William of Malmesbury's Life of St Wulstan Bishop of Worcester*, trans. J.H.F.Peile (Oxford, Basil Blackwell, 1934), 64–5: 'They used to buy men from all England and carry them to Ireland in the hope of gain: nay, they even set forth for sale women whom they had themselves gotten with child. You might well groan to see the long rows of young men and maidens whose beauty and youth might move the pity of a savage, bound together with cords, and brought to market to be sold.'

3. North, 216–17; see also *A Young Squire of the Seventeenth Century:*

from the papers (A.D. 1676–1686) of Christopher Jeaffreson, ed. John Cordy Jeaffreson (Hurst & Blackett, 1878), I. 317–20.

4. Richard Savage, *London and Bristol Compar'd: A Satire Written in Newgate, Bristol* (M.Cooper, 1744), 7.
5. *The Social Survey of Merseyside*, ed. D.C.Jones (1934), I. 17.
6. [J.Wallace], *A General and Descriptive History . . . of the Town of Liverpool* (1795), 229, 229n.
7. [John Macky], *A Journey through England: In Familiar Letters from a Gentleman Here, to his Friend Abroad*, II, third edition (J.Pemberton, 1732), 149.
8. *Liverpool Memorandum-Book* [1752].
9. H[enry]. L[eigh]. B[ennett]., in *DNB*, XIV. 396. See also Revd Josiah Bull, *John Newton of Olney and St. Mary Woolnoth: An Autobiography and Narrative* (Religious Tract Society, [1868]), 43.
10. *The Journal of a Slave Trader (John Newton) 1750–1754*, ed. Bernard Martin and Mark Spurrell (Epworth Press, 1962), 71: 'By the favour of Divine Providence made a timely discovery to day that the slaves were forming a plot for an insurrection . . . put the boys in irons and slightly in the thumbscrews to urge them to a full confession.'
11. [John Newton and William Cowper], *Olney Hymns, in three books* (W.Oliver, 1779), 72–3.
12. William Cowper, 'Pity for Poor Africans', first published in the *Northampton Mercury*, 9 August 1788, and reprinted, with some changes, in his *Poems* (J.Johnson, 1800), I. 404–5.
13. William Cowper, 'Charity', *Poems* (J.Johnson, 1782), 187.
14. For Newton's evidence to the 1788 official inquiry into the slave trade, see *HCSP of the Eighteenth Century*, LXIX (George III: Report of the Lords of Trade on the Slave Trade 1789, pt 1), 118.
15. Thomas Clarkson, *The History of the Rise, Progress, and Accomplishment of the Abolition of the African Slave-Trade by the British Parliament* (Longman, Hurst, Rees, & Orme, 1808), I. 327.
16. J.Latimer, *The Annals of Bristol in the Eighteenth Century* (1893), 472–3; see also I.V.Hall, 'Whitson Court Sugar House, Bristol, 1665–1824', *Transactions of the Bristol and Gloucestershire Archaeological Society*, LXV (1944), 74 n. 128.
17. C.M.MacInnes, *A Gateway of Empire* (1939), 206.
18. E.Donnan, *Documents Illustrative of the History of the Slave Trade to America* (1930–5), II. 468.
19. *The Bristol Poll-Book* [1781], p. iii; *HCSP of the Eighteenth Century*, LXIX. 124–5; *Matthews's New Bristol Directory, For the Year, 1793–4*, [3]; Latimer, *Annals of Bristol in the Eighteenth Century*, 476–7; MacInnes, *Gateway*, 335–6; *The Trade of Bristol in the Eighteenth Century*, ed. W.E.Minchinton (Bristol Record Society, XX, 1957), 60 n. 7.
20. Charles Henry Cave, *A History of Banking in Bristol from 1750 to 1899* (Bristol, W.Crofton Hemmons, 1899), 9; L.S.Pressnell, *Country*

Banking in the Industrial Revolution (Oxford, Clarendon Press, 1956), 239. Tyndall was a partner of Isaac Hobhouse (Latimer, *Annals of Bristol in the Eighteenth Century*, 145).

21. [Henry] R[ichard]. Fox Bourne, *English Merchants: Memoirs in illustration of the progress of British commerce* (Edward Bentley, 1866), II. 16–18; *Accounts of Slave Compensation Claims; for the colonies of Jamaica*, etc. (*HCSP*, 1837–8, XLVIII), p. 68, claim 404 (£2,938 17*s.* 4*d.* for 156 slaves), p. 69, claim 578 (£2,542 4*s.* 8*d.* for 127 slaves), p. 169, claim 1601 (jointly with Thomas Kingston, £2,159 16*s.* 7*d.* for 40 slaves), p. 168, claim 1604 (jointly with Thomas Kingston, £6,622 18*s.* 7*d.* for 130 slaves).
22. T[homas]. S[eccombe]., in *DNB*, X. 936.
23. A.P.Wadsworth and J. de L.Mann, *The Cotton Trade and Industrial Lancashire 1600–1780* (1931), 216 n. 2. For a brief biography of Thomas Johnson, see Romney Sedgwick, *The House of Commons 1715–1754* (HMSO, 1970), II. 180–1.
24. In 1752, Richard Gildart & Sons owned the *Middleham* (captain John Welch, capacity 320 slaves), *Prince William* (John Valentine, 200), and *Rider* (Michael Rush, 300). James Gildart & Co. owned 'at least 26 vessels, mostly of New England build or trade' (Robert Craig and Rupert Jarvis, *Liverpool Registry of Merchant Ships* (Remains Historical and Literary Connected with the Palatine Counties of Lancaster and Cheshire, 3rd ser. XV, Manchester, Chetham Society, 1967), p. xxxvii), including, in 1752, the *Antigua Merchant* (captain Robert Thomas, capacity 200 slaves) and *James* (John Sacheverill, 120). Cf. *Liverpool Memorandum-Book* [1752]. For a brief biography of Richard Gildart, see Sedgwick, II. 63.
25. C.N.Parkinson, *The Rise of the Port of Liverpool* (1952), 96. In 1752, John Welch & Co. owned the *Africa* (captain — Hallison, capacity 250 slaves), *Barclay* (John Gadson, 450), *Ferret* (Joseph Welch, 50), *Judith* (Nicholas Southworth, 350), and *Priscilla* (William Parkinson, 350). John Knight & Co. owned the *Fanny* (captain William Jenkinson, capacity 120 slaves), *Jenny* (Thomas Darbyshire, 450), *Knight* (William Boates, 400), and *Little Billy* (Thomas Dickenson, 60). George Campbell & Co. 'held property in at least 36 vessels, occasionally as sole owner but often in combination with others (Craig and Jarvis, p. xxxvii). In 1752 the Campbell ships included the *Barbadoes Merchant* (captain John Wilson, capacity 400 slaves), *Dolphin* (Joseph Pederick, 200), and *Grace* (captain not identified, 400). Cf. *Liverpool Memorandum-Book* [1752]. For Foster Cunliffe & Sons, see the following note.
26. Matthew Gregson, *Portfolio of Fragments, relative to the History & Antiquities of the County Palatine and Duchy of Lancaster* (Liverpool, G.F.Harris's Widow & Brothers, 1817), 178; Joseph Foster, *Pedigrees of the County Families of England*, I, Lancashire (privately printed, 1873), 'Pedigree of Cunliffe, of Cunliffe and Whycollar';

L.B.Namier, 'Anthony Bacon, M.P., an Eighteenth-Century Merchant', *Journal of Economic and Business History*, II (1929–30), 21 n. 2; H[enry].R[ichard].F[ox].B[ourne]., 'The Merchant Princes of England', chap. xiv, *London Society*, VIII (1865),268–9; Bourne, *English Merchants*, II. 57, 63–4. Foster Cunliffe & Sons 'owned or part-owned at least 26 vessels' (Craig and Jarvis, p. xxxvii), including, in 1752, the *Bulkeley* (captain Christopher Baitson, capacity 350 slaves), *Bridget* (—— Hayston, 250), *Foster* (Edward Cropper, 200), and *Ellis and Robert* (R.Jackson, 300). Cf. *Liverpool Memorandum-Book* [1752]. 'The holdings of these well-known Liverpool merchants were often almost inextricably interwoven', and George Campbell had a part share in another of the Cunliffe ships, the *Cunliffe* (Craig and Jarvis, p. xxxvii). There is a brief biography of Sir Ellis Cunliffe in Sir L.Namier and J.Brooke, *The House of Commons 1754–1790* (1964), II. 285, and one of Charles Pole in Namier and Brooke, III. 305.

27. *Gore's Liverpool Directory* (1796), 203; Gregson, 178; Bourne, *English Merchants*, II. 64.

28. Bourne, *English Merchants*, II. 61, 63, 78–9; Leo H. Grindon, *Manchester Banks and Bankers: Historical, Biographical, and Anecdotal* (Manchester, Palmer & Howe, 1877), 42, 44, 79; H.A.Ormerod, 'Extracts from the Private Ledger of Arthur Heywood of Liverpool Merchant and Banker', *Transactions of the Historic Society of Lancashire and Cheshire*, CIII (1951 [1952]), 103–11; Pressnell, 236; 'The Heywood Story', *Three Banks Review*, no. 85 (March 1970), 50–60; E.J.T.Acaster, 'Benjamin Heywood, Sons & Co: Bankers in Manchester 1788–95', *Three Banks Review*, no. 119 (September 1978), 47–57. In 1752, Arthur and Benjamin Heywood owned the *Phœbe* (captain William Lawson, capacity 280 slaves); cf. *Liverpool Memorandum-Book* [1752]. The Heywoods were among the first in Britain to import slave-grown cotton from the United States (E.Williams, 'The Golden Age of the Slave System in Britain', *Journal of Negro History*, XXV (1940), 70).

29. *Liverpool Memorandum-Book* [1752]; Donnan, II. 492n.

30. Anne Holt, *Walking Together: A Study in Liverpool Nonconformity 1688–1938* (George Allen & Unwin Ltd, 1938), 155.

31. The slave-trading mayors of Liverpool were: Robert Armitage (1738), Peter Baker (1795), Joseph Bird (1746), John Blackburn (1760), Bryan Blundell (1721, 1728), George Campbell (1763), James Crosbie (1753), Foster Cunliffe (1716, 1729, 1735), Robert Cunliffe (1758), Ralph Earle (1769), Thomas Earle (1787), James Gildart (1750), Richard Gildart (1714, 1731, 1736), Charles Goore (1754, 1767), William Gregson (1762), John Hughes (1727), Richard Hughes (1756), Thomas Leyland (1798, 1814, 1820), Richard Norris (1700), Charles Pole (1785), William Pole (1733, 1778), Samuel Staniforth (1812), Thomas Staniforth (1797), John Tarleton (1764), Edward Trafford (1742), and John Williamson (1761).

Thomas Johnson was mayor in 1695, before he became a slave-merchant.

32. [Wallace], 230–1; Wadsworth and Mann, 228; A.G.Hopkins, *An Economic History of West Africa* (1973), 96; H.A.Gemery and J.S.Hogendorn, 'Technological Change, Slavery, and the Slave Trade', in *The Imperial Impact: Studies in the Economic History of Africa and India*, ed. Clive Dewey and A.G.Hopkins (Athlone Press for the Institute of Commonwealth Studies, 1978), 256.
33. Vera M. Johnson, 'Sidelights on the Liverpool Slave Trade, 1789–1807', *Mariner's Mirror*, XXXVIII (1952), 276; *Gore's Liverpool Directory* (1790 etc.), *passim*.
34. Herbert S. Klein, 'The English Slave Trade to Jamaica, 1782–1808', *Economic History Review*, 2nd ser. XXXI (1978), 43, table 10.
35. W.F.Crick and J.E.Wadsworth, *A Hundred Years of Joint Stock Banking* (1936), 411.
36. Crick and Wadsworth, 414.
37. Pressnell, 177, 517; Rondo Cameron and others, *Banking in the Early Stages of Industrialization: A study in comparative economic history* (Oxford University Press, 1967), 26.
38. Bourne, *English Merchants*, II. 294–5; John Hughes, *Liverpool Banks & Bankers 1760–1837* (Liverpool, Henry Young &Sons, 1906), 61, 63n., 86n., 169–78; Crick and Wadsworth, 141, 144, 408–16; Pressnell, 50, 236, 362, 419.
39. Hughes, 129; F.E.Hyde, 'The Growth of Liverpool's Trade, 1700–1950', in *A Scientific Survey of Merseyside*, ed. W. Smith (1953), 153 n. 2; *Gore's Liverpool Directory* (1825), 6, 7.
40. Francis E. Hyde, *Liverpool and the Mersey: an economic history of a port 1700–1970* (Newton Abbot, David & Charles, 1971), 18.
41. Hughes, 61, 171 (Thomas Leyland), 95 (Arthur and Benjamin Heywood), 107–8 (William Gregson), 129–30 (Thomas and Samuel Staniforth), 133 (Francis Ingram), 138 (Jonas Bold), 141 (Joseph Daltera), 166 (Richard Hanly). See also: Pressnell, 49; Hyde, *Liverpool and the Mersey*, 18.
42. Hughes, 198; Pressnell, 50; Hyde, *Liverpool and the Mersey*, 19. Moss was later chairman of the committee promoting the Liverpool and Manchester Railway, deputy chairman of that railway, and chairman of the Liverpool and Birmingham Railway (Hughes, 197–8; Crick and Wadsworth, 145).
43. Hyde, *Liverpool and the Mersey*, 19.
44. R.Stewart-Brown, *Liverpool Ships in the Eighteenth Century* (University Press of Liverpool, Hodder & Stoughton Ltd., 1932), 126–7.
45. S.G.Checkland, 'Finance for the West Indies, 1780–1815', *Economic History Review*, 2nd ser. X (1957–8), 465.
46. A Genuine 'Dicky Sam', *Liverpool and Slavery: An Historical Account of the Liverpool–African Slave Trade* (Liverpool, A.Bowker & Son, 1884), 15.

47. Reprinted as *The Correspondence between John Gladstone, Esq., M.P., and James Cropper, Esq., on the Present State of Slavery in the British West Indies* (Liverpool, West India Association, 1824). See also John Gladstone, *A Statement of Facts connected with the present state of slavery in the British sugar and coffee colonies* (Baldwin & Cradock, 1830).
48. Bourne, *English Merchants*, II. 303.
49. This is the calculation of S.G.Checkland, *The Gladstones: A Family Biography 1764–1851* (Cambridge University Press, 1971), 320–1. See also *Accounts of Slave Compensation Claims* (*HCSP*, 1837–8, XLVIII), p. 58, claims 534 (£5,624 3*s*. 1*d*. for 300 slaves) and 534A (£1,038 7*s*. 5*d*. for an unstated number, approximately 35, out of a joint claim in respect of 106 slaves), p. 121, claims 650 (£10,278 5*s*. 8*d*. for 193 slaves), 656 (£14,721 8*s*. 11*d*. for 272 slaves), and 687 (£22,443 19*s*. 11*d*. for 415 slaves).
50. R.E.Carlson, *The Liverpool & Manchester Railway Project 1821–1831* (1969), 48 n. 2. For John Gladstone, see also S.G.Checkland, 'John Gladstone as Trader and Planter', *Economic History Review*, 2nd ser. VII (1954–5), 216–29.
51. *Fortunes Made in Business* (Sampson Low, Marston, Searle & Rivington, 1884–7), II. 130.
52. *Hansard's Parliamentary Debates*, 3rd ser. vol. 17 (1833), cols. 1345–6. Liverpool MPs who 'all spoke forcibly in the Commons against regulation and abolition' of the slave trade (F.E.Sanderson, 'Liverpool and the Slave Trade: a Guide to Sources', *Transactions of the Historic Society of Lancashire and Cheshire*, CXXIV (1972), 165) were Richard Pennant, Lord Penrhyn (MP, 1767–80, 1784–90), Bamber Gascoyne (1780–96), his brother Isaac Gascoyne (1796–1832), and Banastre Tarleton (1790–1806, 1807–12). For Pennant, see pp. 467–8 n. 18 above. For a brief biography of Bamber Gascoyne, see Namier and Brooke, II. 492.
53. W.E.Gladstone's 1832 election address in Newark, as quoted by Philip Magnus, *Gladstone: A Biography* (John Murray, 1954), 15.

London as a slave port: the West India lobby

1. C.Wilson, *England's Apprenticeship 1603–1763* (1965), 175–6.
2. K.G.Davies, *The Royal African Company* (1957), 67.
3. R.B.Sheridan, 'The Commercial and Financial Organization of the British Slave Trade, 1750–1807', *Economic History Review*, 2nd ser. XI (1958–9), 263; cf. R.B.Sheridan, *Sugar and Slavery* (1973), 293 ('involved' here changed to 'implicated').
4. R.B.Sheridan, 'The Sugar Trade of the British West Indies' (unpublished London University PhD thesis, 1951), 76, as quoted by R.Davis, *The Rise of the English Shipping Industry* (1962), 270; D.W.Thoms, 'The Mills Family: London Sugar Merchants of the Eighteenth Century', *Business History*, XI (1969), 10.

5. Sheridan, 'The Commercial and Financial Organization of the British Slave Trade', 263; Sheridan, *Sugar and Slavery*, 294.
6. K.G.Davies, 'The Origins of the Commission System in the West India Trade', *Transactions of the Royal Historical Society*, 5th ser. II (1952), 91–2.
7. S.G.Checkland, 'Finance for the West Indies, 1780–1815', *Economic History Review*, 2nd ser. X (1957–8), 466–7.
8. [John Oldmixon], *The British Empire in America, Containing The History of the Discovery, Settlement, Progress and present State of all the British Colonies, on the Continent and Islands of America* (John Nicholson etc., 1708), II. 47–8. Oldmixon's reliability is defended by Pat Rogers, 'An Early Colonial Historian: John Oldmixon and *The British Empire in America*', *Journal of American Studies*, VII (1973), 113–23. For Sir John Bawden, see Davies, 'The Origins of the Commission System in the West India Trade', 105–6, and Sheridan, *Sugar and Slavery*, 286–7.
9. Davies, 'The Origins of the Commission System in the West India Trade', 106. For Sir John Eyles, see also R.Sedgwick, *The House of Commons 1715–1754* (1970), II. 21.
10. Richard Pares, 'A London West-India Merchant House 1740–1769', in *Essays Presented to Sir Lewis Namier*, ed. R.Pares and A.J.P.Taylor (Macmillan & Co. Ltd., 1956), 102. This essay is reprinted in R.Pares, *The Historian's Business and Other Essays*, ed. R.A. and Elisabeth Humphreys (Oxford, Clarendon Press, 1961), [198]–226.
11. Pares, 'A London West-India Merchant House', 102–4.
12. *CSP, Colonial Ser. America and West Indies 1720–1721*, sect. 713, p. 486 (Samuel Cox, president of the Barbados Council, to the Council of Trade and Plantations, 8 November 1721: 'Mr Henry Lascells Collector who by being one of the chiefest shippers of sugers to private persons as well as the King, ships the good sugers received for duty to his private correspondents at high prices, and buys french sugers at low rates and ships to the King for duty'); *Calendar of Treasury Papers, 1720–1728*, 97–8; *Calendar of Treasury Books and Papers, 1742–1745*, 527–8, 716, 731, 784; Louis Knott Koontz, *Robert Dinwiddie: his career in American Colonial Government and Westward Expansion* (Glendale, Calif., Arthur H. Clark Company, 1941), [67]–94; J.H.Parry, 'The Patent Offices in the British West Indies', *English Historical Review*, LXIX (1954), 213–15; Pares, 'A London West-India Merchant House', 77–9; Sedgwick, II. 199. For a brief biography of William Smelt, see Sedgwick, II. 426–7.
13. Pares, 'A London West-India Merchant House', 93. John Sharpe sat for Callington, Cornwall, 1754–6; see Sir L.Namier and J.Brooke, *The House of Commons 1754–1790* (1964), III. 428.
14. Pares, 'A London West-India Merchant House', 89, 107.
15. Pares, 'A London West-India Merchant House', 105, 102. For the

house of Lascelles, see also Sheridan, *Sugar and Slavery*, 292, 296–9. For a brief biography of Henry Lascelles, see Sedgwick, II. 199–200. For brief biographies of Edwin Lascelles, see Sedgwick, II.198–9, and Namier and Brooke, III. 22–3.

16. *Accounts of Slave Compensation Claims* (*HCSP*, 1837–8, XLVIII), p. 5, claim 23 (£2,599 0*s*. 4*d*. for 112 slaves), p. 8, claim 147 (£4,286 19*s*. 3*d*. for 232 slaves), p. 172, claim 211 (£6,486 1*s*. 6*d*. for 292 slaves), p. 187, claims 2769 (£3,291 11*s*. 4*d*. for 176 slaves) and 2770 (£5,810 5*s*. 6*d*. for 277 slaves). Pares ('A London West-India Merchant House', 102) refers to another plantation in Barbados, owned by 'the heirs of Henry Lascelles', with apparently 188 slaves; I have not succeeded in tracing the amount of compensation paid for these.

17. A.T.Gary, 'The Political and Economic Relations of English and American Quakers (1750–1785)' (unpublished University of Oxford D.Phil. thesis, 1935), fol. 506. David Barclay of Walthamstow and Youngsbury, brother of the founder of Barclay's Bank, did set free (after the founder's death) 32 slaves in Jamaica who had been given them to settle a debt. See David Barclay, *An Account of the Emancipation of the Slaves of Unity Valley Pen, in Jamaica* (William Philips, 1801); Lieut.-Col. Hubert F. Barclay and Alice Wilson-Fox, *The Barclays in Scotland and England from 1810 to 1933* (A History of the Barclay Family, pt III, St Catherine Press, 1934), 243; Thomas E. Drake, *Quakers and Slavery in America* (Yale Historical Publications, Miscellany, LI, New Haven, Yale University Press, 1950), 122.

18. Gary, fol. 506; R.F.Bourne, *English Merchants* (1866), II. 239–42; W.P.C[ourtney]., in *DNB*, III. 192. See also T.S. Ashton, *An Economic History of England: The 18th Century* (Methuen & Co. Ltd, 1955), 138: 'Francis Baring had been trained by Samuel Touchet, who knew the ropes.' Sir Francis Baring sat for Grampound (1784–90), Chipping Wycombe (1794–6 and 1802–6), and Caine (1796–1802). It was Lord Shelburne who styled him 'the Prince of Merchants'; see Victor Nolte, *Fifty Years in Both Hemispheres; or, Reminiscences of a Merchant's Life* (Trubner & Co., 1854), 158. For a brief biography of Baring, see Namier and Brooke, II. 47–8.

19. Checkland, 'Finance for the West Indies', 464.

20. W. Marston Acres, *The Bank of England from Within* (Oxford University Press, 1931), I. 154–5; J.A.Giuseppi, 'Pannyaring on the Coast; Some Account of Ventures in the African Slave Trade in the Early Years of the Eighteenth Century', *The Old Lady of Threadneedle Street*, XXVI/117 (March 1950), 320–4. Humphry Morice was MP for Newport (1713–22) and Grampound (1722–31); for a brief biography, see Sedgwick, II. 277.

21. Sir Joseph G. Broodbank, *History of the Port of London* (Daniel O'Connor, 1921), I. 115, 116, 117; Acres, II. 620, 622; Sir John Clapham, *The Bank of England: A History* (Cambridge, University

Press, 1944), I. 199, 200; R.Pares, *A West-India Fortune* (1950), 178, 262; Checkland, 'Finance for the West Indies', 463–4.

22. Broodbank, I. 115, 116; Acres, II. 622; Clapham, I. 263.
23. 'The Trials of Job', *Three Banks Review*, no. 24 (December 1954), 25. Nathaniel Bayly was MP for Abingdon (1770–4) and Westbury (1774–9); for a brief biography, see Namier and Brooke, II. 67–8.
24. Edmund Sheridan Purcell, *Life of Cardinal Manning, Archbishop of Westminster* (Macmillan & Co., 1895), I. 6–7; *Caribbeana*, ed. V.L.Oliver (1910–19), I. 241–8, 293–4; Acres, I. [291] n. 4, II. 622; Checkland, 'Finance for the West Indies', 464; Richard B. Sheridan, 'The West India Sugar Crisis and British Slave Emancipation, 1830–1833', *Journal of Economic History*, XXI (1961), 542–3.
25. Clapham, I. 206.
26. *Remarks on the Letter address'd to two great men* [1760], 46.
27. *Collections of the Massachusetts Historical Society* [1st ser. VI] (1799), 195; *Jasper Mauduit: Agent in London for the Province of the Massachusetts-Bay, 1762–1765* [ed. Charles G. Washburn] (Massachusetts Historical Society Collections, LXXIV, 1918), 144n.
28. *Jasper Mauduit* [ed. Washburn], 149n.
29. *Gentleman's Magazine*, XXXVI (1766), 229.
30. Robert Heysham sat for Lancaster (1698–1715) and London (1715–22); his brother William sat for Lancaster (1705–16). For brief biographies, see Sedgwick, I. 136.
31. Stapleton sat for Oxfordshire (1727–40); for a brief biography, see Sedgwick, I. 441–2. Codrington sat for Minehead (1737–8) and his son sat for Beverley (1747–61) and Tewkesbury (1761–92); for brief biographies see Sedgwick, I. 563, 564.
32. Checkland, 'Finance for the West Indies', 464 and n. 6. Pulteney sat for Hedon (1705–34) and Middlesex (1734–42). For a brief biography, see Sedgwick, II. 375–6.
33. University College Library, Bangor, Penrhyn 1255, as quoted by J.Lindsay, *A History of the North Wales Slate Industry* (1974), 48. For Pennant, see pp. 467–8 n. 18 above.
34. *Caribbeana*, ed. Oliver, IV. 95; Sheridan, *Sugar and Slavery*, 61. For brief biographies of these members of the Beckford family, see Sedgwick, I. 451–2, and Namier and Brooke, II. 73–9. For William Beckford senior see also Lucy Sutherland, 'The City of London in Eighteenth-Century Politics', in *Essays Presented to Sir Lewis Namier*, ed. Pares and Taylor, 65–6.
35. *The Letters of Philip Dormer Stanhope, 4th Earl of Chesterfield*, ed. Bonamy Dobrée (Eyre & Spottiswoode, 1932), VI. 2832.
36. Lillian M. Penson, 'The London West India Interest in the Eighteenth Century', *English Historical Review*, XXXVI (1921), 374–5; Lillian M. Penson, *The Colonial Agents of the British West Indies: a study in colonial administration mainly in the eighteenth century*

(University of London Press Ltd, 1924), 230. The Barbadian Sir James Modyford acted as agent for Jamaica while on a visit to England in 1664–6, but this was a temporary appointment; see Frank Cundall, *The Governors of Jamaica in the Seventeenth Century* (West India Committee, 1936), pp. xviii, 22.

37. Penson, *Colonial Agents*, 167–8 and App. ii, 250–4.
38. F.W.Pitman, *The Development of the British West Indies* (1917), [242]–270, [334]–360.
39. Alex[r] Forrow, *The Thames and its Docks: a lecture* (Spottiswoode & Co., 1877), 47; Broodbank, I. 101–3. See also Walter M. Stern, 'The First London Dock Boom and the Growth of the West India Docks', *Economica*, n.s. XIX (1952), 59–77. Hibbert was MP for Seaford, Sussex (1806–12).
40. Penson, 'The London West India Interest in the Eighteenth Century', 378–9, 386–7.
41. Penson, *Colonial Agents*, 198; Davies, 'The Origins of the Commission System in the West India Trade', 90. No minutes of the society's meetings seem to have been kept before 1769.
42. *Gentleman's Magazine*, LIX (1789), i. 334.
43. Penson, *Colonial Agents*, 231. The best and most detailed recent account of the West India lobby will be found in Sheridan, *Sugar and Slavery*, 58–71.

Competition

1. *Journal of the Commissioners for Trade and Plantations from January 1749–1750 to December 1753* (HMSO, 1932), 15, 22. For Exeter and Dartmouth, see F.C.Prideaux Nash, 'Extracts from a Slaver's Log', *Mariner's Mirror*, VI (1920), 3–10.
2. E.Donnan, *Documents Illustrative of the History of the Slave Trade to America* (1930–5), III, 479; R.Craig and M.M.Schofield, 'The Trade of Lancaster in William Stout's Time', in *The Autobiography of William Stout of Lancaster 1665–1752*, ed. J.D.Marshall (Manchester, Chetham Society, 3rd ser. XIV, 1967), 49n.
3. M.M.Schofield, 'The Slave Trade from Lancashire and Cheshire Ports outside Liverpool *c.*1750–*c.*1790', *Transactions of the Historic Society of Lancashire and Cheshire*, CXXVI (1976 [1977]), 48–51.
4. Schofield, 33, 35, 47.
5. Schofield, 37, 35, 50, 37.
6. British Library Add. MS. 14,035 (Papers of the Board of Trade and Plantations 1710–1781), fol. 168r.
7. Schofield, 56, 60.
8. Schofield, 38, 40.
9. G.Williams, *History of the Liverpool Privateers* (1897), 482–4; Robert Craig, 'Shipping and Shipbuilding in the Port of Chester in the Eighteenth and Early Nineteenth Centuries', *Transactions of the Historic Society of Lancashire and Cheshire*, CXVI (1964 [1965]), 45.

10. Schofield, 41–2.
11. Schofield, 33, 35, 43–6.
12. Schofield, 35, 33.
13. C. Duncan Rice, *The Rise and Fall of Black Slavery* (Macmillan, 1975), 145.
14. 'An Early Glasgow–West Indian Miscellany', *Three Banks Review*, no. 54 (June 1962), 37.
15. Ruth Bourne, *Queen Anne's Navy in the West Indies* (Yale Historical Publications, Miscellany, XXXIII, New Haven, Yale University Press, 1939), 91; *Bishop* [Gilbert] *Burnet's History of his own time*, V (Oxford, Clarendon Press, 1823), 90; *Journals of the House of Lords*, XVII (1701–4), 507–11.
16. Bourne, 240 n. 50.
17. *CSP, Colonial Ser. America and West Indies, 1712–1714*, sect. 238, p. 123; Bourne, 255.
18. *CSP, Colonial Ser. America and West Indies, 1717–1718*, sect. 566, p. 271; sect. 681, p. 346.
19. Richard Pares, *War and Trade in the West Indies 1739–1763* (Oxford, Clarendon Press, 1936), 22.
20. J.Latimer, *The History of the Society of Merchant Venturers of the City of Bristol* (1903), 181.

Quality control

1. A Genuine 'Dicky Sam', *Liverpool and Slavery* (1884), 15. For the branding of slaves, see also pp. 53 and 472 n. 35 above and pp. 495–6 n. 35 below.
2. John Atkins, *A voyage to Guinea, Brasil, and the West-Indies; In His Majesty's Ships, the Swallow and Weymouth* (Cæsar Ward & Richard Chandler, 1735), 179–80.
3. Richard Ligon, *A true & exact history Of the Island of Barbados* (Humphrey Moseley, 1657), 46.
4. [J. Oldmixon], *The British Empire in America* (1708), II. 117. For the notorious sale by 'scramble', see *HCSP of the Eighteenth Century*, LXXII (George III, Minutes of Evidence on the Slave Trade 1790, pt 2), 307–8 (evidence of Alexander Falconbridge).
5. William Weston, *The Complete Merchant's Clerk; or, British and American Compting-House* (R.Griffiths, 1754), ii. 41.
6. Messrs George & Robert Tod & Co. to Captain Thomas Nuttall, 1 July 1806, as quoted by Charles R. Hand, 'The *Kitty's Amelia*, the last Liverpool Slaver', *Transactions of the Historic Society of Lancashire and Cheshire*, LXXXII (1930), 73.
7. E.Donnan, *Documents Illustrative of the History of the Slave Trade to America* (1930–5), II. 327.
8. Donnan, II. 444–5; also quoted, in part, in C.M.MacInnes, *Bristol and the Slave Trade* (1963), 12.

9. Sir William Young, Bart., 'A Tour through the several islands of Barbadoes, St. Vincent, Antigua, Tobago, and Grenada', in Bryan Edwards, *An Historical Survey of the Island of Saint Domingo* [ed. Sir W. Young] (John Stockdale, 1801), 269–70. The *Pilgrim* was owned by John Anderson & Co. (*The Trade of Bristol in the Eighteenth Century*, ed. W.E.Minchinton (1957), 60), the *Aeolus* by Thomas Staniforth and others (R.Craig and R.Jarvis, *Liverpool Registry of Merchant Ships* (1967), 119).
10. As quoted by W.F.Crick and J.E.Wadsworth, *A Hundred Years of Joint Stock Banking* (1936), 416.
11. R.Pares, *A West-India Fortune* (1950), 123.
12. David Galenson, 'The Slave Trade to the English West Indies, 1673–1724', *Economic History Review*, 2nd ser. XXXII (1979), 246, table 4; H.S.Klein, 'The English Slave Trade to Jamaica, 1782–1808', *Economic History Review*, 2nd ser. XXXI (1978), 31, table 4; H.S.Klein, *The Middle Passage* (1978), 151, 162n. ('Child mortality was uniformly high from all regions, 159 per 1,000 for boys and 225 per 1,000 for girls'); Herbert S. Klein and Stanley L. Engerman, 'Slave Mortality on British Ships, 1791–1797', in *Liverpool, the African Slave Trade, and Abolition: Essays to illustrate current knowledge and research*, ed. Roger Anstey and P.E.H.Hair (Historic Society of Lancashire and Cheshire, Occasional Ser. ii, 1976), 119 ('the death rate for children exceeded the adult rate by a considerable margin'). It is hard to account for the assertion of L.J.Ragatz, in *The Old Plantation System in the British Caribbean* [1925], 64, and *The Fall of the Planter Class in the British Caribbean, 1763–1833* (1928), 86, that 'cargoes contained few children'; Klein, 'The English Slave Trade to Jamaica, 1782–1808', 30, table 3, shows that in 1791–8, of slaves transported to the West Indies in British slavers, 20·7 per cent from Sierra Leone, 13·7 per cent from the Bight of Biafra, 13·1 per cent from Congo-Angola, 11·8 per cent from the Windward Coast, 9·9 per cent from the Gold Coast, 9·8 per cent from Senegambia, 6·0 per cent from the Bight of Benin, and 10·5 per cent of those of unknown provenance, were children.
13. Death rate of slaves in passage in British slavers averaged 23·6 per cent in 1680–8: see *HCSP of the Eighteenth Century*, LXX. 198; R.P.Thomas and R.N.Bean, 'The Fishers of Men: the Profits of the Slave Trade', *Journal of Economic History*, XXXIV (1974), 897; Klein, *The Middle Passage*, 64. There was a gradual decline between then and the early 1790s, though variance around the average was always high. R.Anstey, *The Atlantic Slave Trade and British Abolition 1760–1810* (1975), 31, 414–15, gives averages of 8·5 per cent for 1769–87, 9·6 per cent for 1791, and 8·4 per cent for 1792. Then came a drop in the last 16 years of the trade, caused partly by Dolben's regulating Act (1788), partly by the payment of £100 to the master and £50 to the surgeon in respect of each cargo where

mortality was under 2 per cent. For the 1790s, see Klein and Engerman, 'Slave Mortality on British Ships, 1791–1797', [113]–125.

14. J.H.Hodson, 'The Letter Book of Robert Bostock, a Merchant in the Liverpool Slave Trade, 1789–1792', *Liverpool Libraries, Museums & Arts Committee Bulletin*, III/1–2 (July–October 1953), 50, 41, 56; cf. G.Chandler, *Liverpool Shipping: a short history* (1960), 169. In 1789 Robert Bostock owned the *Kite* (captain Stephen Bowers), *Little Ben* (captain James Fryer, capacity 75 slaves), *Bess* (William Doyle, 200), and *Jemmy* (Edward Williams, 138).

15. G.Williams, *History of the Liverpool Privateers* (1897), 601; C.M.MacInnes, 'The Slave Trade', in *The Trade Winds*, ed. C.N.Parkinson (1948), 263.

16. J.Latimer, *The Annals of Bristol in the Eighteenth Century* (1893), 146.

17. *HCSP of the Eighteenth Century*, LXXIII (George III: Minutes of Evidence on the Slave Trade 1790), 123ff. (evidence of Isaac Parker, who had been a seaman on the *Black Joke*). Jonathan Press, *The Merchant Seamen of Bristol 1747–1789* (Bristol branch of the Historical Association, 1976), 9, argues perplexingly that much of the ill-treatment 'may well have been due to the need to keep costs down rather than to personal animosity'.

18. As quoted by MacInnes, 'The Slave Trade', 252.

19. Ragatz, *Old Plantation System*, 65; Ragatz, *Fall of the Planter Class*, 87. For mortality among crews of British slavers, see Anstey, *Atlantic Slave Trade*, 32 n. 95: 'Of 12,263 original crew members on 350 Liverpool and Bristol slavers, 1784–90, 2643 died on the voyage – i.e. 21·6%'. This calculation is based on muster rolls summarized in *HCSP of the Eighteenth Century*, LXXXII (George III: Slave Trade 1791 and 1792), 290–4. See also Philip D. Curtin, 'Epidemiology and the Slave Trade', *Political Science Quarterly*, LXXXIII (1968), 190–216; Philip D. Curtin, 'The Atlantic Slave Trade 1600–1800', in *History of West Africa*, ed. J.F.Ajayi and Michael Crowder, I (Longman, 1971), 255. Many of the seamen who survived went blind (Press, 13).

20. *Memoirs of the Late Captain Hugh Crow of Liverpool* (Longman, Rees, Orme, Brown, & Green, 1830), 169n.

21. *HCSP of the Eighteenth Century*, LXIX. 135, 132 (evidence of James Arnold). Cf. G.F.Dow, *Slave Ships and Slaving* (1927), 163.

22. T.Clarkson, *The History of the Rise, Progress, and Accomplishment of the Abolition of the African Slave-Trade* (1808), I. 298–301. The *Brothers* was owned by James Jones, warden of Bristol's Society of Merchant Venturers in 1794; see Commander J.W.Damer Powell, *Bristol Privateers and Ships of War* (Bristol, J.W. Arrowsmith, 1930), 303, and *The Trade of Bristol in the Eighteenth Century*, ed. Minchinton, 173. Sydenham Teast gave evidence to the Privy Council inquiry into the slave trade; see *HCSP of the Eighteenth Century*, LXIX. 141–2.

23. *HCSP of the Eighteenth Century*, LXIX. 138 (evidence of William James, according to whom 'the Captains of Guineamen are tolerable in their first sailing; their Cruelty begins to shew itself on their Arrival upon the Coast, but after they have been there a little Time it has no Bounds').
24. Clarkson, I. 310–18.
25. Clarkson, I. 196, 323–4. For this and the preceding three paragraphs, see also the chapter 'Treatment of the Sailors' in Alexander Falconbridge, *An Account of the Slave Trade on the Coast of Africa* (J.Philips, 1788), 37–50. The author, who had served as surgeon on a slaver, gave evidence to the 1788 inquiry (*HCSP of the Eighteenth Century*, LXIX. 120–1).
26. Clarkson, I. 377, 409–10.
27. Sir James A. Picton, *City of Liverpool: Municipal Archives and Records, from A.D. 1700 to the Passing of the Municipal Reform Act, 1835* (Liverpool, Gilbert G. Walmsley, 1886), 191.
28. Rev. R[aymund]. Harris, *Scriptural Researches on the Licitness of the Slave-trade*, etc. (John Stockdale, 1788), p. [iii]. To the second edition, published in the same year, Harris added 'scriptural directions for the proper treatment of slaves'.
29. Harris, 54. Cf. T.Baines, *History of the Commerce and Town of Liverpool* (1852), 472–4.
30. Picton, 216. In 1796 the city's thanks and a piece of plate valued at 100 guineas were presented to Mr P.W.Branker for his unremitting labours in defending the slave trade and for procuring its continued existence under reasonable restrictions (MacInnes, 'The Slave Trade', 252); this was a reference to the Dolben Act of 1788 designed to improve the conditions under which slaves were shipped.
31. As quoted by A Genuine 'Dicky Sam', 8.
32. Clarkson, I. 375–7.
33. Falconbridge, 23.
34. *HCSP of the Eighteenth Century*, LXIX. 125 (evidence of James Arnold: 'That many of the Slaves would not eat, and that he had always seen them on such Occasions flogged in an unmerciful Manner; the Captain [Joseph Williams] being generally the Executioner himself, and delighting in such Operations'); cf. the edited version in Dow, 173. The flogging to death of a woman slave who had refused to eat was the subject of at least one local broadside; see the British Library's collection of 'Broadsides Printed at Bristol' (pressmark 1880 c. 20), vol. I, no. 304.
35. R.Brooke, *Liverpool as it was during the last Quarter of the Eighteenth Century* (1853), 235: 'When the author was a boy he has seen branding irons, with letters or marks for branding slaves, exhibited for sale in the shops of Liverpool.' In the early part of the eighteenth century the children of black slaves were branded at the age of three; see A.P.Kup, 'Instructions to the Royal African Company's factor at

Bunce, 1702', *Sierra Leone Studies*, n.s. no. 5 (December 1955), 50. On the Codrington estate in Barbados, operated by the Society for the Propagation of the Gospel, newly arrived black slaves were until 1732 branded on the breast with the word SOCIETY in large letters; see J.H.Bennett, Jr, *Bondsmen and Bishops* (1958), 27.

36. G. Williams, 473n.

37. Granville Sharp, Letter Book, 34, as quoted by J. Walvin, *Black and White* (1973), 60.

Black people in the slave ports

1. T.Clarkson, *The History of the Rise, Progress, and Accomplishment of the Abolition of the African Slave-Trade* (1808), I. 375.

2. *Farley's Bristol Newspaper*, 31 August 1728, as quoted by J.Latimer, *The Annals of Bristol in the Eighteenth Century* (1893), 147.

3. *Bristol Journal*, 23 June 1750, as quoted by Latimer, 147.

4. *Bristol Intelligencer*, 12 January 1754, as quoted by Latimer, 147.

5. *Felix Farley's Bristol Journal*, 2 August 1760, p. [3].

6. *Bristol Journal*, 20 June 1767, as quoted by Latimer, 147–8.

7. *Bristol Journal*, 9 January 1768, as quoted by Latimer, 148.

8. H.Smithers, *Liverpool, its Commerce, Statistics, and Institutions* (1825), 105; [James Stonehouse], *Pictorial Liverpool* ([Liverpool], Henry Lacey, [*c.*1844]), 67 ('One street in town were [*sic*] sales were made, was nicknamed "Negro Street" '); James M. Walthew, *A Lecture on the Rise and Progress of Liverpool* (Liverpool, Gilbert G. Walmsley, 1865), 48 ('Negro Row' was 'a street chiefly occupied by African merchants'); A Genuine 'Dicky Sam', *Liverpool and Slavery* (1884); [5]; G.Williams, *History of the Liverpool Privateers* (1897), 474.

9. As quoted by J.A.Picton, *Memorials of Liverpool* (1873 [1872]), I. 225.

10. *Liverpool Chronicle*, as quoted by A Genuine 'Dicky Sam', 9. No date is given.

11. Unidentified Liverpool newspaper dated 17 June 1757, as quoted by J.Hughes, *Liverpool Banks & Bankers 1760–1837* (1906), 141.

12. *Williamson's Liverpool Advertiser*, 24 June 1757, as quoted by G.Williams, 475.

13. *Williamson's Liverpool Advertiser*, 12 September 1766, as quoted by Picton, I. 225. A Genuine 'Dicky Sam', 10, dates this advertisement 8 September 1766.

14. *Liverpool Chronicle*, 15 December 1768, as quoted, *BSB*, 6.

15. *Williamson's Liverpool Advertiser*, 20 August 1756, as quoted by G.Williams, 474.

16. *HCSP of the Eighteenth Century*, LXIX. 83–4; C[arl]. B[ernhard]. Wadström, *An Essay on Colonization, particularly applied to the western coast of Africa* (G.Nicol etc., 1794–5), II. 228; Philip D. Curtin, *The Image of Africa: British Ideas and Action, 1780–1850* (Macmillan & Co. Ltd, 1965), 14.

17. John Haggard, *Reports of cases argued and determined in the High Court of Admiralty*, II (Saunders & Benning, 1833), 105.
18. Unidentified newspaper, as quoted by John Ashton, *Social Life in the Reign of Queen Anne Taken from Original Sources* (Chatto & Windus, 1882), I. 81.
19. *Daily Journal*, no. 2410 (28 September 1728), [2].
20. *Daily Advertiser*, no. 4410 (11 December 1744), [2]; no. 4412 (13 December 1744), [2].
21. *Public Advertiser*, no. 6747 (9 June 1756), [3].
22. *Public Advertiser*, no. 8510 (11 February 1762), [3].
23. *Gentleman's Magazine*, XXXIII (1763), 45.
24. *Public Advertiser*, no. 10747 (8 April 1769), [4]; no. 10786 (29 May 1769), [4].
25. *Public Advertiser*, no. 10944 (28 November 1769), [3].
26. *Gazetteer and New Daily Advertiser*, no. 12,250 (18 April 1769), [2].
27. *Daily Advertiser*, no. 4410 (11 December 1744), [2]; no. 4414 (16 December 1744), [2]; no. 4415 (17 December 1744), [3]; no. 4416 (18 December 1744), [2].
28. *The London Gazette*, no. 5086 (13–17 January 1712 [1713]).
29. *The London Gazette*, no. 5343 (2–5 July 1715).
30. C.M.MacInnes, *Bristol and the Slave Trade* (1963), 7–8. There is a slightly different transcription in C.M.MacInnes, *England and Slavery* (1934), 108, and a photograph in N.File and C.Power, *Black Settlers in Britain 1555–1958* (1981), 54.
31. *Felix Farley's Bristol Journal*, 15 November 1746, as quoted by Latimer, 147.
32. *General Advertiser*, no.4151 (8 April 1748), [2]; no. 4152 (9 April 1748), [2]. *A List of the Free-Holders and Free-Men Who Voted at the Election for Members of Parliament For the City and County of Bristol* (Bristol, Felix Farley, [1744]), 76, shows Josiah Ross, in the parish of 'St Mary Redclift', as a soap-maker.
33. *Bristol Journal*, 12 March 1757, as quoted by Latimer, 147.
34. *Bristol Journal*, as quoted by Latimer, 147. No date is given.
35. *Bristol Journal*, 22 September 1757, as quoted by Latimer, 147.
36. *Bristol Journal*, 15 April 1758, as quoted by Latimer, 147.
37. Unidentified newspaper, dated 14 April 1759, as quoted by Latimer, 147.
38. Unidentified newspaper, as quoted by Ashton, I. 81.
39. Unidentified newspaper, as quoted by Ashton, I. 81.
40. Unidentified newspaper, as quoted by Ashton, I. 81.
41. *Public Advertiser*, no. 6714 (4 May 1756), [3]; no. 6715 (5 May 1756), [2]; no. 6716 (6 May 1756), [2].
42. *Public Ledger*, II/568 (4 November 1761), 1054.
43. *Public Ledger*, II/617 (31 December 1761), 1250.
44. *Public Ledger*, II/589 (28 November 1761), 1138.
45. *Public Ledger*, II/591 (1 December 1761), 1146.

46. *Public Ledger*, II/614 (28 December 1761), 1239.
47. *Public Ledger*, II/616 (30 December 1761), 1247.
48. *Gazetteer and New Daily Advertiser*, no. 12,577 (24 June 1769), [2].

The slave ports' self-image

1. *Public Advertiser*, no. 17724 (27 April 1791), [4].
2. Peter Marshall, *The Anti-Slave Trade Movement in Bristol* (Bristol branch of the Historical Association, 1968), 22–3.
3. M.Craton, *Sinews of Empire* (1974), 156.
4. W[illiam].Moss, *The Liverpool Guide*, second edition (Liverpool, W.Jones, 1797), 127–9.
5. 'Robin Hood', 'The Liverpool Slave Trade', *The Commercial World and Journal of Transport*, 25 February 1893, pp. 8–10, 4 March 1893, p. 3, as quoted by E.Williams, *Capitalism and Slavery*, third impression (1972), 64.
6. George Chandler, *Liverpool* (Batsford, 1957), 306.
7. G.Williams, *History of the Liverpool Privateers* (1897), 473–4.
8. Sir William Watson, 'Thoughts on revisiting a centre of commerce where a vast cathedral church is being erected', *New Poems* (John Lane, 1909), 119.

4. The black community takes shape

Early black organizations

1. Cf. Granville Sharp, *A representation of the Injustice and Dangerous Tendency of Tolerating Slavery; or of admitting the least claim of Private Property in the Persons of Men, in England* (Benjamin White & Robert Horsfield, 1769), 76–7: those advocating the maintenance of slavery in England urged the considerable advantage that attached to black slaves 'because no wages are paid, whereas, free Servants are not only cloathed and boarded at the master's expence . . . but receive wages into the bargain'. For the demand for wages and its role in slave resistance and self-emancipation, see p. 204 above.
2. Aleyn Lyell Reade, *Francis Barber: the Doctor's Negro Servant* (Johnsonian Gleanings, pt II, privately printed, 1912), 4. For Francis Barber, see pp. 424–6 above.
3. James Northcote, *Supplement to the Memoirs of . . . Sir Joshua Reynolds, Knt.* (Henry Colburn, 1815), p. lii.
4. R.B.Cunninghame Graham, *Doughty Deeds: An Account of the Life of Robert Graham of Gartmore, Poet & Politician, 1735–1797* (Heinemann, 1925), 82, 85, 164.
5. John Heneage Jesse, *George Selwyn and his Contemporaries* (Richard Bentley, 1844), IV. 409.
6. Cecil Aspinall-Oglander, *Admiral's Wife: being the life and letters of The*

Hon. Mrs. Edward Boscawen from 1719 to 1761 (Longmans, Green, 1940), 124.

7. Lord Edmond Fitzmaurice, *Life of William, Earl of Shelburne, afterwards first Marquess of Lansdowne* (Macmillan, 1875–6), II. 181.
8. *A Complete Collection of State Trials and Proceedings for High Treason and Other Crimes and Misdemeanors*, comp. T.B.Howell, XX (Longman, Hurst, Rees, Orme & Brown etc., 1814), col. 79.
9. *Gentleman's Magazine*, XXXIV (1764), 493.
10. As quoted by Folarin Shyllon, *Black People in Britain 1555–1833* (Oxford University Press for Institute of Race Relations, 1977), 102.
11. Shyllon, 102.
12. B.N.Turner, 'Account of Dr. Johnson's Visit to Cambridge, in 1765', *New Monthly Magazine*, X/59 (1 December 1818), 386.
13. *Boswell's Life of Johnson*, ed. George Birkbeck Hill and L.F.Powell (Oxford, Clarendon Press, 1934–64), III. 200.
14. *The Servants Pocket-Book* (1761), 18, as quoted by J.J.Hecht, *Continental and Colonial Servants in Eighteenth Century England* (1954), 54.
15. *London Chronicle*, XV/1116 (14–16 February 1764), 166. White people were not as a rule excluded from these 'black hops', however. We read of an Englishwoman who, having paid a shilling entrance fee, 'beheld . . . a lovely African, blooming with all the hue of the warm country that gave him birth, and fell at that instant a sacrifice to the charms of the well made sooty frizeur [i.e. hairdresser]' (*Harris's List of Covent-Garden Ladies; or, Man of Pleasure's Kalender, For the Year, 1788* ('H.Ranger', [*c.*1788]), 84).
16. *London Chronicle*, XXXI/2413 (20–23 June 1772), 598. The report added: 'No sight could be more pleasantly affecting to the feeling mind than the joy which shone at that instant in these poor men's sable countenances.'
17. *London Packet*, no. 418 (26–29 June 1772), as quoted by Hecht, 49.
18. *St. James's Evening Post*, no. 1695 (19–22 March 1726), as quoted by Hecht, 49.
19. *The Diary of John Baker, Barrister of the Middle Temple, Solicitor-General of the Leeward Islands*, ed. Philip C. Yorke (Hutchinson, 1931), 208.
20. Samuel Bowden, *Poems on Various Subjects; with some Essays in Prose, Letters to Correspondents, &c., and a Treatise on Health* (Bath, Leake & Frederick, 1754), 183.
21. *London Packet*, no. 607 (27–29 August 1773), as quoted by Hecht, 48.
22. *Crónica Politica y Literaria de Buenos Aires*, no. 24 (3 May 1827), as quoted by Ricardo Rodríguez Molas, 'La música y la danza de los Negros en el Buenos Aires de los siglos XVIII y XIX', *Historia*, II/7 (1957), 116–17. See also George Reid Andrews, *The Afro-Argentines of Buenos Aires, 1800–1900* (Madison, University of Wisconsin Press, 1980), 138–55.

23. Philip Thicknesse, *A Year's Journey through France and Part of Spain*, second edition (W.Brown, 1778), II. 108.
24. [Edward Long], *Candid Reflections Upon the Judgement lately awarded by the Court of King's Bench, in Westminster-Hall, On what is commonly called the Negroe-cause* (T.Lowndes, 1772), 47.
25. Sir John Fielding, *Extracts from such of the Penal Laws, as Particularly relate to the Peace and Good Order of this Metropolis*, new edition (T.Cadell, 1768), 144–5. Italics in the original.
26. John Fielding, *An Account of the Origin and Effects of a Police Set on Foot by His Grace the Duke of Newcastle* (A.Millar, 1758), 44.
27. Cf. George Rudé, 'The London "Mob" of the Eighteenth Century', *Historical Journal*, II (1959), [1]–18, reprinted in his *Paris and London in the Eighteenth Century: Studies in Popular Protest* (Collins, [1970]), [283]–318. See also the chapter on 'The City Mob' in E.J.Hobsbawm, *Primitive Rebels: Studies in Archaic Forms of Social Movement in the 19th and 20th Centuries* (Manchester University Press, 1959), 108–25, and (for a warning against loose employment of the terms 'mob' and 'riot') E.P.Thompson, 'The Moral Economy of the English Crowd in the Eighteenth Century', *Past and Present*, no. 50 (February 1971), [76]–136.
28. Rudé, 'The London "Mob" of the Eighteenth Century', 14; Rudé, *Paris and London in the Eighteenth Century*, 312.

Black people at work

1. V.Sackville-West, *Knole and the Sackvilles* (1922), 191. Cf. John Steegmann, *The Rule of Taste from George I to George IV* (Macmillan, 1936), 39: 'Chinese boys, for a time, were almost more in demand than negroes, though as yet neither the Blenheim spaniel nor the Italian greyhound had been ousted by the Pekinese.'
2. G.B.Wood, 'A Negro Trail in the North of England', *Country Life Annual*, 1967, p. 42.
3. See Lady Victoria Manners and Dr G.C.Williamson, *John Zoffany, R.A.: his life and works: 1735–1810* (John Lane, 1920), pls. facing pp. 106, 244; William Gaunt, *The Great Century of British Painting: Hogarth to Turner*, second editon (Phaidon, 1978), pls. 131, 113; Ronald Paulson, *Hogarth's Graphic Works*, revised edition (New Haven, Yale University Press, 1970), II. pl. 271.
4. Cf. James Northcote, *Memoirs of Sir Joshua Reynolds, Knt.* (Henry Colburn, 1813), 117.
5. Paulson, II. pl. 128. Black servants made an appearance in the English novel somewhat later – as, for instance, Cesar Gum in Douglas Jerrold's *St. Giles and St. James* (1846), Sambo in Thackeray's *Vanity Fair* (1847–8) (for Sambo as a name see p. 501 n. 9 below) and Gumbo in Thackeray's *The Virginians* (1857–9). They were also the subject of religious chapbooks; see, e.g., [Legh

Richmond], *The Negro Servant* (Edinburgh, [*c.*1804]), reprinted in his *Annals of the Poor*, fifth edition (J.Nisbet, 1826).

6. C.G.Woodson, 'Some Attitudes in English Literature', *Journal of Negro History*, XX (1935), 29.
7. Cf. the description of the vain man by Plato's and Aristotle's pupil Theophrastus (372–287 BC): 'He takes vast pains to be provided with a black servant, who always attends him in public' (W.H.D.Rouse, *A Book of Characters from Theophrastus* etc. (Blackie & Son, 1930), 38). I am grateful to Professor J.S.Cumins for this reference.
8. 'Marmaduke Milton, Esq.', *St. James's Street, a poem, in blank verse* (J.Debrett & E.Harlow, 1790), 14. This poem is sometimes attributed to Charles Dunster.
9. Thomas Whitehead, *Original Anecdotes of the late Duke of Kingston and Miss Chudleigh* (S.Bladon, 1792), 86–90. Sambo could well have been his real name. It is a family name among the Hausa of northern Nigeria, as are Sambu among the Mandinka (Manding) of The Gambia and Samb and Samba among the neighbouring Wolof; see David Dalby, 'The African element in American English', in *Rappin' and Stylin' Out: Communication in Urban Black America*, ed. Thomas Kochman (University of Illinois Press, 1972), 184–5.
10. *Reminiscences of Henry Angelo, with memoirs of his late father and friends* (Henry Colburn, 1828–30), I. 446–52; F.Shyllon, *Black People in Britain* (1977), 41–3.
11. As quoted in Sackville-West, 191.
12. W.M.Thackeray, *The Four Georges* (Smith, Elder, & Co., 1856), 38, 52.
13. 'The Black Man', *All the Year Round*, n.s. XIII (1874–5), 491.
14. David Green, 'A Capful o' Crabs', *Countryman*, XLVIII (1953), 40. Thomas Dyche was a London schoolmaster and lexicographer, whose *Guide to the English Tongue* (Sam. Butler, 1707) had gone into more than 100 editions by 1800.
15. *The Letters of Philip Dormer Stanhope*, ed. B.Dobrée (1932), II. 54.
16. M. Dorothy George, *London Life in the XVIIIth Century* (Kegan Paul, 1925), 134.
17. Copy in Corporation of London Records Office, as quoted by J.Walvin, *The Black Presence* (1971), 65.
18. C.B.Wadström, *An Essay on Colonization* (1794–5), II. 228; George, 137.
19. George, 134. Cf. Millicent Rose, *The East End of London* (Cresset Press, 1951), 71: 'In the eighteenth [century], there were many non-European faces to be seen among the people of the waterfront, . . . mainly of Negroes and Mulattoes of African descent.' For a black person in Ratcliff in 1690, see p. 22 above. Chinese seamen do not seem to have reached east London until the 1780s; see Virginia Berridge, 'East End Opium Dens and Narcotic Use in Britain'.

London Journal, IV (1978), [3], and cf. Ng Kwee Choo, *The Chinese in London* (Oxford University Press, 1968), 5, 16.

20. Michael Banton, *The Coloured Quarter: Negro Immigrants in an English City* (Jonathan Cape, 1955), 23.
21. *St. James's Evening Post*, no. 1721 (21–24 May 1726), as quoted by J.J.Hecht, *Continental and Colonial Servants in Eighteenth Century England* (1954), 36.
22. There seems to be no evidence for the assertion, in Norman Leys, *Kenya* (Hogarth Press, 1924), 367, that 'in the eighteenth century a quarter of the seamen in the British Navy were coloured'. Indeed, according to Pares, the use of black men both in English privateers and in ships of the Royal Navy was rare in the first half of the century. Nevertheless, although Admiral Sir Thomas Frankland condemned the use of what he called 'the woolly race' in warships, and wished to discourage it by selling all black men, free or enslaved, found on board French privateers, the *Downdall* privateer of Jamaica had 15 black men in the crew and the *Queen Anne* had 20, apparently in the 1740s (Richard Pares, 'The Manning of the Navy in the West Indies, 1702–63', *Transactions of the Royal Historical Society*, 5th. ser. XX (1937), 31–2, 32n., reprinted in R.Pares, *The Historian's Business*, ed. R.A. and E.Humphreys (1961), [173], 174n.). 'A London Curate', in an obituary notice of Dr Herbert Mayo, rector of St George in the East, Wapping, for 38 years in the second half of the eighteenth century, wrote of him: 'He was particularly kind to the negroes and uninstructed men of colour; who, employed generally on board of ship, occasionally resided in his parish, which is full of sea-faring people. I suppose no clergyman in England ever baptized so many black men and Mulattoes; nor did he at any time baptize them without much previous preparation' (*Orthodox Churchman's Magazine*, II (1802), 30).
23. *Herrn Zacharias Conrad von Uffenbach Merkwürdige Reisen durch Niedersachsen, Holland und Engelland* [ed. J.G.Schelhorn] (Ulm & Memmingen, Johann Friederich Gaum, 1753–4), II. 532, 536; *London in 1710: from the Travels of Zacharias Conrad von Uffenbach*, trans. and ed. W.H.Quarrell and Margaret Mare (Faber & Faber, 1934), 88, 91.
24. 'Collectanea: or, A collection of advertisements and paragraphs from the newspapers, Relating to various subjects', comp. Daniel Lysons (British Library pressmark, C.103.k.11), I. 107r, 120r.
25. Sir John Barrington, *Personal Sketches of his own Times* (Henry Colburn, 1827–32), II. 208.
26. Christopher Fyfe, *A History of Sierra Leone* (Oxford University Press, 1962), 31–2.
27. *Harris's List of Covent-Garden Ladies . . . For the Year, 1788*, 84.
28. *The* Endeavour *Journal of Joseph Banks 1768–1771*, ed. J.C.Beaglehole (Angus & Robertson, 1962), I. 220–2; James Cook,

'An Account of a Voyage round the World, in the Years MDCCLXVIII, MDCCLXIX, MDCCLXX, and MDCCLXXI', in *An Account of the Voyages undertaken by the order of his present Majesty, for making Discoveries in the Southern Hemisphere*, ed. John Hawkesworth (W.Strahan & T.Cadell, 1773), II. 46–52.

29. *Daily Advertiser*, no. 10796, as quoted by Hecht, 37; C.M.MacInnes, *England and Slavery* (1934), 108; and cf. p. 473 n. 43 above.

30. John Thomas Smith, *Nollekens and his Times* (Henry Colburn, 1828), II. 96, 15, 21.

31. John Jackson, *The History of the Scottish Stage* (Edinburgh, Peter Hill, 1793), 350.

32. Uffenbach, II. 532; *London in 1710*, ed. Quarrell and Mare, 88.

33. Paulson, II. pls. 141, 142.

34. *Nocturnal Revels: or, The History of King's-Place, and Other Modern Nunneries*, second edition (M.Goadby, 1779), II. 98–102.

35. *Boswell: The Ominous Years 1774–1776*, ed. Charles Ryskamp and Frederick A. Pottle (William Heinemann Ltd, 1963), 118. I am grateful to Deirdre Toomey for this reference.

36. *Harris's List of Covent-Garden Ladies . . . For the Year, 1788*, pp. x, 77.

37. *Harris's List of Covent-Garden Ladies . . . for the Year 1793*, 82–3. About the year 1830 'a black girl, called Ebony Bet' was working in the flagellation brothel of Mrs Theresa Berkley, 28 Charlotte Street, Portland Place; see Pisanus Fraxi [H.S. Ashbee], *Index librorum prohibitorum* (privately printed, 1877), pp. xliii–xliv.

Asians in Britain

1. See James M. Holzman, *The Nabobs in England: a study of the returned Anglo-Indian, 1760–1785* (New York, 1926).

2. *Memoirs of William Hickey*, ed. Alfred Spencer (Hurst & Blackett Ltd, 1913–25), IV. 397.

3. Suresh Chandra Ghosh, *The Social Condition of the British Community in Bengal 1757–1800* (Leiden, E.J.Brill, 1970), 111; Revd William Tennant, *Indian Recreations; consisting chiefly of strictures on the domestic and rural economy of the Mahommedans and Hindoos* (Edinburgh, John Anderson etc., 1803), I. 62.

4. Dennis Kincaid, *British Social Life in India 1608–1937* (George Routledge & Sons Ltd, 1938), 83.

5. H.E.Busteed, *Echoes from Old Calcutta, being chiefly reminiscences of the days of Warren Hastings, Francis, & Impey* (Calcutta, Thacker, Spink & Co., 1882), 120n.; W.H.Carey, *The Good Old Days of Honorable John Company; being curious reminiscences illustrating manners and customs of the British in India* (Simla, Argus Press, 1882–7), II. [71]–73; D.R.Banaji, *Slavery in British India* (Bombay, D.B.Taraporevala Sons & Co., [1933]), 6–8. H.A.Stark, *Calcutta in Slavery Days* (Calcutta, H.W.B.Moreno, 1917), 3, while accepting that there were 'a great many African slaves' in eighteenth-century Calcutta, finds it hard to believe that they were bred there. The African presence in India dated from at least the twelfth century, and Africans had begun to enter India in sizeable numbers at least as early as the thirteenth. In the late fifteenth there were some 8,000 African slaves in Bengal, most of them soldiers. See: *The Cambridge History of India*, III, *Turks and Afghans*, ed. Lt-Col. Sir Wolseley Haig (Cambridge, University Press, 1928), 268; D.K.Bhattacharya, 'Indians of African Origin', *Cahiers d'études africaines*, X (1970), [579]–582; Joseph E. Harris, *The African Presence in Asia: Consequences of the East African Slave Trade* (Evanston, Ill., Northwestern University Press, 1971), *passim*, noting prices of African and other slaves in Calcutta at p. 35; Vasant D. Rao, 'The Habshis: India's unknown Africans', *Africa Report*, XVIII/5 (September–October 1973), 35–8; Graham W. Irwin, *Africans Abroad: A Documentary History of the Black Diaspora in Asia, Latin America, and the Caribbean During the Age of Slavery* (New York, Columbia University Press, 1977), 137–67.

6. Sophie Wittwe von la Roche, *Tagebuch einer Reiser durch Holland und England* (Offenbach am Main, Ullrich Weiss & Carl Ludwig Brede, 1791), 266, 519, 491; *Sophie in London, 1786*, trans. Clare Williams (Jonathan Cape, 1933), 126, 272, 257.
7. [Vittoria Caetani,] Duchess of Sermoneta, *The Locks of Norbury: the story of a remarkable family in the XVIIIth and XIXth centuries* (John Murray, 1940), 53–4.
8. *Memoirs of William Hickey*, ed. Spencer, II. 228, 244, 262, 275, 292–3; III. 150.
9. *Annual Register*, 1773, pp. 110–11.
10. Mrs. [Eliza] Fay, *Original Letters from India* [second edition] (Calcutta, 1821), 358–9; ed. E.M.Forster (Hogarth Press, 1925), 242, 284.
11. *London Chronicle*, LXXXVIII/6488 (11–14 October 1800), 363.
12. *Daily Advertiser*, no. 1990 (11 June 1737); no. 3993 (4 November 1743); both as quoted by J.J.Hecht, *Continental and Colonial Servants in Eighteenth Century England* (1954), 53.
13. *The Tatler*, no. 132 (9–11 February 1709 [1710]).
14. *Daily Advertiser*, no. 12566 (4 April 1771); no. 19341 (24 November 1790); both as quoted by Hecht, 51.
15. *Daily Advertiser* no. 8713 (15 December 1758), as quoted by Hecht, 50.
16. *Daily Advertiser*, no. 5947 (31 January 1750 [1751]), as quoted by Hecht, 50.
17. *Daily Advertiser*, no. 13387 (17 November 1773), [2]; *Morning Post, and Daily Advertiser*, no. 1555 (15 October 1777), [3]; *Morning Post, and Daily Advertiser*, no. 1586 (20 November 1777) [3].
18. 'Collectanea', comp. D.Lysons, I. 223v.

Black musicians

1. J.-L.-A.Huillard-Bréholles, *Historia diplomatica Friderici Secundi* (Paris, Henri Plon, 1852–61), V. 676; Arthur Haseloff, *Die Bauten der Hohenstaufen in Unteritalien*, I (Leipzig, Karl W. Hiersemann, 1920), 114; Edmund A. Bowles, 'Eastern Influences on the use of trumpets and drums during the Middle Ages', *Anuario Musical*, XXVI (1971), 21.
2. Henry George Farmer, *Handel's Kettledrums and other papers on military music* (Hinrichsen Edition Ltd, 1950), [103].
3. O.Wright, 'Music', in *The Legacy of Islam*, second edition, ed. Joseph Schacht and C.E.Bosworth (Oxford, Clarendon Press, 1974), 503; cf. Henry George Farmer, 'Oriental Influences on Occidental Military Music', *Islamic Culture*, XV (1941), [235]–242.
4. Henry George Farmer, *Historical Facts for the Arabian Musical Influence* (William Reeves, [1930]), 18; Farmer, 'Oriental Influences on Occidental Military Music', 236. These kettledrums had bowl-shaped bodies of leather, copper, wood, or clay, covered with animal skins, were generally played with two sticks, and were often played in pairs. Like the buisine, they were regarded as a symbol of feudal rank and privilege and were used in musical entertainments, tournaments, and battles. They arrived in England towards the end of the thirteenth century. See James Blades and Jeremy Montagu, *Early Percussion Instruments from the Middle Ages to the Baroque* (Oxford University Press, 1976), 1–2.
5. British Library Add. MS. 27,695, fol. 13r, reproduced in monochrome in: *The Palæographical Society: Facsimiles of Manuscripts and Inscriptions*, ed. E.A.Bond and E.M.Thompson (1873–83), III. pl. 150; Blades and Montagu, p. [x]; *L'Image du noir dans l'art occidental*, ed. Ladislas Bugner, II. ii: *Les Africains dans l'ordonnance chrétienne du monde (xiv*[e]*–xvi*[e] *siècle)* (Paris, Bibliothèque des arts, 1979), 98. Other pictures of black musicians in Europe in the fourteenth to sixteenth centuries can be studied in this last magnificent publication.
6. [Diego Ortíz de Zúñiga], *Annales eclesiasticos y seculares de la muy noble, y muy leal ciudad de Sevilla* (Madrid, Imprenta Real, 1677), 374.
7. Gomes Eannes de Azurara, *Chronica do descobrimento e conquista de Guiné* [1453] (Paris, J.P.Aillaud, 1841), 133; Arthur Helps, *The Spanish Conquest in America* (John W. Parker and Son, 1855–61), I. 37–8; cf. the version in Gomes Eannes de Azurara, *The Chronicle of the Discovery and Conquest of Guinea*, trans. Charles Raymond Beazley and Edgar Prestage (Hakluyt Society, 1896–9), I. 81.
8. Robert Stevenson, 'The Afro-American Musical Legacy to 1800', *Musical Quarterly*, LIV (1968), 497 and n. 66.
9. Anthony Pasquin [i.e. John Williams], *The Life of the Late Earl of Barrymore* (H.D.Symonds, 1793), 70.
10. *The History of the Royal Buckhounds*, comp. J.P.Hore (Newmarket, the compiler, 1895), 321 and n., with an engraving of Cato on p. 322.

11. [Henry Mackenzie and others], *The Lounger*, second edition (Edinburgh and London, A. Strahan etc., 1787), II. 2.
12. *Harris's List of Covent-Garden Ladies . . . For the Year, 1788*, 84.
13. Revd James Woodforde, *The Diary of a Country Parson*, ed. John Beresford (Oxford University Press, 1924–31), II. 334–5.
14. Major J.T.Gorman, 'Drummers and the Leopard-skin', *Sunday Times*, no. 5299 (2 November 1924), 10; J.Paine, 'The Negro Drummers of the British Army', *Royal Military College Magazine & Record*, XXXIII (1928), 22.
15. Scott, *Old Mortality* (1816), chap. 12.
16. Cecil C. P. Lawson, *A History of the Uniforms of the British Army*, I (Peter Davies, 1940), 117–18; J.D.Stewart, *Sir Godfrey Kneller* (1971), 66.
17. Henry George Farmer, *The Rise and Development of Military Music* (Wm Reeves, [1912]), 74.
18. Major T.J.Edwards, 'The Romance of Military Bands', *Cavalry Journal*, XX (1930), 95.
19. *News Letters of 1715–16*, ed. A. Francis Steuart (W. & R. Chambers, Limited, 1910), 63–4.
20. Revd Percy Sumner, 'Army Inspection Returns – 1753 to 1804', *Journal of the Society of Army Historical Research*, III (1924), 244.
21. L.E.Buckell, 'The 4th Queen's Own Dragoons, 1802', *Journal of the Society for Army Historical Research*, XXXV (157), 143–4 and pl. facing p. 143; Cecil C. P. Lawson, *A History of the Uniforms of the British Army*, IV (Norman Military Publications, 1966), 43–4 and fig. 35 (p. 45). According to Buckell (143 n. 1) trumpeters replaced drummers in this regiment in 1768; Charles ffoulkes, *Arms & Armament: An historical survey of the weapons of the British army* (George G. Harrap & Co. Ltd, 1945), 113, dates this change 1766.
22. Capt. Sir George Arthur, Bart., *The Story of the Household Cavalry* (Archibald Constable & Co. Ltd, 1909–26), pl. facing I. 344. A portrait of the Royal Horse Guards' black trumpeter, painted by David Morier, *c.* 1751, shows him wearing a tricorn hat and a pale sky-blue coat laced with red and white lace; see Cecil C. P. Lawson, *A History of the Uniforms of the British Army*, II (Peter Davies, 1941), 151.
23. Lawson, II. 151.
24. John Pine, *The Procession and Ceremonies Observed at the Time of the Installation of the Knights Companions of the Most Honourable Military Order of the Bath: Upon Thursday, June 17, 1725* (W.Innys etc., 1730), p. iv.
25. Farmer, 'Oriental Influences on Occidental Military Music', 239.
26. Cymbals were introduced into the European orchestra in 1680 by Nicolaus Strungk in his opera *Esther* (Blades and Montagu, 18).
27. Henry George Farmer, 'Turkish Influence in Military Music',

Journal of the Society for Army Historical Research, XXIV (1946), 181, reprinted in Farmer, *Handel's Kettledrums*, 45; J.A.Kappey, *Military Music: A History of Wind-Instrumental Bands* (Boosey & Co., [1894]), 82. This effect was scored for by Haydn, Mozart, and Mahler (Blades and Montagu, 22).

28. The triangle entered the European orchestra in the Hamburg Opera in 1710. Mozart used it in *Die Entführung aus dem Serail* (1782), Haydn in his 'Military' Symphony (1794), and Beethoven in his Choral Symphony (1824) – in each case as an imitation of 'Janissary' music (Blades and Montagu, 14).

29. *A Descriptive Catalogue of the Musical Instruments recently exhibited at the Royal Military Exhibition*, comp. Capt. C.R.Day (Eyre & Spottiswoode, 1891), 233.

30. Farmer, *Handel's Kettledrums*, 4n. The Turkish word apparently survives only in the expression *çalgi çağanak*, 'a noisy musical party'.

31. Farmer, 'Turkish Influence in Military Music', 182; Farmer, *Handel's Kettledrums*, 45.

32. Farmer, 'Oriental Influences on Occidental Military Music', 240. Ladies were portrayed playing on these instruments, and pianofortes were specially made with attachments sounding drum, triangle, and tambourine, as in Joseph Smith's 1799 patent.

33. Farmer, 'Turkish Influence in Military Music', 182; Farmer, *Handel's Kettledrums*, 46; Henry George Farmer, *History of the Royal Artillery Band 1762–1953* (Royal Artillery Institution, 1954), 53.

34. Farmer, 'Oriental Influences on Occidental Military Music', 240.

35. Cf. John F. Szwed and Roger D. Abrahams, 'After the Myth: Studying Afro-American Cultural Patterns in the Plantation Literature', *Research in African Literatures*, VII (1976), 220–1, reprinted in *African Folklore in the New World*, ed. Daniel J. Crowley (Austin and London, University of Texas Press, 1977), 74–5.

36. Farmer, 'Turkish Influence in Military Music', 182 (here omitting the word 'orchestral'); Farmer, *Handel's Kettledrums*, 46.

37. Col. L.I.Cowper, *The King's Own* (Oxford, for the Regiment, 1939), I. 195; Col.H.C.B.Rogers, *The British Army of the Eighteenth Century* (George Allen & Unwin Ltd, 1977), 43.

38. But not in animal skins, despite the assertions of Reginald F. Healy, 'Military Music and Military Musicians', *United Service Magazine*, n.s. LIII (1916), 429; Gorman, 'Drummers and the Leopard-skin'; Edwards, 'The Romance of Military Bands', 95; and H.G.Farmer and James Blades, 'Janissary music', in *The New Grove Dictionary of Music and Musicians*, ed. Stanley Sadie (Macmillan, 1980), IX. 497. See W.G.F.Boag, 'Animal Skins: A suggested origin for the use of skins as part of the dress of drummers', *Bulletin, Military Historical Society*, XXVII (1977), 65 ('Despite a very thorough search of contemporary prints, paintings and documents I have been unable to discover one single reference to negro bandsmen wearing animal skins . . . The use of these adornments does not seem to pre-date the latter half of the 19th century . . . The drummers of the regiments of Foot Guards, which regiments were amongst the first to employ negroes, have never used skins at all') and 69 ('The weight of such evidence as I have been able to discover would suggest that skins of bears, tigers, leopards, jaguars etc. is [*sic*] really a Victorian innovation').

39. Paine, 'The Negro Drummers of the British Army', 22.

40. H[ugh]. Everard, *History of Thos. Farrington's Regiment subsequently designated The 29th (Worcestershire) Foot 1694 to 1891* (Worcester, Littlebury & Co., 1891), 55, 74, 122, 221, 355, 358, 375. In 1864 an old ex-sergeant, discharged in 1823, walked 19 miles to see the regiment's colours, and remarked 'that he did not see any black drummers, and that in his time they were all blacks' (Everard, 526n.).

41. Paine, 'The Negro Drummers of the British Army', 21–2.

42. Robert A. Marr, *Music for the People: A Retrospect of the Glasgow International Exhibition, 1888 with an account of the rise of choral societies in Scotland* (Edinburgh and Glasgow, John Menzies & Co., 1889), 94.

43. C. ffoulkes, 'Notes on Early Military Bands', *Journal of the Society for Army Historical Research*, XVII (1938), 194. See also Lieut-Gen. Sir. F.W.Hamilton, *The Origin and History of the First or Grenadier Guards* (John Murray, 1874), II. pl. 3, facing p. 267, showing a black drummer in the regiment, 1792.

44. Ralph Nevill, *British Military Prints* (Connoisseur Publishing Co., 1909), 44.

45. Revd Percy Sumner, 'Jean Baptiste, Cymbal Player of the Scots Fusilier Guards, 1832', *Journal of the Society for Army Historical Research*, XXII (1943–4), [1].

46. Paine, 'The Negro Drummers of the British Army', 23; Boag, 66.

47. J.Paine, 'Cavalry Bands', *Cavalry Journal*, XX (1930), 337.

48. Farmer, *Rise and Development of Military Music*, 78. Russell Braddon, *All the Queen's Men: The Household Cavalry and the Brigade of Guards* (Hamish Hamilton, 1977), 143, says there were four. Trombones were added to the military band towards the end of the eighteenth century; see Adam Carse, 'The Prince Regent's Band', *Music & Letters*, XXVII (1946), 149.

49. W.T.Parke, *Musical Memoirs; comprising an Account of the General State of Music in England* (Henry Colburn & Richard Bentley, 1830), II. 240–2.

50. Revd Percy Sumner, 'Cox & Co., Army Agents: Uniform Items from their Ledgers: Part II. – Infantry', *Journal of the Society for Army Historical Research*, XVII (1938), 139.

51. Sumner, 'Jean Baptiste', [1].

52. Paine, 'The Negro Drummers of the British Army', 23.

53. Nevill, p. xliii. For a picture of the black drummer in the Royal

Fusiliers band, *c.*1789, see Cecil C. P. Lawson, *A History of the Uniforms of the British Army*, III (Norman Military Publications, 1961), pl. 2, facing p. 67.

54. Lawson, III. pl. 3, facing p. 149.

55. *Notes and Queries*, 1st ser. XII (1855), 121.

56. Henry George Farmer, 'The Band of H.M. Scots Guards', *Musical Standard*, n.s. XIX/385 (17 June 1922), 193.

57. Maj.-Gen. Sir F.Maurice, *The History of the Scots Guards from the Creation of the Regiment to the Eve of the Great War* (Chatto & Windus, 1934), II. 264; Sumner, 'Jean Baptiste', [1], according to whom there is a portrait of Baptiste at Windsor Castle.

58. *Journal of the Society for Army Historical Research*, XXVII (1949), 90.

59. Henry George Farmer, 'The Royal Artillery Band: Fresh Light on its History', *Journal of the Society for Army Historical Research*, XXIII (1945), 94; Farmer, *History of the Royal Artillery Band*, 102.

60. Sumner, 'Cox & Co., Army Agents', 137, 141. See also Cecil C. P. Lawson, *A History of the Uniforms of the British Army*, V (Kaye & Ward Limited, 1967), 47: 'The musicians of the 3rd Foot Guards are shown in illustrations of a child's book under the title of *The Duke of Gloucester's Band.* The Duke was Colonel of the Regiment from 1806 to 1834 . . . The negroes wear scarlet, gold laced jackets, white pantaloons with gold lace, short white gaiters, red head-dress with white turban, two white feathers and one red one.'

61. *Fourteenth Report of the Society for the Suppression of Mendicity* (1832), [41]–42.

62. Lawson, V. 51.

63. John Wm Burrows, *The Essex Yeomanry* (Essex Units in the War 1914–1919, III, Southend-on-Sea, [1926]), [71]; a portrait of this drummer by H.Martens is reproduced in colour, facing p. 72 (and in monochrome in Nevill, 25).

64. Farmer, *Rise and Development of Military Music*, 75; Farmer, *History of the Royal Artillery Band*, 54.

65. Everard, 375.

66. Farmer, 'Turkish Influence in Military Music', 182 ('discreetly' here appearing as 'discreet'; 'discretely' seems to be meant); Farmer, *Handel's Kettledrums*, 46.

67. 'A Ramble round the Military Exhibition: An Old Bandsman's Notes', *British Bandsman and Orchestral Times*, III (1889–90), 243.

68. Farmer, *Rise and Development of Military Music*, 77.

69. *Christ. Fried. Dan. Schubart's Ideen zu einer Ästhetik der Tonkunst*, ed. Ludwig Schubart (Vienna, J.V.Degen, 1806), 332. I am grateful to Alan Unwin for translating this passage for me.

70. Paine, 'The Negro Drummers of the British Army', 21.

71. Farmer, *History of the Royal Artillery Band*, 54. There is an echo of this in an essay by Leigh Hunt describing Horse Guards Parade: 'The blacks toss up their cymbals in the sun; the little triangle-boys emulate their long legs'; see [James Henry Leigh Hunt], 'The Wishing-Cap. No. XII. St James's Park', *The Examiner*, no. 863 (16 August 1824), 517.

72. *Ipswich Journal*, no. 605 (15 September 1750), [2].
73. *Ipswich Journal*, 1761, as quoted by G.O. Rickword, 'Black Drummers in the Army', *Journal of the Society of Army Historical Research*, IV (1925), 136.
74. *Ipswich Journal*, no. 3133 (14 August 1790), [2].
75. *Ipswich Journal*, no. 3308 (2 April 1796), [3].
76. Col. H.C.B.Rogers, *Wellington's Army* (Ian Allan Ltd, 1979), 39; and see Thomas Simes, *The Military Medley: Containing the most necessary rules and directions for attaining a Competent Knowledge of the Art*, second edition (1768), plan 11, showing 'Musick. Drum[rs]. Fifers.' by the colours in the centre of the square.
77. Henry George Farmer, 'Our Bands in the Napoleonic Wars', *Journal of the Society for Army Historical Research*, XL (1962), 38; Henry George Farmer, *British Bands in Battle* (Hinrichsen Edition, [1965]), 16.
78. *Western Flying-Post; or Sherborne and Yeovil Mercury, and General Advertiser*, XXXII/1646 (21 August 1780), [3]. See also S.J.W.Kerr, *Records of the 1st Somerset Militia (3rd. Bn. Somerset L.I.)* (Aldershot, Gale & Polden Ltd, [1931]), 26.
79. Nevill, p. xxi. Here and in the version of the anecdote given by Paine, 'The Negro Drummers of the British Army', 22, the bandsman concerned is said to have been Martinique-born Francis, of the Grenadier Guards. Both versions use the spelling 'dat' for 'that'.

5. Eighteenth-century voices

Ukawsaw Gronniosaw

1. *A Narrative of the Most remarkable Particulars in the life of James Albert Ukawsaw Gronniosaw, an African prince, As related by himself* (Bath, S.Hazard [*c.* 1770]), [7].
2. *A Narrative*, 19.
3. *A Narrative*, 26.
4. *A Narrative*, 32.
5. *A Narrative*, 33–4.
6. *A Narrative*, 39.
7. *A Narrative*, 43.
8. *A Narrative*, 43–4.
9. *A Narrative*, 47–8.
10. *A Narrative*, 48.
11. *A Narrative*, Preface, pp. [iv], vi.
12. *A Narrative*, 49.

13. F.Shyllon, *Black People in Britain* (1977), [169].

Phillis Wheatley

1. Her only predecessor was Jupiter Hammon, who published a broadside poem in 1761 and another, in praise of Phillis Wheatley, in 1778. See Oscar Wegelin, *Jupiter Hammon: American Negro poet: Selections from his writings and a bibliography* (Heartman's Historical Ser. no. 13, New York, Chas. Fred. Heartman, 1915); Vernon Loggins, *The Negro Author: his development in America* (New York, Columbia University Press, 1931), 9–16; Benjamin Brawley, *Early Negro American Writers: Selections with Biographical and Critical Introductions* (Chapel Hill, University of North Carolina Press, 1935), 21–2; Sidney Kaplan, *The Black Presence in the Era of the American Revolution 1770–1800* (Greenwich, Conn., New York Graphic Society Ltd, 1973), 171–8.
2. H.W.Debrunner, *Presence and Prestige* (1979), 169.
3. 'Extracts from the Journal of C.J.Stratford', *Proceedings of the Massachusetts Historical Society*, [XIV] (1876–7), 389.
4. [Margaretta Matilda Odell], *Memoir and Poems of Phillis Wheatley, a Native African and a Slave* (Boston, Geo. W. Light, 1834), [9].
5. M.A.Richmond, *Bid the Vassal Soar: Interpretive Essays on the Life and Poetry of Phillis Wheatley (ca. 1753–1784) and George Moses Horton (ca. 1797–1883)* (Washington, DC, Howard University Press, 1974), 12, 70–1, suggests that Phillis Wheatley was a Fula from Senegambia, who might well have been familiar with Arabic script before being transported.
6. Benjamin Brawley, *The Negro in Literature and Art in the United States* (New York, Duffield & Company, 1918), 13.
7. Brawley, *The Negro in Literature and Art*, 13.
8. [Odell], 11.
9. Phillis Wheatley, *Poems on various subjects, religious and moral* (A.Bell, 1773), 18; *The Poems of Phillis Wheatley*, ed. Julian D. Mason, Jr (Chapel Hill, University of North Carolina Press, 1966), 7.
10. Benjamin Quarles, *The Negro in the American Revolution* (Chapel Hill, University of North Carolina Press for the Institute of Early American History and Culture, 1961), 189.
11. *London Magazine*, XLII (1773), 456.
12. *Monthly Review*, XLIX (1773), 459.
13. All eight reviews are reprinted in Mukhtar Ali Isani, 'The British Reception of Wheatley's *Poems on Various Subjects*', *Journal of Negro History*, LXVI (1981), 144–9. 'In every case', Isani points out (p. 145), 'at least one poem was reprinted as a sample of its quality.'
14. William H. Robinson, *Phillis Wheatley in the Black American Beginnings* (Broadside Critics Ser. no. 5, Detroit, Broadside Press, 1975), 11.
15. Julian D. Mason, Jr, in *Poems of Phillis Wheatley*, ed. Mason, p. xxi.
16. Robinson, 30–1.

17. 'To the University of CAMBRIDGE, in NEW-ENGLAND', Wheatley, 15; *Poems of Phillis Wheatley*, ed. Mason, 5.
18. Wheatley, 114–15; *Poems of Phillis Wheatley*, ed. Mason, 54–5. 'S.M.' was Scipio Moorhead, slave to the Revd John Moorhead (Brawley, *The Negro in Literature and Art*, 103).
19. Robinson, 62.
20. [M.M.Odell and G.W.Light], 'Memoir', in [Odell], 23. See also, for Phillis Wheatley, John W. Cromwell, *The Negro in American History: Men and women eminent in the evolution of the American of African descent* (Washington, DC, American Negro Academy, 1914), 77–85; Loggins, 16–29; Brawley, *Early Negro American Writers*, 31ff.; Kaplan, 150–70.

Ignatius Sancho

1. *Letters of the late Rev. Mr. Laurence Sterne, To his most intimate Friends*, ed. Mrs. [Lydia] Medalle (T.Becket, 1775), III. 22–3; *Letters of Laurence Sterne*, ed. Lewis Perry Curtis (Oxford, Clarendon Press, 1935), 282; [Joseph Jekyll], 'The Life of Ignatius Sancho', in *Letters of the late Ignatius Sancho, an African* (J.Dodsley etc., 1782), I. p. vi; *Letters of the late Ignatius Sancho*, ed. Paul Edwards (Dawsons of Pall Mall, 1968), Introduction, p. xvi, facsimile reprint, p. iv.
2. [Jekyll], in *Letters of Sancho* (1782), I. p. vii; *Letters of Sancho* (1968), p. ii.
3. [Jekyll], in *Letters of Sancho* (1782), I. pp. vii-viii; *Letters of Sancho* (1968), p. iii.
4. Paul Edwards, Introduction to *Letters of Sancho* (1968), p. viii. The collections are: *Minuets Cotillons & Country Dances for the Violin, Mandolin, German Flute, & Harpischord*, Composed by an African, Most humbly Inscribed to his Grace Henry Duke of Buccleugh, &c, &c, &c. (Printed for the Author, [*c.*1765]); *A Collection of New Songs*, Composed by an African, Humbly Inscribed to the Honble Mrs James Brudenell by her most humble Devoted & obedient Servant The Author [*c.*1770]; *Minuets for the Violin Mandolin German-Flute and Harpsichord*, Compos'd by an African, Book 2^d^, Humbly Inscribed to the Right Honble John Lord Montagu of Broughton (Richd Duke, [*c.*1770]). For Sancho as composer, see Josephine Wright, 'Ignatius Sancho (1729–1780), African Composer in England', *Black Perspective in Music*, VII/2 (Fall 1979), [133]–145.
5. Vols. III and IV of Sterne's *Sermons* had been published six months before, vols. VI and VII of *Tristram Shandy* in the previous year.
6. *Critical Review*, XXI (1766), 282.
7. *Letters of Sterne* (1775), III. 23–5; cf. the version edited by Sterne, in *Letters of Sterne* (1935), 282–3.
8. *Letters of Sterne* (1775), III. 27–8; cf. *Letters of Sterne* (1935), 285–6.
9. *Letters of Sterne* (1775), III. 31–2; cf. *Letters of Sterne* (1935), 340.

10. *Letters of Sterne* (1775), III. 36; cf. *Letters of Sterne* (1935), 370.
11. [Jekyll], in *Letters of Sancho* (1782), I. p. xi; *Letters of Sancho* (1968), p. v.
12. *Letters of Sancho* (1782), II. 204, 205–6; *Letters of Sancho* (1968), 295, 296.
13. J.T.Smith, *Nollekens and his Times* (1828), I. 28–9.
14. Andrew Knapp and William Baldwin, *Criminal Chronology; or, The New Newgate Calendar* (Liverpool, Nuttall, Fisher, and Dixon, 1809–10), III. 445, 447. I am grateful to Liz Willis for this reference.
15. *Letters of Sancho* (1782), II. 169, 170, 171–4; *Letters of Sancho* (1968), 269, 270, 270–3.
16. *Letters of Sancho* (1782), [editorial note], p. ii.
17. Robin Hallett, *The Penetration of Africa: European enterprise and exploration principally in northern and western Africa up to 1830*, I, *To 1815* (Routledge & Kegan Paul, 1965), 147–8.
18. *Monthly Review*, LXIX (1783), 492n., 497.
19. F. Shyllon, *Black People in Britain* (1977), 191.
20. H[enri].[Baptiste] Grégoire, *De la littérature des Nègres* (Paris, Maradan, 1808), 252, 255, corrected by Edwards, Introduction to *Letters of Sancho* (1968), pp. v–vi. J[ohn]RW[illis], 'New Light on the Life of Ignatius Sancho: Some Unpublished Letters', *Slavery & Abolition*, I/3 (December 1980), [345]–358, includes a facsimile of a letter, dated 29 February 1820, from Sancho's daughter Elisabeth to William Stevenson, a friend of the family, accompanying the presentation of Gainsborough's portrait of Sancho.
21. *Letters of Sancho* (1782), I. 113, 180; II. 14; I. 174, 39; *Letters of Sancho* (1968), 83, 130, 156, 125, 30.
22. *Letters of Sancho* (1782), II. 116, 167; I. 140; II. 126; *Letters of Sancho* (1968), 231, 268, 101, 238.
23. *Letters of Sancho* (1782), II. 155; *Letters of Sancho* (1968), 259.
24. *Letters of Sancho* (1782), I. 140; *Letters of Sancho* (1968), 101.
25. *Letters of Sancho* (1782), II. 86–7; *Letters of Sancho* (1968), 209–10.
26. *Letters of Sancho* (1782), II. 92; *Letters of Sancho* (1968), 214.
27. *Letters of Sancho* (1782), I. 200; *Letters of Sancho* (1968), 143.
28. *Letters of Sancho* (1782), II. 98; *Letters of Sancho* (1968), 218.

Ottobah Cugoano

1. H.W.Debrunner, *Presence and Prestige* (1979), 166.
2. Ottobah Cugoano, *Thoughts and sentiments on the evil and wicked traffc of the slavery and commerce of the human species, humbly submitted to the Inhabitants of Great-Britain* (1787), 7–12.
3. How he was freed is not clear. Debrunner, 166, following H.Grégoire, *De la littérature des Nègres* (1808), says he was 'ransomed' by 'Lord Hoth' and brought to London in 1780; Cugoano's own account is different, as Paul Edwards points out in his introduction to

the facsimile reprint, *Thoughts and Sentiments on the Evil of Slavery* (Dawsons of Pall Mall, 1969), p. v.

4. Prince Hoare, *Memoirs of Granville Sharp, Esq.* (Henry Colburn & Co., 1820), 247–8.
5. Robert W. July, *The Origins of Modern African Thought: Its development in West Africa during the nineteenth and twentieth centuries* (Faber & Faber, 1968), 21.
6. C.Fyfe, *A History of Sierra Leone* (1962), 13; July, 40; Edwards, Introduction to Cugoano, *Thoughts and Sentiments* (1969), pp. vii–xii; F.Shyllon, *Black People in Britain* (1977), 173.
7. Cugoano (1787), 17.
8. Cugoano (1787), 73.
9. Cugoano (1787), pp. iii, 103.
10. Cugoano (1787), 103–4.
11. Cugoano (1787), 109–10, 112, 130, 132.
12. Fyfe, 13.
13. Cugoano (1787), 121–2, 133–5.
14. Cugoano (1787), 75–7. The significance of this passage is pointed out by Imanuel Geiss, *The Pan-African Movement*, trans. Ann Keep (Methuen & Co. Ltd, 1974), 9.
15. *Parliamentary History*, XXX. cols. 659, 660.
16. Robert Isaac and Samuel Wilberforce, *The Life of William Wilberforce* (John Murray, 1838), III. 182.
17. Wilberforce, I. 344.
18. Shyllon, 175.
19. Wilberforce, I. 152–3.
20. Edwards argues (Introduction to Cugoano (1969), p. xii) that the 1791 edition is not an abridgement, but the text from which the 1787 edition had been expanded.
21. [Ottobah Cugoano], *Thoughts and sentiments on the evil of slavery or, The nature of servitude as admitted by the law of God, compared to the modern slavery of the Africans in the West-Indies* (The Author, 1791), [47].
22. Grégoire, 215–16. I have used the contemporary translation, *An Enquiry concernng the intellectual and moral faculties and literature of Negroes* (Brooklyn, Thomas Kirk, 1810), 189. The anti-slavery writer Wilson Armistead wrote of Cugoano in 1848: 'In him we may behold talents without much literary cultivation, to which a good education would have given great advantage' (Wilson Armistead, *A Tribute for the Negro: being a vindication of the moral, intellectual, and religious capabilities of The Coloured portion of Mankind* (Manchester, William Irwin, 1848), as quoted by Debrunner, 166).
23. Geiss, 9, 40.
24. Paul-Marc Henry, 'Pan-Africanism; a dream come true', *Foreign Affairs*, XXXVII (1958–9), 445.

25. Cf. George Shepperson, 'Notes on Negro American influences on the emergence of African nationalism', *Journal of African History*, I (1960), [299]–300, 312.

Olaudah Equiano

1. Paul Edwards, Introduction to *Equiano's Travels* (Heinemann Educational Books, 1967), p. xi; Paul Edwards, Introduction to *The Life of Olaudah Equiano or Gustavus Vassa the African* (Dawsons, 1969), I. pp. xx–xxi, lxxiv n. 31.
2. *The Interesting Narrative of the Life of Olaudah Equiano, or Gustavus Vassa, the African: written by himself* (The Author, [1789]), I. 98–9.
3. *Interesting Narrative*, I. 106.
4. *Interesting Narrative*, I. 116.
5. *Interesting Narrative*, I. 176–8.
6. *Interesting Narrative*, II. 122–3.
7. *Interesting Narrative*, II. 222.
8. *Interesting Narrative*, II. 231.
9. *Interesting Narrative*, II. 234–6. Cf. Equiano's letter to Cugoano, *Public Advertiser*, no. 16496 (4 April 1787), [3].
10. [Captain] Tho. B^{n}. Thompson to Commissioners of the Navy, 21 March 1787: copy in PRO T1 643/305.
11. Commissioners of the Navy to Treasury, 23 March 1787, PRO T1 643/304.
12. Edwards, Introduction to *Equiano's Travels*, p. xii.
13. *Public Advertiser*, no. 16583 (14 July 1789), [3].
14. Thomas Hardy to Revd Mr Bryant of Sheffeld, 8 March 1792: copy in British Library Add. MS. 27,811 ('Original Letter Book of the (London) Corresponding Society'), fols. 4v–5r; cf. the edited version in *Memoir of Thomas Hardy, Founder of, and Secretary to, the London Corresponding Society* (James Ridgway, 1832), 15.
15. *Memoir of Thomas Hardy*, 15.
16. Lydia Hardy to Thomas Hardy, 2 April 1792, PRO TS 24/12/1.
17. G.I.Jones, 'Olaudah Equiano of the Niger Ibo', in *Africa Remembered*, ed. P.D.Curtin (1967), 61.
18. *The Journal of the Rev. John Wesley, A.M.*, ed. Nehemiah Curnock and others (Charles H. Kelly, 1909–16), VIII. 128.
19. *Monthly Review*, LXXX (1789), 551–2.
20. *General Magazine and Impartial Review*, III (1789), 315.
21. P.Hoare, *Memoirs of Granville Sharp* (1820), 236; Edwards, Introduction to *Life of Equiano*, I. pp. lvi–lvii.
22. *The Diary; or Woodfall's Register*, no. 24 (25 April 1789), [3].
23. The letters signed by the 'Sons of Africa' are conveniently assembled in F.Shyllon, *Black People in Britain* (1977), App. ii, [267]–272.
24. [James Tobin], *Cursory Remarks upon the Reverend Mr. Ramsay's Essay*

on The Treatment and Conversion of African Slaves in the Sugar Colonies (G. & T. Wilkie, 1785), 118n.; *Public Advertiser*, no. 16754 (28 January 1788), [1]–[2].

25. *Public Advertiser*, no. 16761 (5 February 1788), [1]–[2].
26. *Public Advertiser*, no. 16754 [*sic*] (31 March 1788), [1]; cf. the version in Shyllon, 251–3.
27. John Alfred Langford, *A Century of Birmingham Life: or, A Chronicle of Local Events, From 1741 to 1841* (Birmingham, E.C.Osborne, 1868), I. 440–1.
28. *The Interesting Narrative of the Life of Olaudah Equiano*, sixth edition (The Author, 1793), 359; Edwards, Introduction to *Life of Equiano*, I. p. xiv.
29. *Gentleman's Magazine*, LXII (1792), i. 384.
30. Reproduced in N.File and C.Power, *Black Settlers in Britain* (1981), [55].
31. *Interesting Narrative*, sixth edition, pp. [xviii]–xxxiv.
32. Equiano to Revd G.Walker, 27 February 1792, as quoted by Edwards, Introduction to *Life of Equiano*, I. p. xiv.
33. Thomas Digges to Mr. O'Brien, Carrickfergus, 25 December 1791, in *Interesting Narrative*, sixth edition, p. xii.
34. *Oracle*, no. 909 (25 April 1792), [3]; *Star*, no. 1,248 (27 April 1792), [3].
35. *Interesting Narrative*, sixth edition, p. vi.
36. *Interesting Narrative*, sixth edition, p. iv.
37. Granville Sharp to his niece Jemima, 22 February 1811, as quoted by Edwards, Introduction to *Equiano's Travels*, p. xv.
38. I owe this last sentence to S. Kaplan, *The Black Presence in the Era of the American Revolution 1770–1800* (1973), 206.

6. Slavery and the law

The legal pendulum

1. John Rushworth, *Historical Collections*, II (John Wright & Richard Chiswell, 1680), i. 468; *Judicial Cases concerning American Slavery and the Negro*, ed. Helen Tunnicliff Catterall (Washington, DC, Carnegie Institution of Washington, 1926–37), I. 1, 9.
2. Jos. Keble, *Reports in the Court of Kings Bench at Westminster* (Thomas Dring etc., 1685), III. 785; *Les Reports de S[r]. Creswell Levinz* (S.Keble etc., 1702), ii. 201; *The Reports of Sr. Creswell Levinz, Knt.*, second edition (D.Browne etc., 1722), ii. 201; Sir Bartholomew Shower, *The Second part of the reports of cases and Special Arguments, argued and adjudged in the Court of King's Bench* (D.Browne etc., 1720), 177; *The English Reports*, LXXXIII (Edinburgh, William Green & Sons, etc., 1908), 518; Catterall, I. 9, 10 n. 2.

3. Lord Mansfield, as quoted by Capel Lofft, *Reports of cases adjudged in the Court of King's Bench* (William Owen, 1776), 8; *A Complete Collection of State Trials*, comp. T.B.Howell, XX (1814), col. 70.
4. Robert Lord Raymond, *Reports of Cases Argued and Adjudged in the Courts of King's Bench and Common Pleas*, second edition (J.Worrall etc., 1765), I. 147; *English Reports*, XCI (1909), 994; Catterall, I. 10.
5. [Guy Miège], *The New State of England Under Their majesties K. William and Q. Mary* (1691), ii. 268.
6. Will of Thomas Papillon, 1700–01, Kent Archives v 1015. T. 44, as quoted by J.Walvin, *Black and White* (1973), 42, 50.
7. Thomas Carthew, *Reports of cases Adjudged in the Court of King's Bench* (R.Gosling etc., 1728), 396–7; Raymond, I. 147; *English Reports*, XCI. 994; Catterall, I. 10–12.
8. William Salkeld, *Reports of cases Adjudg'd in the Court of King's Bench* (J.Walthoe etc., 1717–18), II. 666; *English Reports*, XCI. 566–7; Catterall, I. 2–3, 11.
9. Lord Mansfield, as quoted by Lofft, 8; *State Trials*, comp. Howell, XX. col. 70; Catterall, I. 3.
10. William Maxwell Morison, *The decisions of the Court of Session* (Edinburgh, Archibald Constable & Company, 1811), XXXIII–XXXIV. 14547; Catterall, I. 3, 12.
11. Charles Ambler, *Reports of Cases argued and determined in the High Court of Chancery* (A.Strahan etc., 1790), 76–7; *English Reports*, XXVII (1903), 47–9; Catterall, I. 3–4, 12–13.
12. [Solomon] Bolton, *The Present State of Great Britain and Ireland*, eleventh edition (J.Brotherton etc., 1758), i. 173.
13. Robert Henley Eden, *Reports of cases argued and determined in the High Court of Chancery, from 1757 to 1756* (Charles Hunter etc., 1818), II. 127; *English Reports*, XXVIII (1903), 844–5; Catterall, I. 4, 13.

Granville Sharp challenges the slave-owners

1. The bill of sale is quoted in P.Hoare, *Memoirs of Granville Sharp* (1820), 34–5n.
2. Sharp, as quoted, *BSB*, 21.
3. Sharp, as quoted, *BSB*, 21.
4. Sharp, as quoted, *BSB*, 22.
5. Sharp, as quoted, *BSB*, 23.
6. Sharp, as quoted, *BSB*, 30.
7. Sharp, as quoted, *BSB*, 39.
8. G.Sharp, *A representation of the Injustice and Dangerous Tendency of Tolerating Slavery* (1769), 79, 29, 104–5.
9. James Bradshawe, undated letter to Granville Sharp, in Hardwicke Papers, as quoted, *BSB*, 37–8.
10. Sharp, as quoted, *BSB*, 42.

11. Sharp, as quoted, *BSB*, 43.
12. Sharp, as quoted, *BSB*, 51.
13. T.Clarkson, *History of the Rise, Progress and Accomplishment of the Abolition of the Slave Trade* (1808), I. 75; Hoare, 69n.
14. Hoare, 56n; *BSB*, 46.
15. *BSB*, 15, 169, 234. Mansfield's black slave-servant was called Dido Elizabeth Lindsay.
16. As quoted by Edward Lascelles, *Granville Sharp and the Freedom of Slaves in England* (Humphrey Milford, 1928), 29.
17. Clarkson, I. 76.

The Somerset case

1. As quoted, *BSB*, 43.
2. William Blackstone, *Commentaries on the Laws of England* (Oxford, Clarendon Press, 1765–9), I. 123.
3. W.Blackstone, *Commentaries on the Laws of England*, second edition (Oxford, Clarendon Press, 1766–9), I. 127.
4. This is conclusively argued by Shyllon, *BSB*, [55]–76. He clinches his argument with this quotation from [Sir James Stephen], 'The Clapham Sect', *Edinburgh Review*, LXXX (1844), 264, reprinted in his *Essays in Ecclesiastical Biography* (Longman, Brown, Green, & Longmans, 1849), II. 316: 'Three of the infallible doctors of the Church at Westminster – Yorke, Talbot, and Mansfield – favoured the claim [of David Lisle in the case of Jonathan Strong]; and Blackstone, the great expositor of her traditions, hastened, at their bidding, to retract a heresy on this article of the faith into which his uninstructed reason had fallen.'
5. By far the best account of the Somerset case is Shyllon's, in *BSB*, [82]–124. The summary in *Judicial Cases concerning American Slavery and the Negro*, ed. H.T.Catterall (1926–37), I. 14–18, is, for various reasons, unsatisfactory.
6. P.Hoare, *Memoirs of Granville Sharp* (1820), 77n.; cf. Charles Stuart, *A Memoir of Granville Sharp* (New York, American Anti-Slavery Society, 1836), 11.
7. *Gazetteer and New Daily Advertiser*, no. 13,480 (13 May 1772), [4]; *BSB*, 95.
8. Hoare, 84; *BSB*, 95.
9. Francis Hargrave, *A Complete Collection of state-trials, and proceedings for high-treason*, XI (J.F. & C.Rivington etc., 1781), 346; *State Trials*, comp. T.B. Howell, XX (1814), cols. 59–60; *BSB*, 97.
10. *State Trials*, comp. Howell, XX. col. 69; *BSB*, 101.
11. Hoare, 89; *BSB*, 102–3.
12. Hoare, 89; *State Trials*, comp. Howell, XX. col. 71; *BSB*, 104.
13. *State Trials*, comp. Howell, XX. cols. 74–5; *BSB*, 104.

14. *Gazetteer and New Daily Advertiser*, no. 13,489 (23 May 1772), [4]; *BSB*, 105.
15. *State Trials*, comp. Howell, XX. col. 79; *BSB*, 106.
16. *State Trials*, comp. Howell, XX. col. 79; Cecil Fifoot, *Lord Mansfield* (Oxford, Clarendon Press, 1936), 361.
17. *Gazetteer and New Daily Advertiser*, no. 13,491 (26 May 1772), [4]; *BSB*, 116.
18. *BSB*, 119–22.
19. *Morning Chronicle and London Advertiser*, no. 962 (23 June 1772), [2]; *BSB*, 108.
20. As quoted by Granville Sharp, *The Just Limitation of Slavery in the Laws of God, compared with The unbounded Claims of the African Traders and British American Slaveholders* (B.White etc., 1776), App. 8, pp. 67–9; *BSB*, 108–10. There are serious omissions from the version in *State Trials*, comp. Howell, XX. cols. 80–2; Sharp had a shorthand writer in court, and his version is confirmed by contemporary newspaper reports. The italics and other emphasis are his.
21. *BSB*, 110.
22. See Jerome Nadelhaft, 'The Somersett Case and Slavery: Myth, Reality, and Repercussions', *Journal of Negro History*, LI (1966), 193–208. And note the air of surprise with which J.R.Pole of Churchill College, Cambridge, 'Slavery and revolution: the conscience of the rich', *Historical Journal*, XX (1977), 505–6 n. 4, reports his having learnt that 'even in the light of Somerset, residence in England did not make a slave free if that slave left British shores without compulsion'; that 'James Somerset was the only slave freed by Lord Mansfield's famous decision'; and that 'both slavery and slave sales continued in Britain'.
23. *London Chronicle*, XXXIII (1773), 597; *BSB*, 167.
24. Hannah More to Horace Walpole, July 1790, in William Roberts, *Memoirs of the life and correspondence of Mrs. Hannah More*, second edition (L.B.Seeley & Sons, 1834), II. 235.
25. *Bristol Journal*, 8 December 1792, as quoted, *BSB*, 170.

Slavery and the Scottish law

1. W.M.Morison, *Decisions of the Court of Session* (1811), XXXIII–XXXIV. 14545; *State Trials*, comp. T.B.Howell, XX (1814), col. [1]n.; *Judicial Cases concerning American Slavery and the Negro*, ed. H.T.Catterall (1926–37), I. 13; *BSB*, [177].
2. John Millar, *The origin of the distinction of ranks; or, An inquiry into the circumstances which give rise to influence and authority, in the different members of society* (J.Murray, 1779), 361–2.
3. Morison, XXXIII–XXXIV. 14545–9; *State Trials*, comp. Howell, XX. cols. [2]–7n.; Catterall, I. 18–19; *BSB*, [177]–183.
4. *Boswell's Life of Johnson*, ed. G.B.Hill and L.F.Powell (1934–64), V.

82–3: 'How curious it was to see an African in the north of Scotland, with little or no difference of manners from those of the natives.'

Mass murder on the high seas

1. See *BSB*, 158–64.
2. The account that follows is based on P.Hoare, *Memoirs of Granville Sharp* (1820), 236–47 and App. VIII, pp. xvii–xxi; Henry Roscoe, *Reports of cases argued and determined in The Court of King's Bench*, III (S.Sweet etc., 1831), 232–5; and *BSB*, [184]–209. See also Robert Weisbord, 'The case of the Slave-Ship "Zong", 1783', *History Today*, XIX (1969), 561–7.
3. Such heroism left an indelible record of the slaves' attitude to their captors' barbarities. In 1767 Jamaican slaves smiled contemptuously while being burnt alive (*London Magazine*, XXXVI (1767), 258).
4. G[eorge]. Gregory, *Essays Historical and Moral* (J.Johnson, 1785), 307n.
5. *Gazetteer, and New Daily Advertiser*, no. 21027 (3 May 1796), [3]; Charles Durnford and Edward Hyde East, *Reports of cases argued and determined in the Court of King's Bench*, VI (J.Butterworth, 1796), 656–9; *English Reports*, CI. 756–7; *BSB*, 207–9.

The Grace Jones case

1. This account is based on J.Haggard, *Reports of cases argued and determined in the High Court of Admiralty*, II (1833), 94–134; *Reports of State Trials*, n.s. II (1889), cols. 273–304; *BSB*, [210]–229.
2. *BSB*, 212.
3. *The Times*, no. 13,310 (20 June 1827), 3.
4. Haggard, II. 100–1; *Reports of State Trials*, n.s. II. cols. 279–80; *BSB*, 212.
5. Haggard, II. 115; *Reports of State Trials*, n.s. II. col. 291; *BSB*, 222, 229.
6. Haggard, II. 128–9; *Reports of State Trials*, n.s. II. col. 300; *BSB*, 229.
7. *Antigua Free Press*, IV/174 (14 December 1827), [2]. I owe this and the following two references to *BSB*, 218–19, 219, 213–14.
8. *Royal Gazette* (Kingston, Jamaica), L/2 (5–12 January 1828), Postscript, p. [17].
9. *New Times*, no. 9146 (9 November 1827) [2].

7. The rise of English racism

Race prejudice and racism

1. W.D.Jordan, *White over Black* (1968), 80.
2. A distinction between race prejudice ('essentially irrational and . . . in large measure sub-conscious') and racialism ('a rationalized

ideology based upon what is purported to be irrefutable scientific fact') is drawn by Charles H. Lyons, *To Wash an Aethiop White: British Ideas about Black African Educability 1530–1860* (New York, Teachers College Press, 1975), p. x.

3. Cf. A.J.Barker, *The African Link* (1978), [41].

The demonology of race

1. See Don Cameron Allen, 'Symbolic Color in the Literature of the English Renaissance', *Philological Quarterly*, XV (1936), 83–4; P.J.Heather, 'Colour Symbolism: Part I', *Folk-Lore*, LIX (1948), 169–70; Harry Levin, *The Power of Blackness: Hawthorne Poe Melville* (Faber & Faber, 1958), 35–6; Harold R. Isaacs, 'Blackness and whiteness', *Encounter*, XXI (1963), 12–14; W.D.Jordan, *White over Black* (1968), 7–8; Alan James, ' "Black": an inquiry into the pejorative associations of an English word', *New Community*, IX (1981–2), 19–30; Mary Searle-Chatterjee, 'Colour symbolism and the skin – some notes', *New Community*, IX (1981–2), 31–5.
2. Jordan, *White over Black*, 6, 9; cf. Winthrop D. Jordan, *The White Man's Burden: Historical origins of racism in the United States* (New York, Oxford University Press, 1974), 5.
3. Jeffrey Burton Russell, *Witchcraft in the Middle Ages* (Ithaca and London, Cornell University Press, 1972), 113–14.
4. Iohn Day, *Law-trickes, or, Who would have thought it* (Richard More, 1608), Act V, sig. G4v.
5. T[homas]. H[eywood]., *The fair maid Of The West: or, A Girle worth gold: The second part* (Richard Royston, 1631), Act I, sig. C2v.
6. Reginald Scot, *The discouerie of witchcraft* (1584), 455–6.
7. *The Revelations of Saint Birgitta*, ed. William Patterson Cumming (Early English Text Society, Original Ser. no. 178, 1929), 43.
8. Scot, 535.
9. S[amuel]. H[arsnet]., *A Declaration of egregious Popish Impostures* (Iames Roberts, 1603), 177, 178.
10. [Samuel Butler], *Hudibras: The Second Part* (John Martyn & James Allestry, 1664), 30.
11. T[homas]. H[erbert]., *A relation of some yeares travaile, begunne Anno 1626: Into Afrique and the greater Asia* (William Stansby & Jacob Bloome, 1634), 8; [Thomas Herbert], *Some yeares travels into divers Parts of Asia and Afrique* (Iacob Blome & Richard Bishop, 1638), 11.
12. H[erbert]., *A relation* (1634), 8.
13. 'The plott of The first parte of Tamar Cam', in *The Plays of William Shakespeare . . . with the corrections and illustrations of various commentators* (J.Johnson etc., 1803), III. ii, facing p. 414; *Henslowe Papers*, ed. Walter W. Greg (A.H.Bullen, 1907), 148; W.W.Greg, *Dramatic Documents from the Elizabethan Playhouses: Reproductions & Transcripts* (Oxford, Clarendon Press, [1931]), vii.
14. Ben Ionson, *Volpone Or The Foxe* (Thomas Thorpe, 1607), sig. C4v.

15. Jordan, *White over Black*, 29.
16. Edward Topsell, *The Historie of foure-footed beastes* (William Iaggard, 1607), 10, 12–13, 16, 4.
17. [James VI of Scotland], *Daemonologie, in forme of a Dialogue* (Edinburgh, Robert Walde-graue, 1597), 19.
18. Topsell, 12.
19. R.Iobson, *The Golden Trade* (1623), 153.
20. H[erbert].,*A relation* (1634), 17.
21. [Thomas Herbert], *Some years travels into divers part of Africa, and Asia the Great*, fourth impression (R.Scot etc., 1677), 18.
22. See Conway Zirkle, 'The Knowledge of Heredity before 1900', in *Genetics in the 20th Century: Essays on the Progress of Genetics during its First 50 Years*, ed. L.C.Dunn (New York, Macmillan Company, 1951), 40: 'Apes . . . were supposedly derived from the cross of a human being with some unknown quadruped. The height of absurdity seems to have been reached by Burzurgh-ibn-Shahrizar (ca. 954) who described the manatee as a hybrid between an Arab and a fish.'
23. John Bodin, *Method for the Easy Comprehension of History*, trans. Beatrice Reynolds (Records of Civilization – Sources and Studies, XXXVII, New York, Columbia University Press, 1945), 105. This is a translation of I[ean]. Bodin, *Methodus, ad facilem historiarum cognitionem* (Paris, apud Martinem Iuuenem, 1566).
24. Thomas Phillips, 'A Journal of a Voyage . . . to . . . Africa; And . . . Barbadoes', in *A Collection of Voyages and Travels*, [comp. Awnsham and John Churchill], VI (John Walthoe, 1732), 211.
25. Morgan Godwyn, *The Negro's and Indians advocate, Suing for their Admission into the Church: or A Persuasive to the Instructing and Baptizing of the Negro's and Indians in our Plantations* (J.D., 1680), 12.
26. J.Atkins, *A voyage to Guinea, Brasil, and the West-Indies* (1735), 108.
27. [Georges-Louis Leclerc, comte de Buffon], *Histoire naturelle, générale et particulière*, XIV (Paris, Imprimerie royale, 1766), 3 ('un singe aussi haut, aussi fort que l'homme, aussi ardent pour les femmes que pour ses femelles'), 31 (L'appetit véhément des singes mâles pour les femmes . . . les mélanges forcés ou volontaires des Négresses aux singes, dont le produit est rentré dans l'une ou l'autre espèce'); *Natural History, general and particular*, [trans. William Smellie], VIII (Edinburgh, William Creech, 1780), 40, 65 (I have emended this translation).
28. [James Burnet, Lord Monboddo], *Of the origin and progress of language*, I (Edinburgh, A.Kincaid & W.Creech, 1773), 234–5; second edition (Edinburgh, J.Balfour, 1774), 262n.
29. Chauncey Brewster Tinker, *Nature's Simple Plan: a phase of radical thought in the mid-eighteenth century* (Oxford University Press, 1922), 16.

30. [Burnet], *Origin and progress of language*, I (1773), 239. See also Arthur O. Lovejoy, 'Monboddo and Rousseau', *Modern Philology*, XXX (1932–3), 283ff.

31. [Burnet], *Origin and progress of language*, I, second edition (1774), 289, 270, 345, 290, 276, 346.

32. [James Burnet, Lord Monboddo], *Antient Metaphysics: or, The science of universals*, II (T.Cadell, 1782), 125; III (T.Cadell, 1784), 41.

33. [Burnet], *Origin and progress of language*, I, second edition (1774), 277, 334.

34. Cf. Jordan, *White over Black*, 237; David Brion Davis, *The Problem of Slavery in Western Culture* (Ithaca, N.Y., Cornell University Press, 1966), 455.

35. *Othello*, seventh Arden edition, ed. M.R.Ridley (1958), I. i. 126.

36. Iohn Leo [Africanus], *A geographical historie of Africa*, trans. Iohn Pory (Georg. Bishop, 1600), 38, 42. This was a translation of the *Descrittione dell' Africa*, published in Venice in 1550 as vol. I of G.B.Ramusio's collection of travels. Cf.Samuel Purchas, *Hakluytus Posthumus or Purchas His Pilgrimes* (Glasgow, James MacLehose & Sons, 1905–7), V. 353, 359.

37. E.Jones, *Othello's Countrymen* (1965), p. [vii].

38. Bodin, 143, 106.

39. [G.K.Hunter], 'Elizabethans and foreigners', in *Shakespeare in his own age*, ed. Allardyce Nicoll (Shakespeare Survey, XVII, Cambridge, University Press, 1964), 51, reprinted (with some changes) in G.K.Hunter, *Dramatic Identities and Cultural Tradition: Studies in Shakespeare and his contemporaries* (Liverpool University Press, 1978), 29. Cf. Eldred D. Jones, 'The Physical Representation of African Characters on the English Stage during the 16th and 17th Centuries', *Theatre Notebook*, XVII (1962–3), 18–19: 'The plays of the Elizabethan and Jacobean period used African characters to an extent that is still not fully recognised . . . Altogether I have listed about thirty-six plays and masques of the 16th and 17th centuries in which African characters were used in one way or another. Some of the titles of lost plays, *Mully Mullocco* and *Mahomet* for example, suggest that there may have been more plays which used African characters.' Actors playing these parts were painted black with what Isabel, in *Lust's Dominion*, calls 'the oil of hell'; see *Lust's Dominion; or, The Lascivious Queen: a Tragedie* (Robert Pollard, 1657), V. v, sig. G7v. For a detailed discussion of *The Battle of Alcazar*, *Titus Andronicus*, and *Lust's Dominion*, see Jones, *Othello's Countrymen*, 40–68.

40. Francis [Bacon], *New Atlantis: A Worke vnfinished*, 26, in Francis [Bacon], *Sylva sylvarum or A Naturall History In ten Centuries* (W.Lee, 1627). In C.H.Lyons, *To Wash an Aethiop White* (1975), 5, this vision is unaccountably granted to 'an "unholy hermit" '.

41. 'The strange aduentures of Andrew Battell of Leigh in Essex', in Samuel Purchas, *Purchas his Pilgrimes* (Henrie Fetherstone, 1625), II. 973; cf. Purchas (1905–7), VI. 376.
42. 'A description and historicall declaration of the golden Kingdome of Guinea', in Purchas (1625), II. 927; cf. Purchas (1905–7), VI. 251.
43. Iobson, 52.
44. *The Golden Coast, or A Description of Guinney* (S.Speed, 1665), 76.
45. John Ogilby, *Africa, being an accurate description of the regions of Ægypt*, etc. (the Author, 1670), 451.
46. William Smith, *A New Voyage to Guinea* (John Nourse, [1744]), 221–2, clearly copied from a similar passage in Willem Bosman, *Nauweurige beschryving van de Guinese Goud-, Tand- en Slave-Kust* (Utrecht, Anthony Schouten, 1704), I. 197, as translated in William Bosman, *A New and Accurate Description of the Coast of Guinea* (James Knapton, 1705), 206–7.
47. *The Decades of the newe worlde or west India* [ed. R.Eden] (1555), fol. 355v; cf. R.Hakluyt, *The Principal Navigations . . . of the English Nation* (1903–5), VI. 167; *Europeans in West Africa*, ed. J.W.Blake (1942), II. 338.
48. H[erbert]., *A relation* (1634), 10.
49. Ogilby, 452.
50. Bosman (1704), I. 113; Bosman (1705), 117.
51. [J. Oldmixon], *The British Empire in America* (1708), II. 118.
52. Hugh Jones, *The Present State of Virginia* (J.Clarke, 1724), 37.
53. James Houstoun, *Some New and Accurate observations Geographical, Natural and Historical: Containing a true and impartial account of the Situation, Product, and Natural History of the Coast of Guinea* (J.Peele, 1725), 33–4. Houstoun was for a time physician to the Royal African Company and chief surgeon at Cape Coast Castle.
54. R.Ligon, *A true & exact history Of the Island of Barbados* (1657), 53.
55. [Herbert], *Some yeares travels* (1638), 11.
56. John Seller, *A new systeme: of Geography* (John Seller, [1685]), 90.
57. Bosman (1704), I. 113; Bosman (1705), 117.
58. [Oldmixon], II. 119.
59. H.Jones, 38.
60. Ligon, 51.
61. Richard Hakluyt, *The principal navigations, voiages, traffiques and discoueries of the English Nation* (George Bishop etc., 1598–1600), II. ii. 25; cf. Hakluyt (1903–5), VI. 184; *Europeans in West Africa*, ed. Blake, II. 367.
62. Jean Mocquet, *Voyages en Afrique, Asie, Indes orientales, & occidentales* (Rouen, Iean Caillové, 1645), 74–5; Jean Mocquet, *Travels and Voyages into Africa, Asia, and America*, trans. Nathaniel Pullen (William Newton etc., 1696), 45.

63. William Strachey, *The Historie of Travell into Virginia Britania* [1612], ed. Louis B. Wright and Virginia Freund (Hakluyt Society, 2nd ser. CIII, 1953), 71.
64. H.Jones, 3.
65. Don Cameron Allen, *The Legend of Noah: Renaissance Rationalism in Art, Science, and Letters* (Illinois Studies in Language and Literature, XXXIII/3–4, Urbana, University of Illinois Press, 1949), 119.
66. Gilbert Génébrard, *Chronographiæ Libri Quatuor* (Leyden, sumptibus Ioannis Pillehotte, 1609), 26–7.
67. Guillaume Postel, *De Originibus* (Basle, per Ioannem Oporinum, [1553], 96ff.; Guillaume Postel, *Cosmographicae disciplinae compendium* (Basle, per Ioannem Oporinum, 1561), 37ff.
68. Agostino Tornielli, *Annales sacri & Profani* (Frankfurt, apud Ioannem Theobaldum Schon Wetterum, 1611), I. 133ff.
69. [George Best], *A true discourse of the late voyages of discouerie, for the finding of a passage to Cathaya, by the Northvveast* (Henry Bynnyman, 1578), sig. f4r–f4v; cf. Hakluyt (1903–5), VII. 264.
70. *The Athenian Oracle: Being an Entire Collection of all the Valuable Questions and Answers in the old Athenian Mercuries* [ed. J.Dunton], III (Andrew Bell, 1704), 380.
71. P[eter]. H[eylyn]., *Microcosmus, or A little description of the great world* (Oxford, Iohn Lichfield & Iames Short, 1621), 379.
72. Peter Heylyn, *Μικροκοσμος: A little description of the great world*, third edition (Oxford, William Turner & Thomas Huggins, 1627), 771.
73. Peter Heylyn, *Cosmographie, in four books: containing the Chorographie and History of the whole world* (Anne Seile, 1666), 1004.
74. [Isaac La Peyrère], *Præadmitæ: sive Exercitatio super Versibus duodecimo, decimotertio, & decimoquarto, capitis quinti Epistolæ D. Pauli ad Romanos* ([Amsterdam?], 1655); *Men before Adam: or A Discourse upon the twelfth thirteenth, and fourteenth Verses of the Fifth Chapter of the Epistle of the Apostle Paul to the Romans* (1656).
75. 'Nouvelle Division de la Terre, par les différentes Espéces ou Races d'hommes qui l'habitent, envoyé par un fameux Voyageur à Monsieur ***** à peu près en ces termes', *Le Journal des sçavans*, 1684, pp. 85–9; trans. T.Bendyshe, 'The History of Anthropology', App. I, in *Memoirs Read Before the Anthropological Society of London*, I (1863–4), 360–4.
76. Edward Tyson, *Orang-Outang, sive Homo Sylvestris: or, The anatomy of a pygmie compared with that of a Monkey, an Ape, and a Man* (Thomas Bennet, 1699), 55. For Tyson, see M.F.Ashley Montagu, *Edward Tyson, M.D., F.R.S. 1650–1708 and the rise of human and comparative anatomy in England: A Study in the History of Science* (Memoirs of the American Philosophical Society, XX, Philadelphia, 1943).
77. [Johann] Meckel [the elder], 'Nouvelles observations sur l'épiderme et le cerveau des Négres', *Histoire de l'Académie royale des sciences et*

belles lettres [Berlin], XIII (1757), 71: 'Le sang du Négre . . . étoit si noir, qu'au lieu de rougir le linge, comme le sang le fait ordinairement, il le noircissoit. Il semble donc que les Négres fassent presque une autre espece d'hommes, par rapport à la structure intérieure.'

78. See Arthur O. Lovejoy, *The Great Chain of Being: A Study of the History of an Idea* (Cambridge, Mass., Harvard University Press, 1936).
79. John Atkins, *The Navy-Surgeon: or, A Practical System of Surgery* (Cæsar Ward & Richard Chandler, 1734), App., 23, 24.
80. Atkins, *A voyage to Guinea*, 39. Atkins was soon taken to task for undermining the biblical view of humanity's creation. See *A New General Collection of Voyages and Travels* [comp. John Green] (Thomas Astley, 1745–7 [1743–7]), II. 270: 'With Mr. *Atkins*'s Leave, this is not to be a little heterodox, but in a great Degree so.'
81. Ligon, 54–5. See also Wylie Sypher, *Guinea's Captive Kings: British Anti-Slavery Literature of the XVIIIth Century* (Chapel Hill, University of North Carolina Press, 1942; reprinted New York, Octagon Books, 1969), 122ff.; and Davis, 10–13.
82. Mrs. A[phra]. Behn, *Oroonoko: or, the Royal Slave: A True History* (Will. Canning, 1688), 20–1.
83. Davis, 481. See also Eva B. Dykes, *The Negro in English Romantic Thought: or A Study of Sympathy for the Oppressed* (Washington, DC, The Associated Publishers, Inc., 1942), 2–3; R.Anstey, *The Atlantic Slave Trade and British Abolition* (1975), 145ff.; Douglas A. Lorimer, *Colour, Class and the Victorians: English attitudes to the Negro in the mid-nineteenth century* (Leicester University Press, 1978), 23–4.
84. Joseph Jones, 'The "Distress'd" Negro in English Magazine Verse', *Studies in English*, no. 17 (University of Texas Bulletin, no. 3726, 8 July 1937), 103; see also Dykes, *passim*.
85. Phillips, 'A Journal of a Voyage', 219.

Plantocracy racism

1. As quoted, [J.E.V.Crofts], 'Enthusiasm', in *Eighteenth Century Literature: an Oxford Miscellany* (Oxford, Clarendon Press, 1909), 130.
2. M.Godwyn, *The Negro's and Indians advocate* (1680), 61.
3. Morgan Godwyn, *Trade preferr'd before religion, and Christ made to give place to Mammon: Represented in a Sermon Relating to the Plantations* (B.Took & Isaac Cleave, 1685), Preface, p. 1: 'A *Negro*, whose Owner resided somewhere near *Bristol* . . . addressed himself to the Minister, beseeching Baptism . . . All which soon after arriving to the Master's jealous ear, he, with . . . terrible Menaces, dehorted the Minister [i.e. advised him not to]; adding withal, this insolent enquiry, *Whether he would baptize his Horse?* But perceiving that the

Minister little regarded his Menaces or Arguments, he goes home and instantly chains the *Negro* under the Table among his Dogs.' This slave had himself baptized all the same – and was promptly shipped out to the plantations.

4. Thomas Fuller, *The Holy State* (Cambridge, John Williams, 1642), 129.
5. *A Journal or Historical Account of the Life, Travels, Sufferings, Christian Experiences and Labour of Love in the Work of the Ministry, of that Ancient, Eminent and Faithful Servant of Jesus Christ, George Fox*, I (Thomas Northcott, 1694), 361; G[eorge]. F[ox]., *Gospel Family-Order, being a short discourse concerning the Ordering of Families, both of Whites, Blacks and Indians* (1676), 13–14. See also T.E.Drake, *Quakers and Slavery in America* (1950), 4, 5–8.
6. Richard Baxter, *A Christian Directory: Or, A Summ of practical theologie, and cases of conscience* (Nevill Simmons, 1673), ii. 557–8.
7. 'Philotheus Physiologus' [Thomas Tryon], *Friendly Advice to the Gentlemen-Planters of the East and West Indies* (Andrew Sowle, 1684), 75, 82, 85.
8. Godwyn, *The Negro's and Indians advocate*, Preface, sigs. A7r, A5v.
9. Godwyn, *Trade preferr'd before Religion*, Preface, p. 1.
10. Godwyn, *The Negro's and Indians advocate*, Preface, sig. A7r–A7v; pp. 1–2, 38–9, 3.
11. Godwyn, *The Negro's and Indians advocate*, 20, 14–19, 13.
12. Godwyn, *The Negro's and Indians advocate*, 28.
13. M[organ]. G[odwyn]., *A Supplement to the Negro's & Indian's advocate* (J.D., 1681), 10. For the skills of black slaves in colonial New England, including livestock care and rice cultivation, see Peter H. Wood, *Black Majority: Negroes in Colonial South Carolina from 1670 through the Stono Rebellion* (New York, Alfred A. Knopf, 1974) and *The Other Slaves: Mechanics, Artisans and Craftsmen*, ed. James E. Newton and Ronald L. Lewis (Boston, G.K.Hall & Co., 1978).
14. Godwyn, *Trade preferr'd before Religion*. Preface, p. 6.
15. [Francis Brokesby], *Some Proposals towards Promoting the Propagation of the Gospel in our American Plantations* (G.Sawbridge & B.Bragg, 1708), 3, 11n.
16. *The Petty Papers: Some unpublished writings of Sir William Petty*, ed. [Henry Fitzmaurice,] Marquis of Lansdowne (Constable & Company Limited, 1927), II. 31.
17. Maurice Cranston, *John Locke: a biography* (Longmans, Green & Co., 1957), 115n., 119–20; D.B.Davis, *The Problem of Slavery in Western Culture* (1966), 118–19; W.D.Jordan, *White over Black* (1968), 440–1; C.H.Lyons, *To Wash an Aethiop White* (1970), 22–3.
18. Jordan, 441.
19. John Locke, *An Essay concerning Human Understanding*, ed. Peter H. Nidditch (Oxford, Clarendon Press, 1975), I. ii. 25, p. 62; IV. vii. 16, pp. 606–7.

20. Léon Poliakov, *The Aryan Myth: a history of racist and nationalist ideas in Europe*, trans. Edmund Howard (Sussex University Press, 1974), 145.
21. David Hume, *Essays Moral, Political, and Literary*, ed. T.H.Green and T.H.Grose (Darmstadt, Scientia Verlag Aalen, 1964), 252n.
22. *London Magazine*, XIX (1750), 317.
23. *The Modern Part of the Universal History*, V (T.Osborne etc., 1760), 658–9, 664, 665.
24. *The Modern Part of the Universal History*, VI (T.Osborne etc., 1760), 581.
25. [William Knox], *Three Tracts respecting the Conversion and Instruction of the free Indians, and Negroe slaves in the colonies: addressed to the venerable Society for Propagation of the Gospel in Foreign Parts* [*c.*1768], 41, 16–18.
26. *London Chronicle*, XVI/1214 (29 September–2 October 1764), 317.
27. *Gentleman's Magazine*, XXXIV (1764), 495.
28. *London Chronicle*, XVIII/1378 (19–22 October 1765), 387.
29. *London Chronicle*, XXIII/2537 (13–16 March 1773), 250; Samuel Martin, *An Essay upon Plantership, Humbly Inscribed to his Excellency George Thomas Esq; Chief Governor of All the Leeward Islands*, fifth edition (T.Cadell, 1773), Preface, pp. xiv–xv.
30. *English Chronicle*, as quoted by J.A.C[annon]. in Sir L.Namier and J.Brooke, *The House of Commons 1754–1790* (1964), II. 406–7.
31. Estwick was assistant agent for Barbados, 1763–78, and agent for Barbados, 1778–92. He was MP for Westbury, Wiltshire, 1779–95, deputy paymaster-general, 1782–3, and paymaster-general from 1784 to his death in 1795. For a brief biography, see Namier and Brooke, II. 406–7.
32. [Samuel Estwick], *Considerations on the Negroe Cause Commonly so called, addressed to the Right Honourable Lord Mansfield, . . . By a West Indian* (J.Dodsley, 1772), 44.
33. Samuel Estwick, *Considerations on the Negroe Cause*, second edition (J.Dodsley, 1773), 73–4.
34. Estwick, *Considerations*, second edition (1773), 74–82.
35. [Edward Long], *Candid Reflections* (1772), 48–9.
36. [Long], *Candid Reflections*, 50.
37. [Long], *Candid Reflections*, 46.
38. [E.Long], *History of Jamaica* (1774), I. 4.
39. [Long], *History of Jamaica*, II. 336, 356, 352–3, 356–70, 371, 374–5, 382–3.
40. George Metcalf, Introduction to E.Long, *History of Jamaica* (Cass Library of West Indian Studies, no. 12, Frank Cass & Co. Ltd, 1970), I. p. [xi].
41. G[ilbert]. Francklyn, *Observations occasioned by the attempts made in*

England to effect the abolition of the slave trade (J.Walter etc., 1789), 4n.; cf. G[ilbert]. Francklyn, *An Answer to the Rev. Mr. Clarkson's Essay on the Slavery and Commerce of the Human Species* (J.Walter etc., 1789), 31–3.

42. [Long], *Candid Reflections*, 60.
43. J.H.Plumb, *England in the Eighteenth Century* (Pelican History of England, 7, Harmondsworth, Penguin Books Ltd, 1955 reprint), 88–9. Much the same comparison – in fact, with the condition of English agricultural workers – was made in 1789 by a former private secretary to the governor of Barbados; see William Dickson, *Letters on Slavery* (J.Phillips etc., 1789), 52–3.
44. *HCSP of the Eighteenth Century*, LXXIII. 232, 239, 242–3 (evidence of Ninian Jeffreys); 305 (evidence of Henry Hew Dalrymple).
45. Davis, 461.
46. Oliver Goldsmith, *An History of the Earth, and Animated Nature* (J.Nourse, 1774), II. 226–8.
47. [Janet Schaw], *Journal of a Lady of Quality*, ed. Evangeline Walker Andrews and Charles McLean Andrews (Yale Historical Publications, Manuscripts and Edited Texts, VI, New Haven, Yale University Press, 1921), 127. The original is unfortunately missing from the British Library's Department of Manuscripts.
48. [Charles Johnstone], *The Pilgrim, or a Picture of Life* (T.Cadell & W.Flexny, 1775), I. 239.
49. [James Tobin], *Cursory Remarks upon the Reverend Mr. Ramsay's Essay on The treatment and conversion of African slaves in the sugar colonies* (G. & T. Wilkie, 1785), 118n.
50. See pp. 108–9 above.
51. P.Thicknesse, *A Year's Journey through France and Part of Spain*, second edition (1778), II. 102–5, 108–11. See also *Memoirs and Anecdotes of Philip Thicknesse* (the author, 1788), I. 279, 282n.: blacks were an inferior order of men, never seen to work 'except now and then to serve the mason, or bricklayer, with mortar'.
52. *The World*, no. 735 (9 May 1789), [2]. For Shyllon's suggestion that this letter was written by Long, see his *Black People in Britain* (1977), 111 n. 29.
53. *Morning Chronicle, and London Advertiser*, no. 6015 (19 August 1788), [2].
54. John Scattergood, *An Antidote to Popular Frenzy, particularly to the present rage for the abolition of the slave-trade* (H.Gardner etc., [1792]), 15, 24.
55. Thomas Atwood, *The History of the Island of Dominica* (J.Johnson, 1791), 212, 266, 255, 272.
56. Bryan Edwards, *The History, Civil and Commercial, of The British Colonies in the West Indies* (John Stockdale, 1793), II. 62, 79, 81. Edwards was MP for Grampound, 1796–1800; for a brief biography see W.P.C[ourtney]., in *DNB*, XVII. 111–13.

57. *Fugitive Thoughts on the African slave trade, interspersed with cursory remarks on the manners, customs, and commerce, of the African and American Indians* (Liverpool, 1792), as quoted by B.Davidson, *Black Mother*, revised edition (1980), 14. This rare pamphlet is listed as no. 2133 in Peter C. Hogg, *The African Slave Trade and its Suppression: a classified and annotated bibliography* (Frank Cass, 1973).

Pseudo-scientific racism

1. Charles R. Lawrence, Foreword to Dorothy Hammon and Alta Jablow, *The Africa That Never Was: Four centuries of British writing about Africa* (New York, Twayne Publishers, Inc., 1970), [3].
2. P.D.Curtin, '"Scientific" Racism and the British Theory of Empire', *Journal of the Historical Society of Nigeria*, II (1960–3), 42.
3. Ralph A. Austen and Woodruff D. Smith, 'Images of Africa and British slave-trade abolition: the transition to an imperialist ideology, 1787–1807', *African Historical Studies*, II (1969), 69–83.
4. P.D.Curtin, *The Image of Africa* (1965), 45. As late as 1857, France's first professor of anthropology, Armand de Quatrefages, quoted both Estwick and Long with reference to the alleged infertility of persons of mixed race; see his 'Du croisement des races humaines', *Revue des deux mondes*, séconde période VIII (1857), 162.
5. Carl Linnaeus, *Systema naturæ per Regna tria naturæ*, tenth edition (Stockholm, Laurentius Saluis, 1758–9), I. 21–2; *The Animal Kingdom, or zoological system of the celebrated Sir Charles Linnæus*, trans. Robert Kerr (J.Murray & R.Faulder, 1792), 45.
6. Nicolaus E. Dahlberg, *Dissertatio botanica metamorphoses plantarum sistens* (Stockholm, Typographia regia, [1755]), 22; Knut Hagberg, *Carl Linnæus*, trans. Alain Blair (Jonathan Cape, 1952), 199, erroneously attributing these words to Linnaeus himself.
7. W.D.Jordan, *White over Black* (1968), 236.
8. C[harles]. Bonnet, *Contemplation de la nature* (Amsterdam, Marc-Michel Rey, 1764), I. 81–2; *The Contemplation of Nature* (T.Longman etc., 1766), I. 68–9. For Bonnet, see Lorin Anderson, 'Charles Bonnet's Taxonomy and Chain of Being', *Journal of the History of Ideas*, XXXVII (1976), 45–58.
9. [Soame Jenyns], *Disquisitions on several subjects* (J.Dodsley, 1782), 10. Jenyns was MP for Cambridgeshire, 1741–54; Dunwich, 1754–8; and Cambridge, 1758–80. For a brief biography, see Sir L.Namier and J.Brooke, *The House of Commons 1754–1790* (1964), II. 681–2.
10. Ioann. Frider. Blumenbach, *De generis humani varietate nativa* (Göttingen, Frid. Andr. Rosenbuschii, [1775]), 41–2; second edition (Göttingen, Viduam Abr. Vandenhoek, 1781), 51–2; third edition (Göttingen, Vandenhoek & Ruprecht, 1795), pp. x–xi, 285–7; Joh. Fr. Blumenbach, *Beyträge zur Naturgeschichte* (Göttingen, Johann Christian Dieterich etc., 1790–1811), I. 79–83, 84–118; *The*

anthropological treatises of Johann Friedrich Blumenbach, trans. and ed. Thomas Bendyshe (Publications of the Anthropological Society of London, 1865), 99, 150–1, 264–6, 302–4, 305–12.

11. [Marie Jean Pierre] Flourens, 'Éloge historique de Jean-Frédéric Blumenbach', *Mémoires de l'Académie Royale des Sciences de l'Institut de France*, XXI (1847), p. xiij, reprinted in [Marie Jean] P[ierre]. Flourens, *Recueil des éloges historiques lus dans les séances publiques de l'Académie des Sciences* (Paris, Garnier Frères, 1856–62), I. 212; 'Memoir of Blumenbach', in *Anthropological treatises of . . . Blumenbach*, trans. and ed. Bendyshe, 57.
12. Blumenbach, *De generis humani varietate nativa*, third edition (1795), 106–8, 304; *Anthropological treatises of . . . Blumenbach*, trans. and ed. Bendyshe, 237–8, 269.
13. Jacques Barzun, *Race: a study in modern superstition* (Methuen & Co. Ltd, 1938), 52–3.
14. *Verhandeling van Petrus Camper, over het natuurlijk verschil der wezenstrekken in menschen van onderscheiden landaart en ouderdom* (Utrecht, B.Wild & J.Altheer, 1791), 47, 32; *The Works of the Late Professor Camper, on The Connexion between the Science of Anatomy and The Arts of Drawing, Painting, Statuary, &c. &c.*, trans. T.Cogan (C.Dilly, 1794), 50, 32.
15. Jordan, 226.
16. See Charles White, *An account of the regular gradation in man, and in different animals and vegetables; and from the former to the latter* (C.Dilly, 1799), 41.
17. S[amuel]. Th[omas]. [von] Sömmerring, *Ueber die körperliche Verschiedenheit des Negers vom Europäer* (Frankfurt & Mainz, Varrentrapp, Sohn & Wenner, 1785), 67.
18. [Henry Home, Lord Kames], *Sketches of the History of Man* (Edinburgh, W.Creech, 1774), I. 38–42, 12. For Kames, see Franklin Thomas, *The Environmental Basis of Society: A study in the history of sociological theory* (New York and London, The Century Co., 1925), 269–70, and Gladys Bryson, *Man and society: The Scottish Inquiry of the Eighteenth Century* (Princeton, N.J., Princeton University Press, 1945), especially pp. 64–6.
19. [Thomas Jefferson], *Notes on the state of Virginia; written in the year 1781 . . . for the use of a Foreigner of distinction* ([Paris], 1782 [1784]), 263–4: 'I advance it . . . as a suspicion only, that the blacks, whether originally a distinct race, or made distinct by time and circumstances, are inferior to the whites in the endowments both of body and mind.'
20. White, 66–7, 79, 83, 134–5, 137–8, App.
21. J[ames]. C[owles]. Prichard, *Researches into the Physical History of Mankind*, third edition (Sherwood, Gilbert, & Piper, 1836–47), II. 97. For this paragraph, see also John S. Haller, *Outcasts from Evolution: Scientific Attitudes of Racial Inferiority, 1859–1900* (Urbana, University of Illinois Press, 1971), 77.

22. Curtin, '"Scientific" Racism and the British Theory of Empire', 50.
23. Michael D. Biddiss, ed., in *Images of Race* (Leicester University Press, 1979), 11.
24. Bernard Semmel, *The Governor Eyre Controversy* (Macgibbon & Kee, 1962), 134–5.
25. V.G.Kiernan, *The Lords of Human Kind: European attitudes towards the outside world in the Imperial Age* (Weidenfeld & Nicolson, 1969), 316.
26. I owe some of these categories to Curtin, '"Scientific" Racism and the British Theory of Empire', 43ff.
27. W[illiam]. Lawrence, *Lectures on physiology, zoology and the Natural History of Man* (J.Callow, 1819), 363, 476, 478, 493.
28. T.K.Penniman, *A Hundred Years of Anthropology*, second edition (Gerald Duckworth & Co. Ltd, 1952), 81–2.
29. George Combe, *A System of Phrenology*, second edition (Edinburgh, John Anderson, jun., 1825), 468–9; John D. Davies, *Phrenology, Fad and Science: A 19th-Century American Crusade* (Yale Historical Publications, Miscellany 62, New Haven, Yale University Press, 1955), 145.
30. W[illiam]. F[rédéric]. Edwards, *Des caractères physiologiques des races humaines considérés dans leurs rapports avec l'histoire* (Paris, Compère Jeune, 1829), 45.
31. Curtin, *Image of Africa*, 363, 235.
32. Combe, 461.
33. Robert Verity, *Changes produced in the nervous system by civilization, considered according to the evidence of physiology and the philosophy of history*, second edition (S.Highley, 1839), 57–8, 69, 29n., 64.
34. See Curtin, '"Scientific" Racism and the British Theory of Empire', 50.
35. J.G.Robertson, 'Carlyle', in *The Cambridge History of English Literature*, XIII (Cambridge, University Press, 1953 reprint), 1; see also George Sampson, *The Concise Cambridge History of English Literature*, third edition (Cambridge, University Press, 1970), 572.
36. [Thomas Carlyle], 'Occasional Discourse on the Negro Question', *Fraser's Magazine*, XL (1849), 676–7, 671; T.Carlyle, *Occasional Discourse on the Nigger Question* (Thomas Bosworth, 1853), 42, 5. Ian Campbell, 'Carlyle and the Negro Question Again', *Criticism*, XIII (1971), 279–90, draws attention to a series of five letters 'On the West Indies Question', signed 'Presbyter', published in the *Dumfries and Galloway Courier*, 1829–30, which Carlyle undoubtedly read and from which he seems to have taken certain ideas for the 'Occasional Discourse'.
37. Michael St. John Packe, *The Life of John Stuart Mill* (Secker & Warburg, 1954), 465; D. [i.e. John Stuart Mill], 'The Negro question', *Fraser's Magazine*, XLI (1850), 25–31.
38. [Thomas Carlyle], 'Shooting Niagara: and after?', *Macmillan's Magazine*, XVI (1867), 321.

39. Thomas Carlyle, 'The New Downing Street', 23, in *Latter-day Pamphlets* (Chapman & Hall, 1850); Thomas Carlyle, *On Heroes, hero-worship, & the heroic in history* (James Fraser, 1841), 362; Thomas Carlyle, *Past and Present* (Chapman & Hall, 1843), 215–18; C[arl]. A[dolph]. Bodelsen, *Studies in mid-Victorian imperialism* (Copenhagen, Gyldendalske Boghandel, 1924), 28.
40. Anthony Trollope, *The West Indies and the Spanish Main* (Chapman & Hall, 1859), 56–7.
41. *Spectator*, no. 1942 (16 September 1865), 1035.
42. Cf. Curtin, ' "Scientific" Racism and the British Theory of Empire', 44.
43. *Hansard's Parliamentary Debates*, 3rd ser. vol. 88 (1846), cols. 165–6.
44. Harry H. Johnston, *A history of the colonization of Africa by alien races* (Cambridge, University Press, 1899), 91–2.
45. Gilbert Murray, 'The exploitation of inferior races in ancient and modern times', in *Liberalism and the Empire* (R. Brimley Johnson, 1900), 156.
46. Thomas Arnold, *Introductory lectures on modern history* (Oxford, John Henry Parker, 1842), 36–9.
47. Curtin, *Image of Africa*, 377.
48. Robert Knox, *The Races of Men: a philosophical enquiry into the Influence of Race over the Destinies of Nations*, second edition (Henry Renshaw, 1852), pp. [v], 243–4, 246. For Knox, see M.D.Biddiss, 'The Politics of Anatomy: Dr Robert Knox and Victorian Racism', *Proceedings of the Royal Society of Medicine*, LXIX (1976), 245–50, and Reginald Horsman, 'Origins of Racial Anglo-Saxonism in Great Britain before 1850', *Journal of the History of Ideas*, XXXVII (1976), 405–7. As Biddiss points out (p. 246), the only recent life of Knox – Isobel Rae, *Knox, the Anatomist* (Oliver & Boyd, 1964) – plays down his racism. Henry Lonsdale, *A Sketch of the Life and Writings of Robert Knox the Anatomist* (Macmillan and Co., 1870), was less reticent: see pp. 305–6, [308]–315.
49. Horsman, 407.
50. *Lancet*, 1865, ii. 627.
51. William Hepworth Dixon, *White Conquest* (Chatto & Windus, 1876 [1875]), II. 372–3.
52. Samuel George Morton, 'On the Size of the Brain in Various Races and Families of Man; with Ethnological Remarks', in J.C.Nott and Geo. R. Gliddon, *Types of Mankind: or, Ethnological Researches* (Trübner & Co., 1854), 301–2; [S.G.Morton], 'Origin of the Human Species', in Nott and Gliddon, 310; J.C.N[ott]., 'Comparative Anatomy of Races', in Nott and Gliddon, 450. These figures differ considerably from Morton's earlier findings.
53. Thomas F. Gossett, *Race: the history of an idea in America* (Dallas, Southern Methodist University Press, 1963), 74. Cf. Christine Bolt, *Victorian Attitudes to Race* (Routledge & Kegan Paul, 1971), 15: 'In

recent times, since it has been demonstrated that the Japanese, American Indians, Eskimoes and Polynesians all frequently have brains larger than those found among Europeans, this line of argument has lost its appeal for the racist.'

54. Thomas Hope, *Essay on the origin and prospects of man* (John Murray, 1831), III. 391–6, 397.
55. 'Notices and Abstracts of Communications', etc., 75, in *Report of the Eleventh Meeting of the British Association for the Advancement of Science . . . 1841* (John Murray, 1842).
56. J.W.Burrow, 'Evolution and Anthropology in the 1860's: the Anthropological Society of London, 1863–71', *Victorian Studies*, VII (1963–4), 143, says this was 'little more than a pretext'.
57. Burrow, 146.
58. James Hunt, 'On the Negro's Place in Nature', *Memoirs of the Anthropological Society of London*, I (1863–4), 51–2; James Hunt, *On the Negro's Place in Nature* (Trübner & Co., 1863), 51–2. The society published 1,000 copies of Hunt's paper; see D.A.Lorimer, *Colour, Class and the Victorians* (1978), 138.
59. James Hunt, 'Address delivered at the Third Anniversary Meeting of the Anthropological Society of London', *Journal of the Anthropological Society of London*, IV (1866), p. lxxviii.
60. For the Morant Bay atrocities, see [Sydney Haldane,] Lord Oliver, *The Myth of Governor Eyre* (Hogarth Press, 1933); C.L.R.James, *A History of Negro Revolt* (*Fact*, no. 18, September 1938), 27; Arvel B. Erickson, 'Empire or Anarchy: the Jamaica Rebellion of 1865', *Journal of Negro History*, XLIV (1959), 99–122; Eric Williams, *British Historians and the West Indies* (Port-of-Spain, P.N.M. Publishing Company Limited, 1964), [62]–120, British edition (André Deutsch, 1966), [87]–153; Bolt, 75–108; Lorimer, [178]–200. For additional references, see Lorimer, 260 n. 2. George H. Ford, 'The Governor Eyre Case in England', *University of Toronto Quarterly*, XVII (1947–8), 219–33, and Semmel, *The Governor Eyre Controversy*, discuss repercussions in Britain.
61. As quoted by Ford, 223.
62. *Report of the Jamaica Royal Commission, 1866* (*HCSP*, 1866, XXX).
63. J.B.Atlay, 'The case of Governor Eyre', *Cornhill Magazine*, XII (1902), 211–12, 215, 217; Malcolm Uren and Robert Stephens, *Waterless horizons: The first full-length study of the extraordinary life-story of Edward John Eyre* (Melbourne, Robertson & Mullens, 1945), 239–40; Ford, 225–6.
64. As reported in *The Times*, no. 25,584 (23 August 1866), 7.
65. Hunt, 'Address . . . at the Third Anniversary Meeting', p. lxxviii.
66. Commander Bedford Pim, *The Negro and Jamaica* (Trübner & Co., 1866), 15, 16, 50, 35, 51, 63.
67. 'The end of the Jamaica prosecution', *Spectator*, no. 2084 (6 June 1868), 666.

68. Lorimer, 149–50.
69. Lorimer, 146.
70. Michael Banton, *Race Relations* (Tavistock Publications, 1967), 37.
71. Herbert Spencer, *Social statics; or, The conditions essential to human happiness specified* (John Chapman, 1851), 322–3.
72. Herbert Spencer, 'The comparative psychology of man', in his *Essays: Scientific, Political and Speculative*, III, third edition (Williams & Norgate, 1878), 425–7.
73. R.H.H[utton]., in *DNB*, II. 395; Walter Bagehot, *Physics and politics, or thoughts on the application of the principles of 'Natural Selection' and 'Inheritance' to political society* (Henry S. King & Co., 1872), 43, 49.
74. Benjamin Kidd, *Social Evolution* (Macmillan & Co., 1894), 45–6, 268.
75. Benjamin Kidd, *The Control of the Tropics* (New York, The Macmillan Company, 1898), 53.
76. 'A Biologist' [i.e. Sir Peter Chalmers Mitchell?], 'A biological view of our foreign policy', *Saturday Review*, LXXXII/2101 (1 February 1896), 119.
77. W. Winwood Reade, *Savage Africa: being the narrative of a tour of equatorial, south-western, and north-western Africa* (Smith, Elder, & Co., 1863), 587.
78. F[raser]. R[ae]., in *DNB*, XLIX. 97; *Hansard's Parliamentary Debates*, 3rd ser. vol. 165 (1862), col. 1449.
79. Francis Galton, *Hereditary genius: an inquiry into its laws and consequences* (Macmillan & Co., 1869), 338, 339, 343, 359.
80. Banton, *Race Relations*, 41.
81. Karl Pearson, *National life from the standpoint of science* (Adam & Charles Black, 1901 [1900]), 42, 43, 19, 24, 62.
82. Cf. Barzun, 69, and E.F.Chidell, *Africa and national regeneration* (Thomas Burleigh, 1904), 62–3: 'Even the Australian native does not disappear soon enough to satisfy everyone. I remember an archdeacon, who was a true bishop to these poor folk, after a visit paid to one of their settlements, expressing the wish from a heart overflowing with kindness, that they would all, being first brought into an appropriate frame of mind, at once depart to a better world.'
83. Horsman, 399.
84. Thomas Carlyle, *Chartism* (James Fraser, 1840), 75.
85. Arnold, 33–5.
86. As quoted by Williams (1966), 49.
87. *Hansard's Parliamentary Debates*, 3rd ser. vol. 151 (1858), col. 1821.
88. Charles Wentworth Dilke, *Greater Britain: A record of travel in English-speaking countries during 1866 and 1867* (Macmillan & Co., 1868), I. 273; II. 406; I. 308.
89. Charles Kingsley, *The Roman and the Teuton* (Cambridge and London, Macmillan & Co., 1864), [324], 338, 340.
90. Charles Kingsley to J.M.Ludlow, December 1849, in *Charles*

Kingsley: his letters and memories of his life [ed. Frances E. Kingsley] (Henry S. King & Co., 1877), I. 222–3.

91. Kingsley to his mother, 25 January 1870, in *Charles Kingsley,* II. 312.

92. Kingsley to his wife, 4 July 1860, in *Charles Kingsley*, II. 107.

93. As quoted by Michael Banton, 'A nineteenth-century racial philosophy: Charles Kingsley', *The Idea of Race* (Tavistock Publications, 1977), 79–80. For Kingsley as racist see also an earlier version of Banton's essay: 'Kingsley's Racial Philosophy', *Theology*, LXXVIII (1975), 22–30.

94. J.R.Seeley, *The Expansion of England* (Macmillan & Co., 1883), 262.

95. Captain Frank E. Younghusband, *The heart of a continent: a narrative of travels in Manchuria* etc. (John Murray, 1896), 396.

96. R.A.Huttenback, 'The British Empire as a "White Man's Country" – Racial Attitudes and Immigration Legislation in the Colonies of White Settlement', *Journal of British Studies*, XIII (1973–4), 109.

97. H.D.Traill, ' "The burden of Egypt", I: The difficulties of withdrawal', *Nineteenth Century*, XXXIX (1896), 549.

98. *The Times*, no. 34,732 (12 November 1895), 6.

99. Basil Williams, *Cecil Rhodes*, new edition (Constable & Company Ltd, 1938), 55.

100. W.T.Stead, ed., in *The Last Will and Testament of Cecil John Rhodes* (*Review of Reviews* office, 1902), 52, 63.

101. *Last Will and Testament of . . . Rhodes*, 58.

102. Lord Milner, *The Nation and the Empire* (Constable & Company Ltd, 1913), pp. 496, xxxv.

103. R.N.Chowdhuri, *International Mandates and Trusteeship Systems: a comparative study* (The Hague, Martinus Nijhoff, 1955), 16.

104. *Speech of Edmund Burke, Esq. on moving his resolution for conciliation with the colonies, March 22, 1775*, second edition (J.Dodsley, 1775), 101; *Mr. Burke's Speech, On the 1st December 1783, on Mr. Fox's East India Bill* (J.Dodsley, 1794), 7–8.

105. George R. Mellor, *British Imperial Trusteeship 1783–1850* (Faber & Faber, 1951), 22–3; Austen and Smith, 69–83; Robin Hallett, 'Changing European Attitudes to Africa', in *The Cambridge History of Africa*, V, ed. John E. Flint (Cambridge University Press, 1976), 490.

106. 'Minutes by Sir T.S.Raffles, on the establishment of a Malay college at Singapore. 1819', in [Lady Sophia Raffles], *Memoir of the life and public services of Sir Thomas Stamford Raffles, F.R.S. &c.* (John Murray, 1830), App., p. [24].

107. *Report from the Select Committee on Aborigines (British Settlements)* (*HCSP*, 1837, VII), 4, 6, 76–81.

108. Hallett, 490.

109. Curtin, *Image of Africa*, 415, 422.

110. Lorimer, 77. Lorimer warns (p. 79) against seeing all evangelicals as racially prejudiced. Missionary attitudes to race are discussed in Bolt, 117ff. For missionaries as agents of imperial expansion, see H. Alan C. Cairns, *Prelude to Imperialism: British Reactions to Central African Society 1840–1890* (Routledge & Kegan Paul, 1965), 239–40.

111. Rt Hon. Sir F.D.Lugard, *The Dual Mandate in British Tropical Africa* (Edinburgh and London, William Blackwood & Sons, 1922), 18, 69, 88.

112. Curtin, ' "Scientific" Racism and the British Theory of Empire', 48–9.

113. Sir Charles Eliot, *The East Africa Protectorate* (Edward Arnold, 1905), 92, 99.

114. Eliot, 122.

115. Lugard, 92.

116. J.D.Fage, *A History of Africa* (Hutchinson, 1978), 375. Chamberlain was 'the first British statesman to prize west African territory highly enough to risk fighting France to get it' (Ronald Robinson and John Gallagher, *Africa and the Victorians: The Official Mind of Imperialism* (Macmillan & Co. Ltd, 1961), 395).

117. Rudyard Kipling, 'Recessional', *The Times*, no. 35,258 (17 July 1897), 13; Kipling, *The Five Nations* (Methuen & Co., 1903), 215.

118. Rudyard Kipling, *The White Man's Burden* (printed for private circulation, 1899), [5]; Kipling, *The Five Nations*, 79.

119. Robert Needham Cust, *A sketch of the modern languages of Africa* (Trübner & Co., 1883), II. 457.

120. Curtin, *Image of Africa*, 382.

121. 'Elia' [Charles Lamb], 'Jews, Quakers, Scotchmen, and other imperfect sympathies', *London Magazine*, IV (1821), 152, 155; [Charles Lamb], *Elia* (Taylor & Hessey, 1823), 134, 143.

122. Philip D. Curtin, 'Anglo-Saxons and the Tar Brush', *Journal of African History*, XII (1971), 673.

123. Reade, 555.

124. Bolt, 210; Lorimer, 16, 226 n. 11.

125. Louis James, 'Tom Brown's Imperialist Sons', *Victorian Studies*, XVII (1973), 97. I owe the following reference to James's paper.

126. *Boys of England*, I (1866–7), 3, 19.

127. J.A.Mangan, 'Images of empire in the late Victorian public school', *Journal of Educational Administration and History*, XII (1980), 31, 37.

128. G.A.Henty, *By Sheer Pluck: a tale of the Ashanti war* (Blackie & Son, 1884 [1885]), 118, For Henty as propagandist of 'the stereotype of blacks as lazy, childlike, without capacity, and still more the feeling of contempt for them', see Guy Arnold, *Held Fast for England: G.A.Henty: imperialist boys' writer* (Hamish Hamilton, 1980), 79–80: 'Henty must take a full share of responsibility for propagating the kind of views which have done such damage to British relations with African or Asian people during the present century. Nor is the retrospective defence of such attitudes – that they were normal for that period in history – really tenable. To suggest that Henty was expressing no more than what half his contemporaries felt is to denigrate his powers and influence. He was a propagandist – for empire and British interests – and a highly successful one, too, in his way . . . As Henty often claimed, he set out to instruct as well as amuse . . . At least some of the racial arrogance which, unhappily, has been so marked a characteristic of British behaviour in what is now termed "The Third World" can be attributed to his influence.' The figure for Henty's sales is taken from Arnold's Preface, p. [xi], where it is attributed to Henty's principal publisher, Blackie. For an excellent survey of the presentation of black people in nineteenth-century fiction for children, see Jake W. Spidle, 'Victorian juvenilia and the image of the black African', *Journal of Popular Culture*, IX (1975–6), 51–65. See also G.D.Killam, *Africa in English Fiction 1874–1939* (Ibadan University Press, 1968).

8. Up from slavery

The black poor

1. Herbert Aptheker, *The Negro in the American Revolution* (New York, International Publishers, 1940), 16–21; B.Quarles, *The Negro in the American Revolution* (1961), [19]–32, 119, [134]–181; S. Kaplan, *The Black Presence in the Era of the American Revolution 1770–1800* (1973), 67–8, reproducing as fig. 35, p. 62, Dunmore's proclamation of 7 November 1775, which will also be found in *American Archives: Fourth Series*, III, ed. Peter Force (Washington, 1840), col. 1385; Mary Beth Norton, 'The fate of some black loyalists of the American Revolution', *Journal of Negro History*, LVIII (1973), 402–3; James W.St.G.Walker, 'Blacks as American Loyalists: The Slaves' War for Independence', *Historical Reflections*, II (1975), [51]–67; Sylvia R.Frey, 'The British and the Black: A New Perspective', *The Historian*, XXXVIII (1975–6), 225–38; James W.St.G.Walker, *The Black Loyalists: The Search for a Promised Land in Nova Scotia and Sierra Leone* (Longman & Dalhousie University Press, 1976), [1]–12; Ellen Gibson Wilson, *The Loyal Blacks* (New York, Capricorn Books etc., 1976), 24–36, 138.
2. Wilson, 138; Stephen J.Braidwood, 'Initiatives and Organisation of the Black Poor 1786–1787' (paper presented to the International Conference on the History of Blacks in Britain, London, 28–30 September 1981), 6. Shadrack Furman's petition is at PRO AO 13/29/658–9.
3. Norton, 'The fate of some black loyalists', 404–6; Walker, 'Blacks as American Loyalists', 64–5; Walker, *The Black Loyalists*, 6; Wilson, 138–9. See also Mary Beth Norton, *The British-Americans: The Loyalist Exiles in England 1774–1789* (Constable, 1974), 226.
4. Norton, 'The fate of some black loyalists', 406 n. 11.

5. *Public Advertiser*, no. 15854 (16 March 1785), [2]–[3].
6. F.Shyllon, *Black People in Britain* (1977), 123–4. In 1788 James Adair, recorder of London, headed the list of subscribers to the Society for the Abolition of the Slave Trade, with a subscription of ten guineas; see *List of the Society, instituted in 1787, For the Purpose of effecting the abolition of the slave trade* (1788), sig. A1r.
7. *Public Advertiser*, no. 16106 (6 January 1786), [4]; no. 16109 (10 January 1786), [4]; no. 16114 (16 January 1786), [4]; no. 16137 (11 February 1786), [2]; *Morning Chronicle, and London Advertiser*, no. 5213 (28 January 1786), [1].
8. Proceedings of the Committee for the Relief of the Black Poor, 10 July 1786, PRO T1 633/133. For the 'Expences of the Sickhouse in Warren Street', see PRO T1 532/360, T1 633/128, T1 633/130, T1 634/26, T1 634/133, T1 635/151. T1 638/229, T1 638/230–2, T1 638/233a.
9. *Morning Post, and Daily Advertiser*, no. 4080 (15 March 1786), [1].
10. *Public Advertiser*, no. 16195 (18 April 1786), [2].
11. *Public Advertiser*, no. 16117 (19 January 1786), [3]; see also, for a similar opinion, no. 16143 (17 February 1786), [2].
12. *Public Advertiser*, no. 16195 (18 April 1786), [2]; Braidwood, 8, 19 n. 27.
13. C.B.Wadström, *An Essay on Colonization* (1794–5), II. 220.
14. C.Fyfe, *A History of Sierra Leone* (1962), 15; I.Geiss, *The Pan-African Movement*, trans. A.Keep (1974), 36.
15. [Granville Sharp], *Short sketch of temporary regulations (until better shall be provided) for the intended settlement on the Grain Coast of Africa, near Sierra Leona* (H.Baldwin, 1786); P.D.Curtin, *The Image of Africa* (1965), 99–102.
16. Memorial of Henry Smeathman to the Lords Commissioners of the Treasury, 17 May 1786, PRO T1 631/135; Norton, 'The fate of some black loyalists', 408; Wilson, 141.
17. Reprinted in Henry Smeathman, *Plan of a settlement to be made near Sierra Leona, on the Grain Coast of Africa* (T.Stockdale etc., 1786), 23; Wadström, II. 210; Norton, 'The fate of some black loyalists', 408; Wilson, 152.
18. John Pugh, *Remarkable occurrences in the life of Jonas Hanway, Esq.* (Payne & Son etc., 1787), 211.
19. Proceedings of the Committee for the Relief of the Black Poor, 7 June 1786, PRO T1 632/105; Norton, 'The fate of some black loyalists', 409.
20. Smeathman, *Plan of a settlement*, 18.
21. Norton, 'The fate of some black loyalists', 409–10.
22. Proceedings, 7 June 1786, PRO T1 632/105–6; reproduced in N.File and C.Power, *Black Settlers in Britain 1555–1958* (1981), 31, 32.

23. Mr Peters . . . Account of Receipts and Expences, 5 September 1786, PRO T1 635/150; Braidwood, 12.
24. Proceedings, 17 May 1786, PRO T1 631/178; Braidwood, 11.
25. Proceedings, 7 June 1786, PRO T1 632/107v; Shyllon, 134.
26. Proceedings, 15 July 1786, PRO T1 633/272–5; Proceedings, 26 July 1786, PRO T1 634/28; Jonas Hanway to Treasury, 28 July 1786, PRO T1 634/117; Petition of 15 Corporals, PRO T1 638/258.
27. Messrs Turnbull, Macaulay & Gregory, Proposals to convey Black Poor to Nova Scotia, 28 July 1786, PRO T1 634/145; Norton, 'The fate of some black loyalists', 412.
28. Proceedings, 31 July 1786, PRO T1 634/135; Proceedings, 4 August 1786, PRO T1 634/312; Norton, 'The fate of some black loyalists', 413.
29. Minutes, 9 October 1786, PRO T1 636/128; Proceedings, 24 October 1786, PRO T1 638/238, reproduced in File and Power, 33.
30. PRO T1 636/128.
31. Proceedings, 14 June 1786, PRO T1 632/112; Wilson 143.
32. Draft at PRO T1 636/130.
33. George Peters to Commissioners of Navy, 6 October 1786, PRO T1 636/127; PRO T1 636/128; PRO T1 636/233; Wilson, 143–4; Braidwood, 13.
34. Wilson, 146.
35. Sam[uel] Hoare to Treasury, 6 December 1787, PRO T1 638/227.
36. *General Evening Post*, no. 8276 (14–16 December 1786), [1].
37. *Public Advertiser*, no. 16418 (3 January 1787), [4].
38. e.g. *Public Advertiser*, no. 16419 (4 January 1787), [3]; no. 16426 (12 January 1787), [4].
39. O.Cugoano, *Thoughts and sentiments on the evil and wicked traffic of the slavery and commerce of the human species* (1787), 142.
40. e.g. *Morning Post, and Daily Advertiser*, no. 4327 (29 December 1786), [3], reproduced in File and Power, [27].
41. *Morning Post, and Daily Advertiser*, no. 4328 (30 December 1786), [2].
42. As quoted by Norton, 'The fate of some black loyalists', 415.
43. Cugoano, 140.
44. Norton, 'The fate of some black loyalists', 416.
45. Norton, 'The fate of some black loyalists', 417–18.
46. Norton, 'The fate of some black loyalists', 418–19; Wilson, 150.
47. Norton, 'The fate of some black loyalists', 419.
48. Braidwood, 12.
49. Norton, 'The fate of some black loyalists', 409.
50. Cugoano, 140.
51. C.H.Fyfe, 'Thomas Peters: History and Legend', *Sierra Leone Studies*, n.s. no. 1 (December 1953), [4]–11; Fyfe, *History of Sierra*

Leone, 32–4, 41–2; Walker, *The Black Loyalists*, 25, 31, 44, 94–6, 105, [115]–138, [145]–151; Wilson, 34, 75, 108–13, 177–86, 231–2, 248–56; Christopher Fyfe, in *The Encyclopaedia Africana Dictionary of African Biography*, II (New York, Reference Publications Inc., 1979), 131–2.

52. Fyfe, *History of Sierra Leone*, 42.

Resistance and self-emancipation

1. Will of Thomas Armstrong, 1822, Record Office, Carlisle, as quoted by J.Walvin, *Black and White* (1973), 50.
2. Douglas A.Lorimer, 'Black Slaves and English Liberty: a Re-examination of Racial Slavery in England' (paper presented to the International Conference on the History of Blacks in Britain, London, 28–30 September 1981), abstract and pp. [1], 2, 4, 7–8, 10, 15, 21.
3. *Gentleman's Magazine*, XXXIV (1764), 493.
4. Sir J.Fielding, *Extracts from such of the Penal Laws, as Particularly relate to the Peace and Good Order of this Metropolis*, new edition (1768), 144. Italics in the original.
5. T.Clarkson, *The History of the Rise, Progress, and Accomplishment of the Abolition of the African Slave-Trade* (1808), I. 78–9.
6. J.J.Hecht, *Continental and Colonial Servants in Eighteenth Century England* (1954), 43.
7. Edward Brathwaite, *The Development of Creole Society in Jamaica 1770–1820* (Oxford, Clarendon Press, 1971), 159.
8. *The Diary and Letters of His Excellency Thomas Hutchinson, Esq.*, ed. Peter Orlando Hutchinson (Sampson Low, Marston, Searle & Rivington, 1883–6), II. 276–7.
9. Lorimer, 14.
10. *Gentleman's Magazine*, XI (1741), 186; Hecht, 39.
11. *Diary and Letters of . . . Thomas Hutchinson*, ed. Hutchinson, II. 274–5; G.Williams, *History of the Liverpool Privateers* (1897), 563–4.
12. Lorimer, 12.
13. And.S.Cunningham, *Rambles in the parishes of Scoonie and Wemyss* (Leven, Purves & Cunningham, [1905], 154–6.
14. Lorimer, 15.
15. Nicholas Rogers, 'London politics from Walpole to Pitt: patriotism and independency in an era of commercial imperialism, 1738–63' (unpublished University of Toronto PhD thesis, 1974), 508–9, as quoted by Robert W.Malcolmson, *Life and Labour in England 1700–1780* (Hutchinson, 1981), 132.
16. Malcolmson, 133.
17. E.P.Thompson, 'Eighteenth-century English society: class struggle without class', *Social History*, III (1978), 154, 158, 165.
18. E.P.Thompson, 'Patrician Society, Plebeian Culture', *Journal of Social History*, VII (1973–4), 400.

19. It follows, therefore, that in Britain as in the United States 'the slave community itself was the heart of the abolitionist movement' (C.L.R.James, 'The Atlantic Slave Trade and Slavery: Some Interpretations of Their Significance in the Development of the United States and the Western World', *Amistad 1*, ed. John A.Williams and Charles F.Harris (New York, Random House, 1970), 147). James continues: 'This is a claim that must seem most extraordinarily outrageous to those who think of abolitionism as a movement which required organizations, offices, officers, financiers, printing presses and newspapers, public platforms and orators, writers and petitions. Yet the center of activity of abolitionism lay in the movement of the slaves for their own liberation.'

Abolitionists and radicals

1. William Edward Hartpole Lecky, *History of European Morals from Augustus to Charlemagne* (Longmans, Green, & Co., 1869), I. 169.
2. Dr.Franz Hochstetter, 'Die wirtschlaftlichen und politischen Motive für die Abschaffung der britischen Sklavenhandels im Jahre 1806/1807', in *Staats- und sozialwissenschaftliche Forschungen*, ed. Gustav Schmoller & Max Sering, XXV/1 (Leipzig, Duncker & Humblot, 1905). See also Franz Hochstetter, 'Die Abschaffung des britischen Sklavenhandels im Jahre 1806/07: Ein Kapitel aus der britischen Schiffahrtspolitik', *Meereskunde: Sammlung volkstümlicher Vorträge*, V/52 (1911).
3. C.L.R.James, *The Black Jacobins: Toussaint Louverture and the San Domingo Revolution* (Secker & Warburg, 1938), 311.
4. E.Williams, *Capitalism and Slavery*, third impression (1972), 149, 152, 178, 210.
5. See, e.g., G.R.Mellor, *British Imperial Trusteeship, 1783–1856* (1951); Roger T. Anstey, 'Capitalism and Slavery: a Critique', *Economic History Review*, 2nd ser. XXI (1968), 307–20; Seymour Drescher, 'Capitalism and abolition: values and forces in Britain, 1783–1814', in *Liverpool, the African Slave Trade, and Abolition*, ed. R.Anstey and P.E.H.Hair (1976), [167]–195; S.Drescher, *Econocide: British Slavery in the Era of Abolition* (1977); Stanley L.Engerman and David Eltis, 'Economic Aspects of the Abolition Debate', in *Anti-Slavery, Religion, and Reform: Essays in Memory of Roger Anstey*, ed. Christine Bolt and Seymour Drescher (Dawson, Archon, 1980), [272]–293. A useful survey of the controversy up to the mid-1970s is Roger Anstey, 'The historical debate on the abolition of the British slave trade', in *Liverpool, the African Slave Trade, and Abolition*, ed. Anstey and Hair, [157]–166.
6. D.B.Davis, *The Problem of Slavery in Western Culture* (1966), 153n.
7. E.Williams, *From Columbus to Castro* (1970), 280–327.
8. *Gentleman's Magazine*, LVIII (1788), ii. 460; see also ii. 311–12, 322, 326, 416, 417, 419, 514, 515.

9. T.Clarkson, *The History of the Rise, Progress, and Accomplishment of the Abolition of the African Slave-Trade* (1808), I. 415–16.
10. As quoted by Donald Read, *The English Provinces* c. *1760–1960: A study in influence* (Edward Arnold, 1964), 41.
11. James Walvin, 'The Impact of Slavery on British Radical Politics: 1787–1838', in *Comparative Perspectives on Slavery in New World Plantation Societies*, ed. Vera Rubin and Arthur Tuden (Annals of the New York Academy of Sciences, CCXCII, 1977), 344. I owe some of the facts and references in this section to this essay of Walvin's, some to its companion-piece, 'The Rise of British Popular Sentiment for Abolition, 1787–1832', in *Anti-Slavery, Religion, and Reform*, ed. Bolt and Drescher, [149]–162. See also James Walvin, 'The Public Campaign in England against Slavery, 1787–1834', in *The Abolition of the Atlantic Slave Trade: Origins and Effects in Europe, Africa, and the Americas*, ed. David Eltis and J.Walvin (University of Wisconsin Press, 1981), 63–79; Seymour Drescher, 'Public Opinion and the Destruction of British Colonial Slavery', in *Slavery and British Society 1776–1846*, ed. J.Walvin (Macmillan Press Ltd, 1982), [22]–48; J.Walvin, 'The Propaganda of Anti-Slavery', in *Slavery and British Society*, ed. Walvin, [49]–68.
12. *Eighth Report of the Directors of the African Institution* (1814), 51–67, listing 519 petitions for abolition of the slave trade presented to the Commons between 9 February and 25 April 1792.
13. Lydia Hardy to Thomas Hardy, 2 April 1792, PRO TS 24/12/1.
14. Read, 42.
15. *The Life and Correspondence of Major Cartwright*, ed. F.D.Cartwright (Henry Colburn, 1826), I. 179.
16. *Annual Register*, 1792, 'The History of Europe', 153.
17. *Annual Register*, 1792, 'The History of Europe', 150–1, 154.
18. *Annual Register*, 1793, 'The History of Europe', 90; *Parliamentary History*, XXX (1792–4), cols. 654–5.
19. R.I. and S.Wilberforce, *Life of William Wilberforce* (1838), II. 18; Earl Leslie Griggs, *Thomas Clarkson: The Friend of Slaves* (George Allen & Unwin Ltd, 1936), 70–1; Sir Reginald Coupland, *Wilberforce*, second edition (Collins, 1945), 127–8; Robin Furneaux, *William Wilberforce* (Hamish Hamilton, 1974), 109.
20. *A Very new pamphlet indeed! Being the truth addressed to the people at large: containing some strictures on the English Jacobins* (1792), 3.
21. *Proceedings of the Public Meeting, held at Sheffield, in the open air, On the Seventh of April, 1794* (Sheffield Constitutional Society, 1794), 22–5.
22. *The Tribune, a periodical publication consisting chiefly of the political lectures of J.Thelwall* (D.I.Eaton etc., 1795–6), II. 167.
23. Samuel Taylor Coleridge, *Lectures 1795 On Politics and Religion*, ed. Lewis Patton and Peter Mann (Collected Works of S.T. Coleridge, I, Routledge & Kegan Paul, 1971), 236–7.
24. Walvin, 'The Impact of Slavery on British Radical Politics', 348.

25. Walvin, 'The Impact of Slavery', 349.
26. *Life and Correspondence of Major Cartwright*, ed. Cartwright, II. 84.
27. Walvin, 'The Rise of British Popular Sentiment for Abolition', 155.
28. 'List of the leadeing [*sic*] Reformers', October 1819, PRO HO 42/197.
29. G.D.H.Cole, *A Short History of the British Working-Class Movement, 1788–1947*, revised edition (George Allen & Unwin Ltd, 1948), 44; E.P.Thompson, *The Making of the English Working Class* (Victor Gollancz Ltd, 1963), 162; T.M.Parssinen, 'The Revolutionary Party in London, 1816–20', *Bulletin of the Institute of Historical Research*, XLV (1972), 267.
30. T.M.Parssinen, 'Association, convention and anti-parliament in British radical politics, 1771–1848', *English Historical Review*, LXXXVIII (1973), 516.

The black radicals

1. *Cobbett's Weekly Register*, XXXVI/8 (6 May 1820), cols. 590–8; *Observer*, no. 1520 (7 May 1820), [4]; *British Luminary and Weekly Intelligence*, no. 84 (7 May 1820), 146.
2. PRO HO 44/4/322, HO 44/5/51, HO 44/5/494–5.
3. PRO HO 44/4/322.
4. PRO HO 44/5/391.
5. PRO HO 44/5/426.
6. PRO HO 44/4/317, HO 44/5/38.
7. PRO HO 44/5/202. Thistlewood later claimed that Davidson 'would have killed right and left' if an attempt had been made to seize the banner (Report of informer Stafford, 24 November 1819, PRO HO 42/199).
8. Percy Bysshe Shelley, *The Masque of Anarchy: A Poem* (Edward Moxon, 1832), 2.
9. 'Precis of Secret Information as furnished by Mr.C. [i.e. John Williamson] from July 1819 to Feby 23, 1820', entry for 14 November 1819, PRO HO 42/197.
10. *The Republican*, II/7 (3 March 1820), 219.
11. PRO HO 44/4/100, HO 44/4/322.
12. 'Precis of Secret Information as furnished by Mr.C.', entry for 18 November 1819, PRO HO 42/197; report of informer BC [i.e. William Sallebanks], 18 November 1819, PRO HO 42/199; report of informer BC, 5 December 1819, PRO HO 42/200; PRO HO 44/4/318, HO 44/5/278, HO 44/5/289.
13. Report of Bow Street constable George Ruthven, 24 February 1820, PRO HO 44/4/74.
14. F.K.Donnelly and J.L.Baxter, 'Sheffield and the English Revolutionary Tradition, 1791–1820', *International Review of Social History*, XX/3 (1975), 419–20.

15. Jurors' lists were 'pricked' to indicate which were 'disloyal' or 'strong friends of the Prisoners' and which 'loyal subjects' or 'very loyal'; see PRO HO 44/6/31–6, and cf. E.P.Thompson, *The Making of the English Working Class* (1963), 468 and n. 1.

16. PRO HO 44/6/206–7. Edwards's key report, dated 22 February 1820, is in PRO HO 42/199. His reports were normally signed 'W——r'.

17. Cf. the report of Bow Street constable R. Birnie, 28 February 1820, PRO HO 44/4/291: 'Davison's [*sic*] Hovel was most carefully searched, but nothing found, there was an officer in possession distraining for Rent.'

18. *The Trials of Arthur Thistlewood, James Ings, John Thomas Brunt, Richard Tidd, William Davidson, and others, for High Treason* (J.Butterworth & Son, 1820), 634–5. I am grateful to Ian McCalman for telling me about this book. See also *Cobbett's Weekly Register*, XXXVI/8 (6 May 1820), cols. 560–6.

19. *British Luminary and Weekly Intelligence*, no. 84 (7 May 1820), 146.

20. PRO HO 44/6/271.

21. Besides the sources already cited, the foregoing account of the Cato Street attempt and Davidson's part in it is based on: *The Trials of Arthur Thistlewood . . . to which is added, a copious account of the execution*, second edition (John Fairburn & T.Dolby, [1820]); *Annual Register*, 1820, 'Chronicle', 29–34, 55–66; W[illiam]. C[ar]r., in *DNB*, LVI. 142–5; Sir Charles Oman, *The Unfortunate Colonel Despard and other studies* (Edward Arnold & Co., 1922), 22–48; John Stanhope, *The Cato Street Conspiracy* (Jonathan Cape, 1962); Thompson, 700ff.; Howard Mackey, '"The Complexion of the Accused": William Davidson, The Black Revolutionary In The Cato Street Conspiracy of 1820', *Negro Educational Review*, XXIII (1972), 132–47 (I am grateful to Ian McCalman for this reference and to the British Library for obtaining a photostat for me); David Johnson, *Regency Revolution: The case of Arthur Thistlewood* (Compton Russell, 1974); V.S.Anand and F.A.Ridley, *The Cato Street Conspiracy* (Medusa Press, 1977); Howard Mackey, in *Biographical Dictionary of Modern British Radicals*, I: *1770–1830*, ed. Joseph O.Baylen and Norbert J.Gossman (Hassocks, Sussex, Harvester Press, 1979), 113–14; I.J.Prothero, *Artisans and Politics in Early Nineteenth-Century London: John Gast and his Times* (Dawson, 1979), 123ff.

22. *The Republican*, II/7 (3 March 1820), [217]–223; III/2 (5 May 1820), 44–5. See also the edited version in Theophila Carlile Campbell, *The Battle of the Press As Told in the Story of the Life of Richard Carlile* (A.& H.B.Bonner, 1899), 78–83.

23. *The Horrors of Slavery: exemplified in The Life and History of the Rev. Robert Wedderburn, V.D.M.* (R. Wedderburn, 1824), 4–9.

24. *Horrors of Slavery*, 10–11.

25. *Horrors of Slavery*, 13–14.
26. *The Axe Laid to the Root, or a Fatal Blow to Oppressors, being an address to the Planters and Negroes of the Island of Jamaica*, no. 1 [1817], cols. 12–13.
27. Report of Thomas Lea and William Plush on meeting at Hopkins Street chapel, 6 October 1819, PRO HO 42/196.
28. Robert Wedderburn, *Truth, Self-supported; or, A refutation of certain doctrinal errors, generally adopted In the Christian Church* (G.Riebau, [*c.*1790]), [3], 4; *The Trial of the Rev. Robt. Wedderburn, (A Dissenting Minister of the Unitarian persuasion,) for blasphemy*, ed. Erasmus Perkins (Mrs Carlile etc., 1820), 7, 8.
29. Thompson, 615.
30. *The 'Forlorn Hope', or A Call to the Supine, To rouse from Indolence and assert Public Rights*, [no. 1, 1817], cols. [1], 4.
31. Report of informer A [i.e. James Hanley], 15 April 1819, PRO HO 42/190; Prothero, *Artisans and Politics*, 110, 360 n. 26.
32. PRO HO 40/7(3)/906–7, HO 40/7(3)/2036–7; Olive D.Rudkin, *Thomas Spence and His Connections* (George Allen & Unwin, 1927), 148–9.
33. Report of informer A, 15 April 1819, PRO HO 42/190; R.Wedderburn, *A few Plain Questions for an Apostate* [1819], *A few lines for a Double-Faced Politician* [1819], copies in PRO HO 42/202.
34. Handbill advertising debate at Hopkins Street chapel, 13 September 1819, copy in PRO HO 42/194; Prothero, *Artisans and Politics*, 110, 115, 121. Allen Davenport helped to form the East London Democratic Association in 1837 'and gave it its extremist and *Citizen* terminology' (Iorwerth Prothero, 'Chartism in London', *Past & Present*, no. 44 (August 1969), 87).
35. Report of John Eshelby on meetings at Hopkins Street chapel, 14 November 1819, PRO HO 42/198.
36. Handbill advertising meeting at Hopkins Street chapel, 16 August 1819, copy in PRO HO 42/192. Italics in the original.
37. Annotated letter from Marlborough Street magistrates to Home Office, 12 August 1819, PRO HO 42/191.
38. Copy in PRO HO 42/193.
39. Handbill advertising debate at Hopkins Street chapel, 13 September 1819, copy in PRO HO 42/194; report of informer BC, 15 September 1819, PRO HO 42/194; report of informer BC, 29 September 1819, PRO HO 42/195; report of informer BC, 4 October 1819, PRO HO 42/196; report of Lea and Plush, 6 October 1819, PRO HO 42/196; report of informer BC, 11 October 1819, PRO HO 42/197; handbill enclosed with report of informer BC, 16 October 1819, PRO HO 42/197; report of Plush and Matthew Matthewson, 18 October 1819, fols. 5–6, PRO HO 42/197; 'Substance of proceedings of the Debating Society held at "Hopkins

Street Chapel" Wednesday Eveng. 3[d] Nov. 1819', PRO HO 42/198; report of Plush and Matthewson, 3 November 1819, fols. 5–6, PRO HO 42/198.

40. Reports of Chetwoode Eustace and Richard Dalton, 3 and 10 November 1819, and of Plush and Matthewson, 9 November 1819, on meetings at Hopkins Street chapel, PRO HO 42/198.
41. J.M.Robertson, *A history of freethought in the nineteenth century* (Watts & Co., 1929), 61. A copy of the very rare *Letter* to the Chief Rabbi is enclosed with report by Dalton on meeting at Hopkins Street chapel, 15 November 1819, PRO HO 42/198.
42. *Axe Laid to the Root*, no. 6 [1817], cols. 92–6.
43. *Axe Laid to the Root*, no. 1 [1817], cols. 4–5, 7–8, 12; no. 2 [1817], col. 26.
44. Report of informer BC, 15 September 1819, PRO HO 42/194; T.M.Parssinen, 'The Revolutionary Party in London, 1816–20', *Bulletin of the Institute of Historical Research*, XLV (1972), 277 n. 3.
45. 'Precis of Secret Information as furnished by Mr. C.', entry for 20 October 1819, PRO HO 42/197; report of informer BC, 22 October 1819, PRO HO 42/197; report of James Hanley, 22 November 1819, PRO HO 42/199.
46. Report of informer BC, 5 August 1819, PRO HO 42/191; 'Precis of Secret Information as furnished by Mr.C.', entry for 5 August 1819, PRO HO 42/197.
47. Cf. William H.Wickwar, *The Struggle for the Freedom of the Press 1819–1832* (George Allen & Unwin Ltd, 1928), 89.
48. *Trial of . . . Wedderburn*, 4.
49. *Trial of . . . Wedderburn*, title-page.
50. *Trial of . . . Wedderburn*, 17–19.
51. Revd Erasmus Perkins, *A few hints relative to the texture of mind, and the manufacture of conscience* (T.Davison, [*c.*1820]), p. vi.
52. Prothero, 'Chartism in London', 87; Parssinen, 281–2. For spenceans in the 1830s, see also Patricia Hollis, *The Pauper Press: A study of working-class radicalism in the 1830s* (Oxford University Press, 1970), 212–14.
53. *Horrors of Slavery*, 24. Joel J.Wiener, *Radicalism and Freethought in Nineteenth-Century Britain: The Life of Richard Carlile* (Contributions in Labor History, no. 13, Westport, Conn. and London, Greenwood Press, 1983), 29 n. 2, says Wedderburn 'gave lectures on theology until as late as 1828', but provides no reference. I am grateful to Nicolas Walter for giving me a copy of this book.
54. I owe this information to J.R.Sewell of the Corporation of London Records Office.

The everyday struggle 1787–1833

1. *Ninth Report of the Directors of the African Institution* (1815), 69–71.

2. G.B.Wood, 'A Negro Trail in the North of England', *Country Life Annual*, 1967, p. 43.
3. Wood, 42–3.
4. 'Collectanea', comp. D.Lysons, I. 82v, 83r.
5. 'Collectanea', I. 84v and recto of following leaf.
6. 'Collectanea', I. 85v, 86r; *Gentleman's Magazine*, n.s. VII (1837), i. 327; Henry Morley, *Memoirs of Bartholomew Fair* (Chapman & Hall, 1859), 483; *The Book of Days: A miscellany of popular antiquities*, ed. R.Chambers (W.R.Chambers, 1863–4), II. 267; *Notes and Queries*, 9th ser. V (1900), 456. Richardson, who died in 1837, desired in his will to be buried in the same grave (J[oseph]. K[night]., in *DNB*, XLVIII. 231).
7. *The Times*, no. 8150 (26 November 1810), [3]; no. 8153 (29 November 1810), [3]; 'Collectanea', I. 100v–103r; Edward Hyde East, *Reports of Cases argued and determined in the Court of King's Bench*, XIII (J.Butterworth & J.Cook, 1811), 195–6; G.Cuvier, 'Extrait d'observations faites sur le cadavre d'une femme connue à Paris et à Londres sous le nom de Vénus Hottentotte', *Mémoires du Muséum d'histoire naturelle*, III (1817), [259]–274 (reprinted in G.Cuvier, *Discours sur les révolutions du globe* (Paris, Passard, 1864), [211]–222); Mrs [Anne] Mathews, *Memoirs of Charles Mathews, comedian* (Richard Bentley, 1838–9), IV. 136–7; *Book of Days*, ed. Chambers, II. 621–2; R.V[erneau]., 'Le centième anniversaire de la mort de Sarah Bartmann', *L'Anthropologie*, XXVII (1916), 177–9; Jean Avalon, 'Sarah, la "Vénus Hottentote" ', *Æsculape*, XVI (1926), [281]–288; Percival R.Kirby, 'The Hottentot Venus', *Africana Notes and News*, VI (1948–9), 55–62; Percival R.Kirby, 'La Vénus Hottentote', *Æsculape*, XXXIII (1952), [14]–21; Percival R.Kirby, 'More about the Hottentot Venus', *Africana Notes and News*, (1952–3), 124–34; Richard D.Altick, *The Shows of London* (Cambridge, Mass., Belknap Press of Harvard University Press, 1978), [268]–272; *Kunapipi*, II/1 (1980), 29 (photograph of the exhibit in the Musée de l'Homme); Bernth Lindfors, 'The Hottentot Venus and other African Attractions in Nineteenth Century England' (paper presented to the International Conference on the History of Blacks in Britain, London, 28–30 September 1981), to which I am indebted for many of the foregoing references.
8. *Report from Committee on the State of Mendicity in The Metropolis* (1815), 41.
9. *Second Report of the Society for the Suppression of Mendicity* (1820), 3; *Third Report* etc. (1821), 3; *Fourth Report* etc. (1822), 4; *Fifth Report* etc. (1823), 5; *Seventh Report* etc. (1825), 13; *Eighth Report* etc. (1826), 14.
10. *Ninth Report of the Society for the Suppression of Mendicity* (1827), 12.
11. M.Banton, *The Coloured Quarter* (1955), 26.

12. *First Report of the Society established in London for the Suppression of Mendicity* (1819), 33; *Second Report* etc. (1820), 32, 29–30.
13. *Fourth Report of the Society for the Suppression of Mendicity* (1822), 9, 52.
14. *Report from Select Committee on the State of Mendicity in The Metropolis* (1816), 15.
15. *Report from Committee on the State of Mendicity in The Metropolis* (1815), 16.
16. *Third Report of the Society for the Suppression of Mendicity* (1821), 27–8.
17. See, e.g., James Grant, *Sketches in London* (W.S.Orr & Co., 1838), 27, 44.
18. Pierce Egan, *Life in London; or The day and night scenes of Jerry Hawthorn, Esq. and his elegant friend Corinthian Tom* (Sherwood, Neely, & Jones, 1821), 347; J[ames]. C[atnach]., *The Death, Last Will, and Funeral of 'Black Billy'*, tenth edition (1823); M.Dorothy George, *Hogarth to Cruikshank: Social change in graphic satire* (Allen Lane The Penguin Press, 1967), 169–70.
19. John Thomas Smith, *Vagabondia; or Anecdotes of mendicant wanderers through the streets of London* (J. and A.Arch etc., 1817), 35; Grant, 26–7.
20. Smith, 36.
21. Smith, 33.
22. Smith, 35.
23. Smith, 26.
24. *Copy of all Correspondence between the Commissioners for the Affairs of India, and any other public Body, relative to the Care and Maintenance of Lascar Sailors, during their Stay in England* (1816), 5.
25. *Lascars and Chinese: A short address to Young Men, of the several orthodox denominations of Christians* (W.Harris etc., 1814), 17; *Copy of all Correspondence*, 13–14.
26. R.I. and S.Wilberforce, *Life of William Wilberforce* (1838), IV. 154.
27. *Report from Committee on Lascars and other Asiatic Seamen* (1815), 4–5.
28. *Copy of all Correspondence*, 14.
29. *Lascars and Chinese*, 3–4, 9–10.
30. *First Report from the Committee On the State of the Police of The Metropolis* (1817), 195.
31. [Benjamin Silliman], *A journal of travels in England, Holland, and Scotland, and of two passages over the Atlantic, in the years 1805 and 1806* (Boston, Mass., Howe & Deforest etc., 1812), I. 210.
32. *Eighth Report of the Directors of the African Institution* (1814), 22–3.
33. *The Intimate Letters of Hester Piozzi and Penelope Pennington 1788–1821*, ed. Oswald G. Knapp (John Lane, 1914), 243.
34. See Joseph Marryat, *More thoughts, occasioned by two publications* (J.M.Richardson & J.Ridgway, 1816), 100ff.; Sanders's preface to *Haytian Papers* (W.Reed, 1816), pp. [i]–vi; Benjamin Quarles, *Black Abolitionists* (New York, Oxford University Press, 1969), 130.

35. Henry Noble Sherwood, 'Paul Cuffe', *Journal of Negro History*, VIII (1923), 177; Quarles, 129–30.
36. John Jeremie, *Four Essays on Colonial Slavery* (J.Hatchard & Son, 1831), 49.
37. Letter of Richard Raikes, 5 July 1815, in Gloucester County Record Office, as quoted by J.Walvin, *Black and White* (1973), 60–1.
38. Marryat, 99–100.
39. *Cobbett's Weekly Political Register*, V/24 (16 June 1804), col. 935.
40. Marryat, 105.
41. Alltud Eifion, *John Ystumllyn neu 'Jack Black'* (Tremadoc, R.Isaac Jones, 1888; reprinted Criccieth, Ngwasg y Castell, 1966). I am grateful to Ziggi Alexander for making a translation of this booklet available to me.
42. See Ian Law and Linda Loy, 'A History of Racism and Resistance in Liverpool, 1760–1960 (Summary)' (paper presented to the International Conference on the History of Blacks in Britain, London, 28–30 September 1981); *A History of Race and Racism in Liverpool, 1660–1950*, comp. Ian Law, ed. June Henfrey (Liverpool, Merseyside Community Relations Council, 1981).

9. Challenges to empire

William Cuffay

1. Asa Briggs, 'Chartists in Tasmania: a note', *Bulletin of the Society for the Study of Labour History*, no. 3 (Autumn 1961), 6, citing Tasmanian public records and thus correcting the statement in [Thomas Martin Wheeler], 'Mr. William Cuffay', *Reynolds's Political Instructor*, I/23 (13 April 1850), [177], that he was 'born . . . on board a merchant ship, homeward bound from the Island of St. Kitts'.
2. [Wheeler], 'Mr. William Cuffay'.
3. Wheeler says he had a son who died in youth, but Cuffay denied this at his trial (*The Times*, no. 19,983 (2 October 1848), 6) and he is described as childless in the Hobart convict department records (George Rudé, *Protest and Punishment: the Story of the Social and Political Protesters transported to Australia 1788–1868* (Oxford, Clarendon Press, 1978), 144).
4. Mark Hovell, *The Chartist Movement*, second edition (Publications of the University of Manchester, Historical Ser. xxxi, Manchester, University Press, 1925), 137.
5. Lieut.-Gen. Sir W.Napier, *The Life and Opinions of General Sir Charles James Napier, G.C.B.* (John Murray, 1857), II. 3.
6. I. Prothero, 'Chartism in London', *Past & Present*, no. 44 (August 1969), 80, 98. Other leaders of the London Chartists in the 1840s, as listed by Prothero, were: John Fussell, Philip M'Grath, John Parker, Ruffy Ridley, Henry Ross, John Simpson, John Skelton, Edmund Stallwood, and T.M.Wheeler.

7. David Goodway, *London Chartism 1838–1848* (Cambridge University Press, 1982), 35. I am grateful to Ken Weller for telling me about this book.
8. Goodway, *London Chartism*, 47.
9. *Northern Star*, V/256 (8 October 1842), 3; William Stevens, *A Memoir of Thomas Martin Wheeler* (John Bedford Leno, 1862), 21; Prothero, 'Chartism in London', 97.
10. *Punch*, XIV (1848), 169, 173, 176, 181, 182–3; XV (1848), 145, 154–5, 160, 168. The phrase from *The Times* is as quoted by [Wheeler], 'Mr. William Cuffay'. For the sacking of Mrs Cuffay, see *Weekly Dispatch*, no. 2423 (16 April 1848), [third edition, 181].
11. *Hansard's Parliamentary Debates*, 3rd. ser. vol. 74 (1844), col. 518.
12. As quoted by Stevens, 27.
13. Alice Mary Hadfield, *The Chartist Land Company* (Newton Abbot, David & Charles, 1970), 21, 35.
14. *The Times*, no. 19,813 (17 March 1848), 7; *Weekly Dispatch*, no. 2423 (16 April 1848), [third edition], 183; Goodway, *London Chartism*, 116.
15. John Saville, in *Dictionary of Labour Biography*, ed. Joyce M. Bellamy and J.Saville, VI (Macmillan, 1982), 78. Saville's essay on Cuffay is the indispensable modern key to his life and to sources of information about him, and I have made grateful use of it throughout this section.
16. R.G.Gammage, *The History of the Chartist Movement, from its commencement down to the present time* (Holyoake, & Co., 1854), 330–1; R.G.Gammage, *History of the Chartist Movement 1837–1854*, revised edition (Newcastle-on-Tyne, Browne & Browne, 1894), 308. The first edition of Gammage has Cuffay seconding Reynolds's amendment; in the revised edition the seconder is identified as Robert Lowery.
17. *Morning Chronicle*, no. 24,479 (6 April 1848), 2.
18. *Weekly Dispatch*, no. 2422 (9 April 1848), 180.
19. *Morning Chronicle*, no. 24,480 (7 April 1848), 6.
20. *Morning Chronicle*, no. 24,483 (11 April 1848), 6.
21. *Illustrated London News*, XII/213 (15 April 1848), 241; *Morning Chronicle*, no. 24,483 (11 April 1848), 6.
22. Goodway, *London Chartism*, 94.
23. *The Times*, no. 19,981 (29 September 1848), 4. Cf. Thomas Frost, *Forty years' recollections: literary and political* (Sampson Low, Marston, Searle, & Rivington, 1880), 149–50; David Goodway, 'Chartism in London', *Bulletin of the Society for the Study of Labour History*, no. 20 (Spring 1970), 15 ('Frost . . . misleads when he names William Cuffay as president of the revolutionary committee and apparent "concocter of the conspiracy" '); Goodway, *London Chartism*, pp. xiv (the insurrectionary plans of 1848 'cannot be dubbed as "Cuffay's conspiracy" '), 94.
24. Frost, 162–3.

25. Frost, 165.
26. *The Times*, no. 19,981 (29 September 1848), 4.
27. *The Times*, no. 19,978 (26 September 1848), 7; *Northern Star*, XI/571 (30 September 1848), 6. See also *Reports of State Trials*, n.s. VII, ed. John E. P. Wallis (1896), cols. 467–84.
28. *The Times*, no. 19,979 (27 September 1848), 6; *Northern Star*, XI/571 (30 September 1848), 6.
29. *Northern Star*, XI/571 (30 September 1848), 7.
30. F.C.Mather, *Public Order in the Age of the Chartists* (Manchester University Press, 1959), 206–7.
31. *The Times*, no. 19,983 (2 October 1848), 4.
32. L'Ami du Peuple, 'To the Working Classes', *Northern Star*, XI/572 (7 October 1848), 5.
33. 'Christopher', 'A word in defence of Cuffey', *Reasoner*, VII (1849), 399.
34. [Wheeler], 'Mr. William Cuffay'.
35. Rudé, 217. For a letter from the Home Office to Mrs Cuffay concerning her passage to Tasmania, see *Northern Star*, XIV/687 (21 December 1850), 1.
36. 'Death of a celebrity', *Mercury* (Hobart Town), XVII/3007 (11 August 1870), [3].
37. 'Death of a celebrity'.
38. *Punch*, XV (1848), 265, reprinted in W.M.Thackeray, *Miscellanies: Prose and Verse* (Bradbury & Evans, 1855–7), I. 126–31.
39. [Charles Kingsley], *Alton Locke, tailor and poet* (Chapman & Hall, 1850), 167, 174, 194.
40. Thomas Martin Wheeler, 'Sunshine and Shadow: a tale of the nineteenth century', chap. xxvii, *Northern Star*, XII/624 (6 October 1849), 3. In a later chapter Wheeler observed that 'so disgusting was the treachery by which the government had lured [Cuffay] and his fellows to their fate, that not by the Chartist body alone, but by the public generally, they were regarded more as martyrs than criminals' (*Northern Star*, XIII/636 (29 December 1849), 3).

Mary Seacole

1. Ziggi Alexander and Audrey Dewjee, *Mary Seacole: Jamaican National Heroine and 'Doctress' in the Crimean War* (Brent Library Service, 1982). The best recent account of Florence Nightingale is F.B.Smith, *Florence Nightingale: Reputation and Power* (Croom Helm, 1982).
2. *The Times*, no. 30,202 (24 May 1881), 5; J. Elise Gordon, 'Mary Seacole – A Forgotten Nurse Heroine of the Crimea', *Midwife Health Visitor & Community Nurse*, XI/2 (February 1975), 47.
3. *Wonderful adventures of Mrs. Seacole in many lands*, ed. W.J.S. (James Blackwood, 1858), 2; Gordon, 47.

4. *Wonderful adventures*, 2–3.
5. *Wonderful adventures*, 7.
6. *Wonderful adventures*, 48.
7. *Wonderful adventures*, 59–63.
8. *Wonderful adventures*, 79.
9. *Wonderful adventures*, 97.
10. Frederick Robinson, *Diary of the Crimean War* (Richard Bentley, 1861), 290.
11. *Wonderful adventures*, 114. Her establishment appears as 'M[rs]. Seacole' on the 'Plan of the British Camp before Sebastopol' in W.H.Russell, *The British Expedition to the Crimea* (G.Routledge & Co., 1858), 328.
12. Alexis Soyer, *Soyer's Culinary Campaign: being historical reminiscences of the late war* (G.Routledge & Co., 1857), 231; Helen Morris, *Portrait of a chef: the life of Alexis Soyer sometime chef to the Reform Club* (Cambridge, University Press, 1938), 165.
13. Frederick Harris D. Veith, *Recollections of the Crimean Campaign and the Expedition to Kinburn in 1855* (Montreal, printed by John Lovell & Son, Limited, 1907), 74–5.
14. Mrs. Tom Kelly, *From the Fleet in the Fifties: a history of the Crimean War* (Hurst & Blackett, Limited, 1902), 162.
15. Piers Compton, *Colonel's Lady & Camp-Follower: the story of women in the Crimean War* (Robert Hale & Company, 1970), 135.
16. Douglas Arthur Reid, *Memories of the Crimean War January 1855 to June 1856* (St. Catherine Press, 1911), 13–14.
17. *Wonderful adventures*, 157.
18. *The Times*, no. 22,170 (27 September 1855), 9; W.H.Russell, *The War: from the death of Lord Raglan to the evacuation of the Crimea* (G.Routledge & Co., 1856), 187–8.
19. *The Times*, no. 22,652 (11 April 1857), 8. I am grateful to Ziggi Alexander for this reference.
20. *The Times*, no. 30,200 (21 May 1881), 7; no. 22,537 (28 November 1856), 8.
21. *The Times*, no. 22,533 (24 November 1856), 7.
22. *Punch*, XXXI (1856), 221.
23. *The Times*, no. 22,744 (28 July 1857), 10.
24. Gordon, 50.
25. W.H.Russell, 'To the Reader', in *Wonderful adventures*, p. viii.
26. Reid, 14.
27. Gordon, 50.
28. *The Times*, no. 30,200 (21 May 1881), 7.

Ira Aldridge

1. Herbert Marshall and Mildred Stock, *Ira Aldridge: The Negro Tragedian* (Rockliff, 1958), 335.
2. Marshall and Stock, 54.

3. [John Cole], *A Critique on the Performance of Othello by F.W.Keene Aldridge, the African Roscius* (Scarborough, for John Cole, 1831).
4. Marshall and Stock, 55.
5. *The Times*, no. 12,718 (11 October 1825), [2].
6. *Globe*, no. 7135 (11 October 1825), [3].
7. *Memoir and Theatrical Career of Ira Aldridge, the African Roscius* (J.Orwhyn, 1849), as quoted by Marshall and Stock, 66.
8. Marshall and Stock, 73.
9. [Cole], [3].
10. Marshall and Stock, 129.
11. *Athenæum*, no. 285 (13 April 1833), 236.
12. Marshall and Stock, 119.
13. Unidentified newspaper, after 10 May 1833, as quoted by Marshall and Stock, 138.
14. Marshall and Stock, 138.
15. As quoted by Marshall and Stock, 141.
16. Marshall and Stock, 175.
17. Théophile Gautier, *Voyage en Russie* (Paris, Charpentier, 1867), I. 54–8.
18. A.I.Bazhenov, as quoted by Marshall and Stock, 232.
19. K.Zvantsev, as quoted by Marshall and Stock, 232.

Samuel Coleridge-Taylor

1. 'A Tribute from Sir Hubert Parry', *Musical Times*, LIII (1912), 638.
2. Jeffrey P. Green, 'A Note on Samuel Coleridge-Taylor (1875–1912)', *Black Music Research Newsletter*, VI/1 (Fall 1983), 4. I am grateful to Green for sending me a photocopy of this paper.
3. William Tortolano, *Samuel Coleridge-Taylor: Anglo-Black Composer, 1875–1912* (Metuchen, N.J., Scarecrow Press, Inc., 1977), p. ix.
4. W.C.Berwick Sayers, *Samuel Coleridge-Taylor, Musician: His Life and Letters* (Cassell & Company, Ltd, 1915), 14–16.
5. Sayers, 26–7; Avril Coleridge-Taylor, *The Heritage of Samuel Coleridge-Taylor* (Dennis Dobson, 1979), 24.
6. J[essie]. F. C[oleridge].-T[aylor]., *A Memory Sketch or personal reminiscences of my husband Genius and Musician S.Coleridge-Taylor 1875–1912* (John Crowther Ltd., [1943]), 14; Harold C. Schonberg, in *New York Times*, CXXII/42,190 (29 July 1973), 43.
7. *Letters to Nimrod: Edward Elgar to August Jaeger 1897–1908*, ed. Percy M. Young (Dennis Dobson, 1965), 3–4; Tortolano, 173–4.
8. Herbert Sullivan and Newman Flowers, *Sir Arthur Sullivan: his life, letters & diaries* (Cassell & Company, Ltd., 1927), 244.
9. Percy M. Young, *Elgar O.M.: A Study of a Musician* (Collins, 1955), 120; cf. A.Coleridge-Taylor, *Heritage*, 46.
10. Sayers, 242.

11. J.F.C[oleridge].-T[aylor]., *Memory Sketch*, 39.
12. S.Coleridge-Taylor to Andrew F. Hilyer, 3 January 1904, as quoted by Tortolano, 75; cf. A.Coleridge-Taylor, *Heritage*, 54.
13. S.Coleridge-Taylor to A.F.Hilyer, 14 September 1904, as quoted by Sayers, 154; Percy M. Young, 'Samuel Coleridge-Taylor, 1875–1912', *Musical Times*, CXVI/1590 (August 1975), 704 (inserting 'will' before 'never'); Tortolano, 73 (omitting 'the' before 'prejudice'); A.Coleridge-Taylor, *Heritage*, 52.
14. For the first two visits to the United States, see Ellsworth Janifer, 'Samuel Coleridge-Taylor in Washington', *Phylon*, XXVIII (1967), 185–96.
15. Sayers, 241.
16. A.Coleridge-Taylor, *Heritage*, 96.
17. Sayers, 262.
18. J.F.C[oleridge].-T[aylor]., *Memory Sketch*, 13, 35, 37.
19. *Croydon Guardian and Surrey County Gazette*, no. 2,243 (10 February 1912), 9; no. 2,244 (17 February 1912), 12. Subsequent correspondence in no. 2,245 (24 February 1912), 12; no. 2,246 (2 March 1912), 8 (letter from Dusé Mohamed [Ali]), 12.
20. Ian Duffield, 'The Dilemma of Pan-Africanism for Blacks in Britain, 1760–1950' (paper presented to the International Conference on the History of Blacks in Britain, London, 28–30 September 1981), 6.
21. J.F.C[oleridge].-T[aylor]., *Memory Sketch*, 38.
22. I.Geiss, *The Pan-African Movement*, trans. A.Keep (1974), 183–4, 192.
23. *African Times and Orient Review*, I/1 (July 1912), 16. 'This touches the root of the matter', commented Ali (p. 13).
24. 'A Tribute from Sir Hubert Parry', 638.
25. Reproduced in *African Times and Orient Review*, I/3 (September 1912), 83.

Challenges from Asia

1. Henry Venn, in Joseph Salter, *The Asiatic in England; Sketches of sixteen years' work among orientals* (Seeley, Jackson, & Halliday, 1873), pp. ii–iii; Salter, 20.
2. R.M.Hughes, in Salter, 9, 12; Salter, 25, 236–9.
3. R.C.Majumdar, *History of the Freedom Movement in India* (Calcutta, Firma K. L. Mukhopadhyay, 1962–3), I. 383. For Raja Ramohan Roy, see also Sophia Dobson Collet, *Life and Letters of Raja Rammohun Roy*, [second edition), ed. Hem Chandra Sarkar (Calcutta, A.C.Sarkar, [1913]); Bimanbehari Majumdar, in *Dictionary of National Biography*, ed. S.P.Sen (Calcutta, Institute of Historical Studies, 1972–4), III. 551–4. For Dwarkanath Tagore, see Hiranmoy Banerjee, in *Dictionary of National Biography*, ed. Sen, IV. 302.
4. S.R.Mehrotra, *The Emergence of the Indian National Congress* (Delhi etc., Vikas Publications, 1971), 14–24.

5. Majumdar, *History of the Freedom Movement*, I. 384.
6. R.P.Masani, *Dadabhai Naoroji: The Grand Old Man of India* (George Allen & Unwin Ltd, 1939), 81.
7. Mehrotra, 223ff.
8. As quoted by Masani, 263.
9. Masani, 263–4.
10. Masani, 266.
11. Masani, [286]. See also *Lord Salisbury's 'Blackman'* (Lucknow, Varma & Brothers Press, 1889); *The First Indian Member of the Imperial Parliament* (Madras, Addison & Co., 1892).
12. Masani, 297.
13. Hyndman to Naoroji, 21 August 1884, as quoted by Masani, 292–3.
14. H.M.Hyndman, 'The Bankruptcy of India', *Nineteenth Century*, IV (1878), [585]–608.
15. For Naoroji's relations with Hyndman, see Masani, 197ff. etc., and Chushichi Tsuzuki, *H.M.Hyndman and British Socialism*, ed. Henry Pelling (Oxford University Press, 1961), 23, 48, 76, 93, 127.
16. As quoted by Masani, 431–2.
17. As quoted by Masani, 432.
18. C.F.Andrews and Girija Mukerji, *The rise and growth of the Congress in India* (George Allen & Unwin Ltd, 1938), 159.
19. As quoted by Masani, 20. For Naoroji, see also V.K.R.V.Rao, in *Dictionary of National Biography*, ed. Sen, III. 220–3.
20. Ram Gopal Sanyal, *A General Biography of Bengal Celebrities* (Calcutta, Uma Churn Chuckerbutty,1889), 35–54; Amvika Charan Mazumdar, *Indian National Evolution*, second edition (Madras, G.A.Natesan & Co., 1917), 131; Manicklal Mukherjee, *W.C.Bonnerjee (The first and eighth President of Indian National Congress)* (Calcutta, Deshbandhu Book Depot, [1944]); Robert G. Gregory, *India and East Africa: A History of Race Relations within the British Empire 1890–1939* (Oxford, Clarendon Press, 1971), 135 (I am grateful to Rosina Visram for this reference); D.P.Sinha, in *Dictionary of National Biography*, ed. Sen, I. 131–3. For Monmohon Ghose, see Sanyal, 16–34; *A Short Life of Manomohan Ghose* (Calcutta, Deva Press, 1896).
21. I am grateful to Rosina Visram for telling me about Bhownagree.
22. Sanyal, 113–40; Sir Surendranath Banerjea, *A Nation in Making: Being the Reminiscences of Fifty Years of Public Life* (Oxford University Press, 1925); R.C.Majumdar, in *Dictionary of National Biography*, ed. Sen, I. 125–8.
23. R[omesh].C[hunder].Dutt, *Three Years in Europe, 1868 to 1871, with an account of a second visit to Europe in 1886*, third edition (Calcutta, S.K.Lahiri & Co., 1890); J.N.Gupta, *Life and Work of Romesh Chunder Dutt C.I.E.* (J.M.Dent & Sons, Ltd, 1911); R[abindra].C[handra].Dutt, *Romesh Chunder Dutt* (New Delhi,

Ministry of Information and Broadcasting, 1968); Bhabatosh Datta (II), in *Dictionary of National Biography*, ed. Sen, I. 396–7.

24. Hem Chandra Sarkar, *A Life of Ananda Mohan Bose* (Calcutta, A.C. Sarkar, 1910); Majumdar, *History of the Freedom Movement*, I. 386; Kshitis Roy, in *Dictionary of National Biography*, ed. Sen, I. 209–10.
25. Amalendu Bose, in *Dictionary of National Biography*, ed. Sen, II. 48–9.
26. Kali Charan Ghosh, *The Roll of Honour: Anecdotes of Indian Martyrs* (Calcutta, Vidya Bharati, 1965), 59.
27. M.R.Jayakar, *The Story of My Life*, I (Bombay etc., Asia Publishing House, 1958), 45–6.
28. As quoted by Majumdar, *History of the Freedom Movement*, II. 318.
29. *Indian Sociologist*, I/8 (August 1905), 31–2.
30. Valentine Chirol, *Indian Unrest* (Macmillan & Co., Limited, 1910), 148.
31. As quoted by Ghosh, 60.
32. Majumdar, *History of the Freedom Movement*, II. 321.
33. D.D.Deshpande, *Life Sketch of Mr. P. M. Bapat* (Poona, V.P.Bapat, 1934); D.V.Kale, in *Dictionary of National Biography*, ed. Sen, I. 135–6.
34. Prithvi Singh Azad, in *Dictionary of National Biography*, ed. Sen, II. 142–4.
35. For Shyamaji Krishnavarma, see Jawaharlal Nehru, *An Autobiography: with musings on recent events in India* (John Lane, 1936), 148–50; Indulal Yagnik, in *Dictionary of National Biography*, ed. Sen, IV. 196–9.
36. David Garnett, *The Golden Echo* (Chatto & Windus, 1953), 144, 145, 147, 149.
37. *Daily News*, no. 19,791 (18 August 1909), 7. This version has been slightly emended to correspond more closely to that in a contemporary leaflet reproduced in Ghosh, pl. 5.
38. For Veer Savarkar, see: Dhananjay Keer, *Veer Savarkar*, second edition (Bombay, Popular Prakashan, 1966); Vidya Sagar Anand, *Savarkar: A Study in the evolution of Indian Nationalism* (C. & A.Woolf, 1967); G.V.Ketkar, in *Dictionary of National Biography*, ed. Sen, IV. 92–5. For Madan Lal Dhingra, see K.L.Malhotra, in *Dictionary of National Biography*, ed. Sen, I. 459–60.
39. John S. Hoyland, *Gopal Krishna Gokhale: His Life and Speeches* (Calcutta, Y.M.C.A. Publishing House, 1933); T.V.Parvate, *Gopal Krishna Gokhale: A narrative and interpretative review of his life, career and contemporary events* (Ahmedabad, Navajivan Publishing House, 1959); Stanley A. Wolpert, *Tilak and Gokhale: Revolution and Reform in the Making of Modern India* (Berkeley and Los Angeles, University of California Press, 1962), listing other sources on Gokhale at p. 354; D.B.Mathur, *Gokhale: a political biography: A Study of His Services and Political Ideas* (Bombay, Manaktalas, 1966), listing other sources on Gokhale at pp. 468–9; T.R.Deogirikar, *Gopal Krishna Gokhale*,

second edition (New Delhi, Ministry of Information and Broadcasting, 1969); N.R.Phatak, in *Dictionary of National Biography*, ed. Sen, II. 73–6; B.R.Nanda, *Gokhale: The Indian moderates and the British raj* (Delhi and London, Oxford University Press, 1977).

40. D.V.Tahmankar, *Lokamanya Tilak: Father of Indian Unrest and Maker of Modern India* (John Murray, 1956), 136. For Hardie's visit to India see also Emrys Hughes, *Keir Hardie* (George Allen & Unwin Ltd, 1956), 148–58; Iain McLean, *Keir Hardie* (Allen Lane, 1975), 127–30; Kenneth O. Morgan, *Keir Hardie: radical and socialist* (Weidenfeld & Nicolson, 1975), 190–5.
41. Independent Labour Party, *Report of the Eighteenth Annual Conference . . . 1910*, 83–4. For Pal, see Amitabha Mukherjee, in *Dictionary of National Biography*, ed. Sen, III. 284–7; Amalendu Prasad Mookerjee, *Social and Political Ideas of Bipin Chandra Pal* (Calcutta, Minerva Associates (Publications) Pvt. Ltd., 1974).
42. Tahmankar, 281–3.
43. Tahmankar, 281.
44. Tahmankar, 288.
45. Dhananjay Keer, *Lokamanya Tilak: Father Of The Indian Freedom Struggle*, second edition (Bombay, Popular Prakashan, 1969), 407.
46. Tahmankar, 288, 290. For Tilak, see also: Wolpert, 228, 259; N.G.Jog, *Lokomanya Bal Gangadhar Tilak* (New Delhi, Ministry of Information and Broadcasting, 1970 reprint); Y.B.Chavan, in *Dictionary of National Biography*, ed. Sen, IV. 352–6.

The rise of Pan-Africanism

1. R.W.July, *The Origins of Modern African Thought* (1958), 21–2, 35–47; I.Geiss, *The Pan-African Movement*, trans. A.Keep (1974), 38–40, 98–100; Ian Duffield, 'The Dilemma of Pan-Africanism for Blacks in Britain, 1760–1950' (1981), [1].
2. Cf. Duffield, 'The Dilemma of Pan-Africanism', 2–3.
3. G.Shepperson, 'Notes on Negro American influences on the emergence of African nationalism', *Journal of African History*, I (1960), 301; George Shepperson, 'Pan-Africanism and "Pan-Africanism": Some Historical Notes', *Phylon*, XXIII (1962), 350; *Negro Social and Political Thought 1850–1920: Representative Texts*, ed. Howard Brotz (New York and London, Basic Books, Inc., 1966), 2–3, 37–111; John Hope Franklin, *From Slavery to Freedom: A History of Negro Americans*, third edition (New York, Alfred A. Knopf, 1967), 291; Harold Cruse, *The Crisis of the Negro Intellectual* (W.H.Allen, 1969), 5, 6n., 491n.; Geiss, *Pan-African Movement*, 86–93, 164–6; Cyril E. Griffith, *The African Dream: Martin R. Delany and the Emergence of Pan-African Thought* (University Park and London, Pennsylvania State University Press, 1975), *passim*.
4. *Proceedings of the Royal Geographical Society of London*, IV (1859–60),

218–21 (paper presented jointly by Delany and the Jamaican Robert Campbell, for whom see the following note); *The Times*, no. 23,674 (17 July 1860), 5; *Morning Chronicle*, no. 29,182 (21 July 1860), 6; *Report of the Proceedings of the Fourth Session of the International Statistical Congress* [ed. William Farr and others] (HMSO, 1861), 12, 207; William Wells Brown, *The Black Man: his antecedents, his genius, and his achievements* (Boston, Mass., James Redpath, 1863), 174–5; *Hansard's Parliamentary Debates*, 3rd ser. vol. 171 (1863), cols. 1227–8; *Diary of George Mifflin Dallas* (Philadelphia, J.B.Lippincott Company, 1892), 407–11; John Donald Wade, *Augustus Baldwin Longstreet: A Study of the Development of Culture in the South* (New York, Macmillan, 1924), 325–8; Jessie Fauset, ' "Rank Imposes Obligation" ', *The Crisis*, XXXIII/1 (November 1926), 9–13; Lewis Einstein, 'Lewis Cass', in *The American Secretaries of State and their Diplomacy*, ed. Samuel Flagg Bemis, VI (New York, Alfred A. Knopf, 1928), 309–11; V.Loggins, *The Negro Author* (1931), 182–7; B.Brawley, *Early Negro American Writers* (1935), 216–19; Benjamin Quarles, 'Ministers without Portfolio', *Journal of Negro History*, XXXIX (1954), 36–9; Shepperson, 'Notes on Negro American influences on the emergence of African nationalism', 301; B.Quarles, *Black Abolitionists* (1969), 140–1; Dorothy Sterling, *The Making of an Afro-American: Martin Robison Delany 1812–1885* (Garden City, NY, Doubleday & Company, Inc., 1971), 209–18; Victor Ullman, *Martin R. Delany: The Beginnings of Black Nationalism* (Boston, Mass., Beacon Press, 1971), 235–41; Griffith, 52–7, 86; D.A.Lorimer, *Colour, Class and the Victorians* (1978), 222. Other Afro-American precursors of Pan-Africanism included Paul Cuffe (see p. 234 above), Henry Highland Garnet (see p. 434 above), and Alexander Crummell (see p. 434 above); see Hollis R.Lynch, 'Pan-Negro Nationalism in the New World, before 1862', in *African History*, ed. Jeffrey Butler (Boston University Papers on Africa, II, 1966), 149–79.

5. Geiss, *Pan-African Movement*, 65, 166–9; Duffield, 'The Dilemma of Pan-Africanism', [1]–2; Michael Rose, *Curator of the dead: Thomas Hodgkin (1798–1866)* (Peter Owen, 1981), 116. Born in Jamaica in 1829 of mixed-race and Scots parentage, Robert Campbell was apprenticed as a printer for five years, became a parish teacher in Kingston, and in 1853 went to New York. In 1855 he was appointed science teacher at the Institute of Colored Youth in Philadelphia. See: Robert Campbell, *A Pilgrimage to my motherland; or, Reminiscences of a sojourn among the Egbas and Yorubas of central Africa, in 1859–60* (William John Johnson, 1861); R.J.M.Blackett, 'Return to the motherland: Robert Campbell, a Jamaican in early colonial Lagos', *Journal of the Historical Society of Nigeria*, VIII (1975–7), 133–43; Richard Blackett, 'Martin R.Delany and Robert Campbell: black Americans in search of an African colony', *Journal of Negro History*, LXII (1977), 1–25.

6. Hollis R.Lynch, *Edward Wilmot Blyden: Pan-Negro Patriot 1832–1912* (Oxford University Press, 1967), [248], 252, 250. See also the review of this book by A.Fajana, *Journal of the Historical Society of Nigeria*, V (1969–71), 447–8.
7. Hollis R. Lynch, 'The attitude of Edward W.Blyden to European imperialism in Africa', *Journal of the Historical Society of Nigeria*, III (1964–7), 249–59; E.A.Ayendele, *The Missionary Impact on Modern Nigeria 1842–1914: A Political and Social Analysis* (Longmans, 1966), 253–4; Geiss, *Pan-African Movement*, 108–9, 150.
8. Lynch, *Edward Wilmot Blyden*, 250–1. For Blyden, see further: July, *Origins of Modern African Thought*, 208–33; Shepperson, 'Notes on Negro American influences', [299]–300; C.Fyfe, *A History of Sierra Leone* (1962), especially pp. 321, 385–6, 389–90, 467–9, 618–19; Shepperson, 'Pan-Africanism and "Pan-Africanism" ', 350; Robert W.July, 'Nineteenth-Century Negritude: Edward W.Blyden', *Journal of African History*, V (1964) [73]–86; Hollis R.Lynch, 'Edward W.Blyden: pioneer West African nationalist', *Journal of African History*, VI (1965), [373]–388; Edith Holden, *Blyden of Liberia: An Account of the Life and Labours of Edward Wilmot Blyden, LL.D. As Recorded in Letters and in Print* (New York etc., Vantage Press, 1967); Kola Adelaja, 'Sources in African Political Thought – 1: Blyden and the impact of religion on the emergence of African political thought', *Présence Africaine,*, 70 (1969), 7–26; J.D.Hargreaves, 'Blyden of Liberia', *History Today*, XIX (1969), 568–73; Edwin S.Redkey, *Black Exodus: Black Nationalist and Back-to-Africa Movements, 1890–1910* (New Haven and London, Yale University Press, 1969), [47]–72, 229–30; *Origins of West African Nationalism*, ed. Henry S.Wilson (Macmillan, 1969), [229]–262 (extracts from Blyden's writings); *Black Spokesman: Selected Published Writings of Edward Wilmot Blyden*, ed. Hollis R.Lynch (Frank Cass & Co. Ltd., 1971); J.Ayondele Langley, *Pan-Africanism and Nationalism in West Africa 1900–1945* (Oxford, Clarendon Press, 1973), 112–14; *Selected Works of Dr. Edward Wilmot Blyden*, ed. Willie A.Givens (Robertsport, Liberia, Tubman Center of African Culture, 1976); Paul Edwards, 'Edward W.Blyden: sense and sentimentality', in *The Commonwealth Writer Overseas: Themes of Exile and Expatriation*, ed. Alastair Niven (Brussels, Librairie Marcel Didier, 1976), 139–50; H.W.Debrunner, *Presence and Prestige* (1979), 371–2. I have not seen Thomas W.Livingstone, *Education and Race: a biography of Edward Wilmot Blyden* (San Francisco, Glendessary Press, 1975), and *Selected Letters of Edward Wilmot Blyden*, ed. Hollis R.Lynch (New York, KTO Press, 1978).
9. Robert July, 'Africanus Horton and the Idea of Independence in West Africa', *Sierra Leone Studies* n.s. no. 18 (January 1966), 2–3; July, *Origins of Modern African Thought*, 114–15.
10. James Africanus B.Horton, *West African countries and peoples, British*

and native: with the requirements necessary for establishing that self-government recommended by the Committee of the House of Commons, 1865; and a vindication of the African race (W.J.Johnson, 1868), [1]–2.

11. Horton (1868), 73.
12. George Shepperson, Introduction to J.A.Horton, *West African Countries and Peoples* (Edinburgh, University Press, 1969), p. xviii.
13. David Kimble, *A Political History of Ghana: The Rise of Gold Coast Nationalism 1850–1928* (Oxford, Clarendon Press, 1963), 537–8; July, 'Africanus Horton and the Idea of Independence in West Africa', 3–16; July, *Origins of Modern African Thought*, 114–29; Shepperson, Introduction to Horton (1969), pp. xviii-xix, xxii; Christopher Fyfe, *Africanus Horton 1835–1883; West African Scientist and Patriot* (New York, Oxford University Press, 1972), *passim*; Ian Duffield, 'Pan-Africanism, rational and irrational', *Journal of African History*, XVIII (1977), 601, 614–15.
14. Kimble, 230–2, 243–5, 550; James S.Coleman, *Nigeria: Background to Nationalism* (Berkeley and Los Angeles, University of California Press, 1958), 186; Langley, 110–11.
15. Duffield, 'Pan-Africanism, rational and irrational', 600.
16. George Shepperson, 'Abolitionism and African political thought', *Transition* (Kampala), II/12 (January–February 1964), 23. For Horton, see further: Fyfe, *History of Sierra Leone*, 294–5, 347, 349, 437, 472; George Shepperson, 'An Early African Graduate', *University of Edinburgh Gazette*, XXXII (1962), 23–6 (I am grateful to the British Library for obtaining for me a photocopy of this paper); L.C.Gwam, 'The Social and Political Ideas of Dr James Africanus Beale Horton, M.D., M.R.C.S., F.R.A.S., F.G.S., 1835–1883', *Ibadan*, no. 19 (June 1964), 10–18; *Africanus Horton: The Dawn of Nationalism in Modern Africa*, ed. Davidson Nicol (Longmans, 1969) (extracts from Horton's writings); *Origins of West African Nationalism*, ed. Wilson, [155]–225 (extracts from Horton's writings); E.A.Ayandele, Introduction to Africanus B.Horton, *Letters on the political condition of the Gold Coast*, second edition (Africana Modern Library, no. 12, Frank Cass & Co. Ltd, 1970); Geiss, *Pan-African Movement*, 67–8, 115, 151; Debrunner, 253–4; C. Magbaily Fyfe and Arthur Abraham, in *The Encyclopaedia Africana Dictionary of African Biography*, II (1979), 76–9.
17. As quoted by R.V.Allen, 'Celestine Edwards: his life, work, and death', *Lux*, V/118 (3 November 1894), 213; V/119 (10 November 1894), 229.
18. As quoted by F.Kingerley, 'Reminiscences of Mr S.J.Celestine Edwards', *Fraternity*, I/15 (15 September 1894), 3.
19. Revd W.Horan, 'Reminiscences of S.J.Celestine Edwards', *Lux*, V/124 (15 December 1894), 313.
20. Ida B.Wells, *Crusade for Justice*, ed. Alfreda M. Duster (Chicago and London, University of Chicago Press, 1970), 124.

21. Duffield, 'The Dilemma of Pan-Africanism', 4.
22. [S.J.Celestine Edwards], 'The Negro Race', *Lux*, I/19 (10 December 1892), 290–1.
23. [S.J.Celestine Edwards], 'The Negro Race and British Protectorate', *Lux*, II/29 (18 February 1893), 34–5.
24. *Lux*, III/68 (18 November 1893), 250.
25. *Lux*, V/108 (25 August 1894), 56.
26. R.V.Allen, 'The Future of Christian Evidences', *Lux*, V/109 (1 September 1894), [67].
27. James Marchant, 'Our Departed Friend: a few words at random', *Lux*, V/109 (1 September 1894), 75.
28. H. Silvester [*sic*] Williams, 'Trinidad, B.W.I.', in *British America* (The British Empire Ser. III, Kegan Paul, Trench, Trubner & Co. Ltd, 1900), 474.
29. *Anti-Slavery Reporter*, 4th ser. XVIII/3 (July–August 1898), 182.
30. *Aborigines' Friend*, November 1897, p. 298, in *Transactions of the Aborigines' Protection Society*, [V] (1896–1900).
31. *New Age*, VII/173 (20 January 1898), 249.
32. *Aborigines' Friend*, March 1898, pp. 348–9, in *Transactions of the Aborigines' Protection Society*, [V] (1896–1900).
33. *The Memorial of the African Association on the distress in the West Indies* (1898).
34. Geiss, *Pan-African Movement*, 178.
35. *Anti-Slavery Reporter*, 4th ser. XIX/2 (March–May 1899), 112.
36. As quoted by Owen Charles Mathurin, *Henry Sylvester Williams and the Origins of the Pan-African Movement, 1869–1911* (Contributions in Afro-American and African Studies, no. 21, Westport, Conn. and London, Greenwood Press, 1976), 49–50.
37. Mathurin, 52, says the oldest document in which the term 'Pan-African' is found is a letter from Williams to J.M.Bourne, dated 11 November 1899. DuBois had asserted in 1897 that if black people were to be a factor in the world's history, it would be through 'a Pan-Negro movement' (W.E.B.DuBois, 'The Conservation of Races', *American Negro Academy Occasional Papers*, no. 2 (Washington, DC, 1897), 10, as quoted by Robert Ernst, 'Negro concepts of Americanism', *Journal of Negro History*, XXXIX (1954), 213).
38. *The Times*, no. 36,188 (7 July 1900), 12.
39. Mathurin, 55.
40. *Report of the Pan-African Conference* (Pan-African Association, 1900), 3, as quoted by Geiss, *Pan-African Movement*, 184–5, and Mathurin, 56.
41. As quoted by Mathurin, 62.
42. 'Who Was Who at the 1900 Pan-African Conference', Mathurin, App., [165]–169.

43. Jeffrey P.Green tells me that Mandell Creighton was on the fringes of the Fabian Society and had been a friend of Beatrice Potter since four years before her marriage to Sidney Webb.

44. *The Times*, no. 36,202 (24 July 1900), 7; no. 36,203 (25 July 1900), 15; no. 36,204 (26 July 1900), 11; *Westminster Gazette*, XVI/2,298 (24 July 1900), 4; XVI/2,299 (25 July 1900), 5; [Louise Creighton], *Life and Letters of Mandell Creighton* (Longmans, Green, & Co., 1904), II. 444; Geiss, *Pan-African Movement*, 185–9; Mathurin, 61–8.

45. Joseph Chamberlain to Charles Dilke, 15 April 1896, as quoted by H.A.Will, *Constitutional Change in the British West Indies 1880–1903* (Oxford, Clarendon Press, 1970), 232. I owe this reference to Mathurin, 71. The 'Address to the Nations of the World' is conveniently reprinted in *Ideologies of Liberation in Black Africa 1856–1970: Documents on modern African political thought from colonial times to the present*, ed. J. Ayo Langley (Rex Collings, 1979), 738–9.

46. [W. T. Stead], 'The Revolt against the Paleface', *Review of Reviews* XXII (1900), 131; Geiss, *Pan-African Movement*, 189–94; J.R.Hooker, *Henry Sylvester Williams: Imperial Pan-Africanist* (Rex Collings, 1975), 35–7; Mathurin, 68–73, 80–1.

47. *Westminster Gazette*, XVI/2,300 (26 July 1900), 4.

48. [Stead], 'The Revolt against the Paleface', 131. Other contemporary accounts of the 1900 conference will be found in: *South Africa*, XLVII/605 (28 July 1900), 197; *Bulletin du Comité de l'Afrique Française*, X/8 (août 1900), 283–4; *Anti-Slavery Reporter*, XX/4 (August–October 1900), 139–41.

49. Mathurin, 79.

50. *The Pan-African*, I/1 (October 1901), pp. [i], [1].

51. *The Pan-African*, I/1 (October 1901), 8.

52. Mathurin, 109.

53. Hooker, 28.

54. Mathurin, 110.

55. While practising in South Africa Williams was interviewed by W.T.Stead; see 'Our Coloured Fellow-Citizens: Mr. S.Williams', *Review of Reviews*, XXXI (1905), 250–1.

56. Mathurin, 132.

57. Hooker, 83–119; Mathurin, 137–59. For Henry Sylvester Williams, see also Clarence G. Contee, *Henry Sylvester Williams and origins of organizational Pan-Africanism: 1897–1902* (Washington, DC, Howard University Department of History, 1973); Mildred C. Fierce, 'Henry Sylvester Williams and the Pan-African Conference of 1900', *Genève-Afrique*, XIV (1975), 106–14.

58. Ian Duffield, 'Dusé Mohamed Ali: his purpose and his public', in *The Commonwealth Writer Overseas*, ed. Niven, 151–3; cf. Duffield, 'The dilemma of Pan-Africanism', 7.

59. Duffield, 'Dusé Mohamed Ali: his purpose and his public', 163–4, 173.

60. For Ali's business relations with Taylor, see Ian Duffield, 'The Business Activities of Dusé Mohamed Ali: an example of the economic dimension of Pan-Africanism, 1912–45', *Journal of the Historical Society of Nigeria*, IV (1967–9), 571–3.
61. Geiss, *Pan-African Movement*, 215. There are reports of the Universal Races Congress in *The Crisis*, II/5 (September 1911), [200]–209, and *African Times and Orient Review*, I/1 (July 1912), 27–30; see also Elliott M. Rudwick, 'W.E.B.DuBois and the Universal Races Congress of 1911', *Phylon Quarterly*, XX (1959), 372–8; Michael D. Biddiss, 'The Universal Races Congress of 1911', *Race*, XIII (1971–2), [37]–46; Langley, *Pan-Africanism and Nationalism in West Africa*, 31–2.
62. Ian Duffield, 'John Eldred Taylor and West African opposition to indirect rule in Nigeria', *African Affairs*, LXX (1971), 255.
63. *African Times and Orient Review*, I/1 (July 1912), pp. [iii], 8, 2.
64. *African Times & Orient Review*, n.s. I/20 (4 August 1914), 450.
65. Duffield, 'Dusé Mohamed Ali: his purpose and his public', 165.
66. Imanuel Geiss, 'Notes on the development of Pan-Africanism', *Journal of the Historical Society of Nigeria*, III (1964–7), 731; cf. Geiss, *Pan-African Movement*, 224–5.
67. Duffield, 'The dilemma of Pan-Africanism', 8. For Marcus Garvey, see Edmund David Cronon, *Black Moses: The story of Marcus Garvey and the Universal Negro Improvement Association* (Madison, University of Wisconsin Press, 1955); A[my]. Jacques Garvey, *Garvey and Garveyism* (Kingston, Jamaica, A. Jacques Garvey, 1963); Richard Hart, 'The Life and Resurrection of Marcus Garvey', *Race*, IX (1967–8), [217]–237, with some corrections and additions on pp. 527–8; W.F.Elkins, 'The influence of Marcus Garvey on Africa: a British report of 1922', *Science & Society*, XXXII (1968), 321–3; Jabez Ayodele Langley, 'Garveyism and African Nationalism', *Race*, XI (1969–70), [157]–172; Robert G. Weisbord, 'Marcus Garvey, Pan-Negroist: The View from Whitehall', *Race*, XI (1969–70), [417]–429; Theodore G. Vincent, *Black power and the Garvey movement* (Berkeley, Calif., Ramparts Press, [1971]); Langley, *Pan-Africanism and Nationalism in West Africa*, 68–71, 92–8; Geiss, *Pan-African Movement*, [263]–282; Tony Martin, *Race First: The Ideological and Organizational Struggles of Marcus Garvey and the Universal Negro Improvement Association* (Contributions in Afro-American and African Studies, no. 19, Westport, Conn. and London, Greenwood Press, 1976); for additional sources, see Daniel T. Williams, *The perilous road of Marcus M. Garvey: a bibliography* (1969), in *Eight Negro Bibliographies*, comp. D.T.Williams (New York, Kraus Reprint Co., 1970), no. 8. For Kobina Sekyi, see Kimble, 545–6, 546 n. 1, 546 n. 4, 547; Samuel Rohdie, 'The Gold Coast Aborigines abroad', *Journal of African History*, VI (1965), [389]–411; J. Ayo Langley, 'Modernization and its malcontents: Kobina Sekyi of Ghana and the

re-statement of African political theory (1892–1956)', *Research Review* (University of Ghana Institute of Africa Studies), VI/3 (1970), 1–61; Langley, *Pan-Africanism and Nationalism in West Africa*, 98–103; L.H. Ofusu-Appiah, in *The Encyclopaedia Africana Dictionary of African Biography*, I (New York, Reference Publications Inc., 1977), 315–17; *Ideologies of Liberation in Black Africa*, ed. Langley, 242–54, 440–6 (extracts from Kobina Sekyi's writings).

68. Barry A. Kosmin, 'J. R. Archer (1863–1932): a Pan-Africanist in the Battersea labour movement', *New Community*, VII (1978–9), 430.
69. *South Western Star*, no. 2,849 (22 July 1932), 5.
70. *South Western Star*, no. 1,873 (7 November 1913), 5.
71. *Daily Mail*, no. 5,486 (5 November 1913), 5.
72. *Daily Chronicle*, no. 16,137 (5 November 1913), 7.
73. *South Western Star*, no. 1,873 (7 November 1913), 5.
74. *Wandsworth Boro' News*, no. 1433 (14 November 1913), 11.
75. *Evening Standard*, no. 27,874 (11 November 1913), 9.
76. As quoted, *Wandsworth Boro' News*, no. 1433 (14 November 1913), 6.
77. *The Crisis*, VII/3 (January 1914), 120, 121; VII/5 (March 1914), 224, 225–6.
78. I owe this information to Jeffrey P. Green.
79. Metropolitan Borough of Battersea, *Annual Report of the Council for the Year ended 31st March, 1907*, 2–3, and the reports for 1910 etc.
80. *South Western Star*, no. 2,849 (22 July 1932), 5.
81. 'African Progress Union', *African Telegraph*, I/8 (December 1918), 89–90.
82. Langley, *Pan-Africanism and Nationalism in West Africa*, 245.
83. I am grateful to Jeffrey P. Green for this information about Dr John Alcindor. A fuller account will appear as Green's contribution to *Pan-African Biography and African History*, ed. Robert A. Hill, to be published in Los Angeles by the UCLA Africa Studies Center.
84. Jeffrey P. Green, *Edmund Thornton Jenkins: The Life and Times of an American Black Composer, 1894–1926* (Contributions to the Study of Music and Dance, no. 2, Westport, Conn. and London, Greenwood Press, 1982), 64–6.
85. Langley, *Pan-Africanism and Nationalism in West Africa*, 75.
86. *West Africa*, II/101 (4 January 1919), 842. See also, for the African Progress Union's inaugural meeting, *African Telegraph*, I/9 (January–February 1919), 111–12; I/11 (April 1919), 162–4, 186–8.

Black workers and soldiers

1. Neil Evans, 'The South Wales race riots of 1919', *Llafur: The Journal of the Society for the Study of Welsh Labour History*, III/1 (Spring 1980), 5.
2. *Cardiff Times and South Wales Weekly News*, 11 October 1902, p. 4; Evans, 6.

3. *South Wales Daily News*, no. 13,787 (2 September 1916), 4; *Western Mail*, no. 15,566 (14 April 1919), 3; Evans, 6.
4. Committee on Distressed Colonial and Indian Subjects, *Minutes of Evidence and Appendices*, Cd 5134 (1910), especially pp. 7, 8, 32, 33, 37, 63.
5. F.Shyllon, 'The Black Presence and Experience in Britain' (paper presented to the International Conference on the History of Blacks in Britain, London, 28–30 September 1981), 8.
6. C.L.Joseph, 'The British West Indies Regiment 1914–1918', *Journal of Caribbean History*, II (May 1971), 113.
7. For Indian troops on the Western front, see *The Empire at war*, ed. Sir Charles Lucas (Oxford University Press, 1921–6), V. [202]–240, and Stanley Wolpert, *A new history of India* (New York, Oxford University Press, 1977), 289.
8. As quoted, *African Times and Orient Review*, V/4 (mid-October 1917), [75].
9. Sir Harry H. Johnston, *The Black Man's Part in the War* (Simpkin, Marshall, Hamilton, Kent, & Co. Ltd, 1917), 46, 102–[108].
10. *Western Mail*, no. 15,566 (14 April 1919), 3.
11. *The Empire at war*, ed. Lucas, II. 335.
12. Ba-Ture, 'The Apes at sea', *Blackwood's Magazine*, CCIII (1918), 539n.
13. *African Times and Orient Review*, VI/3 (mid-September 1918), 32–3; see also 'African Heroes', *African Telegraph*, I/8 (December 1918), 98.
14. *The Empire at war*, ed. Lucas, II. 335.
15. 'The Belmont Hospital Affair', *African Telegraph*, I/8 (December 1918), 94–5.
16. West Indian Contingent Committee Minute Book, 1 November 1918, as cited by W.F.Elkins, 'Hercules and the Society of Peoples of African Origin', *Caribbean Studies*, I/4 (January 1972), 49. I am grateful to Elkins for calling his paper to my attention and kindly lending me a copy of the journal in which it appeared.

10. Under attack

Racism as riot: 1919

1. William P. Samuels to Colonial Office, 30 December 1918, PRO CO 111/621.
2. *African Telegraph*, I/11 (April 1919), 184.
3. As quoted, *African Telegraph*, I/11 (April 1919), 184.
4. Sydney Collins, *Coloured minorities in Britain: Studies in British Race Relations based on African, West Indian and Asiatic Immigrants* (Lutterworth Press, 1957), 36; David Byrne, 'The 1930 "Arab riot"

in South Shields: a race riot that never was', *Race & Class*, XVIII (1976–7), 262.

5. William Scott, Chief Constable of South Shields, to Director of Intelligence, Scotland Yard [Sir Basil Thomson], 17 November 1919, copy in PRO CO 318/352; Byrne, 263–4.
6. *Liverpool Courier*, no. 23,186 (11 June 1919), 5; *Liverpool Echo*, no. 12,319 (11 June 1919), 6; *Liverpool Post & Mercury*, no. 19,976 (12 June 1919), 3; *Manchester Guardian*, no. 22,726 (12 June 1919), 5; Roy May and Robin Cohen, 'The Interaction between Race and Colonialism: A Case Study of the Liverpool Race Riots of 1919', *Race & Class*, XVI (1974–5), 118.
7. John Ritchie to Colonial Office, 13 May 1919, PRO CO 323/819/431–2.
8. Minute signed E.R.D. [i.e. E.R.Darnley, acting principal clerk], 29 May 1919, PRO CO 323/819/429.
9. May and Cohen, 113.
10. *Liverpool Post & Mercury*, no. 19,988 (26 June 1919), 3.
11. *Liverpool Post & Mercury*, no. 19,972 (7 June 1919), 3; no. 19,975 (11 June 1919), 3; no. 19,982 (19 June 1919), 3; *Manchester Guardian*, no. 22,722 (7 June 1919), 11; *Liverpool Echo*, no. 12,318 (10 June 1919),4; *Liverpool Courier*, no. 23,186 (11 June 1919), 5; *Liverpool Weekly Post*, no. 2,142 (14 June 1919), 5; no. 2,143 (21 June 1919), 5; Inspector Hugh Burgess, 'Racial Riots', 18 June 1919, copy in PRO CO 318/352; *African Telegraph*, I/12 (May–June 1919), 209; May and Cohen, 114.
12. Burgess, 'Racial Riots'.
13. *The Times*, no. 42,122 (10 June 1919), 9 (cf. *Manchester Guardian*, no. 22,724 (10 June 1919), 8: 'Whenever a black man shows himself after nightfall he is chased and beaten'); *Liverpool Courier*, no. 23,186 (11 June 1919), 5; *Liverpool Echo*, no. 12, 319 (11 June 1919), 5; *Liverpool Post & Mercury*, no. 19,980 (17 June 1919), 3.
14. *Liverpool Echo*, no. 12,318 (10 June 1919), 4; no. 12,319 (11 June 1919), 6; *Liverpool Courier*, no. 23,186 (11 June 1919), 6; *Manchester Guardian*, no. 22,725 (11 June 1919), 7; *Liverpool Post & Mercury*, no. 19,976 (12 June 1919), 3; no. 19,977 (13 June 1919), 3; no. 19,980 (17 June 1919), 3.
15. *Liverpool Courier*, no. 23,186 (11 June 1919), 4.
16. *Manchester Guardian*, no. 22,726 (12 June 1919), 5.
17. *Liverpool Weekly Post*, no. 2,142 (14 June 1919), 5. There is a brief account of the Liverpool riots of 1919 in Ernest Marke's autobiography *Old Man Trouble* (Weidenfeld & Nicolson, 1975), 25–32.
18. Neil Evans, 'The South Wales race riots of 1919', *Llafur: The Journal of the Society for the Study of Welsh Labour History*, III/1 (Spring 1980), 5.
19. *South Wales Argus*, no. 8445 (7 June 1919), [4]; no. 8446 (10 June

1919), 3; *Monmouthshire Evening Post*, XI/3253 (7 June 1919), 10; XI/3254 (10 June 1919), 7; *South Wales News*, no. 14,646 (9 June 1919), 5; no. 14,647 (10 June 1919), [6]; no. 14,667 (3 July 1919), 9; David Williams, Chief Constable of Cardiff, to Director of Intelligence, Scotland Yard [Sir Basil Thomson], 9 October 1919, copy in PRO CO 318/352; Evans, 13.

20. *South Wales News*, no. 14,649 (12 June 1919), 5; no. 14,651 (14 June 1919), 5; no. 14,684 (23 July 1919), 6; *Western Mail*, no. 15,616 (12 June 1919), 5; Evans, 14–15.

21. *Western Mail*, no. 15,616 (12 June 1919), 5; no. 15,617 (13 June 1919), 5–6; no. 15,640 (10 July 1919), 7; *South Wales News*, no. 14,650 (13 June 1919), 5; no. 14,673 (10 July 1919), 7; Williams to Director of Intelligence, 9 October 1919; Evans, 14–15.

22. *South Wales News*, no. 14,650 (13 June 1919), 5; no. 14,651 (14 June 1919), 5; no. 14,654 (18 June 1919), 6; *Western Mail*, no. 15,617 (13 June 1919), 5; *Liverpool Post & Mercury*, no. 19,978 (14 June 1919), 7; *The Times*, no. 42,146 (14 June 1919), 9; Williams to Director of Intelligence, 9 October 1919; Evans, 16.

23. Richard Pankhurst, 'An early Somali autobiography', *Africa* (Rome), XXXII (1977), 373–4. I am grateful to Dr Pankhurst for telling me about Ismaa'il's autobiography and providing me with this reference.

24. *Western Mail*, no. 15,616 (12 June 1919), 5; no. 15,617 (13 June 1919), 5–6; *Manchester Guardian*, no. 22,727 (13 June 1919), 7; no. 22,728 (14 June 1919), 7; *South Wales News*, no. 14,650 (13 June 1919), 5; no. 14,651 (14 June 1919), 5; no. 14,654 (18 June 1919), 6; no. 14,674 (11 July 1919), 2; Williams to Director of Intelligence, 9 October 1919; Evans, 16.

25. *Western Mail*, no. 15,618 (14 June 1919), 8.

26. *South Wales News*, no. 14,651 (14 June 1919), 5; Evans, 17.

27. Evans, 17.

28. *South Wales News*, no. 14,651 (14 June 1919), 5; no. 14,653 (17 June 1919), 5.

29. Evans, 20.

30. *South Wales News*, no. 14,651 (14 June 1919), 5; no. 14,653 (17 June 1919), 5; *Western Mail*, no. 15,648 (19 July 1919), 7 (with picture of Fennell); Evans, 20.

31. *The Times*, no. 42,204 (13 September 1919), 7.

32. Williams to Director of Intelligence, 9 October 1919.

33. *John Bull*, XXVI/687 (2 August 1919), 8.

34. W.F.Elkins, 'Hercules and the Society of Peoples of African Origin', *Caribbean Studies*, I/4 (January 1972), 52.

35. *South Wales News*, no. 14,684 (23 July 1919), 3; no. 14,688 (28 July 1919), 7; *Western Mail*, no. 15,651 (23 July 1919), 3; no. 15,655 (28 July 1919), 10; Evans, 20–1.

36. *The Times*, no. 42,077 (17 April, 1919), 7.

37. William Samuel to Colonial Secretary, [29 May 1919], PRO CO 318/352.
38. *The Times*, no. 42,133 (30 May 1919), 9; no. 42,140 (1 July 1919), 4.
39. *Western Mail*, no. 15,619 (16 June 1919), 6.
40. *The Times*, no. 42,128 (17 June 1919), 9; *Manchester Guardian*, no. 22,781 (18 June 1919), 6.
41. *Manchester Guardian*, no. 22,780 (17 June 1919), 12.
42. *Who Was Who 1916–1928*, fourth edition (1967), 1130.
43. *The Times*, no. 42,126 (14 June 1919), 8.
44. *The Times*, no. 42,130 (19 June 1919), 8.
45. Allen Hutt, *The Post-War History of the British Working Class* (Victor Gollancz, 1937), [9].
46. J.A.Langley, *Pan-Africanism and Nationalism in West Africa 1900–1945* (1973), 71.
47. Elkins, 'Hercules and the Society of Peoples of African Origin', 53.
48. [Lord Milner], 'Repatriation of Coloured Men' [distributed 24 June 1919], PRO CO 323/814/282–3.
49. Tony Martin, 'Revolutionary Upheaval in Trinidad, 1919: Views from British and American sources', *Journal of Negro History*, LVIII (1973), 318, 321, 322. See also W.F.Elkins, 'Black power in the British West Indies: the Trinidad longshoremen's strike of 1919', *Science & Society*, XXXIII (1969), 71–5; and Ron Ramdin, *From Chattel Slave to Wage Earner: A history of trade unionism in Trinidad and Tobago* (Martin Brian & O'Keeffe, 1982), 54–63.
50. *Riot in Belize (July 1919)* (confidential Colonial Office report, copy in PRO CO 884/13), App. B, p. 28; Robert G.Weisbord, 'Marcus Garvey, Pan-Negroist: The View from Whitehall', *Race*, XI (1969–70), 420; W.F.Elkins, 'A source of black nationalism in the Caribbean: the revolt of the British West Indies Regiment at Taranto, Italy', *Science & Society*, XXXIV (1970), 103.
51. R.J[ohnstone]., 'Memorandum of Certain Occurrences in the Period between 5th July and 14th August 1919', PRO CO 137/733.
52. Elkins, 'Hercules and the Society of Peoples of African Origin', 53.
53. Governor of Leeward Islands to Colonial Secretary, 18 October 1919, PRO CO 318/349.
54. W.F.Elkins, ' "Unrest among the Negroes": A British document of 1919', *Science & Society*, XXXII (1968), 66–79; Weisbord, [419]–429.
55. PRO CO 583/97/269–72.
56. For a full report of the case, see *African Telegraph*, I/14 (December 1919), 283–96.
57. B[asil].H.Thomson, Director of Intelligence, Scotland House, to Major Thornton, 4 December 1919, PRO CO 318/352.
58. 'Inauguration dinner of the Society of African Peoples', *African Telegraph*, I/13 (July–August 1919), 269–71.
59. Police report on F.E.M.Hercules, 4 August 1919, copy in PRO CO 318/351.

60. Thomson to Thornton, 4 December 1919.
61. *Parliamentary Debates*, 5th ser. vol. 123 (1919), col. 37.
62. 'Extracts from Letter No. 76/S.9, dated 12th March, 1921, from Rear Admiral Commanding, 8th Light Cruiser Squadron', App. A, 'Prospects of Unrest or Otherwise in the British West Indies', PRO CO 318/366.
63. F.E.M.Hercules, 'The African and Nationalism', *African Telegraph*, I/8 (December 1918), 84.
64. 'The African Progress Union', *African Telegraph*, I/9 (January–February 1919), 112.
65. Johnstone, 'Memorandum of Certain Occurrences'; Telegram from Acting Governor of Jamaica to Colonial Secretary, received 25 July 1919, PRO CO 318/349.
66. *Liverpool Post & Mercury*, no. 19,980 (17 June 1919), 3.
67. F.E.M.Hercules to Colonial Secretary, 12 June 1919, PRO CO 323/814/123–4.
68. Colonial Secretary to F.E.M.Hercules, draft, 11 July 1919, PRO CO 323/814/127–8.
69. 'Discrimination and Disintegration', *African Telegraph*, I/13 (July–August 1919), 253.
70. John H. Harris, 'Britain's Negro Problem', *Atlantic Review*, CXXXI (1923), 544.

Claude McKay and the 'Horror on the Rhine'

1. Robert C. Reinders, 'Racialism on the Left: E.D.Morel and the "Black Horror on the Rhine" ', *International Review of Social History*, XIII (1968), 2. I am grateful to Brian Pearce for telling me about this paper.
2. H.M.Swanwick, *Builders of Peace: being ten years' history of the Union of Democratic Control* (Swarthmore Press Ltd, 1924), 186, 187. Morel sat for Dundee from 1922 until his death in 1924.
3. Raymond Postgate, *The Life of George Lansbury* (Longmans, Green & Co., 1951), 209.
4. *Daily Herald*, no. 1,313 (10 April 1920), [1], 4.
5. E.D.Morel, *The Horror on the Rhine*, third edition (Union of Democratic Control, 1920), 10; italics in the original.
6. J.W.Kneeshaw, 'The Outlook', *Foreign Affairs*, II/4 (October 1920), 66.
7. *Commonweal*, I/52 (17 April 1920), [1].
8. *Nation*, XXVII/2 (10 April 1920), 37; XXVII/4 (24 April 1920), 104; XXVII/7 (15 May 1920), 197.
9. William Harbutt Dawson, 'Germany and Spa', *Contemporary Review*, CXVIII (1920), 8.
10. Reinders, 27.

11. Wayne Cooper and Robert C. Reinders, 'A Black Briton Comes "Home": Claude McKay in England, 1920', *Race*, IX (1967–8), 68.
12. 'A black man replies', *Workers' Dreadnought*, VII/5 (24 April 1920), 2; cf. Cooper and Reinders, 72. The full text of McKay's letter to Lansbury is reprinted in *The Passion of Claude McKay: Selected Poetry and Prose, 1912–1948*, ed. Wayne F. Cooper (New York, Schocken Books, 1973), 55–7.
13. Claude McKay, *A Long Way from Home* (New York, Arno Press & *New York Times*, 1969 reprint), 75.
14. *Spectator*, no. 4,817 (23 October 1920), 539.
15. McKay, *A Long Way from Home*, 60, 61, 67.
16. Claude McKay, *The Negroes in America*, trans. from the Russian by Robert J. Winter, ed. Alan L. McLeod (Port Washington, NY, and London, Kennikat Press Corp., 1979), 9.
17. McKay, *A Long Way from Home*, 68.
18. McKay, *A Long Way from Home*, 76.
19. *The Passion of Claude McKay*, ed. Cooper, 101.
20. McKay, *A Long Way from Home*, 77.
21. *The Passion of Claude McKay*, ed. Cooper, 89.
22. 'Discontent on the lower deck', *Workers' Dreadnought*, VII/30 (16 October 1920), [1].
23. McKay, *A Long Way from Home*, 82–3.
24. 'Official Labour at Portsmouth', *Workers' Dreadnought*, VII/26 (18 September 1920), [1].
25. Claude McKay, *Home to Harlem* (New York and London, Harper & Brothers, 1928), 7; Claude McKay, *Banjo: A Story without a Plot* (New York and London, Harper & Brothers, 1929), 101.

Defence and counter-attack

1. For the 1919 Pan-African Congress, see: 'The Pan-African Congress', *African Telegraph*, I/10 (March 1919), 142–3; 'Le Congrès Panafricain', *L'Afrique Française*, mars–avril 1919, Supplément (*Renseignements coloniaux*, no. 3 et 4), 53–9; 'The Pan-African Congress', *The Crisis*, XVII/6 (April 1919), 271–4; W.E. Burghardt DuBois, *The World and Africa: An inquiry into the part which Africa has played in world history* (New York, Viking Press, 1947), 10–12, reprinted in *Colonial and Coloured Unity: A Programme of Action: History of the Pan-African Congress*, ed. George Padmore (Manchester, Pan-African Federation, [1947]), 15–17; George Padmore, *Pan-Africanism or Communism? The coming struggle for Africa* (Dennis Dobson, 1956), 119–29; Colin Legum, *Pan-Africanism: a short political guide*, revised edition (New York etc., Frederick A. Praeger, 1965), 28–9, 151–2 (confusingly, Legum calls the 1900 Pan-African Conference the first Congress and the 1919 Congress the second Congress, renumbering subsequent congresses accordingly); Clarence G. Contee, 'Du Bois, the NAACP, and the Pan-African

Congress of 1919', *Journal of Negro History*, LVII (1972), 13–28; J.A.Langley, *Pan-Africanism and Nationalism in West Africa 1900–1945* (1973), 63–8; I.Geiss, *The Pan-African Movement*, trans. A.Keep (1974), 234–40.

2. For the 1921 Pan-African Congress, see: *West Africa*, V/240 (3 September 1921), 988, 990, 992, 994 (and two photographs on p. 1004); 'West Africa and the Pan-African Congress', *African World*, Special West African Monthly Supplement, no. 59 (30 September 1921), pp. xi–xvii; Jessie Fauset, 'Impressions of the second Pan-African Congress', *The Crisis*, XXIII/1 (November 1921), 12–18; Jessie Fauset, 'What Europe thought of the Pan-African Congress', *The Crisis*, XXIII/2 (December 1921), 60, 62–7 (and partial list of delegates, pp. 68–9), DuBois, *The World and Africa*, 236–40; *Colonial and Coloured Unity*, ed. Padmore, 17–22; Padmore, *Pan-Africanism or Communism?*, 129–35; Legum, 29; Langley, 71–83; Geiss, 240–8.
3. For the 1923 Pan-African Congress, see: *West Africa*, VII/354 (10 November 1923), 1352, 1367–8; VII/355 (17 November 1923), [1377]–1378 (and a photograph on p. 1394); 'The Third Pan-African Congress', *The Crisis*, XXVII/3 (January 1924), 120–2; W.E.Burghardt DuBois, 'Pan-Africa in Portugal', *The Crisis*, XXVII/4 (February 1924), 170; DuBois, *The World and Africa*, 241–2; *Colonial and Coloured Unity*, ed. Padmore, 22–3; Padmore, *Pan-Africanism or Communism?*, 139–42; Legum, 29–30; Langley, 84–7; Geiss, 251–6. There was to be one more Pan-African Congress before the Manchester Congress of 1945 (for which see pp. 347–51 above). The fourth congress was held in New York in 1927, and the resolutions passed were very similar to those adopted in 1923. See: 'The Pan-African Congresses', *The Crisis*, XXXIV/8 (October 1927), 263–4; DuBois, *The World and Africa*, 242–3, reprinted in *Colonial and Coloured Unity*, ed. Padmore, 23–4; Padmore, *Pan-Africanism or Communism?*, 142–4; Legum, 20; Langley, 87–8; Geiss, 256–8. Topics beyond this scope of this book are the relations between DuBoisian Pan-Africanism and the movement led by Marcus Garvey, and the Comintern's attitude to both in the 1920s.
4. Geiss, 295. For earlier, local, students' organizations, see pp. 438 and 439 above.
5. *African Times and Orient Review*, IV/3 (mid-March 1917), 49; V/2 (mid-August 1917), 46, 48; V/6 (mid-December 1917), 113.
6. C.F.Hayfron-Benjamin, 'The Union for Students of African Descent: its work in London for Africa', *West Africa*, VIII/404 (25 October 1924), 1179–80 (and a photograph on p. 1169).
7. Philip Garigue, 'The West African Students' Union: a study in culture contact', *Africa*, XXIII (1953), 56.
8. Garigue, 59.
9. Cf. *Negro Year Book: A Review of Events Affecting Negro Life*

1941–1946, ed. Jessie Parkhurst Guzman (Department of Records and Research, Tuskegee Institute, 1947), 584.

10. *The Truth About Aggrey House: An Exposure of the Government Plan for the Control of African Students in Great Britain* (West African Students' Union, 1934), [6]–[7].
11. Geiss, 301.
12. J.S.Coleman, *Nigeria: Background to Nationalism* (1958), 241; cf. *Wãsù*, XI/1 (June 1944), 6; XII/2 (March 1946), 6–7.
13. *Wãsù*, X/1 (May 1943), 7–8.
14. Coleman, 207.
15. Roderick J. Macdonald, 'Dr. Harold Arundel Moody and the League of Coloured Peoples, 1931–1947: A Retrospective View', *Race*, XIV (1972–3), [291]–292.
16. David A. Vaughan, *Negro Victory: The life story of Dr. Harold Moody* (Independent Press Limited, 1950), 27–8, 33, 36.
17. Vaughan, 55.
18. *The Keys*, I/3 (January 1934), p. [ii] of cover.
19. *The Keys*, IV/3 (January–March 1937), p. [ii] of cover.
20. 'Race Prejudice in England', *Negro Worker*, March 1932, as reprinted in *Negro Anthology*, ed. Nancy Cunard (Wishart & Co., 1934), 555.
21. St Clair Drake, 'Value Systems, Social Structure and Race Relations in the British Isles' (unpublished University of Chicago PhD thesis, 1954), as quoted by Macdonald, 294.
22. *The Keys*, III/4 (April–June 1936), 52f.
23. Drake, as quoted by Macdonald, 295.
24. Ras Makonnen, *Pan-Africanism from Within*, ed. Kenneth King (Nairobi etc., Oxford University Press, 1973), 126–7.
25. As quoted by Macdonald, 294.
26. C.L.R.James, 'Abyssinia and the Imperialists', *The Keys*, III/3 (January–March 1936), 32, 39–40.
27. Macdonald, 293.
28. Peter Blackman, 'Editorial', *The Keys*, VII/1 (July–September 1939), 3–4.
29. Macdonald, 298.
30. W. Arthur Lewis, 'Notes on the Trinidad Report', *The Keys*, V/4 (April–June 1938), 80–2. For the 1937 oilfield strike and disturbances, see R.Ramdin, *From Chattel Slave to Wage Earner* (1982), 100ff.
31. *The Times*, no. 48,004 (26 May 1938), 12; no. 48,007 (30 May 1938), 10; no. 48,016 (9 June 1938), 10.
32. *The Keys*, VI/1 (July–September 1938), 10; Vaughan, 89–90.
33. Macdonald, 299, 300.
34. As quoted by Vaughan, 96.
35. As quoted by Vaughan, 96.
36. Vaughan, 97.
37. *League of Coloured Peoples News Letter*, no. 15 (December 1940), 68;

Fernando Henriques, 'Coloured men in civilian defence', *League of Coloured Peoples News Letter*, no. 21 (June 1941), 57–9; *League of Coloured Peoples News Letter*, no. 22 (July 1941), 81.

38. As quoted by Vaughan, 98.

39. *League of Coloured Peoples News Letter*, no. 9 (June 1940), 39.

40. Macdonald, 301.

41. Macdonald, 302.

42. *League of Coloured Peoples News Letter*, no. 23 (August 1941), 117, 119.

43. *Daily Herald*, no. 7597 (16 August 1941), [1]; *Parliamentary Debates*, 5th ser. vol. 374 (1941), cols. 68–9; see also Nancy Cunard and George Padmore, *The White Man's Duty*, second edition (Manchester, Panaf Service Ltd, 1945), 9.

44. Drake, as quoted by Macdonald, 304.

45. *League of Coloured Peoples News Letter*, no. 38 (November 1942), 61.

46. *League of Coloured Peoples News Letter*, no. 38 (November 1942), 34.

47. *League of Coloured Peoples News Letter*, X/59 (August 1944), 73. For Moody, see also Sam Morris, 'Moody – the forgotten visionary', *New Community*, I (1971–2), 193–6.

48. Geiss, 353–4.

49. C.L.R.James, *Spheres of Existence: Selected Writings* (Allison & Busby, 1980), 227. For Padmore, see also James R. Hooker, *Black Revolutionary: George Padmore's Path from Communism to Pan-Africanism* (Pall Mall Press, 1967).

50. Ethel Mannin, *Comrade O Comrade: Or, Low-Down on the Left* (Jarrolds, [1947]), 133–5.

51. E.P.Thompson, 'C.L.R.James at 80', *Urgent Tasks*, no. 12 (Summer 1981), p [iv] of cover.

52. Fredric Warburg, *An Occupation for Gentlemen* (Hutchinson, 1959), 211.

53. 'Biographical Introduction' to C.L.R.James, *The Future in the Present: Selected Writings* (Allison & Busby, 1977), 8.

54. C.L.R.James, *Nkrumah and the Ghana Revolution* (Allison & Busby, 1977), 23.

55. Robert A. Hill, 'In England, 1932–1938', *Urgent Tasks*, no. 12 (Summer 1981), 19, 27. For James, see also: Tony Martin, 'C.L.R.James and the Race/Class Question', *Race*, XIV (1972–3), [183]–193; Alan J. Mackenzie, 'Radical Pan-Africanism in the 1930s: A Discussion with C.L.R.James', *Radical History Review*, no. 24 (Fall 1980), 68–75; Cedric J. Robinson, *Black Marxism: The Making of the Black Radical Tradition* (Zed Press, 1983), 349–415.

56. Makonnen, 139.

57. Makonnen, 143; cf. *The Times*, no. 50,620 (28 November 1946), 2.

58. Makonnen, 162.

59. Jeremy Murray-Brown, *Kenyatta* (George Allen & Unwin Ltd, 1972), 117.

60. Scotland Yard report, 18 June 1929, PRO CO 533/384/9, fols. 86–7.

61. *Sunday Worker*, no. 242 (27 October 1929), 3; Johnstone Kenyatta, 'An African people rise in revolt', *Daily Worker*, no. 17 (20 January 1930), 4; Johnstone Kenyatta, 'A general strike drowned in blood', *Daily Worker*, no. 18 (21 January 1930), 10.

62. Johnstone Kenyatta, 'Unrest in Kenya', *Manchester Guardian*, no. 26,065 (18 March 1930), 6; *The Times*, no. 45,471 (26 March 1930), 12.

63. Murray-Brown, 138.

64. PRO CO 533/501/11.

65. Jomo Kenyatta, *Kenya: The Land of Conflict* (International African Service Bureau Publication no. 3, [Manchester], Panaf Service Ltd, [1945]), 22.

66. Leo Spitzer and LaRay Denzer, 'I.T.A.Wallace-Johnson and the West African Youth League', *International Journal of African Historical Studies*, VI/3 (1973), 413.

67. As quoted by Spitzer and Denzer, 441. Cyril P. Foray, in *The Encyclopaedia Africana Dictionary of African Biography*, II (1979), 159–60, gives a slightly different version.

68. Douglas Jardine to Malcolm MacDonald, 30 June 1938, PRO CO/ 267/665/32208.

69. Leo Spitzer, *The Creoles of Sierra Leone: Responses to Colonialism, 1870–1945* (Madison, University of Wisconsin Press, 1974), 190.

70. *Salneb Publication* (Freetown), ser. 2, no. 98 (20 May 1965).

71. Langley, [326].

72. Langley, [326].

73. *The Autobiography of Kwame Nkrumah* (Edinburgh, Thomas Nelson & Sons Ltd, 1957), 27.

74. Padmore, *Pan-Africanism or Communism?*, 146.

75. James, 'Abyssinia and the Imperialists', 32.

76. S.Rohdie, 'The Gold Coast Aborigines abroad', *Journal of African History*, VI (1965), 398, 400, 402; Geiss, 354.

77. *Parliamentary Debates*, 5th ser. vol. 312 (1936), col. 374.

78. Rohdie, 404.

79. As quoted by Padmore, *Pan-Africanism or Communism?*, 145.

80. J.M.Kenyatta, 'Hands off Abyssinia!', *Labour Monthly*, XVII (1935), 536.

81. Padmore, *Pan-Africanism or Communism?*, 159–60.

82. Padmore, *Pan-Africanism or Communism?*, 147, 148.

83. Makonnen, 116.

84. As quoted by Padmore, *Pan-Africanism or Communism?*, 147.

85. C.L.R.James, as quoted by Roderick J. Macdonald, ' "The Wisers

Who Are Far Away . . . ": The Role of London's Black Press in the 1930s and '40s' (paper presented to the International Conference on the History of Blacks in Britain, London, 28–30 September 1981), 13.

86. As quoted by Langley. 339–40.

87. Makonnen, 161.

88. Langley, 343, citing documents in Gambia Records Office (including Chief Constable E.Canning, Special Branch, Metropolitan Police, to Home Office, 20 December 1939).

89. Geiss, 387.

90. Padmore, *Pan-Africanism or Communism?*, 149n. Padmore includes the West African Students' Union in the list, but there is some doubt about this; see Hooker, 83; Geiss, 513 n. 15. Langley, 343, claims that 'there was some objection from Negro groups in Cardiff to the aims of the Padmore–Makonnen leadership'.

91. Padmore, *Pan-Africanism or Communism?*, 149.

92. Makonnen, 137.

93. Makonnen, 163–4.

94. Makonnen, 163.

95. Padmore to DuBois, 17 August 1945, as quoted by Geiss, 395–6.

96. Hooker, 89.

97. Padmore, *Pan-Africanism or Communism?*, 161.

98. Geiss, 401.

99. Padmore, *Pan-Africanism or Communism?*, 161.

100. Geiss, 401.

101. For the 1945 Pan-African Congress, see: DuBois, *The World and Africa*, 244–5; *Colonial and Coloured Unity*, ed. Padmore, 27–74; Hooker, 94–7; Padmore, *Pan-Africanism or Communism?*, 158–70; Legum, 31–2; Langley, 353–5; Geiss, 398–408.

102. Geiss, 408.

103. Makonnen, 167.

104. Shapurji Saklatvala, 'India in the Labour World', *Labour Monthly*, I (1921), 448–9; K.S.Bhat, 'The Workers' Welfare League of India', *Labour Monthly*, XIII (1931), [777]–779; John Patrick Haithcox, *Communism and Nationalism in India: M.N.Roy and Comintern Policy 1920–1939* (Princeton, N.J., Princeton University Press, 1971), 31; Partha Sarathi Gupta, 'British Labour and the Indian Left, 1919–1939', in *Socialism in India*, ed. B.R.Nanda (Delhi etc., Vikas Publications, 1972), 72 n. 11.

105. Labour Party, *Report of the Twenty-Second Annual Conference . . . 1922*, 175.

106. *Parliamentary Debates*, 5th ser. vol. 159 (1922), col. 113.

107. This account of Shapurji Saklatvala is largely based on the essay by Barbara Nield and John Saville in *Dictionary of Labour Biography*, VI, ed. Joyce M. Bellamy and J.Saville (1982), 236–41, which has a very full list of sources.

108. Emil Lengyel, *Krishna Menon* (New York, Walker & Company, 1962), 82.

109. T.J.S.George, *Krishna Menon: a biography* (Jonathan Cape, 1964), 63.

110. Gupta, 110.

111. George, 84.

112. *The Times*, no. 59,211 (7 October 1974), 14. For Krishna Menon, see also Diwan Chaman Lall, in *Dictionary of National Biography*, ed. Sen, III. 98–101.

Racism as colour bar

1. K.L.Little, 'Colour Prejudice in Britain', *Wasu*, X/1 (May 1943), 28.

2. *West Africa*, V/236 (6 August 1921), 798.

3. Geo. W. Brown, 'Investigation of Coloured Colonial Seamen in Cardiff: April 13th–20th, 1935', *The Keys*, III/2 (October–December 1935), 20.

4. P.C.Lewis and G.W.Brown, 'We too were in Cardiff', *The Keys*, III/1 (July–September 1935), 4.

5. P. Cecil Lewis, 'Cardiff Report – General Survey', *The Keys*, III/2 (October–December 1935), 16.

6. See, besides the references in notes 3 and 4 above, Lewis, 'Cardiff Report – General Survey', 16–18; Harold A. Moody, 'The League of Coloured Peoples and the Problem of the Coloured Colonial Seamen in the United Kingdom', *The Keys*, III/2 (October–December 1935), 22–4; D.A.Vaughan, *Negro Victory* (1950), 75–81.

7. Little, 28.

8. Nancie Hare, 'The prospects for coloured children in England', *The Keys*, V/1 (July–September 1937), 11.

9. Vaughan, 80.

10. 'Vicar's Wife Insults Our Allies', *Sunday Pictorial*, no. 1,434 (6 September 1942), 3.

11. Graham A. Smith, 'Jim Crow on the home front (1942–1945)', *New Community*, VIII/3 (Winter 1980), 318.

12. Smith, 318.

13. *Parliamentary Debates*, 5th ser. vol. 383 (1942), cols. 670–1.

14. *The Times*, no. 49,356 (2 October 1942), 5.

15. Christopher Thorne, 'Britain and the black G.I.s: Racial issues and Anglo-American relations in 1942', *New Community*, III/3 (Summer 1974), 265.

16. United States Coloured Troops in the United Kingdom: Memorandum by the Secretary of State for War, September 1942, PRO PREM 4/26/9 and CAB 66/29, WP(42)441.

17. *The Diaries of Sir Alexander Cadogan O.M. 1938–1945*, ed. David Dilks (Cassell, 1971), 483.

18. PRO CAB 65/28, War Cabinet 140(42), 13 October 1942, pp. 88–90, and War Cabinet 143(42), 20 October 1942, pp. 104–5.
19. 'The Colour Problem as the American sees it', *Current Affairs*, no. 32 (5 December 1942), pp. iii–iv of cover. See also Thomas E. Hachey, 'Jim Crow with a British accent: attitudes of London government officials towards American Negro soldiers in England during World War II', *Journal of Negro History*, LIX (1974), 65–77.
20. As quoted by Smith, 321.
21. As quoted by Smith, 324.
22. *League of Coloured Peoples News Letter*, X/60 (September 1944), 93–4. See also Anthony H. Richmond, *Colour Prejudice in Britain: A study of West Indian Workers in Liverpool, 1941–1951* (Routledge & Kegan Paul Limited, 1954), 90; Ruth Glass and Harold Pollins, *Newcomers: The West Indians in London* (Centre for Urban Studies Report no. 1, George Allen & Unwin Ltd, 1960), 118.
23. *League of Coloured Peoples News Letter*, X1/63 (December 1944), 60.
24. *Manchester Guardian*, no. 30,251 (14 September 1943), 4.
25. *League of Coloured Peoples News Letter*, XII/71 (August 1945), 104.
26. 'These Coloured "Intruders" ', *John Bull*, LXXIX/2067 (26 January 1946), 15.
27. *Parliamentary Debates*, 5th ser. vol. 392 (1943), cols. 390–1.
28. As quoted by Smith, 325.
29. C.L.R.James, *Beyond a Boundary* (Hutchinson, 1963), 110.
30. Gerald Howat, *Learie Constantine* (George Allen & Unwin Ltd, 1975), 44.
31. Sir Donald Bradman, *The Art of Cricket* (Hodder & Stoughton, 1958), 158.
32. Howat, 129.
33. Learie Constantine, *Colour Bar* (Stanley Paul & Co. Ltd, 1954), 147–8.
34. *Evening Standard*, no. 37,368 (19 June 1944), 4; no. 37,370 (21 June 1944), 4; no. 37,376 (28 June 1944), 5; *The Times*, no. 49,887 (20 June 1944), 2; no. 49,889 (22 June 1944), 2; no. 49,895 (29 June 1944), 2; *League of Coloured Peoples News Letter*, X/58 (July 1944), 66; *The Times Law Reports*, LX/23 (4 August 1944), 510–13.
35. *Parliamentary Debates*, 5th ser. vol. 416 (1945–6), col. 753.
36. *Parliamentary Debates*, 5th ser. vol. 449 (1947–8), cols. 607–8, 1416.
37. Constantine, 67. For Constantine, see also Sam Morris, 'Learie Constantine', *New Community*, I (1971–2), 68–70.

Racism as riot: 1948

1. *League of Coloured Peoples News Letter*, XVII/103 (July–September 1948), 82.
2. *Liverpool Echo*, no. 21,372 (10 August 1948), 4; *Liverpool Daily Post*, no. 29,021 (10 August 1948), 3.

3. A.H.Richmond, *Colour Prejudice in Britain* (1954), 103.
4. *Liverpool Echo*, no. 21,365 (2 August 1948), 3; no. 21,366 (3 August 1948), 3, 4; no. 21, 369 (6 August 1948), 3; no. 21,372 (10 August 1948), 3; no. 21,380 (19 August 1948), 4; no. 21,381 (20 August 1948), 4; no. 21,383 (23 August 1948), 4; no. 21,384 (24 August 1948), 4; no. 21,386 (26 August 1948), 3; *Evening Express* (Liverpool), no. 23,983 (3 August 1948), [4]; no. 23,989 (10 August 1948), [1]; no. 23,995 (17 August 1948), [1], [4]; no. 23,997 (19 August 1948), [1]; no. 23,998 (20 August 1948), [1]; no. 24,001 (24 August 1948), [4]; *Liverpool Daily Post*, no. 29,015 (3 August 1948), 3; no. 29,016 (4 August 1948), 3; no. 29,028 (18 August 1948), 3; no. 29,030 (20 August 1948), 3; no. 29,031 (21 August 1948), 3; no. 29,033 (24 August 1948), 3; no. 29,036 (27 August 1948), 3.
5. *League of Coloured Peoples News Letter*, XVII/103 (July–September 1948), 85.
6. Richmond, 104–7.
7. *League of Coloured Peoples News Letter*, XVII/103 (July–September 1948), 85.
8. *Liverpool Daily Post*, no. 29,033 (24 August 1948), 3; no. 29,036 (27 August 1948), 3.
9. *Liverpool Daily Post*, no. 29,017 (5 August 1948), [1]; *Liverpool Echo*, no. 21,368 (5 August 1948), 3; *League of Coloured Peoples News Letter*, XVI/103 (July–September 1948), 84–5.
10. Richmond, 108.

11. The settlers

The post-war immigration

1. *Daily Worker*, no. 5226 (23 June 1948), 3.
2. *Daily Worker*, no. 5244 (14 July 1948), 3.
3. *Evening Standard*, no. 38,608 (21 June 1948), [1].
4. Joyce Egginton, *They Seek a Living* (Hutchinson, 1957), 40–1.
5. Nicholas Deakin and others, *Colour, Citizenship and British Society* (Panther Books, 1970), 283.
6. Anthony H. Richmond, *The Colour Problem: A study of racial relations* (Harmondsworth, Penguin Books, 1955), 240–6.
7. Sheila Patterson, 'A recent West Indian immigrant group in Britain', *Race*, I/2 (May 1960), 27.
8. R.Glass and H.Pollins, *Newcomers: The West Indians in London* (1960), 120.
9. Wallace Collins, *Jamaican Migrant* (Routledge & Kegan Paul, 1965), 57.
10. A.G.Bennett, *Because They Know Not* (Phoenix Press, [1959]), 22.
11. Bhikhu Parekh, 'Asians in Britain: Problem or Opportunity?', in *Five Views of Multi-Racial Britain: Talks on race relations broadcast by BBC TV* (Commission for Racial Equality, 1978), 41.

12. *The Times*, no. 53,084 (9 November 1954), 9.
13. *The Times*, no.. 53,314 (1 September 1955), 8.
14. *The Times*, no. 53,182 (5 March 1955), 6.
15. R.B.Davison, *Commonwealth Immigrants* (Oxford University Press, 1964), 43–4.
16. Davison, 70.
17. See also, for this section, A.H.Richmond, *Colour Prejudice in Britain* (1954), 143–3; Clarence Senior and Douglas Manley, *The West Indians in Britain*, ed. Norman Mackenzie (Fabian Research Ser. 179, Fabian Colonial Bureau, 1956); R.B.Davison, *West Indian Migrants: Social and economic facts of migration from the West Indies* (Oxford University Press for Institute of Race Relations, 1962); Kathleen Hunter, *History of Pakistanis in Britain* (Norwich, Page Bros, [1962]); Rashmi Desai, *Indian Immigrants in Britain* (Oxford University Press, 1963) (I am grateful to Ron Ramdin for telling me about this book); *Colour in Britain*, ed. Richard Hooper (British Broadcasting Corporation, 1965); Harry Goulbourne, 'Black Workers in Britain', *African Review* (Dar es Salaam), VII/2 (1977), 63–75; Stuart Hall, 'Racism and Reaction', in *Five Views of Multi-Racial Britain*, 23–35; John Rex, 'Race in the Inner City', in *Five Views of Multi-Racial Britain*, 9–22; Jenny Bourne, 'Cheerleaders and ombudsmen: the sociology of race relations in Britain', *Race and Class*, XXI (1979–80), [331]–352.

Racism as riot: 1958

1. *Guardian Journal* (Nottingham), no. J41,351/G31,871 (25 August 1958), [1], 5; no. J41,352/G31,872 (26 August 1958), [1]; no. J41,357/G31,877 (1 September 1958), [1]; no. J41,358/G31,878 (2 September 1958), [1]; *The Times*, no. 54,238 (25 August 1958), 8; no. 54,239 (26 August 1958), 4; no. 54,240 (27 August 1958), 4; no. 54,241 (28 August 1958), 4; no. 54,243 (30 August 1958), 7; *Manchester Guardian*, no. 34,886 (28 August 1958), 4; no. 34,889 (1 September 1958), 6; no. 34,902 (16 September 1958), [1]; *Nottingham Evening News*, no. 22,666 (1 September 1958), [1]; no. 22,672 (8 September 1958), [1], 7; *Tribune*, 5 September 1958, p. 6; James Wickenden, *Colour in Britain* (Oxford University Press for Institute of Race Relations, 1958), 28, 30–4.
2. *Manchester Guardian*, no. 34,884 (26 August 1958), 10; no. 34,885 (27 August 1958), 6; no. 34,889 (1 September 1958), [1]; no. 34,890 (2 September 1958), [1], 5; no. 34,893 (5 September 1958), [1]; no. 34,896 (9 September 1958), [1]; no. 34,902 (16 September 1958), [1]; *Tribune*, 5 September 1958, p. 6; 12 September 1958, pp. 6, 7; Wickenden, 39–42; Michael Abdul Malik, *From Michael de Freitas to Michael X* (André Deutsch, 1968), [73]–78.
3. *Evening Gazette* (Middlesborough), no. 29,314 (21 August 1961), [1],

10; no. 29,315 (22 August 1961), [1], 12. I am grateful to Paul Gilroy for telling me about the Middlesborough events.

4. *Report of Proceedings at the 90th Annual Trades Union Congress . . . 1958*, 326.
5. *Tribune*, 5 September 1958, p. [1].
6. Robert Moore and Tina Wallace, *Slamming the Door: The Administration of Immigration Control* (Martin Robertson, 1975), 112.

Surrender to racism

1. As quoted by E.J.B.Rose and others, *Colour and Citizenship: A Report on British Race Relations* (Oxford University Press for Institute of Race Relations, 1969), 229.
2. *Parliamentary Debates*, 5th ser. vol. 649 (1961), col. 803.
3. Gideon Ben-Tovim and John Gabriel, 'The Politics of Race in Britain, 1962 to 1979: A Review of the Major Trends and of the Recent Literature', *Sage Race Relations Abstracts*, IV/4 (November 1979), 2.
4. E.R.Braithwaite, 'The "Colored" Immigrant in Britain', *Dædalus: Journal of the American Academy of Arts and Sciences*, XCVI (1967), 496.
5. Catherine Jones, *Immigration and Social Policy in Britain* (Tavistock Publications, 1977), 122.
6. Stuart Hall, 'The Whites of their Eyes: Racist Ideologies and the Media', in *Silver Linings: Some Strategies for the Eighties: Contributions to the Communist University of London*, ed. George Bridges and Rosalind Brunt (Lawrence & Wishart, 1981), 37.
7. Stuart Hall, 'Racism and Reaction', in *Five Views of Multi-Racial Britain* (1978), 29. For a devastating account of the surrender to racism up to 1965, see Paul Foot, *Immigration and Race in British Politics* (Harmondsworth, Penguin Books, 1965).
8. *Parliamentary Debates*, 5th ser. vol. 701 (1964–5), col. 71.
9. Rose and others, 23.
10. Rose and others, 23.
11. A.Sivanandan, 'Race, Class and the State: The Black Experience in Britain', *Race & Class*, XVII/4 (Spring 1976), 354, reprinted in A.Sivanandan, *A Different Hunger: Writings on Black Resistance* (Pluto Press, 1982), 109.
12. Sivanandan, 'Race, Class and the State', 359; Sivanandan, *A Different Hunger*, 114.
13. A.Sivanandan, 'From resistance to rebellion: Asian and Afro-Caribbean struggles in Britain', *Race & Class*, XXIII/2–3 (Autumn 1981/Winter 1982), 123; reprinted in Sivanandan, *A Different Hunger*, 17.
14. Clifford Hill, *Immigration and Integration: A study of the settlement of coloured minorities in Britain* (Oxford, Pergamon Press Limited, 1970), 153–4.

15. *Parliamentary Debates*, 5th ser. vol. 759 (1967–8), cols. 1295–9, 1314, 1341–2.
16. Dilip Hiro, *Black British, White British* (Eyre & Spottiswoode, 1971), 58.
17. R.Moore and T.Wallace, *Slamming the Door* (1975), 113.
18. Sivanandan, 'From resistance to rebellion', 127; Sivanandan, *A Different Hunger*, 22.
19. Sivanandan, 'From resistance to rebellion', 129–30; Sivanandan, *A Different Hunger*, 25.

12. The new generation

Born at a disadvantage

1. David J. Smith, *Racial Disadvantage in Britain: the PEP Report* (Harmondsworth, Penguin Books, 1977), 13.
2. Harry Goulbourne, 'Black Workers in Britain', *African Review* (Dar es Salaam), VII/2 (1977), 67.
3. Smith, 111, 127, 74–5; Goulbourne, 68.
4. Goulbourne, 68.
5. A.Sivanandan, 'From resistance to rebellion: Asian and Afro-Caribbean struggles in Britain', *Race & Class*, XXIII/2–3 (Autumn 1981/Winter 1982), 150; reprinted in A.Sivanandan, *A Different Hunger* (1982), 49.
6. Smith, 104.
7. Smith, 231, 233.
8. Sivanandan, 'From resistance to rebellion', 134; Sivanandan, *A Different Hunger*, 30.
9. David L. Kirp, *Doing good by doing little: Race and schooling in Britain* (Berkeley, Los Angeles, and London, University of California Press, 1979), 39, 62, 64, 40. I am grateful to Compton Ambrose of the British Library for telling me about this book.
10. Michael Marland, 'A Programme for a Community of Schools', in *Education for the Inner City*, comp. and ed. M.Marland (Heinemann Educational Books, 1980), 202–3.
11. Thomas J.Cottle, *Black Testimony: The Voices of Britain's West Indians* (Wildwood House, 1978), 52.
12. Chris Mullard, *Black Britain* (George Allen & Unwin Ltd, 1973), [145]–146, 154, 156.
13. Mullard, 183. See also, for this section, The Runnymede Trust and The Radical Statistics Race Group, *Britain's Black Population* (Heinemann Educational Books, 1980): this is the most up-to-date survey of discrimination and disadvantage in employment, housing, education, and health and social services, and includes relevant information available up to December 1979.

Police against black people

1. Derek Humphry, *Police Power and Black People* (Panther, 1972), 17, 13.
2. Humphry, 178.
3. *Parliamentary Papers* (1971–2), XXXIV. 72.
4. Humphry, 217.
5. Maureen Cain, *Society and the Policeman's Role* (Routledge & Kegan Paul, 1973), 117–19. See also Paul Gilroy, 'Police and thieves', in Centre for Contemporary Social Studies, *The Empire Strikes Back: race and racism in 70s Britain* (Hutchinson, 1982), [143]–144.
6. *Police against Black People* (*Race & Class* pamphlet no. 6, Institute of Race Relations, 1979).
7. Tony Bunyan, *The History and Practice of the Political Police in Britain*, revised edition (Quartet Books, 1977), 147.
8. *Guardian*, 12 August 1970, p. 5.
9. Ian McDonald, 'Candles for Scotland', *Race Today Review*, December 1980/January 1981, p. 73.
10. Stuart Hall and others, *Policing the Crisis: Mugging, the State, and law and order* (Macmillan, 1978), 39–40.
11. Hall and others, 281.
12. John Solomos and others, 'The organic crisis of British capitalism and race: the experience of the seventies', in Centre for Contemporary Social Studies, *The Empire Strikes Back*, 15.
13. Bunyan, 146.
14. Paul Gilroy, 'You can't fool the youths . . . Race and class formation in the 1980s', *Race & Class*, XXIII/2–3 (Autumn 1981/Winter 1982), 218, 219. See also, for this section, Paul Gordon, *White Law: Racism in the police, courts, and prisons* (Pluto Press, 1983).

Resistance and rebellion

1. *Guardian*, 7 July 1981, p. 10; 8 July 1981, p. 13.
2. 'Background – British racism', *Race & Class*, XXIII/2–3 (Autumn 1981/Winter 1982), 232.
3. 'Background – British racism', 238.
4. 'Background – British racism', 243–4.
5. As quoted, *Daily Mail*, 31 January 1978, p. [1].
6. Detective Chief Superintendent Plowman, as quoted, *New Standard*, 13 April 1981, p. 2.
7. Chief Constable Kenneth Oxford, as quoted, *New Statesman*, CII/2626 (17 July 1981), 8.
8. John Solomos and others, 'The organic crisis of British capitalism and race: the experience of the seventies', in Centre for Contemporary Studies, *The Empire Strikes Back* (1982), 32; cf. James Walvin, 'From the Fringes to the Centre: The Emergence of British

Black Historical Studies' (paper presented to the International Conference on the History of Blacks in Britain, London, 28–30 September 1981), 8.

Appendix F. Birmingham, the metal industries, and the slave trade

1. William Camden, *Britain,or a chorographicall description of the most flourishing Kingdomes, England, Scotland, and Ireland*, trans. Philémon Holland (George Bishop & John Norton, 1610), [pt 1], 567.
2. Henry Hamilton, *The English Brass & Copper Industries to 1800* (Longmans, Green, & Co. Ltd, 1926), 137; cf. *The History of the Birmingham Gun-Barrel Proof House: with notes on the Birmingham gun trade* (Birmingham, Guardians of the Birmingham Proof House, [1947]), 20.
3. 'Artifex' and 'Opifex', *The Causes of Decay in a British Industry* (Longmans, Green, & Co., 1907), 128; *Victoria History of the Counties of England: Warwickshire*, II. 228.
4. *Journals of the House of Commons*, XV (1705–8), 631.
5. *Journals of the House of Commons*, XVI (1708–11), 83, 549.
6. De Witt Bailey and Douglas A. Nie, *English Gunmakers: The Birmingham and Provincial Gun Trade in the 18th and 19th Century* (Arms & Armour Press, 1978), 15.
7. Bailey and Nie, 16.
8. W.H.B.Court, *The Rise of the Midland Industries 1600–1838* (Oxford University Press, 1938), 146.
9. 'Artifex' and 'Opifex', 129; Lord E.Fitzmaurice, *Life of William, Earl of Shelburne* (1875–6), I. 404; J.E.Inikori, 'The import of firearms into West Africa 1750–1807: a quantitative analysis', *Journal of African History*, XVIII (1977), 361, 359.
10. *HCSP of the Eighteenth Century*, LXX (George III: Report of the Lords of Trade on the Slave Trade 1789, pt 2), 196.
11. Bailey and Nie, 15.
12. Gavin White, 'Firearms in Africa: an Introduction', *Journal of African History*, XII (1971), 182 n. 34.
13. 'Artifex' and 'Opifex', 129.
14. White, 181.
15. John D. Goodman, 'The Birmingham Gun Trade', in *The Resources, Products, and Industrial History of Birmingham and the Midland Hardware District*. ed. Samuel Timmins (Robert Hardwicke, 1866), 389–90; Keith Dunham, *The Gun Trade of Birmingham: A short historical note of some of the more interesting features of a long-established local industry* (Birmingham, City of Birmingham Museum and Art Gallery, Department of Science and Industry, 1955), [8], 7.

16. Fitzmaurice, I. 404.
17. John Morfitt, in *Harvest Home: consisting of Supplementary Gleanings*, etc., ed. [Samuel Jackson] Pratt (Richard Phillips, 1805), I. 333.
18. Inikori, 361, 359.
19. Karl Pearson, *The Life, Letters and Labours of Francis Galton* (Cambridge, University Press, 1914–30), I. 32.
20. Barbara M.D. Smith, 'The Galtons of Birmingham: Quaker Gun Merchants and Bankers, 1702–1831', *Business History*, IX (1967), 138 and n. 7; cf. Inikori, 346 n. 6.
21. Pearson, I. 45.
22. Howard L. Blackmore, *British Military Firearms 1650–1850* (Herbert Jenkins, 1961), 139.
23. Smith, 150.
24. R.O.Roberts, 'The Development and Decline of the Copper and Other Non-Ferrous Metal Industries in South Wales', *Transactions of the Honourable Society of Cymmrodorion*, session 1956 (1957), 83.
25. A.H.John, *The Industrial Development of South Wales 1750–1850: an essay* (Cardiff, University of Wales Press, 1950), 108; Peter Mathias, *The First Industrial Nation: An economic history of Britain 1700–1914* (Methuen & Co. Ltd, 1969), 122.
26. D. Trevor Williams, *The Economic Development of Swansea and the Swansea District to 1921* (Social and Economic Survey of Swansea and District, pamphlet no. 4, Cardiff, University of Wales Press Board, 1940), 7.
27. Col. Grant-Francis, *The Smelting of Copper in the Swansea District of South Wales, from the Time of Elizabeth to the Present Day*, second edition (Henry Sotheran & Co., 1881), 113; Hamilton, 248; D.T.Williams, 68; John, 30.
28. Grant-Francis, 113, 117, pl. facing p. 116; Hamilton, 154; D. Owen Evans, 'The Non-Ferrous Metallurgical Industries of South Wales, and Welshmen's Share in their Development', *Transactions of the Honourable Society of Cymmrodorion*, session 1929–30 (1931), 17; D.J.Davies, *The Economic History of South Wales prior to 1800* (Cardiff, University of Wales Press Board, 1933), 134; D.T.Williams, 67–8.
29. Hamilton, 151; D.T.Williams, 67; R.O.Roberts, 'Penclawdd Brass and Copper Works: A Link with the Slave Trade', *Gower*, XIV (1960), 35–43; J.R.Harris, 'Michael Hughes of Sutton: The Influence of Welsh Copper on Lancashire Business, 1780–1815', *Transactions of the Historic Society of Lancashire and Cheshire*, CI (1949), 180.
30. Hamilton, 111, 149–51, 246–8. For the Cheadle Company and its subsidiary the Warrington Company, see T.C.Barker and J.R.Harris, *A Merseyside Town in the Industrial Revolution: St. Helens 1750–1900* (Liverpool, University Press, 1954), 76.
31. Barker and Harris, 76. For Charles Roe, see W.H.Chaloner, 'Charles Roe of Macclesfield (1715–81): an Eighteenth-Century

Industrialist', *Transactions of the Lancashire and Cheshire Antiquarian Society*, LXII (1950–1), 133–56, LXIII (1952–3), 52–86.

32. B.L.Anderson, 'The Lancashire bill system and its Liverpool practitioners: The case of a slave merchant', in *Trade and transport*, ed. W.H.Chaloner and B.M.Ratcliffe (1977), 66.
33. *CSP Colonial Ser. America and West Indies, 1726–1727*, 36–7.
34. Barker and Harris, 81; J.R.Harris, *The Copper King: a biography of Thomas Williams of Llanidan* (Liverpool University Press, 1964), 50; J.R.Harris, 'Copper and Shipping in the Eighteenth Century', *Economic History Review*, 2nd ser. XIX (1966), 566–7; Gareth Rees, 'Copper Sheathing: an Example of Technological Diffusion in the English Merchant Fleet', *Journal of Transport History*, n.s. I (1971), 89–90; David M. Williams, 'Abolition and the Re-deployment of the Slave Fleet, 1807–11', *Journal of Transport History*, n.s. II (1973), 111; Herbert S. Klein, 'The English Slave Trade to Jamaica, 1782–1808', *Economic History Review*, 2nd ser. XXXI (1978), 36 n. 3; Kenneth Davies, 'The Eighteenth Century Copper and Brass Industries of the Greenfield Valley', *Transactions of the Honourable Society of Cymmrodorion*, 1979, pp. 204 n. 4, 211–14.
35. *London Chronicle*, LXIV/4946 (8–10 July 1788), 39; *Journals of the House of Commons*, XLIII (1787–8), 651; *Journals of the House of Lords*, XXXVIII (1787–90), 262.
36. [Thomas Pennant], *The History of the Parishes of Whiteford, and Holywell* (B. & J.White, 1796), 205, 211; K.Davies, 203, 219, 220.
37. Harris, *The Copper King*, 9.
38. Jean Day, *Bristol Brass: A History of the Industry* (Newton Abbot, David & Charles, 1973), 84, 90, 169.

Appendix G. Eighteenth-century biographies

1. [E. Long], *The History of Jamaica* (1774), II. 476.
2. [Long], II. 478–85.
3. Revd James Ramsay, *An Essay on the Treatment and Conversion of African Slaves in the British sugar colonies* (James Phillips, 1784), 238.
4. Thomas Bluett, *Some Memoirs of the Life of Job, the Son of Solomon the High Priest of Boonda in Africa* (Richard Ford, 1734), 22.
5. Douglas Grant, *The Fortunate Slave: An illustration of African slavery in the early eighteenth century* (Oxford University Press, 1968), [159].
6. Bluett, 46.
7. Grant, 90.
8. Francis Moore, *Travels into the Inland Parts of Africa* (J.Stagg, 1738), p. 224, sig. P8v.
9. Moore, p. 208, sig. O8v; Charles Theodore Middleton, *A New and Complete System of Geography* (J.Cooke, 1777–8), I. 295.

10. John Nichols, *Literary Anecdotes of the Eighteenth Century* (Nichols, Son, & Bentley, 1812–15), VI. 90.
11. *The Royal African: or, Memoirs of the Young Prince of Annamboe* (W.Reeve etc., [*c.*1750]), 49.
12. *The Royal African*, 37.
13. Thomas Thompson, *An Account of Two Missionary Voyages By the Account of the Society for the Propagation of the Gospel in Foreign Parts* (Benj. Dod, 1758), 35, 47.
14. *Gentleman's Magazine*, XX (1750), pl. facing p. 272.
15. As quoted by A.L.Reade, *Francis Barber: the Doctor's Negro Servant* (1912), 4.
16. *Boswell's Life of Johnson*, ed. G.B.Hill and L.F.Powell (1934–64), I. 239 n. 1.
17. *Fourth Report of the Royal Commission on Historical Manuscripts* (HMSO, 1874), i. 400; Amos Aschbach Ettinger, *James Edward Oglethorpe: imperial idealist* (Oxford, Clarendon Press, 1936), 309.
18. Sir John Hawkins, *The Life of Samuel Johnson, LL.D.* (J.Buckland etc., 1787), 328 and n.
19. Johnson to Barber, 25 September 1770, in *Boswell's Life of Johnson*, ed. Hill and Powell, II. 115–16.
20. Johnson to Mrs Thrale, 13 September 1777, in *The Letters of Samuel Johnson*, ed. R.W.Chapman (Oxford, Clarendon Press, 1952), II. 205.
21. *Boswell's Life of Johnson*, ed. Hill and Powell, III. 68.
22. *Boswell's Life of Johnson*, ed. Hill and Powell, III. 400.
23. *Gentleman's Magazine*, LXIII (1793), ii. 620.
24. *Autobiography of Miss Cornelia Knight, lady companion to the Princess Charlotte of Wales* (W.H.Allen & Co., 1861), I. 14.
25. Hesther Lynch Piozzi, *Anecdotes of the late Samuel Johnson, LL.D.* (T.Cadell, 1786), 210.
26. Piozzi, 211.
27. Hawkins, 586n.
28. John Smith, 'Memoir of Samuel Barber, a local preacher', *Primitive Methodist Magazine*, X (1829), 82.
29. Barber to the bishop of Dromore, 16 December 1788: draft reproduced in Reade, pl. ii; transcription in Reade, 70.
30. *Gentleman's Magazine*, LXIII (1793), ii. 619–20.
31. *Gentleman's Magazine*, LXXI (1801), i. 190.
32. *European Magazine*, LVIII (1810), ii. 275.
33. Reade, 84.
34. Smith, 128.
35. F.L.Bartels, 'Philip Quaque, 1741–1816', *Transactions of the Gold Coast & Togoland Historical Society*, I (1952–5), [153]; see also Grace Bansa, in *The Encyclopaedia Africana Dictionary of African Biography*, I (1977), 305–6.
36. J.J.Crooks, *Records relating to the Gold Coast Settlements From 1750 to*

1874 (Dublin, Browne & Nolan, Limited, 1923), 28–30; J.J.Crooks, 'Negroes in England in the Eighteenth Century', *Notes and Queries*, CLIV (1928), 173–4.

37. *Gentleman's Magazine*, XXXV (1765), 145.
38. Bartels, 157.
39. Bartels, 155.
40. Bartels, 167.
41. Bartels, 169.
42. C.Fyfe, *A History of Sierra Leone* (1962), 19.
43. P.Hoare, *Memoirs of Granville Sharp, Esq.* (1820), 369n.
44. C.B. Wadström, *An Essay on Colonization* (1794–5), II. 268.
45. Fyfe, 54.
46. Sierra Leone Company report, as quoted by H.A.Rydings, 'Prince Naimbanna in England', *Sierra Leone Studies*, n.s. no. 8 (June 1957), 207. For Nemgbana's life, see also Cyril P.Foray, in *The Encyclopaedia Africana Dictionary of African Biography*, II (1979), 125–6.
47. J.W.Thirlwall, 'The Kreutzer Sonata and Mr. Bridgetower', *Musical World*, XXXVI (1858), 771.
48. Betty Matthews, 'George Polgreen Bridgtower', *Music Review*, XXIX (1968), [22]; *The New Grove Dictionary of Music and Musicians*, ed. S.Sadie (1980), III. 282.
49. Hans Volkmann, *Beethoven in seinen Beziehung zu Dresden* (Dresden, Deutscher Literatur-Verlag, [1942]), 151.
50. Matthews, [22].
51. János Harich, 'Haydn Documenta (1)', *The Haydn Yearbook*, II (1963–4), 15; *Die Tagebücher von Joseph Carl Rosenbaum 1770–1829*, ed. Else Radant (*Das Haydn Jahrbuch*, V, 1968), 110.
52. Josephine R.B.Wright, 'George Polgreen Bridgetower: An African Prodigy in England 1789–99', *Musical Quarterly*, LXVI (1980), 69.
53. H.C.Robbins Landon, *Haydn in England 1791–1795* (Haydn: Chronicle and Works, II, Thames & Hudson, 1976), 66; Wright, 69.
54. *Reminiscences of Michael Kelly of the King's Theatre and Theatre Royal Drury Lane* (Henry Colburn, 1826), I. 332, 344; [Henry Angelo], *Angelo's Pic Nic; or, Table Talk* (John Ebers, 1834), 21–5; Lionel de La Laurencie, 'The Chevalier de Saint-George', *Musical Quarterly*, V (1919), 74–85; Lionel de La Laurencie, *L'École française de violon de Lully à Viotti* (Paris, Librairie Delagrave, 1922–4), II. 449–500; Ellwood Derr, in *The New Grove Dictionary*, XVI. 391–2.
55. Mrs [Charlotte Louisa Henrietta] Papendiek, *Court and Private Life in the Time of Queen Charlotte*, ed. Mrs Vernon Delves Broughton (Richard Bentley & Son, 1887), II. 134–5, 139.
56. Wright, 68.
57. Papendiek, II. 155, 177–8; Wright, 77 n. 38.
58. Wright, 67.

59. *The Letters of Beethoven*, ed. Emily Anderson (Macmillan & Co. Ltd, 1961), I. 90.
60. *Thayer's Life of Beethoven*, ed. Elliot Forbes (Princeton, N.J., Princeton University Press, 1964), I. 332.
61. F.G.E[dwards]., 'George P.Bridgetower and the Kreutzer Sonata', *Musical Times*, XLIX (1908), 307.
62. British Library Add. MS. 27,593 (Reminiscences of Sam.Wesley), fol. 109. Some of Wesley's letters to Bridgtower, written between 1797 and 1815, are preserved in Add. MS. 56,411 (Wesley Manuscript and Letters).
63. Papendiek, II. 179; Volkmann, 152; Wright, 70 n. 16.
64. *Gentleman's Magazine*, LXXXI (1811), ii. 37, 158; Wright, 68 n. 7.
65. E[dwards]., 307.
66. E[dwards]., 307.
67. Reproduced in E[dwards]., 307.
68. *Autobiography of James Silk Buckingham* (Longman, Brown, Green, & Longmans, 1855), I. 166.
69. *Autobiography of Buckingham*, I. 169.
70. *Autobiography of Buckingham*, I. 170–1.
71. *Autobiography of Buckingham*, I. 169.
72. Joseph (born 23 July 1803), Thomas (6 July 1805), James (13 July 1807), Cecilia (21 October 1809), and Benjamin (24 June 1812), who died in infancy. See *The Register of Baptisms, Marriages & Burials of the Parish of Falmouth in the County of Cornwall, 1663–1812*, ed. Susan Elizabeth Gay and Mrs. Howard Fox (Exeter, Devon and Cornwall Record Society, 1914–15 [1908–15]), I. 101, 570, 594, 618, 641, 663; II. 956.
73. These short pieces were published in Truro by Mrs Heard & Sons, in London by Dalamaine & Co. There is a copy in the British Library. See also, for Joseph Emidy, Eileen Southern, *Biographical Dictionary of Afro-American and African Musicians* (Westport, Conn. and London, Greenwood Press, 1982), 127; I am grateful to Ziggi Alexander for telling me about Emidy and giving me this reference.

Appendix H. Visitors, 1832–1919

1. B.Quarles, *Black Abolitionists* (1969), 130–1.
2. *A Narrative of the adventures and escape of Moses Roper from American slavery* (Darton, Harvey, & Sarton, 1837); Loggins, *The Negro Author* (1931), 103–4; D.A.Lorimer, *Colour, Class and the Victorians* (1978), 220.
3. Quarles, *Black Abolitionists*, 131; Jane H. Pease and William H. Pease, *They Who Would Be Free: Blacks' Search for Freedom, 1830–1861* (Studies in American Negro Life, New York, Atheneum, 1974), 49.

4. W[illiam]. Wells Brown, *Three years in Europe; or Places I have seen and people I have met* (Charles Gilpin, 1852), 261–2; W.W. Brown, *The Black Man* (1863), 246–50; Loggins, 131, 132–4; B.Quarles, 'Ministers without Portfolio', *Journal of Negro History*, XXXIX (1954), 30–1; Quarles, *Black Abolitionists*, 131–3; Lorimer, 222.
5. *Narrative of the life of Frederick Douglass, an American slave: written by himself* (Boston, Mass., Anti-Slavery Office, 1845); Brown, *Three years in Europe*, 259–60; Brown, *The Black Man*, 180–7; *Life and times of Frederick Douglass, Written by Himself* (Hartford, Conn., Park Publishing Co., 1882), 236–63; J.W.Cromwell, *The Negro in American History* (1914), 146–7; Loggins, 134–56; B.Brawley, *Early Negro American Writers* (1935), 175–9; Benjamin Quarles, *Frederick Douglass* (Washington, DC, Associated Publishers, Inc., 1948), 38–56; George Shepperson, 'Frederick Douglass and Scotland', *Journal of Negro History*, XXXVIII (1953), 307–21; Quarles, 'Ministers without Portfolio', 31; Philip S. Foner, *Frederick Douglass: a biography* (New York, Citadel Press, 1964), 62–74, 182–3; Quarles, *Black Abolitionists*, 136–7; Pease and Pease, *They Who Would Be Free*, 57–60; Leslie Friedman Goldstein, 'Violence as an instrument for social change: the views of Frederick Douglass (1817–1895)', *Journal of Negro History*, LXI (1976), 61–72; Lorimer, 48–9, 52; H.W.Debrunner, *Presence and Prestige* (1979), 246–7; *The Frederick Douglass Papers: Series One: Speeches, Debates, and Interviews*, I: 1841–46, ed. John W. Blassingame (New Haven and London, Yale University Press, 1979), pp. liii-lxi; Joel Schor, 'The rivalry between Frederick Douglass and Henry Highland Garnet', *Journal of Negro History*, LXIV (1979), 30–8; Nathan Irvin Huggins, *Slave and Citizen: The Life of Frederick Douglass* (Boston, Little, Brown and Company, 1980); Betty Fladeland, ' "Our Cause being One and the Same": Abolitionists and Chartism', in *Slavery and British Society 1776–1846*, ed. J.Walvin (1982), 97, 98. For Douglass's writings and speeches while in Britain, see: *The Life and Writings of Frederick Douglass*, ed. Philip S. Foner (New York, International Publishers, [1967]), I. 115–234; *The Frederick Douglass Papers: Series One*, I, ed. Blassingame, 34–485.
6. *Narrative of William W. Brown, an American slave: written by himself* (Charles Gilpin, 1850); Brown, *Three years in Europe*; William Wells Brown, *Clotel; or, the President's Daughter: A Narrative of Slave Life in the United States* (Partridge & Oakey, 1853); Loggins, 156–73; Brawley, 168–70; Quarles, 'Ministers without Portfolio', 32; William Edward Farrison, *William Wells Brown, author & reformer* (Chicago and London, University of Chicago Press, 1969), especially pp. 145–246; Quarles, *Black Abolitionists*, 135, 137, 141; Lorimer, 46, 48–50.
7. Brown, *The Black Man*, 276–8; Cromwell, 30, 144n.; Loggins 195–7; *A Side-light on Anglo-American Relations, 1839–1858: Furnished by the*

Correspondence of Lewis Tappar and Others with the British and Foreign Anti-Slavery Society, ed. Annie Heloise Abel and Frank J. Klingberg (Lancaster, Pa, Association for the Study of Negro Life and History, Incorporated, 1927), 144 n. 112; Quarles, 'Ministers without Portfolio', 32–3; Quarles, *Black Abolitionists*, 136, 137–8; Lorimer, 222; Debrunner, 244–5. I have not seen Pennington's autobiography, *The Fugitive Blacksmith* (C.Gilpin, 1849).

8. Brown, *Three years in Europe*, 233; A[lexander]. C[rummell]., ' "Africa not under a curse" ', *Christian Observer*, [L] (1850), 600–7, reprinted as 'The Negro Race not under a Curse' in Revd Alex[ander]. Crummell, *The Future of Africa*, second edition (New York, Charles Scribner, 1862), [325]–354; Brown, *The Black Man*, 165–9; W.E.Burghardt Du Bois, *The Souls of Black Folk: Essays and sketches*, second edition (Chicago, A.C.McClury & Co., 1903), [215]–227; Cromwell, 130–8; Loggins, 199–200; *Alumni Cantabrigenses*, comp. J.A.Venn, II. ii (Cambridge, University Press, 1944), 193; Kathleen O'Mara Wahle, 'Alexander Crummell: Black Evangelist and Pan-Negro Nationalist', *Phylon*, XXIX (1968), 388–95; Wilson J. Moses, 'Civilizing missionary: a study of Alexander Crummell', *Journal of Negro History*, LX (1975), 229–51; Otey M. Scruggs, 'We the Children of Africa in This Land: Alexander Crummell', in *Africa and the Afro-American Experience: Eight Essays*, ed. L.A.Williams (1977), 77–95; Lorimer, 77, 219.

9. *The Life of Josiah Henson, formerly a slave, now an inhabitant of Canada, as narrated by himself* (Boston, Mass., Arthur D. Phelps, 1849); *'Uncle Tom's Story of His Life': An Autobiography of the Rev. Josiah Henson*, ed. John Lobb, fortieth thousand (*Christian Age* office, 1877); W.B.Hartgrove, 'The story of Josiah Henson', *Journal of Negro History*, III (1918), 1–21; *A Side-light on Anglo-American Relations*, ed. Abel and Klingberg, 329–30 n. 323; Loggins, 215–17; Brawley, 160–1; Jessie L. Beattie, *Black Moses: The Real Uncle Tom* (Toronto, Ryerson Press, 1957); Quarles, 'Ministers without Portfolio', 33; Lorimer, 220.

10. Brown, *The Black Man*, 149–51; Alex[ander]. Crummell, 'Eulogium on Henry Highland Garnet, D.D.', in *Africa and America: Addresses and Discourses* (Springfield, Mass., Willey & Co., 1891), [269]–305; Cromwell, 126–9; W.M.Brewer, 'Henry Highland Garnet', *Journal of Negro History*, XIII (1928), 36–52; Loggins, 191–5; Quarles, 'Ministers without Portfolio', 33–4; Quarles, *Black Abolitionists*, 138; Jane H. Pease and William H. Pease, *Bound with Them in Chains: A Biographical History of the Anti-Slavery Movement* (Westport, Conn., Greenwood Press, Inc., 1972), 162–90; Joel Schor, *Henry Highland Garnet: A voice of black radicalism in the nineteenth century* (Contributions in American History, no. 54, Westport, Conn. and London, Greenwood Press, 1977), especially pp. 111–25, 167; Lorimer, 222; Schor, 'The rivalry between Frederick Douglass and

Henry Highland Garnet'; Fladeland, 97. I have not seen Earl Ofari, *'Let Your Motto Be Resistance': The Life and Thought of Henry Highland Garnet* (Boston, Mass., Beacon Press, 1972).

11. *Slave life in Georgia: a narrative of the life, sufferings, and escape of John Brown, A Fugitive Slave, now in England*, ed. L.A.Chamerovzow (The editor, 1855), 31–44, 168–70, 231; Lorimer, 39, 54.
12. Samuel Ringgold Ward, *Autobiography of a fugitive Negro: his anti-slavery labours in the United States, Canada, & England* (John Snow, 1855); Cromwell, 36n., 149; Loggins, 173–5; Quarles, 'Ministers without Portfolio', 34; Quarles, *Black Abolitionists*, 138; Lorimer, 48, 50–1.
13. William G. Allen, *American Prejudice against Color: an authentic narrative, showing how easily the nation got into an uproar* (W. & F.G.Cash, 1853); 'Prejudices against Colour', *Anti-Slavery Reporter*, 3rd ser. I (1853), [121]–123; 'Professor G.W. [*sic*] Allen', *Anti-Slavery Reporter*, 3rd ser. I (1853), 154; Loggins, 187–8; Quarles, 'Ministers without Portfolio', 35–6; Quarles, *Black Abolitionists*, 138–9; Lorimer, 47.
14. [William Craft], *Running a thousand miles for freedom; or, The escape of William and Ellen Craft from slavery* (William Tweedie, 1860); Brown, *Three years in Europe*, pp. xxv, 163–4, 173–5, 181, 200; Loggins, 227–8; Quarles, 'Ministers without Portfolio', 36; Quarles, *Black Abolitionists*, 136–7; Lorimer, 47–8, 63.
15. Dorothy B. Porter, 'Sarah Parker Remond, Abolitionist and Physician', *Journal of Negro History*, XX (1935), 287–93; Quarles, 'Ministers without Portfolio', 27–8; Quarles, *Black Abolitionists*, 139–40; Lorimer, 222.
16. As quoted by Quarles, 'Ministers without Portfolio', 39–40; cf. Lorimer, 222. For John Sella Martin, see Brown, *The Black Man*, 241–5.
17. Quarles, 'Ministers without Portfolio', 40–1.
18. *Incidents in the Life of the Rev. J*[eremiah]. *Asher* (Charles Gilpin, 1850); Loggins, 229; Lorimer, 221. I have not seen Asher's *An Autobiography, with Details of a Visit to England* (Philadelphia, The Author, 1862).
19. *Life and Sufferings of Francis Fedric, while in slavery* (Birmingham, Tooks & Jones, 1859); Francis Fedric, *Slave Life in Virginia and Kentucky; or, Fifty Years of Slavery in the southern states of America* (Wertheim, Macintosh, & Hunt, 1863); Lorimer, 220–1.
20. *Narrative of Henry Watson, a fugitive slave*, third edition (Boston, Mass., Bela Marsh, 1850); Lorimer, 221.
21. [Linda Brent], *Incidents in the life of a slave girl: written by herself*, ed. L. Maria Child (Hodson & Son, 1862), especially pp. 176–9; Lorimer, 221.
22. Brown, *Three years in Europe*, 112–13.

23. Brown, *Three years in Europe*, 233.
24. Lorimer, 218.
25. *God's image in ebony: being a series of biographical sketches, facts, anecdotes, etc., demonstrative of the mental powers and intellectual capacities of the negro race*, ed. H.G.Adams (Partridge & Oakey, 1854), 77–80; Lorimer, 215–16.
26. C.Fyfe, *History of Sierra Leone* (1962), 188–9, 261; Lorimer, 218.
27. *Church Missionary Intelligencer*, I (1849–50), 144; Lorimer, 218.
28. Fyfe, 254; *Africa Remembered*, ed. P.D.Curtin (1967), 317–22; Lorimer, 218.
29. Kimble, *A Political History of Ghana* (1963), *passim; Great Britain and Ghana: Documents of Ghana History 1807–1957*, ed. G.E.Metcalfe (Thomas Nelson & Sons Ltd, 1964), 532 n. 2; R.W.July, *The Origins of Modern African Thought* (1968), *passim*; The Honourable Mr Justice Azu Crabbe, *John Mensah Sarbah 1864–1910 (His Life and Works)* (Accra, Ghana Universities Press, 1971); S.Tenkorang, 'John Mensah Sarbah, 1864–1910', *Transactions of the Historical Society of Ghana*, XIV (1973), [65]–78 (pointing out, p. 68, that George Emil Eminsang of Elmina, not Sarbah, was the first qualified Gold Coast lawyer, having been trained in Holland and Germany); L.H.Ofosu-Appiah, in *The Encyclopaedia Africana Dictionary of African Biography*, I (1977), 313–14.
30. Fyfe, 535. See also Fred W. Hooke, *Life Story of an African Knight* (Freetown, [YMCA, 1915]); John D. Hargreaves, *A Life of Sir Samuel Lewis* (Oxford University Press, 1958); July, 304–18; John D. Hargreaves, in *The Encyclopaedia Africana Dictionary of African Biography*, II (1979), 102–4. Dr Richard Pankhurst tells me that the first Ethiopian to come to Britain was Prince Alamayou (son of King Theodore), who was brought in 1868, died in 1879 at the age of 19, and was buried in St George's Chapel (see Lord Amulree, 'Prince Alamayou of Ethiopia', *Ethiopia Observer*, VIII/1 (1970), 8–15); and that the first Ethiopian to come to Britain for study is thought to have been Hakim, known as Dr Martin, who read medicine at Glasgow in 1889–91 (see Dr Richard Pankhurst, 'The Foundations of Education, Printing, Newspapers, Book Production, Libraries and Literacy in Ethiopia', *Ethiopia Observer*, VI/3 (1962), 251–3); I am grateful to Dr Pankhurst for these references.
31. *Anti-Slavery Reporter*, 3rd ser. IX (1861), 19–22; Lorimer, 217.
32. *Anti-Slavery Reporter*, 3rd ser. XIV (1866), 109–10; [Frank Cundall], 'Richard Hill', *Journal of the Institute of Jamaica*, II/3 (July 1896), 223–30; Frank Cundall, *Biographical Annals of Jamaica* (Kingston, Educational Supply Company for the Institute of Jamaica, 1904), 29; Frank Cundall, 'Richard Hill', *Journal of Negro History*, V (1920), 37–44; Lorimer, 216.
33. *Anti-Slavery Reporter*, 3rd ser. XIV (1866), 210; Lorimer, 216.
34. *Anti-Slavery Reporter*, 3rd ser. XIV (1866), 210; Lorimer, 216–17.

35. Cundall, *Biographical Annals of Jamaica*, 33.
36. *Anti-Slavery Reporter*, 3rd ser. III (1855), 186–7; Lorimer, 217.
37. *Anti-Slavery Reporter*, 3rd ser. XVII (1871), 191; Colonel William Johnston, *Roll of Graduates of the University of Aberdeen 1860–1900* (Aberdeen, University Press, 1906), 126; Lorimer, 217.
38. *African Times and Orient Review*, I/11 (May 1913), 361.
39. Louis R. Harlan, 'Booker T. Washington and the White Man's Burden', *American Historical Review*, LXXI (1965–6), 464.
40. Harlan, 463. Bandele Omoniyi, a Nigerian student at Edinburgh University, contributed a series of articles, 'Is British Government in West Africa a Success?', to the *Edinburgh Magazine*, VII/164 (19 January 1907), 1435; VII/165 (26 January 1907), 1453; VII/166 (2 February 1907), [1476]. I have not seen Omoniyi's *A Defence of the Ethiopian Movement* (Edinburgh, J. & J. Gray & Co., 1908). For black students in Edinburgh, see George Shepperson's contribution to *Four Centuries: Edinburgh University Life, 1583–1983*, ed. Gordon Donaldson (University of Edinburgh Press, 1983).
41. Imanuel Geiss, 'Notes on the development of Pan-Africanism', *Journal of the Historical Society of Nigeria*, III (1964–7), 729; I.Geiss, *The Pan-African Movement*, trans. A.Keep (1974), 110–12, 207.
42. Theophilus E. Samuel Scholes, *Glimpses of the Ages; or the 'superior' and 'inferior' races, so-called, discussed in the light of science and history* (John Long, 1905–6), II. 176, 177, 179, 237. Jeffrey P. Green tells me that Scholes's association with the Colwyn Bay Institute is referred to in Thomas Lewis Johnson, *Twenty Eight Years a Slave: or The Story of My Life on Three Continents* (Bournemouth, W.Mate and Co., 1909). Green's research into the life of Johnson, an evangelist who had many connections with leading black personalities at the turn of the century, will, when published, add substantially to our knowledge of this period of black history in Britain.
43. *African Times and Orient Review*, n.s. I/5 (21 April 1914), 98; I/11 (May 1913), 334.
44. 'Conference with Africans', *Journal of the African Society*, XII (1912–13), 428.
45. Geiss, *Pan-African Movement*, 295.
46. I owe the information in this paragraph to Jeffrey P. Green, who kindly gave me a copy of his paper 'Caribbean students in London 1917–1920 and their international connections through the Student Movement House, 32 Russell Square, London', to be published in *Caribbean Studies*.
47. J.B.T.M[arsh]., *The Story of the Jubilee Singers; with their songs* (Hodder & Stoughton, 1875), 70.
48. *The Times*, no. 27,683 (7 May 1873), 5.
49. W.C., 'The Jubilee Singers', *Chambers's Journal*, no. 733 (12 January 1878), 19.

50. M[arsh]., 114, 118; J.B.T.Marsh, *The Story of the Jubilee Singers*, new edition (Hodder & Stoughton, 1885), 120.

51. J.B.T.Marsh, *The Story of the Jubilee Singers* (Hodder & Stoughton, 1902), 104.

52. Thomas Rutling, *'Tom': An Autobiography: with revised Negro melodies* (Torrington, N. Devon, Thos. J. Dyer, [*c.* 1910]); *Robinson's Harrogate . . . and District Directory*, 1906, pp. 93, 295, 663; 1910, p. 516.

53. J.B.T.Marsh, *The Story of the Jubilee Singers*, third edition (Hodder & Stoughton, 1876), 106–8; Geiss, *The Pan-African Movement*, 183, 192.

54. Douglas A. Lorimer, 'Bibles, Banjoes and Bones: Images of the Negro in the Popular Culture of Victorian England', in *In Search of the Visible Past: History Lectures at Wilfrid Laurier University 1973–1974*, ed. Barry M. Gough (Waterloo, Ontario, Wilfrid Laurier University Press, 1975), 40.

55. *An Introduction to Gospel Song*, comp. and ed. Samuel B. Charters (RBF Records RF 5), side 1, track 1.

56. Harry Reynolds, *Minstrel Memories: The Story of Burnt Cork Minstrelsy in Great Britain from 1836 to 1927* (Alston Rivers Ltd., [1928]); Nils Erik Enkvist, *Caricatures of Americans on the English Stage prior to 1870* (Commentationes humanarum litterarum, XVIII/1, Helsingfors, 1951 [1953]), 76–93; George F. Rehin, 'Harlequin Jim Crow: Continuity and Convergence in Blackface Clowning', *Journal of Popular Culture*, IX (1975–6), 687–90. I am grateful to Rehin for kindly sending me a photocopy of his paper.

57. Eileen Southern, *The Music of Black Americans: A History* (New York, W.W.Norton & Company, Inc., 1971), 112; Robert C. Toll, *Blacking Up: The Minstrel Show in Nineteenth-Century America* (New York, Oxford University Press, 1974), 196.

58. Southern, 111–12; Toll, 197.

59. H.Marshall and M.Stock, *Ira Aldridge: The Negro Tragedian* (1958), 150–1.

60. Charles Dickens, *American Notes for general circulation* (Chapman & Hall, 1842), I. 217, 218.

61. *Illustrated London News*, XIII/329 (5 August 1848), 77.

62. As quoted by Marian Hannah Winter, 'Juba and American Minstrelsy', in *Chronicles of the American Dance*, ed. Paul Magriel (New York, Henry Holt & Company, 1948), 50.

63. As quoted by Winter, 50.

64. Winter, 53. For Lane, see also Marshall and Jean Stearns, *Jazz Dance: The Story of American Vernacular Dance* (New York, Schirmer Books, 1979 reprint), 44–7; Toll, 43, 196, 197; Lorimer, 'Bibles, Banjoes and Bones', 39.

65. As quoted by Douglas C. Riach, 'Blacks and Blackface on the Irish Stage, 1830–60', *Journal of American Studies*, VIII (1973), 233–4.

66. Reynolds, 162–7; Toll, 199–200.
67. Reynolds, 164–5.
68. Lorimer, 'Bibles, Banjoes and Bones', 42. For Hague's Georgia Minstrel Troupe, see also Carl Wittke, *Tambo and Bones: A History of the American Minstrel Stage* (Durham, N.C., Duke University Press, 1930), 226.
69. Reynolds, 206; Stearns, 50–1; Southern, [260] (reproducing a playbill for a performance by Haverly's Colored Minstrels at Hengler's Cirque, Glasgow, 24 January 1882), 267; Toll, 206, 215, 223.
70. *The Times*, no. 30,323 (12 October 1881), 8.
71. Reynolds, 206–7; Stearns, 57; Southern, 265–7; Toll, 216–17. John Jay Daly, *A Song in his Heart* (Philadelphia, John C. Winston Company, 1951) is a fictionalized biography of Bland.
72. Reynolds, 201–3, 211–12; Toll, 203, 216, 246. For Weston, see also Winter, 57; Southern, 123. James Bohee died in 1897 at the age of 53 (*The Era Almanack*, 1899, p. 97).
73. Edward S. Walker, 'The spread of ragtime in England', *Storyville*, no. 88 (April–May 1980), [123]–127. I am grateful to Ziggi Alexander for giving me a photocopy of this article.
74. *Era*, LXVII/3,393 (3 October 1903), 15; see also Jeffrey P. Green, '*In Dahomey* in London in 1903', *Black Perspective in Music*, XI/1 (Spring 1983), [23]–40.

Appendix I. Prize-fighters, 1791–1902

1. [Pierce Egan], *Boxiana; or Sketches of ancient and modern Pugilism* (G.Smeeton, 1812), 466; [Francis Dowling], *Fistiana; or, The oracle of the ring* (Wm. Clement, jun., 1841), 200; Nat Fleischer, *Black Dynamite: The Story of the Negro in the Prize Ring from 1782 to 1938* (The Ring Athletic Library, 14–16, New York, C.J.O'Brien, 1938), I. [18]–19.
2. For Bill Richmond, see [Egan], *Boxiana* (1812), 212; *The Fancy*, II (1826), [535]–540; [Dowling], 229; Henry Downes Miles, *Pugilistica: being one hundred and forty-four years of the history of British boxing* (Weldon & Co., [1880–1]), I. 289–301; Fleischer, *Black Dynamite*, I. [21]–32; Nat Fleischer, *The Heavyweight Championship: An Informal History of Heavyweight Boxing from 1719 to the Present Day*, revised edition (New York, G.P.Putnam's Sons, [1961]), 28–31; H.W.Debrunner, *Presence and Prestige* (1979), 235–6. For Young Richmond, see [Dowling], 229; Fleischer, *Black Dynamite*, I. [71]–73.
3. *The Times*, no. 8410 (30 September 1811), [3]; 'Collectanea', comp. D.Lysons, IV. 217r, 218r; [Egan], *Boxiana* (1812), 360–71; *The Fancy*, I (1821–2), [489]–502; [Dowling], 212; Miles, I. 254–8, 278–88; Fred Henning, *Fights for the Championship: The men and their times* (*Licensed Victuallers' Gazette* office, [1902]), II. 16–45; Jeffery

Farnol, *Epics of the Fancy: A vision of old fighters* (Sampson Low, Marston & Co.., Ltd, [1928]), 84–92; Fleischer, *Black Dynamite*, I. [33]–45; Denzil Batchelor, *Big Fight: The Story of World Championship Boxing* (Phoenix House Ltd, 1954), 42–4; Fleischer, *Heavyweight Championship*, 31–3; Dennis Prestidge, *Tom Cribb at Thistleton Gap* (Melton Mowbray, Brewhouse Publications, 1971); Debrunner, 236–8.

4. [Dowling], 230–1; Miles, I. 305; Fleischer, *Black Dynamite*, I. [51]–53.
5. [Dowling], 243; Miles, II. 177–82; Fleischer, *Black Dynamite*, I. [46]–50.
6. Pierce Egan, *Boxiana*, revised edition (Sherwood, Neely, & Jones, 1818–24), III. 37–42; [Dowling], 196; Miles, I. 308–10; II. 181–2; Fleischer, *Black Dynamite*, I. [64]–66.
7. [Dowling], 192.
8. [Dowling], 136.
9. [Dowling], 213.
10. *Bell's Life in London, and Sporting Chronicle*, XI/361 (3 June 1832), [3].
11. [Dowling], 212; Fleischer, *Black Dynamite*, I. [54]–63.
12. As quoted by Fleischer, *Black Dynamite*, I. 68.
13. Fleischer, *Black Dynamite*, I. [90]–91.
14. Fleischer, *Black Dynamite*, I. 95.
15. *Bell's Life in London and Sporting Chronicle*, 20 July 1862, p. 7.
16. Fleischer, *Black Dynamite*, I. [86]–89.
17. Fleischer, *Black Dynamite*, III. 276–97.

Suggestions for further reading

This book does not include a formal bibliography. Readers who want more information about a particular person or event will often find relevant books and articles listed in the notes. Thus, for instance, those interested in reading more about Marcus Garvey will find some of the literature about him listed in note 67 on page 564 above. These guides to further reading, which make no pretension to completeness, are identified as such in the index.

The following suggestions are intended for readers who need guidance of a more general nature.

Earlier general histories should not be neglected. Nigel File and Chris Power, *Black Settlers in Britain 1555–1958* (Heinemann Educational Books, 1981), though primarily intended for school pupils, has had a deservedly wide sale to older people, too: it is clearly written, well illustrated, and furnished with helpful brief guides to further information. Its shortcomings are noted by Chris Mullard in *Immigrants & Minorities*, II/1 (March 1983), 89–90. Kenneth Little's pioneering *Negroes in Britain* (Kegan Paul, Trench, Trubner & Co. Ltd, 1947) is still of great value. Edward Scobie's *Black Britannia: A history of blacks in Britain* (Chicago, Johnson Publishing Co., 1972) and James Walvin's *Black and White: The Negro and English Society 1555–1945* (Allen Lane, 1973) are stimulating, though both should be used with caution, as should Walvin's *The Black Presence: a documentary history of the Negro in England, 1550–1860* (Orbach & Chambers, 1971).

For the eighteenth century, F.O.Shyllon's *Black People in Britain 1555–1833* (Oxford University Press for Institute of Race Relations, 1977) is a rich mine of information, as is his earlier and better-organized *Black Slaves in Britain* (Oxford University Press for Institute of Race Relations, 1974), to which chapter 6 of this book owes a considerable debt. These are now joined by Paul Edwards and James Walvin, *Black Personalities in the Era of the Slave Trade* (Macmillan, 1983), which unfortunately I did not see until I had finished work on this book. For the mid-nineteenth century, Douglas A. Lorimer's *Colour, Class and the Victorians* (Leicester University Press, 1978) is thoughtful and suggestive.

The Pan-African movement and its connections with Britain are discussed in two books that should be read in conjunction: J. A. Langley's *Pan-Africanism and Nationalism in West Africa 1900–1945* (Oxford, Clarendon Press, 1973) and Imanuel Geiss's *The Pan-African Movement* (Methuen, 1974), a translation of a work first published in German in 1968.

Several biographies and autobiographies of interest are referred to in the notes above, and others are promised. Ziggi Alexander and Audrey Dewjee have in preparation an edition of Mary Seacole's *Wonderful Adventures*; Ian Duffield is working on a biography of Dusé Mohamed Ali; C.L.R.James's promised autobiography will be one of the major publishing events of the decade. Owen Charles Mathurin's *Henry Sylvester Williams and the Origins of the Pan-African Movement, 1869–1911* (Westport, Conn. and London, Greenwood Press, 1976) throws much light on the black presence in Britain in the early twentieth century, as does Jeffrey P. Green's *Edmund Thornton Jenkins: The Life and Times of an American Black Composer, 1894–1926* (Westport, Conn. and London, Greenwood Press, 1982). James R. Hooker's *Black Revolutionary: George Padmore's Path from Communism to Pan-Africanism* (Pall Mall Press, 1967), Ras Makonnen's *Pan-Africanism from Within* (Nairobi etc., Oxford University Press, 1973), and Ernest Marke's engaging *Old Man Trouble* (Weidenfeld & Nicolson, 1975) together build up a rounded picture of what it was like to be black in Britain during and between the two world wars. Black political thought and activities in Britain in that period are discussed by Cedric J. Robinson in *Black Marxism: The Making of the Black Radical Tradition* (Zed Press, 1983).

For the years since 1948, the serious student will begin with A.Sivanandan's *Coloured Immigrants in Britain: A Select Bibliography* (Institute of Race Relations, Special Series, 1969 and later editions) and *Colored Minorities in Great Britain: a comprehensive bibliography, 1970–1977*, comp. Raj Madan (Westport, Conn., Greenwood Press; London, Aldwych Press Limited; 1979). To keep up with new publications, it is a good plan to glance through each fresh issue of *Sage Race Relations Abstracts*, which from time to time carries helpfully annotated reviews of recent literature: see, e.g., Hazel Waters, 'Guide to the Literature on race relations in Britain 1970–75', I/2 (March 1976), 97–105; and Gideon Ben-Tovim and John Gabriel, 'The politics of race in Britain, 1962 to 1979: A Review of the Major Trends and of the Recent Literature', IV/4 (November 1979), 1–56.

The economic setting is best approached through Eric Williams's *Capitalism and Slavery* (Chapel Hill, University of North Carolina Press, 1944; third impression, André Deutsch, 1972). Those interested in the debate around this book will find some points of departure listed in note 5 on page 542 above.

For the history of black people in Britain as part of the history of black people in Europe as a whole, see Hans Werner Debrunner's *Presence and Prestige: Africans in Europe: A History of Africans in Europe before 1918* (Basel, Basler Afrika Bibliographien, 1979), a thorough, scholarly, and well-illustrated labour of love.

Some of the gaps in this cursory reading-list are due to gaps in the literature. There is not yet, for example, a satisfactory history of Asians in Britain. One at least of these gaps will be filled by Ron Ramdin's forthcoming history of the black working class in Britain.

Index